Management and Organisational Behaviour

Management & Organisational Behaviour

ELEVENTH EDITION

LAURIE J. MULLINS

WITH **GILL CHRISTY**

PEARSON

Harlow, England • London • New York • Boston • San Francisco • Toronto • Sydney • Auckland • Singapore • Hong Kong
Tokyo • Seoul • Taipei • New Delhi • Cape Town • São Paulo • Mexico City • Madrid • Amsterdam • Munich • Paris • Milan

Pearson Education Limited

Edinburgh Gate
Harlow CM20 2JE
United Kingdom
Tel: +44 (0)1279 623623
Web: www.pearson.com/uk

First published in 1985 in Great Britain under the Pitman imprint (print)
Fifth edition published in 1999 by Financial Times Pitman Publishing (print)
Seventh edition 2005 (print)
Eighth edition 2007 (print)
Ninth edition 2010 (print)
Tenth edition 2013 (print and electronic)
Eleventh edition published 2016 (print and electronic)

ISBN: 978-1-292-08848-8 (print)
       978-1-292-08851-8 (PDF)
       978-1-292-08849-5 (eText)

British Library Cataloguing-in-Publication Data
A catalogue record for the print edition is available from the British Library

Library of Congress Cataloging-in-Publication Data
Names: Mullins, Laurie J.
Title: Management and organisational behaviour / Laurie J. Mulllins.
Description: Eleventh Edition. | New York : Pearson, 2016. | Revised edition of the author's Management and organisational behaviour, 2013.
Identifiers: LCCN 2015038750 | ISBN 9781292088488
Subjects: LCSH: Organizational behavior.
Classification: LCC HD58.7 .M85 2016 | DDC 658--dc23 LC record available at http://lccn.loc.gov/2015038750

10 9 8 7 6 5 4 3 2 1
19 18 17 16

Front cover image: Mike Kiev © Getty Images
Print edition typeset in 10/12pt minionPro-Regular by SPi Global
Print edition printed and bound by L.E.G.O. S.p.A., Italy

NOTE THAT ANY PAGE CROSS-REFERENCES REFER TO THE PRINT EDITION

To Pamela and for our families

Contents in brief

Contents in detail

Part 3
Groups, leadership and management 269

In acknowledgement and appreciation

Special tribute to my wife Pamela and family for their love, continuing support and encouragement.

Special thanks

Thanks and gratitude to friends and colleagues Gill Christy and Peter Scott for their invaluable contribution to the eleventh edition.

Thanks and gratitude also to:

Richard Christy

Mike Crabbe and Mike Timmins

Hugo Misselhorn

Anne Riches

Those managers who kindly gave permission to reproduce material from their own organisations.

The team at Pearson Education including Donna Goddard, Mary Lince, Eileen Srebernik, Rachel Gear, Simon Lake (for always being there), Jess Kneller and colleagues in marketing and sales.

Those who in a variety of ways through their friendship, interest and support have helped with completion of this eleventh edition, including: Marlon Aquino, Di and Mike Blyth; Jenny and Tony Hart; Lynn and Wayne Miller; Francesca Mullins; Bryan Mundy; Christine Paterson.

Reviewers

Thanks and appreciation to the following reviewers, approached by the publishers, for insightful and constructive comments that helped shape this eleventh edition: John Spoerry, Jean-Anne Stewart, Colin Combe, Kathryn Thory, Nicholas Jackson, Kevin Tennent and Claire Williams.

Laurie J. Mullins

About the authors

Laurie Mullins was formerly a principal lecturer at the University of Portsmouth Business School and led the Behavioural and Human Resource Management Group. Laurie has experience of business, local government, university administration and human resource management, and for a number of years was an instructor in the Territorial Army. He has worked with the United Nations Association International Service (UNAIS), Voluntary Service Overseas (VSO), professional and educational bodies including UNISON Education and as external examiner for university courses and professional organisations. Laurie has undertaken an academic exchange at the University of Wisconsin, USA, a visiting fellowship at the Royal Melbourne Institute of Technology University, Australia and was a visiting lecturer in the Netherlands. He is also author of *Essentials of Organisational Behaviour* and co-author of *Hospitality Management and Organisational Behaviour*, both published by Pearson Education.

Gill Christy is a visiting lecturer in Organisational Behaviour/Human Resource Management (OB/HRM) at Portsmouth University. She read History at Cambridge, then trained and worked as a teacher before moving into a career in training and personnel management, achieving membership of the Chartered Institute of Personnel and Development in 1990. Gill spent five years at Southampton City Council before joining Portsmouth Business School in 1992, where she became subject leader for the OB/HRM group and served a term as Head of the Human Resource and Marketing Management Department.

Peter Scott is a senior lecturer at the University of Portsmouth Business School, specialising in organisational behaviour and employee relations. He has previously taught at the University of Bath and Manchester Metropolitan University. Peter's doctoral research was on craft skills and advanced manufacturing technology.

About this book

In an increasingly competitive environment, an understanding of the behaviour and actions of people at work is of particular importance. The activities of an organisation are directed towards the attainment of certain goals and also have social implications. Organisational behaviour is a wide and essentially multidisciplinary field of enquiry and should not be considered in a vacuum but related to the process of management and wider organisational context and environment. **Broadening the scope of the subject matter beyond the concerns of traditional organisational behaviour texts is a distinctive feature of this book, which is especially suitable across a range of different but related modules, including single or double semester units.**

The underlying theme of the book is the need for effective organisational performance and development based on an understanding of the behaviour of people at work and the role of management as an integrating activity. The concepts and ideas presented provide a basis for contrasting perspectives on the structure, operation and management of organisations, and interactions among people who work in them.

Aims of this book

The aims of this book are to:

- relate the study of organisational behaviour with that of management;
- provide an integrated view embracing both theory and practice;
- point out applications of social science and cultural influences, and implications for management action;
- indicate ways in which organisational performance may be improved through better understanding of effective management of people;
- increase awareness of, and sensitivity to, personal skills and employability.

The comprehensive coverage and progressive presentation of contents will appeal to students at undergraduate level or on related professional courses, and to graduate and post-experience students who, through their course of study, wish to enhance their knowledge and understanding of the subject area. The book will hopefully also appeal to those aspiring to a managerial position.

Distinctive format

There is a logical flow to the sequencing of topic areas and each chapter of the book is self-contained, **with appropriate cross-referencing to other chapters.** This provides a flexible approach. Selection and ordering of chapters can be varied to suit the demands of particular courses of study or individual interests.

The book is written with a minimum of technical terminology and the format is clearly structured. Each chapter is supported with illustrations and practical examples and contains:

- a short introduction and learning outcomes;
- critical review and reflections throughout the text;
- a practical management and organisational behaviour in action case study;
- a pictorial concept map;
- a summary of ten key points to remember;
- review and discussion questions;
- an assignment;
- a personal skills and employability exercise;
- a case study;
- detailed notes and references.

For each part of the book there is also an academic viewpoint and integrative case study.

The eleventh edition

The book retains the same underlying aims and approach that have been a hallmark of its success. In response to clear user and reviewer feedback, there is a noticeable reduction in the size of this edition. Based on this feedback, certain subject areas have been integrated into other chapters to provide a more succinct format.

The book is structured in four parts with a total of sixteen chapters.

Following the revised structure, there is considerable reordering throughout. Attention has been focused on the overall plan of the book and sequence of contents between and within chapters. Strategy is now included in Chapter 14: 'Strategy, corporate responsibility and ethics'. Certain chapters are renamed to reflect more accurately their contents. Each chapter has been reworded or substantially rewritten as necessary. Words set in **colour** throughout the main text indicate inclusion in the **Glossary.**

Every effort has been made to balance a smaller text with the inclusion of new material and additional features without detracting from the continuing appeal of the book. These changes provide a new and fresh look while enhancing ease of readability, which is another key feature of the book. In addition:

- There are eleven revised or completely new management and organisational behaviour in action case studies, seven new concept maps and nine revised or completely new assignments.

- The section on personal skills and employability has been rewritten and expanded. There are five completely new end-of-chapter exercises. There is also a review of personal skills and employability at the end of the book.

- There are now an average of ten critical review and reflections throughout each chapter and a summary of ten key points to remember at the end of each chapter.

- All end-of-chapter case studies have been revised and updated where necessary. There are four completely new chapter case studies.

- For each part of the book there is a completely new academic viewpoint.
- The end-of-part integrative case studies have been revised and updated as necessary and there is a completely new case study for Part 4.

Attention continues to be focused on design features and overall appearance to provide a manageable and attractive text with enhanced clarity and user-friendliness.

Personal skills and employability

The Confederation for British Industry (CBI) points out that in an increasingly competitive employment market, employers are looking beyond simple academic achievement when considering applicants for a job or internship.

> *Many now expect to see evidence of other skills and achievements that boost someone's attractiveness as a potential employee. Businesses want graduates who not only add value but who have the skills to help transform their organization in the face of continuous and rapid economic and technological change. All graduates – whatever their degree disciple – need to be equipped with employability skills.*[1]

The UK Commission for Employment and Skills (UKCES) aims to raise UK prosperity and opportunity by improving employment and skills levels across the UK, benefitting individuals, employers, government and society. Recent years have seen attention given by the government and other employment and professional bodies to the importance of the supply and application of skills attainment for the prosperity of the UK economy. For example, the Chartered Institute of Personnel and Development (CIPD) points out that, for individuals, skills determine their employment and earning potential and, for the organisation, skills are vital to current and future demands.[2]

University education and employability

One of the recommendations in a report from the Chartered Management Institute (CMI) on the future of management and leadership is to 'build employability into education'. The report outlines a series of practical proposals to help embed practical management, enterprise and leadership experiences into the world of education: 'The standing of business studies courses should be reviewed to ensure they are relevant, attractive to young people and respected by employers and higher education.'[3]

UKCES reports that higher education is well placed to play its part in helping to overcome the well-documented skills challenge: 'Collaborations between employers and universities have a significant role to play in providing the supply of highly skilled people to meet demand from businesses now and in the future.'[4] **GOV.UK** refers to the need for a better connection to bridge the gap between education and work. Attention should be focused on 'Real results, not exam results. Success should be measured by a wide set of outcomes, including jobs and progression, not just qualifications.'[5]

The Prince's Trust also points out the human cost of skills shortages that could affect levels of productivity and morale among existing workforces.[6]

People management and social skills

A survey report on tomorrow's leaders suggests that managers recognise the potential benefits of management qualifications that help improve young people's practical skills. Managers were asked to select three factors with the biggest impact on their decision-making when recruiting young people. In two-thirds of cases managers highlight personal presentation, three out of five point to academic qualifications and half focus on an individual's ambition: 'This suggests that managers are often looking at characteristics that demonstrate an individual's potential rather than fully fledged skills themselves.'[7]

Unlike technical or practical skills, social skills are more intangible. They are difficult to get a firm hold of, or to define and measure clearly. Social skills are often associated as 'soft skills' and regarded as a natural part of human behaviour. As a result, a common concern with attention to the skills shortage is a lack of focus on people management, social skills and interpersonal behaviour. For example, an important aspect of working with other people and leadership skills is an awareness and acceptance of individual differences and diversity.

The skills imperative

The European Commission has drawn attention to 'the skills imperative' and points out the importance of a skills policy to raising productivity. For the first time, skills are part of the portfolio of a European Commissioner. The EU is promoting a 'learnings outcome' approach focusing on what people actually know, understand and are able to do, no matter where and how they acquired their knowledge, skills and competencies. Focusing on what people can actually do breaks down the divide between the world of education and the world of work. In-demand skills include the ability to plan and manage projects in order to achieve objectives and transversal skills such as language, problem-solving, communication, ability and willingness to keep learning, and the ability to work with others.[8]

Developing your employability skills

Increasingly, graduate recruiters are placing greater emphasis on key interpersonal and social skills, and attitudes. A first step in working harmoniously and effectively with other people is to know and understand yourself and the skill of self-management. Reflecting honestly on your personal strengths and weaknesses should help develop your level of competence. You cannot even begin to think of managing other people until you can effectively manage yourself.

The continual development of employability skills as part of your university education and lifelong learning is important for:

- progressing your personal confidence and self-awareness;
- developing harmonious interpersonal relationships with colleagues and external contacts;
- initial attractiveness for appointment with a potential employer;
- maintaining a competent level of work performance;
- enhancing work motivation and job satisfaction; and
- helping to safeguard your career progression.

Many employers have structured programmes for the continued development of their staff. Your longer-term employment prospects will be enhanced when you are able to demonstrate a genuine and enthusiastic commitment to your own personal development.

Study as an aid to practice

Study is an aid to practice. An underlying aim of this book is to provide an integrated view embracing both theory and practice. The ideas and concepts discussed provide you with opportunities to explore the underlying skills associated with management and organisational behaviour.

As you progress through your studies, reflect upon what you have read and about the importance of social skills, including:

- personal awareness and how you project yourself;
- openness to diversity, equality and inclusion;
- perceiving and understanding other people;
- written, verbal and non-verbal communications;
- social interactions with others and teamworking;
- persuasiveness and leadership;
- personal organisation and time management;
- coping with change;
- coaching and mentoring; and
- working in a multicultural society.

The critical review and reflection sections throughout each chapter are controversial statements to help provoke and inspire personal reflection about areas you have just read. Draw upon the views of your colleagues to share experiences and test not only your assumptions and ideas, but also your skills of group interaction and influencing other people. References to the importance of skills throughout the text, together with the exhibits, case studies and assignments, should serve to stimulate your awareness of the importance of underlying personal and employability skills necessary for effective performance.

You are encouraged to complement your reading by drawing upon your own observations and practical experiences. This can, of course, be from your university. You may also have work experience, even part-time or casual employment, in other organisations to draw upon. In addition, you will have contact with a range of other organisations such as supermarkets, local pubs and shops, banks or building societies, fast food restaurants, service stations, doctors or a dentist surgery. An analytical approach to contemporary examples from your own observations should help further your interest in the subject area.

Bear in mind that opportunities to develop personal skills are not always immediately apparent but embedded into your course of study. Adopt an inquisitive and enquiring mind. Search for both good and bad examples of organisational behaviour and people management, and the manner in which concepts and ideas presented in this book are applied in practice. Make a point of continually observing and thinking about the interpersonal and work-based skills exhibited. Use this awareness and knowledge to enhance development of your own employability skills and aid career progression.

Monitor and assess your development

It is recommended strongly that you maintain a portfolio of what you have learned in your personal development and the employability skills you have attained or enhanced during your course of study. This can provide a useful basis of discussion with a potential employer.

You may find it useful to assess progression of your personal skills and employ-ability by reviewing your learning and development under the broad headings shown in the illustration.

Personal skills and employability exercises

Critical self-reflection is a positive activity that can challenge narrow preconceived thought processes, encourage creativity and provide a valuable personal learning and development experience.

At the end of each chapter there is a personal skills and employability exercise. This is designed to encourage you to think about further development of your social and work-based skills.

At the end of the book is a review of features within the text that relate to employ-ability skills. You are encouraged to examine the extent to which you have enhanced your personal awareness and knowledge, and are better prepared to demonstrate your employability skills and aid your career progression.

References

1. 'Boosting employability skills', CBI, http://cbi.org.uk (accessed 17 December 2014).
2. 'Skills policy in the UK: Factsheet', CIPD, January 2014.
3. 'MANAGEMENT 2020: Leadership to unlock long-term growth', The Commission on the Future of Management and Leadership, CMI, July 2014, p. 12.
4. 'Forging Futures: Building higher level skills through university and employer collaboration', UKCES, September 2014.
5. 'Growth Through People', UKCES, 25 November 2014.
6. 'The Skills Crunch', Prince's Trust, 2014.
7. Woodman, P. and Hutchings, P. 'Tomorrow's Leaders', CMI, March 2011.
8. 'The Skills Imperative', Social Agenda, *European Commission Magazine on Employment and Social Affairs,* No. 41, July 2015, pp.14–20.

Publisher's acknowledgements

We are grateful to the following for permission to reproduce copyright material:

Figures

Figure 1.3 adapted from *Management*, 8th ed., pub. South-Western, a part of Cengage Learning, Inc. (Hellriegel, D., Slocum, J.W., Jr. and Woodman, R.W. 1998) p.6, reproduced by permission; Figures 1.5, 3.10, 4.6, 5.5, 7.12, 10.6, 12.3, 15.6, 16.7 Copyright © 2011 The Virtual Learning Materials Workshop, Courtesy of Virtual Learning Materials Workshop; Figure 1.7 from *Organisational Behaviour: Individuals, Groups and Organisation*, 4th ed., Financial Times Prentice Hall (Brooks, I. 2008) p.272, Pearson Education Ltd; Figures 2.2, 8.3, 9.7, 14.3 Copyright © 2008 The Virtual Learning Materials Workshop, Courtesy of Virtual Learning Materials Workshop; Figure 3.1 from *Human Resource Management in the Public Sector*, Kwansei Gakuin University Press (Smart, P. and Inazawa, K. 2011) p.21, reproduced with permission; Figure 3.7 from *Strategic Management*, 7th ed., Pearson Education Ltd. (Lynch, R. 2015) p.73, Exhibit 3.1; Figure 3.11 from *How to tackle work-related stress*, publication INDG430, October (Health and Safety Executive 2009), Contains public sector information published by the Health and Safety Executive and licensed under the Open Government Licence; Figure 4.4 adapted from *The Structure of Human Abilities* (Vernon, P.E. 1950) Copyright © 1950 Methuen & Co., reproduced by permission of Taylor & Francis Books UK; Figure 4.5 from Hay Group. Copyright © 1999 Hay Group Limited. All rights reserved. Reproduced with permission; Figure 5.4 from *Assessment Issues in Higher Education*, October, Department of Employment (Atkins, M.J., Beattie, J. and Dockrell, W.B. 1993) p.51, Department for Employment and Learning, Contains public sector information licensed under the Open Government Licence v2.0; Figure 6.4 from *Can You Believe Your Eyes?*, Robson Books (Block, J.R. and Yuker, H.E. 2002) p.163, reproduced with permission of Pavilion Books; Figure 6.7 from *Introduction to Psychology*, 6th ed., McGraw-Hill (King, R.A. 1979) Figure 10.22, p.339, reproduced with permission from the author, Professor Richard King; Figure 6.11 from *Odd Perceptions* (Gregory, R.L. 1986) p.71, Copyright © 1986 Methuen, reproduced by permission of Taylor & Francis Books UK; Figure 6.12 from *Interactive Behaviour at Work*, 3rd ed., Financial Times Prentice Hall (Guirdham, M. 2002) p.162, Pearson Education Ltd; Figure 6.13 Copyright © 2009 The Virtual Learning Materials Workshop, Courtesy of Virtual Learning Materials Workshop; Figure 6.14 from Nick Fitzherbert, www.fitzherbert.co.uk, reproduced with permission; Figure 7.4 reproduced with permission from Andrzej A. Huczynski and David A. Buchanan, *Organizational Behaviour*, Pearson Education (eighth edition), p.293; Figure 7.13 from Knowledge Workers: The New Management Challenge, *Professional Manager*, Institute of Management, November, 1994, p.13 (Tampoe, M.), Reproduced with permission from Chartered Management Institute; Figure 7.15

from J. Richard Hackman and Greg R. Oldham, *Work Redesign*, 1st Ed. ©1980. Reprinted and Electronically reproduced by permission of Pearson Education, Inc. New York; Figure 8.1 from *Beyond the Team*, Butterworth-Heinemann (Belbin, R.M. 2000) Copyright © 2000. Reproduced with permission from Belbin, www.belbin. com; Figure 8.5 from *Interactive Behaviour at Work*, 3rd ed., Financial Times Prentice Hall (Guirdham, M. 2002) p.119, Pearson Education Ltd; Figure 9.2 from *Action-Centred Leadership*, Gower Press (Adair, J. 1979) p.10, Reproduced with permission from John Adair; Figure 9.3 from How to Choose a Leadership Pattern, *Harvard Business Review*, May/June 1973, p.167 (Tannenbaum, R. and Schmidt, W.H.), Copyright © 1973 by Harvard Business School Publishing Corporation; all rights reserved; Figure 9.4 adapted from *A Theory of Leadership Effectiveness*, McGraw-Hill (Fiedler, F.E. 1967) p.146, Reproduced with permission from Fred E. Fiedler; Figure 9.8 from A Good Fit is Essential, *Professional Manager*, Vol.15, No.3, May, p.38 (Cutler, A. 2005), Reproduced with permission from the Chartered Management Institute and Alan Cutler; Figure 10.2 from *Management, Organisation and Employment Strategy* (Watson, T.J. 1986) p.29, Copyright © 1986 Routledge and Kegan Paul, reproduced by permission of Taylor & Francis Books UK; Figure 10.9 from Managers Charter, https://civilservice.blog.gov.uk/wp-content/uploads/sites/86/2014/09/Annex-C-Managers-Charter.pdf, Contains public sector information licensed under the Open Government Licence (OGL) v3.0.http://www.nationalarchives.gov.uk/doc/open-government-licence; Figures 11.11, 13.7 Copyright © 2012 The Virtual Learning Materials Workshop, Courtesy of Virtual Learning Materials Workshop; Figure 11.12 from *Strategic Management*, 6th ed., Financial Times Prentice Hall (Lynch, R. 2012) p.464, Pearson Education Ltd; Figure 11.13 from *Industrial Organization: Theory and Practice*, 2nd ed., Oxford University Press (Woodward, J. 1980) p.128, by permission of Oxford University Press; Figure 11.14 from Reed Business Information, Copyright © Reed Business Information Ltd., reprinted with permission; Figure 11.15 from Gray, *Organizational Behavior: Concepts and Applications*, 4th ed. © 1988. Reprinted and Electronically reproduced by permission from Pearson Education Inc. New York; Figure 13.3 from *Organization: Contemporary Principles and Practice*, Blackwell Publishing (Child, J. 2005) p.121 © 2005 by John Child, Reproduced with permission of Blackwell Pub in the format Republish in a book via Copyright Clearance Center; Figure 13.4 reprinted with the permission of The Free Press, a Division of Simon & Schuster, Inc., from *A Comparative Analysis of Complex Organizations: On Power, Involvement, and Their Correlates*, Revised and Enlarged Edition by Amitai Etzoni. Copyright © 1975 by Amitai Etzoni; copyright renewed © 2003 Amitai Etzoni. All rights reserved; Figure 14.2 from *Organisational Behaviour and Analysis*, 4th ed., Financial Times Prentice Hall (Rollinson, D. 2008) p.56, Pearson Education Ltd; Figure 15.1 from *Organizational Change*, 4th ed., Financial Times Prentice Hall (Senior, B. and Swailes, S. 2010) p.161, Pearson Education Ltd; Figure 15.2 from *Organisational Behaviour and Analysis: An Integrated Approach*, 4th ed., Financial Times Prentice Hall (Rollinson, D. 2008) p.592, Pearson Education Ltd; Figure 15.3 from *Exploring Strategy*, 10th ed., Pearson Education Ltd. (Johnson, G., Whittington, R., Scholes, K., Angwin, D. and Regner, P. 2014) p.156; Figure 15.4 from *The Cultural Imperative: Global Trends in the 21st Century*, Nicholas Brealey (Lewis, R.D. 2007) © 2003 Richard Lewis. Reproduced by permission of Nicholas Brealey Publishing; Figure 16.3 from *Managing*, Financial Times Prentice Hall (Mintzberg, H. 2009) p.197, Reproduced by permission of Henry Mintzberg; Figure 16.6 from Get Engaged, *Management Today*, April, p.40 (De Vita, E. 2007), Reproduced from

Management Today magazine with the permission of the copyright owner, Haymarket Business Publications Limited; Figure 16.8 from Investors in People © Investors in People - UK Commission for Employment and Skills 2015, www.investorsinpeople.co.uk; Figure 16.9 from EFQM Excellence Model, Copyright © 2012 EFQM. The EFQM Excellence Model is a registered trademark of the EFQM. Reproduced with permission; Figure 16.10 from *Organizational Capabilities Matter* © 2012, The Boston Consulting Group (BCG).

Tables

Table 3.1 adapted from Gray, *Organizational Behavior: Concepts and Applications*, 4th Ed. © 1988. Reprinted and Electronically reproduced by permission from Pearson Education, Inc., New York; Table 4.3 adapted from *Identity and the Life Cycle*, Norton (Erikson, E.H. 1980) worksheet table appendix, Copyright © 1980 by W. W. Norton & Company, Inc. Copyright © 1959 by International Universities Press, Inc. Reproduced with permission from W. W. Norton & Company, Inc; Table 4.4 from Feeling and Smiling, *The Psychologist* vol.12, no.1, January, pp.16–19 (Briner, R. 1999), Reproduced with permission from the British Psychological Society; Table 5.1 from The Debate Starts Here, *People Management in Perspective: A Collection of Key Articles Published in the Last Year on Training and Development*, IPD (April 1999), 16–17 (Burgoyne, J., Cunningham, I., Garratt, B., Honey, P., Mayo, A., Mumford, A., Pearn, M., Pedler, M.), reproduced with permission from Peter Honey; Table 8.1 from Belbin © 2015 www.belbin.com; Table 11.1 from *The Analysis of Organizations*, 2nd ed., John Wiley & Sons (Litterer, J. A. 1973) p.339, Reproduced with permission from the estate of Joseph A. Litterer.

Text

Extract on page 10 from *In Praise of Idleness: And Other Essays*, Russell, B. Copyright © 1996 The Betrand Russell Peace Foundation, Routledge Classics Edition pub 2005, reproduced by permission of Taylor & Francis Books UK; Extract on page 14 from *Engaging for Success: Enhancing Performance Through Employee Engagement*, A Report to Government, Department for Business, Innovation and Skills (Macleod, D. and Clarke, N. 2009), © Crown copyright. Contains public sector information licensed under the Open Government Licence (OGL) v3.0. http://www.nationalarchives.gov.uk/doc/open-government-licence/version/3/; Extract on page 15 from *Parkinson's Law*, John Murray Press (Parkinson, C.N. 1958), © C. Northcote Parkinson 1958. Reproduced by permission of John Murray Press, a division of Hodder and Stoughton Limited; Case Study on pages 19–20 from Rachael Jackson, Fred Olsen Cruise Lines; Extract on pages 43–44 from *The End of Management and the Rise of Organizational Democracy*, Jossey-Bass (Cloke, K. and Goldsmith, J. 2002) pp.92–94, Copyright © 2002 by John Wiley & Sons, Inc, Reproduced with permission of John Wiley & Sons, Inc. in the format Republish in a book via Copyright Clearance Center; Case Study on pages 50–51 from Vanguard Consulting Limited, reproduced with permission, http://vanguard-method/net; Exercise on pages 62–63 adapted from DuBrin, Andrew J., *Human Relations: A Job Oriented Approach*, 1st Ed. © 1978. Reprinted and Electronically reproduced by permission of Pearson Education, Inc.,

New York; Case Study on pages 88–89 kindly provided by Hugo Misselhorn, M.O.D. Consulting, South Africa; Extract on page 107 from Virtual worlds as digital workplaces: Conceptualizing the affordances of virtual worlds to expand the social and professional spheres in organizations, *Organizational Psychology Review*, vol. 4. no. 2, pp.175–95 (Koles, B. and Nagy, P. 2014), http://opr.sagepub.com/content/4/2/175. abstract, Copyright © 2014 by Sage Publications. Reprinted by permission of SAGE Publications; Case Study on pages 138–139 from Lloyds Banking Group Diversity and Inclusion Team; Exhibit on pages 139–40 from Office for National Statistics, Source: Office for National Statistics licensed under the Open Government Licence v.3.0; Exhibit on page 167 from Talent Management Team, Lloyds Banking Group, December 2014, reproduced with permission from Dorrie Dowling; Case Study on pages 167–68 from Dan Robertson; Extract on page 173 from Friends in high places, *Management Today*, October, p.50 (Garrett, A. 2012), http://www.managementtoday .co.uk/news/1150343/Friends-high-places/, reproduced with permission; Case Study on page 187 from *Diversity Resource Handbook* (Portsmouth Hospitals NHS Trust 2013) November, reproduced with permission; Extract on pages 199–200 from *Going Dutch in Beijing: The International Guide to Doing the Right Thing* by Mark McCrum. Copyright © 2008 by Mark McCrum. Reproduced by permission of Profile Books and Used by permission of Henry Holt and Company, LLC. All rights reserved; Case Study on page 226 from *The Happy Manifesto: Make Your Organisation a Great Workplace – Now!* by Stewart Henry. Reproduced with permission of Kogan Page in the format Book via Copyright Clearance Center; Extract on page 261 from Visible tattoos in the service sector: A new challenge to recruitment and selection *Work, Employment and Society*, Vol.29, No. 1, pp.60–78 (Timming, A.R. 2015), http://wes .sagepub.com/content/early/2014/07/30/0950017014528402, Copyright © 2015 by Sage Publications. Reprinted by permission of SAGE Publications; Quote on pages 277–78 from *Kaizen Strategies for Winning Through People*, Financial Times Prentice Hall (Cane, S. 1996) p.131, Pearson Education Ltd; Case Study on page 287 from Remote control – how to manage homeworkers – Take-home lessons: Tips from remote workers and their bosses, *Management Today*, 1 March, p.49 (Kennett, M 2011), http://www.managementtoday.co.uk/features/1055794/Remote-control-manage-homeworkers/, reproduced with permission; Extract on page 317 from Debate: The changing face of the leader, *Management Today*, 3 June (Nair, L. 2013), http://www.managementtoday.co.uk/features/1182986/debate-changing-face-leader/, reproduced with permission; Extract on pages 326–27 from *Leadership in Organizations*, 6th ed., Pearson Education (Yukl, G. 2006) © 2006. Reprinted and electronically reproduced by permission of Pearson Education, Inc., New York; Case Study on pages 337–38 from Aidan Alston, Talent and Diversity Manager, Post Office Ltd; Extract on pages 359–60 reproduced from *Management Today*, March, 2012, p.52, with the permission of the copyright owner, Haymarket Media Group Limited; Case Study on page 361 from Fareham Borough Council; Case Study on pages 383–84 from http://www.ukrd.com/news/latest-ukrd-news/629214/double-2012-sunday-times-success-for-ukrd-group/, Reprinted with permission of UKRD Group Limited; Extract on page 386 from Are Good Citizens Good Transformational Leaders as Well? An Employee-Centric Perspective on Transformational Leadership, *Group & Organization Management*, vol.40, no. 1, pp. 62–87 (Marinova, S., Van Dyne, L. and Moon, H. 2015), doi: 10.1177/1059601114561257, copyright © 2015, Sage Publications. Reprinted by permission of SAGE Publications; Extract on pages 389–90 from Shaping the Future, *The Guardian*, 06/10/2004 (Vidal, J.), Copyright Guardian News &

Media Ltd. 2015; Extract on page 397 from Whose Side Are You On?, *Professional Manager*, November,1997, p.3 (Rawson, M.), Reprinted by permission of CMI, Copyright © CMI. All rights reserved; Case Study on pages 410–411 from Investors in People content provided by the UK Commission for Employment and Skills www.investorsinpeople.co.uk © investors in People – UK Commission for Employment and Skills 2013; Case Study on pages 450–451 from The Enemy Within: Negotiating on Monitoring and Surveillance, *Workplace Report*, no. 97, December pp.15–16 (Labour Research Department 2011); Extract on pages 461–63 from *EBEAM: Evaluating the Benefits of Electronic Assessment Management* (Ellis, C. and Reynolds, C. 2013) http://jiscdesignstudio.pbworks.com/w/file/fetch/66830875/EBEAM%20Project%20report.pdf, with permission from Professor Cath Ellis; Extract on pages 497–98 from Osland, Joyce S.; Kolb, David A.; Rubin, Irwin M. *Organizational Behavior: An Experiential Approach*, 7th ed., © 2001. Reprinted and Electronically reproduced by permission of Pearson Education, Inc., New York; Extract on page 507 from www.dontyoubelieveitblog.com, Reproduced with permission of Alastair Dryburgh, leading contrarian consultant and author of Everything You Know About Business is Wong, www.dontyoubelieveitblog.com, originally published in Management Today; Extract on page 509 from The John Lewis Partnership, www.johnlewispartnership.co.uk; Case Study on page 514 from CSR is Good for Brands, *Management Today*, May 2011, p.69 (McWilliam, G. 2011), reproduced from Management Today with the permission of the copyright owner, Haymarket Media Group Limited; Extract on pages 515–16 from United Nations Global Compact, https://www.unglobalcompact.org/news/381-09-05-2013; Extract on pages 530–31 from *Head and Heart of Leadership*, Reach Publishers, SA (Misselhorn, A. 2012) p.86, Reproduced with permission; Case Study on page 549 from Paola Fonseca, Manager at TMF Costa Rica, case was published originally in ICSA Global Outlook, a supplement to the May 2011 issue of Chartered Secretary magazine, with permission from Governance + Compliance Magazine, www. icsa.org.uk; Exhibit on page 551 from Creating a Positive Organizational Climate in a Negative Economic One, *Forum Corporation* (Atkinson, T. and Frechette, H.), www.trainingindustry.com/media, accessed 8 October 2011, Forum Corporation; Case Study on pages 555–56 from '*MANAGEMENT 2020*', *Commission on The Future of Management and Leadership* Chartered Management Institute, July 2014 (Green, H.) p.33, www.managers.org.uk/management2020, reproduced with permission from the Chartered Management Insitute; Extract on page 560 from Implementing an Effective Change Programme, *Management Checklist 040*, Chartered Management Institute, September 2014, Available via ManagementDirect – see http://www.managers.org.uk/getmanagementdirect; Extract on pages 562–63 adapted from Material in this section reproduced with kind permission of Anne Riches, creator of The Almond Effect® and author of CLUES:Tips, strategies and examples for change leaders. (For further information see www. AnneRiches.com); Extract on pages 563–564 from *Management Challenges for the 21st Century* (Drucker, P.F. 1999) p.73, Copyright © 1999 Butterworth-Heinemann, reproduced by permission of Taylor & Francis Books UK; Extract on page 581 from Rosemary Stewart, *Managers and Their Jobs*, published 1988, Macmillan, p.123 reproduced with permission of Palgrave Macmillan; Case Study on page 591 from Investors In People content provided by the UK Commission for Employment and Skills www.investorsinpeople.co.uk, Reproduced with permission, Investors in People; Extract on page 592 from EFQM, reproduced with permission from EFQM; Case Study on page 596 from Investors in People content provided by the UK Commission for Employment and Skills, www.investorsinpeople.co.uk, Reproduced with permission, Investors in People; Extract on page 607 from Efficacy, Moral Meaningfulness, and Moral Courage: A Quasi-experimental Study, *Journal of Business Ethics*, no.124, pp. 67–80 (May, D.R., Luth, M.T. and Schwoerer, C.E. 2014) © Springer Science+Business Media Dordrecht 2013. With permission of Springer; Extract on pages 609–10 from Flexible working boosted my business, *Telegraph*, 27/06/2014 (Timpson, J.), http://www.telegraph.co.uk/finance/businessclub/management-advice/10930476/John-Timpson-In-25-years-I-want-to-say-HS2-was-a-good-idea.html, copyright © Telegraph Media Group Limited 2014; Extract on pages 610–11 from Timpson has key to giving ex-convicts a second chance, *Telegraph*, 22/08/2013 (Osborne, A.), http://www.telegraph.co.uk/finance/newsbysector/retailandconsumer/10266250/Timpson-has-key-to-giving-ex-convicts-second-chance.html, copyright © Telegraph Media Group Limited 2013; Exercise on pages 614–15 reproduced with permission from Hugo Misselhorn, M.O.D. Consulting. August 2014.

Photographs

(Key: b-bottom; c-centre; l-left; r-right; t-top)

29 Press Association Images: Michael Stephens (r); Franka Bruns (l). 64 Getty Images: Bloomberg via Getty Images. 104 Press Association Images: AP Photo / H.O. 109 Magnum Photos Ltd: © Steve McCurry / Magnum Photos. 115 Fotolia.com: BillionPhotos.com (tc). 176 Alamy Images: Caroline Penn. 215 Getty Images: David Samuel Robbins. 257 Photofusion Picture Library: Paul Ridsdale. 263 Press Association Images: Adrian Wyld. 265 Press Association Images: Seth Wenig. 266 Press Association Images: Jean / Empics Entertainment. 269 Shutterstock.com: jugulator (tc). 306 Shutterstock.com: Graham Taylor. 344 Shutterstock.com: Tupungato. 383 UKRD Group Limited. 394 Shutterstock.com: amasterphotographer (tc). 431 Courtesy of Waitrose Ltd. 461 Shutterstock.com: Igor Normann. 499 Getty Images: John MacDougall / AFP / Getty Images. 532 Alamy Images: Simon Rawles. 567 Getty Images: Marco Luzzani / Stringer. 603 Co-operative. 609 Alamy Images: © Andrew Paterson. 1,2,34,69 Pearson Education Ltd: violetkaipa (1/tc)
Cover images: *Front:* Getty Images: Mike Kiev

PART 1
The organisational setting

CHAPTER 1
Understanding organisational behaviour

In an increasingly global and competitive business environment, particular attention must be given to organisational effectiveness. It is people who are the organisation. It is important to recognise the main influences on behaviour in work organisations, the effective management of the human resource and the nature of the people–organisation relationship.

Learning outcomes

After completing this chapter you should have enhanced your ability to:

- explain the nature and main features of organisational behaviour;
- detail contrasting perspectives on orientations to work and the work ethic;
- evaluate the nature and importance of the psychological contract;
- explain the relevance of the Peter Principle and Parkinson's Law;
- outline the importance of management as an integrating activity;
- assess the impact of globalisation and the international context;
- debate the significance of culture for organisational behaviour.

Critical review and reflection

Although a commonly used term, organisational behaviour is a misnomer. Rarely do all members act collectively in such a way as to represent the behaviour of the organisation as a whole. In practice, we are talking about the attitudes and actions of individuals or small groups within the organisation.

What do YOU see as the significance of this comment? What term would YOU suggest best explains the subject area of organisational behaviour?

The significance of organisational behaviour

A major report from the Chartered Management Institute (CMI) on the state of UK management and leadership points out that the UK lags behind its competitors in terms of productivity and management practice and reminds us that: 'At its heart, the art of management is the art of managing people.'

> *But, worryingly, this is where British managers fall down most. We need a change in attitude in the UK, whereby management is seen as a highly professional role where integrity is seen as a virtue, and where ethics are valued as highly as profitability.*[1]

Increasing recognition is given to the demand not only for technical skills alone, but also for good people skills as a basis of organisational effectiveness. The importance of skills including understanding human behaviour and interpersonal skills is a wide and frequent source of attention, including government agencies such as The UK Commission for Employment and Skills (UKCES), The Department of Business Innovation & Skills, and other bodies such as the Prince's Trust, the Advisory, Conciliation and Arbitration Service (ACAS) and professional institutes. Against this backdrop the study of organisational behaviour can be seen of even greater significance.

> *Organisational Behaviour is one of the most complex and perhaps least understood academic elements of modern general management, but since it concerns the behaviour of people within organisations it is also one of the most central . . . its concern with individual and group patterns of behaviour makes it an essential element in dealing with the complex behavioural issues thrown up in the modern business world.*[2]

Vecchio suggests three reasons for studying organisational behaviour:

- **Important practical applications** that follow from an understanding and knowledge of organisational behaviour and the ability to deal effectively with others in an organisational setting.
- **Personal growth** and the fulfilment gained from understanding our fellow humans. Understanding others may also lead to greater self-knowledge and self-insight.
- **Increased knowledge** about people in work settings, for example the identification of major dimensions of leadership leading to the design leadership training programmes in organisations.[3]

At its most basic level, **organisational behaviour** (OB) is concerned with the study of the behaviour of people within an organisational setting. It involves the understanding, prediction and control of human behaviour. Common definitions of organisational behaviour are generally along the lines of: **the study and understanding of individual and group behaviour and patterns of structure in order to help improve organisational performance and effectiveness.**

However much of a cliché, the inescapable fact is that people are the main resource of any organisation. Without its members, an organisation is nothing; an organisation is only as good as the people who work within it. In today's increasingly dynamic, global and competitive environment, understanding human behaviour at work and effective management of the people resource are even more important for organisational survival and success.

A managerial approach

There is a multiplicity of interrelated factors that influence the decisions and actions of people as members of a work organisation. The scope for the examination of organisational behaviour is therefore very wide. It has always been a feature of this book to acknowledge that while the role, responsibilities and actions of management are, of course, subject to debate, what cannot be denied is the growing importance of effective management, however it is perceived, to the successful performance of work organisations. Clearly, organisational behaviour does not encompass the whole of management. Equally clearly, however, there is a close relationship between organisational behaviour and management theory and practice. Some writers still appear critical of a managerial approach to organisational behaviour. What is also apparent, however, is that in recent years a number of books on organisational behaviour have paid increasing attention to aspects of management and managerial behaviour.

Critical review and reflection

The best way to appreciate the nature and applied skills of organisational behaviour is when study of the subject area is related to an understanding of the importance of management to effective work organisations.

To what extent do YOU support this contention? Do YOU believe a managerial approach is an aid to YOUR future career ambitions?

A multidisciplinary perspective

The bottom line is that sooner or later every organisation has to perform successfully if it is to survive. In order to study the behaviour of people at work it is necessary to understand inter-relationships with other variables that together comprise the total organisation. Whatever the approach, the study of organisational behaviour cannot be undertaken entirely in terms of a single discipline. It is necessary to recognise the influences of a multidisciplinary, behavioural science perspective.

Although there are areas of overlap among the various social sciences and related disciplines such as economics and political science, the study of human behaviour can be viewed in terms of three main disciplines – **psychology, sociology** and **anthropology.** All three disciplines have made an important contribution to the field of organisational behaviour (*see* Figure 1.1).

A **psychological** approach has its main emphasis on the individuals of which the organisation is comprised. The main focus of attention is on the individual as a whole person, or what can be termed the 'personality system', including, for example, perception, attitudes and motives. Psychological aspects are important but by themselves provide too narrow an approach for the understanding of management and organisational behaviour. Our main concern is not with the complex detail of individual differences and attributes per se, but with the behaviour and management of people within an organisational setting.

A **sociological** approach has a broader emphasis on human behaviour in society. Sociological aspects can be important. The main focus of attention is on the analysis of social structures and positions in those structures – for example, the relationship between the behaviour of leaders and followers. A number of sociology writers seem set on the purpose of criticising traditional views of organisation and management. Many of the criticisms and limitations to which such writers refer are justified and help promote healthy academic debate. However, much of the argument tends to be presented in the abstract and is lacking in constructive ideas on how, in practical terms, action can be taken to improve organisational performance.

Anthropologists are more concerned with the science of humankind and the study of human behaviour as a whole. As far as organisational behaviour is concerned, the main focus of attention is on the cultural system, the beliefs, customs, ideas and values within a group or society, and the comparison of behaviour among different cultures – for example, the importance to Muslim women of wearing trousers to work. People learn to depend on their culture to give them security and stability and they can suffer adverse reactions to unfamiliar environments.

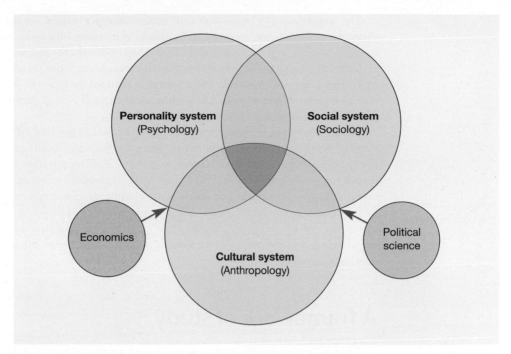

Figure 1.1 Organisational behaviour: a multidisciplinary approach

The contribution of relevant aspects of psychology, sociology and anthropology underpins the field of organisational behaviour. In terms of the applications of behavioural science to the management of people, we need also to consider the relevance and applications of philosophy, ethics and the law.

Interrelated influences on behaviour

This multidisciplinary perspective provides contrasting but related approaches to the understanding of human behaviour in organisations and presents a number of alternative pathways and levels of analysis. For our purposes, the study of organisational behaviour embraces broad parameters within which a number of interrelated dimensions can be identified – the individual, the group, the organisation and the environment – which collectively influence behaviour in work organisations.

The individual – organisations are made up of their individual members. The individual is a central feature of organisational behaviour, whether acting in isolation or as part of a group, in response to expectations of the organisation, or as a result of the influences of the external environment. Where the needs of the individual and the demands of the organisation are incompatible, this can result in frustration and conflict. It is the role of management to integrate the individual and the organisation and to provide a working environment that permits the satisfaction of individual needs as well as the attainment of organisational goals.

The group – groups exist in all organisations and are essential to their working and performance. The organisation comprises groups of people, and almost everyone in an organisation will be a member of one or more groups. Informal groups arise from the social needs of people within the organisation. People in groups influence each other in many ways and groups may develop their own hierarchies and leaders. Group pressures can have a major influence over the behaviour and performance of individual members. An understanding of group structure and behaviour complements knowledge of individual behaviour and adds a further dimension to the study of organisational behaviour.

The organisation – individuals and groups interact within the structure of the formal organisation. Structure is created to establish relationships between individuals and groups, to provide order and systems and to direct the efforts of the organisation into goal-seeking activities. It is through the formal structure that people carry out their organisational activities to achieve aims and objectives. Behaviour is influenced by patterns of structure, technology, styles of leadership and systems of management through which organisational processes are planned, directed and monitored.

The environment – applications of organisational behaviour and the effective management of people at work take place in the context of the wider environmental setting, including the changing patterns of organisations and work. The organisation functions as part of the broader external environment, which affects the organisation through, for example, internationalisation, technological and scientific development, economic activity, social and cultural influences, governmental actions, and corporate responsibility and ethical behaviour. The increasing rate of change in environmental factors has highlighted the need to study the total organisation and the processes by which the organisation attempts to adapt to the external demands placed upon it.

A framework of study

The use of separate topic areas is a recognised academic means of aiding study and explanation of the subject. In practice, however, the activities of an organisation and the role of management cannot be isolated neatly into discrete categories. The majority of actions are likely to involve a number of simultaneous functions that relate to the total processes within an organisation. Consider, for example, a manager briefing departmental staff on a major unexpected, important and urgent task. Such a briefing is likely to include consideration of goals and objectives, organisation and role structures, management systems, known problem areas, forms of communications, delegation and empowerment, teamwork, leadership style, motivation and control systems. The behaviour of the staff will be influenced by a combination of individual, group, organisational and environmental factors.

Topics studied in organisational behaviour should not be regarded, therefore, as entirely free-standing. Any study inevitably covers several aspects and is used to a greater or lesser extent to confirm generalisations made about particular topic areas. Reference to the same studies to illustrate different aspects of management and organisational behaviour serves as useful revision and reinforcement and provides a more integrated approach to your study.

In order to study the behaviour of people at work it is necessary to understand interrelationships with other variables that together comprise the total organisation. As has been said before, the bottom line is that sooner or later every organisation has to perform successfully if it is to survive. (**Organisational performance and effectiveness are discussed in Chapter 16.**)

The study of organisational behaviour embraces, therefore, an understanding of the interactions among:

- the nature and purpose of the organisation, its aims and objectives;
- formal structure and role relationships;
- the tasks to be undertaken and technology employed;
- organisational processes and the execution of work;
- the human element, informal organisation and behaviour of people;
- the process of management as an integrating and co-ordinating activity;
- social responsibilities and business ethics;
- the external environment of which the organisation is part; and
- the need for organisation success and survival.

This provides us with a basic, but convenient, framework of study (*see* Figure 1.2).

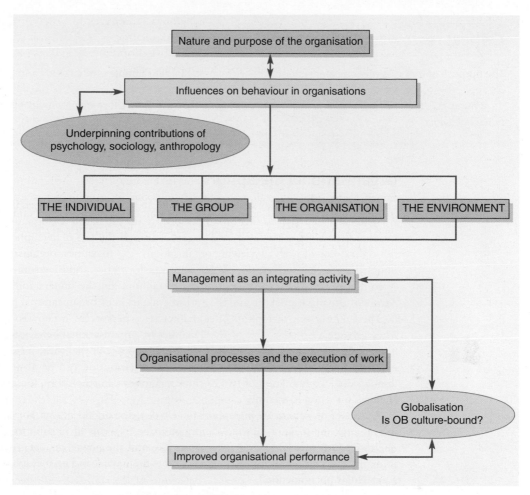

Figure 1.2 Organisational behaviour (OB): a basic framework of study

Relevance of theory

You should not be put off by the use of the word 'theory' in your studies. Most rational decisions are based on some form of theory. Theory provides a sound basis for action and contains a message on how managers might behave. This will influence attitudes towards management practice and lead to changes in actual patterns of behaviour. It further provides a conceptual framework and gives a perspective for the practical study of the subject. Together they lead to a better understanding of factors influencing patterns of behaviour in work organisations and applications of the process of management.[4] As *McGregor* expresses it:

> *Every managerial act rests on assumptions, generalizations, and hypotheses – that is to say, on theory. Our assumptions are frequently implicit, sometimes quite unconscious, often conflicting; nevertheless, they determine our predictions that if we do a, b will occur. Theory and practice are inseparable.[5]*

Patching suggests that all managers who think about what they do are practical students of organisational theory:

> *Theory is not something unique to academics, but something we all work with in arriving at our attitudes, beliefs and decisions as managers. It seems obvious to most of us that some theories are better than others. Many managerial discussions which we undertake in meetings focus upon trying to agree upon which theory will be best for a particular decision.[6]*

Critical review and reflection

The purpose of theory is often misunderstood. Theory helps in building a framework of study and generalised models applicable to a range of different organisations or situations.

What is YOUR view? How does a knowledge of underlying theory help YOUR study of management and organisational behaviour?

Organisational metaphors

Organisations are complex social systems that can be defined and studied in a number of ways. A significant approach to this broad perspective on the nature of organisations and organisational behaviour is provided by *Morgan*. Through the use of metaphors, Morgan identifies eight different ways of viewing organisations – as machines, organisms, brains, cultures, political systems, psychic prisons, flux and transformation, and instruments of domination. According to Morgan, these contrasting metaphors aid the understanding of the complex nature of organisational life and the critical evaluation of organisational phenomena.[7]

These contrasting metaphors offer an interesting perspective on how to view organisations. They provide a broader view of the dynamics of organisational behaviour and how to manage and design organisations. However, Morgan points out that these metaphors are not fixed categories and are not mutually exclusive. An organisation can be a mix of each and predominantly a combination of two or three metaphors. Furthermore, these combinations may change over a period of time.

A number of writers use metaphors to help describe organisations. For example, in discussing the role and logic of viewing the organisation in terms of metaphors, *Drummond* raises questions such as what an organisation is like and the power of metaphors in shaping our thinking, but also points out that all metaphors are partial and no metaphor can explain fully a particular phenomenon.[8]

Realities of organisational behaviour

However one looks at the nature or disciplines of organisational behaviour it is important to remember, as *Morgan* points out, 'the reality of organisational life usually comprises numerous different realities!'[9]

Hellriegel et al. suggest:

> One way to recognise why people behave as they do at work is to view an organisation as an iceberg. What sinks ships isn't always what sailors can see, but what they can't see.[10]

The overt, formal aspects focus only on the tip of the iceberg (organisation). It is just as important to focus on what you can't see – the covert, behavioural aspects (*see* Figure 1.3).

Egan refers to the importance of the shadow side of the organisation: that is, those things not found on organisation charts or in company manuals – the covert, and often undiscussed, activities of people, which affect both the productivity and quality of the working life of an organisation.[11] As *Howes* points out, the fiercest battles of the workplace may seem trivial yet they are nothing of the sort. Underlying and unresolved disputes can brew animosity and resentment, and halt production.

> Forget disagreements over strategies or policy – many of the bitterest workplace battles are fought over the prosaic matters of air conditioning and in-office music.[12]

Watson reminds us that the biggest challenge we face when trying to analyse or to manage organisations is that they do not actually exist.

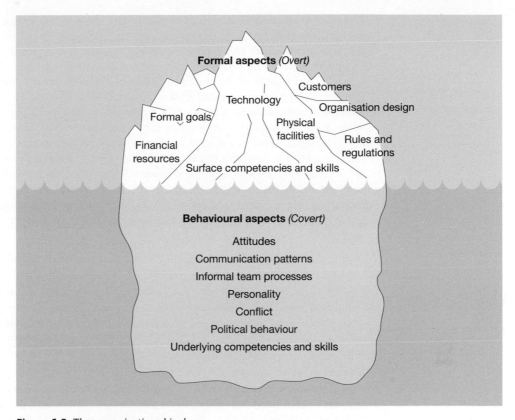

Figure 1.3 The organisational iceberg

Source: From Hellriegel, D., Slocum, J. W., Jr. and Woodman, R. W. *Management*, eighth edition, South-Western Publishing (1998), p. 6. Reproduced by permission.

The organisation in which you work or study is not something you can see, hear, touch, smell, kick, kiss or throw up in the air. And this is not just because you might be a relatively junior member of that organisation. The top managers of the organisation are no more capable than you are of relating to the organisation as if it existed in a straightforward way. This, in fact, is one of the most fascinating aspects of organisational and managerial work – and its essential ambiguity.[13]

Looking outside organisations

Wilson suggests that the meaning of the term 'organisational behaviour' is far from clear. She challenges what constitutes organisational behaviour and questions whether we should be interested only in behaviour that happens within organisations. There is a reciprocal relationship in what happens within and outside organisations. Wilson suggests that we also look outside of what are normally thought of as organisations and how we usually think of work. We can also gain insight into organisational life and behaviour by looking at what happens in rest and play, considering emotion and feeling, considering the context in which work is defined as men's or women's work and looking at less organised work – for example, work on the fiddle and the meaning of work for the unemployed.[14] These suggestions arguably add an extra dimension to the meaning and understanding of organisational behaviour.

What is work?

In a classic 1932 essay 'In Praise of Idleness', *Bertrand Russell* puts forward an interesting view that the road to happiness and prosperity lies in an organised diminution of work.

First of all: what is work? Work is of two kinds: first, altering the position of matter at or near the earth's surface relatively to other such matter; second, telling other people to do so. The first kind is unpleasant and ill paid; the second is pleasant and highly paid. The second kind is capable of indefinite extension: there are not only those who give orders, but those who give advice as to what orders should be given. Usually two opposite kinds of advice are given simultaneously by two organised bodies of men, this is called politics. The skill required for this kind of work is not knowledge of the subjects as to which advice is given, but knowledge of the art of persuasive speaking and writing, i.e. of advertising. Throughout Europe, though not in America, there is a third class of men, more respected than either of the classes of workers, there are men who, through ownership of land, are able to make others pay for the privilege of being allowed to exist and to work. These landowners are idle, and I might therefore be expected to praise them. Unfortunately their idleness is only rendered possible by the industry of others; indeed their desire for comfortable idleness is historically the source of the whole gospel of work. The last thing they have ever wished is that others should follow their example.[15]

Whatever your view of this essay, what is clear is how the nature of work itself has changed over the past eighty years. From work primarily as a wage and means of survival to the growth and power of trade unions, an emphasis on manufacturing and apprenticeship with repetitive mundane work, few professionally qualified managers and the development of business schools, labour disputes, discord and mass industrial relations, broadening work horizons but times of uncertainty, rapid pace of change, working longer and harder, more flexible working, and the impact of information technology.[16]

Donkin, however, maintains that for most citizens everywhere work remains about earning a living and not much else.[17] For most people today, work in one form or another is clearly a major part of their lives, and many people spend a large proportion of their time working.

Orientations to work and the work ethic

People differ in the manner and extent of their involvement with, and concern for, work. From information collected about the work situation, organisational participation and involvement with work colleagues, and life outside the organisation, *Goldthorpe et al.* identified three main types of orientation to work: instrumental, bureaucratic and solidaristic.[18]

- Individuals with an **instrumental orientation** define work not as a central life issue but in terms of a means to an end. There is a calculative or economic involvement with work and a clear distinction between work-related and non-work-related activities.

- Individuals with a **bureaucratic orientation** define work as a central life issue. There is a sense of obligation to the work of the organisation and a positive involvement in terms of a career structure. There is a close link between work-related and non-work-related activities.

- Individuals with a **solidaristic orientation** define the work situation in terms of group activities. There is an ego involvement with work groups rather than with the organisation itself. Work is more than just a means to an end. Non-work activities are linked to work relationships.

Opportunities and choices

According to *Bunting,* although some people in poorly paid jobs requiring long hours do not have other options, for the majority there is a degree of choice in how hard they work. People make their own choices. If they want to work hard, or if they wish to opt out and live the good life, it is up to them.[19] As the number of baby-boomers (born between 1946 and 1963 and typified by a search for security) declines and the proportion of Generation Y (born between 1980 and 1995 and typified by travel first, then a career) increases, this will have a further impact on the future world of work.[20] (**See also a fuller discussion in Chapter 3.**)

Some people may well have a set motivation to work, whatever the nature of the work environment. However, different work situations may also influence the individual's orientation to work. For example, the lack of opportunities for teamwork and the satisfaction of social expectations may result in an instrumental orientation to work and a primary concern for economic interests such as pay and security. In other situations where there are greater opportunities to satisfy social needs, membership of work groups may be very important and individuals may have a more solidaristic orientation to work. This often appears to be the case, for example, with people working in the hospitality industry.

A sense of identity

Work can help fulfil a number of purposes including providing the individual with a sense of identity. Many people see themselves primarily in terms of their career and what they do at work. It defines who they are. *Waller* suggests that work inevitably plays a key role in shaping identity, and at least there you are challenging yourself, developing and learning.

> *In the knowledge economy, where responsibilities morph and working hours are flexible, the boundaries between work and free time blur, and it's hard for many of us to tell when we're off-duty. It follows that if people are getting absorbed by their work-life, they expect their job to help them to discover and develop themselves. Identity can be linked to such basics as the satisfaction of a job well done – yet in a modern economy, work is rarely actually 'finished'.[21]*

For some people who do not necessarily have any financial motivation, work appears to provide a sense of purpose and a structure to their day. It is often even explained as 'a reason to get up in the morning'.

Cultural influences

National culture is also a significant influence on orientations to work. For example, *Reeves* comments on the importance of conversation for effective organisational relationships but how this is resisted in the UK work culture.

> *The Protestant version of the work ethic prevails, implying heads-down work, focused agendas, punctuality, efficiency. In French and Spanish offices, it takes the first hour to kiss everyone, the second to discuss local gossip and the third to pop out for a coffee and croissant. In Britain, these activities would count as sexual harassment, time-wasting and absenteeism. Many firms have built cafés or break out areas and then discovered people are too scared to use them for fear of looking work-shy.[22]*

McCrum refers to a key division in the international world as that between those who live to work and those who work to live.

> *The American appetite for putting work first, even to the extent of giving up weekends, will not be understood in much of mainland Europe or Latin America. Here, regular time off is regarded as essential for family and friends and a go-getting 'familiarisation weekend' would be particularly unwelcome. In the East, of course, the Japanese take their work just as seriously as the Americans.[23]* **(Work/life balance is discussed in Chapter 3.)**

Critical review and reflection

An individual's orientation to work and underlying work ethic is the strongest influence on his or her motivation and organisational performance. The actions of management have only minimal effect.

To what extent do YOU agree with this contention and to what extent is it true for YOU? How would YOU explain YOUR own orientation to work and the work ethic?

Social exchange theory

An important feature that underlies the behaviour and interrelationships of people at work is that of **social exchange theory**. Rooted in cultural anthropology and economics, the central premise of social exchange theory is that a fundamental feature of human interaction is the exchange of social and material resources.[24] Social behaviour is determined by an exchange process. When people enter into a relationship with some other person, there is the expectation of obtaining some kind of reward or benefit in exchange for giving something to the other person in return. Individuals will seek to achieve a positive balance for themselves by maximising the benefits and minimising the costs of such exchanges. Social exchanges are influenced by a complex web of power relationships and as a result are not always equal but have an uneven balance of outcomes.[25]

Exchanges are viewed in terms of a subjective cost–benefit analysis. Benefits and costs can be financial, material, time, social, status, emotional or opportunistic. In different relationships there will be different expectations of the content and balance of the exchange, for example between a senior manager and subordinate or between fellow team members. The level of satisfaction from the exchange will depend not just upon the actual outcomes but on the individual's expectation of likely outcomes. The perceived outcomes of a present relationship may also be viewed in consideration of both past relationships and potential future relationships. The nature of social exchanges impacts upon many other subject areas including the psychological contract, individual differences and diversity, communications, equity theory of motivation, group behaviour, leadership and management, control and power, and organisational culture.

The psychological contract

One significant aspect of organisational behaviour, which has its roots in social exchange theory and the relationship between the individual and the process of management, is the concept of the **psychological contract**. This is not a written document or part of a formal agreement but implies a series of mutual expectations and satisfaction of needs arising from the people–organisation relationship. The psychological contract covers a range of expectations of rights and privileges, duties and obligations that have an important influence on people's behaviour. It is also an important factor in the socialisation of new members of staff to the organisation. Early experiences of the people–organisation relationship have a major effect on an individual's perception of the organisation as a place to work and the quality of management, and can have a major influence on job satisfaction, attitude and levels of performance.

The nature and extent of individuals' expectations vary widely, as do the ability and willingness of the organisation to meet them. It is difficult to list the range of implicit expectations that individuals have; these expectations also change over time. They are separate from any statutory requirements placed upon the organisation; they relate more to the idea of social responsibility of management (**discussed in Chapter 14**). The organisation will also have implicit expectations of its members. The organisational side of the psychological contract places emphasis on expectations, requirements and constraints that may differ from, and may conflict with, an individual's expectations. Some possible examples of the individual's and the organisation's expectations are given in Figure 1.4.

Process of balancing

It is unlikely that all expectations of the individual or of the organisation will be met fully. There is a continual process of balancing, and explicit and implicit bargaining. The nature of these expectations is not defined formally, and although the individual member and the organisation may not be consciously aware of them, they still affect relationships between them and have an influence on behaviour. *Stalker* suggests that successful companies are those that have the ability to balance the unwritten needs of their employees with the needs of the

INDIVIDUALS' EXPECTATIONS OF THE ORGANISATION

- Provide safe and hygienic working conditions.
- Make every reasonable effort to provide job security.
- Attempt to provide challenging and satisfying jobs, and reduce alienating aspects of work.
- Adopt equitable human resource management policies and procedures.
- Respect the role of trade union officials and staff representatives.
- Consult fully with staff and allow genuine participation in decisions that affect them.
- Implement best practice in equal opportunity policies and procedures.
- Reward all staff fairly according to their contribution and performance.
- Provide reasonable opportunities for personal development and career progression.
- Treat members of staff with respect.
- Demonstrate an understanding and considerate attitude towards personal problems of staff.

ORGANISATIONAL EXPECTATIONS OF THE INDIVIDUAL

- Uphold the ideology of the organisation and the corporate image.
- Work diligently in pursuit of organisational objectives.
- Adhere to the rules, policies and procedures of the organisation.
- Respect the reasonable authority of senior members of staff.
- Do not take advantage of goodwill shown by management.
- Be responsive to leadership influence.
- Demonstrate loyalty, respect confidentiality and not betray positions of trust.
- Maintain harmonious relationships with work colleagues.
- Do not abuse organisational facilities such as email or Internet access.
- Observe reasonable and acceptable standards of dress and appearance.
- Show respect and consolidation to customers and suppliers.

Figure 1.4 The psychological contract: possible examples of individual and organisational expectations

company. Such companies use a simple formula of Caring, Communicating, Listening, Knowing, Rewarding:

- **Caring** – demonstrating genuine concern for individuals working in the organisation.
- **Communicating** – really talking about what the company is hoping to achieve.
- **Listening** – hearing not only the words but also what lies behind the words.
- **Knowing** – the individuals who work for you, their families, personal wishes, desires and ambitions.
- **Rewarding** – money is not always necessary; a genuine thank-you or public recognition can raise morale.[26]

The changing nature of organisations and individuals at work has placed increasing pressures on the awareness and importance of new psychological contracts. *Ghoshal et al.* suggest the new management philosophy needs to be grounded in a very different moral contract with people. Rather than being seen as a corporate asset from which value can be appropriated, people are seen as a responsibility and a resource to be added to. The new moral contract also demands much from employees, who need to abandon the stability of lifetime employment and embrace the concept of continuous learning and personal development.[27]

Critical review and reflection

Differences in status and power mean that the psychological contract is always balanced in favour of the organisation. Managers will expect individuals to display loyalty and commitment, and put in extra hours, effort and performance. Individuals can only hope for some commensurate fair reward now or later.

To what extent do YOU agree with this contention? How far are the expectations YOU have of the psychological contract met by YOUR university or organisation?

The nature of human behaviour in organisations

It is convenient, here, to consider two sets of observations on the nature of organisational behaviour and what may actually happen, in practice, in organisations: the Peter Principle and Parkinson's Law. Although presented in a satirical manner, these observations nevertheless make a serious and significant point about the management and functioning of organisations and the actual nature and practice of organisational behaviour.

The Peter Principle

This is concerned with the study of occupational incompetence and the study of hierarchies. The analysis of hundreds of cases of occupational incompetence led to the formulation of the **Peter Principle**, which is:

> *In a hierarchy every employee tends to rise to their level of incompetence.*[28]

Employees competent in their position are promoted and competence in each new position qualifies for promotion to the next highest position until a position of incompetence is reached. The principle is based on perceived incompetence at all levels of every hierarchy – political, legal, educational and industrial – and ways in which employees move upwards through a hierarchy and what happens to them after promotion.

Among the many examples quoted by *Peter* are those from the teaching occupation. C, a competent student, teacher and head of department, is promoted to assistant principal and being intellectually competent is further promoted to principal. C is now required to work directly with higher officials. By working so hard at running the school, however, C misses important meetings with superiors and has no energy to become involved with community organisations. C thus becomes regarded as an incompetent principal.

Means of promotion

Peter suggests two main means by which a person can affect their promotion rate, 'Pull' and 'Push':

- Pull is an employee's relationship – by blood, marriage or acquaintance – with a person above the employee in the hierarchy.
- Push is sometimes manifested by an abnormal interest in study, vocational training and self-improvement.

In small hierarchies, Push may have a marginal effect in accelerating promotion; in larger hierarchies the effect is minimal. Pull is, therefore, likely to be more effective than Push.

> *Never stand when you can sit; never walk when you can ride; never Push when you can Pull.*[29]

Parkinson's Law

A major feature of **Parkinson's Law** is that of the 'rising pyramid' – that is, 'work expands so as to fill the time available for its completion.'[30] General recognition of this is illustrated in the proverb, 'It is the busiest person who has time to spare.' There is little, if any, relationship between the quantity of work to be done and the number of staff doing it. Underlying this general tendency are two almost axiomatic statements:

- An official wants to multiply subordinates, not rivals.
- Officials make work for each other.

Parkinson goes on to give the following example. If a civil servant, *A,* believes he is over-worked, there are three possible remedies: (i) resignation; (ii) ask to halve the work by having it shared with a colleague, *B;* or (iii) seek the assistance of two subordinates, *C* and *D.* The first two options are unlikely. Resignation would involve loss of pension rights, while sharing work with a colleague on the same level would only bring in a rival for promotion. So *A* would prefer the appointment of two junior members of staff, *C* and *D.* This would increase *A*'s status. There must be at least two subordinates, so that by dividing work between *C* and *D, A* will be the only person to understand the work of them both. Furthermore, each subordinate is kept in order by fear of the other's promotion.

When, in turn, *C* complains of overwork, *A,* with the agreement of *C,* will advise the appointment of two assistants, *E* and *F.* However, as *D*'s position is much the same and, to avoid internal friction, two assistants, *G* and *H,* will also be recommended to help *D.* There are now seven people, *A, C, D, E, F, G* and *H,* doing what one person did before, and *A*'s promotion is almost certain. With the seven people now employed, the second stage comes into operation. The seven people make so much work for each other that they are all fully occupied and *A* is actually working harder than ever.

Among other features of organisational practice that Parkinson discusses are: principles of personnel selection; the nature of committees; personality screen; high finance; the 'Law of Triviality', which means (in a committee) that the time spent on any agenda item will be in inverse proportion to the sum involved; the layout of the organisation's administration block; and 'injelitis' – the disease of induced inferiority.

Relevance of observations

Despite the light vein of Parkinson's writing, the relevance of his observations can be gauged from comments in the Introduction by HRH The Duke of Edinburgh.

> The most important point about this book for serious students of management and admin-istration is that it illustrates the gulf that exists between the rational/intellectual approach to human organisation and the frequent irrational facts of human nature . . . The law should be compulsory reading at all business schools and for all management consultants. Management structures solve nothing if they do not take the facts of human nature into proper consideration, and one of the most important facts is that no one really likes having to make decisions. Consequently structures may generate a lot of activity but little or no useful work.[31]

Positive organisational behaviour

A different approach to organisational behaviour is that of positive organisational behaviour (POB), which takes a functionalist or positivist approach. In recent years increasing attention has been given to **positive psychology**, which is defined broadly as 'the scientific study of what makes life most worth living'. Although arguably originated by *Maslow* in his hierarchy of needs theory in 1954 (**see Chapter 7**), positive psychology is associated with the work of *Martin Seligman* in 1998.[32] Rather than focus on finding out what was wrong with people – the 'disease' model – positive psychology complements traditional psychology by focusing on determining how things go right and how to enhance people's satisfaction and well-being. According to *Peterson*, among the major concerns of positive psychology are:

positive experiences like happiness and engagement, positive traits like character strengths and talents, positive relationships like friendship and love, and the larger institutions like family and school that enable these.

Peterson goes on to suggest that the topic of morale can also be placed under the positive psychology umbrella. Morale is used as a cognitive, emotional and motivational stance towards the goals and tasks of a group. In the same way that life satisfaction is an indicator of individual well-being, morale is an indicator of group well-being.[33]

Applications to the work situation

To what extent can positive psychology be applied to the work organisation? *Wong and Davey* maintain that each day, in every organisation, huge amounts of valuable resources are wasted because of human problems, wrong policies or poor training. The focus of leadership needs to be shifted from process and outcome to people and the development of social/emotional/spiritual capital. However, although positive psychology can be introduced into the workplace, they question the ability of managers to apply this to employees in a meaningful way.[34]

Positive organisational behaviour is defined by *Luthans* as:

The study and application of positively oriented human resource strengths and psychological capacities that can be measured, developed and effectively managed for performance improvement in today's workplace.

This definition incorporates many existing concepts from the domains of attitudes, personality, motivation and leadership.[35]

Donaldson and Ko maintain that the primary emphasis of POB is in the workplace and the accomplishment of work-related outcomes and performance improvement. Studies of POB have been conducted at the micro- and meso-levels of analysis using survey research and tend to develop from individual to group to organisational levels of analysis. There appears to be potential to invigorate research and applications in the traditional fields of industrial psychology and organisational behaviour.[36]

POB has been subject to much critique. According to *Wright and Quick*, for example, there still exists some measure of confusion regarding just what constitutes the realm of 'positive' behaviour, and what distinguishes the positive organisational agenda from organisational behaviour in general. However, despite the sceptics and critics, Wright and Quick believe that the role of positive organisational movement will continue to grow and prosper, and gain significant attention in the applied sciences.[37]

The changing world of work organisations

Increasing business competitiveness, globalisation, shifting labour markets, rapid technological progress, the move towards more customer-driven markets, a 24/7 society and demands of work/life balance have led to a period of constant change and the need for greater organisational flexibility. The combination of these influences is transforming the way we live and work. And this clearly has significant implications for management and organisational behaviour. It is important to understand how organisations function and the pervasive influences that they exercise over the behaviour and actions of people.

The power and influence of private and public organisations, the rapid spread of new technology and the impact of various socio-economic and political factors have attracted increasing attention to the concept of corporate responsibilities and business ethics (**discussed in Chapter 14**). Increasing attention is also being focused on the ethical behaviour that underlies the decisions and actions of people at work.

A summary of the changing context of work, including topics discussed in subsequent chapters, is set out in the concept map shown in Figure 1.5.

THE CHANGING CONTEXT OF WORK

- TRADITIONAL V. EMERGENT WORK CONTEXTS
- EMPLOYEE SKILLS IN THE NEW ORGANISATION
- WORK/LIFE BALANCE
- FLEXIBLE WORKING RIGHTS

FLEXIBLE WORKING RIGHTS

Anyone can ask their employer to allow flexible working patterns, but in the UK the government has introduced a statutory right in order to encourage applications. This legal framework allows someone to request flexible working if the person:

- is an employee with 26 or more weeks' service and
- has a child under the age of six (or disabled child under 18) and
- is responsible for that child and is applying to care for that child

_or_

- is someone caring for an adult living at the same address as the employee

IF THESE CONDITIONS ARE MET, THE EMPLOYER MUST GIVE THE REQUEST "SERIOUS CONSIDERATION". EMPLOYERS CAN REFUSE ON CERTAIN "BUSINESS GROUNDS" DESCRIBED IN THE LEGISLATION

Remember – employees sometimes just need time away from work to pursue their own personal interests!

TRADITIONAL & EMERGENT WORK CONTEXTS COMPARED

Some observed differences between traditional & emergent organisations include the following:

NOTE 1: THESE ARE TENDENCIES – EXCEPTIONS CAN OFTEN BE FOUND

NOTE 2: THE NATURE OF THE ORGANISATIONS MAY DEMAND WORK (TRADITIONAL APPROACH)

CHARACTERISTIC	TRADITIONAL	EMERGENT
Organisation structure (1)	Many management layers	Few management layers
Organisation structure (2)	Hierarchical	Flexible
Career path for employees (1)	Heavily organisation influenced	Principally based on individual's own plans
Career path for employees (2)	Based in very few organisations	Based in many organisations
Employee development	Largely restricted to current job	Aimed at future as well as current job
Organisation output	Product/service based	Knowledge based
Management style (1)	More formal	More relaxed
Management style (2)	Inward-looking	More broadly based on outside society
Decisionmaking	Often hierarchical	Frequently collective
Workplace	Office location based	Field or home based

EMPLOYEE SKILLS IN THE NEW ORGANISATION

Emergent organisations tend to have fewer management positions. One implication for employees is that in addition to their own technical or professional expertise a working competency is needed in such topics as:

- **Clerical and administrative work** – because support staff are increasingly seen as an unwarranted overhead expense
- **Information & Communications Technology (ICT)** – because emerging organisations are highly dependent on new technologies
- **Advanced personal communication systems** – especially for field or embossed workers
- **'Customer-facing' skills** – because employees increasingly deal with customers/clients
- **Financial skills** – to help in understanding the business as a whole
- **Change-coping and change management capabilities** – because rapid changes in the business are a common feature

WORK/LIFE BALANCE

Early trades unions demanded that on working days a worker should have:

'Eight hours work, eight hours leisure, and eight hours sleep'

FACTORS ASSOCIATED WITH INCREASED EMPHASIS ON THE WORK SITUATION

- Deep interest in the nature of the work itself
- Income a high priority
- Employee unempowered and not confident
- Organisation norms expect attendance
- Organisation pay dictated by time attendance
- Employee has home problems and would rather be at work.

FACTORS ASSOCIATED WITH INCREASED EMPHASIS ON LIFE OUTSIDE WORK

- Formal recognition by the organisation that employees have commitments other than work (including child/elderly people care)
- Employee outputs based on results, not time attended
- Excellent organisational ICT systems, enabling easy communication with employees
- Organisation climate resulting in confident employees

Figure 1.5 The changing context of work

Source: Copyright © 2011 The Virtual Learning Materials Workshop. Reproduced with permission.

Management as an integrating activity

Whatever the individual's orientations to work, or the nature of the work organisation or cultural influences, it is through the process of management that the efforts of members of the organisation are co-ordinated, directed and guided towards the achievement of its goals. Management is the cornerstone of organisational effectiveness (*see* Figure 1.6).

It is important always to remember that it is people who are being managed, and people should be considered in human terms. Unlike physical resources, the people resource is not owned by the organisation. People bring their own perceptions, feelings and attitudes towards the organisation, systems and styles of management, their duties and responsibilities, and the conditions under which they are working. Human behaviour is capricious and scientific methods or principles of behaviour cannot be applied with reliability. It is also widely observed that you cannot study the behaviour of people without changing it. At the heart of successful management is the problem of integrating the individual and the organisation, and this requires an understanding of both human personality and work organisations.[38]

Providing the right balance

People and organisations need each other. Management is an integral part of this relationship. It is essentially an integrating activity that permeates every facet of the organisation's operations and should serve to reconcile the needs of people at work with the requirements of the organisation. Management should endeavour to create the right balance between the interrelated elements that make up the total organisation and to weld these into coherent patterns

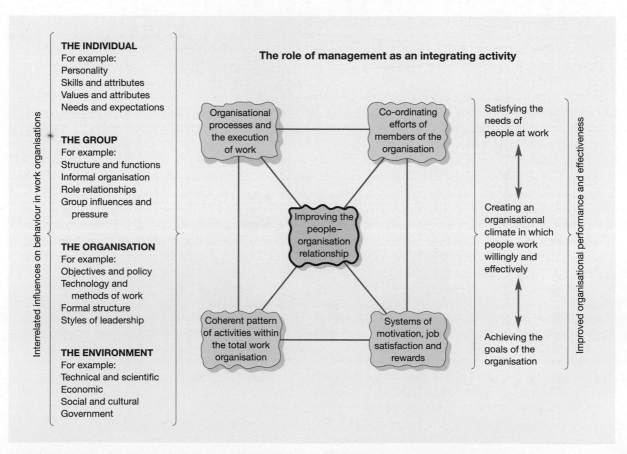

Figure 1.6 Management as the cornerstone of organisational effectiveness

of activity best suited to the external environment in which the organisation is operating. Consideration must be given to developing an organisational climate in which people work willingly and effectively.

According to *Gratton*, for example:

> *When people are engaged and committed they are more likely to behave in the interests of the company and they have less need to be controlled and measured. In essence, engaged people can be trusted to behave in the interests of the company, in part because they perceived their interests to be the same as, or aligned with, the interests of the company.*[39]

The style of management adopted can be seen as a function of the manager's attitudes towards people and assumptions about human nature and behaviour (**discussed in Chapter 10**).

Critical review and reflection

Performance of people at work is determined predominantly by the idiosyncratic behaviour of individuals and a complex combination of social factors and unofficial working methods. In reality, managers have only limited influence.

What is YOUR opinion? How would YOU describe the situation in YOUR own university or organisation?

Management and organisational behaviour in action case study
Fred. Olsen Cruise Lines

An increasingly significant sector of the hospitality and leisure industry is that of cruise ships. The number of holidaymakers choosing a holiday at sea continues to rise, with a record 1.7 million UK holidaymakers taking an ocean cruise in 2014.

In an ever-growing and continually evolving cruise industry, the delivery of a memorable personal service experience is particularly significant as an integral part of organisational effectiveness. Goods and services alone are no longer enough and, in addition to providing a consistently high-quality product, cruise companies need to differentiate themselves by an emotional engagement with customers and the highest levels of customer service.[40]

Fred. Olsen Cruise Lines is one of the only family-run cruise lines in the world, with sailing experience going back over 160 years. Fred. Olsen has stylish, contemporary ships built 'on a human scale', with capacities between 800 and 1,350 guests, departing from ten regional UK ports. The ships are large enough to provide the facilities desired by guests, but small enough to enable a close exploration of a wide range of exciting destinations. Emphasis is on a comfortable, friendly atmosphere, with a 'country house hotel' feel, delivered 'with a smile', by caring and attentive crew. Guests are welcomed as individuals in a relaxed, familiar ambience. Among a number of recent accolades, Fred. Olsen Cruise Lines was awarded the prestigious *Which?* 'Recommended Provider' status in the influential consumer body's first-ever cruise survey and the coveted 'Gold Trusted Merchant Accreditation' by independent review site Feefo for 2014 and 2015.

Successful cruise management is a combination of travel agency, hotel and leisure activities, on-board entertainment and organised tours. It entails a complex and involved series of processes, both at sea and in different ports of call, and is unlike that experienced in hardly any other business organisation. Some particular factors to consider include, for example:

- continual heavy guest occupancy and usage, with rapid turnover, mass entry and exit;
- 'people logistics' – attending to the complex transportation needs of guests pre- and post-cruise, and logistics of a broad variety of shore excursions in different locations;
- wide range of on-board activities and events throughout the day and evening;
- highest standards of safety and maintenance, logistics and tender operations;
- relationships with head office, technical department, port authorities, pilots, etc;

- expectations of high-quality cuisine, design and mix of menus, special dietary requirements;
- crew from a diverse range of cultures and backgrounds, with long periods away from home and families;
- health and hygiene, with large numbers of guests and crew in continual close contact;
- crew resource deployment and rotation planning, with unavailability of additional agency or temporary staff, as with land-based organisations, and need for flexible working practices in response to the demands of the business;
- accommodating annual leave requirements, flights for some members of the crew, and managing opportunities for time on shore;
- changeover of crew at the end of contracts – maintaining continuity within the business.

Cruising is associated with a high level of service delivery, and based on preconceived expectations passengers can be very demanding. Passenger satisfaction is dependent to a very large extent on day-to-day contact with – and care and attention from – members of the crew. Crew members work long hours, in often difficult and demanding conditions, and are away from their homes, and in many cases young families, for up to nine months. Management's concern and support for the welfare of its crew are of prime importance. At the same time, the nature of cruising demands attention to a safe and secure environment, for both passengers and crew. This demands a management structure with clear lines of authority, directed leadership and good order. Strong discipline must be maintained at all times.

Fred. Olsen prides itself on providing exceptional service by anticipating, meeting and exceeding its guests' expectations when they are on board its ships. Despite the continually evolving and highly competitive nature of the industry, Fred. Olsen attracts a high level of 'repeat guests' – that is, loyal customers who have cruised with the company at least once before. On a typical Fred. Olsen cruise, more than half of the guests are repeat customers, which is one of the highest return rates of any major cruise line. A particularly noticeable feature of passenger feedback is the extremely favourable and complimentary comments regarding the level of attention from courteous and always smiling crew members.

Gratuities to crew members are an accepted custom throughout the cruise industry. Tips are a recognised feature of the reward system for good performance. It is up to passengers to opt out of payment or vary the amount. The high number of Fred. Olsen crew members returning to complete further contracts (varying between six and nine months), and who have been engaged over many years with the company, is testament to both crew and passenger levels of satisfaction.

Source: Thanks to Rachael Jackson, Fred. Olsen Cruise Lines, **www.fredolsencruises.com**

Tasks

1. Explain particular features of organisational behaviour raised by this case study.
2. What do you think are the most important factors that explain the high level of repeat guests on Fred. Olsen cruise ships?
3. The company has a particular attraction for discerning, traditional guests. What additional considerations do you think this creates for both crew and management?
4. Discuss specific ways in which this case draws attention to the importance of the people–organisation relationship.

Globalisation and the international context

One major challenge facing managers today arises from what many commentators have identified as an increasingly international or **global** business environment. In broad terms, **globalisation** refers to organisations integrating, operating and competing in a worldwide economy. The organisations' activities are more independent across the world, rather than confined nationally. The following factors are frequently cited as potential explanatory factors underlying this trend:

- improvements in international information and communication facilities leading to an increased consciousness of differences in workplace attitudes and behaviour in other societies;

- international competitive pressure – for example, the emergence of newly industrialised and/or free-market nations including, for example, the Far East region and former communist bloc countries;
- increased mobility of labour;
- international business activity, for example: overseas franchising or licensing agreements; outsourcing of business units to other countries (call centres provide a topical example); direct foreign investment and the activities of multinational corporations that, by definition, operate outside national boundaries;
- greater cross-cultural awareness and acceptance of the advantages of diversity.

Globalisation will also impact on the nature of social responsibilities and business ethics. As organisations, and especially large business organisations, adopt a more global perspective this will have a significant effect on the broader context of management and organisational behaviour.

The future of globalisation

Globalisation has been subjected to much criticism, in part at least due to lack of clarity as to its exact meaning and to the confusion about organisations that are very large scale (such as Walmart in the USA) but have only a small proportion of their operations on a global basis. Globalisation has also become the subject of demonstrations and has been blamed for escalating inequalities in the developing world and endangering regional cultures. There appears to be a return to strong nationalistic tendencies in countries such as the USA and France.

Child points out that globalisation is a complex phenomenon and the term is used in so many different ways it is in danger of losing any useful purpose. Globalisation is a trend rather than a condition that necessarily already exists, it is not spreading evenly across the world and many unsubstantiated and sweeping claims have been made: 'The trend towards globalisation is a strong one, but it remains to be seen how far and how fast it will spread. It has powerful opponents.'[41]

By contrast, *McLean* maintains that globalisation is here to stay – it will not go away and if anything will get worse: 'We must face the realism that the world, and indeed organisations and the way they are managed, will never be the same. We must encompass these changes and harness the opportunities they present.'[42]

French, however, reminds us that social trends are, by their very nature, fluctuating. For example, it is quite possible that the trend for global flows of workers may decrease in importance or even be reversed in the future.[43]

Cultural environment

Whatever the extent of globalisation, there are clear implications for organisational behaviour in accommodating international dimensions of management and cultural differences. The importance of people in business understanding cultural differences is illustrated by IBM, which publishes for members of staff a comprehensive guide to the main dimensions of culture and business, and an introduction to concepts, tips, resources and tools for building cross-cultural competencies across national, organisational, team and interpersonal barriers.

Another advantage of adopting a cross-cultural approach to the study of organisational behaviour, and to the management of people more generally, lies in the recognition of variations in workplace attitudes and behaviour between individuals and groups in different cultural contexts.

As an example, in the USA there is a strong commitment to the organisation (the corporation) and work and career are taken very seriously (as the author has experienced for himself). Hard work is accepted as part of the American way of life and good timekeeping is important. It is a long-hours culture and generally there is little concern for the work/life balance. There is a strong emphasis on political correctness and little banter or humour at work (again as the author found out to his cost), especially not in formal meetings. Americans do not like self-deprecation and find it strange that the British are prepared to laugh at themselves.

In China there is an enormous bureaucracy, and hierarchy is an important indication of authority. In the business world you may need to deal with several ascending levels of management before reaching the senior manager. There can be an apparent lack of courtesy – and rather than being taken as given, respect and trust have to be earned. There is a strong superior–subordinate relationship, with staff often undertaking menial tasks for their boss.[44]

In Japan and Korea, where society tends to be male dominated, in the business world men are more likely to be taking the main role in setting agendas, communications and decision-making.

In examining the centrally important topic of motivation, *Francesco and Gold* inform their readers: 'Managers must develop organizational systems that are flexible enough to take into account the meaning of work and the relative value of rewards within the range of cultures where they operate.'[45]

According to *Hare,* we need to embrace the opportunities international management brings. All countries have their issues, but whatever the customs, differences and similarities, most cultures recognise the need to get something done. Successful international management boils down to five simple principles:

1. Listen well so you understand the rationale, motivations and outcomes desired by the other party.
2. Take time to do your research and homework.
3. Be courteous and polite, and mindful of local manners and customs.
4. Develop good working relationships through trust and respect.
5. Embrace the opportunities from international management.[46]

Critical review and reflection

National culture is not only an explanation of human beliefs, values, behaviours and actions, it is arguably the most significant feature underlying the study of management and organisational behaviour.

To what extent do YOU support this contention? What examples can YOU give in support of your view? What effect does national culture have in YOUR university or organisation?

Is organisational behaviour culture-bound?

While it can be valuable to apply organisational behaviour concepts to diverse cultural settings, it should also be borne in mind that some **universal** theories and models may, in reality, contain important culturally derived assumptions. When examining classical frameworks for understanding organisation structure (**discussed in Chapter 2**), *Schneider and Barsoux* point out: 'Theories about how best to organise – Max Weber's (German) bureaucracy, Henri Fayol's (French) administrative model, and Frederick Taylor's (American) scientific management – all reflect societal concerns of the times as well as the cultural background of the individuals.'[47] That writers on work organisations may themselves be influenced by their own cultural backgrounds when compiling their work is unsurprising: however, equally it should not be ignored.

More significant still is the possibility that whole topics within organisational behaviour, per se, may be underpinned by a particular culturally derived frame of reference. *French* examines the extent to which universally applicable pressures or logics effectively rule out significant cultural variations in formal organisational arrangements, such as bureaucracy, as opposed to culture itself viewed as a variable within a range of factors influencing structure.[48]

Culture as understanding

For our most basic common link is that we all inhabit this small planet, we all breathe the same air, we all cherish our children's future, and we are all mortal.

John F. Kennedy, 10 June 1963

There are a number of very good reasons why we could usefully understand cultural difference (and similarity) at work, based on new awareness contributing to our own effectiveness and moreover to the accomplishment of organisational goals. It could also be true to say that an appreciation of culture and its effects may be of intrinsic value. There could therefore be advantages to cross-cultural awareness, which include:

- increased self-awareness;
- sensitivity to difference and diversity;
- questioning our own assumptions and knowledge;
- lessening ignorance, prejudice and hatred.

However, it would be wrong to think that increased cross-cultural awareness or activity will automatically bring about any of these outcomes.

Brooks is one of several commentators who draw our attention to the interlinked nature of culture and commonly held values. Figure 1.7 illustrates the interplay between relevant factors affecting any one national culture.[49] You may wish to consider how these factors have combined to shape your own 'home' culture and that of one other country with which you are familiar.

Above all, those aspects of organisational behaviour that focus on individual differences and diversity, groups and managing people are the most clearly affected by culture and it is essential to take a cross-cultural approach to the subject. (**Organisation culture is discussed in Chapter 15.**)

Critical review and reflection

Despite obvious advantages from an appreciation of culture differences and its effects, it is not easy for everyone to feel comfortable working in a multicultural environment.

To what extent are YOU aware of, and sensitive to, cultural differences? What is YOUR experience of studying in a multicultural environment at your university? What benefits have YOU gained?

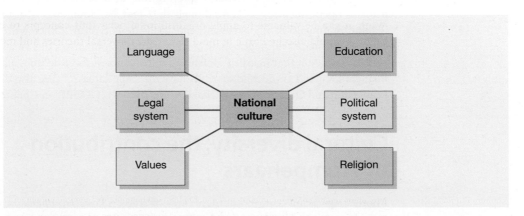

Figure 1.7 Factors affecting national culture

Source: From Brooks, I. *Organisational Behaviour: Individuals, Groups and Organisation,* fourth edition, Financial Times Prentice Hall (2009), p. 272. Reproduced with permission from Pearson Education Ltd.

Five dimensions of culture: the contribution of Hofstede

Geert Hofstede is one of the most significant contributors to the body of knowledge on culture and workplace difference. His work has largely resulted from a large-scale research programme in the late 1960s and early 1970s involving employees from the IBM Corporation, initially in forty countries. In focusing on one organisation Hofstede felt that the results could be more clearly linked to national cultural difference. Arguing that culture is, in a memorable phrase, **collective programming** or **software of the mind,** Hofstede initially identified four dimensions of culture: power distance, uncertainty avoidance, individualism and masculinity.[50]

- **Power distance** relates to the *social distance among people* depending upon management style, hierarchical structure, willingness of subordinates to disagree with superiors, and the educational level and status accruing to particular roles.
- **Uncertainty avoidance** refers to the extent to which members of a society feel threatened by *ambiguity or unusual situations* or accepting of risks and uncertainty.
- **Individualism** describes the relatively *individualistic or collectivist ethic* evident in that particular society, for example the degree of respect for individual freedom or commitment to group membership.
- **Masculinity** refers to a continuum between *'masculine' characteristics,* such as assertiveness and competitiveness, *and 'feminine' traits,* such as caring, a stress upon the quality of life and concern with the environment.

A fifth dimension of culture, **long-term/short-term orientation,** was originally labelled 'Confucian work dynamism'. This dimension developed from the work of *Hofstede and Bond* in an attempt to locate Chinese cultural values as they impacted on the workplace.[51] Countries that scored highly on Confucian work dynamism or long-term orientation exhibited a strong concern with time along a continuum and were therefore both past and future oriented, with a preoccupation with tradition but also a concern with the effect of actions and policies on future generations.

Evaluation of Hofstede's work

Extremely influential, the seminal work of Hofstede has been criticised from certain quarters, for example for its simplicity and limited practical application. In common with other writers in this area, there is a focus on the national rather than the regional level. The variations within certain countries, for example Spain, can be more or less significant. Again in common with other contributors, Hofstede's classifications include medium categories that may be difficult to operationalise, accurate though they may be. Some may also find the masculinity/femininity dimension unconvincing and itself stereotypical. Other writers have questioned whether Hofstede's findings remain current. *Holden* summarises this view: 'How many people have ever thought that many of Hofstede's informants of three decades ago are now dead? Do their children and grandchildren really have the same values?'[52] **(See also discussion on Global Leadership and Organizational Behavior Effectiveness (GLOBE) in Chapter 9.)**

Cultural diversity: the contribution of Trompenaars

Another significant contributor to this area of study is *Fons Trompenaars,* whose later work is co-authored with *Charles Hampden-Turner.*[53] Trompenaars' original research spanned fifteen years, resulting in a database of 50,000 participants from fifty countries. It was supported by cases and anecdotes from 900 cross-cultural training programmes. A questionnaire method comprised a significant part of the study, which involved requiring participants to consider their underlying norms, values and attitudes. The resultant framework identifies seven areas in which cultural differences may affect aspects of organisational behaviour:

- Relationships and rules. Here societies may be more or less **universal,** in which case there is relative rigidity in respect of rule-based behaviour, or **particular,** in which case the importance of relationships may lead to flexibility in the interpretation of situations.
- Societies may be more oriented to the **individual** or **collective.** The collective may take different forms: the corporation in Japan, the family in Italy or the Catholic Church in the Republic of Ireland. There may be implications here for such matters as individual responsibility or payment systems.
- It may also be true that societies differ in the extent to which it is thought appropriate for members to show emotion in public. **Neutral** societies favour the 'stiff upper lip', while overt displays of feeling are more likely in **emotional** societies.
- In **diffuse** cultures, the whole person would be involved in a business relationship and it would take time to build such relationships. In a **specific** culture, such as the USA, the basic relationship would be limited to the contractual. This distinction clearly has implications for those seeking to develop new international links.
- **Achievement**-based societies value recent success or an overall record of accomplishment. In contrast, in societies relying more on **ascription,** status could be bestowed through such factors as age, gender or educational record.
- Trompenaars suggests that societies view **time** in different ways, which may in turn influence business activities. The American dream is the French nightmare. Americans generally start from zero and what matters is their present performance and their plan to 'make it' in the future. This is 'nouveau riche' for the French, who prefer the *ancien pauvre;* they have an enormous sense of the past.
- Finally it is suggested that there are differences with regard to attitudes to the **environment.** In Western societies, individuals are typically masters of their fate. In other parts of the world, however, the world is more powerful than individuals.

Trompenaars' work is based on lengthy academic and field research. It is potentially useful in linking the dimensions of culture to aspects of organisational behaviour that are of direct relevance, particularly to people approaching a new culture for the first time.

High- and low-context cultures

A framework for understanding cultural difference has been formulated by *Ed Hall;* his work is in part co-authored with *Mildred Reed Hall*.[54] Hall conceptualises culture as comprising a series of 'languages', in particular:

- language of time;
- language of space;
- language of things;
- language of friendships;
- language of agreements.

In this model of culture Hall suggests that these 'languages', which resemble shared attitudes to the issues in question, are communicated in very different ways according to whether a society is classified as a 'high'- or 'low'-context culture.

The features of **'high'-context societies,** which incorporate Asian, African and Latin American countries, include the following:

- a high proportion of information is 'uncoded' and internalised by the individual;
- indirect communication styles – words are less important;
- shared group understandings;
- importance attached to the past and tradition;
- a 'diffuse' culture stressing the importance of trust and personal relationships in business.

'Low'-context societies, which include the USA, Australia, the UK and the Scandinavian countries, exhibit contrasting features including the following:

- a high proportion of communication is 'coded' and expressed;
- direct communication styles – words are paramount;
- past context is less important;
- a 'specific' culture stressing importance of rules and contracts.

Other countries, for example France, Spain, Greece and several Middle Eastern societies, are classified as 'medium' context.

The importance of organisational behaviour

As part of the *Financial Times Mastering Management* series, *Wood*, in his discussion of the nature of organisational behaviour, suggests that in its concern for the way people behave in an organisational context, organisational behaviour can be regarded as the key to the whole area of management.

> *Is the study of behavior in organizations important? I think it is vital. What the social sciences, humanities and the arts are to university education, OB is to business school education. The more technical a manager's training, the more important organizational behavior becomes. It is arguably the one area that can carry the burden of bringing the collective wisdom of human history into the decision-making calculus of developing managers. And this is no trivial task.[55]*

In the Foreword to Cloke and Goldsmith's thought-provoking book *The End of Management*, *Bennis* claims that a distinct and dramatic change is taking place in the philosophy underlying organisational behaviour, calling forth a new concept of humanising organisations.

> *This new concept is based on an expanded knowledge of our complex and shifting needs, replacing an oversimplified, innocent, push-button idea of humanity. This philosophical shift calls for a new concept of organizational values based on humanistic-democratic ideals, which replace the depersonalized, mechanistic value system of bureaucracy. With it comes a new concept of power, based on collaboration and reason, replacing a model based on coercion and threat . . . The real push for these changes stems from the need not only to humanize organizations but to use them as crucibles for personal growth and self-realization.[56]*

Robbins and Judge remind us that there are few, if any, simple and universal principles that explain organisational behaviour, but that understanding organisational behaviour has never been more important for managers than it is today.

> *For instance, the typical employee in more developed countries is getting older; more and more women and people of color are in the workplace; corporate downsizing and the heavy use of temporary workers are severing the bonds of loyalty that historically tied many employees to their employers; and global competition is requiring employees to become more flexible and to learn to cope with rapid change. The war on terror has brought to the forefront the challenges of working with and managing people during uncertain times. In short, there are a lot of challenges and opportunities today for managers to use OB concepts.[57]*

Critical review and reflection

A noticeable feature of organisational behaviour is the invariable difficulty in identifying a single solution to a particular situation. The absence of one *right answer* not only makes study of the subject complex and frustrating, but also brings into question the value of studying the subject at all.

What are YOUR views? Do YOU feel frustrated by the study of organisational behaviour?

Ten key points to remember

1 At the heart of management is the art of managing people. Increasing attention is focused on good people skills as a basis of organisational effectiveness.

2 Organisational behaviour (OB) is broadly concerned with the study of the behaviour of people within an organisational setting and is of even greater significance.

3 It is necessary to recognise a multidisciplinary approach. Organisational behaviour can be viewed in terms of interrelated aspects of the individual, the group, the organisation and the environment

4 People differ in the manner and extent of their involvement with, and concern for, work. Different situations influence the individual's orientation to work and the work ethic.

5 The psychological contract implies a series of informal mutual expectations and satisfaction of needs arising from the people–organisation relationship.

6 Two important observations on the nature of human behaviour and what may actually happen in organisations are the Peter Principle and Parkinson's Law.

7 A major challenge facing managers today arises from an increasingly international or global business environment that also impacts on social responsibilities and ethics.

8 This highlights the need for a cross-cultural approach to the study of organisational behaviour and understanding the impact of national culture.

9 There are clear implications for organisational behaviour in accommodating dimensions of cultural differences, and the study and understanding of workplace behaviour.

10 There are few absolute principles that explain organisational behaviour, but in its concern for the behaviour of people it has never been more important for managers.

Review and discussion questions

1 Give your own explanation of the meaning, significance and scope of organisational behaviour.

2 Explain reasons for a multidisciplinary approach and suggest main headings under which factors influencing behaviour in work organisations can best be identified.

3 To what extent do you believe people are identified and perceived according to the nature of the work they undertake? Where possible give actual examples in support of your answer.

4 Discuss with supporting examples the nature and significance of (i) social exchange theory *and* (ii) the psychological contract.

5 Explain the extent to which you can identify with examples of organisational practices relating to (i) the Peter Principle *and* (ii) Parkinson's Law.

6 Discuss critically the role of management as an integrating activity. Give your views on the nature and importance of managerial work today.

7 Give your own views on the changing nature of the work organisation and specific changes that you foresee in the next ten years. How do you feel about the possible changes?

8 Why is it increasingly important for managers to adopt an international approach? What do you see as the future impact of globalisation?

9 Debate fully the importance and potential difficulties of national culture to the study of management and organisational behaviour. Where possible, give your own examples.

10 Discuss critically what you believe are the main factors to bear in mind with, and particular difficulties presented by, the study of organisational behaviour.

Assignment

It is often said that people are every organisation's most import asset. This is perfectly true but people are not like other assets. As well as being valuable in their own right – in terms of performance, skills and creativity – it is individual employees who bind every other aspect of working life together.

('The People Factor – engage your employees for business success', ACAS, March 2014, p. 4)

Working in small groups, discuss critically:

1 What this statement actually means to you and fellow members of your group.
2 What exactly is meant by 'individual employees binding every other aspect of working life together'?
3 The extent to which members of staff in your own university appear to be valued as an important asset.
4 Shared experiences within your group of any other work situations, with good and/or bad examples.
5 Why is it that, although the importance of people as the most important asset is often preached by organisations, this rarely seems to be the reality.
6 How this assignment relates to your study of organisational behaviour.
7 An agreed written group report on your findings and conclusions.

Personal skills and employability exercise

Objectives

Completing this exercise should help you to enhance the following skills:

- Obtain a clearer picture of your own and other people's attitudes to studying.
- Explore the likely importance of work to you and your orientation to work.
- Relate responses to your personal learning and development.

Exercise

Form into small groups, preferably including any colleagues whom you have not yet got to know very well and/or from a different ethnicity. Discuss openly and honestly how you each feel regarding your attitude, enthusiasm and motivation towards studying. *For example:*

1 What do you find most satisfying about studying?
2 What do you find least satisfying about studying?
3 How well are you able to concentrate on your studies?
4 To what extent do you enjoy studying for its own sake or only as a means to an end?
5 What do you find most distracting or difficult about your studies?
6 Is it possible to learn how to improve the skill of studying?
7 What rewards most encourage you in your studying?
8 At what time of the day and for how long at a time do you usually study best?

9 Do you prefer to fit studies around leisure time or enjoy leisure more if you have studied first?

10 What is the single most important feature of effective studying?

Discussion

- How do your responses compare with those of your colleagues? Do any of the responses surprise you?
- To what extent do you believe the responses are a true indication of work ethic? What do you see as the characteristic traits of a person with a healthy work ethic?
- How far do you agree with the contention that 'we are employed for our skills but valued for our attitudes'?

Case study
Virgin Atlantic and Ryanair

Source: Franka Bruns/AP/Press Association Images   *Source:* Michael Stephens/PA Archive/Press Association Images

Michael O'Leary (left) and Richard Branson (right) have both created very successful airline companies, but their organisational cultures and values are very different from each other.

This case examines two organisations that have many similarities as well as a number of significant differences. The essential technology and systems behind each organisation may be very similar, but the nature and style of management and its consequent impact on the way people working in these organisations think, feel and behave has created very different organisational cultures. So what are the similarities, and what are the differences?

The most obvious similarity is that both Virgin Atlantic and Ryanair operate in the UK passenger air transport industry. Virgin's air transport business was founded by Richard Branson in 1984[58] and Michael O'Leary took over as chief executive at Ryanair, a small Irish airline, in 1985.[59] Both started life in competition with major national flag-carrier airlines (British Airways and Aer Lingus respectively) and grew to be major challengers to these established companies. As they grew, their scale of operations brought them into competition with a much larger number and range of airlines operating from the UK: Branson's Virgin Atlantic competes with some major intercontinental companies such as American Airlines and Qantas; O'Leary

competes with the likes of Flybe and EasyJet in the short-haul market. Both Branson, who was born in 1950, and O'Leary, who is ten years younger, are individuals with strong and distinctive personalities, who have a relentless appetite for media presence and who make extensive use of themselves in their frequent marketing communications. They are readily engaged in advertising stunts, often appear on the news media in relation to stories about the industry, and their faces and personalities are powerfully associated with their companies.

Charting different courses

There are, however, some major differences. Firstly, they differ in their choice of markets. Virgin's air transport business originated in the long-haul, mainly transatlantic market, which might be highly profitable but is also extremely competitive. As the business grew, offshoots were founded as independent companies – for instance, Virgin Australia and the ambitious project for the world's first spaceline, Virgin Galactic,[60] which remains live despite the loss of the first vehicle, Enterprise, in November 2014. Ryanair started as a short-haul carrier and has remained so, focusing on European destinations from a small number of airports in the UK and Eire. Its competitive positioning is also very different. Ryanair is well known as 'The Low Cost Airline'; the first thing that hits you in its publicity material is the price[61] and this is very clearly the core of its business strategy. The 'no frills' approach means just that; even the in-flight food is limited to sandwiches and costs extra. Virgin, by contrast, attracts passengers by offering a superior experience and is firmly positioned at the quality end of the market. Publicity material emphasises style and comfort but with a touch of humour,[62] and there is a range of in-flight extras which, even at the economy end of the price range, includes a full meal and drinks service and a range of entertainment including e-books.

As was noted, both men love publicity stunts and often use humour in their public communications. Branson is usually smiling and in poses that indicate fun and a desire to show close links with his staff and popularity with employees, customers and the public in general. O'Leary is much more likely to be acerbic, critical and uses what might euphemistically be called 'colourful' language in his public statements. He seems to care little about public opinion of him as an individual, and has been in trouble with the Advertising Standards Authorities in the UK and Eire on more than one occasion. The appointment of Kenny Jacobs to head the company's first television advertising campaign in 2013, however, set Ryanair on a slightly different course. While still highlighting its low prices, the new (and cheaply shot) advertising campaign heralded the introduction of allocated seating, an additional carry-on bag and a slicker booking website. These moves, along with the cancellation of its annual 'girlie' calendar, suggested the company was aiming for a family market; and the continued rise in profits during 2014[63] showed that being 'nice' could indeed pay off.[64]

The brand values are also very different. Virgin, as a collection of businesses, does everything from running trains to selling wine via mobile phones and financial services. All these enterprises are linked by the single powerful central image of the founder and the characteristic red livery. Ryanair does one thing and one thing only, but in doing so sets an almost buccaneering tone, readily taking on authorities such as the British Airports Authority over its charging practices (characteristically direct, O'Leary observed that 'people have to pay £10 for the privilege of getting on and off this rain-sodden and weather-beaten island')[65] and European Union bureaucrats, for instance in a spectacularly damning account of EU competition policy in a speech at the EU's own Innovation Convention on 6 December 2011.[66] Branson

has certainly had his conflicts with British Airways, notably over the 'dirty tricks' affair of the early 1990s, but is not likely to challenge governments. Virgin tries hard to build customer loyalty and gain repeat business through brand-related service values; Ryanair's repeat business (and for some customers the Ryanair experience is one that inspires the thought 'never again') is on price, not loyalty to the brand. These differences have a significant effect on the nature of employment relations and the psychological contract between the two companies and their employees.

Working for Richard and Michael

The brand image and the treatment of customers by each company have a bearing on the nature of organisational relationship with staff, and vice versa. Aspects of organisational behaviour therefore show through in a variety of interconnected ways to create consistent and very different cultures.

At Virgin Atlantic, cabin crew are there to be helpful and welcoming; they are important projectors of the brand image and their job is partly to encourage the all-important customer loyalty that generates continuing profit. The importance of staff as carriers of company values is clearly reflected in the recruitment material and other statements about the nature of work at Virgin Atlantic.

> Virgin Atlantic brings together all manner of people in all manner of roles, all playing a crucial role in the smooth running of a very complex operation. But whoever you are and wherever you join us, you'll never stop thinking of our customers and what we can do for them. From frontline cabin crew to IT analysts, everyone here plays a role in delivering the Virgin brand. That means using initiative, taking responsibility for your actions and being ready to support those around you at all times. Similarly, you'll play your part in maintaining the friendly, unconventional professionalism that makes Virgin Atlantic such a unique place of work.[67]

The recruitment process is lengthy and includes a group interview that acts as a filter for further tests before job offers are made. Training programmes for cabin crew and other staff are run from a dedicated training centre, and there is a wide range of benefits for full-time staff including seven free flights a year, private pensions and medical schemes and discounted goods and services across the Virgin group.

At Ryanair, the cabin crew start by working for a supplier organisation called Crewlink. You can discover if you qualify to apply for a job by answering a series of ten online questions. Successful applicants for cabin crew posts are trained at Crewlink's Hahn centre in Germany, and are expected to pay an upfront charge of €2,349 for the six-week course; or it can be offset against the initial year's salary at a total cost of €2,949. In either case, accommodation during the course is a further €700. Successful graduates get a three-year contract with Crewlink to work on Ryanair flights on a shift work basis and are not expected to have to make overnight stops at its destinations. Post-tax starting salary is said to be 'competitive', with experienced supervisory staff able to earn up to €30,000 pa. Staff must be flexible in terms of their work location across the thirty plus European centres, and Crewlink does not guarantee work if individuals specify a preferred work location.[68]

By comparison with long haul, a short-haul operation involves very tight turnaround times and Ryanair aims for twenty minutes. New aircraft have been commissioned with non-reclining seats that do not have magazine pockets (the required passenger safety instructions are fixed to seat backs), facilitating cleaning and cutting time on the ground. This creates a very different pace and set of pressures on the workforce compared with those at Virgin, which is likely to have higher staffing

levels and to give crew longer rest breaks in the destination locations between flights. The nature of customer relations, by contrast, might be more demanding at Virgin than at Ryanair; staff and customers are together for longer and the brand image must be maintained.

Complaints and horror stories can be found about work at both organisations; however, Ryanair is subject to a more systematic and organised campaign of criticism for its employment practices by trade union organisations. In past years the International Transport Workers' Federation ran a major campaign on its website, the purpose of which was to pressurise the management at Ryanair into accepting the role of trade unions in representing the workforce – to no avail.

Both organisations have been successful. Ryanair continues to turn in significant profits in a sector that is prone to disruption and is holding its own during recession.[69] Virgin, unusually, suffered annual losses in 2012 and 2013, partly because of increased fuel costs, but has embarked on a two-year recovery programme and seems on course to return to profitability in 2015.[70] But the cultures and values that get them off the ground could hardly be more different.

Tasks

1 Some writers, such as Morgan, use metaphors to help us understand the nature of organisational behaviour. Identify one of Morgan's metaphors that you think might be applied appropriately to Virgin and one to Ryanair, and then develop two of your own, one for each organisation. How would you explain your choices?

2 Critically evaluate both organisations in terms of either social exchange theory or the notion of the psychological contract given in the chapter.

3 Identify the different demands that might be made of managers to achieve organisational effectiveness in each business (you could use Figure 1.6 as a framework). What are the implications for the role and development of managers in each case?

4 Ryanair has recently considered entering the transatlantic market, and Virgin set up 'Little Red', which operates short-haul domestic flights in the UK. What might be the implication of these changes for the management of cabin staff in each company?

Notes and references

1. 'MANAGEMENT 2020: Leadership to unlock long-term growth', The Commission on the future of management and leadership, CMI, July 2014, p. 14.

2. 'Introduction to Module 6, Organisational Behaviour', *Financial Times Mastering Management*, FT Pitman Publishing (1997), p. 216.

3. Vecchio, R. P. *Organizational Behavior: Core Concepts*, sixth edition, Dryden Press (2005).

4. See, for example, Billsberry, J. 'There's Nothing So Practical as a Good Theory: How Can Theory Help Managers Become More Effective?', in Billsberry, J. (ed.) *The Effective Manager: Perspectives and Illustrations,*

Sage (1996), pp. 1–27; and Naylor, J. *Management,* second edition, Financial Times Prentice Hall (2004), pp. 13–15.

5. McGregor, D. *The Human Side of Enterprise,* Penguin (1987), p. 6.

6. Patching, K. *Management and Organisation Development,* Macmillan Business (1999), p. 11.

7. Morgan, G. *Creative Organisation Theory,* Sage (1989), p. 26.

8. Drummond, H. *Introduction to Organisational Behaviour,* Oxford University Press (2000).

9. Morgan, G. *Creative Organisation Theory,* Sage (1989), p. 26.

10. Hellriegel, D., Slocum, J. W. and Woodman, R. W. *Organizational Behavior,* eighth edition, South-Western Publishing (1998), p. 5.

11. Egan, G. 'The Shadow Side', *Management Today,* September 1993, pp. 33–8.

12. Howes, L. 'The Real Workplace Battle', *Professional Manager,* Winter 2014, pp. 60–3.

13. Watson, T. J. *Organising and Managing Work,* second edition, Financial Times Prentice Hall (2006), p. 55.

14. Wilson, F. M. *Organisational Behaviour and Work: A Critical Introduction,* second edition, Oxford University Press (2004), pp. 1–2.

15. Bertrand Russell 'In Praise of Idleness' by Richard Nordquist, http://grammar.about.com/od/classicessays/a/praiseidleness. htm (accessed 27 June 2012).

16. 'Modern World of Work', BBC 2 Television, March 2011.

17. Donkin, R. *The Future of Work,* Palgrave Macmillan (2010).

18. Goldthorpe, J. H., Lockwood, D., Bechofer, F. and Platt, J. *The Affluent Worker,* Cambridge University Press (1968).

19. Bunting, M. *Willing Slaves,* HarperCollins (2004).

20. Stern, S. 'My Generation', *Management Today,* March 2008, pp. 40–6.

21. Waller, D. 'Are You What You Do?', *Management Today,* October 2008, pp. 42–6.

22. Reeves, R. 'Reality Bites', *Management Today,* March 2003, p. 35.

23. McCrum, M. *Going Dutch in Beijing,* Profile Books (2007), p. 153; see, for example, Robbins, S. P. and Judge, T. A. *Organizational Behavior,* thirteenth edition, Pearson Prentice Hall (2009).

24. Homans, G. C. 'Social Behaviour as Exchange', *American Journal of Sociology,* vol. 63, no. 6, 1958, pp. 597–606; see also Thibaut, J. W. and Kelley, H. H. *The Social Psychology of Groups,* Wiley (1959).

25. Blau, P. *Exchange and Power in Social Life,* Wiley (1964); see also Bacharach, S. B. and Lawler, E. J. *Power and Politics in Organizations,* Jossey-Bass (1980).

26. Stalker, K. 'The Individual, the Organisation and the Psychological Contract', *British Journal of Administrative Management,* July/August 2000, pp. 28–34.

27. Ghoshal, S., Bartlett, C. A. and Moran, P. 'Value Creation: The New Millennium Management Manifesto', in Chowdhury, S. (ed.) *Management21C,* Financial Times Prentice Hall (2000), pp. 121–40.

28. Peter, L. J. and Hull, R. *The Peter Principle,* Pan Books (1970), p. 22.

29. Ibid., p. 56.

30. Parkinson, C. N. *Parkinson's Law,* Penguin Modern Classics (2002), p. 14.

31. HRH The Duke of Edinburgh, 'Introduction' to Parkinson, C. N. *Parkinson's Law,* Penguin Modern Classics (2002), pp. 9–10.

32. Seligman, M. E. P. and Csikszentmihalyi, M. 'Positive Psychology: An introduction', *American Psychologist,* vol. 55, no. 1, 2000, pp. 5–14.

33. Peterson, C., Park, N. and Sweeney, P. J. 'Group Well-Being: Morale from a Positive Psychology Perspective', *Applied Psychology: An International Review,* vol. 57, 2008, p. 20.

34. Wong, T. P. and Davey, M. A. 'Best Practices in Servant Leadership', School of Global Leadership & Entrepreneurship, Regent University, July 2007; Gable, S. H. and Haidt, J. 'What (and Why) is Positive Psychology?', *Review of General Psychology,* vol. 9, no. 2, 2005, pp. 103–10.

35. Luthans, F. 'Positive organizational behaviour: Developing and managing psychological strengths', *Academy of Management Executive,* vol. 16, no. 1, 2002, pp. 57–72.

36. Donaldson, S. I and Ko, L. 'Positive organizational psychology, behaviour and scholarship: A review of emerging literature and evidence base', *Journal of Positive Psychology,* vol. 5, no. 3, 2010, pp. 177–91.

37. Wright, T. A. and Quick, J. C. 'The role of positive-based research in building the science of organizational behaviour', *Journal of Organizational Behavior,* vol. 30, 2009, pp. 329–36.

38. See, for example, Argyris, C. *Integrating the Individual and the Organisation,* Wiley (1964).

39. Gratton, L. *The Democratic Enterprise,* Financial Times Prentice Hall (2004), p. 208.

40. Wong, A. 'The role of emotional satisfaction in service encounters', *Managing Service Quality,* vol. 14, no. 5, 2004, pp. 365–76.

41. Child, J. *Organisation: Contemporary Principles and Practice,* Blackwell (2005), p. 30.

42. McLean, J. 'Globalisation Is Here to Stay', *Manager, The British Journal of Administrative Management,* June/July 2006, p. 16.

43. French, R. *Cross-Cultural Management in Work Organisations,* second edition, Chartered Institute of Personnel and Development (2010), p. 4.

44. See, for example, Slater, D. 'When in China . . . ', *Management Today,* May 2006, pp. 46–50.

45. Francesco, A. M. and Gold, B. A. *International Organizational Behavior,* second edition, Pearson Prentice Hall (2005), p. 140.

46. Hare, C. 'We need to embrace the opportunities international management brings', *Management Today,* May 2012, p. 62.

47. Schneider, S. C. and Barsoux, J, *Managing Across Cultures,* second edition, Financial Times Prentice Hall (2003) p. 167.

48. French, R. *Cross-Cultural Management in Work Organisations,* second edition, Chartered Institute of Personnel and Development (2010).

49. Brooks, I. *Organisational Behaviour: Individuals, Groups and Organisation,* fourth edition, Financial Times Prentice Hall (2009), p. 286.

50. Hofstede, G. *Culture's Consequences: International Differences in Work-Related Values,* Sage (1980).

51. Hofstede, G. and Bond, M. H. 'The Confucius Connection: From Cultural Roots to Economic Growth', *Organisational Dynamics,* Spring 1988, pp. 4–21.

52. Holden, N. J. *Cross-Cultural Management: A Knowledge Management Perspective,* Financial Times Prentice Hall (2002), p. 51.

53. Trompenaars, F. and Hampden-Turner, C. *Riding the Waves of Culture,* second edition, Nicholas Brearley (1999).

54. Hall, E. T. and Hall, M. R. *Understanding Cultural Differences,* Intercultural Press (1990).

55. Wood, J. 'Deep Roots and Far From a "Soft" Option', *Financial Times Mastering Management,* Financial Times Pitman Publishing (1997), p. 217.

56. Bennis, W. 'Foreword', in Cloke, K. and Goldsmith, J. *The End of Management and the Rise of Organisational Democracy,* Jossey-Bass (2002), p. ix.

57. Robbins, S. P. and Judge, T. A. *Organizational Behavior,* thirteenth edition, Pearson Prentice Hall (2009) p. 50.

58. Virgin Atlantic, 'All About Us', http://www.virgin-atlantic.com/en/us/allaboutus/ourstory/history.jsp

59. Creaton, S. *Ryanair – How a Small Irish Airline Conquered Europe*, Aurum (2004).

60. Virgin Galactic, http://www.virgingalactic.com/

61. For instance, at the Ryanair website www.ryanair.com

62. For instance, see its James Bond parody of 2011; or the 'Lion's Den' advert for business travellers, http://www.virgin-atlantic.com/gb/en/the-virgin-experience/let-it-fly.html

63. Ryanair Corporate, http://corporate.ryanair.com/news/news/150202-ryanair-reports-q3-profit-of-49m-guidance-rises-to-840m-850m/?market=en

64. Topham, G. 'Nicely does it', *Guardian,* 23 December 2014, http://www.theguardian.com/business/2014/dec/23/ryanair-richly-rewarded-transformation

65. Allen, K. 'Ryanair reduces Stansted flights by 14%', *Guardian,* 22 July 2009, p. 24.

66. Available on YouTube, http://www.youtube.com/watch?v=p4HYSsrlcq8&list=PL70F799CB0BB756EE&index=2&feature=plpp_video

67. Virgin Atlantic, 'Working for Us', http://www.virgin-atlantic.com/en/gb/careers/workingforus/index.jsp

68. Crewlink, www.crewlink.ie

69. Ryanair website, Investor pages, http://corporate.ryanair.com

70. Virgin Atlantic corporate website press releases, http://www.virgin-atlantic.com/gb/en/footer/media-centre/press-releases/financial-results.html

CHAPTER 2
Approaches to organisation and management

Organisational behaviour is a discursive subject and much has been written about it. The study of organisations, their structure and management has therefore to proceed on a broad front. The comparative analysis of different approaches will yield benefits to the manager. Identification of major trends in management and organisational theory, and the work of leading writers, provide a perspective on concepts and ideas discussed in more detail in other chapters.

Learning outcomes

After completing this chapter you should have enhanced your ability to:

- provide a framework in which to study different approaches to organisation and management;
- identify major trends in the development of organisational behaviour and management thinking;
- evaluate the relevance of different approaches to present-day work organisations;
- debate the significance and value of the idea of postmodernism;
- assess the relevance of study of different approaches to organisation and management;
- debate benefits of management theory and influences on management practice;
- establish a basis for consideration of aspects of management and organisational behaviour discussed in subsequent chapters.

Critical review and reflection

Criticism of the study of theory or history of management is misjudged. More attention to the ideas of leading writers, and to evolutions in management and organisational behaviour, would help improve understanding and performance.

How would YOU attempt to defend this assertion to a group of sceptical managers? What benefits do YOU expect to gain from a study of management theory?

Developments in management and organisational behaviour

A central part of the study of organisational behaviour is the development of management thinking and what might be termed management theory. (**See also Chapter 1.**) Managers reading the work of leading writers on the subject might see in their thoughts, ideas and conclusions a message about how they should behave. This will influence their attitudes towards management practice and bring about change in behaviour.

Writing on organisation and management, in some form or another, can be traced back thousands of years.[1] Also, *Shafritz* makes an interesting observation about the contribution of William Shakespeare (1564–1616):

> *While William Shakespeare's contribution to literature and the development of the English language have long been acknowledged and thoroughly documented, his contribution to the theory of management and administration have been all but ignored. This is a surprising oversight when you consider that many of his plays deal with issues of personnel management and organizational behavior.[2]*

However, the systematic development of management thinking is viewed, generally, as dating from the end of the nineteenth century with the emergence of large industrial organisations and the ensuing problems associated with their structure and management.[3]

Importance of management theory

The study of management theory is important for the following reasons:

- It helps to view the interrelationships between the development of theory, behaviour in organisations and management practice.
- An understanding of the development of management thinking helps in understanding principles underlying the actual process of management and reasons for the attention given to main topic areas.
- Management theories are interpretive and evolve in line with changes in the organisational environment.
- Many of the earlier ideas are of continuing importance to the manager and later ideas on management tend to incorporate earlier ideas and conclusions.

However, if action is to be effective, the theory must be adequate and appropriate to the task and to improved organisational performance. It must be a 'good' theory. To be of any help to the practising manager, theory has to be appropriate. For example, *Lee* refers to:

> *the danger of adopting theories because they are teachable, rather than because they are effective . . . [however,] without appropriate theory, there would be very little communication of the insights of scientific theory to practising managers.[4]*

Crainer points out that although management is active, not theoretical, it is nothing without ideas.

> *Nothing is so practical as a good theory. Ideas drive management as surely as the immediate problems which land on managers' desks or which arrive via their e-mail. Decisions have to be based on ideas as well as instinct. Without ideas managers flit desperately from crisis to crisis. They cannot know where they are going, why they are doing something or what they will achieve, without the vital fuel of ideas.[5]*

Framework of analysis

In order to help identify the main trends in the development of organisational behaviour and management theory, it is helpful to categorise the ideas and work of writers into various 'approaches', based on their views of organisations, their structure and management.

Management theory is a complex area of study in which it is possible to identify a large number of writers and a wide range of comparative and/or conflicting points of view.

There are, therefore, many ways of categorising the various approaches. For example, *Skipton* attempts a classification of eleven main schools of management theory.[6] Whatever form of categorisation is adopted, it is possible to identify a number of other approaches, or at least sub-divisions of approaches, and cross-grouping among the various approaches. The choice of a particular categorisation is therefore largely at the discretion of the observer and the demands of the reader.

For convenience, the following analysis revolves around a framework based on four main approaches, shown in Figure 2.1. Although a simplistic process, it provides a useful framework in which to direct study and focus attention on the progression of ideas concerned with improving organisational performance:

- classical – including scientific management and bureaucracy;
- human relations – including neo-human relations;
- systems;
- contingency.

Attention is also drawn to other 'approaches' or ideas, including technology, decision-making, social action and postmodernism. *See* Figure 2.3 below.

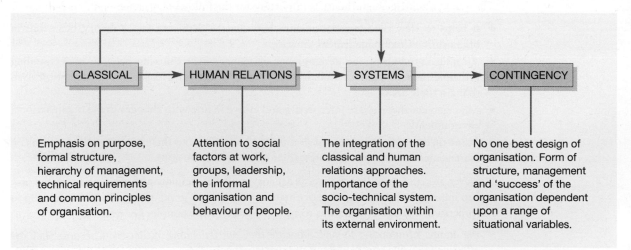

Figure 2.1 Main approaches to organisation, structure and management

Critical review and reflection

It is often claimed that what leading writers say is an important part of the study of management and organisational behaviour. Others say these different ideas are too abstract, are little more than short-term fads and have little practical value.

What do YOU think? To what extent do YOU expect to learn about the realities of management and organisational behaviour from the work of leading writers?

The classical approach

The **classical** writers thought of the organisation in terms of its purpose and formal structure. Emphasis is on planning of work, technical requirements of the organisation, principles of management, and the assumption of rational and logical behaviour. The analysis of organisation in this manner is associated with work carried out initially in the early part of the last century, by such writers as Taylor, Fayol, Urwick and Brech. Such writers were laying the foundation for a comprehensive theory of management.

A clear understanding of the purpose of an organisation is seen as essential to understanding how the organisation works and how its methods of working can be improved. Identification of general objectives would lead to the clarification of purpose and responsibilities at all levels of the organisation and to the most effective structure. Attention is given to division of work, clear definition of duties and responsibilities, and maintaining specialisation and co-ordination. Emphasis is on a hierarchy of management and formal organisational relationships.

Sets of principles

The classical writers (also variously known as the formal or scientific management writers – although scientific management is really only a part of the **classical approach**) were concerned with improving the organisation structure as a means of increasing efficiency. They emphasised the importance of principles for the design of a logical structure of organisation. Their writings were in a normative style and they saw these principles as a set of 'rules' offering general solutions to common problems of organisation and management. Most classical writers had their own set of principles but among the most publicised are those of *Fayol* and *Urwick*.

Fayol identified five managerial activities: planning, organising, command, co-ordination and control, together with a set of principles of management. Fayol recognised that there was no limit to the principles of management but in his writing advocated fourteen[7] (**as discussed in Chapter 10**).

Urwick originally specified eight principles of the requirements of the formal organisation, but these were revised to ten in his later writing.[8]

Brech attempts to provide a practical approach to organisation structure based on tried general principles as opposed to concentration on specific cases or complex generalisations of little value to the practising manager. He sets out the various functions in the organisation and the definition of formal organisational relationships.[9] Although clearly a strong supporter of the formal approach in some of his views such as, for example, on the principle of span of control, Brech is less definite than other classical writers and recognises a degree of flexibility according to the particular situation.

Brech does place great emphasis, however, on the need for the written definition of responsibilities and the value of job descriptions as an aid to effective organisation and delegation. This work builds on the ideas of earlier writers, such as Urwick, and therefore provides a comprehensive view of the classical approach to organisation and management.

Evaluation of the classical approach

The classical writers have been criticised generally for not taking sufficient account of social factors and for creating an organisation structure in which people can exercise only limited control over their work environment. The idea of sets of principles to guide managerial action has also been subject to much criticism. For example, *Simon* writes:

> *Organisational design is not unlike architectural design. It involves creating large, complex systems having multiple goals. It is illusory to suppose that good designs can be created by using the so-called principles of classical organisation theory.*[10]

Research studies have also expressed doubt about the effectiveness of these principles when applied in practice.[11]

However, the classical approach prompted the start of a more systematic view of management and attempted to provide some common principles applicable to all organisations. These principles are still of relevance in that they offer a useful starting point in attempting to analyse the effectiveness of the design of organisation structure. However, the application of these principles must take full account of the particular situational variables of each individual organisation and the psychological and social factors relating to members of the organisation.

Major sub-groupings

Two major 'sub-groupings' of the classical approach are **scientific management** and bureaucracy.

Critical review and reflection

Whatever the nature of modern organisations, attention must still be given to essential principles of effective structure and management. Any criticism should be directed not at the need for such principles but at the manner in which they are implemented by managers.

What is YOUR view? How effectively are the principles of structure and management applied in YOUR university or organisation?

Scientific management

Many of the classical writers were concerned with the improvement of management as a means of increasing productivity. Emphasis was on the problem of obtaining increased productivity from individual workers through the technical structuring of the work organisation and the provision of monetary incentives as the motivator for higher levels of output. A major contributor to this approach was *F. W. Taylor* (1856–1917), the 'father' of scientific management.[12] Taylor believed that in the same way that there is a best machine for each job, so there is a best working method by which people should undertake their jobs. All work processes could be analysed into discrete tasks and that by scientific method it was possible to find the 'one best way' to perform each task. Each job was broken down into component parts, each part timed and the parts rearranged into the most efficient method of working.

Principles to guide management

Taylor was concerned with finding more efficient methods and procedures for co-ordination and control of work, and a believer in the rational–economic needs concept of motivation. If management acted on his ideas, work would become more satisfying and profitable for all concerned. Workers would be motivated by obtaining the highest possible wages through working in the most efficient and productive way. He set out a number of principles to guide management. These principles are usually summarised as:

- the development of a true science for each person's work;
- the scientific selection, training and development of workers;
- co-operation with workers to ensure work is carried out in the prescribed way;
- hierarchical structures of authority and close supervision;
- clear division of tasks and responsibility between management and workers.

In his famous studies at the Bethlehem Steel Corporation, Taylor applied his ideas on scientific management to a group of seventy-five men loading pig iron. Taylor selected a Dutch labourer, Schmidt, whom he reported as a 'high-priced' man with a reputation for placing a high value on money, and of limited mental ability. By following detailed instructions on when to pick up the pig iron and walk, and when to sit and rest, and with no back talk, Schmidt increased his output from 12½ tons to 47½ tons per day. He maintained this level of output throughout the three years of the study. In return Schmidt received a 60 per cent increase in wages compared with what was paid to the other men. One by one other workers were selected and trained to handle pig iron at the rate of 47½ tons per day and in return they received 60 per cent more wages. Taylor drew attention to the need for the scientific selection of the workers. When the other labourers in the group were trained in the same method, only one in eight was physically capable of the effort of loading 47½ tons per day, although there was a noticeable increase in their level of output.

Reactions against scientific management

There were strong criticisms of, and reaction against, scientific management methods from the workers who found the work boring and requiring little skill. Despite these criticisms, Taylor attempted to expand the implementation of his ideas in the Bethlehem Steel Corporation. However, fears of mass redundancies persuaded the management to request Taylor to moderate his activities. Yet Taylor's belief in his methods was so strong that he would not accept management's interference and eventually they dispensed with his services. Continued resentment and hostility against scientific management led to an investigation of Taylor's methods by a House of Representatives Committee, which reported in 1912. The conclusion of the committee was that scientific management did provide some useful techniques and offered valuable organisational suggestions, but gave production managers a dangerously high level of uncontrolled power.

Taylorism as management control

Taylor placed emphasis on the content of a 'fair day's work' and optimising the level of workers' productivity. A major obstacle to this objective was 'systematic soldiering' and what Taylor saw as the deliberate attempt by workers to promote their best interests and to keep employers ignorant of how fast work, especially piece-rate work, could be carried out.

According to *Braverman,* scientific management starts from the capitalist point of view and method of production, and the adaptation of labour to the needs of capital. Taylor's work was more concerned with the organisation of labour than with the development of technology. A distinctive feature of Taylor's thought was the concept of management control.[13] Braverman suggests Taylor's conclusion was that workers should be controlled not only by the giving of orders and maintenance of discipline, but also by removing from them any decisions about the manner in which their work was to be carried out. By division of labour, and by dictating precise stages and methods for every aspect of work performance, management could gain control of the actual process of work. The rationalisation of production processes and division of labour tends to result in the de-skilling of work and this may be a main strategy of the employer.[14]

Cloke and Goldsmith also suggest that Taylor was the leading promoter of the idea that managers should design and control the work process scientifically in order to guarantee maximum efficiency. He believed in multiple layers of management to supervise the work process and in rigid, detailed control of the workforce.

Taylor's theories justified managerial control over the production process and removed decision making from employees and from owners as well. The increasingly authoritative operational role of management diminished the direct involvement of owners in day-to-day decision making. Managers saw this as an opportunity to solidify their power and adopted Taylor's ideas wholesale. In the process, they affirmed efficiency over collaboration, quantity over quality, and cost controls over customer service.[15]

Relevance of scientific management

Taylor's work is often criticised today, but it should be remembered that he was writing at a time of industrial reorganisation and the emergence of large, complex organisations with new forms of technology. He believed his methods would lead to improved management–labour relations and contribute to improved industrial efficiency and prosperity. Workers were regarded as rational–economic, motivated directly by monetary incentives linked to the level of work output.

Among the criticisms are those by *Rose*. Taylor regarded workers from an engineering viewpoint and as machines, but the one best way of performing a task is not always the best method for every worker. The reduction of physical movement to find the one best way is not always beneficial and some 'wasteful' movements are essential to the overall rhythm of work. Rose also argues that the concept of a fair day's pay for a fair day's work is not purely a technical matter. It is also a notion of social equity and not in keeping with a scientific approach.[16]

According to *Drucker,* however, the central theme of Taylor's work was not inefficiency but the need to substitute industrial warfare with industrial harmony. Taylor sought to do this through:

- higher wages from increased output;
- the removal of physical strain from doing work the wrong way;
- development of the workers and the opportunity for them to undertake tasks they were capable of doing; and
- elimination of the 'boss' and the duty of management to help workers.

Frederick Winslow Taylor may prove a more useful prophet for our times than we yet recognize . . . Taylor's greatest impact may still be ahead . . . the under-developed and developing countries are now reaching the stage where they need Taylor and 'scientific management' . . . But the need to study Taylor anew and apply him may be the greatest in the developed countries.[17]

Impetus to management thinking

Whatever the opinions on scientific management, Taylor and his disciples left to modern management the legacy of such practices as work study, organisation and methods, payment by results, management by exception and production control.

Taylor did give a major impetus to the development of management thinking and the later development of organisational behaviour. For example, *Crainer and Dearlove* suggest that although Taylor's theories are now largely outdated, they still had a profound impact throughout the world and his mark can be seen on much of the subsequent management literature.[18] And *Stern* goes a stage further:

The 'scientific management' of Frederick Taylor . . . shaped the first coherent school of thought with application to the industrialised world. He was our first professional guru and Taylorism – with its twin goals of productivity and efficiency – still influences management thinking 100 years on.[19]

Principles of Taylor's scientific approach to management appear still to have relevance today. We can see examples of Taylorism alive and well, and management practices based on the philosophy of his ideas. As an example, large hotel organisations often make use of standard recipes and standard performance manuals, and it is common for housekeeping staff to have a prescribed layout for each room, with training based on detailed procedures and the one best way. Staff may be expected to clean a given number of rooms per shift, with financial incentives for additional rooms.[20]

Modern customer call centres can also be seen to exhibit many features of Taylorism.[21] The strict routine, uniformity, clearly specified tasks, detailed checklists and close control in fast food restaurants such as McDonald's also suggest close links with scientific management.

It is difficult to argue against the general line of Taylor's principles but they are subject to misuse. What is important is the context and manner in which such principles are put into effect. There is arguably one best way *technically* to perform a job – for example, with factory assembly line production in particular. However, account needs to be taken of human behaviour. People tend to have their preferred way of working and the need for variety and more interesting or challenging tasks. Provided work is carried out safely and to a satisfactory standard and completed on time, to what extent should management *insist* on the 'one best way'?

It seems that Taylor did not so much ignore (as is often suggested) but was more *unaware* of the complexity of human behaviour in organisations and the importance of the individual's feelings and sentiments, group working, managerial behaviour and the work environment. However, we now have greater knowledge about social effects within the work organisation and about the value of money, incentives, motivation, and job satisfaction and performance.

Critical review and reflection

Despite strong criticisms of scientific management, in the right circumstances the underlying concepts still have relevance and much to offer work organisations today. It is just that many commentators appear reluctant to admit this openly.

What do YOU think? Where do YOU think scientific management could be applied to the best overall effect in YOUR university or organisation?

Bureaucracy

A form of structure to be found in many large-scale organisations is **bureaucracy.** *Weber,* a German sociologist, showed particular concern for what he called 'bureaucratic structures', although his work in this area came almost as a side issue to his main study on power and authority.[22] He suggested that 'the decisive reason for the advance of bureaucratic organization has always been its purely technical superiority over any other form of organization'. Weber pointed out that the definition of tasks and responsibilities within the structure of management gave rise to a permanent administration and standardisation of work procedures, notwithstanding changes in the actual holders of office.

The term 'bureaucracy' has common connotations with criticism of red tape and rigidity, though in the study of organisations and management it is important that the term is seen not necessarily in a depreciative sense but as applying to certain structural features of formal organisations. Weber analysed bureaucracies not empirically but as an 'ideal type' derived from the most characteristic bureaucratic features of all known organisations. He saw the development of bureaucracies as a means of introducing order and rationality into social life.

Main characteristics of bureaucracies

Weber did not actually define bureaucracy but did attempt to identify the main characteristics of this type of organisation. He emphasised the importance of administration based on expertise (rules of experts) and administration based on discipline (rules of officials).

- The tasks of the organisation are allocated as official duties among the various positions.
- There is an implied clear-cut division of labour and a high level of specialisation.
- A hierarchical authority applies to the organisation of offices and positions.
- Uniformity of decisions and actions is achieved through formally established systems of rules and regulations. Together with a structure of authority, this enables the co-ordination of various activities within the organisation.
- An impersonal orientation is expected from officials in their dealings with clients and other officials. This is designed to result in rational judgements by officials in the performance of their duties.
- Employment by the organisation is based on technical qualifications and constitutes a life-long career for the officials.[23]

The four main features of bureaucracy are summarised by *Stewart* as **specialisation, hierarchy of authority, system of rules** and **impersonality.** Stewart sees the characteristic of impersonality as the feature of bureaucracy that most distinguishes it from other types of organisations. A bureaucracy should not only be impersonal but be seen to be impersonal.[24]

Robbins and Judge emphasise standardisation as the key concept that underlies all bureaucracies.

> *The bureaucracy is characterized by highly routine operating tasks achieved through specialization, very formalized rules and regulations, tasks that are grouped into functional departments, centralized authority, narrow spans of control, and decision making that follows the chain of command . . . However, it does have its advantages. The primary strength of the bureaucracy lies in its ability to perform standardized activities in a highly efficient manner.[25]*

Criticisms of bureaucracy

Weber's concept of bureaucracy has a number of disadvantages and has been subject to severe criticism:

- The over-emphasis on rules and procedures, record keeping and paperwork may become more important in its own right than as a means to an end.
- Officials may develop a dependence upon bureaucratic status, symbols and rules.
- Initiative may be stifled, and when a situation is not covered by a complete set of rules or procedures there may be a lack of flexibility or adaptation to changing circumstances.
- Position and responsibilities in the organisation can lead to officious bureaucratic behaviour. There may also be a tendency to conceal administrative procedures from outsiders.
- Impersonal relations can lead to stereotyped behaviour and a lack of responsiveness to individual incidents or problems.

Restriction of psychological growth

One of the strongest critics of bureaucratic organisation, and the demands it makes on the worker, is *Argyris*.[26] He claims that bureaucracies restrict the psychological growth of the individual and cause feelings of failure, frustration and conflict. Argyris suggests that the organisational environment should provide a significant degree of individual responsibility and self-control, commitment to the goals of the organisation, productiveness, and work and an opportunity for individuals to apply their full abilities.

A similar criticism is made by *Caulkin*, who refers to the impersonal structure of bureaucracy as constructed round the post rather than the person and the ease with which it can be swung behind unsocial or even pathological ends.

> *The overemphasis on process rather than purpose, fragmented responsibilities and hierarchical control means that it's all too easy for individuals to neglect the larger purposes to which their small effort is being put.*[27]

A number of writers refer to 'adhocracy' as the opposite of bureaucracy. **Adhocracy** is a flexible, loosely structured, adaptable, organic and informal form of organisation. According to *Morgan*, adhocracy is an organic form of organisation, highly suited for the performance of complex and uncertain tasks. It is frequently used for research and development.[28] *Waterman* sees adhocracy as any form of organisation that cuts across normal bureaucratic lines to capture opportunities, solve problems and get results.[29] *Mintzberg* views adhocracy as the project organisations build around project teams of experts, with senior managers linking and dealing to secure the projects.[30]

Critical review and reflection

It is difficult to envisage how large-scale organisations, especially within the public sector, could function effectively without exhibiting at least some of the features of a bureaucracy. Demands for alternative forms of structure are unrealistic.

How would YOU attempt to justify the benefits of bureaucratic structures? To what extent would YOU be comfortable working in a bureaucratic organisation?

Evaluation of bureaucracy

Growth of bureaucracy has come through the increasing size and complexity of organisations and associated demand for effective administration. Effective organisation is based on structure and delegation through different layers of the hierarchy. The work of the classical writers has given emphasis to the careful design and planning of organisation structure and the definition of individual duties and responsibilities. Greater specialisation and the application of expertise and technical knowledge have highlighted the need for laid-down procedures.

Bureaucracy is founded on a formal, clearly defined and hierarchical structure. However, with rapid changes in the external environment, de-layering of organisations, empowerment and greater attention to meeting the needs of customers, there is an increasing need to organise for flexibility. For example, the crisis IBM experienced in the 1980s/1990s over the market for personal computers is explained at least in part by its top-heavy corporate structure, cumbersome organisation and dinosaur-like bureaucracy.[31]

According to *Cloke and Goldsmith*, management and bureaucracy can be thought of as flip sides of the same coin. The elements of bureaucracy generate organisational hierarchy and management, while managers generate a need for bureaucracy.

> *Bureaucracies provide a safe haven where managers can hide from responsibility and avoid being held accountable for errors of judgement or problems they created or failed to solve. In return, managers are able to use bureaucratic rules to stifle self-management and compel employees to follow their direction . . . Yet bureaucratic systems can be broken down and transformed into human-scale interactions. We have seen countless managers recreate themselves as leaders and facilitators, employees reinvent themselves as responsible self-managing*

team members, and bureaucracies transform into responsive, human-scale organizations. Alternatives to organizational hierarchy are both practical and possible.[32]

By their very nature, bureaucracies have always tended to attract criticism. Much of this criticism is valid, but much also appears unfair. For example, according to *Drucker:*

Whenever a big organization gets into trouble – and especially if it has been successful for many years – people blame sluggishness, complacency, arrogance, mammoth bureaucracies. A plausible explanation? Yes. But rarely the relevant or correct one.[33]

Need for alternative structures

As organisations face increasing global competitiveness and complex demands of the information and technological age, the need arises for alternative forms of corporate structure and systems. For example, there appears to be a particular dilemma for management in personal service industries. The underlying characteristics of bureaucracy would seem to restrict personal service delivery, which requires a flexible approach, responsiveness to individual requirements and the need for initiative and inventiveness.[34]

Ridderstråle points out that in the past century the hallmark of a large company was hierarchy, which rests on principles at odds with the new strategic requirements. 'Bureaucracies allowed people with knowledge to control ignorant workers. Now, new structures are needed as knowledge spreads.' Ridderstråle suggests four specific ways in which high-performing organisations have responded to increasingly complex knowledge systems by developing organisational solutions that depart from the traditional bureaucratic model:

- more decentralised and flatter structures in order that quick decisions can be taken near to where the critical knowledge resides;
- the use of more than a single structure in order that knowledge may be assembled across the boundaries of a traditional organisation chart;
- converting companies into learning organisations and giving every employee the same level of familiarity with personnel and capabilities;
- broader sharing of expertise and knowledge, which may be located in the periphery where little formal authority resides.[35]

Stewart suggests that more organisations today contain mainly, or a considerable number of, professionals. Such organisations will still have bureaucratic features, but there is more reliance on professional discretion and self-regulation than on control through rules and regulations.[36]

Public-sector organisations

However, despite new forms of organisation that have emerged, many writers suggest that bureaucracy is still relevant today as a major form of organisation structure.[37] In the case of public-sector organisations, in particular, there is a demand for uniformity of treatment, regularity of procedures and public accountability for their operations. This leads to adherence to specified rules and procedures and to the keeping of detailed records. In their actual dealings with public-sector organisations, people often call for what amounts to increased bureaucracy, even though they may not use that term. The demands for equal treatment, for a standard set of regulations that applies to everyone and that decisions should not be left to the discretion of individual managers are, in effect, demands for bureaucracy.

Green argues that, although bureaucracies are becoming less and less the first-choice format for organisational shape, there is still a place for bureaucracy in parts of most organisations and especially public-sector organisations such as local authorities and universities. The use and implementation of tried and tested rules and procedures helps to ensure essential values and ethics, and that necessary functions are run on a consistent and fair basis.[38] New forms of information technology, such as electronic transactions processed from home or public access terminals, are likely to change processes of government service delivery, administrative workloads and the nature of bureaucracy.[39]

Human relations approach

The main emphasis of the classical writers was on structure and the formal organisation, but during the 1920s greater attention began to be paid to the social factors at work and to the behaviour of employees within an organisation – that is, the **human relations approach.**

The Hawthorne studies

The turning point in the development of the human relations movement ('behavioural' and 'informal' are alternative headings) came with the famous studies at the Hawthorne plant of the Western Electric Company near Chicago (1924–32) and the subsequent publication of the research findings.[40] Among the people who wrote about the Hawthorne studies was Elton Mayo (1880–1949), who is often quoted as having been a leader of the researchers. However, there appears to be some doubt as to the extent of Mayo's actual involvement.[41]

There were four main phases to the Hawthorne studies:

- the illumination experiments;
- the relay assembly test room;
- the interviewing programme;
- the bank wiring observation room.

Illumination experiments

The original investigation was conducted on the lines of the classical approach and was concerned, in typical scientific management style, with the effects of the intensity of lighting upon the workers' productivity. The workers were divided into two groups, an experimental group and a control group. The results of these tests were inconclusive as production in the experimental group varied with no apparent relationship to the level of lighting, but actually increased when conditions were made much worse. Production also increased in the control group although the lighting remained unchanged. The level of production was influenced, clearly, by factors other than changes in physical conditions of work. This prompted a series of other experiments investigating factors of worker productivity.

Relay assembly test room

In the relay assembly test room the work was boring and repetitive. It involved assembling telephone relays by putting together a number of small parts. Six women workers were transferred from their normal departments to a separate area. Researchers selected two assemblers who were friends, then chose three other assemblers and a layout operator. The experiment was divided into thirteen periods during which the workers were subjected to a series of planned and controlled changes to their conditions of work, such as hours of work, rest pauses and provision of refreshments. The general environmental conditions of the test room were similar to those of the normal assembly line.

During the experiment the observer adopted a friendly manner, consulting the workers, listening to their complaints and keeping them informed. Following all but one of the changes (when operators complained that too many breaks made them lose their work rhythm) there was a continuous increase in the level of production. The researchers formed the conclusion that the extra attention given to the workers and the apparent interest in them shown by management were the main reasons for the higher productivity. This has become famous as the 'Hawthorne effect'.

Interviewing programme

Another significant phase of the experiments was the interviewing programme. The lighting experiment and the relay assembly test room drew attention to the form of supervision as a contributory factor to the workers' level of production. In an attempt to find out more about the workers' feelings towards their supervisors and their general conditions of work, a large interviewing programme was introduced. More than 20,000 interviews were conducted before the work was ended because of the Depression.

Initially, interviewers approached their task with a set of prepared questions, relating mainly to how the workers felt about their jobs. However, this produced only limited information. As a result, the style of interviewing was changed to become more non-directive and open ended. There was no set list of questions and the workers were free to talk about any aspect of their work. The interviewers set out to be friendly and sympathetic. They adopted an impartial, non-judgemental approach and concentrated on listening.

Using this approach, interviewers found out far more about workers' true feelings and attitudes. They gained information not just about supervision and working conditions, but also about the company itself, management, work group relations and matters outside of work such as family life and views on society in general. Many workers appeared to welcome the opportunity to have someone to talk to about their feelings and problems and to be able to 'let off steam' in a friendly atmosphere. The interviewing programme was significant in giving an impetus to present-day human resource management and the use of counselling interviews, and highlighting the need for management to listen to workers' feelings and problems. Being a good listener is arguably even more important for managers in today's work organisations and it is a skill that needs to be encouraged and developed.[42]

Bank wiring observation room

Another experiment involved the observation of a group of fourteen men working in the bank wiring room. It was noted that the men formed their own informal organisation with sub-groups or cliques, and natural leaders emerging with the consent of the members. The group developed its own pattern of informal social relations and 'norms' of what constituted 'proper' behaviour. Despite a financial incentive scheme where the workers could receive more money the more work produced, the group decided on a level of output well below the level they were capable of producing. Group pressures on individual workers were stronger than financial incentives offered by management. The workers believed that if they increased their output, management would raise the standard level of piece rates. The importance of group 'norms' and informal social relations are discussed later (**see Chapter 8**).

Evaluation

The Hawthorne studies have received much criticism, for example on methodology and on failure of the investigators to take sufficient account of environmental factors – although much of this criticism is with the value of hindsight. The human relations writers have been criticised generally for the adoption of a management perspective, their 'unitary frame of reference' and their over-simplified theories.[43] Other criticisms of the human relations approach are that it is insufficiently scientific and that it takes too narrow a view. It ignores the role of the organisation itself in how society operates.

Sex power differential

There are a number of interpretations of the results of the Hawthorne studies, including the possible implications of the 'sex power differential' between the two groups. In the bank wiring room, where output was restricted, the group was all male. In the relay assembly room, where output increased, all members were young unmarried women. All except one were living at home with traditional families of immigrant background. In the work environment of the factory, women had been subjected to frequent contact with male supervisors and therefore 'the sex power hierarchies in the home and in the factory were congruent'. It is suggested, therefore, that it was only to be expected that the women agreed readily to participate with management in the relay assembly test room experiment.[44]

Importance of the Hawthorne studies

Whatever the interpretation of the Hawthorne studies, they generated significant new ideas concerning the importance of work groups and leadership, communications, output restrictions, motivation and job design. The studies undoubtedly marked a significant step forward in providing further insight into human behaviour at work and the development of management thinking. They are regarded as one of the most important of social science investigations and the foundation of the human relations approach to management and the development of organisational behaviour.

Supporters of the classical approach adopted a more managerial perspective and sought to increase production by rationalisation of the work organisation. By contrast, the human relations movement has led to ideas on increasing production by humanising the work organisation and strove for a greater understanding of people's psychological and social needs at work as well as improving the process of management.

Recognition of the informal organisation

The human relations approach also recognised the importance of the informal organisation, which will always be present within the formal structure. This informal organisation will influence the motivation of employees who will view the organisation for which they work through the values and attitudes of their colleagues. Their view of the organisation determines their approach to work and the extent of their motivation to work well or otherwise.

In a review of humane approaches to management, *Crainer* asserts: 'The Hawthorne Studies were important because they showed that views of how managers behaved were a vital aspect of motivation and improved performance. Also, the research revealed the importance of informal work groups.'[45]

Human relations writers demonstrated that people go to work to satisfy a complexity of needs and not simply for monetary reward. These writers emphasised the importance of the wider social needs of individuals and gave recognition to the work organisation as a social organisation and the importance of the group, and group values and norms, in influencing individual behaviour at work. It has been commented that the classical school was concerned about 'organisations without people' and the human relations school about 'people without organisations'.

Critical review and reflection

The human relations approach makes all the right noises, with an emphasis on humane behaviour, considerate management and recognition of the informal organisation. However, it is more about what people would like to believe and ignores the realities of the actual working environment.

What is YOUR opinion? To what extent have YOU experienced a genuine human relations approach in a work organisation?

Neo-human relations

Certainly there were shortcomings in the human relations approach, and assumptions that evolved from studies such as the Hawthorne studies were not necessarily supported by empirical evidence. For example, the contention that a satisfied worker is a productive worker was not always found to be valid. However, the results of the studies and subsequent attention given to the social organisation and to theories of individual motivation gave rise to the work of those writers in the 1950s and 1960s who adopted a more psychological orientation. New ideas on management theory arose and a major focus of concern was the personal adjustment of the individual within the work organisation and the effects of group relationships and leadership styles.

This group of writers is often (and more correctly) categorised separately under the heading of **neo-human relations.** The works of these writers are examined later in more detail (**in Chapter 7 and Chapter 10**) but summarised briefly here.

Some leading contributors

A major impetus for the neo-human relations approach was the work of *Maslow* who, in 1943, put forward a theoretical framework of individual personality development and motivation based on a hierarchy of five levels of human needs: physiological, safety, love, esteem and self-actualisation at the highest level.[46] The work of Maslow provides a link with the earlier human relations approach.

Among the best-known contributors to the neo-human relations approach are *Herzberg* and *McGregor.* Herzberg isolated two different sets of factors affecting motivation and satisfaction at work. One set of factors comprises those that, if absent, cause dissatisfaction, and concerned basically the job environment. However, to motivate workers to give of their best, proper attention must be given to a different set of factors, the 'motivators' or 'growth' factors concerned with job content.[47] McGregor argued that the style of management adopted is a function of the manager's attitudes towards human nature and behaviour at work. He put forward two suppositions called Theory X and Theory Y, which are based on popular assumptions about work and people.[48]

Other major contributors to the neo-human relations approach are *Likert,* whose work includes research into different systems of management;[49] *McClelland,* with ideas on achievement motivation;[50] and *Argyris,* who considered the effects of the formal organisation on the individual and psychological growth in the process of self-actualisation.[51] Argyris's major contributions include his work on organisational learning and on effective leadership.[52]

The neo-human relations approach has generated a large amount of writing and research, not only from original proposers but also from others seeking to establish the validity of their ideas. This has led to continuing attention given to such matters as organisation structuring, group dynamics, job satisfaction, communication and participation, leadership styles and motivation. It has also led to greater attention to the importance of interpersonal interactions, the causes of conflict and recognition of employee relations.

The systems approach

Criticisms of earlier approaches to organisation are based in part on the attempt to study the activities and problems of the organisation solely in terms of the internal environment. The classical approach emphasised the technical requirements of the organisation and its needs – 'organisations without people'; the human relations approach emphasised the psychological and social aspects, and the consideration of human needs – 'people without organisations'. The **systems approach** attempts to reconcile these two earlier approaches and the work of the formal and informal writers.

Systems theory is not new and has been used in the natural and physical sciences for a number of years. One of the founders of this approach was the biologist *Ludwig von Bertalanffy*, who used the term 'systems theory' in an article published in 1951 and who is generally credited with having developed the outline of General Systems Theory.[53] The systems approach to organisation has arisen, at least in part, therefore, from the work of biologists, and *Miller and Rice* have likened the commercial and industrial organisation to the biological organism.[54]

From a business perspective, organisations are analysed as 'systems' with a number of interrelated sub-systems. Attention is focused on the total work organisation and the interrelationships of structure and behaviour, and the range of variables within the organisation. The idea is that any part of an organisation's activities affects all other parts. The systems approach encourages managers to view the organisation both as a whole and as part of a larger environment. (**The view of the organisation as an open system is discussed later in Chapter 3.**)

Socio-technical system

The idea of socio-technical systems arose from the work of *Trist* and others, of the Tavistock Institute of Human Relations, in their study of the effects of changing technology in the coal-mining industry in the 1940s.[55] The traditional method of working was small, self-selecting groups of miners working together, as an independent team, on one part of the coal face – the 'single place' or 'shortwall' method. The increasing use of mechanisation and the introduction of coal-cutters and mechanical conveyors enabled coal to be extracted on a 'longwall' method. Shift working was introduced, with each shift specialising in one stage of the operation – preparation, cutting or loading.

However, the new method meant a change in the previous system. Technological change had brought about changes in psychological and sociological properties of the old method of working. There was a lack of co-operation between different shifts and, within each shift, an increase in absenteeism, scapegoating and signs of greater social stress. The 'longwall' method was socially disruptive and did not prove as economically efficient as it could have been with the new technology.

The researchers saw the need for a socio-technical approach in which an appropriate social system could be developed in keeping with the new technical system. The result was the 'composite longwall' method, with more responsibility to the team as a whole and shifts carrying out composite tasks, the reintroduction of multiskilled roles and a reduction in specialisation. The composite method was psychologically and socially more rewarding and economically more efficient than the 'longwall' method.

The **socio-technical system** is concerned with the interactions between the psychological and social factors and the needs and demands of the human part of the organisation, and its structural and technological requirements. The 'socio-technical' system directs attention to the transformation or conversion process itself, to the series of activities through which the organisation attempts to achieve its objectives. Recognition of the socio-technical approach is of particular importance today. People must be considered as at least an equal priority along with investment in technology. For example, *Lane et al.* point out that major technological change has brought about dramatic changes in worker behaviour and requirements. It is people who unlock the benefits and opportunities of information and communications technology.[56]

Technological determinism

The socio-technical system provides a link between the systems approach and a sub-division, sometimes adopted – the **technology approach**. Writers under the technology heading attempt to restrict generalisations about organisations and management and emphasise the effects of varying technologies on organisation structure, work groups and individual performance and job satisfaction. This is in contrast with the socio-technical approach, which did not regard technology, per se, as a determinant of behaviour.

Under the heading of the technology approach could be included the work of such writers as: *Walker and Guest* (effects of the assembly line production method on employee behaviour);[57] *Sayles* (relationship between technology and the nature of work groups);[58] *Blauner* (problems of 'alienation' in relation to different work technologies);[59] and *Turner and Lawrence* (technology and socio-culture)[60]. (**Technology and organisations is examined in Chapter 12.**)

Critical review and reflection

The underlying principles and ideas of the socio-technical systems and technological determinism approaches are of particular relevance and assistance to the practical manager.

To what extent do YOU agree with this assertion? As a manager, how would YOU envisage drawing upon YOUR understanding of these approaches?

Management and organisational behaviour in action case study
'Vanguard Method' for systems thinking

A different, more recent approach to thinking on management applied to service organisations is that of the 'Vanguard Method', which is based on the pioneering work of, among others, W. Edwards Deming, Chris Argyris and Taiichi Ohno. Ohno, the father of the Toyota Production System, drew attention to managers' lack of control on the shop floor and to the importance of continuous revisions, and his ideas gave rise to concepts such as total quality management and just-in-time. Ohno viewed the work organisation as an integrated system, with the focus on flow throughout the system rather than on individual functions. As *Seddon* notes: 'In Ohno's philosophy each person's work is connected to the needs of customers, as opposed to arbitrary and counterproductive measures of activity.'[61]

Vanguard helps organisations change from command and control thinking to a systems thinking on the design and management of work.

Command and control thinking		Systems thinking
Top-down, hierarchy	**Perspective**	Outside-in system
Functional specialisation and procedures	**Design of work**	Demand, value and flow
Contractual	**Attitude to customers**	What matters?
Separated from work	**Decision-making**	Integrated with work
Output, targets, activity, standards: related to budget	**Measurement**	Capability, variation: related to purpose
Contractual	**Attitude to suppliers**	Co-operative
Control budgets, manage people	**Management ethos**	Learn through action on the system
Extrinsic	Assumptions about motivation	Intrinsic

Emphasis is placed on the customer and measurement of success as opposed to targets of expected performance. The consequences are improved service to customers, at lower costs and improved morale. Service is different to manufacturing. In simple terms, there is inherently greater variety in customer demand, hence the need to design to absorb that variety. Vanguard recommends that service organisations avoid the 'tools' developed for 'lean manufacturing' as they do not apply well in service organisations.

Intrinsic to the Vanguard Method is the transfer of expertise to people (managers and staff) in the organisation. Vanguard uses 'sensei', people who are experts in both intervention theory (how you make a change) and systems theory (how to analyse and design work). Vanguard senseis are experts in the 'what' (how a systems design improves performance) and the 'how' (how to make this change).

Steps in the Vanguard Method

Understanding the distinctions – Top management must understand what it means to change from command and control to systems thinking.

Scoping – Assessing the scope for improvement; knowledge about customer demand, revenue and service flows, waste and the causes of waste; the potential scope and value of making this change in practical terms.

Check – People who do the work to be given technical support and check their understanding of the what and why of performance as a system.

Measures and method – In parallel with 'check', managers work on the relationship between measures and method, understanding the need to change and use of measures for managing and improving performance.

Prototyping – The 'check' team and managers work on measures and establish a prototype of the redesign. The purpose is to develop the redesign and determine anticipated economies.

Leader's review – In order to make informed choices about benefits from adopting the new systems design and authorises preparation for implementation.

Proof of concept – Prototype is extended and developed to handle all customer demands; the consequential improvements are tracked with new (system) measures while management develop a new budgeting and management information system.

Constancy of purpose – Leadership of the change with the top management team including, in particular, roles and measures. Clarity about future state and means of implementation.

Implementation – Here a choice can be made: establishing a working pilot (a complete redesign but limited in volume or scope); or making a complete change to the organisation.

Changes to policy and practice – Review matters of policy and practice. Typically they will include budgeting, HR policy and practice, interpretation of regulations and IT.

Finding out what matters to your customers – Having redesigned and improved your service, it is a natural extension to step over the boundary and learn about what matters to your customers. The work leads to new services, designed with customers.

Source: Thanks to David Puttick, Vanguard. Reproduced with permission. http://vanguard-method.net/

Tasks

1. What is your view on a systems approach and the Vanguard Method?
2. To what extent do you believe systems thinking can be applied effectively to production organisations?
3. How do you think managers are likely to react to an ethos of learning through action on the system? What potential difficulties do you see?

The contingency approach

The classical approach suggested one best form of structure and placed emphasis on general sets of principles, while the human relations approach gave little attention at all to structure. In contrast, the **contingency approach** shows renewed concern with the importance of structure as a significant influence on organisational performance. The contingency approach, which can be seen as an extension of the systems approach, highlights possible means of differentiating among alternative forms of organisation structures and systems of management. There is no one optimum state. For example, the structure of the organisation and its 'success' are dependent, that is contingent upon, the nature of tasks with which it is designed to deal and the nature of environmental influences.

The most appropriate structure and system of management is therefore dependent upon the contingencies of the situation for each particular organisation. The contingency approach implies that organisational theory should not seek to suggest one best way to structure or manage organisations, but should provide insights into the situational and contextual factors that influence management decisions. Situational variables may be identified in a number of ways and include type of organisation and its purpose, culture, size, technology and environment. Contingency models of organisation and management are discussed later (**see Chapter 11**).

A summary of management theory and some links with other chapters are set out in the concept map in Figure 2.2.

Other approaches to the study of organisations

The fourfold framework of classical, human relations, systems and contingency approaches provides a helpful, although rather simplistic, categorisation. The study of organisations, their structure and management is a broad field of enquiry. Depending on the views and preferences of the writer, other possible main approaches include decision-making and social action.

Decision-making approach

The systems approach involves the isolation of those functions most directly concerned with the achievement of objectives and the identification of main decision areas or sub-systems. Viewing the organisation as a system emphasises the need for good information and channels of communication in order to assist effective decision-making in the organisation. Recognition of the need for decision-making and the attainment of goals draws attention to a sub-division of the systems approach, or a separate category – that of the **decision-making (decision theory) approach.** Here the focus of attention is on managerial decision-making and how organisations process and use information in making decisions.

Successful management lies in responding to internal and external change. This involves the clarification of objectives, the specification of problems and the search for and implementation of solutions. The organisation is seen as an information-processing network with numerous decision points. An understanding of how decisions are made helps in understanding behaviour in the organisation. Decision-making writers seek to explain the mechanisms by which conflict is resolved and choices are made.

Some leading writers

Leading writers on the decision-making approach include *Barnard, Simon* and *Cyert and March*. The scope of the decision-making approach, however, is wide and it is possible to identify contributions from engineers, mathematicians and operational research specialists in addition to the work of economists, psychologists and writers on management and organisation.

Barnard stressed the need for co-operative action in organisations. He believed that people's ability to communicate, and their commitment and contribution to the achievement of a common purpose, were necessary for the existence of a co-operative system.[62] These ideas were developed further by Simon. He sees management as meaning decision-making and his concern is with how decisions are made and how decision-making can be improved. Simon is critical of the implication of 'man' as completely rational and proposes a model of 'administrative man' who, unlike 'economic man', 'satisfices' rather than maximises. Administrative decision-making is the achievement of satisfactory rather than optimal results in solving problems.[63]

Economic models of decision-making, based on the assumption of rational behaviour in choosing from known alternatives in order to maximise objectives, can be contrasted with

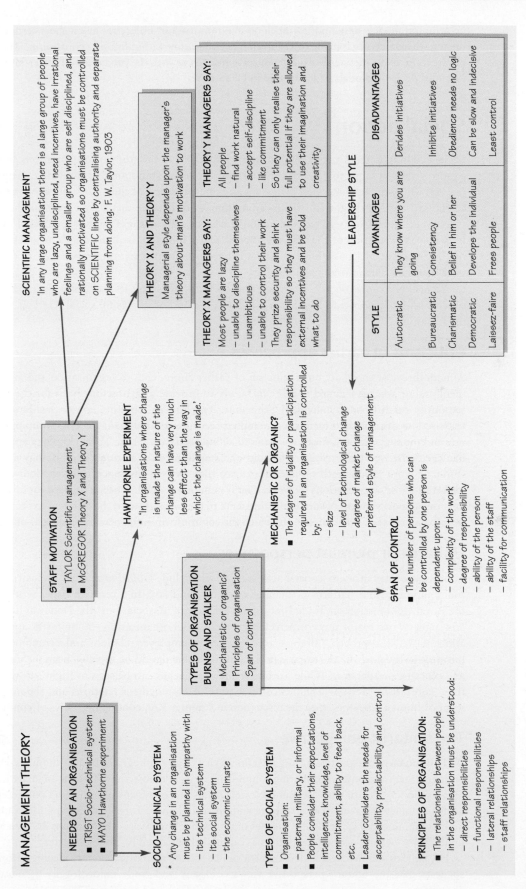

Figure 2.2 Concept map of management theory

Source: Copyright © 2008 The Virtual Learning Materials Workshop. Reproduced with permission.

behavioural models based not so much on maximisation of objectives as on short-term expediency, where a choice is made to avoid conflict and to stay within limiting constraints. Managers are more concerned with avoiding uncertainties than with the prediction of uncertainties.[64] (See also decision models of leadership in Chapter 9.)

Social action

Social action represents a contribution from sociologists to the study of organisations. Social-action writers attempt to view the organisation from the standpoint of individual members (actors) who will each have their own goals and interpretation of their work situation in terms of the satisfaction sought and the meaning that work has for them. The goals of the individual, and the means selected and actions taken to achieve these goals, are affected by the individual's perception of the situation. Social action looks to the individual's own definition of the situation as a basis for explaining behaviour. Conflict of interests is seen as normal behaviour and part of organisational life.

According to *Silverman,* 'The action approach . . . does not, in itself, provide a theory of organisations. It is instead best understood as a method of analysing social relations within organisations.'[65]

Criticisms of earlier approaches

A main thrust of social action is criticism of earlier approaches to organisation and management and of what is claimed to be their failure to provide a satisfactory basis for the explanation or prediction of individual behaviour. The human relations approaches have been criticised because of their focus on generalised theories of good management, group psychology and the suggestion of needs common to all individuals at work. The technology approach has been criticised for attributing feelings of alienation to the nature of technology and the status of work groups rather than an analysis that focused on concern for the individual's expectations of, and reactions to, work. The systems approach has been criticised for failure to examine the orientation of individual members to the organisation, the different expectations people have of their work or ways in which the environment influences expectations of work.

Unitarist or pluralist perspectives

Important contributors to a social action approach include *Goldthorpe et al.* (industrial attitudes and behaviour patterns of manual workers)[66] and *Fox.* In a research paper written for the Royal Commission on Trade Unions and Employers' Associations (the Donovan Report), Fox suggests two major ways of perceiving an industrial organisation – a 'unitarist' approach and a 'pluralist' approach.[67] In the search for effective employee relations and a common commitment to the goals of the organisation, consideration should be given to both the unitarist and pluralist perspectives. While neither of the approaches can be seen as 'right' or 'wrong', these contrasting views will influence the nature of employment relations and the management of human resources. (See the discussion in Chapter 3 on contrasting views of conflict.)

The unitarist perspective

With the **unitarist perspective** the organisation is viewed as an integrated and harmonious whole, with managers and other staff sharing common interests and objectives. There is an image of the organisation as a team with a common source of loyalty, one focus of effort and one accepted leader. Conflict is perceived as disruptive and unnatural and can be explained by, for example, poor communications, personality clashes or the work of agitators. Trade unions are seen as an unnecessary evil and restrictive practices as outmoded or caused by trouble-makers.

HR policies and managerial development can be seen as reflecting a unitary ideology. *Horwitz* suggests that the unitary perspective views company and trade union loyalty as mutually exclusive. He raises the question of human resource management (HRM) as a reformation of a unitarist managerial ideology. Developments in HRM, in seeking to optimise co-operation and organisational loyalty, can be seen as imposing new forms of control. A managerial approach to facilitating organisational goals and the direct involvement of employees furthers a unitary perspective and can mask an underlying distaste for unionism.[68]

The pluralist perspective

An alternative view suggested by *Fox* is the **pluralist perspective**, which views the organisation as made up of powerful and competing sub-groups with their own legitimate loyalties, objectives and leaders.[69] These competing sub-groups are almost certain to come into conflict. From the pluralist perspective, conflict in organisations is seen as inevitable and induced, in part, by the very structure of the organisation. Conflict is not necessarily a bad thing but can be an agent for evolution, and internal and external change.

Restrictive practices may be seen as a rational response from a group that regards itself as being threatened. The role of the manager would be less commanding and enforcing, and more persuading and co-ordinating. Fox suggests that the pluralist perspective is a more realistic frame of reference. He argues the importance of viewing work situations through the different groups involved rather than attempting a wished-for unitarist approach.

Critical review and reflection

The study of social action may be popular with academics but too much attention is given to the easy option of criticising other approaches. Social action theory offers little that is constructive or of positive value to the practical manager.

What is YOUR view? Can YOU present a counter argument? How much benefit do YOU derive from the study of social action?

Action theory

A theory of human behaviour from an 'action approach' is presented by *Bowey*.[70] She suggests that action theory, systems theory and contingency theory are not necessarily incompatible approaches to the understanding of behaviour in organisations. It would be possible to take the best parts of the different approaches and combine them into a theory that would model empirical behaviour and also facilitate the analysis of large numbers of people in organisations.

The three essential principles of action theory can be summarised as below:

- Sociology is concerned not just with behaviour but with 'meaningful action'.
- Particular meanings persist through reaffirmation in actions.
- Actions can also lead to changes in meanings.

Bowey suggests these three principles apply mainly to explanations of individual, or small-scale, behaviour. She gives four additional concepts, taken from systems theory, on which analysis of large-scale behaviour can be based. These concepts are redefined in accordance with an action approach.

- **Role** – this is needed for the analysis of behaviour in organisations. It explains the similar actions of different people in similar situations within the organisation and the expectations held by other people.
- **Relationships** – this is needed to explain the patterns of interaction among people and the behaviours displayed towards one another.

- **Structure** – the relationships among members of an organisation give rise to patterns of action that can be identified as a 'transitory social structure'. The social factors, and non-social factors such as payment systems, methods of production and physical layout, together form the behavioural structure.
- **Process** – human behaviour can be analysed in terms of processes, defined as 'continuous interdependent sequences of actions'. The concept of process is necessary to account for the manner in which organisations exhibit changes in structure.

The three principles of action theory, together with the four additional concepts from systems theory, provide an action approach to the analysis of behaviour in organisations. Bowey goes on to illustrate her theory with case studies of five different types of organisations, all in the restaurant industry.

Postmodernism

With the development of the information and technological age a more recent view of organisations and management is the idea of **postmodernism.** *Cooper and Burrell* refer to the contrasting postmodern view of 'organisation less the expression of planned thought and calculative action and a more defensive reaction to forces intrinsic to the social body which constantly threaten the stability of organised life'.[71]

In the 1990s, writers such as *Clegg* described the postmodern organisation in terms of the influence of technological determinism and structural flexibility, premised on niches, multi-skilled jobs marked by a lack of demarcation, and more complex employment relationships including subcontracting and networking.[72]

Postmodernism rejects a rational systems approach to our understanding of organisations and management and to accepted explanations of society and behaviour. Postmodern organisations are perceived as highly flexible and responsive, with decentralised decision-making, fluid, less hierarchical structures and with the ability to change quickly to meet present demands.

Generalised sociological concept

The idea of postmodernism is, however, not easy to explain fully in clear and simple terms. It is arguably more of a generalised sociological concept rather than a specific approach to organisation and management. There is even some discussion of two connotations, and theories or philosophies of the concept depending on whether the term is hyphenated or not.[73] Perhaps understandably, therefore, the concept of postmodernism appears to have little interest or appeal to the practical manager. Indeed *Watson,* for example, questions the value of labelling more flexible forms of bureaucratic structure and culture as postmodern or post-bureaucratic and differentiating these from the modernist bureaucratic organisation.

> *The labelling of more flexible forms of bureaucratic structure and culture as 'postmodern' or 'post-bureaucratic' is unhelpful. It is unrealistic to suggest that there is something new occurring to work organisations at the level of the basic organising principle. There is no postmodern or post-bureaucratic organisational form available to us that is **essentially** different from the modernist bureaucratic organisation. We are indeed seeing different mixes of direct and indirect management control attempts as the world changes. But the world was always changing. Probably from the very beginning of industrialisation there has been a mixing of direct and indirect controls with emphases in one direction and then the other being made at different times.[74]*

Nevertheless, postmodernist organisation can arguably be seen as a healthy challenge to more traditional approaches. It puts forward alternative interpretations of rationality, credibility and ambiguity, and a thoughtful critical perspective on disorders in work organisations, and reminds us of the complexities in our understanding of management and organisational behaviour.

An outline of developments in management theory is set out in Figure 2.3.

Critical review and reflection

The idea of postmodernist organisation can be likened to the 'Emperor's new clothes'. It is easy to champion the idea in the classroom but in reality it is too abstract and vague, and lacks any real adaptive value for the practical manager.
How would YOU attempt to challenge this assertion?

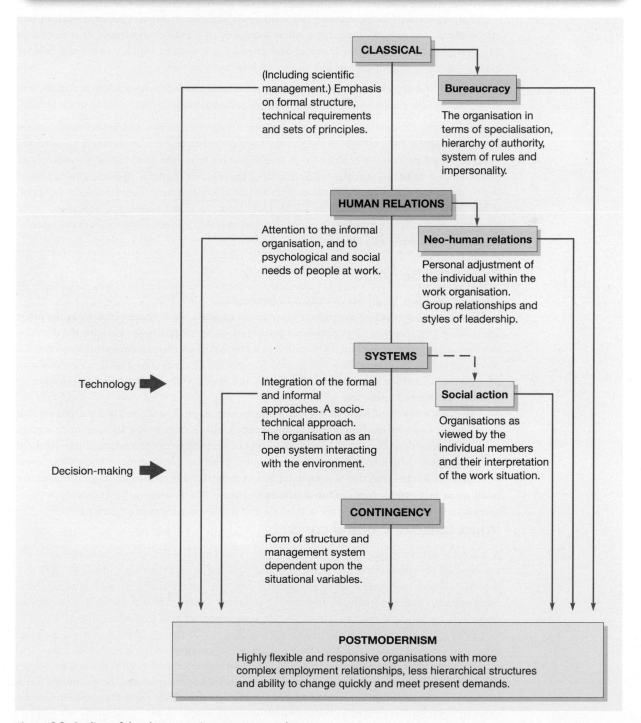

Figure 2.3 Outline of developments in management theory

Relevance to management and organisational behaviour

The different possible categorisations are not necessarily a bad thing; they illustrate the discursive and complex nature of the study and practice of management and organisational behaviour. Discussion on the various categorisations of approaches and the identification of individual writers within a particular approach can provide a useful insight into the subject.

Whatever form of categorisation is adopted, the division of writers on organisation and management into various approaches offers a number of positive advantages. It is helpful in the arrangement and study of material and provides a setting in which to view the field of management and organisational behaviour. As *Miner* points out:

> Schools of management thought are very much a reality, and the management student who approaches the field without at least a minimal understanding of them does so at some risk.[75]

A review of the different approaches helps in organisational analysis and in the identification of problem areas. For example, is the problem one of structure, of human relations or of the socio-technical process? It enables the manager to take from the different approaches those ideas that best suit the particular requirements of the job. For example, in dealing with a problem of structure, the ideas of the classical writers or of contingency theory might be adopted. When there is a problem relating to HRM, ideas from the human relations movement might be of most value. If the problem is one of environmental influence, insights from the systems approach might prove most helpful.

Caveats to be noted

There are, however, a number of caveats to be noted.

The various approaches represent a progression of ideas, each building on from the other and adding to it. Together they provide a pattern of complementary studies into the development of management thinking. The different approaches are not in competition with each other and no one approach should be viewed as replacing or superseding earlier contributions. Many ideas of earlier writers are still of relevance today and of continuing importance in modern management practice.

Any categorisation of individual writers into specific approaches is inevitably arbitrary and not all writers can be neatly arranged in this manner. This is only to be expected. Such writers are expounding their current thoughts and ideas in keeping with the continual development of management theory and changes in management practice. The comment made about some management writers that they are saying different things at different times might therefore be taken more as a compliment than as a criticism.

Importance of cultural contexts

A major criticism of the attempt to define generalised models of management theory is the assumption of national culture. *Schneider and Barsoux* draw attention to how the different theories on how to organise all reflect societal concerns of the times, as well as the cultural backgrounds of the individuals. Different approaches reflect different cultural assumptions regarding, for example, human nature and the importance of task and relationships.[76]

Cheng et al. also question the universality of theories of management and organisational behaviour on the grounds that they have not adequately addressed the factor of culture: 'Traditionally, the greatest aspiration of researchers is to discover objective, universalistic principles of behaviour. The tacit assumption behind this is that these principles may be discovered without reference to cultural contexts.' Cheng *et al.* conclude that while there may be some universality to organisation structures, for example the need for some form of hierarchy whatever its shape may be, different national cultures frequently give those structures different meanings.[77]

Value of management theory

Whatever the value of management theory, clearly no single approach to organisation and management provides all the answers. It is the comparative study of different approaches that will yield benefits to the manager. A knowledge and understanding of management theory will help with an awareness and appreciation of the complexities of modern work organisations.

Reporting on a twelve-year study of the knowledge and use of management concepts in technical organisations, *Flores and Utley* suggest that a look back at the theories and principles that have been taught in the past could give an indication of the success of any new approach and help prepare today's and tomorrow's managers for the future.[78] And *Stern* has this to say:

> Management thinkers still have a lot to tell us. You don't have to believe everything they say, but they may at least offer stimulation; they might provoke senior managers into abandoning complacency and trying to see problems in a new light.[79]

There is undoubtedly much scepticism about, and criticism of, management gurus. For example, in a cynical and provocative feature in *The Times*, *Billen* suggests that the tide is turning against the gurus and their gobbledegook.

> In the past two decades, management theory, once rejected in Britain by both management and unions, has been deliberately imposed on almost every aspect of commercial and public life . . . It would be a brave new world without such gobbledegook in it but – to use a management theorist's phrase – an empowered one, too. Managers would be chosen not for their ability to bandy jargon with their superiors but for their empathy, pragmatism, experience and decisiveness with their staff.[80]

However, according to *McLean:*

> Of course, management theories have often been the subject of discourse and criticism. Some critics see organisational philosophies as management fads that will be replaced by new ones as other theories are proposed. That may well be the case, but it is good for management theories to evolve, because organisations change, the environment changes, and as a result, management practices and techniques change . . . Theories provide us with valuable insights into how we can be more understanding, influential and ultimately more successful in managing organisations and the turbulent dynamic environments in which they operate . . . you of course, may have a different view![81]

There are no definitive or final solutions to the problems of organisations. The nature of work organisations and the environment in which they operate is becoming increasingly complex and subject to continual change. However, at least we do understand more about the dynamics of management and organisational behaviour as a basis for the analysis of human behaviour in organisations.[82] *Stern* suggests that 'Management is both science and art, and the trick of it lies in separating the good ideas from the bad, knowing when to be scientific and when to be artful.'[83]

Conceptual thinking and management theory

In an interesting discussion on learning classic management theories, *Robinson and Francis-Smythe* draw attention to the importance of conceptual thinking for managers and how far knowledge of formal academic theory helps in the discharge of managerial responsibilities. The overwhelming majority of established senior managers will be hard-pressed to identify a single significant occasion of decision-making guided by direct reference to a particular management theory. Even if names of respected theorists can be recalled, managers will be hard-pressed to provide a succinct explanation of their theories. Robinson and Francis-Smythe question what happens to all the theory that managers are exposed to during their training and education.

> *When in the light of their recognition-based decision-making, managers are asked to explain the role that academic theory plays in their approach to managing, they will frequently assert that it 'must' exert a subtle, covert, subconscious, or even subliminal influence over them. Whilst it would be easy to dismiss this as 'wishful thinking', there is good evidence to suggest that these assertions may actually be true . . . The inability to 'name' either a theory or a theoretician should not be taken to imply a failure to understand the theory in a more gener- alised, more abstract, more conceptual way.*

Robinson and Francis-Smythe suggest that academic knowledge is not, per se, a key profes- sional requirement or an important aspect of managerial competence. Rather it will serve to underpin the process of building a repertoire of concepts that will be held in long-term memories in the way most likely to facilitate subsequent retrieval, good managerial moves and solutions to managerial challenges.[84]

There are, then, many aspects to management. There are no simple solutions, no one best way to manage. However, study of different approaches to organisations, their structure and management is still important for the manager and remains an indispensable part of the job.

Critical review and reflection

The historical study of different approaches to organisations and the development of management theory have little practical relevance. It is no more than a luxury for students and the time could be spent better on the study of more important topic areas.

How would YOU present a counterargument? To what extent has YOUR study of management theory been of per- sonal value to YOU as a potential manager?

Ten key points to remember

1 A central part of the study of organisational behaviour is the development of management thinking and what might be termed 'management theory'

2 The work of leading writers can be categorised into various 'approaches' based on their views of organisations, their structure and management.

3 The classical writers placed emphasis on purpose and structure, technical requirements of the organisation, and assumption of rational and logical behaviour.

4 The human relations writers emphasised the informal organisation, group relationships, and the psychological and social needs of people at work.

5 The systems approach focuses attention on the interactions between technical and social vari- ables and influences of the external environment.

6 Contingency theory highlights possible means of differentiating between alternative forms of structures and systems of management.

7 It is possible to identify a number of other approaches or sub-divisions of approaches including technology decision-making, social action and postmodernism.

8 Whatever form of categorisation is adopted, there are a number of positive advantages but also criticisms and caveats to be noted, including cultural contexts.

9 A knowledge and understanding of management theory will help with an awareness and appreciation of the complexities of modern work organisations.

10 Ideas and instinct are both important to managers. It is necessary to view interrelationships among the development of theory, behaviour in organisations and management practice.

Review and discussion questions

1 Detail fully how you would attempt to identify and analyse developments in management and organisational behaviour.

2 Assess critically the relevance of scientific management to present-day organisations. To what extent does your university exhibit features of scientific management?

3 Argue a positive case for bureaucratic structures. Select a large-scale organisation of your choice and suggest ways in which it displays characteristics of a bureaucracy.

4 What are the main conclusions that can be drawn from the Hawthorne studies? Discuss critically the relevance of these studies for management and organisational behaviour today.

5 Evaluate the application of the systems approach to the analysis of work organisations. Suggest an example of a work situation in which the systems approach might be appropriate.

6 Contrast approaches to improving organisational performance based on attention to technical and structural requirements with those based on concern for psychological and social factors.

7 Explain what is meant by a social action approach. Assess critically the practical relevance of 'action theory'.

8 Discuss critically the practical value and relevance of the postmodernist view of organisations.

9 Present a detailed argument for the potential benefits to managers from a study of management theory.

10 Outline briefly what you believe are the major trends in organisation and management since the beginning of this century. Which *one* writer do you most associate with, and why?

Assignment

1 Specify the *most important key features* associated with the methods of operation, structure and management of each of the following organisations:
- six-star luxury international hotel
- major civil service department
- medical research university
- maternity hospital
- motor-car manufacturer

- large comprehensive school
- maximum-security prison
- leisure centre

2 Then, working in small groups:
  (i) Compare and discuss your list of features.
  (ii) How much agreement was there among members of your group?
  (iii) What conclusions do you draw?
  (iv) How does the assignment link with your knowledge of different approaches to organisations and management?

Personal skills and employability exercise

Objectives

Completing this exercise should help you to enhance the following skills:

- Knowledge about the future direction of your work career.
- Recognition of the type of job and work you would enjoy.
- Awareness of the type of organisation structure in which you would feel comfortable working.

Exercise

Answer each question 'mostly agree' or 'mostly disagree'. Assume that you are trying to learn something about yourself. Do not assume that your answer will be shown to a prospective employer.

		Mostly agree	Mostly disagree
1	I value stability in my job.	❑	❑
2	I like a predictable organisation.	❑	❑
3	The best job for me would be one in which the future is uncertain.	❑	❑
4	The army would be a nice place to work.	❑	❑
5	Rules, policies and procedures tend to frustrate me.	❑	❑
6	I would enjoy working for a company that employed 85,000 people worldwide.	❑	❑
7	Being self-employed would involve more risk than I am willing to take.	❑	❑
8	Before accepting a job, I would like to see an exact job description.	❑	❑
9	I would prefer a job as a freelance house painter to one as a clerk for the Department of Motor Vehicles.	❑	❑
10	Seniority should be as important as performance in determining pay increases and promotion.	❑	❑
11	It would give me a feeling of pride to work for the largest and most successful company in its field.	❑	❑

	Mostly agree	Mostly disagree
12 Given a choice, I would prefer to make £40,000 per year as a vice president in a small company to £50,000 as a staff specialist in a large company.	❑	❑
13 I would regard wearing an employee badge with a number on it as a degrading experience.	❑	❑
14 Parking spaces in a company lot should be assigned on the basis of job level.	❑	❑
15 If an accountant works for a large organisation, he or she cannot be a true professional.	❑	❑
16 Before accepting a job (given a choice), I would want to make sure that the company had a very fine programme of employee benefits.	❑	❑
17 A company will probably not be successful unless it establishes a clear set of rules and procedures.	❑	❑
18 Regular working hours and holidays are more important to me than finding thrills on the job.	❑	❑
19 You should respect people according to their rank.	❑	❑
20 Rules are meant to be broken.	❑	❑

Source: Adapted from DuBrin, A. J. *Human Relations: A Job Oriented Approach*, 1st Ed., Reston Publishing/Prentice Hall (1978), pp. 296–7. Copyright © 1978. Reproduced with permission from Pearson Education Inc.

You should then consider the further information supplied to you individually by your tutor.

Discussion

- After receiving feedback from your tutor, share and compare your responses in a small-group situation and attempt to obtain group consensus on the answers.
- How far did members relate the questions to different ideas or studies on the structure and management of work organisations?
- To what extent do you think personal skills and employability are influenced by the type of organisation structure?

Case study
Not being evil: Google

For many people, California-based Google is the most prominent example of a twenty-first-century company. Founded in 1998 by Larry Page and Sergei Brin, it grew very rapidly to become the world's best-known search engine, accompanied by a proliferation of other ventures. The company's name has achieved the rare distinction of becoming a verb in its own right – these days, we google, rather than search (and probably more often than we hoover). The company's 2014 revenue was $66 billion[85] and, in 2015, the two founders were listed by *Fortune* magazine as nineteenth and twentieth in its list of the world's billionaires.[86] This spectacular growth has been achieved by a company whose informal motto is 'Don't Be Evil'. How do the two ideas – commercial success and avoiding evil – work together in practice, and how well will the company be able to respond to the challenges that lie ahead in this turbulent market?

→

A Street View of Google
Source: Bloomberg via Getty Images

In commercial terms, the predominant contributor has been advertising revenues derived from the Google Internet search operation, which is based upon the highly successful PageRank technology developed by the founders. In common with all of the competitive search engines, the Google Internet search service looks free to users, to the extent that this added value is probably now taken for granted by most. But Google's success in its core business has been accompanied by a steady flow of new and intriguing ideas. For example, it is now completely routine to be able to search images as well as text, to call up detailed maps of anywhere on the planet, to switch to a satellite view or increasingly to photographic images at street level. The YouTube facility, acquired by Google in 2006, allows free access to a vast database of video clips uploaded by organisations and individuals. Google's email service has grown rapidly and its Google+ service is aimed at the social networking market. In what used to be the separate mobile phone market, Google's Android system, as well as Google's range of phones and tablets, are engaged in a fierce battle with Apple's iPhone and iPad.

Google's rapid diversification looks like the very opposite of the 'stick to the knitting' recommendation in a best-selling strategy book twenty-five years earlier.[87] In diversifying, any company is choosing to serve new types of customers in unfamiliar markets and with the opposition of new incumbent competitors, all of which tends to increase the total risk for the company, as well as placing its core resources under strain. However, Google claims in its philosophy statement that this diversity stems from the application of its one core competence: search.[88] From the outset, Google has actively sought out new opportunities and has deliberately fostered a culture to preserve and encourage this restlessness. As Tim Harford observes, Google fully expects most of its new ideas to fail, but its future lies with the ideas that do not fail.[89] In a 2014 interview,[90] Google's two founders commented that a key role of the company was to integrate diversity, in order that the services have a recognisable Google 'feel'.

Growing pains?

How, then, can these cultural values be preserved as a company grows and changes? From its beginnings in a garage, Google had grown by the end of 2014 into a global corporation employing more than 53,000 worldwide and operating out of seventy offices in forty countries around the world.[91,92] It has, however, managed to retain its reputation for an informal and quirky style: for example, the company famously encourages its employees to spend 20 per cent of each working week working on projects that interest them, rather than their main responsibilities. The many accounts of life in its Googleplex headquarters describe the mixture of working hard and playing hard – video games, pool tables, pianos and other leisure facilities are provided and commitment levels are expected to be very high. As can be seen from the examples of Google recruitment questions that can be found in Internet posts, the company is looking for very bright recruits who can think quickly, imaginatively and unconventionally.

In the tough competitive environments in which Google operates, it is hardly surprising that some have questioned how well its 'Don't Be Evil' motto is holding up. Google attracted fierce criticism for its decision to comply with the Internet censorship laws in the People's Republic of China for the search services it provides in that country. As can be seen from the company's transparency statement, the censorship question is a continuing issue for Google (and other similar companies) in many parts of the world.[93] There have also been concerns about privacy and data security, and Google was one of a number of multinational companies criticised for tax avoidance in the UK, a claim it rejects emphatically.[94]

How does Google's strength and culture equip it to deal with the market challenges it now faces? The first part of the answer is to re-examine the assumptions behind the story so far. As Kahneman points out in his book *Thinking Fast and Slow*,[95] we should beware of seeing the story of Google's development as something from which reliable, more general lessons can be learned. Making reference to Nassim Taleb's concept of *narrative fallacy,*[96] he warns against underestimating the role of luck (i.e. alongside hard work, inspiration and talent) in the way it turned out – we should take care to notice the things that did not happen, as well as the well-documented events that make up the story. Above all, we should be cautious about any notion of using our 'understanding' of the story so far to predict the future. This must be doubly so when the future in question is that of the global information industry.

Gentle giant or robber baron?

Google's success has been based upon its mastery of Internet search, which has established it as a powerful global player, both while the Internet was growing around the world and in the later phases of user-generated content and the growth of social networking. But the next challenge is posed by the growing preference of users to access the Internet and its services via mobile smartphones, a change of format that threatens the standard models of revenue generation for a number of players, including Google. The effect of this is that those who want to remain major players have to build up their mobile capabilities.[97] For some years, the smartphone sector has been a fierce (and often litigious) battle between Apple's iPhone and devices based on Google's Android operating system. As the *New York Times* put it in 2012:[98]

> *Last year, for the first time, spending by Apple and Google on patent lawsuits and unusually big-dollar patent purchases exceeded spending on research and development of new products, according to public filings.*

As commentator Bryan Appleyard observes, Android is open – given away free to phone manufacturers – while Apple's is not.[99] Some see this same open/closed contrast in the corporate cultures of the two giants.[100]

From one point of view, consumers around the world have done very well from this competitive melee, with a succession of amazing devices at affordable prices. On the other hand, some (for example *The Economist*),[101] are more critical of the contemporary IT giants, drawing parallels between their plans and the late-career behaviours of the early 20th century US industrialists (Carnegie, Rockefeller, Harriman etc) known as 'robber barons.'

> *'We're charmed by their corporate mantras – for example "Don't be evil" (Google) or "Move fast and break things" (Facebook). In their black turtlenecks and faded jeans they don't seem to have anything in common with Rupert Murdoch or the grim-faced, silk-hatted capitalist bosses of old. . .*
>
> *What gets lost in the reality distortion field that surrounds these technology moguls is that, in the end, they are fanatically ambitious, competitive capitalists. They may look cool and have soothing bedside manners, but in the end these guys are in business not just to make money, but to establish sprawling, quasi-monopolistic commercial empires. And they will do whatever it takes to achieve those ambitions.'*[102]

It is perhaps futile to speculate about how this complex market will look in just a few years. In the twentieth century, much competition took place between well-established large players (say, Ford and General Motors) in market domains characterised by stability and predictability. Twenty-first-century competition is different – technologies and market definitions are endlessly shifting and changing, bringing new players into contention with each other and raising the stakes for all concerned. Google's spectacular success in its relatively short existence so far has given it commercial strength and its culture has given it the flexibility to deal with rapid change.

Tasks

1 Examine the organisational development of Google using two of the four main analytical models in Figure 2.1. Which do you think offers the best explanation of the company's development, and why?

2 What are the main challenges that Google faced in attempting not to 'be evil' as it expanded into new and unfamiliar territories and markets? How might local managers throughout the world create a corporate culture based on this motto?

3 Is Google a 'postmodern' organisation or, in essence, no more than a globalised bureaucracy? Present the arguments on each side of the case.

4 If you were to research the degree to which growth and change has affected the organisational behaviour of Google employees, which theoretical approach would you choose as the basis for your enquiry? Explain and justify your choice.

Notes and references

1. See, for example, George, C. S. *The History of Management Thought,* second edition, Prentice Hall (1972).

2. Shafritz, J. M. *Shakespeare on Management,* Carol Publishing Group (1992), p. xi.

3. For a review of management thinking see, for example, Sheldrake, J. *Management Theory: From Taylorism to Japanization,* International Thomson Business Press (1996); see also Flores, G. N. and Utley, D. R. 'Management Concepts in Use – A 12-Year Perspective', *Engineering Management Journal,* vol. 12, no. 3, 2000, pp. 11–17.

4. Lee, R. A. 'There is Nothing so Useful as an Appropriate Theory', in Wilson, D. C. and Rosenfeld, R. H. *Managing Organisations: Text, Reading and Cases,* McGraw-Hill (1990), p. 31.

5. Crainer, S. *Key Management Ideas,* third edition, Financial Times Prentice Hall (1998).

6. Skipton, M. D. 'Management and the Organisation', *Management Research News,* vol. 5, no. 3, 1983, pp. 9–15.

7. Fayol, H. *General and Industrial Management,* Pitman (1949); see also Gray, I. Henri Fayol's *General and Industrial Management,* Pitman (1988).

8. Urwick, L. *Notes on the Theory of Organization,* American Management Association (1952).

9. Brech, E. F. L. *Organisation: The Framework of Management,* second edition, Longman (1965).

10. Simon, H. A. *Administrative Behaviour,* third edition, Free Press (1976), p. xxii.

11. Woodward, J. *Industrial Organization: Theory and Practice,* second edition, Oxford University Press (1980).

12. Taylor, F. W. *Scientific Management,* Harper & Row (1947). Comprises 'Shop Management' (1903), 'Principles of Scientific Management' (1911) and Taylor's testimony to the House of Representatives' Special Committee (1912).

13. Braverman, H. *Labor and Monopoly Capital,* Monthly Review Press (1974).

14. For a study of employers' labour relations policies, including comments on the work of Braverman, see Gospel, H. F. and Littler, C. R. (eds) *Managerial Strategies and Industrial Relations,* Heinemann Educational Books (1983).

15. Cloke, K. and Goldsmith, J. *The End of Management and the Rise of Organizational Democracy,* Jossey-Bass (2002), p. 27.

16. Rose, M. *Industrial Behaviour,* Penguin (1978), p. 31; see also Rose, M. *Industrial Behaviour,* second edition, Penguin (1988), ch. 2.

17. Drucker, P. F. 'The Coming Rediscovery of Scientific Management', *The Conference Board Record,* vol. 13, June 1976, pp. 23–7; reprinted in Drucker, P. F. *Towards the Next Economics and Other Essays,* Heinemann (1981).

18. Crainer, S. and Dearlove, D. *Financial Times Handbook of Management,* second edition, Financial Times Prentice Hall (2001).

19. Stern, S. 'Guru Guide', *Management Today,* October 2001, pp. 83–4.

20. See also Mullins, L. J and Dossor, O. P. *Hospitality Management and Organisational Behaviour,* fifth edition, Pearson Education (2013).

21. See, for example, Beirne, M., Riach, K. and Wilson, F. 'Controlling business? Agency and constraint in call centre working', *New Technology, Work and Employment,* vol. 19, no. 2, 2004, pp. 96–109.

22. Weber, M. *The Theory of Social and Economic Organization,* Collier Macmillan (1964).

23. Blau, P. M. and Scott, W. R. *Formal Organizations,* Routledge & Kegan Paul (1966).

24. Stewart, R. *The Reality of Management,* third edition, Butterworth–Heinemann (1999).

25. Robbins, S. P. and Judge, T. A. 'Organizational Behavior', thirteenth edition, Pearson Prentice Hall (2009), p. 561.

26. Argyris, C. *Integrating the Individual and the Organization,* Wiley (1964).

27. Caulkin, S. 'Faceless Corridors of Power', *Management Today,* January 1988, p. 65.

28. Morgan, G. *Images of Organization,* second edition, Sage (1997).

29. Waterman, R. *Adhocracy: The Power to Change,* W.W. Norton (1994).

30. Mintzberg, H. *Managing,* Financial Times Prentice Hall (2009).

31. Tibballs, G. *Business Blunders,* Robinson Publishing (1999).

32. Cloke, K. and Goldsmith, J. *The End of Management and the Rise of Organizational Democracy,* Jossey-Bass (2002), pp. 92–4.

33. Drucker, P. F. *Classic Drucker,* Harvard Business School Press (2006), p. 22.

34. See Mullins, L. J. and Dossor, P. *Hospitality Management and Organisational Behaviour,* fifth edition, Pearson Education (2013).

35. Ridderstråle, J. 'Business Moves Beyond Bureaucracy', in Pickford, J. (ed.) *Financial Times Mastering Management 2.0,* Financial Times Prentice Hall (2001), pp. 217–20.

36. Stewart, R. *The Reality of Management,* third edition, Butterworth–Heinemann (1999).

37. See, for example, Wilson, F. A. *Organizational Behaviour: A Critical Introduction,* Oxford University Press (1999).

38. Green, J. 'Is Bureaucracy Dead? Don't Be So Sure', *Chartered Secretary,* January 1997, pp. 18–19.

39. See, for example, Waller, P. 'Bureaucracy Takes New Form', *Professional Manager,* May 1998, p. 6.

40. There are many versions of the Hawthorne experiments. Among the most thorough accounts is that by Roethlisberger, F. J. and Dickson, W. J. *Management and the Worker,* Harvard University Press (1939); see also Landsberger, H. A. *Hawthorne Revisited,* Cornell University Press (1958).

41. See, for example, Rose, M. *Industrial Behaviour,* second edition, Penguin (1988).

42. See, for example, Buggy, C. 'Are You Really Listening?', *Professional Manager,* July 2000, pp. 20–2.

43. Silverman, D. *The Theory of Organisations,* Heinemann (1970).

44. Stead, B. A. *Women in Management,* Prentice Hall (1978), p. 190.

45. Crainer, S. *Key Management Ideas: Thinkers That Changed the Management World,* third edition, Financial Times Prentice Hall (1998), p. 111.

46. Maslow, A. H. 'A Theory of Human Motivation', *Psychological Review,* vol. 50, no. 4, 1943, pp. 370–96.

47. Herzberg, F. W., Mausner, B. and Snyderman, B. B. *The Motivation to Work,* second edition, Chapman and Hall (1959).

48. McGregor, D. *The Human Side of Enterprise,* Penguin (1987).

49. Likert, R. *New Patterns of Management,* McGraw-Hill (1961); see also Likert, R. *The Human Organization,* McGraw-Hill (1967); Likert, R. and Likert, J. G. *New Ways of Managing Conflict,* McGraw-Hill (1976).

50. McClelland, D. C. *Human Motivation,* Cambridge University Press (1988).

51. Argyris, C. *Understanding Organizational Behavior,* Tavistock (1960); and *Integrating the Individual and the Organization,* Wiley (1964).

52. See, for example, Caulkin, S. 'Chris Argyris', *Management Today,* October 1997, pp. 58–9.

53. Bertalanffy, L. von 'Problems of General Systems Theory: A New Approach to the Unity of Science', *Human Biology,* vol. 23, no. 4, 1951, pp. 302–12.

54. Miller, E. J. and Rice, A. K. *Systems of Organization,* Tavistock (1967).

55. Trist, E. L., Higgin, G. W., Murray, H. and Pollock, A. B. *Organizational Choice,* Tavistock (1963).

56. Lane, T., Snow, D. and Labrow, P. 'Learning to Succeed with ICT', *British Journal of Administrative Management,* May/June 2000, pp. 14–15.

57. Walker, C. R. and Guest, R. H. *The Man on the Assembly Line,* Harvard University Press (1952); see also Walker, C.

R., Guest, R. H. and Turner, A. N. *The Foreman on the Assembly Line,* Harvard University Press (1956).

58. Sayles, L. R. *Behaviour of Industrial Work Groups,* Wiley (1958).

59. Blauner, R. *Alienation and Freedom,* University of Chicago Press (1964).

60. Deutsch, S. E. 'Industrial Jobs and the Worker: An Investigation of Response to Task Attributes by Arthur Turner and Paul Lawrence', *Technology and Culture,* vol. 7, no. 3, 1966, pp. 436–8.

61. Seddon, J. *Freedom from Command & Control: A better way to make the work work,* Vanguard Consulting Ltd (2005).

62. Barnard, C. *The Functions of the Executive,* Oxford University Press (1938).

63. Simon, H. A. *The New Science of Management Decision,* revised edition, Prentice Hall (1977).

64. Cyert, R. M. and March, J. G. *A Behavioural Theory of the Firm,* second edition, Blackwell (1992).

65. Silverman, D. *The Theory of Organisations,* Heinemann (1970), p. 147.

66. Goldthorpe, J. H., Lockwood, D., Bechhofer, F. and Platt, J. *The Affluent Worker,* Cambridge University Press (1968).

67. Fox, A. *Industrial Sociology and Industrial Relations,* HMSO (1966).

68. Horwitz, F. M. 'HRM: An Ideological Perspective', *International Journal of Manpower,* vol. 12, no. 6, 1991, pp. 4–9.

69. Fox, A. *Industrial Society and Industrial Relations,* HMSO (1966).

70. Bowey, A. M. *The Sociology of Organisations,* Hodder & Stoughton (1976).

71. Cooper, R. and Burrell, G. 'Modernism, Postmodernism and Organizational Analysis: An Introduction', *Organization Studies,* vol. 9, no. 1, 1988, pp. 91–112.

72. Clegg, S. R. *Modern Organizations: Organization Studies in the Postmodern World,* Sage (1990).

73. See, for example, Legge, K. *Human Resource Management: Rhetorics and Realities,* Macmillan Business (1995).

74. Watson, T. J. *Organising and Managing Work,* second edition, Financial Times Prentice Hall (2006), p. 271.

75. Miner, J. B. *Management Theory,* Macmillan (1971), p. 145; see also Miner, J. B. *Theories of Organizational Behaviour,* Holt, Rinehart and Winston (1980), ch. 1.

76. Schneider, S. C. and Barsoux, J. *Managing Across Cultures,* second edition, Financial Times Prentice Hall (2003).

77. Cheng, T., Sculli, D. and Chan, F. 'Relationship Dominance – Rethinking Management Theories from the Perspective of Methodological Relationalism', *Journal of Managerial Psychology,* vol. 16, no. 2, 2001, pp. 97–105.

78. Flores, G. N. and Utley, D. R. 'Management Concepts in Use – A 12-year Perspective', *Engineering Management Journal,* vol. 12, no. 3, 2000, pp. 11–17.

79. Stern, S. 'Guru Guide', *Management Today,* October 2001, p. 87.

80. Billen, A. 'Goodbye to Glib Gurus and Their Gobbledegook', *The Times,* 9 March 2009.

81. McLean, J. 'Management Techniques and Theories', *Manager, The British Journal of Administrative Management,* August/September 2005, p. 17.

82. See, for example, Klein, S. M. and Ritti, R. R. *Understanding Organizational Behavior,* second edition, Kent Publishing (1984), ch. 1.

83. Stern, S. 'The Next Big Thing', *Management Today,* April 2007, p. 50.

84. Robinson, L and Francis-Smythe, J. 'Managing to abstraction', *Professional Manager,* vol. 19, no. 5, 2010, pp. 36–8[TS5].

85. https://investor.google.com/earnings/2014/Q4_google_earnings.html (accessed 24 February 2015).

86. http://www.forbes.com/billionaires/list/#tab:overall (accessed 24 February 2015).

87. Peters, T. and Waterman, R. H. *In Search of Excellence,* Harper and Row (1982).

88. http://www.google.com/about/company/philosophy/ (accessed 24 February 2015).

89. Harford, T. *Adapt: Why success always starts with failure,* Abacus, Kindle edition (2012), p. 233.

90. http://bgr.com/2014/07/07/google-vs-apple-products-strategy/ (accessed 24 February 2015).

91. http://www.google.com/about/company/facts/locations/ (accessed 24 February 2015).

92. http://en.wikipedia.org/wiki/Google (accessed 24 February 2015).

93. http://www.google.com/transparencyreport/removals/government/ (accessed 24 February 2015).

94. http://www.theguardian.com/technology/2013/apr/22/google-eric-schmidt-tax-avoidance (accessed 24 February 2015).

95. Kahneman, D. *Thinking Fast and Slow,* Penguin (2011), p. 199 *et seq.*

96. Taleb, N. N. *The Black Swan,* Penguin (2008), p. 62 *et seq.*

97. Appleyard, B. 'In the Beginning Was Google', *Sunday Times,* 29 July 2012, http://bryanappleyard.com/in-the-beginning-was-google/ (accessed 24 February 2015).

98. http://www.nytimes.com/2012/10/08/technology/patent-wars-among-tech-giants-can-stifle-competition.html?pagewanted=all&_r=0 (accessed 24 February 2015).

99. Appleyard, B. 'In the Beginning Was Google', op. cit.

100. http://www.think-act.com/blog/2013/google-vs-apple-a-tale-of-two-strategies/ (accessed 24 February 2015).

101. Briefing: 'Robber barons and silicon sultans', *The Economist,* 3 January 2015, p. 49.

102. Naughton, John (2012) 'New-tech moguls: the modern robber barons?', *The Guardian,* 1 July 2015.

CHAPTER 3
The organisational environment

Applications of organisational behaviour and management take place not in a vacuum but within the context of a particular organisational setting and environment. The organisation is a complex social system and the sum of many interrelated variables. It is important to understand the main features that affect the structure, management and functioning of the work organisation, and which influence the lives of its members.

Learning outcomes

After completing this chapter you should have enhanced your ability to:

- explain the perspectives and main types of formal organisations;
- examine the organisation in terms of an open-systems model;
- analyse the main features of a work organisation;
- explain the features and importance of the formal and informal organisation;
- review the nature and outcomes of organisational conflict;
- explore the sources and impact of stress at work;
- assess the importance of work/life balance and the organisation of the future.

Critical review and reflection

Recognition of the importance of the organisational environment and underlying realities of the work situation is an essential part of the study of management and organisational behaviour.

To what extent do YOU agree with this statement? Think critically about the environment of YOUR own university and the realities of student life.

Perspectives of the organisation

Organisations in one form or another have always been an integral feature of human civilisation. Although the origins of modern organisations can be traced back thousands of years, organisations evolve continually and those of today are clearly very different. The beginning of the twentieth century, with the emergence of large corporate entities, and the work of writers such as Frederick Taylor on scientific management and Max Weber on bureaucracy, drew attention to the importance of the work organisation.[1]

Organisations are an integral part of society, involving both public and private sectors and including the voluntary and communities sector. All organisations have some function to perform. Through collaborative action, members of an organisation can achieve a synergistic effect and enable objectives to be achieved that could not be attained by the efforts of individuals on their own. There are many different types of organisations that come in all forms, shapes and sizes, and set up to serve a number of purposes and to meet a variety of needs. Not only are there many different types of organisations, but cultural differences in countries can reflect different conceptions of what actually is an organisation.[2]

Classification of organisations

In order to relate the study of management and organisational behaviour to one particular type of organisation as distinct from another, it is helpful to group similar types of organisations together. This enables generalisations to be made on the basis of certain characteristic features of organisations within a particular grouping. Organisations can be distinguished by, for example, their nature and type, goods or services provided, size, aims and objectives, and the people who are employed by or who work in them. Organisations can, therefore, be classified in a number of ways and different writers have emphasised particular features of organisations.

A common classification of organisations is by major purpose. This leads to a distinction between, for example:

- **economic** – such as business firms;
- **mutual** – employee-owned, such as co-operatives or building societies;
- **public service** – such as government departments, local authorities and hospitals;
- **social enterprise** – social or environmental concerns such as fair trading;
- **protective** – such as the military, trade unions and police forces;
- **social or associative** – such as clubs and societies;
- **religious** – such as churches, monasteries and mosques;
- **political** – such as political parties, pressure groups;
- **educational** – such as universities, colleges and training centres; and
- **voluntary and community** – such as Citizens Advice Bureaux, RNLI or hospital radio. These organisations along with those not-for-profit are also called the third sector.

Such distinction, however, tends to lack refinement, and not all organisations fit simply into one classification. Social-enterprise organisations have both social and financial objectives. Many universities combine business consultancy with teaching. Some hospitals are concerned as much with training and/or research as with treatment of patients. One could debate the main purpose of a prison: is it, for example, corrective, protective, penal or educational? The main purpose of a trade union is seen, presumably, as protection of the interests of its members through their wages and working conditions, but many trade unions also have strong social, educational and political interests. Many organisations serve more than one goal, but although they are multi-purpose organisations it is usually possible to identify one predominant goal (or purpose) by which the organisation can be classified, however crude this classification may be.

Private- and public-sector organisations

Organisations can, traditionally, be distinguished in terms of two generic groups: private-enterprise organisations and public-sector organisations. The distinction can be made broadly on the basis of ownership and finance, and the profit motive. **Private-enterprise organisations** are owned and financed by individuals, partners or shareholders in a joint-stock company, and are accountable to their owners or members. They vary widely in nature and size, and in the type and scope of goods and services provided. The main aim is of a commercial nature, such as profit, return on capital employed, market standing or sales level.

Public-sector organisations are created by government and include, for example, municipal undertakings and central government departments, which do not have profit as their goal. Municipal undertakings such as local authorities are 'owned' by the council-tax payers and business ratepayers and financed by council taxes, business rates, government grants, loans and charges for certain services. Central government departments are 'state owned' and financed by funds granted by Parliament. Public-sector organisations have political purposes and do not distribute profits. Any surplus of revenue over expenditure may be reallocated through improved services or reduced charges. The main aim is a service to, and the well-being of, the community.

Smart and Inazawa suggest that although the size, scope and structure of the public sector differ extensively between different countries, there are seven common features that define the public sector in terms of seven main aspects of activity[3] (*see* Figure 3.1).

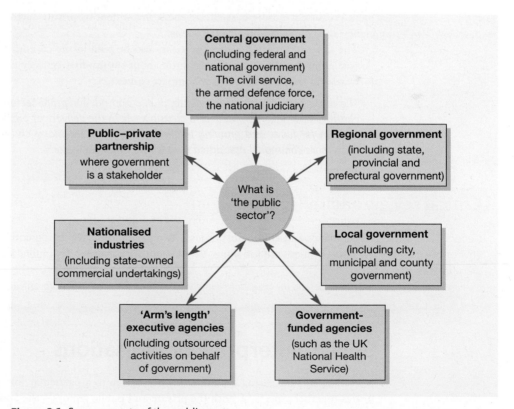

Figure 3.1 Seven aspects of the public sector

Source: From Smart, P. and Inazawa, K. *Human resource management in the public sector*, Kwansei Gakuin University Press (2011), p. 21. Reproduced with permission.

The private–public interface

The extent of the state ownership of public-sector operations, or of their **privatisation,** and the balance between commercial and social interests are determined by the government of the day. Exposure to competition and demands for economical and high-quality services have prompted local authorities to place greater emphasis on practices of business management.

In spite of the fashion for applying private-sector techniques in government, *Saunders* questions whether business and government are really comparable and whether business methods can win similar positive results for the public services. There are huge differences between business and government, and they have different objectives. When it comes to notoriously complex and multidimensional challenges such as providing healthcare and education, just how far will the commercial metaphor stretch? Although some skills are transferable, strategically, the operations of state and commerce remain poles apart.[4]

As an adviser to both the Labour Party and the Coalition, *Morrell* suggests that while the public sector cannot be run like a business, it could be a lot more businesslike.[5] (**Management in private-enterprise and public-sector organisations is discussed in Chapter 10.**)

Not-for-profit organisations

The increasing scale of privatisation and the blurring of commercial interests and social interests have led to an alternative classification of organisations: those run for **profit;** and those clearly **not for profit.** Not-for-profit organisations include on the one hand charities, private societies and most religious organisations, and on the other hand National Health Service (NHS) hospitals, universities, prisons, and most government and local authority departments. However, even in not-for-profit public-sector organisations there has been increased government pressure to ensure cost-effectiveness, investment by private-sector involvement, and efficiency and economy in their operations.

The same blurring of distinctions can also be seen in the case of charities. For example, *Arnott* points out that there is very little about twenty-first-century charities that is straightforward and they exist in a highly complex context.

> *The old distinctions between private, public and not-for-profit sectors have been blurred as charities have taken on an ever-increasing role in the delivery of public services. Tough competition for funds and growing public scrutiny have led many charities to adopt practices once more commonly associated with the commercial sector.*[6]

Critical review and reflection

Generalised models of organisation serve no useful purpose. All organisations have their unique culture and working environment and no two organisations are the same. The skill of the manager is to understand clearly what takes place in their own organisation.

How would YOU attempt to defend this assertion? How would YOU explain YOUR own university or organisation?

Social-enterprise organisations

In recent years increasing attention has been given to a particular form of organisation that brings together aspects of both the private and public sectors – the **Social-enterprise organisation.** Although such organisations function as companies, their main concern is with the community in general rather than with shareholder value or specific public interest. Social-enterprise organisations promote the well-being of society but are not charities, and they suggest elements of both capitalism and socialism.

Unlike not-for-profit organisations, social-enterprise organisations have a triple bottom line, trading in goods and/or services with social, environmental and financial objectives. However, as the name suggests, they have a primary concern with a social purpose and the creation of social value. Social enterprises are very diverse and may take a number of different forms including community enterprises, farmers' markets, leisure trusts, recycling, transport and energy, provision of local services, and job creation and training. In the public sector there are many examples of social enterprises in primary and community health, care and welfare services.[7]

A particular example of a social-enterprise organisation is Grameen Bank, which provides microcredit loans without collateral to rural villages in Bangladesh (see the case study at the end of this chapter). Another example is Jamie Oliver's project 'Fifteen', which offered disadvantaged young people opportunities for a career in the restaurant industry.

Other well-known examples include the Eden Project, The Big Issue, Café Direct and Divine Chocolate. Social-enterprise organisations are also developing internationally. A common theme is empowering people and harnessing their skills and abilities. In Singapore there is a non-profit 'Social Innovation Park' that acts as a form of incubator for start-up social enterprises, including a dance centre that channels profits to bursaries for low-income students, cooking and deportment lessons for plus-sized people, and opportunities for individuals with untapped talents to showcase their original creations or to perform a dance or song. An example of social enterprise in the Arabian Gulf is Sidab women in Oman who have mastered the formation of their own small business to market their sewing and photography, Omani home cooking and henna applications.

According to *Lucas,* there is an unprecedented level of interest in social enterprise as an alternative, more sustainable future business model. With increasing pressure on public-sector spending, the demand for social-enterprise services is increasing. However, two important issues that could hold back social enterprises are access to funding and the need for leadership and management skills to build business capacity.[8] The European Commission also recognises the increasing potential of social enterprises as pioneers in developing new markets and creating sustainable jobs. However, entrepreneurs may lack business skills and there is a lack of measurement of the social value generated.[9]

Common features of organisations

Whatever their classification, all organisations have their own individual character, culture and sense of identity, and differ in their attributes, processes and methods of working. However, despite the differences, it must be remembered that all organisations are structures of people. Through collaborative action members can achieve a synergistic effect. They exist in order to achieve objectives and to provide satisfaction for their members. There are at least three common features of any organisation: people, objectives and structure.

It is the interaction of **people** in order to achieve **objectives** that forms the basis of an organisation. Some form of **structure** is needed by which people's interactions and efforts are channelled and co-ordinated. We can add to these a fourth factor: management.

Some process of **management** is required by which the activities of the organisation, and the efforts of its members, are directed and controlled towards the pursuit of objectives.

Effectiveness of the organisation will be dependent upon the quality of its people, its objectives and structure, and the resources available to it. The interrelationship of people, objectives and structure, together with the efficient use of available non-human and human resources, will determine the success or failure of the organisation and the extent of its effectiveness (*see* Figure 3.2).

Differences in applications

Despite these common features, the structure, management and functioning of individual organisations will vary because of differences in their nature and type, respective goals and objectives, and the behaviour of the people who work in them.

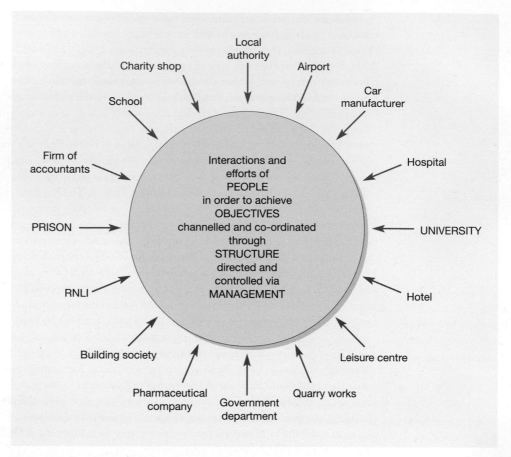

Figure 3.2 Common features of organisations

Consider just two types of organisations towards the opposite ends of a possible continuum – say, a maximum security prison and a university largely concerned with academic research – as a framework on which to focus attention. We can appreciate readily that although both types of organisation will be concerned with the basic activities of organisation and management, their goals and objectives, actual procedures and methods of operation, structure, systems and style of management, and orientation and behaviour of members will differ considerably (*see* Figure 3.3).

The organisation as an open system

Organisations differ in many important respects but they also share common features, and can be viewed as open systems that take inputs from the environment (outputs from other systems) and through a series of activities transform or convert these inputs into outputs (inputs to other systems) to achieve some objective (*see* Figure 3.4). By adopting the systems view of organisations, we can identify principles and prescriptions of organisation and management that apply to business organisations in general. Differences in the application and operation of these principles and prescriptions between one organisation and another are largely a matter only of degree and emphasis.

In terms of the **open-systems model**, the business organisation, for example, takes in resources such as people, finance, raw materials and information from its environment, transforms or converts these and returns them to the environment in various forms of outputs such

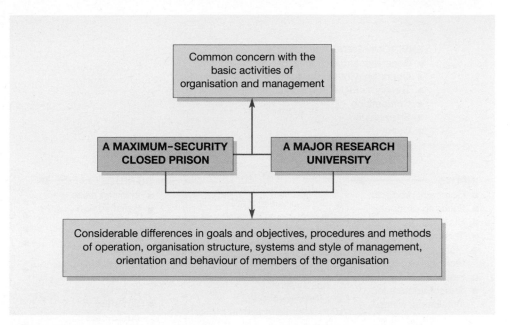

Figure 3.3 The nature of organisations

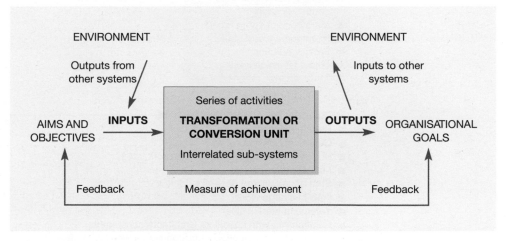

Figure 3.4 The open-systems model of organisations

as goods produced, services provided, completed processes or procedures in order to achieve certain goals such as profit, market standing, level of sales or consumer satisfaction.

Applying the systems model, the same form of analysis can be applied to all types of organisations. This provides a common point of reference and enables us to take a general approach to the study of organisations, to analyse them and to derive general principles and prescriptions.

An example of the open-systems model applied to the environment-systems division of a major heating and ventilation company is given in Figure 3.5.

Interactions with the environment

The structure, management and functioning of an organisation are determined not only by internal considerations and choices, but also influenced strongly by a range of volatile **external environmental factors.** In order to be effective and maintain survival and growth, the

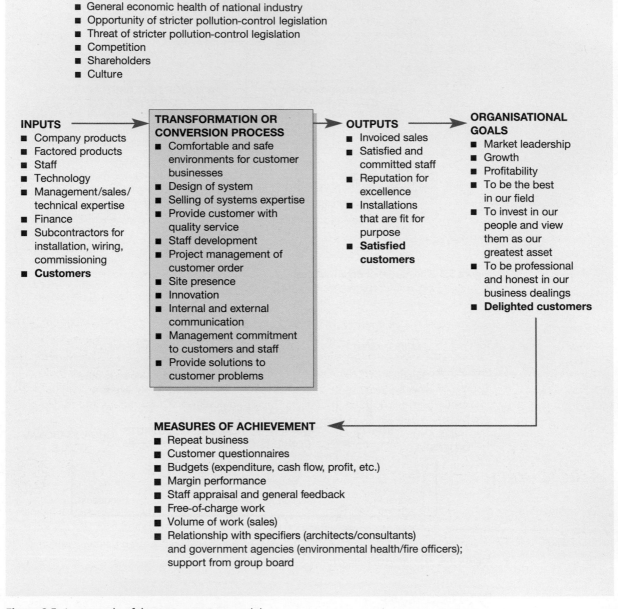

ENVIRONMENTAL INFLUENCES
- General economic health of national industry
- Opportunity of stricter pollution-control legislation
- Threat of stricter pollution-control legislation
- Competition
- Shareholders
- Culture

INPUTS
- Company products
- Factored products
- Staff
- Technology
- Management/sales/ technical expertise
- Finance
- Subcontractors for installation, wiring, commissioning
- **Customers**

TRANSFORMATION OR CONVERSION PROCESS
- Comfortable and safe environments for customer businesses
- Design of system
- Selling of systems expertise
- Provide customer with quality service
- Staff development
- Project management of customer order
- Site presence
- Innovation
- Internal and external communication
- Management commitment to customers and staff
- Provide solutions to customer problems

OUTPUTS
- Invoiced sales
- Satisfied and committed staff
- Reputation for excellence
- Installations that are fit for purpose
- **Satisfied customers**

ORGANISATIONAL GOALS
- Market leadership
- Growth
- Profitability
- To be the best in our field
- To invest in our people and view them as our greatest asset
- To be professional and honest in our business dealings
- **Delighted customers**

MEASURES OF ACHIEVEMENT
- Repeat business
- Customer questionnaires
- Budgets (expenditure, cash flow, profit, etc.)
- Margin performance
- Staff appraisal and general feedback
- Free-of-charge work
- Volume of work (sales)
- Relationship with specifiers (architects/consultants) and government agencies (environmental health/fire officers); support from group board

Figure 3.5 An example of the open-systems model

organisation must respond to the opportunities and challenges, and the risks and limitations, presented by the external environment of which it is part.

The increasing rate of change in major environmental factors (technical, economic, social and governmental) has highlighted the need to study the total organisation and to adopt a systems approach. In addition to these major environmental factors, there is a multiplicity of constantly changing environmental influences that affect the operation of an organisation (*see* Figure 3.6). In order to understand the operations of organisations, and to improve organisational performance, it is necessary to consider how they achieve an internal and external balance and how they are able to adapt to changes in their environment and the demands placed upon them.[10]

Figure 3.6 Environmental influences on the organisation

Consider, for example, how the management and operation of a large comprehensive school might be affected by such external influences as government proposals for reform of education, changing demographic trends, the general economic climate, advances in information technology, changing views of the role of education in society, greater diversity of people in the catchment area, reports from Her Majesty's Inspectors, increased health and safety concerns, social networking, representations from employers' associations and trade unions, parent groups and equality campaigners.

Critical review and reflection

The ability to respond effectively to external environmental factors is clearly the single most important managerial skill influencing the successful performance and long-term survival of any organisation.
To what extent do YOU agree with this statement? Relate this claim to YOUR own university and/or organisation.

PESTEL analysis

Organisational performance and effectiveness will be dependent upon the successful management of the opportunities, challenges and risks presented by changes in the external environment. One popular technique for analysing the general environment is a **PESTEL analysis** – that is, Political, Economic, Socio-cultural, Technological, Environmental and Legal influences. As an example, *Lynch* presents the main issues that might be considered when undertaking a PESTEL analysis (*see* Figure 3.7).[11]

Worthington and Britton refer to the complexity of the external environment.

External influences are almost infinite in number and variety and no study could hope to consider them all. For students of business and for managers alike, the requirement is to recognise the complexity of the external environment and to pay greater attention to those influences which appear the most pertinent and pressing for the organisation in question, rather than to attempt to consider all possible contingencies.[12]

Political future

- Political parties and alignments at local, national and European or regional trading-bloc level
- Legislation, e.g. on taxation and employment law
- Relations between government and the organisation (possibly influencing the preceding items in a major way and forming a part of future strategic management)
- Government ownership of industry and attitude to monopolies and competition

Socio-cultural future

- Shifts in values and culture
- Change in lifestyle
- Attitudes to work and leisure
- 'Green' environmental issues
- Education and health
- Demographic changes
- Distribution of income

Economic future

- Total GDP and GDP per head
- Inflation
- Consumer expenditure and disposable income
- Interest rates

- Currency fluctuations and exchange rates
- Investment – by the state, private enterprise and foreign companies
- Cyclicality
- Unemployment
- Energy costs, transport costs, communications costs, raw materials costs

Technological future

- Government and EU investment policy
- Identified new research initiatives
- New patents and products
- Speed of change and adoption of new technology
- Level of expenditure on R&D by organisation's rivals
- Developments in nominally unrelated industries that might be applicable

Environmental future

- 'Green' issues that affect the environment and impact on the company
- Level and type of energy consumed – renewable energy?
- Rubbish, waste and its disposal

Legal future

- Competition law and government policy
- Employment and safety law
- Product safety issues

Figure 3.7 Checklist for a PESTEL analysis
Source: Lynch, R. *Strategic Management*, seventh edition, Pearson Education (2015), p. 73.

Analysis of work organisations

All organisations need clear aims and objectives that will determine the nature of inputs, the series of activities to achieve outputs and the realisation of organisational goals. Feedback about the performance of the system, and the effects of its operation on the environment, is measured in terms of achieving aims and objectives.

Basic principles of organisation and management apply in any series of activities in any organisation. For example:

- attention must be given to the design of a suitable structure;
- common elements of management – clarification of objectives, planning, organising, directing and control – apply to a greater or lesser extent in all cases;
- execution of essential financial, legal, human resources and administrative functions.

These common features make possible the application of general principles of management and organisational behaviour (including, for example, in both a prison and a university) and the meaningful study of organisational theory. While general principles and prescriptions apply to all organisations, differences in their aims and objectives, organisational goals and environmental influences highlight alternative forms of structure, management, methods of operation and behaviour of people employed by or working in different types of organisations.

Organisational sub-systems

Within the organisation (system) as a whole, each of the different transformation or conversion activities may themselves be viewed as separate **organisational sub-systems**. A framework of five main interrelated sub-systems as a basis for the analysis of work organisations can be identified as:

- **Task** – the goals and objectives of the organisation: the nature of inputs and outputs, and the work activities to be carried out in the transformation or conversion process.
- **Technology** – the manner in which the tasks of the organisation are carried out and the nature of work performance: the materials, systems and procedures, and equipment used in the transformation or conversion process.
- **Structure** – patterns of organisation, lines of authority, formal relationships and channels of communication among members: the division of work and co-ordination of tasks by which the series of activities is carried out.
- **People** – the nature of the members undertaking the series of activities: for example, their attitudes, skills and attributes; needs and expectations; interpersonal relations and patterns of behaviour; group functioning and behaviour; informal organisation and styles of leadership.
- **Management** – co-ordination of task, technology, structure and people, and policies and procedures for the execution of work: corporate strategy, direction of the activities of the organisation as a whole and its interactions with the external environment. (*See* Figure 3.8.)

The framework of five main interrelated sub-systems – task, technology, structure, people and management – provides a useful basis for the analysis of organisational performance and effectiveness. Attention should be focused on the total work organisation and on the interrelationships between the range of variables that affect organisational performance.

Contingency models of organisation

Irrespective of the identification of sub-systems, the nature and scale of the series of activities involved in converting inputs to outputs will differ from one organisation to another in terms of the interrelationships between technology, structure, methods of operation and the nature of environmental influences. 'Contingency' models of organisation highlight these interrelationships and provide a further possible means of differentiation between alternative forms of organisation and management. The contingency approach takes the view that there is no one best, universal form of organisation. There are a large number of variables, or situational factors, that influence organisational performance. (**Contingency models are examined in Chapter 11.**)

Critical review and reflection

The traditional analysis of an organisation is usually based upon the structure and efficiency of individual departments. However, this leads to blinkered sectional interests rather than to the interrelationships and co-ordination of sub-systems of the organisation as an integrated whole.

What do YOU see as the relevance of the traditional form of analysis?

Task   – the nature of the work activities to be carried out
Technology – the manner in which activities are carried out
Structure   – patterns of organisation and formal relationships within which activities are
                  carried out
People   – the nature of members undertaking the activities
Management – effective co-ordination of the sub-systems and direction of activities of the
                  organisation as a unified whole

Figure 3.8 Organisational sub-systems

Formal and informal organisations

So far we have been looking at the nature of formal organisations – that is, organisations deliberately planned and structured to meet stated objectives.

A **formal organisation** has been defined by *Schein* as:

> *the planned co-ordination of the activities of a number of people for the achievement of some common, explicit purpose or goal, through division of labour and function, and through a hierarchy of authority and responsibility.*[13]

An organisation is a pattern of roles and a blueprint for their co-ordination. The object of co-ordination is activities, not people.

The formal organisation is:

- deliberately planned and created;
- concerned with the co-ordination of activities;

- hierarchically structured with stated objectives; and
- based on certain principles such as the specification of tasks and defined relationships of authority and responsibility.

An organisation chart may give a representation of the formal structure. Other examples of the formal organisation are rules and regulations, policy manuals, standing orders and job descriptions. The formal organisation can exist independently of the membership of particular individuals.

The informal organisation

The formal organisation can be distinguished from the informal organisation – the difference between them is a feature of the degree to which they are structured. A major feature of organisational life is that whatever the type or nature of an organisation or its formal structure, an **informal organisation** will always be present (*see* Figure 3.9). The informal organisation arises from the interaction of people working in the organisation, their psychological and social needs, and the development of groups with their own relationships and norms of behaviour, irrespective of those defined within the formal structure.

- The informal organisation is flexible and loosely structured.
- Relationships may be left undefined.
- Membership is spontaneous with varying degrees of involvement.

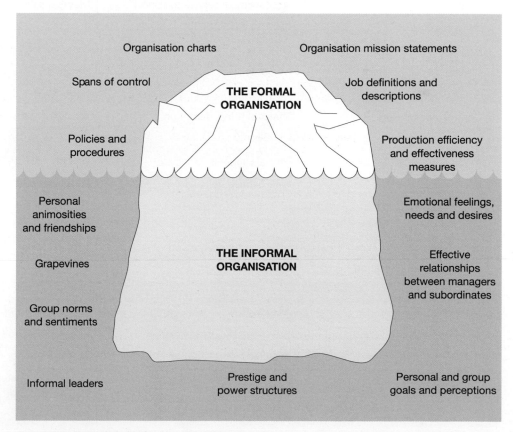

Figure 3.9 Formal and informal organisations

Source: Lysons, K. 'Organisational Analysis', supplement to Manager, The British Journal of Administrative Management, No. 18, March/April 1997. Reproduced with permission of The Institute of Administrative Management.

Group relationships and norms of behaviour exist outside the official structure, and the informal organisation may, therefore, be in conflict with the aims of the formal organisation. A summary of differences between the formal and the informal organisation is given in Table 3.1.

Functions of the informal organisation

The informal organisation can serve a number of important functions. It provides for:

- **satisfaction of members' social needs** and a sense of personal identity and belonging;
- **additional channels of communication** – for example, through the 'grapevine', where information of importance to particular members is communicated quickly;
- **means of motivation** – for example, through status, social interaction, peer rating, variety in routine or tedious jobs, and informal methods of work.

Table 3.1 Comparison of the formal and the informal organisation

Characteristic	Formal organisation	Informal organisation
1 Structure		
A Origin	Planned	Spontaneous
B Rationale	Rational	Emotional
C Characteristics	Stable	Dynamic
2 Position terminology	Job	Role
3 Goals	Profitability or service to society	Member satisfaction
4 Influence		
A Base	Position	Personality
B Type	Authority	Power
C Flow	Top-down	Bottom-up
5 Control mechanisms	Threat of firing, demotion	Physical or social sanctions (norms)
6 Communication		
A Channels	Formal channels	Grapevine
B Networks	Well-defined, follow formal lines	Poorly defined, cut across regular channels
C Speed	Slow	Fast
D Accuracy	High	Low
7 Charting the organisation	Organisation chart	Sociogram
8 Miscellaneous		
A Individuals included	All individuals in work group	Only those 'acceptable'
B Interpersonal relations	Prescribed by job description	Arise spontaneously
C Leadership role	Assigned by organisation	Result of membership agreement
D Basis for interaction	Functional duties or position	Personal characteristics, ethnic background, status
E Basis for attachment	Loyalty	Cohesiveness

Source: Adapted from Gray, J. L. and Starke, F. A. *Organizational Behavior: Concepts and Applications*, fourth edition, Merrill Publishing Company (1988) © 1988, p. 432. Reprinted and electronically produced with permission from Pearson Education Inc.

- **feeling of stability and security,** and through informal 'norms' of behaviour can exercise a form of control over members;
- **means of highlighting deficiencies or weaknesses** in the formal organisation – for example, areas of duties or responsibilities not covered in job descriptions, or outdated systems and procedures.

The informal organisation may also be used when formal methods would take too long, or not be appropriate, to deal with an unusual or unforeseen situation.

> *Buying a coffee machine and water cooler could be the most important investments a company ever makes in its future. For it's at these social hubs of office life that the real business often gets done, as part of a casual chat or chance meeting.*[14]

The informal organisation, therefore, has an important influence on the morale, motivation, job satisfaction and performance of staff. It can provide members with greater opportunity to use their initiative and creativity in both personal and organisational development. Covert and informal activities may also have economic consequences for the organisation in terms of added values and/or costs that escape ordinary accounting procedures.[15] (**The importance and nature of groups, and reasons why people form into groups, both formal and informal, are discussed in Chapter 8.**)

Friendships and relationships at work

One particular aspect of the informal organisation that has received increasing attention is the possible effects of personal friendships and relationships at work, and potential conflict between the informal and formal organisation. For example, according to *Vernon*, while work is one of the best sources of friends as well as the most desirable place to have them, the trouble is that friendships at work are full of ambiguities. For friendships, the trouble with work is that you are there to be useful: to do something for a client, team or boss. Professional friendships will always be influenced and possibly determined by the utility factor.[16] Potential conflict between personal freedom and team performance is discussed later (**see Chapter 8**).

The Code of Conduct for the Royal Bank of Scotland includes the following:

> *While the Group entirely respects the right of every one of us to form friendships and personal relationships at work, there will be occasions when it will be appropriate to tell your manager about a relationship that may impact on your work by creating a conflict of interest.*[17]

Critical review and reflection

Study of the planning and structure of the formal organisation is largely a waste of time. In reality it is the nature and working of the informal organisation that ultimately determines the operation and effectiveness of any work organisation.

Based on YOUR own experience, to what extent do YOU agree with this assertion? What practical examples can YOU give?

Underlying realities of work organisations

Conflict and stress are two underlying realities of work organisations that have a significant influence on management and organisational behaviour. The two forces of conflict and stress are often interrelated. Conflict in many of its forms can have a contributory influence on stress, and people under stress may be more inclined to experience situations of conflict.

Organisational conflict

Most of us will understand what is commonly meant by organisational conflict and be aware of its existence and effects. Conflict can be related to power and politics, or managerial style and leadership. But conflict can also arise from many different situations or actions and is a term that can be defined and interpreted in a number of ways. For our purpose we can see **conflict** as behaviour intended to obstruct the achievement of some other person's goals. Conflict is based on the incompatibility of goals and arises from opposing behaviours. It can be viewed at the individual, group or organisation level. *Ackroyd and Thompson* use the term 'organizational misbehaviour' to refer to 'anything you do at work which you are not supposed to'. Management establish boundaries that distinguish acceptable and non-acceptable behaviour from employees. The actions of employees are then judged as falling one side or the other of these boundaries.[18]

Common definitions of conflict tend to be associated with negative features and situations that give rise to inefficiency, ineffectiveness or dysfunctional consequences. The traditional view of conflict is that it is bad for organisations. Conflict is perceived as disruptive and unnatural and represents a form of deviant behaviour that should be controlled and changed. Clearly, extreme cases of conflict in organisations can have very upsetting, or even tragic, consequences for some people and have adverse effects on organisational performance. Conflict situations can give rise to excessive emotional or physical stress.

According to ACAS, conflict in the workplace can be divided into three categories: **organised conflict,** which manifests itself as strike action or action short of strike, wildcat strikes, occupations etc.; **overt individual conflict,** such as formal grievances raised over working conditions; and **latent conflict,** where the signs of unrest, discontent and disengagement are expressed through increased absence levels and higher turnover of personnel, a drop in performance and more fractious interpersonal relationships between managers and the managed, which can lead to an increase in bullying and harassment.[19]

Contrasting perspectives of conflict

It might be expected that a healthy organisational climate would be reflected by complete harmony in working relationships, loyalty and common commitment to the goals and objectives of the organisation. This view of work organisations as 'happy families' is perhaps a worthwhile and creditable ideal and as such appears to be implied by a number of management writers. (**See also the discussion in Chapter 10.**)

Drucker, for example, makes the following point:

> *Any business enterprise must build a true team and weld individual efforts into a common effort. Each member of the enterprise contributes something different, but they must all contribute towards a common goal. Their efforts must all pull in the same direction, and their contributions must fit together to produce a whole – without gaps, without friction, without unnecessary duplication of effort . . . The manager must know and understand what the business goals demand of him in terms of performance, and his superior must know what contribution to demand and expect of him – and must judge him accordingly. If these requirements are not met, managers are misdirected. Their efforts are wasted. Instead of teamwork, there is friction, frustration and conflict.*[20]

Unitarist and pluralist perspectives

Such traditional views appear to imply a **unitarist perspective** of the organisation (**discussed in Chapter 2**). The natural state of the organisation is viewed as an integrated, co-operative and harmonious whole. There is an image of the organisation as a team with a common source of loyalty and one focus of effort. But if one accepts the idea of a pluralist perspective to work organisations, conflict is not necessarily a bad thing but can be an agent for evolution and internal and external change. The pluralist manager is more likely to accept that conflict in organisations requires careful handling and attempt to reconcile rival interests.

The radical perspective

The **radical perspective** is associated with the ideas of writers such as Karl Marx and the structuralist approach to organisations and management.[21] It challenges the traditional view of conflict in society and sees organisations in terms of disparity in power and control between owners and workers. Conflict is an inherent feature of the unequal nature of organisational life and a means of bringing about change.[22] Collective bargaining is not seen as particularly helpful in a system stacked against the workers. Conflict is a natural part of the class struggle.

According to the radical approach, the design of organisation structure, management systems and the choice and use of technology all form part of the struggle for power and control within the work organisation. Greater attention should be given to relationships between the formal and informal aspects of the organisation and the study of conflict between the needs of the individual and those of the organisation, and between workers and management.

Broader interpretation of conflict

A more recent view of conflict is the **interactionist perspective,** which believes that conflict is a positive force and necessary for effective performance. This approach encourages a minimum level of conflict within the group in order to encourage self-criticism, change and innovation, and to help prevent apathy or too great a tolerance for harmony and the status quo.[23]

Conflict per se is not necessarily good or bad but an inevitable feature of organisational life and should be judged in terms of its effects on performance. Even if organisations have taken great care to try to avoid conflict, it will still occur. Conflict will continue to emerge despite management attempts to suppress it.

The current view appears to recognise that conflict can be interpreted more broadly than in the traditional view. *Townsend* sees conflict as a sign of a healthy organisation – up to a point.

> *A good manager doesn't try to eliminate conflict; he tries to keep it from wasting the energies of his people . . . If you're the boss and your people fight you openly when they think you're wrong – that's healthy. If your people fight each other openly in your presence for what they believe in – that's healthy. But keep all the conflict eyeball to eyeball.*[24]

Constructive conflict

Conflict, then, is not necessarily a bad thing. It can be seen as a 'constructive' force, and in certain circumstances it can be welcomed or even encouraged. Healthy conflict can help generate innovation and be seen as an aid to incremental improvement in organisation design and functioning, and to the decision-making process. Conflict can be an agent for evolution, and for internal and external change. Properly identified and handled, it can help to minimise the destructive influences of the win–lose situation.

In a discussion of conflict at board level, *Dunne* refers to the destructive force of failure to manage conflict. However, if the board focuses on a combination of the right strategy, right resources and right governance, and executives on strategic options, delivering the business plan and operational and financial integrity, then there is a much better chance of achieving a healthy degree of constructive conflict and sustained high performance.[25]

Conflict and 'difficult people'

The idea of conflict as inevitable is discussed by *Irvine,* who suggests that if you ask a group of managers about the nature and level of conflict they experience, the majority will tell you honestly that, apart from the odd minor tiff, there is not much conflict about. There are, however, 'difficult people'.

> *Perhaps our reluctance to identify, and then directly address, conflict within organisations is based upon the widely held belief that conflict is inevitable, negative and unmanageable. There is a tendency to see conflict as a result of one person's personality. Conflict may be inevitable, but how dramatically situations could be changed if we could also view it as positive and manageable! What if we think of these situations as raising **questions of difference?** What if we were to make a shift away from blaming individuals and their personalities, recognizing instead that it is through normal human interaction that outward expressions of difference are produced?*[26]

According to *Mannering,* conflicts, misunderstandings and personality clashes are usually at the root of the problem when employees become unhappy at work. There is an erosion of our social framework, and the work environment has become more competitive with pressure to have the best jobs and gadgets. People are placed into teams with people they would possibly never choose to associate with. Mannering suggests that people can be 'difficult' for a number of reasons, but it is important not to concentrate on the negative points. Negativity is the most difficult behaviour to overcome or change as it constantly undermines what the team is trying to achieve.

In order to help defuse conflict, it is important to draw a fine line between firm management and aggressive behaviour. Humour may help defuse a situation but it is more important to stay calm and professional. Improved communications and relationships may help but if someone is determined not to co-operate, then there will be conflict. Mannering makes the point that although you cannot please everyone all the time, avoidance is not an option for dealing with difficult people. Managers must develop solid coping mechanisms and do their best in the particular situation.[27]

Critical review and reflection

There are many positive outcomes from conflict that demonstrate commitment and enthusiasm about work activities. Properly managed, conflict can be an energising and vitalising force within groups and the organisation. Managers should therefore be encouraged to invoke constructive conflict.

To what extent do YOU think potential benefits of constructive conflict are outweighed by negative aspects? How would YOU attempt to manage conflict?

Sources of conflict

There are many potential sources of organisational conflict, including those summarised as follows:

- **Differences in perception** – We all see things in different ways and have our own set of values, beliefs and opinions. Differences in perception result in individuals attaching different meanings to the same stimuli. As perceptions become a person's reality, value judgements can be a potential major source of conflict. (**The importance of perception is discussed in Chapter 6.**)

- **Limited resources** – Most organisational resources are limited, and individuals and groups have to fight for their share – for example, at the time of the allocation of the next year's budget or when cutbacks have to be made. The greater the limitation of resources, then usually the greater the potential for conflict. In an organisation with reducing profits or revenues, the potential for conflict is likely to be intensified.

- **Departmentalisation and specialisation** – Most work organisations are divided into departments with specialised functions. Because of familiarity with the manner in which they undertake their activities, managers tend to turn inwards and to concentrate on the achievement of their own particular goals. When departments need to co-operate, this is a frequent source of conflict. Differing goals and internal environments of departments are also a potential source of conflict, for example between task and element function (**discussed in Chapter 11**). In her study of management organisation of firms in this country, *Woodward* comments on the bad relationships between accountants and other managers. One reason for this hostility was the bringing together of two quite separate financial functions. People concerned with works accounting tended to assume responsibility for end results that were not properly theirs; they saw their role as a controlling and sanctioning one rather than as a servicing and supportive one. Line managers resented this attitude and retaliated by becoming aggressive and obstructive.[28]

- **Nature of work activities** – Where the activities of one person are dependent upon the work of others there is potential for conflict. For example, a worker is expected to complete the assembly of a given number of components each day but must rely on another worker forwarding the part-assembled components in good time. If reward and punishment systems are perceived to be based on performance levels, then the potential for conflict is even greater. If the work of a department is dependent upon the output of another department, a similar situation could arise, especially if this situation is coupled with limited resources.

- **Role conflict** – A role is the expected pattern of behaviours associated with members occupying a particular position within the structure of the organisation. In practice, the manner in which people actually behave may not be consistent with their expected pattern of behaviour. Problems of role incompatibility and role ambiguity arise from inadequate or inappropriate role definition and can be a significant source of conflict. (**Role conflict is discussed in Chapter 8.**)

- **Inequitable treatment** – A person's feeling of unjust treatment, for example in the operation of HR policies and practices or in reward and punishment systems, can lead to tension and conflict. For example, according to the equity theory of motivation (**discussed in Chapter 7**), the perception of inequity will motivate a person to take action to restore equity, including changes to inputs or outputs, or through acting on others.

- **Violation of territory** – People tend to become attached to their own 'territory' – for example, to their own area of work, clients to be dealt with, or to their own room, chair or parking space. Jealousy may arise over other people's territory, such as size of room, company car, allocation of an assistant or other perks or through access to information or through membership of groups.[29] Ownership of territory may be conferred formally, for example by organisation charts, job descriptions or management decisions; it may be established through procedures, such as circulation lists or membership of committees; or it may arise informally, for example through group norms, tradition or perceived status symbols. The place where people choose to meet can have a significant symbolic value. For example, if a subordinate is summoned to a meeting in a manager's office this might be taken to mean that the manager is signalling higher status. If the manager chooses to meet at the subordinate's place of work, or on neutral territory, this may be a signal that the manager wishes to meet the subordinate as an equal. If a person's territory is violated this can lead to the possibility of retaliation and conflict.

- **Environmental change** – Changes in an organisation's external environment, such as economic depression, increased competition, government intervention, new technology or changing social values, can cause major areas of conflict. For example, a fall in demand for, or government financial restrictions on, enrolments for a certain discipline in higher education can result in conflict over the allocation of resources. If the department concerned is a large and important one and led by a powerful head, there could be even greater potential for conflict.

Other potential sources of conflict

There are many other potential sources of organisational conflict, including:

- **individual** – such as attitudes, personality characteristics or particular personal needs, illness or stress;
- **personal friendships,** relationships and romance in the workplace – and potential conflict between the informal and formal organisation, discussed above;
- **group** – such as group skills, team roles, patterns of interaction and group norms;
- **organisation** – such as communications, authority structure, leadership style, managerial behaviour; and
- **the age gap** – *Hart* discusses how relationships between older employees and younger managers, where experience is on one side and power on the other, can lead to conflict.

The problem for the inexperienced manager in conflict with an older employee is that it is all too easy to label someone 'difficult' rather than intelligently trying to explore the reasons behind their behaviour. If steps are not taken to improve the relationship both manager and employee can end up feeling threatened and undermined.[30]

Management and organisational behaviour in action case study
Based on real events

The production manager (Jack), quality control manager (Josh) and planning manager (Jill) work for a company producing PVC raw materials for customers making a variety of PVC products, such as clothing, tarpaulins, seat covers, plastic containers, etc. Here is a conversation on the shop floor between them concerning a customer complaint about the PVC raw materials.

Josh: I wish your department would give more attention to quality, Jack. We can only do a 10% check on quality from our random sampling. Now we have this complaint from a customer about quality on a batch we produced last week. And the boss is real mad . . . was real mad when I told him.

Jack: Why the heck didn't you come to me first? . . . This puts me in a bad light before I have a chance to investigate and do something. You have assumed that the factory is to blame. . . it could have been . . .

Josh: You always have some excuse and start blaming others . . . like blaming me for poor quality-control checks. You've even put pressure on our department to be retrained, or even fired, for poor quality-control, when you know we are under pressure with increased sales. Have you forgotten . . . ?

Jack: [Interrupts] Why don't you let me finish my sentence before you cut in and attack me?

Josh: Well you're always finding fault with me. So now you know what it's like. Anyway, what did you want to say?

Jack: I wanted to suggest that our complicated delivery schedule can cause confusion.

Josh: It's you chaps that make it complicated. I've already checked with Jill on planning and also checked despatch. There was nothing wrong with the order. This is clearly a production mess up . . .

Jack: Well I'm going to check with Jill's schedule anyway to make sure we have got the right production schedule . . .

Josh: Go ahead . . . perhaps you will be able to blame Jill.

Jack: What the hell are you talking about? . . . Who said anything about blame? I'm just trying to get to the facts before taking the rap for something we didn't do.

Josh: Well I don't know about that Jack. As I walk through the plant, I'm not convinced that some of your supervisors and operators really pay enough attention to quality and the correct operating procedures.

Jack: You're a real pain in the arse Josh! [Shouting]
Josh: So are you . . . [Shouting]
Jill walks in and notices the tension.
Jill: What's the problem chaps?
Jack: Josh is blaming production for a quality problem from a customer complaint and. . .
Josh: Not blaming, simply stating a fact that. . .
Josh: That's absolute bull!
Jill: It seems that you chaps have two problems. A problem with the job – the complaint – and a problem with your conflict. I can't see you solving the complaint until you manage your conflict better.

Source: Kindly provided by Hugo Misselhorn, M.O.D. Consulting, South Africa.

Tasks

1. What do you see as the underlying cause of the conflict between Jack and Josh?
2. If you were Jill, how would you encourage Jack and Josh to investigate the complaint?
3. How would you attempt to avoid further conflict?

The management of conflict

Much has been written about the implications of conflict as a social process. While recognising the importance of this debate, it is not the intention here to enter into a detailed discussion of the ideologies of conflict. The important point is not so much the extent to which it is possible to create a totally harmonious working environment, or whether competing sub-groups and conflict are seen as inevitable consequences of organisation structure, but how conflict, when found to exist, is handled and managed.

Although a certain amount of organisational conflict may be seen as inevitable, there are a number of ways in which management can attempt to avoid harmful effects of conflict. Many of these ideas will be discussed in later chapters. The strategies adopted will vary according to the nature and sources of conflict outlined above. Bear in mind that managing conflict takes time and effort, but attempting to establish a climate of mutual trust, consideration and respect is worthwhile.

- **Clarification of goals and objectives** – Continual refinement and communication of goals and objectives, role definitions and performance standards will help to avoid misunderstandings and conflict. Focusing attention on superordinate goals that are shared by the parties in conflict may help to defuse hostility and lead to more co-operative behaviour.
- **Resource distribution** – Although it may not always be possible for managers to increase their allocated share of resources, they may be able to use imagination and initiative to help overcome conflict situations: making a special case to higher management; greater flexibility to transfer funds between budget headings; or delaying staff appointments in one area to provide more money for another area.
- **HR policies and procedures** – Careful and detailed attention to just and equitable HR policies and procedures may help reduce areas of conflict. Examples are: job analysis; systems of reward and punishment; appeals, grievance and disciplinary procedures; arbitration and mediation; recognition of trade unions and their officials; and training managers in coaching and negotiation skills.
- **Non-monetary rewards** – Where financial resources are limited, it may be possible to pay greater attention to non-monetary rewards, such as: job design; more interesting, challenging or responsible work; increased delegation or empowerment; improved equipment; flexible working hours; attendance at courses or conferences; unofficial perks; or more relaxed working conditions.

- **Development of interpersonal/group process skills** – This may help engender a better understanding of one's own behaviour, the other person's point of view, communication processes and problem-solving. Attention to body language may also assist people to work through conflict situations in a constructive manner. Where possible, encourage addressing disputes early on a one-to-one basis.
- **Group activities** – Attention to the composition of groups and to factors that affect group cohesiveness may reduce dysfunctional conflict. Overlapping group membership with a 'linking-pin' process, and the careful selection of project teams or task forces for problems affecting more than one group, may also be beneficial.
- **Leadership and management** – A more participative and supportive style of leadership and managerial behaviour is likely to assist in conflict management: showing an attitude of respect and trust; encouraging personal self-development; and creating a work environment in which staff can work co-operatively. An open-door policy and identifying potential causes of disputes may help avoid conflict.
- **Organisational processes** – Conflict situations may be reduced by attention to such features as: the nature of the authority structure; work organisation; patterns of communication and sharing of information; democratic functioning of the organisation; and unnecessary adherence to bureaucratic procedures and official rules and regulations.
- **Socio-technical approach** – Viewing the organisation as a socio-technical system, in which psychological and social factors are developed in keeping with structural and technical requirements, will help in reducing dysfunctional conflict.

Conflict resolution

An ACAS policy paper on managing conflict and individual employment disputes concludes that:

> *While the scale and direction of individual workplace conflict is both contested and difficult to measure, there has been less disagreement as to the potentially damaging effects for both the individuals and organisations involved. Furthermore, there has been a degree of consensus that changes in the structures of workplace representation and the changing balance between the responsibilities of HR and line management have a significant impact on the capacity of organisations to resolve difficult issues in the workplace.*[31]

From an analysis of five case studies, ACAS found that in larger organisations effective conflict management revolves around informal social processes, underpinned by high-trust relationships between key organisational stakeholders. However, these relationships are threatened by more centralised models of HR, and the lack of confidence and capability of line managers to deal with difficult issues. Evidence suggests conflict management was seen as a lower-order skill and the support of senior managers was crucial. There is need for developing structures of employee representation and increased investment in developing the skills and confidence of line managers. The analysis highlights the importance of communications between managers and staff and the positive role of performance management systems and employee engagement in conflict situations.[32]

Critical review and reflection

Potential for interpersonal conflict should be accepted as a reality of organisational behaviour. HR has limited influence. The only effective way to mitigate adverse effects of conflict is through recruiting members of staff with the inherent skills and ability to manage people and social interactions at work.

Do YOU agree? If asked at interview, how would YOU attempt to demonstrate YOUR skill at managing people?

Organisational stress

In addition to organisational conflict, a major and related influence on the work/life balance (discussed later in this chapter) is the extent to which employees suffer from organisational stress. **Stress** is a complex and dynamic concept. It is a possible source of tension and frustration, and can arise through a number of interrelated influences on behaviour, including individual, group, organisational and environmental factors (discussed in Chapter 1).

York contends that, despite all the business-speak, people get seriously vague when it comes to definitions, and raises the question: what is stress? Is it a new name for an old-fashioned condition such as unhappiness or overwork, or is it peculiar to our uniquely pressured times? York suggests there is something in the idea that stress is not just about hard work or unhappiness, but about conflict, confusion and frustration. It is about the anxiety generated by multi-tasking and balancing priorities, meeting contradictory demands, about knowing where to start and papering over the cracks when you want to do too much.[33]

Scepticism

Understandably perhaps, there is a level of scepticism about the amount of attention given to stress, and a number of press and other articles feature the 'myth' of work stress. For example, an interesting report from the Institute for Social and Economic Research suggests that claims of workplace pressure may be misplaced. Levels of job satisfaction and mental distress vary systematically according to the day of the week on which respondents are interviewed. Stress appears to disappear on Friday and Saturday. When genuine dissatisfaction was found, it tended to be because employees were working too few or too many hours. However, the main cause of stress was money difficulties, caused by unemployment or debt. The research casts a question mark over the generous compensation regularly handed out by the courts to employees claiming they suffer from stress.[34]

Randall comments that 'Whichever lawyer first hit on the idea of promoting stress as either a reason for not going to work or a way to make others cough up could hardly have done more damage to Britain's work ethic than if he or she had arranged a quintupling of dole payments.'[35]

Despite the scepticism, however, an increasing number of surveys report perceived or actual increases in levels of stress and contend that stress at work is one of the biggest problems in European companies and one of the major adverse influences on the quality of working life and work performance. There have also been a number of highly publicised reports of successful legal claims based on the effects of stress.

A CBI survey on absence and workplace health reported that, although non-work-related anxiety/stress/depression was then a major cause of long-term illness absence, 29 per cent of absences were attributed to work-related stress and it is on the increase.[36]

Causes of stress

Whatever the effects, it is generally acknowledged that stress is potentially part of everyday working life. It occurs for a variety of reasons, including individual differences and types of personality, occupation and actual stressful nature of the job (whether working in the private or public sector) and organisational conflict (discussed earlier in this chapter). External economic pressures, such as a result of recession, also account for an increase in stress.

Other sources of stress at work include the following:

- **Restructuring of organisations** and reductions in staffing levels resulting from demands for improved business competitiveness and lower operating costs have placed greater pressures on remaining staff.

- **The long-hours culture,** increased workloads and work intensification, together with unreasonable deadlines.
- **Excessive rules and regulations** and greater bureaucratic burdens, especially among professional groups.
- **Developments in information and communications technology (ICT)** that mean staff are far more constantly and easily contactable and expected to deliver everything faster. This can lead to greater pressure on individuals, a reluctance to switch off and a blurring between work and home life.
- **Organisational changes** such as redundancies and the loss of key members of staff that place extra demands on managers.
- **Authoritarian styles of leadership and management.** For example, as *Cooper* points out: 'one of the key factors which contribute to employees being stressed at work and suffering from ill health is their line manager'.[37]
- **Interpersonal relationships at work,** especially with team colleagues; poor communications; office politics.
- **Lack of empowerment and autonomy over control of work.** Stress is often caused by the hierarchical structure of the organisation or lack of delegation and empowerment.
- **Organisation structure and role relationships.** Lack of clarity about expected patterns of behaviour, or role conflict, is a potential source of stress (**discussed in Chapter 8**).

Cultural differences

To what extent do causes of stress vary according to different cultures? There is some evidence to suggest that the incidence of stress does not vary noticeably among different cultures. For example, Type A personalities (**discussed in Chapter 4**) exhibit similar levels of stress across the UK, Hungary, Italy, Israel and the USA.[38] From a study of European Canadians, East Asian Canadians and Japanese exchange students, *Tweed et al.* identified variations between culture and ways of coping with stressful events.[39] Another study of a diverse set of countries across the Anglo world, China and Latin America suggests that stress caused by long work hours can be mitigated by a strong social support network, such as families or friends.[40]

Stress or pressure: is stress necessarily to be avoided?

According to the Health and Safety Executive (HSE), people get confused about the difference between pressure and stress: 'We all experience pressure regularly – it can motivate us to perform at our best. It is when we experience too much pressure and feel unable to cope that stress can result.'[41] HSE defines work stress as: 'The adverse reaction people have to excessive pressures or other types of demand placed on them at work.' Stress is not an illness – it is a state. However, if stress becomes too excessive and prolonged, mental and physical illness may develop. Stress can hit anyone at any level of the business and recent research shows that work-related stress is widespread and is not confined to particular sectors, jobs or industries.[42]

A certain amount of stress may not necessarily be seen as a bad thing and may perhaps even help promote a higher level of intensity and motivation to get work done. It is arguable that stress is a normal motivating factor and, in moderation and in short spells, stress may be good for you. It is important to bear in mind, however, that stress is potentially very harmful. But what is the distinction between pressure and stress? 'Pressure' can be seen as a positive factor that may be harnessed to help people respond to a challenge and function more effectively. 'Stress' may be regarded as a continuous negative response arising from extreme pressure or other demands and the individual's inability to cope.

According to *Cobb,* the issue of pressure is a complex one, though some small changes can make all the difference in assisting you. Cobb refers to two separate aspects of stress:

- pressure that comes from outside, for example working to imposed deadlines when you have many other tasks to perform as well, which places emphasis on your planning skills;
- pressure from within and self-imposed, for example if you are a perfectionist and everything has to be just so in your work, which suggests you should look at why you have developed this attitude and learn to be a little easier on yourself.[43]

Stress is a very personal experience, as is the response of each individual to it and their beliefs about how best to cope with the causes and effects. *Gwyther* points out that although stress appears to have become public health enemy number one and is viewed as the culprit of myriad complaints, the term is bandied about far too readily and there is a need to stand back and attempt to get things into some sort of perspective. A measure of stress is natural. A degree of stress at work is no unhealthy thing and without it nothing would ever get done.[44]

However, it is important to bear in mind that although management may believe that a moderate level of stress can be a spur to increased work performance, employees are unlikely to perceive this in the same way and will dispute what is regarded as an acceptable level of stress or excessive pressure. As ACAS points out, while some amount of stress can be useful as a spur to motivation it is important to avoid the adverse reaction. This can include physical symptoms such as headaches, stomach problems and muscle tension, and mental symptoms such as anxiety and depression. These reactions can be extremely debilitating and result in reduced productivity, absenteeism and poor morale in the workplace.[45]

A summary of the nature and causes of stress is given in the concept map in Figure 3.10.

Critical review and reflection

People may be busy and under pressure, but stress is far too much an overused word. Stress has become something of a fashion and many people appear to compete for who is most stressed. The biggest danger is that the more people talk about stress, the more likely they will really become stressed.

What are YOUR honest views? Do YOU feel the need to talk about stress?

Coping with stress

There are a number of measures by which individuals and organisations can attempt to reduce the causes and harmful effects of stress. There are also many suggested techniques to help individuals bring stress under control – for example, changing one's viewpoint, identifying causes of distress, effective time management (**discussed in Chapter 16**), expanding one's social network, laughing and telling jokes, relaxation training, working on stress reduction and appreciating that some stress can be useful. However, there are not always easy remedies for stress and much depends upon the personality of the individual.

Techniques such as relaxation therapy may help some people, although not others, but still tend to address the symptoms rather than the cause. Organisations also need to give greater attention to training, support and counselling and to the work organisation and job design. However, *Briner* suggests that talking therapies certainly can be useful in some circumstances, but if problems of high-level stress-related issues are caused by a poor working environment or poor management, then counselling is unlikely to help or, if it does, the effects are likely to be only short-lived.[46]

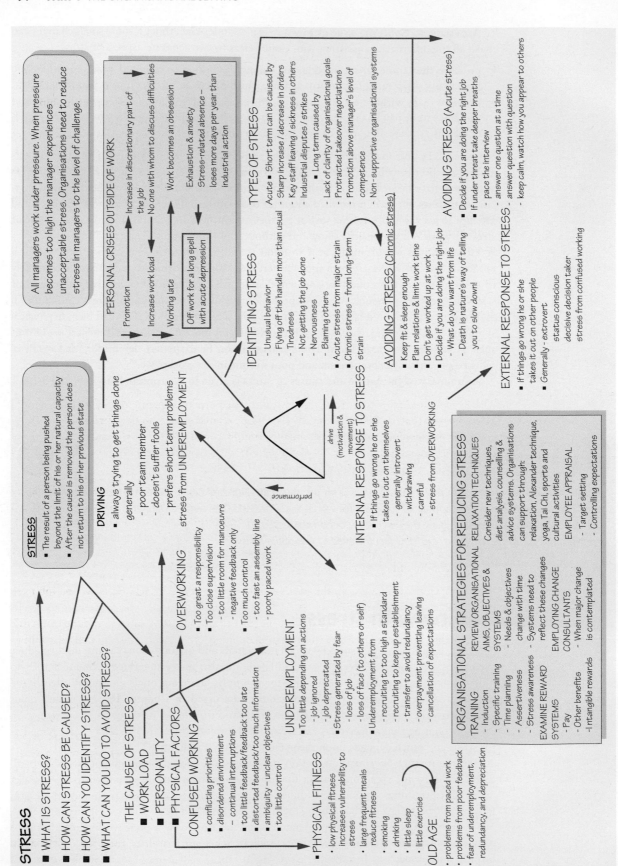

Figure 3.10 Stress

Effective communications and conversation

Effective two-way communications at all levels of the organisation are clearly important in helping to reduce or overcome the level of stress. Staff should feel able to express their true feelings openly and know they will be listened to. However, in addition to good communications, *Reeves* refers to the importance of conversation for maintaining relationships and suggests a case for a conversation culture. The ability to hold good-quality conversations is becoming a core organisational and individual skill. Unlike communication, conversations are intrinsically creative and roam freely across personal issues, corporate gossip and work projects: 'Conversations are a defence against stress and other mental health problems. People with good social relationships at work are much less likely to be stressed or anxious.'[47]

A growing number of organisations are introducing an email-free day to encourage staff to use the telephone or walk across the corridor to talk more with one another.

Informing members of staff in the first place about what is happening, especially at times of major change, involving them proactively in the change process and allowing people to feel in control and exercise their own discretion reduce uncertainty and can help minimise the potential for stress. Managers can do much to create a psychologically supportive and healthy work environment. Treating people with consideration, respect and trust, giving full recognition and credit, getting to know members of staff as individuals and placing emphasis on end results can all help to reduce stress. Managers should attempt to be role models, and through their language and body language indicate to others that they are dealing effectively with their own work pressures.

EU framework agreement

The European Commission states that work-related stress is one of the biggest health and safety factors that we face in Europe today. Work-related stress can be approached on different levels – individual worker, work organisation, national and EU level. Aside from the legal obligations, stress is a problem for the individuals, their work organisation and society, and work-related stress problems are increasing.

> At European Union level, social partners have negotiated agreement on work-related stress to identify and prevent or manage problems. The agreement identifies a number of anti-stress measures, dealing primarily with management and communication such as clarifying company objectives and the role of individual workers; ensuring adequate management support for individuals and teams; matching responsibility and control over work; improving work organisation and processes, working conditions and environment.[48]

According to the Commission, the most common causes of work-related stress are: job reorganisation or job insecurity (72 per cent), hours worked or workload (66 per cent), unacceptable behaviour such as bullying or harassment (59 per cent), lack of support to fulfil one's role (57 per cent), lack of clarity on roles or responsibilities (52 per cent) and limited possibilities to manage one's own work patterns (46 per cent).

Moreover, employees affected by stress are not in a position to deploy full potential and contribute as much as they could to the development of the company for which they work – not to mention the human costs and lifelong repercussions of psychosocial diseases for the employees concerned and their families.

The Commission also draws attention to the gap between the legal obligations of EU employers to manage stress and psychosocial risk at the workplace and practices actually observed. Numerous examples confirm work-related stress can be approached in the same manner as other health and safety issues.[49]

HSE Management Standards

According to HSE, 'Well-designed, organised and managed work is good for us but when insufficient attention to job design, work organisation and management has taken place, it can result in **work related stress.**' HSE has developed the Management Standards approach to tackling work-related stress; these standards represent a set of conditions that, if present, reflect a high level of health, well-being and organisational performance. They are based on the familiar 'Five steps to risk assessment' model, requiring management and staff to work together.[50] *See* Figure 3.11.

Use of kaizen principles

Another interesting approach to reducing stress is through the use of the Japanese kaizen principles (**see also Chapter 16**). According to *Scotchmer,* applying the kaizen 5S method (translated into English as Sort, Straighten, Shine, Standardise and Sustain) can help increase efficiency and productivity, raise morale and lower an individual's stress levels: 'The busier you are the tidier your desk should be; that is if you wish to get ahead and deliver more with less stress.'[51]

Individual needs and expectations

Rigby points out that stress at work is getting worse, and the problem for those who would seek an easier life is that big-money jobs generally come with a big chunk of hassle attached. People suffering from high stress at work should try switching to a job more in tune with their

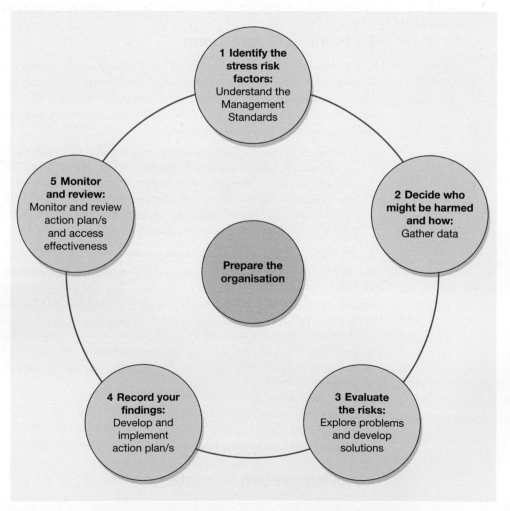

Figure 3.11 The Management Standards approach: five steps to risk assessment

Source: Health and Safety Executive, 'How to tackle work-related stress', publication INDG430, October 2009.

individual needs and expectations. Rigby suggests five prescriptions for those seeking a lower-stress job and a healthier, more satisfying work/life balance.

- **Stability and security** – Consider professional jobs, those requiring specialised technical knowledge or jobs in obscure sectors such as industry and food technology.
- **Personal contact** – Forging strong relationships with customers and colleagues can be great for stress relief, but avoid front-line contact with overbearing customer-care departments or call centres.
- **Right kind of boss** – Unless you have a good boss, look for a job that gets you out on your own a lot or allows flexible working, or become self-employed.
- **Change, pressure and perception** – Look for firms changing fast because they are leading the way, but avoid working for a firm where change is imposed because it is trying to catch up. Consider also the public perception of how far the job is important or socially useful.
- **Potential for fulfilment** – Even if the work is hard and long, look for jobs that are creative or engaging or provide a sense of worth or satisfaction.[52]

Critical review and reflection

Suggestions for coping with a high level of stress, for example adjusting your viewpoint, changing your job or relaxation therapy, may be well intended but are difficult to implement and have little adaptive value. Stress is predominately a feature of a person's personality and must be accepted as such.

What do YOU think? How well does YOUR personality allow YOU to cope with stress?

Work/life balance

We have looked at the importance, nature and some main features of work organisations as an integral feature of human civilisation. But what role do, or should, organisations play in the lives of their staff or with broader concerns for the work/life balance? What are the ethical considerations and how much also depends upon the individual's orientations to work? (**Discussed in Chapter 1.**)

It is not easy to determine the extent to which attention to the quality of working life and the work/life balance is based on the exercise of a genuine social responsibility and a moral or ethical motivation (**discussed in Chapter 14**) or based primarily on the pursuit of economic efficiency and motivated through good business practice and enlightened self-interest. But to what extent should the work/life balance form part of the ethical concern or underlying values of an organisation? Opinions appear to be divided. For example, *Sternberg,* while recognising the importance of treating employees ethically, does not support the belief that a business should be run for the benefit of its employees or should, by action or by omission, encourage employees to have inappropriate expectations of the business.

> *Despite widespread notions to the contrary, it is not the role of business to give meaning to the lives of its employees or to provide social welfare or full employment; business is not a substitute for family or community, the church or the state.*[53]

The European Commission, however, still stresses the importance of helping people to improve their work/life balance, and continues to unveil a series of packages to update existing EU legislation. The Commission also draws attention to the interactions between work/life balance and public policy.

> *While the choices that people make when combining the professional, private and family aspects of their lives are primarily personal, the way in which they balance these competing*

demands has direct consequences for public policy. It influences, for example, the number of children people choose to have, or if they decide to work or not. At the same time, public policy itself influences these choices: the existence of public provision of care for children and other dependents, for instance, or legal rights to family related leave.[54]

Meaning in people's lives

Popular press articles often suggest that work is still a large component of what gives meaning to people's lives and give examples of big lottery or pools winners staying in work and often in their same, even apparently routine, jobs. Other surveys and reports continue to suggest that the workplace is no longer a central feature of social activity. For a majority of people the main reason for work remains the need for money to fulfil the necessities of life. However, much still appears to depend on the extent of an individual's social contacts and activities outside of the work situation.

A *European Industrial Relations Review* points out that work/life balance is an issue of growing concern within the UK:

> *The declining influence of trade unions in regulating the employment relationship, job insecurity, the extension of operating and opening hours, and the impact of new forms of information and communications technology on work are just some of the factors that have made it increasingly difficult for workers to balance their work and their personal lives.*[55]

Is work/life balance still important?

Many staff still have specific places of work and agreed times in which to undertake their duties. However, technology and the Internet allow for greater flexibility in work schedules. So-called knowledge workers, who work from home on computers, with greater control over their roles and work times, arguably have improved motivation and productivity. But, in a thought-provoking article, *Reeves* questions the extent to which progress has been made in establishing a healthy equilibrium between our working day and personal time and if work/life balance is still an issue or already past its sell-by date. The phrase has been contested for the presumption that life is better than work and that the two are separable in a clear-cut way that allows a calculation of 'balance' between them.

Continuing concern with the issue cannot be explained simply with reference to working hours. Work/life balance is moving towards a concern with flexibility and parenting. It taps into a desire for greater autonomy at work, a shift in gender roles within the family, the possibilities of technology and an intensification of working life. The conclusion from Reeves is:

> *It would be a shame if work/life balance faded away into the dustbin of business jargon. Underneath its banal-sounding aspirations are some deep-seated, radical challenges to organisations and to individuals. If work/life balance means anything of value at all, it is a clarion call for a better quality of life, for better parenting and, above all, for greater personal autonomy. It seems to me that work/life balance is either a crusade for human freedom or it is nothing.*[56]

ACAS points out that the pace of change is now more rapid than ever, and with organisations under constant pressure to match the requirements of customer and business there is a need for work/life balance and flexible working.[57] (**Flexible patterns of working are discussed in Chapter 11.**)

The Department for Business Innovation & Skills (BIS) draws attention to the continuing importance of family structure and work satisfaction.

> *The issue of how to promote the balance of work and family responsibilities is a major policy concern and has deserved increasing scholarly activity attention in recent years. As this report has shown the relationship between the labour market and the household is an important*

determinant in understanding people's living conditions in current society. Particularly, this is the case for women who traditionally have assumed most of the duties in the rearing of children while in the last few decades have increasingly been incorporated in the labour market to pursue a professional career.

BIS points out that work/life balance policies play an important role in worker satisfaction and this effect seem to be gender neutral. Male workers in 'family-friendly' environments also experience higher levels of job satisfaction and involvement.[58]

Business Link also emphasises the business benefits of improved work/life balance. It can enable employees to feel more in control of their working life and lead to increased productivity, lower absenteeism and a happier, less stressed workforce.

Introducing employment practices that encourage a healthier work/life balance for your employees can bring real benefits to your business. Flexible working and work/life balance policies will also foster a more positive perception of you as an employer. This can lead to better relations with your employees and greater staff loyalty, commitment and motivation, reducing staff turnover and recruitment costs.[59]

A family-friendly model

According to *Black*, employers that promote a healthy work/life balance maximise productivity and optimise their corporate performance. In order to attract the best staff there is a rise in the family-friendly employer offering best packages to staff including flexible working conditions and characteristics to promote a happy and healthy work/life balance. Black suggests five, not mutually exclusive, reasons: the commercial reality of flexible working; the contribution of female leadership; advantages of diversity; an aid to recruitment; and demographic changes. Black also suggests three parts to a family-friendly model:

- **Culture** – the first and most important aspect and this comes from managers; you need someone very senior and on message.
- **Emotional and developmental** – helping parents to get clarity on choices they make, including one-to-one coaching programmes, mentoring schemes and online maternity coaching packages.
- **Practical** – practical solutions to support the right culture and clarity on priorities, for example parents' network, provisions for childcare and elderly care support. A downside to more flexible working patterns is old networks of friends and families do not work as they used to.[60]

The workplace of the future

The evolving nature of work organisations and the social context has led to a climate of constant change and the need for greater organisational flexibility. Managers need to be aware of new psychological contracts and to adopt alternative styles of management. *Cloke and Goldsmith* refer to the rise of organisational democracy. There is a demand for alternative organisational practices, and a far-reaching transformation has already begun, based on the idea that management as a system fails to open the heart or free the spirit. The age of management is coming to an end and the real push for the future is for more authentic human relationships and the humanisation of organisations as crucibles for personal growth and development.[61]

Generation X and Generation Y

Management Today commissioned a survey from FreshMinds looking at the future world of work and the contrasting attitudes and perspectives of three different generations and age groups:

- the confident, footloose, wire-free **Generation Y** (born between 1980 and 1995 and typified by travel first, then a career);

- the mellow **baby-boomers** (born between 1946 and 1963 and typified by a search for security); and
- the pig-in-the-middle **Generation X** (born between 1964 and 1980 and typified by after the slog, the rewards).

From the online survey of 1,000 people, supplemented by three extensive focus-group sessions, emerges 'a complex picture of a workforce in a state of flux, struggling to come to terms with the changed realities of today'. This new world of work is termed 'Work 2.0'. As the number of baby-boomers declines and the proportion of Generation Y increases this will have an impact on the work environment.

Generation X have another three decades at work, but this is a different world of work from the one they entered fifteen or so years ago and there is less confidence and few guarantees about their financial future.

By contrast, **Generation Y** will have fewer problems in adapting to the changed realities of the twenty-first century. For example, they are likely to be more technologically sophisticated.

Encouraging the three different age groups to work happily as a team will require imagination on all sides and competent management. For example, the influence of the Second World War on the baby-boomers and the search for security is not something understood readily by Generations X or Y. The message from Alistair Leathwood, Managing Director of FreshMinds Talent, is that the rules of engagement at work have changed: 'Work 2.0 signals a new social contract between employers and employees – one premised upon short-term commitment, flexibility and, most importantly, one where the employee's loyalty to their employer is not expected to be any greater than what little the employer provides to its staff.'[62]

Although these generational characteristics are broad stereotypes and differences will clearly exist between individuals, they may help provide an understanding of contrasting work orientations and attitudes, job security and work/life balance; and with implications for social interactions, motivation, and styles of leadership and management.[63]

Aside from Generations X and Y and the baby-boomers, as people live and work longer there will be a wider spread of age groups in the workforce.

The future of the workplace

As part of a round-table debate hosted by the Royal College of Art, *Gwyther* comments on the future of the workplace.

> *The idea of the workplace is in a state of flux, which is down to a variety of factors: cost, carbon, technology, sustainability and culture. People still accept that it's very important for an organisation to have a clear definition of what it is and how to go efficiently about achieving its aims, but how does the working environment play its part? The workplace is becoming more fragmented – people aren't working together under the same roof as they were 20 years ago. What effect will that have on the culture of an organisation? Is it a weakness that people aren't communicating face to face on a regular basis?[64]*

Topics in subsequent chapters will discuss further the changing nature and structure of work organisations, employment and social interactions.[65]

Critical review and reflection

The rapidly changing nature of employment demands new ways of looking at the world of work organisations. Traditional management models are completely outdated and should no longer form part of classroom discussion.

What do YOU think? How would YOU present a convincing counterargument?

Ten key points to remember

1 Applications of organisational behaviour and process of management take place not in a vacuum but within the context of an organisational setting.

2 Organisations are set up to serve a variety of purposes and needs. Common features in any organisation are people, objectives, structure and management.

3 Organisations can be viewed as open systems with sub-systems of task, technology, structure, people and management in interaction with the external environment.

4 Whatever the nature of the formal structure, an informal organisation will always be present and arises from the interactions of people, their psychological and social needs.

5 The informal organisation serves a number of important functions and has a significant influence on the morale, motivation, job satisfaction and performance of staff.

6 Conflict is a reality of management and organisational behaviour. There are contrasting perspectives of conflict and it can be seen to have both positive and negative outcomes.

7 Stress at work is a potential source of mental and physical ill-health. However, a certain amount of pressure may arguably help promote a higher level of performance.

8 The effective management of both conflict and stress demands a supportive work environment, skilled managers and a climate of mutual trust, respect and consideration.

9 Increasing attention is focused on the role organisations play in the lives of staff and with broader concerns for the work/life balance and for meaning in people's lives.

10 It is important to be aware of the changing nature of the workforce of the future, including the significance of generation and age gaps.

Review and discussion questions

1 How would you define an organisation and why do work organisations exist?

2 Discuss critically the extent to which differences among various organisations limit the value of the study of management and organisational behaviour.

3 What are the common features in any organisation? Give your view on how successfully these features interrelate to influence the effectiveness of your own university.

4 Assess critically the practical value to both the student and the manager of adopting an open-systems view of organisational analysis.

5 Distinguish between the formal and the informal organisation and explain their main characteristics. What functions are served by the informal organisation?

6 To what extent do you accept the view that conflict is an inevitable feature of management and organisational behaviour?

7 Debate critically the extent to which you believe that stress is a major concern in modern work organisations.

8 Discuss whether you believe that stress is contagious and is influenced by the behaviour and actions of other people.

9   Why do you think increasing attention is being given to the work/life debate? Is this attention justified? As a manager, what steps would you take to help improve the quality of working life for staff?

10 Set out in detail how you see the nature of organisations of the future. What do you think is the *single* most significant change?

Assignment

Work in small groups as directed by your tutor.

From the classification of organisations at the beginning of this chapter, select one organisation of your choice from *any five* of the ten classifications.

Now, for *each* of your chosen five organisations, identify three:

a. significance features characteristic of the organisation;
b. areas of work or responsibility with potential for a high level of conflict; and
c. likely potential causes of stress.

How much agreement is there among members of your group?

What conclusions do you draw from the assignment?

Personal skills and employability exercise

Objectives

Completing this exercise should help you to enhance the following skills:

*   Understand factors that impact upon work conflict and stress.
*   Assess benefits from your course of study.
*   Participate in preparing a plenary report.

Exercise

PART 1 – Look back at the Management and organisational behaviour in action case study in this chapter. To what extent can you relate the situation in this case to potential sources of conflict discussed in the text of the chapter, such as:

*   differences in perception;
*   limited resources;
*   departmentalisation and specialisation;
*   nature of work activities;
*   role conflict;
*   inequitable treatment; and
*   violation of territory?

PART 2 – Think of any stressful situation you have experienced during either your university studies or any type of work experience you have had. Explain fully the nature of the situation and the causes, symptoms and consequences, and how you attempted to deal with the situation. How successful were you?

Now, explore fully the extent to which you can relate the contents and discussion in this chapter to the situation you experienced.

PART 3 – Share and discuss your findings in a small-group situation and elect a spokesperson to report back in plenary session.

Discussion

- How far have you been able to relate your course of study to actual situations of conflict and stress?
- To what extent do you perceive any relationship between conflict, stress and gender or ethnicity?
- How would you best prepare your university colleagues to deal with potential conflict and stress in the work environment?

Case study
Grameen Bank: a business that really helps the poor

The issue of Third World poverty is one that is rarely far from Western headlines, sometimes as the result of a particular humanitarian crisis or natural disaster, but often in association with debates about the effects of globalisation, and in particular the impact of global business activities on individuals and communities in poor countries. It is an issue that inspires heated argument, as well as demands for money, or action, or both. Discussion of the trading position of Third World countries in a global context often tends to focus on the behaviour of specific business organisations and the 'ethical' status of their activities in poorer parts of the world. The high-street fashion chains are frequently in the firing line about subcontracting their manufacturing operations to exploitative or irresponsible local employers, and the collapse of the Rana Plaza factory near Dhaka, Bangladesh, in April 2013, which left over 1,000 of its workers dead and another 2,500 injured, propelled this issue into the headlines.[66] Some participants in the debate question whether business can ever truly be 'ethical' because its very existence depends upon acts of exploitation. So can business ever really help improve the condition of poor people in developing countries?

When considering such issues, it is important to remember that poverty is not the same thing as helplessness. The development of the Grameen Bank, a Bangladeshi banking business, illustrates one way in which ingenuity coupled with enterprise can present an alternative to charity and government aid as a route out of poverty.

Why banks are important to the poor

The development of any successful enterprise relies not only on the ingenuity, creativity and hard work of the individual entrepreneur, but also on a number of social and economic preconditions, including such things as property rights and the ability to amass or borrow capital for investment in equipment and materials.[67] Borrowing power among the poor is very limited, as they are unlikely to be able to provide adequate security for loans from a commercial lending institution such as a bank. Without the ability to purchase the tools of their trade or raw materials, many individual workers remain dependent upon friends, family, moneylenders or employers to loan them what they need, often at extortionate rates and at the risk of physical violence if repayments are not made on time. Poor workers are therefore generally unable to amass sufficient funds to become independent economic operators. This situation of dependency upon an employer or other intermediary for both paid work and the means to do the work is often described as 'debt bondage' or 'debt peonage'. The effect of such structures is often to ensure that the poorest in society remain unable, by their own efforts, to break free from a form of servitude that stifles more general economic growth.

Mohammed Yunus and the Grameen Bank

Traditional banks developed from places where rich people were able to deposit their money safely, into commercial institutions where customers' money is used to make loans to other customers. In the earlier stages of their development they competed for the business of large customers such as companies and wealthy individuals, since these were low-risk borrowers and provided high-growth prospects. Until the standardisation and automation of many banking operations, most working-class people in developed economies did not have ready access to banking services. For poor people in developing countries, access to commercial banking services, including loans, remains a remote prospect indeed.

Mohammed Yunus and the Grameen Bank he founded won the 2006 Nobel Peace Prize
Source: AP Photo/H.O./Press Association Images

Mohammed Yunus is a Bangladeshi economist who, after studying and working in the USA, returned home to become an economics professor at the University of Chittagong. He became familiar with the problems of poor local people, mainly women, in his lunchtime strolls around the city of Dhaka, and realised that many of the people he met would be greatly helped by the injections of very small amounts of capital, as little as $US1–2. He developed the idea of a specific type of what is usually termed 'microcredit', and in 1976, using $26 of his own money, began to make very small loans to poor local women so that they could invest in animals or materials that would enable them to make money. Such tiny loans were out of the question for standard commercial banks because of the high administrative costs relative to the investment, the lack of loan security and impossibility of proper credit referencing. Thus he invented a new type of organisation: a low-cost, local operation that runs from the homes and community centres of the village (*grameen* literally means 'village'). The loans are unsecured so rely on local knowledge and trust, and need to be very precisely targeted. Both the investors and the creditors of Grameen Bank know each other, and members meet regularly to monitor the progress of business, including loan repayments. Social capital is the mainstay of the banks, and borrowers are highly involved in loan decisions and the general operation of the banks. This social nexus leads to a very unusual feature of the banks, which is their policy of making loans only to the very poor, and, in the vast majority of cases, to women, who are generally more trustworthy in their handling of money than men. Yunus believes that this type of credit can lead to significant change in the status of

poor individuals, and can help provide a route out of extreme poverty without reliance on external sources of money.

> *The first and foremost task of development is to turn on the engine of creativity . . . This is why Grameen Bank offers the poor not handouts or grants but credit – loans they must repay, with interest, through their own productive work. This dynamic makes Grameen Bank sustainable. Loan repayments supply funds for future loans, to the same individuals or to new bank members, in an ever-expanding cycle of economic growth. It also helps the poor demonstrate to themselves that they can change their world for the better – and it gives them the tools to do just that, for themselves . . . To me, the essence of development is changing the quality of life of the bottom half of the population. And that . . . must also include the enabling environment that lets individuals explore their own creative potential.[68]*

The system proved highly successful; the 2012 annual report recorded 2,567 branches throughout Bangladesh, with over 8.3 million members; the overwhelming majority (96 per cent) of the borrowers were women.[69] Yunus himself was awarded a Nobel Peace Prize for his anti-poverty work in 2006.

Growth and change

The Grameen business model, small-scale, local and trust-based with a focus on helping the poorest members of a community, has inspired many other microcredit organisations worldwide – for example, FINCA (the Foundation for International Community Assistance), which took root in Latin America during the 1980s.[70] However, the schemes are not beyond criticism, and some commentators see the structure as a form of social control. A political row between the Bangladeshi prime minister and Yunus about the governance of the bank led to a legal challenge to his continuation as managing director (a court found that he had exceeded the official retirement age) and he resigned from the bank in May 2011.

Despite this, Yunus remains actively involved with many offshoot organisations that are linked to the Grameen philosophy, but independent of the bank itself. One such is Grameenphone, which initially enabled local women to set themselves up as 'village phone ladies' by purchasing a mobile phone with a Grameen Bank loan, and then renting it out for local use. From its inception in 1997, this initiative has brought communication technology to rural areas that are otherwise largely isolated; villagers can make contact with friends and relatives, but also with hospitals and other services. It has also improved the market position of Grameenphone customers who are engaged in other sorts of work. An example is described by Roland Buerk, in a BBC report on one of the Grameen 'telephone ladies', Roshinara Begum, in the Bangladeshi village of Kalimajani. One of her customers is local fish farmer, Mohammed Abul Hashem, who uses the phone service to order food and supplies from the capital. He is quoted as explaining that:

> If the phone wasn't here then I'd have to travel to Dhaka. It's a very long and unpleasant journey. Now I can use the phone I am saving time and it makes my business more competitive.[71]

Grameenphone entered into a profitable partnership with the Norwegian telecoms company Telenor, which provides both the technical knowledge and the equipment to run the network successfully. It is now the largest mobile phone network in Bangladesh, with over 50 million subscribers and a network that reaches 99 per cent of the population. It remains committed to supporting economic development in the area by increasing access to the Internet and other services:

> Grameenphone also invests in various corporate social responsibility activities such as remote medical services and an innovative Internet school program that brings education to rural villages that were previously without access to teachers. Our commitment to empower and build societies is unwavering. We will continue to work to enhance the lives of our 50 million customers in Bangladesh and 160 million customers in Asia by focusing on our Internet for All mission and delivering tailored solutions that meet the needs of our users.[72]

Yunus believes that the financial crisis of 2007–8 has created a worldwide appetite for change and a growing interest in the notion of 'social enterprise'. His skill and reputation are drawing global companies such as Danone, Adidas and BASF into joint ventures that combine business with a social purpose, such as producing nutrient-rich yoghurt, affordable footwear and mosquito nets to combat malaria.[73] His local initiative may, in the long run, have global consequences.

Tasks

1 Two of the significant features of the Grameen Bank are its focus on helping individuals to achieve independence and its strong preference for loans to women. What problems might this cause, and what risks does it take, in the communities and societies (mainly Islamic) where it operates?

2 Read the section in the chapter about the idea of the 'social enterprise' and research some examples. Contrast this system of work organisation with that of a more traditional commercial business using the open-systems model of a business organisation (Figure 3.4), explaining how the difference might affect each aspect of the model.

3 In 2006 the French dairy company Danone set up Grameen Danone Foods, a social business enterprise, which was a 'unique initiative to bring daily healthy nutrition to low-income, nutritionally deprived populations in Bangladesh'[74] by building factories in Bangladesh to manufacture the product. Carry out a PESTEL analysis for this initiative. Would you have made the same decision?

4 How far do the concepts of the 'formal' and the 'informal' organisation (as illustrated in Figure 3.9 and Table 3.1) apply to this case?

Notes and references

1. For an account of developments in organisations, see Peters, G. 'Creating the Modern Organization', in Crainer, S. and Dearlove, D. (eds) *Financial Times Handbook of Management*, second edition, Financial Times Prentice Hall (2001), pp. 24–45.

2. Schneider, S. C. and Barsoux, J. *Managing Across Cultures*, second edition, Financial Times Prentice Hall (2003).

3. Smart, P. and Inazawa, K. *Human resource management in the public sector*, Kwansei Gakuin University Press (2011).

4. Saunders, A. 'Why Can't Government Be More Like Business?, *Management Today*, October 2010, pp. 42–3.

5. Morrell, P. 'The Accidental Civil Servant', *Management Today*, January 2013, pp. 40–3.

6. Arnott, J. 'Cause and Ethics', *Chartered Secretary,* December 2002, pp. 22–4.

7. See, for example, 'Social Enterprises as a New Type of Employer', *Employment Relations Matters,* ACAS, issue 11, June 2008, pp. 3–5.

8. Lucas, E. 'Businesses that "put back" are bucking the trend', *Professional Manager,* vol. 18, no. 5, 2009, pp. 26–8.

9. 'The Lessons from the Ground', *Social Agenda,* European Commission, No. 32, February 2013.

10. For a more detailed discussion of environmental influences, see, for example, Worthington, I. and Britton, C. *The Business Environment,* fifth edition, Financial Times Prentice Hall (2006).

11. Lynch, R. *Strategic Management,* sixth edition, Pearson Education (2012).

12. Worthington, I. and Britton, C. *The Business Environment,* fifth edition, Financial Times Prentice Hall (2006), p. 13.

13. Schein, E. H. *Organizational Psychology,* third edition, Prentice Hall (1988), p. 15.

14. Law, S. 'Beyond the Water Cooler', *Professional Manager,* January 2005, p. 26.

15. Egan, G. 'The Shadow Side', *Management Today,* September 1993, pp. 33–8.

16. Vernon, M. 'Office Friends: Who needs them?', *Management Today,* September 2005, pp. 59–61.

17. 'Integrity Matters: Our Code of Conduct', Royal Bank of Scotland Group, July 2011.

18. Ackroyd, S. and Thompson, P. *Organizational Misbehaviour,* Sage (1999).

19. Podro, S. 'Riding out the storm: managing conflict in a recession and beyond', ACAS Policy Discussion Paper, ACAS, March 2010.

20. Drucker, P. F. *The Practice of Management,* Heinemann Professional (1989), p. 119.

21. For an account of the Marxist critique, see, for example, Johnston, R. 'Hidden Capital', in Barry, J., Chandler, J., Clark, H., Johnston, R. and Needle, D. (eds) *Organization and Management: A Critical Text,* International Thomson Business Press (2000), pp. 16–35.

22. Salaman, G. *Class and Corporation,* Fontana (1981).

23. See, for example, Robbins, S. P. and Judge, T. A. *Organizational Behavior,* thirteenth edition, Pearson Education (2009).

24. Townsend, R. *Further Up the Organisation,* Coronet Books (1985), p. 39.

25. Dunne, P. 'Balance on the board', *Governance + Compliance,* April 2014, pp. 24–7.

26. Irvine, L. 'Conflicts of Interest', *Manager, The British Journal of Administrative Management,* March/April 1998, pp. 8–10.

27. Mannering, K. 'Working with "Prickly" People', *Professional Manager,* vol. 19, no. 1, 2009, pp. 32–4.

28. Woodward, J. *Industrial Organization: Theory and Practice,* second edition, Oxford University Press (1980), p. 113.

29. See, for example, James, J. *Body Talk at Work,* Piatkus (2001).

30. Hart, J. 'Mind the Gap', *Professional Manager,* November 2002, pp. 22–3.

31. Saundry, R. *et al.* 'Reframing Resolution – Managing Conflict and Resolving Individual Employment Disputes in the Contemporary Workplace', ACAS Policy Discussion Paper, ACAS, March 2014, p. 12.

32. Saundry, R. and Wibberley, G, 'Workplace Dispute Resolution and the Management of Individual Conflict – A Thematic Analysis of Five Case Studies', ACAS Research Paper, June 2014.

33. York, P. 'Getting a Grip on Stress', *Management Today,* October 2001, p. 105.

34. Taylor, M. 'Tell Me Why I Don't Like Mondays', Working Paper of the Institute for Social and Economic Research, October 2002.

35. Randall, J. 'Home Truths', *Management Today,* June 2001, p. 31.

36. 'Healthy returns? Absence and workplace health survey 2011', CBI, May 2011.

37. Cooper, C. L. 'A different approach', *Chartered Secretary,* July 2010, p. 16.

38. Liu, C., Spector, P. E., and Shi, L. 'Cross-National Job Stress: A Quantitative and Qualitative Study', *Journal of Organisational Behavior,* February 2007, pp. 209–39.

39. Tweed, R. G., White, K. and Lehman, D. R. 'Culture, stress and coping: Internally and externally targeted control strategies of European Canadians, East Asian Canadians and Japanese', *Journal of Cross-Cultural Psychology,* vol. 35, no. 6, 2004, pp. 652–8.

40. Spector, P. E. 'A Cross-National Comparative Study of Work-Family Stressors, Working Hours and Well-Being: China and Latin America versus the Anglo World', *Personnel Psychology,* Spring 2004, pp. 119–42.

41. Health and Safety Executive 'How to tackle work-related stress', INDG430, October 2009.

42. **http://www.hse.gov.uk/stress** (accessed 14 October 2014).

43. Cobb, K. 'Handling Pressure: Developing skills for mangers to stay resilient', *Manager, British Journal of Administrative Management,* Winter 2011, pp. 24–5.

44. Gwyther, M. 'Stressed for Success', *Management Today,* January 1999, pp. 22–6.

45. *ACAS News,* issue 11, Spring 2008.

46. Briner, R. 'Ask the experts', *Professional Manager,* July/ August 2011, p. 38.

47. Reeves, R. 'Reality Bites', *Management Today,* March 2003, p. 35.

48. 'Coping with stress at work', *Social Agenda,* European Commission magazine on employment and social affairs, March 2009, pp. 7–10.

49. 'Stress at work – Mind the gap', *Social Agenda,* European Commission, No. 36, February 2014.

50. Health and Safety Executive 'How to tackle work-related stress', INDG430, October 2009.

51. Scotchmer, A. 'A Place For Everything and Everything in Its Place', *Professional Manager,* vol. 16, no. 1, 2007, pp. 30–1.

52. Rigby, R. 'Under Pressure', *Management Today,* March 2010, pp. 50–2.

53. Sternberg, E. *Just Business: Business Ethics in Action,* second edition, Oxford University Press (2000), pp. 124–5.

54. 'Juggling Act: How the EU is Helping People Improve Their Work–Life Balance', *Social Agenda,* European Commission, No. 19, December 2008, pp. 15–20.

55. 'Work–Life Balance: Evidence from Across the UK', *European Industrial Relations Review,* issue 380, September 2005, p. 27.

56. 'Reeves, R. 'Still Juggling After All These Years', *Management Today,* June 2007, pp. 36–43.

57. 'Flexible working and work-life balance', ACAS, September 2010.

58. Perez, A. M. 'Family structure and work satisfaction: Can work-life balance policies foster happiness in the workplace?', Department for Business Innovation & Skills, November 2009.

59. 'Meet the need for work/life balance', Business Link, **www.businesslink.gov.uk/bdotg** (accessed 26 October 2011); Armitage, K. 'Can We Really Achieve a Life/Work Balance?', *British Journal of Administrative Management,* July/August 2001, pp. 14–15.

60. Black, B. 'Family Friendly', *Governance + Compliance,* January 2014, pp. 52–3.

61. Cloke, K. and Goldsmith, J. The End of Management and the Rise of Organizational Democracy, Jossey-Bass (2002).

62. Stern, S. 'My Generation', *Management Today,* March 2008, pp. 40–6.

63. See, for example, Searle, I. 'Out with the old, in with the new', *Governance + Compliance,* October 2013, pp. 20–2.

64. Gwyther, M. 'The future of the workplace', *Management Today,* June 2011, pp. 57–9.

65. See, for example, Hazelhurst, J. 'The Way We Work Now', *Management Today,* June 2013, pp. 46–9.

66. North, A. 'Dhaka Rana Plaza collapse: Pressure tells on retailers and government', BBC News website, 14 May 2013, **http://www.bbc.co.uk/news/world-asia-22525431** (accessed 9 February 2015).

67. De Soto, H. *The Mystery of Capital,* Black Swan (2001).

68. Yunus, M. *Creating a World without Poverty,* PublicAffairs (2007), p. 56.

69. Grameen Bank, Annual Report 2012, **www.grameen.com** (accessed 9 February 2015).

70. FINCA website, **http://www.finca.org/site/ c.6fIGIXMFJnJ0H/b.6088193/k.BE5D/Home.htm** (accessed 9 February 2015).

71. Buerk, R. '"Telephone Ladies" Connect Bangladesh', BBC News website, 26 November 2005, **http://news.bbc. co.uk** (accessed 9 February 2015).

72. Telenor Group press report, 14 October 2014, **http:// www.telenor.com/media/articles/2014/grameenphone- reaches-50-million-customers/** (accessed 9 February 2015).

73. Fontanella-Khan, J. 'Yunus expands joint venture companies', FT.com website, 16 February 2012 (accessed 9 February 2015).

74. Danone Group press release, 7 November 2006, **http:// www.danone.com/uploads/tx_bidanonepublications/ FR_ZZ_MY_01.pdf** (accessed 9 February 2015).

Academic viewpoint

Below you will find the title and abstract of a recent article in an academic journal that explores a topic relevant to the chapters in Part 1.

Koles, B. and Nagy, P. 'Virtual worlds as digital workplaces: Conceptualizing the affordances of virtual worlds to expand the social and professional spheres in organizations', *Organizational Psychology Review,* vol. 4. no. 2, 2014, pp. 175–95. doi: 10.1177/2041386613507074

Abstract

The primary aim of the current paper is to explore ways in which organizations can benefit from virtual environments to expand their social and professional spheres. Applying the theory of third places to virtual worlds, our conceptual model incorporates practical organizational affordances within three composite dimensions. First, we propose that through their unique, supportive and neutral environments, virtual worlds may reduce the prevalence of social hierarchies, via decreasing the emphasis on predetermined ranks, stereotypes, and cultural or geographic variation. Second, we posit that via encouraging open communication within the form of synchronous and real-time interactions, virtual worlds enable efficient teamwork and collaborative learning. Finally, we emphasize that these friendly, secure, and supportive environments may contribute to the reduction of certain work-related stressors, and in turn promote professional development activities. We conclude by discussing practical implications and future research directions.

Commentary

The authors start by noting that rapid technological advancements and their widespread adoption means that today's work organisations are increasingly complex, fragmented and decentralised. This poses major challenges for management. They also note that while organisations have often started to use social networks (Facebook, Twitter, etc.) as tools for communication and management, they have generally been slow to create full-scale virtual worlds or 'third spaces' – neutral areas remote from both work and home that are readily accessible, allow social exchange between highly diverse individuals and that are characterised by fun and playfulness. Their study seeks to apply the main principles of virtual worlds to work organisations. They conclude that the levelling, 'safe' and relatively stress-free environment of virtual worlds could be highly beneficial to the management of today's organisation, particularly where people work across a variety of cultures, social groups and time zones.

The article might prompt you to consider some of the following questions.

- The authors suggest that virtual worlds can break down many of the barriers of social difference. To what extent do you agree? What new social divisions might use of a virtual world create, and how?
- The psychological effects of participation in virtual worlds are viewed by the authors as stress reducing and positive. Do you think this is always the case? What problems might result from being connected to the virtual version of an organisation?
- Can virtual organisations replace physical or 'real' organisations? What are the cultural, social and environmental factors that might affect the degree to which an organisation can exist in virtual form?

Part 1 Case study
Indian Railways: lifeline to the nation

On 16 April 1853, and to the reverberations of a 21-gun salute, a 14-carriage railway train steamed out of Bori Bunder station in Bombay (Mumbai) to carry its 400 passengers the 21 miles (34 km) to nearby Thane. This was the inaugural journey on a railway system that, over the last 160 years, has grown into an operation that transports almost 23 million passengers around India – *every day*. This astonishing number of journeys is made possible by a network connecting over 7,000 stations by 64,600 km of track, served by over 9,500 locomotive engines and approximately 2.4 million wagons. The system also carries over 1,000 million tonnes of freight around the country annually. No wonder Indian Railways is known as the 'lifeline to the nation'.[1]

Hooking up the lifeline

As in England, where the railway system had its origins, railways in India were initially built rapidly but piecemeal by private companies. Yet their potential to transform and unify this diverse country of (now) well over 1,200 million people in 29 states with 15 official languages (excluding English)[2] was realised by Madhav Rao, an Indian Chief Minister of State, towards the end of the nineteenth century:

What a glorious change the Railway has made in long and neglected India! . . . Populations which had been isolated for unmeasured ages, now easily mingle in civilised confusion. In my various long journeys it has repeatedly struck me that if India is to become a homogeneous nation, and is ever to achieve solidarity, it must be by means of the Railways as a means of transport, and by means of the English language as a medium of communication.[3]

In 1924 the entire network, including its construction, operation and financing, was brought under the control of the British Indian government, paving the way for its nationalisation in 1951 just four years after Indian independence. It remains a state-run public utility monopoly, but one of such significance that it has its own government ministry (run by a government minister and two ministers of state) and a Railway Board; and it has its own annual budget, which is presented to the Indian Parliament independently of the main national government budget.

Indian Railways' structure can be described as rational and hierarchical (*see* the figure). The main operation of running the seventeen geographic zones (their track, locomotives, stations, signalling, passenger and freight services, as well as the stations' finances and personnel) falls to zone general managers who report to the Railway Board; and the zones are further split into seventy-one divisions, each headed by a divisional railway manager who reports to the relevant zone's general manager. Further down the hierarchy, each station is in the care of a station manager. In addition to the zone general managers, there are general managers in charge of the main production units (PUs), which include such things as locomotive construction workshops, coach and wheel factories, and rolling stock modernisation works. More general managers are responsible for the electrification project and new line construction. A further key section, headed by a director-general, is the Railway Staff College. Finally, there is a collection of fifteen or more public sector undertakings (PSUs) – semi-autonomous operations which, while still under the control of the Ministry and Board, focus on certain ancillary commercial activities such as catering and tourism, engineering consultancy, information systems and software design, and freight logistics. In many cases the PSUs operate with private investment in the form of private – public partnerships, and sell their expertise commercially to other businesses – for instance, the leasing and export of locomotives to railway systems worldwide. The apparent simplicity and rationality of the structure therefore conceals a plethora of differing activities, skills and operating conditions, not to mention geographic, linguistic and cultural ones.

A country within a country

As we have already seen, the whole organisation is characterised by a collection of mind-boggling statistics, and when it comes to the staff aspects they are no less impressive. Indian Railways has around 1.3 million regular employees, together with 300,000 or so casual workers. The management of the human side of the business is therefore quite a challenge, and one that rests on the shoulders of the relatively small Indian Railways Personnel Service (IRPS), which comprises 320 or so professionals. They are organised to support the numerous zones, divisions and production units of Indian Railways' structure, and are responsible for a number of key activities, namely:

- Establishment and personnel management
- Industrial relations
- Administration of labour laws
- Administration of welfare schemes
- Legal matters pertaining to staff and personnel

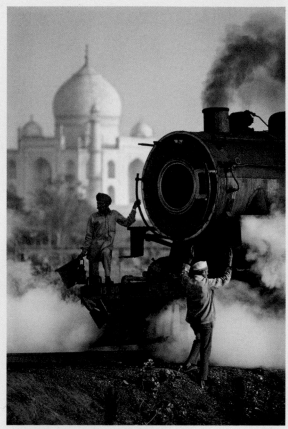

India's lifeline to the nation
Source: © Steve McCurry/Magnum Photos

- Human resource development
- Pension affairs of more than a million retired railway personnel

An idea of the scale of the task can be gleaned from the experience of one IRPS officer who commented that, early in her career, she attended a training course along with professionals from other organisations, both public and private sector:

> we were asked to introduce ourselves, our position and the number of staff we were responsible for. I was one of the last few and when I heard the positions and the number of staff my fellow HR professionals in both the sectors were responsible for, I was surprised. And when I said I was merely a junior personnel officer for the Indian railways responsible for a small division comprising 60,000 staff, everyone else was stunned and asked if this was really true.[4]

Regular staff are organised into four major groupings in descending order of seniority: A, B, C and D. Groups A and B are the managerial staff, and account for 1.3 per

Overview of Indian Railways organisational structure: 2013

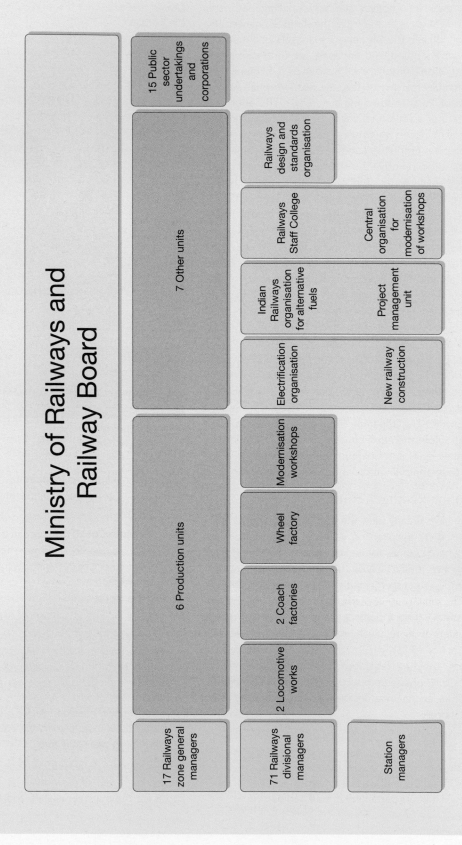

Ministry of Railways and Railway Board

17 Railways zone general managers

71 Railways divisional managers

Station managers

6 Production units

2 Locomotive works

2 Coach factories

Wheel factory

Modernisation workshops

7 Other units

Electrification organisation

Indian Railways organisation for alternative fuels

Railways Staff College

Railways design and standards organisation

New railway construction

Project management unit

Central organisation for modernisation of workshops

15 Public sector undertakings and corporations

cent of the total employed. The IRPS forms part of this layer. Group C staff are by far the largest cohort, and account for around 81 per cent of regular employees, with group D containing the remainder. In groups C and D, two-thirds are employed in the operational side of the organisation and one-third are artisans and work-shop employees. One particular group within the organisation is the security-cum-police force, the Railway Protection Special Force, which has its own uniform and quasi-legal powers. They are charged with maintaining law and order on trains and railway premises, as well as the overall security of the assets and the staff. This is not the only way in which Indian Railways differs from other employers. The organisation owns and maintains schools for the children of railway employees. It runs its own hospitals, banks, co-operative societies, clubs and housing – all available to Indian Railways workers and their families. It runs holiday homes, sports clubs and handicraft centres (where railway workers' families can learn crafts and earn additional income). Indian Railways prides itself on its support for competitive sports at national and international level – Assistant Commercial Manager Sushil Kumar was a wrestling silver medallist and national flag bearer at the 2012 London Olympic Games. Together with significant job security and relatively generous pension arrangements, these features make a job with Indian Railways among the most sought after in the country. Once in, an employee has access to such a wide range of benefits that the 1.3 million and their families are often said to be living in a 'country within a country'.

Getting on board

Recruitment into such desirable employment is, as might be expected of a governmental organisation, a highly formalised process. For group D personnel, recruitment is through national Railway Selection Boards, which co-operate with local employment exchanges to find and select suitable candidates. Group C staff are recruited through one of nineteen Railway Recruitment Boards, which come under the control of an overarching Railway Recruitment Control Board that monitors standards and identifies staffing and skill requirements at national level. This process involves passing formal examinations, and in 2010–11 almost 6,000 candidates were selected by these boards for deployment into relevant posts.

At the higher levels, group A and B staff are also selected through competitive examination, but, as the Railway is a government agency, this process is run by the national Union Public Service Commission, which

recruits all Indian civil servants. Group A and B staff are termed 'gazetted', meaning that notice of their selection has appeared in the nationally published list (or gazette) of public servants. Recruitment to the PSUs is often by secondment of staff from existing zones and divisions, and on a fixed-term basis.

At whatever level, the process additionally includes a full medical examination by doctors of the Indian Railways Hospitals service before staff can be appointed; information is also sought about the background and character of potential appointees. In the vast majority of cases there is a probationary period of one year before appointments are confirmed. Induction and initial training is compulsory, and there is a strong emphasis on service and acceptance of the hierarchy and general regulations governing Indian Railways employee behaviour. For example, railway personnel are expected to be flexible in the sense of being prepared to spend time away from home and family; dutiful in the sense of having regard always for the safety and security of the railway, fellow staff and passengers; and have an 'inner discipline' to enable them to serve the needs of a differing people in a range of circumstances, but always in a responsible manner.

In return, as has been noted, both the employment security and benefits are generous – free rail passes and concessionary fares for family members being seen as highly attractive features of the package – although salaries and wages are usually lower than their private-sector equivalents.

The terms, conditions and pay structures that apply to Indian Railways staff are many and complex. Hours of work are codified in an annex to an Act of Parliament as the 'Railway Servants (Hours of Employment) Rules 1961' and classify types of work according to a set of parameters as 'continuous', 'essentially intermittent' (when an employee may be on duty but not actively working the whole time) or 'intensive (involving strenuous physical activity or periods of high mental concentration), and prescribes the weekly maximum hours accordingly. Managers and certain others are 'excluded' from these maxima, as are the Railway Special Protection Force. A government Pay Commission sets and, periodically, reviews the pay structure and levels, and all employees are placed on a pay scale, receiving annual increments until they reach the upper limit of their scale. There are additional allowances payable (e.g. for night duty, and working in inhospitable or expensive locations), annual leave entitlements are specified, as are retirement and pension conditions and insurance and death-in-service benefits. The 'Establishment Rules'

also extend to matters of conduct and discipline, and so many aspects of management are governed by railway law. Staff are paid monthly, and gazetted staff via bank transfer, although others can choose to be paid in cash. As can be imagined, running a payroll for 1.3 million people with the variety of terms and allowances in force is an enormous challenge, and one that the Ministry of Railways is currently proposing to outsource to a private contractor. Unsurprisingly, there seems to be limited enthusiasm among railway staff for the idea of outsourcing in this way.[5]

In a democracy such as India, the freedom of workers to organise themselves to represent their interests to management is an important one. Indian Railways recognises two main trade unions at national level – the National Federation of Indian Railwaymen and the All India Railway Federation. Contact between management and organised labour is channelled through a twin system: the Permanent Negotiating Machinery (PNM) and the Joint Consultative Machinery (JCM). These operate at divisional and board level, but a governmentally appointed tribunal will hear cases that cannot be resolved by the machinery. These institutions consult and bargain over matters relating to pay and allowances, hours of work, leave entitlements and the classification of grades of workers, but are restricted to considering general principles and do not handle individual cases or grievances. Collective grievances (disputes), however, are part of their remit, and can be highly contentious. In 1960 there was a strike over pay; in 1968 another over the operation of the JCM; and in 1974 a strike of railwaymen contributed to a landslide electoral defeat for the governing Congress Party. However, disputes in 1978 and 1997 that threatened to result in strikes were resolved by the negotiating mechanisms, signalling a more co-operative period in the organisation's history that has since endured. It was, perhaps, the outcome of a sea-change in economic and political life that challenged the very basis of Indian Railways' existence in the last decades of the twentieth century – the move towards global economic liberalisation.

Back on the rails

Indian Railways has not always been a profitable operation. In 2001 the government was considering privatisation as a drastic remedy to a period of sustained and significant losses by the organisation, very much in tune with the economic liberalism sweeping the globe in the wake of the Regan and Thatcher governments in the West. The espousal of free-market, neo-liberal economic policies in the UK and elsewhere resulted in the privatisation of many state-owned organisations

such as telecommunications, energy suppliers and, to a limited extent, transportation. If it were to survive as a state-run enterprise, Indian Railways had to change, and so a strategy of modernisation, in terms of management style and culture as well as the physical asset, was needed to bring the organisation into the twenty-first century and ensure its long-term viability.

The business needed to become more customer orientated, to increase its revenue from both freight and passenger services, and to reduce its liabilities, of which the salary bill formed a large part. It therefore embarked on projects to upgrade the system – track electrification, computerisation of ticketing, mechanisation of track maintenance – and at the same time implement a planned reduction in staff numbers. In 2000–1 Indian Railways had almost 1.55 million regular staff on the payroll, a figure that has been reduced by around 16 per cent over a twelve-year period.[6] Average pay, however, has increased, and the use of productivity-linked bonuses is part of a strategy to improve efficiency within the service. A system of full-blown performance-related pay (PRP) is significantly different from the established scales and grades approach so familiar in public-sector organisations, and as yet moves to introduce PRP are in their early stages.

All of this change relied heavily on the co-operation of staff, both collectively in terms of positive trade union relations and individually in terms of their willingness and capacity to upgrade their skills. This could only be achieved through training and development.

Training and development for railway staff is extensive. In addition to the compulsory induction programme already mentioned, there is a wide variety of types of training available at all levels. For the managers and officers (the gazetted staff), seven Centralised Training Institutes cover specialisms such as engineering of all types (civil, mechanical, electrical), signalling and telecommunications, transport management and, at a specific centre, training for the Railway Protection Force. The spectacularly beautiful Railway Staff College at Vadodara in Gujarat[7] specialises in both general and strategic management, sometimes in collaboration with internationally reputed business and management providers from outside India. A further seven centralised and 300 regional training centres exist to provide routine basic and refresher training, with a strong emphasis on safety to technical non-gazetted staff such as drivers, guards and motormen. Once again, the size of the operation is impressive: 3.4 million non-gazetted and 8,400 gazetted staff benefited from Indian Railways training during 2012–13.[8] Training needs, beyond the routine, are identified during annual appraisals, and railway workers appear to recognise that the number of training programmes has increased in recent years.[9] Efforts are made to test the effectiveness of training programmes by examination (both written and practical) or simulations. There are also moves to encourage local, continuous training within the zones by equipping qualified and experienced staff with training skills via a 'train the trainer' initiative.

Clearly, then, training and development is crucial to achieving the turnaround necessary to keep Indian Railways on track in the twenty-first century:

Human resource development strategies on IR have been re-oriented towards enhancing the competitiveness of the Railways organisations in the context of internal and external changes in the environment. In addition to in-house training, railwaymen are being provided specialized training in other institutions in India and abroad. Railway employees are also encouraged to enhance their knowledge and skills by acquiring higher educational qualifications in the specified areas relevant to their work by granting incentives to them. Efforts are being made to improve the basic infrastructure for training to provide structured training programme in improved learning environment. Manpower planning system has been redesigned to regulate manpower intake with reference to emerging business needs and financial viability of the system.[10]

In the last years of the previous millennium, Indian Railways was a loss-making giant. Today, and for the last ten years, it has been a profitable and internationally renowned engine of national economic growth – and one of the largest commercially operating employers in the world.

Tasks

1. How would you go about researching the organisational behaviour aspects of Indian Railways? Base your answer around the concept of organisational behaviour as a multidisciplinary approach (see Figure 1.1) and explain how you would gather information for each aspect of this approach.

2. How and how far do you think Indian Railways has been affected by the changing nature of work and work organisation since the year 2000? What are the implications for managers, and how should these implications be integrated into managerial training?

3. What does the case of Indian Railways reveal about Indian national culture? Use the Hofstede framework to develop your analysis.

4. Chapter 3 suggests that organisations can be classified according to major purpose. Can Indian Railways be classified in this way? Explain your answer with reference to all ten types of organisational purpose outlined. Which do you think is the best fit for Indian Railways, and why?

5. Using the PESTEL framework (see Figure 3.7), identify significant contextual issues for Indian Railways under each heading. How might the organisation plan to address these issues? To what extent does the framework help to provide an integrated plan?

Note on sources

The main source for this case is a study carried out into the HR aspects of Indian Railways for the Society of Human Resource Management by Vijay Pereira of Portsmouth Business School and published as:

Pereira, V. (2009) 'Managing people in the world's largest commercial employer (Indian Railways): A case study analysis', Society of Human Resource Management, USA. Thought Leaders Symposium Dec. 11–12, 2009 on HRM in India held in Mumbai, India.

Notes and references

1 Indian Railways Annual Report and Accounts 2012–13.
2 CIA World Factbook, **https://www.cia.gov/library/publications/the-world-factbook/geos/in.html** (accessed 25 February 2015).
3 Pereira, V. 'Managing people in the world's largest commercial employer (Indian Railways): A case study analysis', Society of Human Resource Management, USA. Thought Leaders Symposium Dec. 11–12, 2009 on HRM in India held in Mumbai, India.
4 Ibid., p. 9.
5 Ibid.
6 Indian Railways Annual Report and Accounts 2012–13.
7 Website, **http://www.rscbrc.indianrailways.gov.in/** (accessed 25 February 2015).
8 Indian Railways Annual Report and Accounts 2012–13, p. 102.
9 Pereira, V. (2009), op. cit.
10 Indian Railways Annual Report and Accounts 2012–13, p. 101.

PART 2
The individual

CHAPTER 4
Individual differences and diversity

The organisation is a collection of individuals with their own perceptions, feelings and attitudes. Our unique different characteristics and attributes shape our values and what we give and expect to receive from working. People are not homogeneous, and individual differences are the basis of diversity. Effective managers need to match the needs and expectations of the individual with the requirements of the organisation.

Learning outcomes

After completing this chapter you should have enhanced your ability to:

- assess the application of personality studies to the work organisation;
- explain the nature of ability and emotional intelligence;
- detail the nature and significance of attitudes to the workplace;
- assess the value of psychometric tests and assessments;
- explore the nature and importance of diversity management;
- evaluate the business case for diversity and the management of diversity;
- focus on valuing individual differences and factors affecting organisational performance.

Critical review and reflection

You cannot expect to work well with other people unless you are fully aware of your own individual differences and characteristic features. Successful understanding and management of interpersonal relationships can only start with an honest individual self-analysis.

To what extent do YOU agree with this contention? How well do YOU know YOURSELF – both the 'good' and the 'bad'?

Recognition of individuality

The individual is a central feature of organisational behaviour. Organisations are made up of their individual members, whether acting in isolation or as part of a group, in response to expectations of the organisation, or as a result of the influences of the external environment.

Individual differences can foster creativity, enjoyment and satisfaction at work but can also be the potential for conflict and frustration. Managers are required to be competent at selecting and developing individuals who will be valuable to the organisation. They need to be observant about the individuals who are capable of effective performance, have the potential for development and work well with other people within the context of the organisation as a whole. Effective management of people requires not only an understanding of individual employees, but also recognition of the culture of the organisation. What is expected and accepted in one work situation may not be the same in another. For instance, creativity and individuality may be encouraged in one organisation but undermined by bureaucracy in another. Managers also need to be able to recognise, respect and value individual difference and be sensitive to contrasting needs. Finally, managers need to know themselves and understand their uniqueness and the impact of their own personality on others.

Managing relationships at work has always been a key skill, but the speed of change in organisations and the external environment places increasing pressure on individuals at work. Sensitivity to individual needs and differences, especially in terms of their resilience, becomes particularly significant when organisations embark on change initiatives. When change appears to be externally imposed, the management of people takes on a different dimension in terms of the sensitivity required. Such changes may lead to new mindsets, attitudes and perceptions that enable people to cope with and adjust to the different world. Managers will be expected to understand the strains employees feel during times of change, but at the same time deal with their own levels of stress.

How do individuals differ?

Our sense of self is shaped by inherited characteristics and by influences in our social environment. The impact of early family life and the country in which we live have a significant part to play in our identity. Most social scientists would agree that both inherited and environmental factors are important in our development, and the way these factors interact is the key to our adult personality. However, scientists differ with regard to the weight they place on these factors – some believing that our personality is heavily influenced by our inherited characteristics and will never change, others believing the reverse.

But first, what are the differences among individuals? These include:

- ethnic origin
- physique
- gender
- early family experiences
- social and cultural factors
- national culture
- motivation
- attitudes
- personality traits and types
- intelligence and abilities
- perception.

Developmental influences such as ageing and health may also arguably affect personality characteristics.

Some of these characteristics are shared with others – for example, individuals who are from the same ethnic group or who have the same ability levels or who share similar physical attributes such as short-sightedness. But our uniqueness stems from the dynamic ways in which these inherited and environmental factors combine and interact. Central to the way in which it is possible to differentiate between individuals, including their behaviour, actions and performance at work, is an understanding of personality: the heart of individual differences.

The functions of attitudes are discussed later in this chapter. An understanding of the way people learn is fundamental to an appreciation of individual differences and is considered in Chapter 5. The process of perception and communications is examined in Chapter 6. All contribute to a greater understanding of self and others.

Critical review and reflection

Individual differences and behaviour are riddled with complexity and contradictions. Frustrations and conflicts are inevitable. Managers should just accept the reality of the situation and concentrate on the work that needs to be done.

As a manager what would be YOUR reaction to this contention?

Personality

Personality may be viewed as consisting of stable characteristics that explain why a person behaves in a particular way. So, for instance, independence, conscientiousness, agreeableness and self-control are examples of personality characteristics. However, it is only when we see/hear/observe a person that we can gain an understanding of their personality. For example, a person who is independent may show that characteristic by displaying a strong sense of self-sufficiency. We would expect the person to take the initiative and not depend on other people. Furthermore, if the characteristic is 'stable' we can rely on this being a consistent part of the person's behaviour. We would be surprised if the person one day demonstrated autonomy and initiative and the next withdrew and delayed any decisions.

There are times when we might be surprised by somebody's behaviour and feel they are 'acting out of character'. Of course this would be known only if we had an understanding of their 'typical behaviour' in the first place. Individuals may exaggerate or suppress certain personality traits if, for example, they are under stress or influenced by drink/drugs. Managers need to learn the art of 'reading' and understanding people's behaviour in order to manage relationships effectively.

Nomothetic and idiographic approaches

Broadly speaking, personality studies can be divided into two main approaches, labelled nomothetic and idiographic.

The **nomothetic approach** is a measurable and specific perspective that looks at the identification of traits and personality as a collection of characteristics. These characteristics are ones that can be described, identified and measured, and therefore can be subjected to observation and tests. This perspective is especially helpful for managers when they are involved in the selection, training and development of individuals. Nomothetic approaches tend to view environmental and social influences as minimal and view personality as consistent, largely inherited and resistant to change. Although they would not diminish the difficulties that measuring personality brings, nomothetic approaches would claim that it is possible to measure and predict the ways in which personality types would behave, given certain circumstances.

Nomothetic researchers closely align themselves to studies that are 'scientific' in a positivistic sense. (The term 'positivism' refers to the branch of science that is exclusively based on the objective collection of observable data – data that are beyond question.) Such an approach transfers methods used in natural sciences to the social world. Some psychologists are interested in describing and measuring characteristics and comparing individuals' scores. Does this person exhibit more or less than 'average' of this particular trait? Being able to predict behaviour is a major aim and outcome of this approach.

The **idiographic approach** is a holistic and dynamic perspective that insists that managers take into account a 'whole' understanding of the individual at work. This may also require going beyond the study of pure psychology to an understanding of the societal context in which the person lives. These are called idiographic approaches and are particularly pertinent in understanding motivation, career development and team relationships.

Idiographic approaches are concerned with understanding the uniqueness of individuals and the development of the self-concept. They regard personality development as a process that is open to change. They regard individuals as responding to the environment and people around them and see the dynamics of the interactions as playing a critical part in shaping personality. The measurement of traits is seen as largely inappropriate, in that one person's responses may not be comparable with another's. They suggest that personality assessment is not a valid method of understanding the unique ways in which a person understands and responds to the world. The depth and richness of a person's personality cannot be revealed in superficial paper-and-pencil questionnaires. Furthermore, the categories defined by psychologists are too narrow in scope and depth.

Theory and the world of work

The application of theory to the world of work is not always easy and some find the process confusing when theory does not match with their experiences. Psychological investigations emphasise the complexity and variety of individual behaviour, and insist that simple answers and explanations are generally inadequate. The study of personality provides an excellent example of some of the complexities involved in applying psychological theory in practice.

Consider two individuals who share similar characteristics. They are both 24 years old and have lived in the same area; both have a first-class honours degree in pharmacy and they have identical personality assessment profiles. However, we would still predict individual differences with regard to, for example, their attitude and performance in the workplace. The complexities of the process pose a number of questions that interest psychologists and evoke different responses.

Figure 4.1 identifies the links between the dynamics of personality and life's experiences.

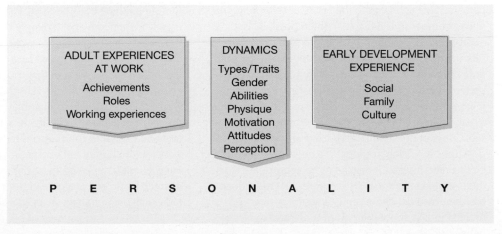

Figure 4.1 To what extent does our personality remain constant?

Uniqueness and similarities

Tables 4.1 and 4.2 focus on two major issues of prime importance in the study of personality. Firstly, is personality a constant throughout our lifetime, which remains resistant to change and circumstances? Secondly, to what extent can we measure and compare individuals on the basis of their personality? This second question assumes that it is possible to distinguish personality characteristics in the first place. Trying to make sense of the nature of personality has resulted in a prolific number of theories, with some psychologists focusing solely on the unique make-up of individuals, others drawing comparisons between individuals or looking for broad similarities in aspirations and goals.

In a work context we tend to be more interested in understanding 'what' an individual's personality is rather than 'why' it is as it is. Furthermore, it is important to understand how various personality characteristics relate to performance at work. The idiographic approach enriches our understanding of 'why' and the nomothetic approach explores the 'what' of personality.

Table 4.1 The role of early experiences – what is their impact?

Environment is significant	Inherited characteristics are significant
Approach taken by idiographic theorists	Approach taken by nomothetic theorists
The personalities of the two pharmacists described above are the culmination of experiences. Their personalities have been shaped by the people around them from their very earliest years. Early family life – the relationship between family members, the size of the family, the rewards and punishments exercised by parents – would have had an influence on the type of person each is now. In other words, the environment and early learning experiences have significantly contributed to their personality development.	The pharmacists inherited a genetic make-up that would remain core and would be resistant to change. Early experiences, while they may shape the person to a certain extent, do not alter the inherited make-up. Intelligence, physical appearances and physiological reactions are 'wired in' from birth – the 'core' of the individual is a 'given'.

Table 4.2 Is it possible to 'measure' an individual's personality?

No, personality is unique	Yes, there are identifiable traits
Approach taken by idiographic theorists	Approach taken by nomothetic theorists
Idiographic approaches do not believe it is possible to put personal characteristics to the test. Our very uniqueness makes comparisons difficult, if not impossible. Is it appropriate to consider the 'strength' of a trait? Our pharmacists may not always reveal their true 'self' – at times circumstances may force them to 'mask' their preferred ways of behaving. Our pharmacists may not reliably report on their own behaviour or there may be a real difference between what they say and what others see. Critics of questionnaires believe answering 'set' questions is 'forcing' responses to questions that may not be relevant. Instead, it may be more appropriate to use open-ended techniques. This ensures that individuals use their own definitions and allows for greater understanding about their motivations and causes of behaviour.	Identifying an individual's personality typically refers to distinguishing traits or types. Personality traits are usually identified by what people do and the behaviour they exhibit, e.g. sociability. Psychologists have designed questionnaires asking people to report on the way they feel or behave. They claim that this is a legitimate way of assessing personality. These self-reporting questionnaires would then be subject to quantitative methods. It is therefore possible to quantify the strength of a person's trait and to enable comparisons to be made with others. Such information then becomes a basis for prediction. For example, if a person has a high score on extroversion, it would be possible to predict the way in which the individual might behave in a given situation.

Critical review and reflection

We know that every person is an individual in their own right, but many theories and models of organisational behaviour still appear to apply to people in general. Rather than looking at similarities among people, we should be more concerned with the study of differences among individuals.

What are YOUR views? What do YOU believe is the value of theories or models of organisational behaviour?

The big five personality factors

Identification of personality traits has been a dominant subject of research in the UK and the USA. There is now a broad body of evidence that suggests that five dimensions provide a common basis by which to capture distinct differences between people. These clusters of traits (not personality types) are known as the 'big five'[1] and sometimes expressed in the acronym OCEAN (or sometimes CANEO):

Openness/closed-mindedness
Conscientiousness/heedlessness
Extroversion/introversion
Agreeableness/hostility
Neuroticism/stability

The big five and work performance

The big five form the basis of standard personality questionnaires that determine positive or negative scores for each dimension. Results from a wide number of studies have shown that these factors can be identified as being significant in measuring the variation between people.[2] Of these, conscientiousness has the highest positive link with high levels of job knowledge and performance across a range of occupations.[3] However, some researchers are critical of the descriptors used.[4]

Bentall suggests they are 'tainted by the investigators' values' and continues: 'I suspect that most people will have a pretty clear idea of where they would like to find themselves on the dimensions of neuroticism, extroversion, openness, agreeableness and conscientiousness.' He questions the ethical and political nature of the scales.[5] The relationship between personality and work performance is also questioned by *Robertson*, who suggests that the only two of the five dimensions that linked consistently with high levels of performance are conscientiousness and emotional stability.[6]

Despite these reservations, the strength and value of the big five model has been extolled in a review by *Lord and Rust,* who conclude:

> *Indeed, the five factor model has become the linchpin that holds personality assessment together, at least within the work context. Without it, how would we generalize with confidence from the validity of one work-based instrument to that of another? Furthermore, the model links the study of assessment instruments within the HR field to research in personality and related areas carried out within clinical and mainstream psychology fields in which the Big Five have also become dominant.*[7]

Support for the big five is also provided by *Luthans and Youssef,* who report that the personality traits have been found to be related strongly to performance and also to:

- **individual-level outcomes** such as happiness and physical and psychological health, spirituality and identity;
- **interpersonal-level outcomes** such as quality of relationships with peers, family and romantic others; and

- **organisational or social-level outcomes** such as occupational choice, satisfaction, performance, community involvement, criminal activity and political ideology.[8]

Moutafi et al. undertook a study of 900 UK managers across ten organisations. Participants completed two personality tests (Revised NEO Personality Inventory and Myers–Briggs Type Indicator (MBTI)) and reported their managerial level in their organisation. Results showed that conscientiousness, extroversion and MBTI intuition were positively correlated with managerial level, and neuroticism, MBTI introversion and sensing were negatively correlated with managerial level. These findings attest to the utility of personality tests used within the occupational community, for selection and assessment of suitability for promotion to senior managerial roles.[9]

Hans Eysenck

Hans Eysenck believed that personality was largely inherited and that we are born with differing physiological tendencies. He identified two major individual differences – *see* Figure 4.2. Eysenck's approach was influenced by the positivistic tradition, with his findings grounded in robust research. His aim was to produce objective evidence of personality differences using large samples of the population.[10] The two dimensions define four distinct personality types:

- stable extroverts (sanguine), with traits such as being talkative, responsive, easygoing, lively, carefree;
- unstable extroverts (choleric), with traits such as being impulsive, changeable, excitable, restless;
- stable introverts (phlegmatic), with traits such as being calm, even-tempered, peaceful, thoughtful;
- unstable introverts (melancholic), with traits such as being anxious, moody, reserved, pessimistic.

Individuals in Eysenck's theory could, therefore, be one of four main personality types. The type would lead to a predisposition of traits that would, itself, lead to the likelihood of certain behaviours. For instance, a person typed as an extrovert would predictably talk over things with someone to help them think it through, while an introvert would prefer to mull it over before talking about the issue. Eysenck developed an instrument to measure personality type called EPQ (Eysenck's Personality Questionnaire).

Although Eysenck's theory appears simplistic, it has an impressive amount of supporting research evidence. His approach has immediate appeal to managers in organisations who are concerned with predicting the future behaviour of their employees, either for selection or promotion. Given the evidence that personality is a useful predictor of behaviour, it is not surprising that the use of psychometric tests has grown substantially over the past decade and that the majority of large companies use occupational tests.[11] (**Further information about testing is given later in this chapter.**)

Figure 4.2 Eysenck's personality dimensions

Raymond Cattell

Cattell's work resembles Eysenck's in the methods used to study personality. He used quantitative, objective techniques in order to analyse his data and followed traditional scientific procedures in order to understand the basic dimensions of personality.[12] He identified two main types of personality traits:

- **surface traits** that seem to cluster together consistently and are observable in behaviour, such as assertiveness;
- **source traits,** such as self-discipline, that can only be inferred and seem to underlie and determine the traits that are likely to 'surface' into behaviour.

Unlike Eysenck, Cattell did not 'type' individuals but used 'traits' as his main personality descriptor. They also differed with regard to the determinants of personality: Eysenck viewed the inherited physiological basis as the main determinant, whereas Cattell was more interested in taking social factors into account when understanding an individual's personality. The original work identified twelve source traits, or primary factors, but was revised to sixteen, which form the basis of the Cattell Sixteen Personality Factor (16PF) Questionnaire. Both theorists have contributed to a lively debate about personality structure and its measurement, and in doing so have advanced the selection techniques available to managers.[13]

Idiographic theoretical approaches

Idiographic approaches emphasise the development of the individual and of individuals' views of themselves – their self-concept. Supporters of idiographic approaches are critical of the nomothetic approach that attempts to categorise individuals on the basis of group data. They argue that the techniques used to collate the group data are questionable and the outcome inappropriate to an understanding of personality. For the idiographic researchers, personality is expressed through the experiences and development of the individual. It cannot be understood outside a social context and has to be studied in the light of individuals' own perceptions of their world.

Idiographic researchers would always take into account the social circumstances of the person, and in particular the relationships with others, family life and social conditions. In early childhood strong personal relationships and unconditional love are essential for later fulfilment and psychological growth. *Carl Rogers'* theory claims that personality is embedded within personal relationships. The process of becoming an adult requires the ability to give and receive unconditional regard – the warmth and respect for the *person,* who they *are,* regardless of how they behave.[14] The phrase 'the looking-glass self' was first discussed in 1902 by *Cooley* – by this he meant that we come to know ourselves through our relationship with others and their reactions to us. Our self-concept is shaped by how others respond to us.[15]

Erik Erikson

Erik Erikson's theory is a good example of the idiographic approach. He viewed personality development as continuing throughout life, and was interested in the effect of experiences on the development of the self-concept and how different individuals resolved personal conflicts.[16] Erikson recognised the importance of early childhood in establishing certain basic concepts of trust, autonomy and initiative, but also claimed that all stages of life produce different tensions and conflicts.

For Erikson, there are eight distinct stages of life, each of which produces different tensions and conflicts that have to be resolved (*see* Table 4.3). Successful resolution of these conflicts produces a healthy personality, whereas difficulties in earlier stages may produce problems

Table 4.3 Erikson's eight stages of personality development

Stage 1	Trust	v.	Mistrust	1st year
Stage 2	Autonomy	v.	Doubt	2–3 years
Stage 3	Initiative	v.	Guilt	4–5 years
Stage 4	Industry	v.	Inferiority	6–11 years
Stage 5	Identity	v.	Role confusion	12–18 years
Stage 6	Intimacy	v.	Isolation	Young adult
Stage 7	Generativity	v.	Self-absorption	Middle age
Stage 8	Integrity	v.	Despair	Old age

Source: Adapted from Erikson, E. H. *Identity and the Life Cycle*, Norton (1980), worksheet table appendix. Copyright © 1980 by W. W. Norton & Company, Inc. Copyright © 1959 by International Universities Press, Inc. Reproduced with permission from W. W. Norton & Company Inc.

later on. Erikson's theory not only makes considerable sense in terms of face validity (i.e. the 'it feels right' factor), but also links with other research indicating that managers' motivations and goals change with age (see also *Hunt*, who identified nine different career/life stages).[17]

Critical review and reflection

The academic study of personality, the idea of nomothetic and idiographic approaches and the work of well-known writers may be of interest in the classroom, but have limited meaning or value to the practical manager.
What is YOUR view? How would YOU attempt to justify the application of theory to the world of work?

Complementary approaches

Some researchers do not fit easily into either of the two broad approaches of nomothetic or idiographic and have their own theories and models of personality development – for example, the work of Carl Jung or the cognitive approach of George Kelly.

Carl Jung

Carl Jung's theory is of particular significance in that it bridges the psychoanalytic approach (of writers such as Sigmund Freud) with modern approaches of personality test design. His theory identifies life energy as concerned with hopes and goals of the future and not just of the past. Jung describes three levels of personality:

- a conscious level (daily reality);
- an unconscious level (contains our unique complexes);
- a collective unconscious level (store of universal and evolutionary experiences).

According to Jung, people have a psychological preference for extroversion or introversion. This basic dichotomy is expanded into four additional factors, namely thinking, sensing, feeling and intuition, which provide a matrix of four personality types:

Sensation-Thinking (ST) Sensation-Feeling (SF)
Intuition-Thinking (NT) Intuition-Feeling (NF)[18]

The Myers–Briggs Type Indicator

Jung is probably best known for his constructs that form the foundation for the MBTI personality indicator. The **Myers–Briggs Type Indicator (MBTI)®** assessment tool was designed by *Isabel Briggs Myers* and *Katherine Briggs*, who applied the rigours of systematic testing to Jung's personality functions and attitudes.[19] Jung identified differences between individuals in terms of their libidinal energy that could flow outwards to the external world (extrovert) or inwards to their inner world (introvert). Personality differences would also be manifest through differing cognitive functions of thinking, feeling, sensation and intuition. The Myers–Briggs assessment added a further dimension of style of living. The MBTI tool has promoted considerable research interest, particularly with regard to the correlation between personality type, occupations and management style (*see* Figure 4.3).

The MBTI assessment tool has been in and out of fashion over the years and there is constant debate about its continuing relevance or usefulness. For example, *Vernon* maintains that Jung's ideas have become an integral part of business and that many do not even realise they were his in the first place. Advocates of Jung's analytical psychology believe his legacy is still underexploited and, despite its risks, MBTI is still the most popular non-clinical measure of personality type.[20]

Kelly's personal construct theory

Kelly's theory of personal constructs does not just consider personality development; it considers the whole person in terms of their perceptions, attitudes and goals. Personality is the individual's way of construing and experimenting with their world, and Kelly was critical of separating the study of personality from the 'whole' person.

The underlying theme of personal construct theory is that people organise their experiences with the world into conceptual classifications called *constructs*. Observation of the behaviour of other people leads to our hypotheses – personal constructs – about the social world. Based on perceptions of, and personal experiences with, their environment, each individual shapes their own unique set of constructs that are important to them. Kelly maintains that these constructs manifest themselves as polar opposites. We develop a wide range of constructs that we can challenge and change over time. How a person organises and prioritises their constructs influences their judgements, actions and decisions

Inherent differences in people's personal constructs can lead to bias in research. *Kelly* developed the Repertory Grid in order to measure an individual's construct of the world. Kelly was thus able to employ a clear and valid measure within an idiographic approach and the repertory technique has become increasingly important as a research tool. It enables the person to use their own constructions of the world but in such a way that they are comparable and measurable.[21]

ISTJ	ISFJ	INFJ	INTJ
Salt of the earth	Behind-the-scenes leader	Oracle for people	Designer of the future
ISTP	**ISFP**	**INFP**	**INTP**
Walking encyclopedia	Gentle spirit	Valued crusader	Blueprinter of ideas
ESTP	**ESFP**	**ENFP**	**ENTP**
Self-starter	Everyone's friend	Spark of energy	Classic entrepreneur
ESTJ	**ESFJ**	**ENFJ**	**ENTJ**
Take-charge leader	Servant leader	Valued spokesperson	Grand-scale organiser

Figure 4.3 Leadership styles and the Myers–Briggs types

Table 4.4 A sequence of work emotions, thought and behaviour

- Jane is asked to carry out a difficult project, usually given only to more experienced colleagues; she feels valued, flattered and trusted – also a little worried
- While working hard on the project her emotions range from excitement and elation to fear and frustration
- She completes the task well and feels proud and relieved
- Jane tells her boss and shows her completed work
- Boss gives no thanks or praise and picks out a trivial error
- Jane then feels resentful and angry and thinks that she will never again 'put herself out' for her boss; also feels exploited
- Thinks about looking for another job
- Doesn't volunteer to do additional tasks any more
- Starts to feel sad and disappointed
- Updates her CV and regularly starts looking at job advertisements

Source: Briner, R. 'Feeling and Smiling', *The Psychologist*, vol. 12, no. 1, January 1999, pp. 16–19. Reproduced with permission from the British Psychological Society.

Emotions at work

Traditionally, workplaces were seen as rational, logical places where emotions were excluded or seen in a negative light. *Hochschild*'s research describes the way in which some jobs require a display of certain emotions – especially those in the service industries, where customer care is inextricably linked with making people feel good. Such work has been labelled as emotional labour and distinguishes between surface acting (displaying emotion without experiencing it) and deep acting (involving thinking and visualising to induce the emotion in the situation).[22]

Briner challenges psychologists to broaden research to throw light on the complexities of emotions in the workplace. He notes that organisations specify the emotions they would like their employees to feel in the mission statements, and in more subtle ways in terms of the rewards and career enhancements people receive when they display appropriate emotions. However, he suggests that little is known about the incidence of emotion at work and the part it plays in work behaviours.[23] The illustration shown in Table 4.4, although simplistic, plots a possible sequence of events and the effects of power of rewards and on psychological well-being.

Note also the discussion on emotional intelligence later in this chapter.

Stress at work

The significance of stress at work is **discussed in Chapter 3.** Personality is a contributing factor in the understanding of stress. Stress is a complex topic: it is individually defined and is intrinsically tied into an individual's perceptual system. Everyone has a range of comfort within which they can feel steady and safe. Stress occurs when each individual feels that they are working outside of that comfort zone. Individuals will differ when they feel discomfort. The effects of stress will differ too; for some, the incidence of stress may energise and activate but for others it may immobilise.

Type A and Type B personalities

Two polar sets of behaviour that link with personality and health have been identified by medical students *Friedman and Rosenman*, who identified recurring patterns of personality in patients suffering from premature heart disease.[23] Individuals with a **Type A personality** are excessively competitive and thrive on hard work and long hours. They work under moderate to high levels of stress and exhibit characteristics such as:

- a high need for achievement;
- extreme competitiveness;
- impatience with obstacles to the completion of tasks;
- aggressiveness;
- a tendency to move and speak rapidly;
- an aversion to idleness;
- restlessness and urgency about time.

Individuals with a **Type B personality** are considered to exhibit the opposite characteristics from Type A. They are not preoccupied with achievement, are easygoing, rarely impatient, not easily frustrated, enjoy leisure time, and move and speak slowly. Type B personalities may still have high levels of drive and ambition but are more relaxed, work at a steady pace and do not exhibit a sense of time urgency.

According to Friedman and Rosenman, Type A personalities are far more vulnerable to heart attacks than Type B personalities. Individuals who have a personality classified as Type A are more likely to suffer from heart disease under severe stress than individuals with a Type B personality. With training, Type A personalities can change to a Type B, provided they are sufficiently aware and find time to implement change strategies.[24] Research also supports the link between stress and Type A personality.[25]

Type A people and team performance

Gratton reports on what happens when Type A people, for whom time urgency is crucial, get to work together with less time-urgent people. Type A people are likely to pay a great deal of attention to the passage of time, constantly check the time remaining and see time as their enemy. Typically they will be very efficient in their use of time, and will use deadlines to prioritise tasks and increase their work pace. Type A people have the potential to keep things moving and active but can have a detrimental impact.[26] A study by *Waller et al.* found that where teams were responsible for completing creative tasks, Type A time-urgent people tended to impose strict, linear schedules on members and this reduced the innovative performance of the team.[27]

Critical review and reflection

Most Type A people are content with their personality characteristics. They welcome a demanding, competitive and challenging work environment, and the link with stress-related illness is exaggerated.

To what extent would YOU dispute this contention? Are YOU a Type A or Type B personality?

Ability and intelligence

Individuals vary with regard to their mental abilities and the extent to which they apply them at work, and different occupations require different skills, competencies and abilities. The 'happy' scenario is one where a match occurs between each individual's abilities and their occupation, but reality suggests that this is not always the case. The extremes include employees, bored rigid with a simple task, who become careless and make a succession of mistakes, and the employees who have been promoted beyond their capability. The result could be stress either for the individuals unable to cope or for their colleagues picking up the debris left behind.

Terminology varies, but **ability** is defined generally as a stable characteristic of a person's capacity for physical or mental performance. **Intelligence** is the ability to undertake constructive thinking, adaption, reasoning and problem-solving.

In a similar vein to the studies of personality, different schools of thought have emerged with regard to the study of abilities. Similar debates to the ones that surround the study of personality have also swirled around the research on intelligence. Is intelligence inherited? Is it constant throughout life? Is it dependent upon our life's experiences, our culture, our education, etc.? What is the nature of intelligence? Can it be measured, and how?

The nature of intelligence

Arguments have raged within psychologists' circles as to the nature of intelligence. Is it dependent on a general overall factor that will have an overarching effect on specific activities? Or are specific activities independent of each other? *Spearman* proposed a two-factor theory of intelligence and suggested that every intellectual task involves a level of mental agility – a general factor (g^{**}) – plus specific abilities (s).[28] This idea, developed by *Vernon,* resulted in a model that placed abilities in a hierarchy (*see* Figure 4.4). Abilities at the lower end of the hierarchy are more likely to correlate, hence if a child has a good vocabulary, the child is more likely to have abilities in reading and also comprehension.[29]

Thurstone claimed seven primary mental abilities that can be separately measured resulting in a profile of scores:

- spatial ability
- perceptual speed
- numerical reasoning
- verbal reasoning
- memory
- verbal fluency
- inductive reasoning.[30]

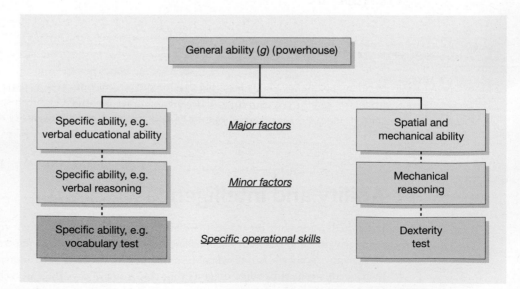

Figure 4.4 A hierarchy of abilities

Source: Adapted from Vernon, P. E. *The Structure of Human Abilities,* Methuen and Co. (1950). Reproduced with permission from Taylor and Francis.

Intelligence – one or many?

Guilford criticised theories that aimed to simplify intelligence into a small number of factors. He devised a model that identified 120 different abilities and suggested that intellectual ability requires individuals to think in one of three dimensions:

- **Content** – What must the individual think about (e.g. meaning of words or numbers)?
- **Operation** – What kind of thinking is the individual required to do (e.g. recognising items, solving a problem, evaluating an outcome)?
- **Product** – What kind of outcome or answer is required (e.g. classifying or reordering items)?[31]

Guilford also expressed concern about the convergent nature of tests that required a single solution or answer. He suggested that tests should also be looking at an individual's ability to produce divergent answers.

Emotional intelligence (EI)

Developed originally by *Salovey and Mayer*,[32] EI (or EQ, for Emotional Quotient) is generally attributed to *Goleman* who, in 1955, published his ground-breaking work. Goleman agreed that the classical view of intelligence was too narrow. He felt that the emotional qualities of individuals should be considered. These, he felt, played a vital role in the application of intelligence in everyday life. He identified the key characteristics as:

> *abilities such as being able to motivate oneself and persist in the face of frustrations; to control impulse and delay gratification; to regulate one's moods and keep distress from swamping the ability to think; to empathise and to hope.*[33]

Emotional intelligence is the sum of a range of interpersonal skills that form the public persona, including the emotional qualities of individuals. Goleman's model outlines five main EI constructs:

- **Self-awareness**
- **Self-regulation**
- **Social skill**
- **Empathy**
- **Motivation.**

Emotional competencies are not innate talents, but rather learned capabilities that must be worked on and can be developed to achieve outstanding performance.

EI has received considerable attention as a key aspect of managing people effectively. Goleman argues for a more empathetic style of management and suggests that EI predicts top performance and accounts for more than 85 per cent of outstanding performance in top leaders.[34] The Hay Group, working with Goleman, has identified eighteen specific competencies that make up the four components of EI and has produced an inventory designed to measure emotional competence (*see* Figure 4.5). The Emotional Competence Inventory defines EI as 'The capacity for recognising our own feelings and those of others, for motivating ourselves and for managing emotions within ourselves and with others.'[35]

Significance of emotional intelligence

Research from the Chartered Management Institute identifies EI as one of the key skills managers and leaders will need in the coming decade.[36] According to *Landale*, it should really be no surprise to find EQ so much in demand.

> *After all, we work in structures which are much flatter than ever. We have to be much faster on our feet with both colleagues and clients and, whatever the team structure, there is increasing proximity for us to build the relationships we need – fast. In this context EQ is the glue that holds people and teams together.*[37]

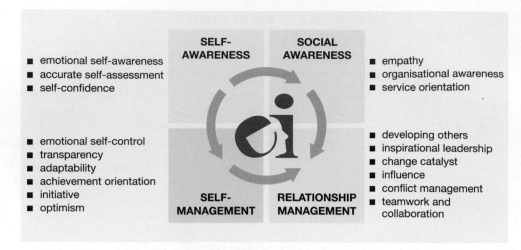

Figure 4.5 Emotional Intelligence Competence Model
Source: Hay Group. Copyright © 1999 Hay Group Limited. All rights reserved. Reproduced with permission.

Venus makes the point that success in the boardroom is not just down to sound business sense and technical competence; interpersonal relationships also play a key role. The set of competencies known as EI are often overlooked in terms of professional success.[38]

Developing EI

Landale refers to the importance of empathy in EI, which involves how a person self-manages and addresses how to engage with the emotions of others, and suggests a six-step process for developing EI:

1. Know what you feel.
2. Know why you feel it.
3. Acknowledge the emotion and know how to manage it.
4. Know how to motivate yourself and make yourself feel better.
5. Recognise the emotions of other people and develop empathy.
6. Express your feelings appropriately and manage relationships.

> *There seems little doubt that managers and leaders who have trained up in EQ have far more initiative in dealing with organizational life than those who don't. Stress will always exist at work, but EQ gives people the tools and ways of thinking to manage it to their advantage.*[39]

According to *Dann,* becoming highly self-aware allows an individual to recognise inner and outer conflict and develop more proactive self-management. Developing greater social awareness allows the fostering of productive relations and a greater degree of engagement between employees and management. A manager with a high EQ benefits both the organisation and the individual.[40]

However, *Alexander* reports on research concerning the negative uses and dark side of EI, and questions what happens when people start using it to manipulate others in order to further their own careers. Those on the dark side of EI will scrutinise the emotions of others but are adept at controlling their own emotional displays. For example, bosses with negative EI in mind may focus on employees' emotions for cynical purposes. Employees looking to profit by dark EI may constantly scrutinise a superior's emotions for ways to enhance how they are estimated by attuning to the superior's state of mind.[41]

Critical review and reflection

It is evident that emotional intelligence (EI) is the single most important predictor of the capacity for effective work performance and professional success. Organisations should concentrate their efforts on identifying and developing EI for all managers.

What is YOUR view? To what extent do YOU have a high level of emotional intelligence?

Attitudes

Another factor that influences and distinguishes individual behaviour is a person's attitudes. So what are **attitudes** and how can they be distinguished from beliefs and values? Attitudes can be defined as providing a state of 'readiness' or tendency to respond in a particular way.[42] **Beliefs** are concerned with what is known about the world; they centre on what 'is', on reality as it is understood. **Values** are concerned with what 'should' be and what is desirable.

There are no limits to the attitudes people hold. Attitudes are learned throughout life and are embodied within our socialisation process. Some attitudes (such as religious beliefs) may be central to us – a core construct – and may be highly resistant to any change, whereas other, more peripheral attitudes may change with new information or personal experiences. Specific events, particularly traumatic ones such as redundancy, may have a dramatic effect on our attitudes.

Gross suggests that 'to convert a belief into an attitude, a "value" ingredient is needed which, by definition, is to do with an individual's sense of what is desirable, good, valuable, worthwhile and so on'. Gross has suggested that whereas 'adults may have thousands of beliefs, they may have only hundreds of attitudes and a few dozen values'.[43] *Hofstede* defines values as a 'broad tendency to prefer certain states of affairs over others'.[44]

The functions of attitudes

Katz has suggested that attitudes and motives are interlinked and, depending on an individual's motives, attitudes can serve four main functions:

- **Knowledge** – One of the major functions is to provide a basis for the interpretation and classification of new information. Attitudes provide a knowledge base and a framework within which new information can be placed.
- **Expressive** – Attitudes become a means of expression. They enable individuals to indicate to others the values that they hold and thus to express their self-concept and adopt or internalise the values of a group.
- **Instrumental** – Held attitudes maximise rewards and minimise sanctions. Hence, attitudes towards other people (or objects) might be held because of past positive (or negative) experiences. Behaviour or knowledge that has resulted in the satisfaction of needs is thus more likely to result in a favourable attitude.
- **Ego-defensive** – Attitudes may be held in order to protect the ego from an undesirable truth or reality.[45]

Employee attitude surveys

Attitude surveys or questionnaires are used by many organisations as a way of attempting to gauge the climate of the organisation and monitor views of members of staff. The Chartered Management Institute defines an employee attitude survey as:

A planned procedure which enables managers to explore employees' opinions both on particular issues, and on the organisation itself, so as to be able to take account of them in the planning process, or make changes that will be beneficial to both the organisation and individuals who work within it.

Surveys can be used to monitor employees' views or gauge effects of a new policy, and provide effective communications or a sounding board. It is crucial that people understand reasons for the survey, the benefits it may have and are assured there are no 'hidden agendas'. Surveys require significant time and resources to administer and evaluate. The frequency should be no more than every eighteen months, and it is important to communicate results of the survey and plans of action to both senior managers and all employees.[46] The usual method of measurement is by adopting a five-point 'Likert scale' that reflects the comparative strength of the attitude.[47] See the example in Table 4.5.

Theories on attitude change stress the importance of **balance** and **consistency** in our psyche. *Heider,* for example, suggests that not only would we find it uncomfortable to hold two conflicting attitudes, but to do so would motivate us to change one of the attitudes in order to reach a balanced state.[48]

Table 4.5 An example of an attitude questionnaire

Please tick one box that most closely represents how you feel about each statement	Strongly disagree				Strongly agree
	1	2	3	4	5
I believe in what OrgCo is trying to achieve	❑	❑	❑	❑	❑
I enjoy discussing OrgCo with people who do not work here	❑	❑	❑	❑	❑
I know how my job contributes to OrgCo's aims and objectives	❑	❑	❑	❑	❑
Good and bad news about what is happening at OrgCo is communicated regularly	❑	❑	❑	❑	❑
My values and those of the organisation are very similar	❑	❑	❑	❑	❑
Right now, staying with OrgCo is a matter of necessity as much as desire	❑	❑	❑	❑	❑
I am constantly interrupted in my work	❑	❑	❑	❑	❑
I enjoy my job	❑	❑	❑	❑	❑
I am encouraged to seek out new training opportunities	❑	❑	❑	❑	❑
My manager discusses with me ways in which I can improve my work performance	❑	❑	❑	❑	❑
OrgCo is serious about removing barriers to ensure equality of opportunity	❑	❑	❑	❑	❑
Staff at OrgCo regularly help and support each other at work	❑	❑	❑	❑	❑
I lack direction from my manager	❑	❑	❑	❑	❑
When things do not go well in our team/department we learn from the experience	❑	❑	❑	❑	❑
Communication within my team is positive and effective	❑	❑	❑	❑	❑
Taking everything into account, I have a high level of job satisfaction with my team	❑	❑	❑	❑	❑

Cognitive dissonance is the term given by *Festinger* to the discomfort felt when we act in a way that is inconsistent with our true beliefs. When there is inconsistency between our behaviour and a consciously held attitude, we experience a feeling of dissonance and we are motivated to reduce its impact.[49]

Critical review and reflection

Changing the behaviour of people is comparatively easy but changes to underlying personality or attitudes are far more difficult. A change in behaviour does not necessarily mean a change in a person's personality or attitudes.

Do YOU believe we should simply concentrate on how to change behaviour and ignore the study of personality and attitudes?

Testing and assessment

Much has been written about the value of selection tests and questionnaires and how they are subject to constant debate with regard to the validity of these measures – that is, do they actually measure what they claim to measure? It should be noted that the word 'test' is often taken to refer to measures of intelligence, achievement and developed abilities, and aptitude for particular tasks. Measures of interests, social attitudes, emotional stability or traits of personality are usually referred to as questionnaires or profiles, or similar. Answers are regarded as common or uncommon, typical or untypical, rather than right or wrong, good or bad.

The word 'test' is therefore usually avoided in such measures, as, for example, the Cattell 16PF Questionnaire. Also, the terms 'personality tests' and 'psychometric tests' are often used interchangeably. Strictly, however, personality tests measure only enduring characteristics of an individual, whereas a psychometric test measures a broader range of all psychological characteristics. Most people will have taken a **psychometric test** of one kind or another by the time they are an adult in employment. Tests may be administered at school or college, or as part of the selection assessment process at work. The use of tests is widespread and growing. They are perceived to be useful as an objective discriminating tool, but they are not without controversies and sensitivities.

For a test to be considered as a psychological instrument it must be **objective, standardised, reliable, valid** and **discriminating** (but not discriminatory). The selection and choice of the test should be based on a number of other key features such as its acceptability, practicality, time, costs, and perceived and actual added value.

Use and limitations of tests

All tests have limitations. Tests can sample behaviour only at one particular moment in time. The information they provide is dependent upon good testing practice and will only add evidence to the decision-making process. Tests will not provide the answer. Some individuals are very nervous and may not perform at their best, and indeed some may feel indignant that they are obliged to take a test at all. Great skill is required, therefore, in the administering of tests or questionnaires and in the interpretation of results. A suitable physical environment is also important. The possible reaction of candidates must be considered. Some might find any form of 'test' something of an ordeal or regard it as an unpleasantness. A major concern with the majority of tests is the doubts about validity and lack of statistically proven reliability.

Goss suggests that the use of personality assessments not only is an infringement of the individual's privacy, but also leads to unfortunate organisational consequences, with 'cloning' as an outcome. Such techniques can be perceived as a form of social engineering and an insidious form of organisational control.[50] Aware of these problems, the British Psychological Society has produced guidelines and codes of practice for users of psychometric tests. Furthermore, evidence is emerging to show that where personality questionnaires have been specifically designed and related to work characteristics, prediction and validity scores are much higher.[51]

Reasons for using psychological tests may be summarised as follows. Tests should be seen as an additional source of information only, but administered properly they can:

- make more systematic and precise decisions about people;
- predict future performance and reduce uncertainty;
- provide more accurate descriptions of people and their behaviour.

However, it must be remembered that:

- tests may be expensive and time consuming;
- without proper professional practice, they can be misused and results abused;
- they may be seen as an intrusion;
- they may be regarded as inappropriate;
- practice may have an effect on test results.

A major consideration in the controversy about the use of psychometric tests is how to avoid any cultural bias. There are still widespread doubts and criticisms about the use and value of personality tests, and continuing debate about their value in predicting performance at work. Even when psychometric tests *are* used, they should not be used in isolation but applied in appropriate circumstances as part of a comprehensive selection process or assessment centre. It is also important to ensure adequate feedback to candidates in the process.

As *Yeung* points out, although there are good personality tests available, personality testing is a completely unregulated market that does not require a licence or any qualifications. There is no legislation to protect people from unscrupulous untrained consultants selling in-house personality tests. The best tests indicate results at one point in time that are found to predict performance at a later date. Without predictive validity, a personality test is essentially worthless.[52]

Critical review and reflection

Despite continuing popularity, so-called personality tests have limited value in predicting suitability for a job or likely work performance. Not only are they a waste of time, but too often tests are used to avoid personal responsibility for judgements and decision-making.

What is YOUR considered opinion? What is YOUR own experience of taking a personality test?

Diversity in the workplace

An integral and essential feature of individual differences is diversity. We have seen from the discussion above that people are not homogeneous. **Diversity** focuses on the multiplicity of differences among people – on the variety of people as heterogeneous groupings. Individual differences are the basis of diversity.

Individual differences and diversity have long been recognised as important for effective team performance, but in recent years greater attention has been given to the management of diversity. Reasons for this include:

- changing social attitudes;
- more global environment and increasing internationalisation;
- influence of the European Commission;

- Equality Act 2010 and equal employment opportunities legislation;
- government action to increase female representation at senior levels;
- demographic changes in the workforce;
- wider customer base;
- shortage of higher-level skills;
- programmes of affirmative action, inclusion and positive discrimination;
- increasing number of women, older and part-time workers in the workforce.

However, valuing differences is easier said than done. It means relating and working with people who hold different perspectives and views, bringing different qualities to the workplace, having different aspirations and different customs and traditions. Differences are challenging; they question people's views, perceptions and attitudes, and require individuals to see things from a different frame of reference.

Diversity is relevant to anything that may affect workplace relationships and achievements. The Chartered Management Institute provides the following description of diversity:

> *The concept of diversity encompasses any sort of difference between individuals. These could be differences in ethnic origin, age, disability, gender, gender identity, sexual orientation, family status, religion, education, social class, and even personality or attitudes. The management of diversity involves developing and implementing inclusive strategies through which a network of varied individuals are integrated into a dynamic workforce.*[53]

From equal opportunities to managing diversity

Equal opportunities relates to legislation intended to outlaw discrimination. The government is committed to protect individuals at work against discrimination. Encouraging a diverse workforce is high on the government's agenda and the reluctant employer is having its hand forced by statutory obligations. Although diversity in the workplace relates to treating everyone equally, it complements and further develops initiatives on equal opportunities. Future demographic patterns present new challenges for managers.

> *Diversity management goes beyond what is required by legislation designed to promote equal opportunities and prevent discrimination. It comprises an approach which recognises and values differences and aims to make positive use of the unique talents and perspectives within the workforce. The focus is on individuals rather than minority groups.*[54]

Employers Network for Equality and Inclusion

Employers Network for Equality and Inclusion (enei) is the UK's leading employer network, covering all aspects of equality and inclusion in the workplace. Enei works with business members and their leaders, covering all aspects of equality and inclusion in the workplace in order to make change happen. Strategic themes are pan-diversity and include:

- **unconscious bias** – its impact on attitudes, behaviours and decision-making;
- **inclusive leadership** – creating inclusive cultures through behaviour change;
- **agile working** – changing the way people work and improve organisational effectiveness;
- **workforce representation** – driving competitive advantage by attracting and retaining diverse talent;
- **access to opportunities** – promoting social mobility and opening up work opportunities;
- **managing diversity and inclusion in a global marketplace** – maximising business performance through the development of talented people working across cultural and geographical boundaries.

Enei recognises that equality and inclusion issues often cut across the 'protected characteristics' defined under the Equality Act 2010 and help employers think about equality and inclusion in a broader sense.[55]

Business case for diversity

As businesses become increasingly global it is even more important for managers to have a sound understanding of diverse countries and workforces. According to ACAS, the business case for diversity – that a more diverse employee base will attract a more diverse customer base and increase sales, improve performance, etc. – is a well-argued one.[56]

A joint report from the CBI and TUC, supported by the Equality and Human Rights Commission, suggests that promoting diversity in the workplace and employing people solely on the basis of their ability can bring many real business benefits. These include:

- increasing employee satisfaction, which helps attract new staff and retain those already there, reduces recruitment costs and can increase productivity;
- understanding better how the company's diverse customers think and what drives their spending habits, or how companies access markets they have not previously been able to tap into so effectively;
- finding enough workers to fill skills gaps in areas with tight labour markets, where there are not enough 'obvious candidates' for the vacancies companies have.

The report also makes clear that diversity can be improved through positive action – such as encouraging applications from types of people who have not in the past applied for jobs, additional training, providing support networks or adapting work practices – but not positive discrimination.[57]

Diversity and management recruitment

The Institute for Employment Studies, in conjunction with the Chartered Management Institute, emphasises the importance of diversity as a strategic priority for retaining and developing key people in an organisation. They draw attention to the different career ambitions of managers from under-represented groups and state that, if organisations want management talent at the top, recruitment approaches must recognise that managers from different ethnic groups are attracted by different benefits. For example, compared with other ethnic groups, black managers were more likely to cite good progression opportunities; Asian managers more likely to cite working for a good employer; managers from mixed backgrounds to cite challenging work; white managers and black managers more likely to mention better work/life balance.[58]

Diversity and social class

Although many firms pat themselves on the back for their diversity policies, *Reeves* suggests that, in fact, social mobility in the UK is in steady decline and class inequality is not dead. If businesses continue to run a 'people like us' strategy when it comes to talent, they risk blunting their own competitive edge.

> *To be blunt: it is perfectly possible to look 'diverse' by hiring and promoting, in sufficient numbers, posh women, posh ethnic minorities and posh gay men and lesbians. All of which is better, for sure, than a monopoly of posh straight white men. But the standard diversity agenda misses the more subtle inequalities of class.*[59]

A summary of equality at work is set out in the concept map in Figure 4.6.

Critical review and reflection

Despite all the rhetoric and claimed advantages of diversity, it is still more about the benefits to business rather than moral or social concerns. In reality, it is little more than another form of political correctness and viewed with scepticism by many members of the workforce.

How would YOU respond to such a claim? What is YOUR experience?

EQUALITY AT WORK

- ■ UNDERLYING CONCEPTS OF EQUALITY
- ■ LEGISLATION AND EQUALITY
- ■ EQUALITY & DIVERSITY COMPARED
- ■ EQUALITIES AND RECRUITMENT & SELECTION
- ■ SOME SIMPLE ACTIONS FOR BETTER EQUALITY

SOME EQUALITY CONCEPTS

In the context of our society, equality means:

- • Treating everyone concerned equally and fairly
- • Not unfairly discriminating against particular individuals or groups
- • Providing equality of opportunity, irrespective of personal background or belief

* Employees
* Customers
* Clients
* Suppliers

LEGISLATION AND EQUALITY

Legislation lays down, in **particular topic areas**, that individuals have the right not to be **unfairly discriminated** against, both in the workplace and outside

These **topic areas** include:
- – Age
- – Disability
- – Gender
- – Race
- – Religion
- – Sexual orientation

Discrimination, as recognised in law, can be DIRECT DISCRIMINATION or INDIRECT DISCRIMINATION

Setting a condition, plainly and openly stated, that means someone in one or more of the categories described in law are excluded from consideration. For example: a job requirement that 'Only fit men should apply'

Setting a condition that means someone in one or more of the categories described in law would find it more difficult to comply with. For example: a job requirement for workers where a minimum height is set could discriminate against some racial types

EQUALITY & DIVERSITY COMPARED

There are close links between the subjects of Equality & Diversity – but they are not the same. Some points of comparison are:

EQUALITY	DIVERSITY
Often: • Externally initiated • Legislation driven • Problem focused • Reacting to situation • Specific focus on particular topics (gender, disability & others)	Frequently: • Internally initiated • Business needs driven • Opportunity focused • Proactive approach • Considers all differences (and combinations of them)

Using the term 'UK Equality Legislation' in an internet search engine will allow detailed information on current legal requirements to be located

Record your decisions relating to equalities (and the reasons for them)

When recruiting, focus on abilities and aptitudes, not stereotypes

Seek opinions from experienced & trusted colleagues

Actively seek equalities training

If in difficulty, seek advice from qualified people

Keep up to date with equalities legislation

POSSIBLE EQUALITY PROBLEMS AT THE DIFFERENT RECRUITMENT & SELECTION STAGES

1 Specify the job
- ■ Setting non-vital requirements that are difficult for minority applicants to meet

2 Specify the person
- ■ Setting non-vital requirements that are difficult for minority applicants to meet
- ■ Excluding certain groups

3 Attract applicants
- ■ Advertising in places not usually accessible to certain groups

4 Prepare short-list
- ■ Excluding applications from minority groups

5 Interview
- ■ Asking questions likely to be more difficult for minority group applicants to answer

6 Select
- ■ Selectors biased against certain groups

These issues can lead to examples of both direct and indirect discrimination

Figure 4.6 Equality at work

Source: Copyright © 2011 The Virtual Learning Materials Workshop. Reproduced with permission.

Diversity management and training

More than ever, effective organisational performance demands an understanding of, and response to, diversity. This necessitates a work climate that respects individual differences and treats all members of staff with dignity and mutual respect. Diversity training will not be effective unless there is active support from the top and it is recognised as a company-wide initiative and part of the core value of the organisation.

Organisations need to manage diversity in a manner that benefits the well-being of all members of staff. Training should involve:

- increasing the awareness and value of diversity;
- education in understanding the culture and values of members of a diverse workforce;
- the ability to communicate effectively with all members of staff – and also customers and suppliers;
- developing the skills of effective diversity management;
- addressing biases, prejudices and stereotypes.

Business in the Community (BITC) is one of the agencies that help businesses to embrace a culture of inclusiveness by promoting equality of opportunity for all staff, irrespective of gender, race, age, disability, sexual orientation and faith.

> *We know that creating diverse and inclusive workplaces is a business imperative, not a nice thing to do. Organisations benefit when they create workplaces which tap into a diverse range of skills and talents . . . We also campaign on the issues which will make the most beneficial difference to individuals, society and our economy.*[60]

Management and organisational behaviour in action case study
Lloyds Banking Group Diversity Programme

At Lloyds Banking Group, diversity and inclusion is central to our business success. Our 25 million customers are very diverse and if we are to be successful, we need to ensure that we understand and can meet their diverse needs. Reflecting the diversity of the UK population in our own workforce helps us to achieve that goal. We are therefore creating an environment where everyone can provide excellent service to our customers and develop their individual careers, whatever their background. Our commitment starts at the top of the organisation, with our Group Executive sponsoring our diversity programme by taking the lead on initiatives that improve both the quality of our customer service and the working environment for our colleagues. Through a range of initiatives and strategies, we work hard to ensure Lloyds Banking Group is inclusive for everyone.

We participate in benchmarking exercises run by national campaigns covering the main diversity strands. These benchmarks independently assess performance, track progress over time and compare performance against other organisations. This kind of external evaluation is extremely important to us and helps Lloyds Banking Group to maintain momentum and continue to strive to retain its leading edge status.

Our policies, programmes and practices are recognised as amongst the best, and the strategy is underpinned by focus on these key actions:

1. **Diversity metrics** – all aspects of the workforce are monitored, analysed and reported on by diversity demographic. Progress is measured half yearly and the diversity interventions in place are measured for effectiveness using key performance indicators.
2. **Colleague research** – extensive quantitative and qualitative research is carried out with colleagues to ensure that strategies in place address their specific needs. In addition, ongoing consultation with employees provides feedback on how well the strategy is working.
3. **Training and development** – our focus is on developing talent and ensuring that all colleagues can progress their careers regardless of gender, ethnicity, disability, sexual orientation, gender identity, religion or age. Personal

development workshops for specific groups are also available, which inspire and motivate attendees to take control of their personal and career aspirations/development.

4. **Top level commitment –** as well as agreeing and committing to the delivery of the diversity programme, our Group Executive Committee and Board monitor progress. In addition, our Group Executives act as sponsors for the organisation's disability, ethnicity, gender, agility and sexual orientation programmes. The power of such top level commitment and the success that can be seen from it is evidenced by us recently receiving the highest score ever awarded to an organisation by the Business Disability Forum. A major contribution to such an accolade is the success of our Workplace Adjustment Programme. This leading edge initiative includes:

  • End-to-end case management with external suppliers who are experts in this field.
  • 30 day Service Level Agreement from initiation of request to completion of adjustments.
  • Central funding of all physical adjustments (IT equipment, software, furniture).
  • Specific guidance on non-physical adjustments (e.g. changes to working patterns, targets, rest breaks).
  • Training and coaching for both colleagues and their line managers around any assistive technology with which they have been provided.

In addition, Lloyds Banking Group deliver personal and career development programmes for staff with impairments or long-term health conditions. These programmes have been specifically tailored to meet the needs of those who live and work with a disability or impairment. Through detailed research, we found that standard training methods on assertiveness, influencing skills, personal empowerment and career development weren't as effective for colleagues with impairments. In addition, our research with disabled staff demonstrated that having access to positive action training had a huge impact on their engagement within the organisation.

Source: Lloyds Banking Group Diversity & Inclusion Team.[61] October 2014

Tasks

1. Discuss how you believe reflecting on workforce diversity can help an organisation achieve its business success.
2. Give your views on the four key actions that underpin Lloyds Banking Group's diversity programme strategy.
3. To what extent do you think there is a high top level of commitment to the disability programme in your university or organisation?

The effective management of diversity will also entail a review of organisational processes and the execution of work. For example, not everyone:

  • shares the same work ethic or seeks the same goals and objectives;
  • responds in the same way to working in a bureaucratic structure;
  • works better in a self-managed group or with a more participative style of management;
  • will fit the same psychometric profile;
  • is motivated in the same way; or
  • reacts the same way to different forms of control.

Diversity management requires time and effort and may well have a high financial cost. There is a general feeling that badly managed initiatives do more harm than good. Managing diversity requires a company-wide philosophy and commitment, a change to organisational culture and supportive systems of management and training.

ONS – equality and diversity policy

The Office for National Statistics (ONS) is committed to being an equal opportunities employer and to achieving equality of opportunity for all employees. ONS values and welcomes diversity and all employees are entitled to work in an environment free from discrimination and harassment.

Our equality and diversity policy aims to ensure that existing employees and applicants for jobs are treated fairly and within the law. No ONS employees or applicants for jobs in ONS should receive less favourable treatment on unjustifiable grounds because of their: sex, marital or civil partnership status, age, race, disability, responsibility for dependants, religion or belief (actual or perceived), sexual orientation (actual or perceived), transgender status, pregnancy, political beliefs, trade union activities, working patterns or contract status.

ONS supports a range of flexible working patterns to enable employees to balance home and work responsibilities and treats people fairly, irrespective of their working arrangements.

Key points of Equality and Diversity work at ONS:

- The Director General of ONS chairs the Equality and Diversity Steering Groups, which set the strategic direction for all equality work, scrutinising, monitoring and staff survey data;
- ONS has diversity champions to cover each of its sites, alongside a senior sponsor for each of its 15 diversity network groups;
- ONS exceeds its statutory equality duties as a public authority and is committed to achieving best practice in promoting equality and eliminating discrimination and harassment. To aid this, ONS participated in a number of equality benchmarking exercises and recently became the first organisation to receive the 'Gold Standard' in the Business Disability Forum's Disability Standard.

Promoting equality is core to the expectations ONS staff should have of ONS as an employer, and in the expectations ONS has of its workforce; all staff are required to have an objective that covers equality and diversity, which forms part of the annual performance review.

ONS has a detailed **Equality and Diversity Strategy (2012–2016)** and four detailed action plans for 2014–2015, which cover:

- Representation of women at senior levels
- Disability Action Plan
- Part-time working Action Plan
- Ethnicity Action Plan.

Source: Office for National Statistics. Crown Copyright material is reproduced under terms of the Click-Use Licence.

Diversity and stereotyping

Diversity also challenges many traditional stereotypes **(discussed in Chapter 6)**. Stereotyping infers that people within a particular perceived category are assumed to share the same traits or characteristics. Stereotypes are a means of making simplified judgements of other people instead of coping with a range of individual stimuli. Stereotyping attributes to all individuals the characteristics or tendencies of the categorisation as a whole. An important feature of managing diversity is an awareness of, and training in, overcoming inaccurate stereotyped perceptions and attributions. A greater understanding of cultural differences in non-verbal communications and body language will help improve interpersonal relationships.

> *There have been instances in my life, both at home and at work, when people have felt I'm a little crazy because I am pushy, outspoken, energetic, competitive, enthusiastic, driven and strong. Crazy, because that's not what's expected of an Asian woman. Crazy, because it's not what the majority of people are like. And crazy, because they think they know me better than I know myself.*

Saira Khan – star of *The Apprentice* television series[62]

Gender diversity

One of the most significant and important aspects of managing diversity is that of gender equality, and the participation of men and women in the workforce.[63] One of our initial perceptions and classifications of another individual is usually the identification of their gender. How does this perception affect our behaviour?

- What difference does it make if our work group is predominantly male or female?
- Do women and men have different experiences at work?
- If organisations are rational and neutral institutions – why should gender make a difference?
- Does it matter that many classic theories have been based on research carried out on men, by male researchers?
- What has been the influence of diversity policies on work behaviour and on the position of women in organisations?

Since 2011, when Lord Davies set a target of achieving 25 per cent women directors for FTSE companies, to now, in 2015, there have been continual media reports on the number of women in senior positions in business. However, as *Bernadette Barber,* for example, points out: 'we have come a long way in the past hundred years but achieving true diversity at all levels of working life is not an easy nut to crack'.[64] However, *Laura Spira and Helen Pitcher* maintain that it is unfortunate that diversity has become synonymous with gender in media discussions. They raise the debatable issue of voluntary or mandatory quotas. Material diversity in the boardroom is not always synonymous with a well-performing board. Although there is some argument to correlate gender diversity with effective performance, this should not ignore other bases for argument.[65]

Managing an ageing workforce

The focus on diversity has drawn attention to managing the generation gap and the increasing numbers of older people in the workforce. The EU refers to the ageing population, to the future shrinking of the working-age population and to the whole world ageing fast. Working longer is not enough. We need to empower older people to participate and contribute to their communities so that they can remain autonomous as long as possible. This requires a more age-friendly and inclusive society.[66]

Now that the UK default retirement age of 65 has been removed there will be an increasing challenge to manage an intergenerational workforce. *Barnes* suggests that, at worst, young workers can see their older colleagues as dinosaurs, set in their ways and blocking creativity, as well as their own path to promotion. Older workers, too, can feel threatened by the energy and technological ease of their younger colleagues or impatient with their brashness and lack of experience. Managers need to recognise and harness differences in skills, motivations and work routines to deliver high-quality output and mutual learning.[67]

According to a report by the CMI and CIPD, there is plenty of encouraging news about managers' attitudes to the ageing workforce and older workers are seen as valuable employees who bring vital skills, knowledge and experience to their jobs. However, organisations still need to work hard with their policies of recruitment, retention and development to prepare for the impact of demographic change.[68]

Earlier (see **Chapter 3**), attention was drawn to three different generations and age groups in the workplace. As people live and work longer there will be a wider spread of age groups in the workforce. *Wilton,* for example, suggests a fourth generation, that of 'Homelanders' born after 9/11 changed the world.

> *That the late Boomers and early Gen X aren't going to be quick to jack it in and buy a boat has key implications for retirement, pensions and health policies. And maybe that's no bad thing. Sometimes amid more high-profile efforts to increase gender and racial diversity in the workplaces, older groups are forgotten.*[69]

Criticisms and limitations

Despite potential benefits from diversity, there are a number of criticisms and perceived limitations. While acknowledging that the positive management of diversity aims to promote an inclusive culture in which individuals are valued and respected, the CMI points out that diversity management should not be mistaken for equal opportunities or be merely a question of legal compliance. Managers should avoid handling diversity issues insensitively, invading employees' privacy, failing to consult and gain commitment throughout the organisation or falling into an 'us' and 'them' mentality.[70]

Individuality and groups

Social interaction is a natural feature of human behaviour, and group working is a major feature of organisational life. Strong and cohesive groups can have beneficial effects for the organisation but there are potential disadvantages. There is arguably a potential conflict with workforce diversity because of the need to consider staff both as individuals and as members of a group. The greater the compatibility of its members and the more homogeneous the group, the greater the danger of the group developing its own sub-culture. Members may display a critical attitude towards people outside the group or members of other groups. Encouraging individuality and at the same time expecting group co-operation and teamwork are potential triggers for tension. **Group cohesiveness is discussed in Chapter 8**.

Diversity can also be threatened by power relationships. The concept of social exchange theory (**discussed in Chapter 1**) suggests that social exchanges are influenced by a complex web of power relationships and, as a result, are not always equal but have an uneven balance of outcomes. Those individuals at the lower end of power relationships, perhaps for example part-time or casual workers or ethnic minorities, may arguably be disadvantaged.

Concern for moral and social issues

A major concern with the increasing attention to diversity is that too much attention is given to the advantages for business rather than to broader moral or social issues and the ethical arguments for equality of treatment.

In arguing the case for combining heterogeneity and homogeneity, *Nordström and Ridderstråle* suggest that although quite often people talk favourably about diversity since it supposedly promotes a better atmosphere and equality, the typical manager is persuaded to change the mix of people at the company for economic reasons: 'The competitive reality is that organisations that are bogged down in issues of race, gender, age, sexual preferences, look and so on, will slip deeper down in the mire.'[71] *Kirton and Greene* believe that the 'business case' should be broadened to include wider issues of social justice and social responsibility.[72]

According to *Lucas*, one of the key messages the experts want to get across is that paying attention to diversity is not just a moral obligation, it is a business imperative.

> *Workers in organisations where diversity is valued generally feel more engaged with their employer and are more likely to stay on board. The organisation will build a reputation as an 'enlightened' employer, and will be able to attract the best people at a time when talent is at a premium. The business can also draw on the expertise of its diverse workforce to create new and improved products and services which will help them get ahead in competitive, global markets.*[73]

Critical review and reflection

Whatever the skills, experience or qualifications of an individual, personality is arguably the most important criterion for employability, subsequent relationships with other people at work, personal development and career progression.

What do YOU think? How large a part does personality play in influencing YOUR behaviour and performance at work?

Ten key points to remember

1 The individual is a central feature of organisational behaviour. Managers need to be competent at selecting and developing individuals of value to the organisation.

2 Individual differences can be the potential source of problems and conflict, and managing interpersonal relationships is riddled with complexity and contradictions.

3 A significant difference among individuals is in terms of their personality – those stable characteristics that explain why a person behaves in a particular way.

4 Discussion of personality concerns uniqueness and similarities. Studies on personality can be divided into two main approaches, nomothetic and idiographic.

5 People vary in their abilities and intelligence. Emotional intelligence (EI) focuses on the range of the individual's interpersonal skills and emotional qualities.

6 Attitudes provide a state of readiness or tendency to respond in a particular way. Assessment of attitudes is vital in selecting potential employees and managers.

7 Psychometric tests and personality questionnaires may help to identify individual characteristics but are subject to doubts and criticisms about their predictive value.

8 Diversity focuses on the multiplicity of individual differences among people. Valuing differences is not easy and demands the effective management of diversity.

9 An increasing number of organisations appear to recognise the business case for diversity but there are potential criticisms, including concern for moral and social issues.

10 Effective organisational performance demands an understanding of, and a response to, a work climate that respects and values individual differences and diversity.

Review and discussion questions

1 Explain fully what you see as the main issues and difficulties relating to the effective management of individuals at work.

2 How would you explain the big five model of personality traits? What value for the practical manager do you place on this model?

3 To what extent do you believe you can relate an individual's personality type to career choice and successful work performance?

4 Explain your understanding of emotional intelligence and discuss critically its significance and applications for work organisations.

5 Why are attitudes difficult to measure and change? Explain your understanding of cognitive dissonance.

6 Relating to your own experience where possible, discuss critically both the potential benefits and limitations of psychometric testing.

7 What questions would you ask to provide an assessment of the individual characteristics of one person from your work or study group? How accurate do you feel your assessment is likely to be?

→

8   To what extent do you see a clear differentiation between equal opportunities and recognition and effective management of diversity in the workplace?

9   Discuss critically the contention that too much attention is given to the advantages for business from managing diversity rather than to broader moral or social concerns.

10   Discuss the significance of individual differences and major ways in which these differences are manifested in the work situation.

ASSIGNMENT

If you're still not sure where you fall on the introvert–extrovert spectrum, you can assess yourself here. Answer each question 'true' or 'false', choosing the answer that applies to you more often than not.*

1 _____ I prefer one-on-one conversations to group activities.
2 _____ I often prefer to express myself in writing.
3 _____ I enjoy solitude.
4 _____ I seem to care less than my peers about wealth, fame, and status.
5 _____ I dislike small talk, but I enjoy talking in depth about topics that matter to me.
6 _____ People tell me that I'm a good listener.
7 _____ I'm not a big risk-taker.
8 _____ I enjoy work that allows me to 'dive in' with few interruptions.
9 _____ I like to celebrate birthdays on a small scale, with only one or two close friends or family members.
10 _____ People describe me as 'soft-spoken' or 'mellow'.
11 _____ I prefer not to show or discuss my work with others until it's finished.
12 _____ I dislike conflict.
13 _____ I do my best work on my own.
14 _____ I tend to think before I speak.
15 _____ I feel drained afrer being out and about, even if I've enjoyed myself.
16 _____ I often let calls go through to voice mail.
17 _____ If I had to choose, I'd prefer a weekend with absolutely nothing to do to one with too many things scheduled.
18 _____ I don't enjoy multitasking.
19 _____ I can concentrate easily.
20 _____ In classroom situations, I prefer lectures to seminars.

Source: Susan Cain, *Quiet: The Power of Introverts in a World That Can't Stop Talking*, Viking an imprint of Penguin Books (2012) pp. 13–14.

(a) Discuss your answers with colleagues. To what extent do they agree with you?
(b) What conclusions do you draw?
Further information may be provided by your tutor

*This is an informal quiz, not a scientifically validated personality test. The questions were formulated based on characteristics of introversion often accepted by contemporary researchers.

Personal skills and employability exercise

Objectives

Completing this exercise should help you to enhance the following skills:

- Mindful of your own attitudes and behaviours towards individual differences.
- Acceptance of the dimensions, benefits and impact of diversity.
- Develop greater respect and empathy towards other people.

Exercise

For each of the following ten statements you are required to make notes in order to indicate *honestly and fully* the extent to which you:

1. Believe in managing diversity for moral and social reasons.
2. Are happy mixing with people from different cultures.
3. Resist stereotyping or profiling individuals into general categories of people.
4. Show patience and understanding when dealing with people whose English language is limited.
5. Accept that positive discrimination can sometimes be fully justified.
6. View diversity as distinctly different from political correctness.
7. Enjoy learning about different cultures and values.
8. Believe that diversity enriches the working lives of all employees.
9. Feel comfortable working closely with a colleague who has a different sexual orientation.
10. Are willing to take orders from someone much younger or much older than yourself, or from the opposite gender.

Discussion

After completing the questionnaire, pair with a colleague – where possible with a different ethnicity, culture, gender or age group – and compare and discuss critically both sets of responses.

- To what extent were you each surprised by the responses or comments from your colleague?
- What do you and your colleague believe are the greatest obstacles to a harmonious, truly diverse workforce? How much consensus between you is there?
- Detail fully in writing what have your learnt about your awareness of, and attitude and adaptability to, diversity.

Case study
B&Q: the business case for diversity

B&Q is the largest chain of DIY (do-it-yourself) stores in the UK, selling materials and equipment for the home improvement and domestic gardening market. The founders, Richard Block and David Quayle, opened their first store in Southampton in 1969, and after nearly twenty years of growth the company was acquired by FW Woolworth and is presently part of the Kingfisher Group. Kingfisher also owns the Brico Depot, Screwfix and Castorama DIY stores and has a 50 per cent stake in the Koçtaş Group in Turkey, giving it a major presence in Europe and Asia. The majority of B&Q stores are in the UK and Ireland and the headquarters remain in Hampshire.

The business has always sourced some of its products from Chinese manufacturers and so had strong links in the Far East from the outset. These links helped the company to expand its sales business into the Far East and, in 1996, it opened a store in Taiwan. In 1999 it moved into mainland China and is now well established in the Chinese market with thirty-nine stores, including the world's largest, B&Q Beijing, which also sells furniture and furnishing materials. The nature of the Chinese property market has also made it viable for the company to offer a fitting and decorating service for customers moving into newly built apartments (called

Is diversity in the workplace simply political correctness? B&Q recognised the value of diversity after a new store staffed by over-50s outperformed its other stores
Source: B&Q plc

'Do-it-for-Me'), thereby expanding its business opportunities through a strategy of vertical integration.

In 2014 it operated 360 stores across the UK and Ireland, although that was set to reduce to 300 during 2015–16 as part of Kingfisher's plan to rationalise its overall business structure.[74] Despite being significantly affected by the drop in the housing market during 2007–9, B&Q continued to perform strongly, and in December 2014 its 'Sharesave' employee ownership scheme announced £3.3 million growth, giving employee investors an average dividend of £1573.[75]

B&Q and the 'demographic time bomb'

As is noted towards the end of this chapter, the UK population is ageing, and the impact of this so-called 'demographic time bomb' began to generate particular concerns during the late 1980s. Some businesses, like B&Q, took a critical look at their current employment practices as a result of predicted shortages in certain parts of the labour market, and the consequent fear of intensified competition between employers for younger workers. This was particularly important for a growing company like B&Q, which might find its expansion plans would be seriously harmed by labour shortages. In 1989, therefore, B&Q management reviewed the workforce, and noted that not only did it have a predominantly young age profile (the majority of staff were aged 16–26), but also staff turnover costs were particularly

high in the 18–20-year-old category. They also noted positive customer feedback about their older staff, who appeared to deliver better customer service, partly because of their own knowledge of DIY.

The company management decided to tackle the problem by challenging widely held views about the disadvantages and problems of employing older workers. Initially, the B&Q board expressed some concerns about the proposal to target older people in the labour market and was naturally cautious about unproven claims of their effectiveness.

In 1990 it seemed to make good common sense to employ older people but a number of stereotypes and issues were raised. Answers were needed to explode these myths.[76]

The concerns and myths about older workers reflected findings in other studies on the subject, such as that reported in 1993 to the Institute of Personnel Management (now the CIPD).[77] These included both positive and negative features; for instance, older workers were seen as more reliable, loyal, conscientious and hard working than younger ones; at the same time they were viewed as less adaptable, especially to new technology, as well as being less able and less motivated to learn or be trained. Other studies have shown that stereotypical views about older workers tend to cluster under general headings of poor performance (including those related to assumptions about age-related physical impairment), absenteeism and turnover.[78] There were also concerns about the relationship between younger and older workers, and particularly those between young managers and older staff members.

B&Q managers decided that it would be important to collect some hard evidence if they were to gain the backing of the business owners. In 1990 B&Q opened a new store in Macclesfield, staffed wholly by workers over 50. The experiment was monitored by a research team from Warwick University, who carried out a study to benchmark the Macclesfield store's performance against a selection of four similar stores during its first year of operation. The results were significant: the Warwick team reported that the Macclesfield store had higher profits, substantially reduced staff turnover, over a third less absenteeism and almost two-thirds less 'shrinkage' (loss to stock as the result of damage or pilfering by staff and customers).[79] Many of the board's concerns had clearly been put to rest; the business case for diversifying the workforce had been supported by the evidence. B&Q therefore began to adopt a positive approach towards the recruitment and employment of an age-diverse workforce. This was more than ten years before age discrimination legislation came into operation in the UK, and fifteen years before the scrapping of the mandatory retirement age. Further research in 1995 confirmed the initial results, leading the company to reaffirm its initial commitment to increasing the age diversity of its workforce. There were clear indications that the policy is about good business in all senses of the words. In 2000 the company became one of the founding members of the Employers Forum on Age (EFA),[80] an independent group of over 200 UK employers that sets out to campaign for and support the cause of employing an age-diverse workforce, and now part of the Employers Network for Equality and Inclusion.[81]

Diversity at B&Q: the growing agenda

Having been successful with its approach to employing the over 50s (25 per cent of its workforce is now over 50), B&Q also recognises the value of a broader approach to diversity. The company website includes statements about its current approach to ethics and respect for the diversity of people.

The commitment of the Group's employees is vital to ensure that high standards of customer care and service are maintained throughout the business. The Group is fully committed to treating its employees and customers with dignity and respect, and to valuing diversity. It is Group policy to:

- *ensure there is no discrimination in employment on the grounds of race, gender, age, disability, marital status, sexual orientation or religious belief;*
- *implement measures in stores to ensure a level of customer service for disabled people equivalent to that offered to non-disabled people; and*
- *maintain a mechanism which customers and employees can use to give feedback on the Group's performance and ensure that all customer comments are analysed, responded to and acted upon.*[82]

B&Q's diversity manager reports directly to the company chief executive, and the Kingfisher board now takes an active interest in the diversity strategy, which extends to a commitment to increase the proportion of women at senior manager and board level. It also includes a strong commitment to cultural diversity, and to people with disabilities as both customers and employees. The company reflects all this in its advertising and publicity material as well as its personnel and management policies, thus making diversity an important part of the business's brand values and public image.

The disability policy was formulated in 1998 and, like the age policy, it links the importance of understanding and integrating disability issues into the business strategy. The twin goals are to remove barriers that make working and shopping at B&Q difficult for disabled people. Similarly, the cultural diversity strategy at B&Q goes beyond simple compliance measures to ensure that the company does not breach the law. In 2001 the company discovered that over 1,000 of its staff were bilingual, and that between them they spoke over sixty languages other than English, including British Sign Language. Staff are actively encouraged to use languages other than English where this can help to understand and respond to customer needs, and many wear language badges to indicate this. The company produces a cultural diversity information pack for use in stores, together with a calendar of religious and cultural festivals, which not only helps staff to understand customers, but assists managers with work scheduling.

What next for B&Q?

The economic downturn and the particular problems in the UK housing market during 2007–9 have clearly had a major impact on the home improvement sector generally. However, B&Q managed to retain its market share and generate a healthy operating profit despite this difficult trading environment. The key to B&Q's strategy is its people; real staff feature heavily in its advertising campaigns and the company is investing in training with in-house versions of City and Guilds retail management qualifications and apprenticeships. This helps ensure all staff have both knowledge and confidence about all key areas of business, from practical DIY skills to understanding finance, and underpins a key corporate objective of:

Creating employment and a brighter future for our people, the environment and wider communities.[83]

Tasks

1 Why did B&Q adopt its present approach to diversity? How far do you agree or disagree with these reasons for its action, and why?

2 Review B&Q's approach in the light of theories about personality. Which of the theoretical approaches do you think might best explain the company's approach to its staff and customers?

→

3 How might the B&Q approach to diversity encourage individuals (both staff and customers) to contribute to the organisation's commercial performance?

4 B&Q operates in a very specific sector, namely retail DIY building and gardening materials and equipment. Would its approach to diversity translate to other types of organisation, for example an online or telephone retail insurance company (e.g. selling motor, travel or home insurance), a car manufacturer or a state-run school or hospital?

Notes and references

1. McCrae, R. R. and Costa, P. T. 'More Reasons to Adopt the Five-Factor Model', *American Psychologist,* vol. 44, no. 2, 1989, pp. 451–2.

2. Bayne, R. 'The Big Five versus the Myers-Briggs', *The Psychologist,* January 1994, pp. 14–17.

3. Barrick, M. R. and Mount, M. K. 'The Big Five Personality Dimensions and Job Performance: A Meta-Analysis', *Personnel Psychology,* Spring 1991, pp. 1–26.

4. Mount, M. K., Barrick, M. R. and Strauss, J. P. 'Validity of Observer Ratings of the Big Five Personality Factors', *Journal of Applied Psychology,* April 1994, p. 272.

5. Bentall, R. P. 'Personality Traits May Be Alive, They May Even Be Well, But Are They Really Useful?', *The Psychologist,* July 1993, p. 307.

6. Robertson, I. 'Undue Diligence', *People Management,* no. 22, November 2001, pp. 42–3.

7. Lord, W. and Rust, J. 'The Big Five Revisited: Where Are We Now? A Brief Review of the Relevance of the Big Five for Occupational Assessment', *Selection and Development Review,* vol. 19, no. 4, 2003, pp. 15–18.

8. Luthans, F. and Youssef, C. M. 'Emerging Positive Organizational Behavior', *Journal of Management,* vol. 33, no. 3, 2007, pp. 321–49.

9. Moutafi, J., Furnham, A. and Crump, J. 'Is Managerial Level Related to Personality? **British Journal of Management, vol. 18, no. 3, 2007, pp. 272–80.**

10. Eysenck, H. J. *Eysenck on Extraversion,* Crosby Lockwood Staples (1973).

11. Mabey, B. 'The Majority of Large Companies Use Occupational Tests', *Guidance and Assessment Review,* vol. 5, no. 3, 1989.

12. Personality tests have been debated by: Bartram, D. 'Addressing the Abuse of Personality Tests', *Personnel Management,* April 1991, pp. 34–9; and Fletcher, C. 'Personality Tests: The Great Debate', *Personnel Management,* September 1991, pp. 38–42.

13. Howarth, E. 'A Source of Independent Variation: Convergence and Divergence in the Work of Cattell and Eysenck', in Dreger, R. M. (ed.) *Multivariate Personality Research,* Claiton (1972).

14. Rogers, C. *A Way of Being,* Houghton Mifflin (1980).

15. Cooley, C. 'The Social Self', in Parsons, T., Shils, E., Naegele, K. D. and Pitts, J. R. (eds) *Theories of Society,* Free Press (1965).

16. Erikson, E. H. *Identity and the Life Cycle,* W.W. Norton (1980).

17. Hunt, J. W. *Managing People at Work: A Manager's Guide to Behaviour in Organisations*, third edition, McGraw-Hill (1992).

18. Jung, C. G. *Analytical Psychology: Its Theory and Practice,* Routledge & Kegan Paul (1968); see also Jacobi, J. *Psychology of C. G. Jung,* seventh edition, Routledge & Kegan Paul (1968).

19. Myers, I. B. *Introduction to Type,* sixth edition, Consulting Psychologists Press (1998); and Myers, K. D. and Kirby, L. K. *Introduction to Type Dynamics and Development,* second edition, Consulting Psychologists Press (2000).

20. Vernon, M. 'Why Jung still matters', *Management Today,* June 2011, pp. 4–50.

21. Kelly, G. A. *The Psychology of Personal Constructs,* W.W. Norton (1955); see also Kelly's theory as described by Bannister, D. and Fansella, F., in *Inquiring Mind: The Theory of Personal Constructs,* Penguin (1971), pp. 50–1.

22. Hochschild, A. R. *The Managed Heart: Commercialization of Human Feeling,* University of California Press (1983).

23. Friedman, M. and Rosenman, R. *Type A Behavior and Your Heart,* Knopf (1974).

24. Rosenmann, R., Friedman, F. and Straus, R. 'A Predictive Study of CHD', *Journal of the American Medical Association,* vol. 89, 1964, pp. 15–22; and Warr, P. and Wall, T. *Work and Well Being,* Penguin (1975).

25. See, for example, Jex, S. M., Adams, G. A., Elacqua, T. C. and Bachrach, D. G. 'Type "A" as a Moderator of Stressors and Job Complexity: A Comparison of Achievement

Strivings and Impatience-Irritability', *Journal of Applied Psychology,* vol. 32, no. 5, 2002, pp. 977–96.

26. Gratton, L., *Hot Spots,* Financial Times Prentice Hall (2007).

27. Ibid., p. 83.

28. Spearman, C. *The Abilities of Man,* Macmillan (1927).

29. Vernon, P. E. *The Structure of Human Abilities,* Methuen (1950).

30. Thurstone, L. L. 'Primary Mental Abilities', *Psychometric Monographs,* no. 1, 1938.

31. Guilford, J. P. *The Nature of Human Intelligence,* McGraw-Hill (1967).

32. Salovey, P and Mayer, J. D. 'Emotional Intelligence', *Imagination, Cognition and Personality,* vol. 9, 1990, pp. 185–211.

33. Goleman, D. *Emotional Intelligence,* Bloomsbury (1996), p. 34.

34. Goleman, D. *Working with Emotional Intelligence,* Bantam Books (1998).

35. Boyatzis, R., Goleman, D. and Hay/McBer, *Emotional Competence Inventory Feedback Report,* Hay Group (1999).

36. 'Management Futures: The World in 2018', Chartered Management Institute, March 2008.

37. Landale, A. 'Must Have EQ', *Manager, The British Journal of Administrative Management,* February/March 2007, pp. 24–5.

38. Venus, D. 'Emotional responses', *Chartered Secretary,* December 2009, pp. 30–1.

39. Ibid.

40. Dann, J. 'Managing Your Emotions', *Professional Manager,* vol. 17, no. 4, 2008, pp. 32–4.

41. Alexander, R. 'The Dark Side of Emotional Intelligence', *Management Today,* April 2011, pp. 46–50.

42. Ribeaux, P. and Poppleton, S. E. *Psychology and Work,* Macmillan (1978).

43. Gross, R. D. *Psychology: The Science of Mind and Behaviour,* Edward Arnold (1987).

44. Hofstede, G. *Culture's Consequences: International Differences in Work-Related Values,* Sage (1980).

45. Katz, D. 'The Functional Approach to the Study of Attitudes', *Public Opinion Quarterly,* issue 21, 1960, pp. 163–204.

46. 'Undertaking Employee Attitude Surveys', Checklist 078, Chartered Management Institute, March 2011.

47. Likert, R. 'A Technique for the Measurement of Attitudes', *Archives of Psychology,* vol. 22, no. 1, 1932, pp. 1–55.

48. Heider, F. 'Attitudes and Cognitive Organization', *Journal of Psychology,* vol. 21, 1946, pp. 107–12.

49. Festinger, L. A. *A Theory of Cognitive Dissonance,* Row, Peterson (1957); reissued by Stanford University Press and Tavistock (1962).

50. Goss, D. *Principles of Human Resource Management,* Routledge (1994).

51. Gibbons, P., Baron, H., Nyfield, G. and Robertson, I. 'The Managerial Performance and Competences', Conference paper given at the British Psychological Society Occupational Psychology Conference, University of Warwick, January 1995.

52. Yeung, R. 'Mind games', *Chartered Secretary,* June 2010, pp. 38–9.

53. 'Managing for Diversity', Checklist 152, Chartered Management Institute, February 2014.

54. Ibid.

55. www.enei.org.uk

56. 'Back to Basics: Acas' Experience of Equality and Diversity in the Workplace', ACAS Policy Discussion Paper no. 5, November 2006.

57. 'Talent not Tokenism: The Business Benefits of Workforce Diversity', CBI and TUC, June 2008.

58. 'Management Recruitment: Understanding Routes to Greater Diversity', Chartered Management Institute, June 2008.

59. Reeves, R. 'Worth not Birth', *Management Today,* September 2013, pp. 36–9.

60. 'Building Diverse Workplaces', Business in the Community, March 2011. See also **www.bitc.org.uk**

61. Information kindly provided by Tim Taylor, Manager Diversity & Inclusion, Lloyds Banking Group.

62. Khan, S. *P.U.S.H. for Success,* Vermilion (2006), p. 230.

63. See, for example, 'What's Keeping Women out of the Top Jobs?', *Social Agenda,* European Commission, no. 16, February 2008, pp. 7–10.

64. Barber, B. 'The diversity barrier', *Governance + Compliance,* April 2014, p. 12.

65. Spira, L. F. and Pitcher, H. 'Questioning quotas', *Governance + Compliance,* April 2014, p. 18.

66. 'Older and more diverse', *Social Agenda,* The European Commission Magazine, no. 26, March 2011, pp. 11–14.

67. Barnes, H. 'Managing the generation gap', *Manager, The British Institute of Administrative Management,* Autumn 2010, p. 30.

68. 'Managing an ageing workforce: How employers are adapting to an older labour market', Chartered Management Institute and Chartered Institute of Personnel and Development, September 2010.

69. Wilton, P. 'Diversity is a Blueprint for Business', *Professional Manager,* Spring 2014, p. 19.

70. 'Managing for Diversity', Checklist 152, Chartered Management Institute, February 2014.

71. Nordström, K. and Ridderstråle, J., 'Funky Inc.,' in Crainer, S. and Dearlove, D. (eds) *Financial Times Handbook of Management,* second edition, Financial Times Prentice Hall (2001), p. 63.

72. Kirton, G. and Greene, A.-M. *The Dynamics of Managing Diversity,* Butterworth–Heinemann (2000).

73. Lucas, E. 'Making Inclusivity a Reality', *Professional Manager,* vol. 16, no. 4, July 2007, pp. 32–5.

74. BBC News, 'B&Q Set to Close About 60 Stores', 31 March 2015.

75. Kingfisher Press Release, 5 December 2014, http://www.kingfisher.com/index.asp?pageid=55&newsid=1081 (accessed 10 February 2015).

76. B&Q 'Is Age a Barrier to Employment? Equality and Diversity; Achieving a Balanced Workforce'.

77. Warr, P. and Pennington, J. *Views about age discrimination and older workers,* Institute of Personnel Management (1993).

78. Stoney, C. and Roberts, M. 'The case for the older worker at Tesco: An examination of attitudes, assumptions and attributes', Carleton University School of Public Policy and Administration Working Paper No. 53, 2003.

79. B&Q 'Is Age a Barrier to Employment? Equality and Diversity; Achieving a Balanced Workforce'.

80. The Employers Forum on Age can be found at www.efa.org.uk

81. The Employers Network for Equality and Inclusion, http://www.enei.org.uk

82. Kingfisher Annual Report and Accounts 2013/14, p. 7, http://www.kingfisher.com/files/reports/annual_report_2014/files/pdf/annual_report_2014.pdf (accessed 20 July 2015).

83. Ibid., p. 7.

CHAPTER 5
Learning and development

Learning and personal development is an implicit feature of management and organisational behaviour. It is important to understand how people learn and develop their knowledge and skills in order to cope effectively with the complex and changing demands of the workplace. Attention must be given to the management of learning within organisations. Managers also need to develop their personal development aspirations with the goals of the organisation.

Learning outcomes

After completing this chapter you should have enhanced your ability to:

- explain the importance of learning and development in organisational behaviour;
- debate the value of different theories and studies about learning;
- assess the nature and importance of learning styles;
- review the importance of knowledge management and its impact on learning;
- explain the nature and importance of creativity in organisations;
- evaluate the importance of mentoring and coaching for learning and development;
- review the effective management of the learning process.

Critical review and reflection

Without learning, individuals will not be able to develop or cope with change and organisations will not survive. Whatever the required knowledge or skills of an individual, the motivation and ability to learn is arguably of greatest importance.

What do YOU think? What does learning mean to YOU and how do YOU learn best?

The importance and significance of learning

Globalisation and technological advances have heightened the pace of change, including the relative importance of different occupations and skills, and transformed the way we live and work. Learning inevitably involves an examination of how change takes place. An understanding of the ways in which people learn and develop is a fundamental feature of organisational behaviour and management. **Learning** is generally defined in terms of the acquisition of knowledge that leads to a relatively permanent change in behaviour, which results from experience. Individuals may experience a temporary change in behaviour because of, for example, maturation or ageing, or short-term factors such as tiredness or alcohol. These temporary changes are of a different nature to those associated with the process of learning, which results in knowledge or a relatively permanent change in behaviour. Learning can be a deliberate and formal process or an unintentional outcome of nature, activity or progression.

An understanding of how people learn is a highly significant area of study and has been of continual interest in the development of psychology as a science. Learning is a function of the inner workings of our mind and has created a number of methodological difficulties. Individuals differ in their learning capabilities, their style and their creative responses.

Imagine, for example, these scenarios:

- a student attending an action learning set;
- a person undertaking a fork-lift truck driving lesson;
- a trainee observing a manager deal with an irate customer;
- a nurse measuring blood pressure for the first time;
- a manager completing a learning portfolio;
- an older employee introduced to a new financial computer system.

These scenarios all share the common feature that learning has taken or is about to take place. They demonstrate that a discussion of learning involves not only knowledge and skills, but also attitudes and social behaviour. Learning implies a different internal state, which may result in **new behaviours and actions** (e.g. a new skill such as taking blood pressure) or **new understanding and knowledge** (e.g. a new subject area such as finance). Sometimes behaviour and knowledge coincide (e.g. learning a language, becoming IT literate); at other times people will learn to act in certain ways without an underlying understanding of the reasons why (e.g. operating machinery without an understanding of its mechanical features).

Individual learning is a lifelong process that is essential if people are to be able to cope with the changing nature of work organisations. *Payne and Whittaker,* for example, stress the importance of skills for the future and **lifelong learning.**

> *Lifelong learning will be the only way to keep abreast of the pace of change in a technological age, requiring flexible labour markets that operate in an increasingly global economy. Lifetime careers will become a rarity in the future, and the way that people are able to deal with this is by reskilling through lifelong learning. Business can only be competitive with a highly skilled, highly educated workforce. Lifelong learning and self-development will increase an individual's employment prospects and provide business with the skills it needs.*[1]

Learning and the social world

Much of what we learn takes place without any necessary deliberations or assessments. Learning can be seen to be a continuous and automatic process, often taking place in a social context. The spontaneous nature of learning can be observed in young children's play as they imitate and model their behaviour and attitudes on the people around them. Learning has an active and dynamic nature. As active participants, we engage and relate to the people around us. Our ability to learn will be affected by both our innate potential and our social experiences.

Learning, therefore, links the individual to the social world and is both a personal and a social experience. Often, learning is an event that is shared with others. The process may be a deliberate sharing of information or guiding behaviour – as, for example, in the parent–child relationship when parents are attempting to socialise the child into acceptable ways of behaving, or in organisations where new members are taught opening phrases when answering the telephone. At other times it is the actual sharing of the learning experience – going through the same learning process – that makes the process challenging and valuable. It is through the support of others that individuals can find both strength and rewards.

Learning occurs in many ways; information or skills may be imparted quite explicitly and at the same time the implicit values and attitudes of the trainer will also be communicated. Learning is a rich experience. At times we may be learning 'incidentally' as we acquire, process and remember information automatically. (**See also the discussion on mentoring as part of the learning process, later in this chapter.**)

> *When learning is work it is ineffective – look at all the executives 'forced' to go on training courses. The learning that sticks has a joy of discovery, playfulness. Many executives have been to brainstorming seminars where an atmosphere of deliberate playfulness often stimulates high levels of executive learning for an hour or so. Corporations of the future are going to need to find ways to extend that hour to cover the entire working day.[2]*

Learning and emotions

Learning implies that an individual has experienced 'something', has stored that experience and is able to refer to and/or use it at a later time. Learning and memory are inextricably linked. There are many factors that influence both the rate and enjoyment of learning (*see* Figure 5.1). The rewards and punishments levelled at us in the past will affect our motivation and attitudes towards learning in the present and the future. Expectations of others and the climate that surrounds us will determine our readiness to learn.

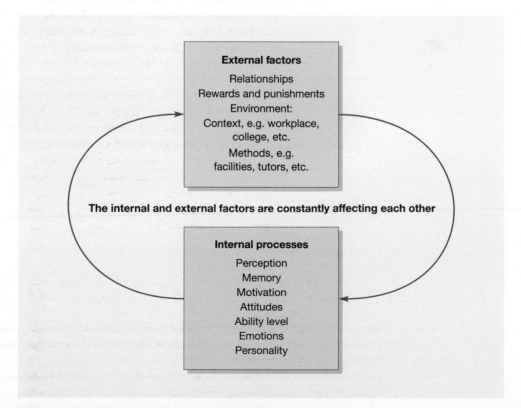

Figure 5.1 Factors influencing the learning process

Feelings generated by the process of learning are very powerful and often tend to be pleasur-able. A sense of achievement that often accompanies the completion of a learning process can lead to an enhancement of an individual's self-worth and esteem. However, learning can also be an uncomfortable experience; it can 'shake an individual's comfort zones'; it can provide new and alarming perceptions and can be disruptive and anxiety-provoking. An illustration of this has been noted by trainers in diversity, who need to challenge individuals' attitudes and perceptions when there is evidence of prejudice:

> *Learning to learn about diversity can be, and may even have to be, a painful process. It is not a comfortable experience to learn that we have prejudices we need to deal with. It is not comfortable to find that our own view of the world is just one of many and those other views are equally valid.*[3]

Critical review and reflection

Testing *what* has been learned is ingrained in our society and accounts largely for the ways in which individuals are compared and judged. This is too short-sighted. Far more attention should be given to *why* or *how* a person has learned.

What is YOUR critical assessment of this contention? How would YOU attempt to monitor the why and how of learning?

A declaration on learning

Eight distinguished scholars on learning in organisations launched a declaration summarising their collective thoughts on the nature of learning, its benefits and what should be done about learning. They singled out learning as a key process for individuals, organisations and for soci-ety as a whole for the twenty-first century. They believe that it is too easy to take learning for granted and treat it as an automatic part of the human condition. They claim that individuals frequently do not organise or plan their learning and they leave the evaluation of learning to chance. Typically, individuals fail to check what exactly they can do better or differently as a result of the learning experience.[4] Two parts of the declaration are shown in Table 5.1.

Organisations and the management of learning

If learning can result in the benefits outlined by *Burgoyne et al.* in Table 5.1, it is clearly in the organisation's best interest to ensure it utilises the knowledge and skills of all its employees. But how do organisations achieve these outcomes? It is surprising to observe that in some organisations learning is still left to chance. The individual employee is expected to 'pick up' behaviour, attitudes and skills. Much learning appears to come about as a natural con-sequence of the demands of the job, overcoming problems and interactions with colleagues. That is, learning achieved through experience.

It becomes difficult, therefore, to separate how learning occurs without taking some account of the relationship between employee and manager and the general climate of the organisation (**discussed in Chapter 15**). In the past, organisations may have relied largely on the stability of the organisation structure for knowledge transmission. Managers would tend to know who to go to for advice and would seek out the older and experienced employees who held the 'know-how'. This knowledge and wisdom, accumulated over years of work, was a precious store of information. However, such a store was rarely formalised or articulated and would be communicated only on an informal basis. Communication to the next generation of employees was an important part of the organisation's culture and socialisation process.

Table 5.1 A declaration on learning: John Burgoyne, Ian Cunningham, Bob Garratt, Peter Honey, Andrew Mayo, Alan Mumford, Michael Pearn, Mike Pedler

Learning: the central issue for the twenty-first century	The benefits
Learning is the most powerful, engaging, rewarding and enjoyable aspect of our personal and collective experience. The ability to learn about learning and become masters of the learning process is the critical issue for the next century	The following benefits assume that the learning in question has both morally acceptable intent and outcome:
Our understanding of learning has generally been restricted to formal teaching and training. It is often seen as unrelated to daily life and work. Systems of accreditation are sometimes used as a way of unfairly discriminating between individuals and are often felt to be irrelevant to real needs. The biggest missed opportunity for policy-makers and leaders is the failure to capitalise on the collective learning ability of people	For individuals • Learning is the key to developing a person's potential • Learning to learn is the key to effective learning • Learning enables the individual to meet the demands of change • The capacity to learn is an asset that never becomes obsolete • Embracing learning helps the individual to acknowledge that learning is more than formal education and training
Organisational leaders need to harness relevant knowledge and experience so that the organisation as a whole and the people who comprise it can learn more effectively. The same principle applies at community, national and international levels. Every person, team and organisation both survives and progresses through the ability to internalise and act upon this fundamental truth	For organisations • Learning increases everyone's capacity to contribute to the success of organisations • Learning enables the organisation to be more effective in meeting its goals • Learning emancipates the organisation through clarification of purpose, vision, values and behaviour • A focus on learning, planned and unplanned, formal and informal, produces a wider range of solutions to organisational issues • Learning helps to achieve a better balance between long-term organisational effectiveness and short-term organisational efficiency
This declaration does not contain all there is to say on the subject of learning. It does, however, reflect the thinking of the eight signatories. The declaration is designed to stimulate and encourage dialogue	For society • Society survives and thrives through learning • A focus on capturing and sharing learning contributes to a more cohesive society • Individual and collective learning reinforces the informed, conscious and discriminating choices that underpin democracy • Learning helps to enhance the capacity of individuals to create a more fulfilled society

Source: Burgoyne, J., *et al.* 'The Debate Starts Here', in *People Management in Perspective: A Collection of Key Articles Published in the Last Year on Training and Development*, IPD (April 1999), pp. 16–17.

Older employees were useful as a source of knowledge and guidance for younger ones. Many held the role of an informal mentor and were much appreciated by their younger subordinates. (**Mentoring and coaching are discussed later in this chapter.**)

Practices such as downsizing and outsourcing have had a major effect on this layer of experienced employees. Not only are relationships disrupted by the restructuring of the business, but also there is the potential for the complete loss of this powerful and important reservoir of knowledge and understanding.

How do people learn?

Early classic studies of learning offer explanations for simple learning situations. The principles arising from these laboratory experiments remain applicable to an understanding of organisational behaviour. The effects of rewards and punishment (the ways in which behaviour can be shaped and modified) have considerable relevance in understanding the motivation of individuals and the culture of organisations. **These are called behaviourist theories.**

Dissatisfaction with the earliest theories led researchers to consider more complex learning situations. **Cognitive theories of learning** have particular application to an understanding of individual differences in learning situations. They offer models that explain the process of learning and take into account different preferences and styles.

Critical review and reflection

The world of computer games is now advancing fast in the new digital culture. They help stimulate literacy, improve problem-solving and develop hand-to-eye co-ordination. Individuals can connect across different continents and in different time zones.

Do YOU agree that the future of learning is clearly playful? To what extent would YOU encourage the use of computer games for students?

Behaviourist approach to learning

Theories of learning have their roots in the history of psychology, and some of the earliest experimental psychologists focused their attention on animal learning and were keen to develop laws of learning. They were interested only in behaviour that could be objectively measured and they designed experiments that maximised key scientific conditions: **control, reliability** and **validity.** A school of psychology called **behaviourism** developed out of these early research studies. As the name suggests, researchers were interested in the study of behaviour and those actions that could be observed, measured and controlled. Ideas and thoughts in people's minds were considered inaccessible to objective, scientific measurement and were therefore excluded from study.

Exercise and association

Watson developed the **Law of Exercise and Association.** This refers to the process that occurs when two responses are connected and repeatedly exercised. Watson was particularly interested in the study of fixed habits and routines.[5] In organisational life we can see evidence of this in the habits and routines at work. These behaviours can become 'locked in', believed to be 'the only way' of completing certain tasks – a part of cultural life; it is as if they are fixed into beds of concrete. Speech is a further illustration of our routine habits. The predictability of a greeting provides acknowledgement of our existence – when people say 'How are you?' they do not expect to be given a rundown of your medical history. The rhetorical question is really saying, 'Hello – I see, acknowledge and recognise you.'

Classical conditioning

Pavlov,[6] working in Russia, developed a theory called **classical conditioning.** His laboratory experiments demonstrated how instinctive reflexes, such as salivation, could be 'conditioned' to respond to a new situation and a new stimulus (*see* Figure 5.2). Pavlov, through his repeated

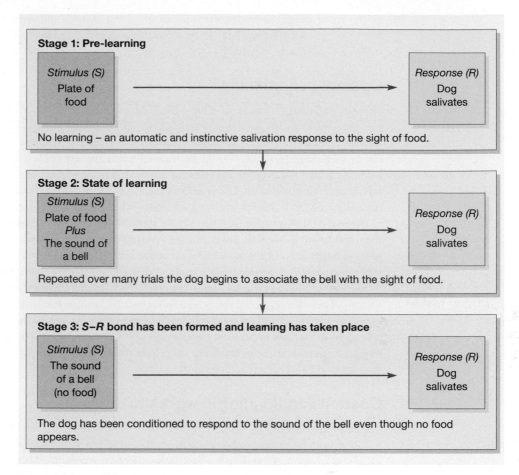

Figure 5.2 Classical conditioning

experimental studies, showed the power and strength of association. How can we relate these experiments on dogs to behaviour at work? There are times when our body responds more quickly than our mind. We may have an initial panic reaction to a situation without necessarily realising why. Physiological reactions may be appropriate in times of stressful situations – our body may be in a state of readiness to run (fight or flight reaction).

At other times our reactions may be 'conditioned' because of previous associations of pain, guilt or fear. Smells and sounds are particularly evocative and may release physiological reactions akin to the Pavlovian experiments. Thus, sitting in a waiting room at the dentist's and hearing the sound of the drill may invoke an increase in our blood pressure or heart rate – nothing to do with any actual pain we may be experiencing. Returning to school for a parents' evening may invoke feelings of 'dread' or 'pleasure' depending on our own childhood experiences of school and its associations. Training for some occupations may depend upon learned associations and automatic reactions, an example being initial military training. If fire drills are to be successful, immediate reaction to the bell or siren is essential.

Law of Effect

Thorndike's work drew attention to the outcomes of learning – **the Law of Effect.** All learning is a process of stimulus–response (S–R). The strength of the S–R link is dependent upon the extent to which the experience is pleasurable. Behaviour that results in a favourable outcome is more likely to be repeated. Thorndike watched animals in new situations and noted how they learned to adapt successfully to the environment. He noted that in his experiments there were no flashes of insight shown but learning would occur by **trial and error**. Over time these correct responses were 'stamped in'. If an action was successful and led to a reward, the behaviour was more likely to be repeated.[7]

Operant conditioning

Skinner advanced the ideas of Thorndike and produced a thesis of **operant conditioning**. Skinner's experiments on animals showed the effects of reward and punishment on animal learning. Unlike classical conditioning, learning was rewarded after the response had occurred. He proved that a response would be learned when the animal associated the behavioural response with a reward (or reinforcement) and could be broken with punishment. Partial reinforcement strengthened the S–R bond and the behaviour was more resistant to extinction. The reward seemed to hold even greater importance when it was given intermittently.[8]

Negative reinforcement was also shown to be powerful. These experiments demonstrated the importance of the S–R bond, but the reward was the prevention of something painful or nasty occurring. *Not* being shocked is the reward in such experiments. Negative reinforcement is not punishment. **Punishment** is trying to break the stimulus–reward bond.

Skinner and his researchers applied operant conditioning theory to many experimental situations. They demonstrated the power and control of simple learning principles: the identification of a stimulus and a reward following a successful response. Skinner and colleagues were able to train animals to perform complex acts by a process known as 'shaping'. Behaviour is shaped through a series of small but successive steps, with rewards given for those responses that approximate the desired end result.

Operant conditioning in work situations

The technique of shaping (modifying and controlling behaviour) and the identification of the S–R bond can be applied to work situations. Illustrations of the power of rewards can be seen in almost any work organisation – for example, bonuses, commission, prizes for reaching sales targets and 'employee of the month' awards.

Intermittent reinforcement is another useful outcome of Skinner's research. If an employee always receives a reward, does its value diminish? Skinner's research would say 'yes'. There is an interesting parallel with this concept in transactional analysis, whereby too many positive verbal comments (called strokes) are described as 'marshmallow throwing'.[9] (**Transactional analysis is discussed in Chapter 6.**)

A difficult problem with the application of operant conditioning is that Skinner was dealing with 'hungry' animals; they had a clear drive to eat and therefore a plate of food was, no doubt, a reward. It is far more complex when we consider **rewards for people**. We may all have our own definitions of a 'reward'. Although money might be a suitable reward for some employees, others may prefer to have 'time out' or a symbolic gesture of the work they have achieved. So having a photograph on public display may be a proud and rewarding moment for some but other employees may be acutely embarrassed. How organisations reward their employees makes a statement about what they value. How different pay practices affect organisational and individual performance is a critical aspect of reward management.

The same principle applies to people's perception of punishment. Inappropriate behaviour at work can be punished directly by, for example, withholding rewards or by initiating the company's disciplinary procedure. Some managerial actions may be perceived as punishment, for example being sent on a training course or not being sent on an international assignment. Whether the punishment is real or perceived, it is likely to cause feelings of resentment in the mind of the employee. Hence, punishment results in negative psychological outcomes. Although the employee may comply with requirements, it is likely that resentment will lead to anger and/or apathy and psychological revenge.

Some organisations endeavour to exercise tight control over their employees' language and behaviour. Training new employees is a form of 'shaping' behaviour in line with written training objectives. As employees demonstrate their responses, they may be rewarded with a tick in the training box or a 'badge' that they wear on their clothing. Learning occurs incrementally, with the task divided into sub-goals, each with its own reward. Sometimes shaping can occur in training centres where peer assessment can add further power to the modification process. **See also the discussion on organisational behaviour modification in Chapter 7.**

Social learning

Supporters of the behavioural school appear to have neglected the influence of broader social interactions. Developing the work of Skinner, *Bandura* drew attention to the importance of environmental influences on observable behaviour. **Social learning theory** is based on the premise that people learn by observing and interacting with others and through imitation. Even aggressive behaviour can arguably be learned by imitation. The concept of **self-efficacy** refers to a person's perception of themselves and a belief in their ability to act in a particular way and successfully achieve a task.[10] People with a high level of self-efficacy tend to exhibit high work performance without becoming stressed.

People learn by watching others. The term 'modelling' was coined by *Miller and Dollard* to explain learning by imitating others and 'role models' as a label for those individuals who are held up as examples of good practice.[11] So, the trainees observing how to prepare a soufflé will imitate the actions of their role model. Interpersonal skills can also be learned by observation, and new recruits, by watching others, will 'pick up' the habits and techniques of those around them. Miller and Dollard's research brought attention to cognitive functions of thinking, perception, attention and memory in addition to behavioural responses. So, for instance, a trainee watching a supervisor deal with a customer complaint would need to attend to the customer's emotions, note the reaction of the supervisor and learn how the 'lessons' of this interaction could be applied to another situation.

Social learning also relates to standards of behaviour and action expected from members of the organisation by observing and imitating, for example working within the hierarchical structure, how to address other members of staff, physical appearanceor or acceptance of the psychological contract.

Critical review and reflection

Social learning theory is a simplification. Not all learning is a direct result of imitating others. Indeed, the concept of self-efficacy suggests that people with a strong belief in their own ability will discover and learn much for themselves.
What is YOUR view of the validity of social learning theory? Do YOU have a high level of self-efficacy?

Cognitive theories of learning

Focusing only on behaviour is useful but limited and cannot explain all forms of learning. The understanding and application of basic factual knowledge can arguably be learned through operant conditioning, for example computer-based training for call-centre staff. However, more advanced levels of learning require more active brain processes. The inner mind has particular relevance to understanding how, what and why people learn. Personality, perceptions, motivations and attitudes will all play their part in helping or hindering the learning process.

Behaviourism cannot easily explain the natural curiosity that humans have, the great desire to learn, to make sense of their environment and to feel competent in activities. Neither can it explain the extent of incidental learning that takes place. Observing changes in behaviour is only part of the learning process. To understand how and why people learn, attention must be given to myriad individual factors including plans, ambitions and goals.

Research conducted in the last century highlighted the fact that the process of learning was more complex than simple S–R associations. *Tolman* showed that rats allowed to wander freely through a maze to find food were capable of learning an image (a cognitive map) of the maze that they would use at a later time if their initial route was blocked.[12]

Learning styles

Learning styles indicate various approaches to, or methods of, learning and the ways in which people learn. This approach recognises that individuals have their own learning style and strategy. This influences how people prefer to learn. Some cognitive theorists have emphasised the cyclical nature of learning and its active nature. *Davis*[13] claims that 'experiential learning is an integration and alteration of thinking and doing'. Although there are a number of models of learning style, two of the best known and useful are that of David Kolb and that of Honey and Mumford.

The Kolb learning cycle

Kolb's learning cycle (*see* Figure 5.3) is typical of this approach and is one used frequently in the management literature.[14] It provides useful insights into the nature of learning:

- It demonstrates that there is no end to learning but only another turn of the cycle.
- Learners are not passive recipients but need actively to explore and test the environment.
- It identifies the importance of reflection and internalisation.
- It is a useful way of identifying problems in the learning process.

The approach emphasises the importance of the synthesis between individuals' behaviour and the evaluation of their actions. Reflection on what has been learned in order to experiment with new situations and to become aware of new possibilities is a vital part of the learning process. This is the very essence of **action learning**: going through the cycle that learners are exposed to, applying, reflecting and testing out their learning. This encourages in individuals

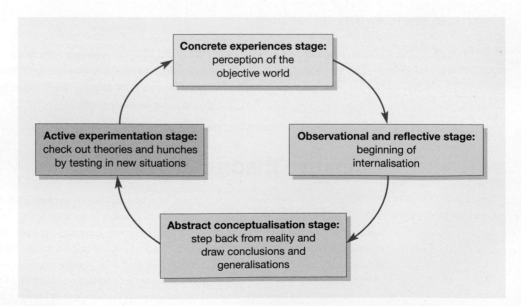

Figure 5.3 Kolb's learning cycle

habits compatible with the notion of lifelong learning. It is therefore no surprise that Kolb addresses his ideas to managers and suggests that experiential learning will enable managers to cope with change and complexity.

Kolb and his colleagues suggest that partnerships between education and industry should create feedback loops that enable interactions between ideas and action – certainly ideas that fit well into a learning organisation framework and into the concept of knowledge management, considered below.

Action learning

Learning includes social learning and also has a reflective element as members are asked to reflect on their experience and learning. Typically, **action learning** involves a small group of learners (action learning set) meeting regularly to undertake a practical, organisational-based project. It is based on real work issues and designed to help develop both the manager and the organisation. Action learning involves participants working together to find solutions to actual problems and reflecting on their experiences.

According to the CIPD, action learning can enhance the way people learn. Group members may increase their capacity to respond to new situations. By drawing on real work practices and working together, the set can encourage group members to apply new ideas to their role and help make changes to their current or future roles, or tackle joint projects.[15] Action learning can therefore be seen as relevant to group development and performance.

The emphasis is on learning and self-evaluation by doing, with advice and support from tutors and other course members. It is therefore essentially a learner-driven process. Action learning can be contentious compared with traditional programmed knowledge of development. There may be no formal structure and the process demands flexibility, with attention focused on questioning and challenging. The process can be daunting for some people and a supportive atmosphere is essential. However, *Gitsham* maintains that experiential learning is one of the most effective ways to build leadership skills: 'Action learning and learning through projects where you are in the real world engaging with people is very valuable.'[16]

Yukl refers to action learning as an approach often used for combining formal training with learning from experience. An alternative approach is to link projects to a process of mutual coaching and mentoring. Project participants identify their own learning objects and the group meets periodically to devise solutions to problems, evaluate progress and discuss what was learned.[17]

Honey and Mumford styles of learning

When applying the learning cycle to the study of individual differences, Kolb demonstrated that individuals may have a preference for one of the key stages, and therein lies their learning style. His work, developed by *Honey and Mumford*, has been applied to managerial behaviour.[18] Kolb identified four different styles of learning:

- **accommodative** – strong preference for concrete experiences and active experimentation (hands-on);
- **divergent** – preference for concrete experiences, but to reflect on these from different perspectives;
- **assimilative** – prefers to swing between reflection and conceptualisation and will use inductive reasoning to develop new theory;
- **convergent** – prefers to apply ideas, will take an idea and test it out in practice.

Honey and Mumford simplified Kolb's learning cycle and refined his learning-style questionnaire. They also identify four learning styles and associated patterns of behaviour:[19]

- **Activists – What's new? I'm game for anything.** Activists are enthusiastic, flexible and open-minded. They like the challenge of new experiences, but can become bored with long-term routine procedures. Activists enjoy the here and now. They tend to think first and consider consequences later.

- **Reflectors – I'd like time to think about this.** Reflectors are cautious and slow to reach conclusions. They stand back and observe and like to think things through carefully. By collection and analysis they maintain a big-picture perspective. At discussions and meetings, reflectors prefer to adopt a low profile and take a back seat.
- **Theorists – How does this relate to that?** Theorists are logical and disciplined, and value rationality and objectivity. They assimilate disparate facts in order to understand coherent theories. Theorists tend to be perfectionists and reject subjectivity, lateral thinking or flippancy.
- **Pragmatists – How can I apply this in practice?** Pragmatists like to experiment and seek and try new ideas or theories. They enjoy challenges and problem-solving. Pragmatists are practical, down to earth, quick to make decisions and quickly bored with long-term discussions.

The researchers claim that an understanding of one's learning style will enhance learning effectiveness, whether as a trainee or as a tutor. Although all styles are necessary, individuals tend to be more comfortable with and focus on one particular style. An integrated and effective learner will be equipped to manage all four styles, even though the learner may have a preference for one. Knowing your learning style may help avoid repeated mistakes by attempting activities to enhance alternative styles. For example, if you tend to 'jump in at the deep end', consider spending time reflecting on experiences before taking action.

Other studies

Other studies have also shown links between personality and learning and have found, for example, that introverts and extroverts differ with respect to punishment and reward. Whereas introverts are more likely to be affected by punishment, extroverts' performance is enhanced by reward.[20] They also differ with respect to their retention of short- and long-term material; extroverts tend to have a better performance at short-term intervals whereas the reverse is true for introverts.

Studies using the Myers–Briggs Type Indicator (**discussed in Chapter 4**) also reveal differences in learning preferences for the sixteen personality types. Such differences indicate that introverts work best if they can think before participating or ask questions before completing tasks or exercises, whereas extroverts work best if they can interact in a small group and/or talk the lesson over with other individuals. However, some of the interesting research has been completed on the interaction between trainer and trainee. Thus, an extroverted trainer who is also high on 'sensing' may positively evaluate students who are active, energetic and practical, but may overlook the thoughtful, introspective and conceptual students.[21] Such studies highlight the necessity for trainers not only to be sensitive to the personality needs of the group of trainees, but also to be aware of the impact their own personality has on the learning experience.

Mayo and Lank suggest that organisations need to recognise the simple fact that different people learn in different ways and should take the following actions:

- give people the opportunity to discover their most natural learning style;
- offer learning opportunities that suit people with different learning styles;
- recognise the need to complete the full learning cycle;
- help people to translate the learning cycle into an upwards continuous spiral of learning.[22]

Complex models of learning

Given the complexity of learning, how can managers make the best sense of the theories, concepts and frameworks? Models of learning such as that shown in Figure 5.4 are inevitably complex. However, the model might stimulate questions and could help in the preparation and design of learning programmes. For example, has sufficient consideration been given to the abilities of employees, learning styles and the best methods to be used?

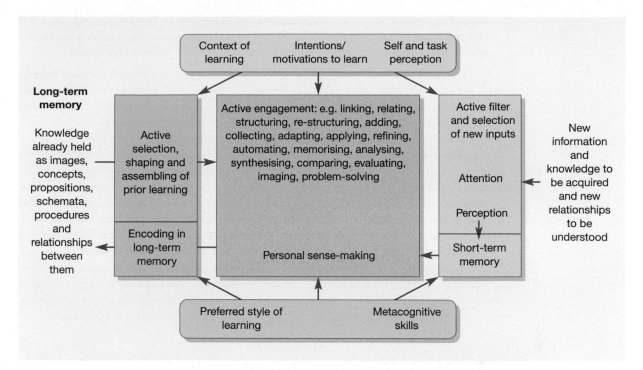

Figure 5.4 A cognitive model of learning
Source: From Atkins, M. J., Beattie, J. and Dockrell, W. B. *Assessment Issues in Higher Education,* Department of Employment (October 1993) p. 51. © Crown Copyright 1993. Crown copyright material is reproduced under terms of the Click-Use Licence.

Critical review and reflection

Learning is an instinctive process and people will only learn if they want to. Psychological studies of how people learn and learning styles have limited relevance in the classroom and even less practical application to the work situation.

How would YOU present a counterargument? How well do YOU learn?

E-learning

Learning via technology – **e-learning** – is now a global phenomenon and is central to many organisations. It is not difficult to see why online learning is growing in popularity. It offers the opportunity to provide a standard message to a large number of widely geographically dispersed people with the minimum disruption to their working and private lives. And, where large numbers of learners are involved, learning materials delivered online can bring the cost per learner to negligible proportions. Thus, learning becomes more accessible than ever before. There is an increasing use of technology as a means of enhancing the learning situation.

The Chartered Management Institute provides the following explanation of e-learning:

The facilitation of learning through the Internet, or an intranet. E-learning, short for electronic learning, is a development from computer-based training, and comprises self-contained learning materials, and resources, that can be used at the pace, and convenience, of the learner. An e-learning package normally incorporates some form of test which can demonstrate how much an e-learner has assimilated from a course, as well as some form of monitoring to enable managers to check the usage of the system e-learning. Successful e-learning depends largely on self-motivation of individuals to study effectively. Since it is Internet-based, it has the potential to respond to a company's rapidly changing needs, and offer new learning opportunities relevant to a company's new position very quickly.[23]

E-learning can be used in a variety of contexts with varying amounts of personal interaction. For example, with some university courses the majority of study is undertaken online with minimal attendance at campus or face-to-face tuition. However, in business organisations, technological and culture barriers appear to hinder the widespread uptake of online learning.

For many students, there are a number of potential benefits associated with e-learning including: open access to education and flexibility in location and timing; quicker delivery of training; individuals can proceed at their own pace; acquiring computer skills; and monitoring and feedback on activities. Potential disadvantages include: concerns over quality of content; maintaining motivation and danger of procrastination; and lack of teamworking and social interaction.

The challenge involved in e-learning is not simply teaching in a different way. Rather, it means rethinking the whole nature of the teaching/learning process. It is clear that e-learning is more appropriate for the acquisition of knowledge and there are doubts about its application to training in social skills. Despite all of these reservations, as communications technology develops and as people want to learn exactly what they need to know, with the minimum disruption to their lives, e-learning will become an increasingly significant part of training, either pre-course preparation or post-course evaluation and refreshment of knowledge.

Knowledge management

As mentioned previously, it is clearly in the best interests of the organisation to develop the knowledge and skills of its employees. Learning at the individual or group level impacts on the learning, development and performance of the organisation as a whole, and the process of learning is influenced by the general climate of the organisation. An increasingly important aspect of organisational performance is the idea of **knowledge management.** This is usually defined in terms of a range of practices or processes to identify, create, distribute and share knowledge throughout the organisation.[24] Growth will continue as more collaborative IT applications become available. Knowledge management is related to business strategy, IT, human resource management and people management, and can therefore be linked to organisational learning (**discussed in Chapter 16**).

Explicit and tacit knowledge

Nonaka argues that competitive advantage is founded in the ability of companies to create new forms of knowledge and translate this knowledge into innovative action. He says that 'the one sure source of lasting competitive advantage is knowledge', and describes the different kinds of knowledge that exist in organisations and the ways in which knowledge can be translated into action.[25] Nonaka distinguishes explicit and tacit knowledge.

- **Explict knowledge** is that held consciously in mental focus by an individual. It is easily communicated, quantified and available to others in various forms such as language, mathematical expression or printed matter.
- **Tacit knowledge,** however, is internalised and an individual may not be consciously aware of it. It is personal and specific to the individual and more akin to wisdom that is inarticulate, understood but rarely described. Although more problematic, because it is not so easily disseminated, tacit knowledge is arguably as important as explicit knowledge.

According to Nonaka, those companies able to use both kinds of knowledge will make the creative breakthroughs. He suggests that the knowledge-creating companies systematically ensure that the tacit and explicit feed into each other in a spiral of knowledge. Tacit knowledge is converted into explicit knowledge by articulation and that explicit knowledge is used within an individual's cognitive understanding by a process of internalisation. It perhaps is no surprise that 'knowledge management' has been the subject of hype in the management literature and has been extolled as the route to the holy grail of competitive advantage.

The importance of knowledge management

Tan argues that managing knowledge is now the issue for business in the twenty-first century. He suggests that:

> A successful company is a knowledge-creating company: that is one which is able consistently to produce new knowledge, to disseminate it throughout the company and to embody it into new products or services quickly.[26]

Santosus and Surmacz suggest that a 'creative approach to knowledge management (KM) can result in improved efficiency, higher productivity and increased revenues in practically any business function'.[27]

A substantial number of benefits have been identified by researchers of KM that no doubt have contributed to the surge of interest. *Kerr* identifies seven reasons why KM is an important area:

- business pressure on innovation;
- inter-organisational enterprises (e.g. mergers, takeovers, etc.);
- networked organisations and the need to co-ordinate geographically dispersed groups;
- increasingly complex products and services with a significant knowledge component;
- hyper-competitive marketplace (decreasing life cycles and time to market);
- digitisation of business environments and IT revolution;
- concerns about the loss of knowledge due to increasing staff mobility, staff attrition and retirements.[28]

The Chartered Management Institute points out that knowledge has become a key strategic asset in a knowledge-based economy, and every organisation that values knowledge must invest in developing the best strategy for identifying and applying the knowledge assets it needs to succeed.

> Managing knowledge systematically and professionally can bring many benefits to an organisation. These include the ability to learn from past failures and avoid repeating them or reinventing solutions which have previously proved to be inadequate. KM can also be a driver of new ideas leading to the creation of new products, services and solutions.[29]

McLean suggests that although many early management techniques have been relegated to the vaults of history, KM shows no sign of disappearing from boardroom discussion. KM has become a major driver of organisational change and wealth creation.

> Knowledge management aims to empower individuals and organisations to deal with real-life problems and issues which they face on a day-to-day basis. It also challenges them to identify ways in which they can 'know what they know' and use that conscious knowledge to assist their organisations to be a competitive force against rivals.[30]

Embedded within the business

From an examination of the changing shape of knowledge-sharing practices in organisations, *Burton* refers to an argument about whether (KM) is dead or that it is a 'live' discipline that has adapted and evolved. Pure KM focuses on unlocking the knowledge in people's heads for the greater corporate good, or simply getting those people working and talking together, often cross-functionally, for the greater corporate good.

Criticisms of KM include that it can morph into a version of content management; it rapidly becomes a specialist discipline with practitioners talking in abstract terms; and many of its supporters have become over-theoretical and insufficiently focused on tangible business benefit. Principles of KM need to be built into a company's overall business strategy and require the buy-in of senior management.

> *Most companies now realise that knowledge management is something that has to be embedded within the business. It is not something where you can bring in a specialist team and they will manage all your knowledge for you.*[31]

The success of KM would depend on the culture of the organisation and its priority in sharing learning and knowledge, and has roots in the learning organisation (**discussed in Chapter 16**).

Critical review and reflection

Knowledge management (KM) appears to be widely accepted as an important feature of improved organisational performance. However, in reality it is a very nebulous concept. KM means different things to different people and it is difficult to implement in a meaningful and rewarding way.

What is YOUR opinion of the practical value of KM? How effective is KM in your own university or organisation?

Talent management

Recent years have seen the emergence of the concept of **talent management** as a strategic approach to gaining competitive advantage. The Chartered Management Institute defines talent management in its broadest terms as 'the selection, development, engagement and retention of individuals, who are seen to be of particular value to an organisation':

> *The development of talented employees can be one of the most profitable investments an organization makes. As long-term organizational performance is achieved primarily through a focus on people, it is fundamental that talented personnel are identified, nurtured and, most importantly, retained within an organization. Investment in 'human capital' develops the skills, knowledge and vision needed to take an organization forward and can help to meet strategic objectives, maintain competitive advantage within the marketplace and ensure the long-term success and viability of the organisation.*[32]

Talent management is inextricably linked with the human capital management approach, with these particularly valuable individuals being seen as assets who should be invested into via development, appropriate planned deployment and engagement and retention initiatives. The competitive advantage secured is normally measured through indicators such as improved retention and succession planning of high performers, an increased reputation as an employer of choice, making the organisation more attractive to work in for external talent, and other factors such as increased diversity of the workforce and ultimately the success of the organisation.

Talent management needs to be aligned to the direction of the organisation and it needs senior management endorsement if it is to succeed. Line managers need to understand the concept and be encouraged to view talent in their own teams as a corporate resource rather than be concerned about their local deployment and workload issues.

Blass refers to the difficulty in finding a clear definition of talent management. The process may differ between organisations and the same activity can result in different actions and/or outcomes. However, Blass refers to the importance of a clear strategic perspective that shapes the way an organisation takes to talent management and how it is viewed, implemented and operationalised.[33]

Managing future talent

A report from the CIPD, in conjunction with the TUC and ACAS, draws attention to the development and support of young talent in the world of work. It is crucial that when a young person first enters the workplace, the experience sets them up for a long and successful career.

For a young person, the experience of entering the workplace, adjusting to working life, and learning and performing new tasks can be a daunting prospect. It is important that line managers responsible for young talent provide the right support and structure, and maintain good communications.[34]

Talent management at Lloyds Banking Group

At Lloyds Banking Group the purpose of talent management is to ensure the long-term sustainability of the Group by creating diverse and credible pipelines of successors. The approach focuses on creating opportunities for conversations to drive effective succession planning at all levels in the Group. In its application, talent is defined as a factor of (current) performance and (future) potential.

Current performance is assessed through the individual balanced scorecard, which is linked directly to the organisation's scorecard via team and business unit scorecards. Future potential is assessed against the Group's Indicators of Potential. These factors are jointly assessed by line managers and individuals through the annual talent review process and result in colleagues being assigned a talent rating.

Development is largely self-managed within a broad framework of solutions, and individual suitability and growth is regularly reviewed to ensure that core/critical business capability requirements are met, as well as individual needs.

Source: Talent Management Team, Lloyds Banking Group. December 2014. Reproduced with permission.

Management and organisational behaviour in action case study
Tapping into diverse talent: Career Watch at EY

EY provides global services in four main areas: assurance, tax, transactions and advisory. It helps clients retain the confidence of investors, manage their risk, strengthen their controls and achieve potential. EY is a global partnership employing 175,000, including 8,500 across the UK and Republic of Ireland. Research shows that if EY attracts and retains the best talent and develops people, it will be able to offer more innovative client solutions, thus winning in the market and building its brand and reputation, while also helping to attract even more talent.

People statistics identified:

1. Representation of women and ethnic minorities at junior levels is 50 per cent and 25 per cent, while representation at partner level is 17 per cent and 4 per cent respectively.
2. Performance ratings are not always distributed in a representative way.
3. Promotions are not proportional to the gender and ethnicity of the population from which promotions are made.
4. In the people survey women are less satisfied than men with career questions and ethnic minorities less satisfied than white people in questions on careers and inclusive behaviours.
5. The Career Watch programme's effectiveness was questioned.

In 2012 Career Watch changed the target audience from senior women and ethnic minorities to those at manager level and became a two-year sponsorship programme targeting high-performing female and ethnic minority managers. Participants are paired with a partner in their business with the intention that they are promoted to senior manager by the end of the two years. Objectives for Career Watch are to:

- retain diverse talent into leadership;
- remove and/or avoid roadblocks in people's career journeys;
- develop both the watchee and watcher;
- provoke organisational learning and change.

Career Watch is a one-to-one relationship programme which includes high-quality masterclasses on relevant topics (i.e. sponsorship, ethnic minority careers and gender differences in the workplace). It is led by a partner in each of the four main business units, thus ensuring the business owns the diverse pipeline of future leaders. These partners have shown leadership by introducing each of the sessions for their service line and sharing their own personal experience by recounting stories and experiences.

Checkpoint conference calls with watchers and watchees after six months, a detailed analysis of people statistics after twelve months and a survey of watchees showed that those on Career Watch:

- improved or maintained their performance rating (80 per cent compared with 39 per cent of peers);
- were promoted (41 per cent compared with 22 per cent);
- were retained in the firm (90 per cent compared to 70 per cent);
- would recommend Career Watch to others (over 80 per cent);
- felt it had fully met or exceeded their expectations (69 per cent);
- believe that it has increased their engagement with EY, supported them with obstacles and improved their leadership skills (more than half of watchees).

Source: Dan Robertson, Diversity and Inclusion Director, Employers Network for Equality and Inclusion. Reproduced with permission.

Tasks

1. Explain what you think are reasons for the kind of people statistics such as those identified at EY.
2. Give your own views on the Career Watch programme as a means of attracting and retaining talent.
3. Discuss what you see as the best way to attract greater talent from a diverse and inclusive workplace.

Critical review and reflection

University courses should be designed less around knowledge of academic disciplines and more to take account of the skills and abilities necessary in the workplace and for career advancement.
To what extent does YOUR course of study enable you to develop and express your potential organisational talents?

Creativity

With a continuing complex, turbulent and uncertain environment, a creative organisational culture is essential in order to maintain competitive advantage. For organisations to be innovative, creative solutions are required. Organisations need to recruit employees with the potential for both development and creativity. There are numerous definitions of **creativity** but it is defined generally, for example by *Goodman*, in terms such as 'the process of generating new ideas or concepts' or more specifically such as 'the application of imaginative thought which results in innovative solutions to many problems'.

Goodman suggests that: 'Actively creative people have a talent for getting to the heart of a problem. They are not confused by detail and by the need to invoke standard approaches.' There tends to be consensus in the literature that suggests such individuals have a desire for originality, non-conformity and the opportunity to experiment and express new ideas. A difference can also be drawn between those people who are productive in terms of the number of ideas they can create and those individuals who have entrepreneurial capabilities and are able to bring the ideas to the marketplace.[35]

Creativity is often linked with innovation but this term is generally associated with the development of new products or services. For example, *Gurteen* views creativity as essentially about generating ideas while innovation is about implementing these ideas and turning them into reality.[36]

The importance of managing creativity is emphasised by, for example, the Chartered Management Institute:

> *An organisation's ability to innovate by developing and utilising people's creativity and generating new ideas is considered a key to competitive advantage, particularly in the context of rapid change in business and society. It is vital for organisations to foster and manage creativity and innovation on an ongoing basis to help them achieve and sustain success.*[37]

Promoting a culture of creativity

The importance of creativity as a management skill has received increasing attention in recent years, lending a so-called soft edge of organisational behaviour to the business literature. Strategic management writers suggest that managers will be required to go beyond rational/logical thinking and use their senses of feeling, creativity and intuition to create businesses for the future. The Creative Model of management is:

> *built on the philosophical assumption that the real world which surrounds the organisation is a dynamic construct enacted by the members of the organisation over time . . . they will require a diverse group of senior managers able to perceive the world differently, yet able to participate in a process that transcends these different views to enact a complex organisational reality.*[38]

Such a view suggests that personality, sensitivity, creativity and communication skills are going to be the requirements of managers in the future. It also requires managers to be proactive in their search for root causes to problems and be imaginative in solving them.

In order to promote creativity employees must feel motivated and there must be a supporting environmental climate and organisation structures. Managers and supervisors need to adopt a style of behaviour and leadership based on openness, respect and trust that encourages the generation and implementation of new ideas. **See transformational or creative leadership in Chapter 9.**

Imaginative thought may lead to new ways of seeing things that may be novel for the person or completely novel in time. According to *Burton*, 'creativity is often viewed as a talent which resides only in a few and many managers will not see it necessarily as part of their role. In the 21ˢᵗ Century workplace, as well as building on existing knowledge, we need to develop new cultures which focus on developing creativity in everyone.' Burton refers to two parts of our imagination: **synthetic imagination,** which enables us to analyse previous and imagined scenarios based on that experience and knowledge; and **creative imagination,** which enables us to develop completely new and different ideas and concepts to solve problems and achieve goals.

> *Traditional management culture often trusts what comes from the synthetic imagination above the creative imagination, as these ideas have evidence and experience to back them up. Organisations moving from good to great, however are learning to trust ideas from the creative imagination as well.*[39]

Lucas comments that:

> *Organisations are toying with improvisation to help managers work together better in teams, release creativity and improve their presentation skills. However the key to gaining acceptance is getting past people's scepticism about its value in the workplace. Rigid structures are all very well but they can and do inhibit free thinking, which is vital for creativity, improving business performance and engaging with your audience.*[40]

Blocks to creativity

Managers often lack confidence in their ability to be creative and organisations may set up a number of blocks. It is therefore understandable that creativity is suppressed and devalued.

Goodman suggests six common blocks to personal creativity:

- **Perceptual** – habitual responses, stereotyping and reliance on past instructions and experiences.
- **Emotional** – fear, anxiety about looking foolish in front of others or making errors.

- **Process** – lack of technique or skills in process; a quick grasp at a solution.
- **Communication** – style, method or skills unsuitable for dealing with problems.
- **Environmental** – facilities, stress factors, mindsets of others that inhibit responses.
- **Cultural** – culture and attitudes not facilitative; too risky and open-ended.[41]

A distinction can be made in Goodman's list between the first four features, which are aspects of the individual's psyche and repertoire of skills, and the last two, which are functions of the culture of the organisation. Unless there is a culture of creativity and interest in reconstruction, it is more likely that individuals will use their creativity and resourcefulness outside the organisation or against the organisation rather than for the organisation.

Despite the doubts and blocks, learning to be creative is encouraged by many writers through exercises and activities to stretch and develop imagination in wild and novel ways – often referred to as 'thinking outside the box'. **These include procedures such as lateral thinking and brainstorming, discussed in Chapter 8.**

Creativity and context

Rickards et al. see creativity as a complex and compelling area of study that is as difficult to define as it is to achieve. In a thought-provoking series of contemporary articles, they explore how creativity can be better understood and used in a range of contexts, including innovation and entrepreneurship, environmental influences, knowledge management, personal creativity and structured interventions. Rickards *et al.* refer to creativity occurring within particular contexts, two of the most important being cultural and organisational. These do not act merely as influences and determinants, however, but instead are also influenced by creativity: 'It is simplistic to think that contexts are always the influence and creative thinking the result. Instead, interplay implies that environments act on and are influenced by creative people and their efforts.'[42]

Critical review and reflection

Traditional methods of student assessment are too rigid and restrictive in responses expected from students. The underlying search for standard answers effectively stifles or even penalises originality and creativity.
What are YOUR views? To what extent do you believe YOUR creativity is stifled?

Mentoring and coaching

Organisations need to offer learning and development opportunities that simultaneously challenge and support, together with effective procedures that enable people to harness their potential. This requires creativity to engage and motivate people emotionally to operate at their limits. So, how are employees to learn and acquire the skills that are necessary to further their career progression and/or to be effective managers? An integral part of this process is the role of mentoring and coaching.

Both mentoring and coaching are concerned with helping individuals to take responsibility for their learning and development. Although there is confusion about the two terms, which are often used interchangeably, practitioners usually perceive a clear difference.

Mentoring aims to facilitate each individual's capability and potential, to enhance their performance and to achieve their ambitions and career progression. Mentors are there to offer advice, guidance, support and feedback. Mentoring tends to focus on long-term development and the mentor is typically not the line manager but an expert in an area or a leader within the organisation. Rapport and confidentiality are essential for either relationship to work effectively. Mentoring can also serve as a means of socialisation and encouraging a sense of membership.

Coaching is a supportive relationship aimed at developing the individual's self-awareness. Coaching is usually a line-management function with focus on knowledge and skills relating to specific tasks or activities that can be monitored and measured. There is an emphasis on performance. However, a coach does not 'fix' someone or solve their problems or assume an 'expert's' position; rather they try to draw out the wisdom from within.

Managers have always been informal mentors and coaches – some relishing this role with the required portfolio of skills, some being more hesitant and others having a negative influence and acting as a 'block' rather than a steer to their subordinates. One of the joys of managing others is to know that you have helped others develop and grow. Mentoring is widely regarded today as a two-way process with benefit to both parties. Mentors often comment on the pleasure of being in touch with other people, what they themselves have learned and the opportunity to reflect on their own abilities and leadership style. (**Management development is discussed in Chapter 16.**)

Benefits of mentoring and coaching

The potential benefits of an organisation developing a mentoring and coaching culture seem to be well recognised.

According to *Whitaker*, mentoring is becoming increasingly popular as a powerful personal development and empowerment tool and as an effective way of helping people to progress in their careers. Mentoring traditionally described a relationship in which a more experienced work colleague used greater knowledge and understanding to support the development of a more junior or inexperienced member of staff.

> *Nowadays, however, a mentor is more than that. A mentor can help the mentee find the right direction and develop solutions to career issues. Mentors will usually rely on having had similar experiences to gain an empathy with the mentee and an understanding of their issues . . . Mentoring is to support and encourage people to manage their own learning in order that they may maximise their potential, develop their skills, improve their performance and become the person they want to be.[43]*

Garrett suggests that mentoring is evolving from a casual arrangement to a vital tool for creating the next generation of leaders.

> *Mentoring has become so well established that it is virtually a way of life within many businesses, one of the key ways in which the baton is passed from one generation to the next. And its potency is acknowledged in the increasing use of mentoring to promote diversity within organisations; it can help to furnish a route map to the top that might not previously have existed.[44]*

ACAS refers to the success of coaching, shadowing and mentoring systems in developing conflict management capacity among line and operational managers.[45]

Coaching is used to help a person move forward. It is about change and focuses on results. It is therefore no surprise that many organisations are turning to coaching.

Despite some criticisms about the unethical process, the potential benefits of an organisation developing a coaching culture seem to be well recognised. According to *Hodgson*, for example:

> *One of the unique benefits that coaching offers is a 'safe place' where individuals can openly discuss the challenges they face and put in place a firm development plan to help them overcome any obstacles. This can help them accelerate their own personal performance as well as that of their business.[46]*

See the use of neuro-linguistic programming (NLP) as part of coaching in Chapter 6.

A summary of formal mentoring is set out in the concept map of Figure 5.5.

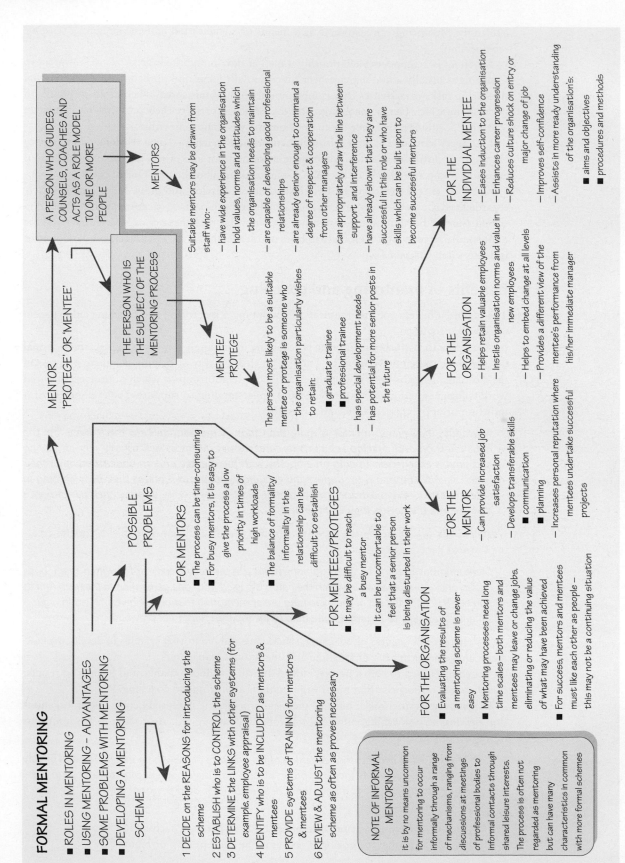

FORMAL MENTORING

- ROLES IN MENTORING
- USING MENTORING – ADVANTAGES
- SOME PROBLEMS WITH MENTORING
- DEVELOPING A MENTORING SCHEME

MENTOR
'PROTEGE' OR 'MENTEE'

A PERSON WHO GUIDES, COUNSELS, COACHES AND ACTS AS A ROLE MODEL TO ONE OR MORE PEOPLE

MENTORS

Suitable mentors may be drawn from staff who:–
- have wide experience in the organisation
- hold values, norms and attitudes which the organisation needs to maintain
- are capable of developing good professional relationships
- are already senior enough to command a degree of respect & cooperation from other managers
- can appropriately draw the line between support and interference
- have already shown that they are successful in this role or who have skills which can be built upon to become successful mentors

THE PERSON WHO IS THE SUBJECT OF THE MENTORING PROCESS

MENTEE/PROTEGE

The person most likely to be a suitable mentee or protege is someone who
- the organisation particularly wishes to retain:
  - graduate trainee
  - professional trainee
- has special development needs
- has potential for more senior posts in the future

FOR THE ORGANISATION
- Helps retain valuable employees
- Instils organisation norms and value in new employees
- Helps to embed change at all levels
- Provides a different view of the mentee's performance from his/her immediate manager

FOR THE INDIVIDUAL MENTEE
- Eases induction to the organisation
- Enhances career progression
- Reduces culture shock on entry or major change of job
- Improves self-confidence
- Assists in more ready understanding of the organisation's:
  - aims and objectives
  - procedures and methods

POSSIBLE PROBLEMS

FOR MENTORS
- The process can be time-consuming
- For busy mentors, it is easy to give the process a low priority in times of high workloads
- The balance of formality/informality in the relationship can be difficult to establish

FOR MENTEES/PROTEGES
- It may be difficult to reach a busy mentor
- It can be uncomfortable to feel that a senior person is being disturbed in their work

FOR THE MENTOR
- Can provide increased job satisfaction
- Develops transferable skills
  - communication
  - planning
- Increases personal reputation where mentees undertake successful projects

1 DECIDE on the REASONS for introducing the scheme
2 ESTABLISH who is to CONTROL the scheme
3 DETERMINE the LINKS with other systems (for example, employee appraisal)
4 IDENTIFY who is to be INCLUDED as mentors & mentees
5 PROVIDE systems of TRAINING for mentors & mentees
6 REVIEW & ADJUST the mentoring scheme as often as proves necessary

FOR THE ORGANISATION
- Evaluating the results of a mentoring scheme is never easy
- Mentoring processes need long time scales – both mentors and mentees may leave or change jobs, eliminating or reducing the value of what may have been achieved
- For success, mentors and mentees must like each other as people – this may not be a continuing situation

NOTE OF INFORMAL MENTORING

It is by no means uncommon for mentoring to occur informally through a range of mechanisms, ranging from discussions at meetings of professional bodies to informal contacts through shared leisure interests.
The process is often not regarded as mentoring but can have many characteristics in common with more formal schemes

Figure 5.5 Formal mentoring

Unilever's global mentoring programme

Unilever's global mentoring programme started in 2009 to fulfil the specific business objective of accelerating more women into senior leadership positions. 'Before, mentoring was quite informal,' says global talent manager Katherine Ray. 'This was designed to speed up the transition between certain high-level roles.'

Patricia Corsi, Unilever's brand development director for laundry products in Europe, joined the programme two years ago, and when her first mentor left the company she was paired with Pier Luigi Sigismondi, Unilever's chief supply chain officer and a member of the worldwide executive board.

Corsi, who came to the UK from Brazil four years ago, says: 'I wanted to have an opportunity to learn from a much more experienced professional and to get a different point of view on my career next steps.' She was also eager to learn from someone who had made a similar geographic move – Sigismondi is originally from Italy and has worked in Venezuela – and had some specific management issues to discuss. She explains: 'Sometimes you have a situation where you have to influence stakeholders. I wanted to find out how to convey one message, how do I make this message really strong and convincing?'

Sigismondi says the first meeting was not about formal objectives, however, but about getting to know each other. 'It's important that you treat your mentee as a person, not as an employee,' he says. 'So we started talking about ourselves, and this was the biggest surprise for her, because she was never expecting me to be myself and to actually tell her about what my challenges are where I sit,'

The pair have met every couple of months during the year for two hours at a time, and Corsi makes a point of preparing carefully for each meeting. She says: It's important he feels I am committed to this programme and I really value his time, which I know is precious.'

For his part, Sigismondi says it is essential in any mentoring relationship to have 'rules of engagement': there must be a mutual interest, a clear commitment to invest the time, and respect. But he also believes that to be most effective, mentoring crosses the boundary of the merely professional, and explores deeper personal questions. 'That unleashes many of the self-confidence issues that you need to face in order to grow professionally.'

His approach, he says, is to come to each meeting with a fresh perspective that Corsi will not have considered: 'It keeps her thinking after the meeting on how to improve, how to see things differently and how to grow as a person.' And Corsi says: 'The value is immense, not just because he's on the Unilever board, but because Pier Luigi is a very inspiring person.'

She concludes: 'Knowing people believe in you drives you to do more and better. I'm very reassured about my role in Unilever, how the company sees me, and I have clarity on where I'm going. I really, really treasure this relationship with my mentor.'

Source: Garrett, A. (2012) Friends in high places, *Management Today,* October 2012, p. 50. **www.managementtoday.com** Reproduced with permission

Applications of learning theory to organisations

Some of the major areas where it is possible to apply theories of learning include the following:

Self-development
- Learning what to 'do' (e.g. skills and knowledge).
- Learning how to 'be' (role behaviour).
- Learning the ropes (socialisation process and culture) and the social rules (norms and attitudes).

Development of others
- Personal development – training others and developing their potential (including skills of mentoring and coaching).
- Development of planned learning events.

Development of learning culture
- Policy development – developing policies for 'learning organisations'; coping with changes and development; enabling 'loose', creative and lateral thinking.

Critical review and reflection

Despite claims about benefits to the individual from coaching, in reality too much attention is given to improving organisational performance. There should be a stronger focus on personal development, learning life skills and the ability to adapt to change.

To what extent can YOU argue against this assertion? What is YOUR experience of coaching or what would YOU expect to gain from coaching?

Ten key points to remember

1 An understanding of ways in which people learn and develop is a dynamic concept and fundamental feature of organisational behaviour and management.

2 Learning takes place in a variety of ways and a range of situations. Lifelong learning is essential to cope with the changing nature of work organisations.

3 The behaviourist approach to learning was interested only in the study of behaviour and those actions that could be observed, measured and controlled.

4 Major studies include classical conditioning, the Law of Effect and operant conditioning. Social learning theory draws attention to the influence of social interactions and imitation.

5 The cognitive approach gives attention to ways in which people learn. Two major models include the Kolb learning cycle and the Honey and Mumford styles of learning.

6 It is difficult to separate how learning occurs without taking account of the employee and manager relationship and the general organisational climate.

7 Learning via technology (e-learning) is central to many organisations. It arises in a number of forms and can be used in a variety of different contexts.

8 An increasingly important aspect of effective organisational performance is the idea of knowledge management, which is linked to organisational learning.

9 In order to maintain competitive advantage the importance of a creative organisational culture has received increasing attention in recent years.

10 Mentoring and coaching may contribute to an organisational climate in which individuals take responsibility for their own learning and development.

Review and discussion questions

1 Explain fully what you understand by the nature and significance of learning and personal development.

2 Explain fully the extent to which you can identify with the individual benefits of learning set out in a 'declaration of learning' in Table 5.1.

3 Give your own detailed interpretation of the learning process, including how *you* best learn.

4 Evaluate critically the relevance today of the behaviourist theories of learning.

5   How would you explain social learning theory *and* the concept of self-efficacy?

6   Discuss the extent to which you identify with (i) the Kolb learning cycle *and* (ii) the Honey and Mumford styles of learning.

7   Debate critically the practical applications and benefits of knowledge management to an organisation of your choice.

8   To what extent could you argue that, despite apparent popularity, the lack of direct face-to-face interaction severely limits the value of e-learning?

9   Discuss the contention that most university courses expect standard responses from students with insufficient allowance for originality or creative thinking.

10 Why is mentoring and coaching becoming a more common form of learning and development in organisations? Discuss critically the likely implications.

Assignment

A study by US psychologists suggested that you remember and recall more from writing notes by longhand rather than into a laptop or tablet computer.

Arrange for members of your seminar group to watch a video recording of a lecture they have not seen previously.

Ensure half the group have only pen and paper and half a laptop or tablet to make notes during the recording or immediately after.

Thirty minutes later, chair a meeting with the group where you ask a series of recall and comprehension questions based on the recording.

- What conclusions do you draw and to what extent do they support the original study?
- What, if any, are the implications for the process of learning and development?
- Be prepared to report back in plenary session.

Personal skills and employability exercise

Objectives

Completing this exercise should enable you to enhance the following skills:

- Participate meaningfully in a role play activity.
- Demonstrate the skills required in coaching and mentoring.
- Show sensitivity in your personal relationships with other people.

Exercise

Role play: manager/supervisor

You are a manager in the accounts department. Graeme, one of your most energetic people, has asked for some of your time and is coming to see you in a couple of minutes. You are not sure what it is about but you would like to take the opportunity to talk to him about the amount of work he takes on. He takes on anything that needs doing and is always the first to volunteer for new projects. This has been particularly so over the past few months and you are beginning to be concerned about his health. He looks pretty drained at the moment.

You obviously want his enthusiasm to remain high but you do not want a stressed or burnt-out employee. Decide how you will approach the issue and how you might get him to moderate the workload.

Role play: employee/Graeme

You have been in the accounts department for six years now and really love your job. In fact, since you and your long-term partner split up a few months ago you have really thrown yourself into your work. It is nothing for you to work late into the evening and quite often at weekends. There are so many exciting things to get involved with that there is not enough time to do as much as you would like. Besides, your social life is not exactly buzzing at the moment and you have never got hooked into any particular hobbies or pastimes. Your manager has always been full of praise for your performance, consistently giving you a high rating on your objectives. You have also made rapid progress during your time in the department.

You have felt a bit drained recently and find it hard to switch off. You have asked to see your manager about an exciting new piece of work you have heard about. You would really like to get involved in it. You do not want to give up your other stuff, though.

Discussion

- What do you believe is the best training method for developing coaching and mentoring skills?
- How would you attempt to ensure the transparency necessary for good coaching while maintaining confidentiality about personal circumstances?
- Debate critically what you have learned from undertaking this activity.

Case study
VSO

In 2008 the charity Voluntary Service Overseas (VSO) celebrated its fiftieth birthday with an event in the Royal Festival Hall involving some of the 30,000 VSO volunteers past and present. Unlike charities that work by sending money abroad to support projects or provide direct financial aid, VSO sends people, their energy and their expertise to partner organisations in the developing world. It is a significant aspect of the UK's work for overseas development, and in 2013–14 the UK government provided almost £50 million (approximately 75 per cent) of VSO's income.[47] VSO has come a long way since the first dozen young people took 'a year between' school and university during 1958–9 to head for Nigeria, Ghana and Sarawak with the aim of offering:

service that would not only make a positive contribution to those countries but would constitute an experience of inestimable benefit to many of our young people.[48]

Not only has it grown (by 2014 it had placed over 40,000 volunteers in developing countries around the world)[49] but its structure and emphasis have changed in line with globalisation, economic development and new challenges. One thing that has not changed, however, is the importance of and value placed on learning and knowledge sharing, which is at the centre of VSO's mission.

The structure and emphasis of VSO's practices has changed in line with globalisation but the value of learning and knowledge sharing remains at the core of its mission

Source: © Caroline Penn / Alamy Stock Photo

The gap year

The phrase 'year between' was coined by a sub-editor of the *Sunday Times* on 23 March 1958. It was used in the headline given to a letter from the Bishop of Portsmouth that had been written in collaboration with Alec and Moira Dickson, the three founders of what became VSO.

In it they suggested that some of the school leavers who found themselves having to wait before university places became available (the ending of national service had created a bottleneck) could both offer something and benefit from a spell collaborating in projects for education, youth work and community development in poorer areas of the world. Dickson had worked in Nigeria and Iraq for the government and for UNESCO, and he and his wife had also spent time in Sarawak, so he understood the opportunities first hand. What inspired him was the idea that young people without specialist training, expertise or technical skills could offer help on a more equal footing than in the usual types of aid project, which Western experts managed and ran. The idea took root; just over a dozen 18–19 year olds signed up to the adventure, and the idea of the 'gap year' had been born.

Yesterday, today, tomorrow

VSO today is different in many respects from its 1958 self. In its foundation year the average age of the UK-recruited volunteers was 18; they expected to be placed for a year and were mainly involved in teaching (usually English) and healthcare. This remained broadly characteristic of the volunteer group for the first ten years of operation, but by 2008 things had changed. The 1,500 plus active volunteers had an average age of 41; they were recruited in Asia and Africa as well as in the UK and the average stay was two years.

In the early years of the new millennium, VSO revised its strategy and approach to reflect the changing needs of the developing world. Many developing countries now have their own source of school leavers and graduates so the focus is now on sharing skills for future professionals rather than providing immediate, direct services. In 2006 it announced that it would be attempting to recruit experienced head teachers and education managers rather than newly qualified teachers in order to focus on helping governments and training colleges to improve schools in developing countries; a number have since travelled to Rwanda, Namibia and Ghana to do just this.[50] At the same time it launched an appeal to recruit senior-level managers who could work with government departments and private businesses, even if only for a short period of a few weeks, to help with such things as developing IT, tourism, financial and HR management systems.[51] However, it has not abandoned its traditional base, and is working with the government and other volunteering organisations to support an initiative that provides opportunities for 18–25 year olds with limited expertise – the International Citizen Service (ICS).[52]

While education workers still comprise the largest professional group among VSO volunteers, there is a growing emphasis on activities to ensure a secure and sustainable livelihood for poor people, focusing on agriculture, food and natural resource management. One of the next most important areas of activity for the charity is HIV and AIDS-related work, with volunteers training 23,800 local health, HIV and AIDS practitioners in Africa, Asia and Mongolia during 2013–14.[53]

Learning from experience

From the outset, VSO saw that learning had to be reciprocal between volunteers and host organisations. The history of the movement offers a wealth of anecdotes and stories which suggest that the learning is very much a two-way process.[54] While volunteers can be, and are, prepared for many aspects of their experience through briefings and training activities prior to leaving the UK, some things just have to be learned the hard way. Culture shock was recognised as a major risk from the outset – especially since VSO has always maintained that a volunteer goes:

> not as a crusader, still less as a social revolutionary, and least of all as a representative or advocate of some British or Western 'way of life', but as an assistant, to work within an established framework and for objectives already formulated by the local authority which the volunteer undertakes to serve.[55]

Learning to fit in, therefore, is crucial, and misunderstandings or ignorance about significant cultural norms can create unforeseen risks.[56] Later there are 're-entry' problems; many volunteer diaries tell of reluctance to leave their host communities and the anticipated difficulty of fitting back into a more structured life at home with far less autonomy and responsibility than they experienced during their placement.

In the early years, culture shock was often exacerbated by isolation, since most placements were in remote and inaccessible areas where communication was difficult and infrequent. While satellite technology may have helped resolve some of these difficulties, the lack of reliable infrastructure (electricity in particular) still means that volunteers can feel very 'alone'. However, communication is at the heart of learning, which remains the core of VSO's mission.

Writing in 2004, two information and learning professionals with VSO described the importance of a professional approach to learning and knowledge transfer.[57] They outline the creation of a 'knowledge map' of the organisation's often fragmented and locally stored expertise which can be the basis of a catalogue for volunteers to search as and when they need it. The concept has been integrated into the training and support system for volunteers via the VSO 'Learning Hub', a web-based intranet resource which contains information, briefing materials and language training, and which connects both current and past volunteers through online discussion forums. Volunteers have password-protected access to the site, which is introduced during the six-stage induction and initial training programme.[58] The Learning Hub additionally contains a dedicated section for returners, enabling volunteers to prepare for the transition when coming home, but also capturing their knowledge and experience for future volunteers.

Sharing skills, changing lives

Of course, the volunteers themselves should learn as much as their hosts, and return to the UK with new-found or honed skills. As Mark Goldring, former VSO Chief Executive, remarked in a press interview:

> Returned volunteers are better at improvisation and problem solving. They have better interpersonal, cross-cultural and management skills.[59]

The recession too had an impact on VSO, with the organisation experiencing double the usual number of enquiries in the last three months of 2008.[60] Clearly there is value in being able to add a spell of voluntary work to a CV in a tough jobs market, and we should remember that poorer countries have suffered from the recession too, perhaps more acutely than wealthier ones, so volunteers still have much to offer. A final thought about the role of volunteering in the modern world comes from a piece by an Australian volunteer turned development academic.

> At its worst, international volunteering can be imperialist, paternalistic charity, volunteer tourism or a self-serving quest for career and personal development on the part of well-off Westerners . . . At its best, I argue, international volunteering brings benefits (and costs) to individual volunteers and the organisation with which they work, at the same time as providing the space for an exchange of technical skills, knowledge and cross-cultural experience in developing communities.[61]

Tasks

1 Research VSO's six-stage pre-placement briefing programme for new volunteers available on the VSO website **http://www.vso.org.uk/volunteer/supporting-you/training-and-orientation**. What types of learning do you think are involved? Who do you think should be involved in its delivery, and why?

2 How could an understanding of learning styles improve the effectiveness of the volunteer training programme? Explain the practical implications this would have for the way the programme is run.

3 How effective do you think a knowledge management system like the VSO Learning Hub can be in capturing and transferring both *explicit* and *tacit* types of knowledge? Is it more suited to one than the other?

4 What employability skills do you think might be developed in young people who have limited work experience by the International Citizen Service scheme? How can VSO and other organisations ensure these skills are transferred back to the volunteers' home environments afterwards?

Notes and references

1. Payne, E. and Whittaker, L. *Developing Study Skills*, second edition, Financial Times Prentice Hall (2006), p. xxi.

2. Crainer, S. and Dearlove, D. *Financial Times Handbook of Management*, third edition, Pearson Education (2004), p. 750.

3. Clements, P. and Jones, J. *The Diversity 'Training Handbook': A Practical Guide to Understanding and Changing Attitudes*, Kogan Page (2002), p. 9.

4. Burgoyne, J., Cunningham, I., Garratt, B., Honey, P., Mayo, A., Mumford, A., Pearn, M. and Pedler, M. 'The Debate Starts Here', in *People Management in Perspective: A Collection of Key Articles Published in the Last Year on Training and Development*, IPD (1999), pp. 16–17.

5. Watson, J. B. *Behaviourism*, JB Lippincott (1924).

6. Pavlov, I. *Conditioned Reflexes*, Oxford University Press (1927).

7. Thorndike, E. L. *The Fundamentals of Learning,* Teachers College (1932).
8. Skinner, B. F. *Science and Human Behaviour,* Macmillan (1953); and Skinner, B. F. *About Behaviourism,* Jonathan Cape (1974).
9. Stewart, S. and Joines, V. *TA Today: A New Introduction to Transactional Analysis,* Lifespace Publishing (1987).
10. Bandura, A. *Social Learning Theory,* Prentice Hall (1977).
11. Miller, N. E. and Dollard, J. C. *Personality and Psychotherapy,* McGraw-Hill (1950).
12. Tolman, E. C. *Purposive Behaviour in Animals and Men,* The Century Co. Appleton–Century Crofts (1932).
13. Davis, L. *Experience-Based Learning within the Curriculum,* Council for National Academic Awards (1990).
14. Kolb, D. A. *Experiential Learning: Experience as the Source of Learning and Development,* Prentice Hall (1985).
15. 'Action Learning Factsheet', CIPD, July 2009.
16. Gitsham, M. in conversation with Lucas, E. 'Learning With a Helping Hand', *Professional Manager,* vol. 18, no. 5, 2009, pp. 22–5.
17. Yukl, G. *Leadership in Organizations,* seventh edition, Pearson Prentice Hall (2010).
18. Honey, P. and Mumford, A. *The Manual of Learning Styles,* third edition, Honey (1992).
19. Honey, P. 'Styles of Learning', in Mumford, A. (ed.) *Handbook of Management Development,* fourth edition, Gower (1994).
20. Eysenck, M. 'Learning, Memory and Personality', in Eysenck, H. J. (ed.) *A Model of Personality,* Springer (1981), pp. 169–209.
21. Hirsch, S. K. *Using the Myers–Briggs Type Indicator in Organisations,* second edition, Consulting Psychologists Press (1991).
22. Mayo, A. and Lank, E. *The Power of Learning: A Guide to Gaining Competitive Advantage,* IPD (1994), pp. 135–6.
23. 'Knowledge Management', Checklist 166, Chartered Management Institute, February 2013.
24. See, for example, Scarborough, H. and Swan, J. *Case Studies in Knowledge Management,* IPD (1999).
25. Nonaka, I. 'The Knowledge Creating Company', in Starkey, K. (ed.) *How Organizations Learn,* International Thomson Business Press (1996), pp. 18–32.
26. Tan, J. 'Knowledge Management – Just More Buzzards?' *Manager, The British Journal of Administrative Management,* March–April 2000, pp. 10–11.
27. Santosus, M. and Surmacz, J. 'The ABCs of Knowledge Management', *CIO Magazine,* 23, May 2001.
28. Kerr, M. 'Knowledge Management', *Occupational Psychologist,* no. 48, May 2003, pp. 24–6.
29. 'Knowledge Management', Checklist 166, Chartered Management Institute, February 2013.
30. McLean, J. 'Does your organisation know what it knows?', *Manager, The British Journal of Administrative Management,* Spring 2009, pp. 32–33.
31. Burton, G. 'Knowledge Empowered', *Manager,* Spring 2013, pp. 28–31.
32. 'Talent Management'. Checklist 227, Chartered Management Institute, June 2011.
33. Blass, E. 'Talent for the Downturn', *Professional Manager,* vol. 18, no. 2, March 2009, pp. 26–8.
34. 'Managing Future Talent: A guide for employers', CIPD, February 2014.
35. Goodman, M. *Creative Management,* Prentice Hall (1995), p. 86.
36. Gurteen, D. 'Knowledge, creativity and innovation,' *Journal of Knowledge Management,* vol. 2, no. 1, 1998, pp. 5–13.
37. 'Managing Creativity', Checklist 177, Chartered Management Institute, May 2013.
38. Hurst, D. K., Rush, C. and White, R. E. 'Top Management Teams and Organisational Renewal', in Henry, J. (ed.) *Creative Management,* Sage (1991), pp. 232–53.
39. Burton, L. 'Creativity and Innovation: The power of imagination', *Manager, The British Journal of Administrative Management,* Autumn 2009, p. 25.
40. Lucas, E. 'Work: Unlimited', Professional Manager, vol. 19, no. 4, 2010, pp. 22–5.
41. Goodman, M. *Creative Management,* Prentice Hall (1995).
42. Rickards, T., Runco, M. A. and Moger, S. (eds) *The Routledge Companion to Creativity,* Routledge (2009).
43. Whitaker, H. ' Speak the same language', *Governance + Compliance,* April 2014, pp. 54–5.
44. Garrett, A. 'Friends in High Places', *Management Today,* October 2012, pp. 48–51.
45. Saundry, R and Wibberley, G. 'Workplace Dispute Resolution and the Management of Individual Conflict – A Thematic Analysis of Five Case Studies', Research Paper 06/14, ACAS, 2014.
46. Hodgson, M. 'The early bird catches the worm', *Training Journal,* 1 May 2014, pp. 61–4.
47. VSO: Annual Report and Financial Statements for the year ended 31 March 2014.
48. Adams, M. Voluntary Service Overseas: The Story of the First Ten Years, Faber and Faber (1968), p. 48.
49. VSO, **http://www.vso.org.uk/about** (accessed 11 February 2015).
50. BBC News, 15 June 2009, 'Heads learn from Africa challenge' (accessed 8 August 2012).
51. VSO, **http://www.vso.org.uk/volunteer/opportunities/management-business-it/index.asp** (accessed 11 February 2015).
52. VSO, **http://www.vso.org.uk/volunteer/opportunities/vso-ics-for-18–25-year-olds** (accessed 11 February 2015).

53. VSO Health, HIV and IADS Capability Statement, July 2015, http://www.vsointernational.org/sites/vso_international/files/vso_health_hiv_and_aids_capability_statement_2015.pdf (accessed 5 August 2015).

54. Stories and blogs can be found on the VSO website, http://www.vso.org.uk/about/stories

55. Adams, M., op. cit., p. 89.

56. For instance, the episode of Gillian Gibbons – not a VSO worker – who, in 2007, found herself jailed in Sudan for allowing her primary school class to name a teddy bear 'Mohammed'. See an interview about her experience at http://news.bbc.co.uk/1/hi/world/middle_east/8010407.stm (accessed 11 February 2015).

57. Gilmour, J. and Stancliffe, M. 'Managing knowledge in an international organisation: the work of Voluntary Services Overseas (VSO)', *Records Management Journal,* vol. 14, no. 3, 2004, pp. 124–8.

58. For details of the programme and the Learning Hub see the VSO website http://www.vso.org.uk/volunteer/supporting-you/training-and-orientation (accessed 11 February 2015).

59. Gould, M. 'Leading Questions Interview with Mark Goldring, 6 June 2007, in the *Guardian,* http://www.guardian.co.uk/society/2007/jun/06/guardiansocietysupplement2 (accessed 8 August 2012).

60. Thorpe, A. 'Recession sends volunteer numbers soaring', *Observer,* 21 December 2008.

61. Devereux, P. 'International volunteering for development and sustainability: Outdated paternalism or a radical response to globalisation?', *Development in Practice,* vol. 18, no. 3, 2008, pp. 357–70.

CHAPTER 6
Perception and communication

The process of perception is at the root of our understanding, behaviour and actions. Knowledge and awareness of the perceptual process can help develop insights about ourselves and interactions with others. The words we use and speak, the way we look and the body language we display communicate our view of the world. Managers need to understand the importance of perception and communications in guiding behaviour and for effective personal and work relationships with others.

Learning outcomes

After completing this chapter you should have enhanced your ability to:

- explain the nature and importance of the perceptual process;
- detail internal and external factors that provide meaning to the individual;
- explain the importance of perceptual illusions, and impression management;
- identify difficulties in perceiving other people, including non-verbal communications;
- explain the importance of language and communications in perception;
- evaluate the relevance of neuro-linguistic programming and transactional analysis;
- assess the nature and significance of perceptual distortions and errors.

Critical review and reflection

People differ as individuals. Even confronted with exactly the same situation this will give rise to a variety of responses, behaviours and actions. There is no way managers can cope with such a range of individual perspectives so the study of perception is largely a waste of time.

What are YOUR views? What do YOU expect to gain from a study of perception?

The importance of understanding perception

The significance of individual differences is particularly apparent when focusing on the process of **perception.** Although general theories of perception were first proposed during the last century, the importance of understanding the perceptual process is arguably even more significant today. We all have our own, unique picture or image of how we see the 'reality' of the world around us, and our own way of looking at and understanding our environment and the people within it. This is a complex and dynamic process.

We do not passively receive information, we analyse and judge it, and place significance on certain information and disregard other information as worthless. We may also be influenced by our expectations so that we perceive what we expect to 'see' or 'hear'. A situation may be the same, but the interpretation of that situation by two individuals may be vastly different. Perception is at the root of organisational behaviour; any situation can be analysed in terms of its perceptual connotations. Consider, for instance, the following situation.

A member of senior management has sent an email to departmental managers asking them to provide statistics of overtime worked within their section during the past six months and projections for the next six months. Mixed reactions could result:

- One manager may see it as a reasonable and welcome request to provide information in the hopeful expectation that this will help lead to improved staffing levels.
- Another manager may be extremely upset and suspect the information will be used by senior management to order cutbacks in future overtime in order to reduce staffing costs.
- A third manager may see it as an unreasonable demand, intended only to enable management to exercise closer supervision and control over the activities of the section.
- A fourth manager may have no objection to providing the information but be suspicious that it may lead to possible intrusion into the running of the section.
- Yet another manager may see it as a positive action by management to investigate ways of improving efficiency throughout the organisation.

Each of the departmental managers has their own different perception of the email, which could be influenced, for example, by their working relationship with senior management or previous experiences. Their perceived reality and understanding of the situation provokes individual reactions. In addition, there are likely to be mixed reactions to the use of email as the means of communication in this instance.

The perceptual process

It is not possible to have an understanding of perception without taking into account its sensory basis. We are not able to attend to everything in our environment; our sensory systems have limits. The physical limits therefore insist that we are selective in our attention and perception. Early pioneer work by psychologists has resulted in an understanding of universal laws that underlie the perceptual process. It seems that we cannot help but search for meaning and understanding in our environment. The way in which we categorise and organise this sensory information is based on a range of factors including the present situation, our emotional state and any experiences of the same or a similar event.

Selectivity in attention and perception

Some information may be considered highly important to us and may result in immediate response. In other instances, the information may be simply 'parked' or assimilated in other ideas and thoughts. Some of our 'parked' material may be forgotten or, indeed, changed and reconstructed over time.[1] We should be aware of the assumptions that are made throughout the perceptual process, below our conscious threshold. We have learned to take for granted certain constants in our environment. We assume that features of our world will stay the same and thus we do not need to spend our time and energy seeing things afresh and anew. We make a number of inferences throughout the entire perceptual process. Although these inferences may save time and speed up the process, they may also lead to distortions and inaccuracies.

Perception as information processing

It is common to see the stages of perception described as an information-processing system (*see* Figure 6.1): (top-down) information (stimuli) (Box A) is selected at one end of the process (Box B), then interpreted (Box C) and translated (Box D), resulting in action or thought patterns (Box E). However, it is important to note that such a model simplifies the process and although it makes it easy to understand, it does not do justice to the complexity and dynamics of the process. In certain circumstances, we may select information out of the environment because of the way we categorise the world. The dashed line illustrates this 'bottom-up' process.

For instance, if a manager has been advised by colleagues that a particular trainee has managerial potential, the manager may be specifically looking for confirmation that those views are correct. This process has been known as 'top-down' because the cognitive processes are influencing the perceptual readiness of the individual to select certain information. This emphasises the active nature of the perceptual process. We do not passively digest the information from our senses, but actively attend to and indeed, at times, seek out certain information. (See also the discussion on self-fulfilling prophecy below.)

Meaning to the individual

The process of perception explains the manner in which information (stimuli) from the environment around us is selected and organised to provide meaning for the individual. Perception is the mental function of giving significance to stimuli such as shapes, colours, movement, taste, sounds, touch, smells, pain, pressures and feelings. Perception gives rise to individual behavioural responses to particular situations.

Despite the fact that a group of people may 'physically see' the same thing, they each have their own version of what is seen – their perceived view of reality. Consider, for example, the image (published by W. E. Hill in *Puck*, 6 November 1915) shown in Figure 6.2. What do

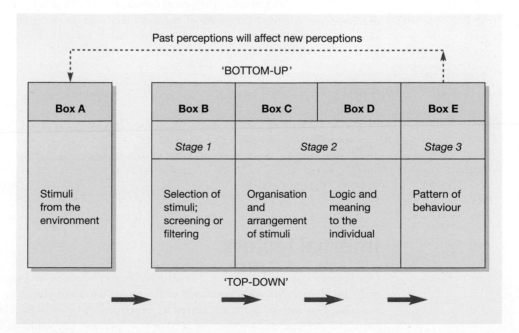

Figure 6.1 Perceptions as information processing

Figure 6.2

you see? Do you see a young, attractive, well-dressed woman? Or do you see an older, poor woman? Or can you now see both? **And who can say with certainty that there is just the one, 'correct' answer?**

Why do we attend to certain stimuli and not to others? There are two important factors to consider in this discussion. The process of perceptual selection is based both on internal characteristics relating to the state of the individual and on the environment and influences external to the individual.

Critical review and reflection

In order to develop our perceptual abilities the first step is recognition and understanding of the process that we determine of our selection and attention of the stimuli around us.

To what extent do YOU identify with this statement? What stimulus factors most catch YOUR attention and selection?

Internal factors

Our sensory systems have limits. For instance, our eyes receive and convert light waves into electrical signals that are transmitted to the visual cortex of the brain and translated into meaning. Our sensory system is geared to respond to changes in the environment. This has particular implications for the way in which we perceive the world and it explains why we are able to ignore the humming of the central heating system but notice instantly a telephone ringing. The term used to describe the way in which we disregard the familiar is 'habituation'.

Sensory limits or thresholds

As individuals we may differ in terms of our sensory limits or thresholds. People differ not only in their absolute thresholds, but also in their ability to discriminate between stimuli. For instance, it may not be possible for the untrained to distinguish between different types of wine but this would be an everyday event for the trained sommelier. We are able to learn to discriminate and are able to train our senses to recognise small differences between stimuli. It is also possible for us to adapt to unnatural environments and learn to cope.[2] We may also differ in terms of the amount of sensory information we need to reach our own comfortable equilibrium. Some individuals would find loud music at a party or gig uncomfortable and unpleasant, whereas for others the intensity of the music is part of the total enjoyment. Likewise, if we are deprived of sensory information for too long this can lead to feelings of discomfort and fatigue.

Psychological factors

Psychological factors will also affect what is perceived. These internal factors, such as personality, learning and motives, will give rise to an inclination to perceive certain stimuli with a readiness to respond in certain ways. This has been called an individual's perceptual set (*see* Figure 6.3).

Differences in the ways individuals acquire information have been used as one of four scales in the Myers–Briggs Type Indicator (**discussed in Chapter 4**). They distinguish individuals who 'tend to accept and work with what is given in the here-and-now, and thus become realistic and practical' (sensing types), from others who go beyond the information from the senses and look at the possible patterns, meanings and relationships. These 'intuitive types' 'grow expert at seeing new possibilities and new ways of doing things'. Myers and Briggs stress the value of both types and emphasise the importance of complementary skills and variety in any successful enterprise or relationship.[3]

Needs of the individual

The needs of each individual will affect their perceptions. For example, a manager deeply engrossed in preparing an urgent report may screen out ringing telephones, the sound of computers, people talking and furniture being moved in the next office, but will respond readily to the smell of coffee brewing. The most desirable and urgent needs will almost certainly affect

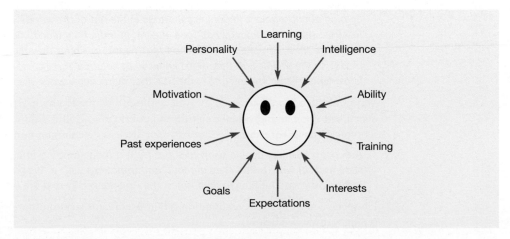

Figure 6.3 Factors affecting an individual's perceptual set

an individual's perceptual process. Members of a church choir might well form a perception of the minister quite different from that of a parishioner seeking comfort after the recent death of a close relative.

The 'Pollyanna Principle' claims that pleasant stimuli will be processed more quickly and remembered more precisely than unpleasant stimuli. However, it must be noted that intense internal drives may lead to perceptual distortions of situations (or people) and unwillingness to absorb certain painful information. (**Perceptual distortions are considered later in the chapter.**)

Learning from experiences has a critical effect throughout all stages of the perceptual process. It will affect the stimuli perceived in the first instance, and then the ways in which those stimuli are understood and processed, and finally the response that is given. For example, it is likely that a maintenance engineer visiting a school for the first time will notice different things about it than will a teacher attending an interview or a child arriving on the first day. The learning gained from experiences colours what is seen and processed.

Cultural differences

The ways in which people interact are also subject to cultural differences and such differences may be misconstrued. There are many ways of describing **culture**, but the following definition from *Schein* helps relate culture to diversity and perception.

> *A pattern of basic assumptions – invented, discovered or developed by a given group as it learns to cope with its problems of external adaptation and internal integration – that has worked well enough to be considered valuable and therefore to be taught to new members as the correct way to perceive, think and feel in relation to these problems.[4]*

Embarrassment and discomfort can occur when emotional lines are broken. This was demonstrated in an American study that researched the experience of Japanese students visiting the USA for the first time. The researchers felt that the Japanese students faced considerable challenges in adapting to the new culture. Some of the surprises that the students reported related to social interaction:

> *Casual visits and frequent phone calls at midnight to the host room-mate were a new experience to them. The sight of opposite-sex partners holding hands or kissing in public places also surprised them . . . That males do cooking and shopping in the household or by themselves, that fathers would play with children, and that there was frequent intimacy displayed between couples were all never-heard-of in their own experiences at home.[5]*

In certain cultures, such as the USA, it is 'normal' to explain all details clearly, explicitly and directly. In other cultures the 'spelling out' of all the details is unnecessary and embarrassing.

> *McCrum refers to a joke circulated on the Web by disaffected UN staff. A worldwide survey was conducted by the UN. The only question asked was: 'Would you please give your honest opinion about solutions to the food shortage in the rest of the world?' The survey was a failure. In Africa they didn't know what 'food' meant; in India they didn't know what 'honest' meant; in Europe they didn't know what 'shortage' meant; in China they didn't know what 'opinion' meant; in the Middle East they didn't know what 'solution' meant; in South America they didn't know what 'please' meant; and in the USA they didn't know what 'the rest of the world' meant.[6]*

Ways in which words are used and the assumptions made about shared understanding are dependent upon an individual's culture and upbringing. Cultural differences often lead to stereotypical views. For example, *Stewart-Allen* discusses a common mindset about Americans:

> *American business people seem to suffer from a long-standing image problem abroad. The stereotypical view is that they are loud and impatient with a 'bigger is better' attitude; they lecture others about how to do business the American way and are insular in outlook.*

However, a more accurate assumption is that Americans lack international exposure.[7] (**Stereotyping is discussed below.**)

Management and organisational behaviour in action case study
Diversity Resource Handbook

Portsmouth Hospitals NHS Trust has produced a comprehensive 'Diversity Resource Handbook' intended to provide members of staff with practical advice and guidelines on delivering a sensitive service to the diverse community it serves. Good communication is fundamental to providing a good quality service. If the correct meaning is not conveyed via effective communication, we risk inducing feelings of confusion, frustration, isolation and perhaps anger. It is important not only to be aware of the appropriate naming systems, but to use them effectively.

Using the right terminology is extremely important, particularly when referring to disability, because the words you use reflect your attitudes and beliefs. The key towards working towards acceptable language is firstly to see the person and not their disability, or background, and choose language that aims to include and value people with a disability. The booklet sets out advice and guidelines on age, disability, race, religious and cultural issues, major world religions, interpreting and translating, sexual orientation and gender, and aids to communication.

The booklet draws attention to the importance and realities of perceptual awareness, including:

Awareness in a multicultural society – some guidelines

Be aware that in some communities it may not be the custom to shake hands, especially amongst women.

Be sensitive to the difficulties that may be caused for ethnic minorities by using jargon and slang.

Be sensitive to using colloquialisms or terms of endearment that may cause offence, e.g. love, dear or darling.

Be aware that in some communities a woman may feel uncomfortable or may not wish to be in a room with a man who is not a relative.

Be aware that an act of comfort, such as putting an arm around a person, may cause embarrassment or offence.

Appreciate cultural differences in body language – for example, looking away instead of maintaining eye contact is not necessarily a sign of dishonesty or disrespect, in some communities it may be the opposite.

Ask for the individual's personal and family name. Don't ask someone what his or her Christian name or surname is.

Just because someone responds to questions in English they may not fully understand what is being said.

Don't underestimate the influence of your own cultural background on your unconscious perceptions and behaviours.

Source: Extracts from Portsmouth Hospitals NHS Trust, *Diversity Resource Handbook*, November 2013. Reproduced with permission.

Tasks

1. What do you think of the idea of an NHS Diversity Resource Handbook? Would you recommend a similar handbook for your own university or organisation?
2. Give your own examples of the importance and realities of perceptual awareness.
3. Discuss how you would attempt to improve awareness of perception and communication in a multicultural society.

Critical review and reflection

The overriding obstacles to effective perception and communication are lack of understanding cultural differences and inappropriate use of language.

From YOUR own experience to what extent do YOU agree with this contention? How much are YOU aware of cultural differences and YOUR own use of language?

External factors

Knowledge, familiarity or expectations about a given situation or previous experiences will influence perception. External factors refer to the nature and characteristics of the stimuli. There is usually a tendency to give more attention to stimuli that are, for example:

- bright
- novel
- repeated
- in strong contrast to their background.

Any number of these factors may be present at a given time or in a given situation. The use of these stimuli is a key feature in the design of advertising. (Think of your own examples.) It is the **total pattern** of the stimuli together with the **context** in which they occur that influence perception. For example, it is usually a novel or unfamiliar stimulus that is more noticeable, but a person is more likely to perceive the familiar face of a friend among a group of people all dressed in the same-style uniform (*see* Figure 6.4).[8]

We are all familiar with the expression 'what on earth is that doing here?'. The sight of a fork-lift truck on the factory floor in a manufacturing organisation is likely to be perceived quite differently from one in the corridor of a university. Consider another example: the sight of a jet ski (left temporarily by a neighbour moving house) in the garage of a person known

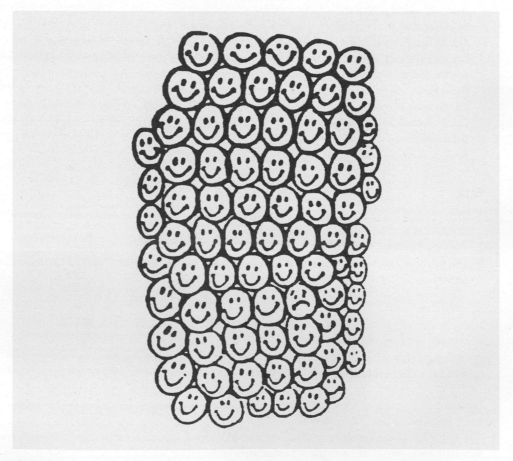

Figure 6.4 Is everybody happy?
Source: Block, J. R. and Yuker, H. E. *Can You Believe Your Eyes?*, Robson Books (2002), p. 163.

to be scared of water is likely to elicit such a remark. Yet the sight of numerous jet skis on the beach is likely to pass without comment. The word 'terminal' is likely to be perceived differently in the context of: (i) a hospital, (ii) an airport, or (iii) a computer firm. Consumer psychologists and marketing experts apply these perceptual principles with extraordinary success for some of their products.

Organisation and arrangement of stimuli

The Gestalt School of Psychology led by Max Wertheimer claimed that the process of perception is innately organised and patterned. It described the process as one that has built-in field effects. In other words, the brain can act like a dynamic, physical field in which interaction among elements is an intrinsic part. The Gestalt School produced a series of principles, which are still readily applicable today. Some of the most significant include the following:

- figure and ground
- grouping
- closure.

Figure and ground

The figure and ground principle states that figures are seen against a background. The figure does not have to be an object; it could be merely a geometrical pattern. Figure and ground relationships are often reversible, as in the popular example shown in Figure 6.5. What do you see first? Do you see a white chalice (or small stand shape) in the centre of the frame? Or do you see the dark profiles of twins facing each other on the edge of the frame? Now look again. Can you see the other shape?

The figure and ground principle has applications in occupational situations. It is important that employees know and are able to attend to the significant aspects (the figure) and treat other elements of the job as context (background). Early training sessions aim to identify and focus on the significant aspects of a task. Managerial effectiveness can also be judged in terms of chosen priorities (the figure). Stress could certainly occur for those employees who are uncertain about their priorities and are unable to distinguish between the significant and less significant tasks. They feel overwhelmed by the 'whole' picture.

Figure 6.5

Grouping

The grouping principle refers to the tendency to organise shapes and patterns instantly into meaningful groupings or patterns on the basis of their proximity or similarity. Parts that are close in time or space tend to be perceived together. For example, in Figure 6.6a, the workers are more likely to be perceived as nine independent people, but in Figure 6.6b, because of the proximity principle, the workers may be perceived as three distinct groups of people. Consider the importance of the layout of the room and tables for a large wedding reception and the perception of people in terms of both the table where they are sat and with whom they are grouped!

Taxi firms often use the idea of grouping to display their telephone number. In the example below, which of the following numbers – (a), (b) or (c) – is most likely to be remembered easily?

(a) 347 474   (b) 347474   (c) 34 74 74

Similar parts tend to be seen together as forming a familiar group.

In the following example there is a tendency to see alternate lines of characters – crosses and noughts (or circles). This is because the horizontal similarity is usually greater than the vertical similarity. However, if the page is turned sideways the figure may be perceived as alternate noughts and crosses in each line.

× × × × × × × ×
○ ○ ○ ○ ○ ○ ○ ○
× × × × × × × ×
○ ○ ○ ○ ○ ○ ○ ○

It is also interesting to note that, when asked to describe this pattern, many people refer to alternate lines of noughts and crosses – rather than crosses and noughts.

There is also an example here of the impact of cultural differences, mentioned earlier. The author undertook a teaching exchange in the USA and gave this exercise to a class of American students. Almost without exception the students described the horizontal pattern correctly as alternate rows of crosses and noughts (or zeros). The explanation appears to be that Americans do not know the game as 'noughts and crosses' but refer to it as 'tic-tac-toe'.

Closure

There is also a tendency to complete an incomplete figure – to fill in the gaps (mentally) and to perceive the figure as a whole. This creates an overall and meaningful image for the individual rather than an unconnected series of lines or blobs.

In the example in Figure 6.7[9] most people are likely to see the blobs as either the letter B or the number 13, possibly depending on whether at the time they had been more concerned with written material or dealing in numbers. However, for some people the figure may be described in terms of just a series of eleven discrete blobs, or perceived as some other (to them) meaningful pattern/object. According to Gestalt theory, perceptual organisation is instant and spontaneous. We cannot stop ourselves making meaningful assumptions about our environment.

(a)   (b)

Figure 6.6

Figure 6.7
Source: King, R. A. *Introduction to Psychology*, 6th edition, McGraw-Hill (1966).
Figure 10.22, p.339. Reproduced with permission from the author, Professor
Richard King.

The Gestaltists emphasised the ways in which the elements interact and claimed that the new
pattern or structure perceived had a character of its own, hence the famous phrase 'the whole
is more than the sum of its parts'.

Perceptual illusions

Here are some examples to help you judge your perceptive skills. In Figure 6.8 try reading aloud
the four words. It is possible that you find yourself 'caught' in a perceptual set that means that
you tend to pronounce 'machinery' as 'MacHinery', as if it too were a Scottish surname.

In Figure 6.9, which of the centre blue circles is the larger – A or B?

M – A – C – D – O – N – A – L – D
M – A – C – P – H – E – R – S – O – N
M – A – C – D – O – U – G – A – L – L
M – A – C – H – I – N – E – R – Y

Figure 6.8

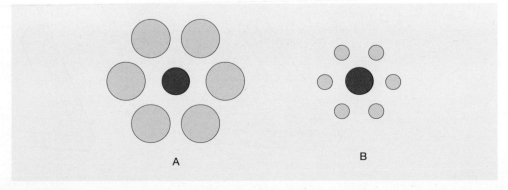

Figure 6.9

Although you may have guessed that the two centre circles are in fact the same size, the circle on the right (B) may well **appear** larger because it is framed by smaller circles. The centre circle on the left (A) may well **appear** smaller because it is framed by larger circles.

In Figure 6.10 try saying the *colour* of the word, *not* the word itself.

The physiological nature of perception has already been discussed briefly, but it is of relevance here in the discussion of illusions. Why does the circle on the right in Figure 6.9 look bigger? Why is it difficult to say the colour, not the word? These examples demonstrate the way our brain can be fooled. Indeed, we make assumptions about our world that go beyond the pure sensations our brain receives.

Beyond reality

Perception goes beyond the sensory information and converts patterns to a three-dimensional reality that we understand. This conversion process, as we can see, is easily tricked. We may not be aware of the inferences we are making as they are part of our conditioning and learning. The Stroop experiment shown in Figure 6.10 illustrates this perfectly.[10]

An illustration of the way in which we react automatically to stimuli is the illusion of the impossible triangle (*see* Figure 6.11).

Even when we know the triangle is impossible we still cannot stop ourselves from completing the triangle and attempting to make it meaningful. We thus go beyond what is given and make assumptions about the world, which in certain instances are wildly incorrect. Psychologists and designers may make positive use of these assumptions to project positive images of a product or the environment. For instance: colours may be used to induce certain atmospheres in buildings; designs of wallpaper or texture of curtains may be used to create feelings of spaciousness or cosiness; and packaging of products may tempt us to see something as bigger or perhaps more precious.

BLUE	GREY	YELLOW	MAUVE
BLACK	ORANGE	GREEN	RED
WHITE	PURPLE	BLUE	BROWN

Figure 6.10

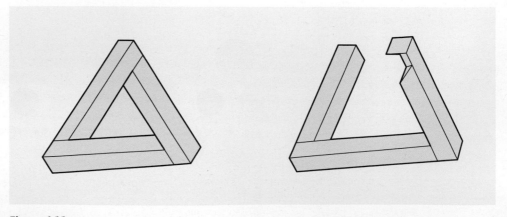

Figure 6.11
Source: Gregory, R. L. *Odd Perceptions*, Methuen (1986), p. 71. Reprinted by permission of the publishers, Routledge, a division of Taylor & Francis Ltd.

Impression management

In some situations we all attempt to project our attitudes, personality and competence by paying particular attention to our appearance and the impact this may have on others. This has been labelled 'impression management'.[11] The selection interview is an obvious illustration. Some information is given more weight than other information when an impression is formed. It would seem that there are central traits that are more important than others in determining our perceptions.

What information do we select and why? The social situation consists of both verbal and non-verbal signals. Non-verbal signals include:

- bodily contact
- proximity
- orientation
- head movements
- facial expressions
- gestures
- posture
- direction of gaze
- dress and appearance
- non-verbal aspects of speech.

Verbal and non-verbal signals are co-ordinated into regular sequences, often without the awareness of the parties. The mirroring of actions has been researched and is called 'postural echoing'.[12] There is considerable evidence to indicate that each person is constantly influencing the other and being influenced.[13]

Lucas refers to the importance of the 'personal brand' that we all have.

You may not be aware of it and you probably haven't consciously developed it, but it's what drives how you are perceived at work and how successful you are in your daily dealings with colleagues and clients. Your personal brand is about the way you come across to others. It's about the messages you send with the way you dress, the tone of your voice and your body language.[14]

Rigby points out that although it would be good to think all managers view staff as equal and judged only on results, there are still plenty of ways in which people discriminate. Eleven factors that can hold back your career are:

- dress sense
- appearance
- body modification
- accent
- education
- parentage
- height
- hair
- weight
- politics
- religion.[15]

Despite becoming somewhat clichéd, *Everett* reminds us of the truth of the expression that 'you never get a second chance to make a first impression'. It takes five to seven seconds to make a first impression.

To begin with, the person we are meeting will take in our non-verbal impact, beginning with our body language and then our dress and appearance. That will be followed by the quality or clarity of our voice, and thirdly what we say. This does not mean that image is more important than content – far from it, we need real substance too . . . Making a positive first impression sounds like common sense, but it is not common practice. Bring it into your conscious thoughts every day and manage that instant portrayal of your person brand more effectively.[16]

Research by *Willis and Todorov* demonstrated that an exposure time of no more than a tenth of a second is sufficient to form an impression of a stranger from their facial appearance. Longer exposure time increases confidence in judgements but does not alter significantly the first impression.[17]

Dress code and culture

The meanings we ascribe to these non-verbal signals are rooted in our culture and early socialisation. Thus it is no surprise that there are significant differences in the way we perceive such signals. For instance, dress codes differ in degrees of formality. *Schneider and Barsoux* summarise some interesting cultural differences:

> *Northern European managers tend to dress more informally than their Latin counterparts. At conferences, it is not unlikely for the Scandinavian managers to be wearing casual clothing, while their French counterparts are reluctant to remove their ties and jackets. For the Latin managers, personal style is important, while Anglo and Asian managers do not want to stand out or attract attention in their dress. French women managers are more likely to be dressed in ways that Anglo women managers might think inappropriate for the office. The French, in turn, think it strange that American businesswomen dress in 'man-like' business suits (sometimes with running shoes).[18]*

Ziolo discusses how the collective set of each generation differs due to different life experiences, work ethic and culture. Even if we have to make large generalisations, an understanding of sartorial trends of each generation can lead to a better understanding of the culture that guides them.

> *Even if you are not a dedicated follower of fashion what you wear is defined not just by your individual tastes but also by the societal and cultural experiences of your era. With most senior managers and executives hailing from the old school, clothing is not an expression of self, but a business uniform identifying the divide between the professional self and the self at leisure – therefore, a suit is the norm. Younger employees are less likely to make this distinction, seeing work much more part of what defines them, where expression of personality matters.[19]*

Critical review and reflection

Popular sports, film or television celebrities often appear to have a far greater impact on perception, communications and behaviour of people at work than any textbook, manager or training course.
   Why do YOU think this is the case and is it necessarily a bad thing? To what extent does this apply to YOU?

Organisation and judgement

The way in which we organise and make judgements about what we have perceived is, to a large extent, based on experiences and learning. It is important to be aware of the inferences and assumptions we make that go beyond the information given. We may not always be aware of our pre-set assumptions but they will guide the way in which we interpret the behaviour of others. In the same way that we make assumptions, about the world of objects and go beyond the information provided, we also make critical inferences about people's characteristics and possible likely behaviours.

A manager might well know more about person A, a member of staff who has become or was already a good friend, who is seen in a variety of social situations and with whom there is a close relationship, than about person B, another member of staff in the same section as A and undertaking similar duties, but with whom there is only a formal work relationship and a limited social acquaintance. These differences in relationship, information and interaction might well influence the manager's perception if asked, for example, to evaluate the work performance of A and B.

Judgement of other people can also be influenced by perceptions of such stimuli as:

- role or status
- occupation

- ethnicity, gender and age
- physical factors and appearance
- non-verbal communication and body language (**discussed below**).

Physical characteristics and appearance

There are frequent popular surveys and articles that refer to the suggestion that tall people, both men and women, are more likely to be successful both socially and professionally. For example, *Cohen* comments that taller people who look down on shorter colleagues are perceived to have confidence and respect. In an interesting account celebrating the lives of tall people, Cohen maintains that height is a pivotal piece of identity and the most defining force in our lives. Height determined her choice of sports (swimming), boyfriends (tall), social circle (tall), my college (tall), and my personality (big enough to fill the tall).[20]

An example is the appointment (June 2009) of the Speaker of the House of Commons, John Bercow, who is 5 ft 6 in tall (1.68 m). This appointment prompted newspaper articles about 'heightism' and perceptions about the 'shorter man'.[21]

In the work situation there are similar comments that taller people have better promotion prospects and earn higher salaries than short people. (We leave you to make your own judgement about this claim!)

In a discussion of physical attributes and good leadership, *Dib* suggests that 'we seem to associate the effectiveness of leaders with certain personality traits, which are in turn assumed as a consequence of their looks'. Examples are gender, hair colour, face, height, ethnicity and weight.

> *Of course there is no scientific evidence of correlation between height and intelligence, or height and the ability to lead people. Yet tall people are massively overrepresented in leadership roles. Similarly, other illogical preferences on hair colour, weight and facial features have nestled into our subconscious through societal, cultural and historical channels, and continue to affect the decisions we make and the leaders we turn to.*

Dib reports that there are convincing arguments for why we need to confront and overhaul ingrained preconceptions and stereotypes.[22] (**Stereotyping is discussed below.**)

Note also that *Mintzberg* includes 'tall' in a composite list of basic managerial qualities.[23] (**See Figure 16.3 in Chapter 16.**)

Framing

The term 'framing' is used to explain how we interpret particular circumstances. Rather like a picture frame, we place into the frame our particular perspective, focus and colour on things. So if we are feeling happy our experience is being 'framed' in a positive way. What is in the 'frame' will depend on what is filtered in or out. Whether we look at a difficult situation as a 'problem' or as an opportunity, or whether we see a mistake as a terrible failure or as a learning moment, will depend on how we have 'framed' the experience. If we are in a good mood we may only filter in messages from our environment that confirm our happy state; we may create an inner dialogue in which our inner voice is reaffirming why we are feeling so content. We may also be visualising a situation in which we are successful and these thoughts are establishing neural pathways. Helping people to reframe situations can be part of the mentoring and coaching process (**see Chapter 5**).

Critical review and reflection

We often mask what we really feel, act in ways that cover our true emotions and speak words that we do not really mean. In our dealings with other people we need to look beyond what is seen and heard and delve beneath the surface.

To what extent do YOU mask YOUR feelings and emotions? How do YOU think we can best judge the true beliefs and intentions of other people?

Perceiving other people

There are a number of well-documented difficulties that arise when perceiving other people. Many of these problems occur because of our limitations in selecting and attending information. This selectivity may occur because:

- we already know what we are looking for and are therefore 'set' to receive only the information that confirms our initial thoughts;
- previous training and experience have led us to shortcut and see only a certain range of behaviours;
- we may group features together and make assumptions about their similarities.

The Gestalt principles apply equally well to the perception of people as to the perception of objects. Thus we can see, for example, that if people live in the same geographical area, assumptions may be made about not only their wealth and type of accommodation, but also their attitudes, their political views and even their type of personality.

> To interact effectively (present ourselves and communicate appropriately, influence others, work with them in relationships and groups or lead them) we must have a grasp of what others are thinking and feeling, including their motives, beliefs, attitudes and intentions. In social perception, accuracy and differentiation are essential but difficult. Achieving them may be linked to the complexity of a person's system of cognitive constructs.[24]

The way we see others, the habits we have formed, the associations we have made and the assumptions we make lead us to make errors and distortions when perceiving others. The focus of the following section is to examine the perception of people and to consider the impact this has on the management and development of people at work. The principles of perceptual differences explained earlier apply to the way we perceive others. Some examples might be as follows:

- **Grouping** – The way in which a manager may think of a number of staff, for example either working in close proximity, or with some common feature such as all IT staff, all graduate trainees or all older workers; as a homogeneous group rather than a collection of individuals, each with their own separate identity and characteristics.
- **Figure and ground** – A manager may notice a new recruit and set the recruit apart from the group because of particular characteristics such as age, appearance or physical features.
- **Closure** – The degree to which unanimity is perceived and decisions made or action taken in the belief that there is full agreement with staff when, in fact, a number of staff may be opposed to the decision or action.

A manager's perception of the workforce will influence attitudes in dealing with people and the style of managerial behaviour adopted. The way in which managers approach the performance of their jobs and the behaviour they display towards subordinate staff are likely to be conditioned by predispositions about people, human nature and work. An example of this is the style of management adopted on the basis of McGregor's Theory X and Theory Y suppositions (**discussed in Chapter 10**). In making judgements about other people it is important to try to perceive their underlying intent and motivation, not *just* the resultant behaviour or actions.

The perception of people's performance can be affected by the organisation of stimuli. In employment interviews, for example, interviewers are susceptible to contrast effects and the perception of a candidate may be influenced by the rating given to immediately preceding candidates. Average candidates may be rated highly if they follow people with low qualifications, but rated lower when following people with higher qualifications.[25]

Recognising assumptions held and testing these out requires a heightened level of critical reflection. Many leadership and management development courses start with a 'self-awareness and diagnostic' module intended to help participants understand and recognise their style and preferences and the impact on others. Courses that take a more challenging stance will encourage managers to question their existing frames of mind and challenge them constantly to re-evaluate their purpose, strategies and action.

Dynamics of interpersonal perception

Unlike the perception of an object that just exists, when you perceive another individual they will react to you and be affected by your behaviour – the dynamics are all-important. This interaction is illustrated in the following quotation:

> *You are a pain in the neck and to stop you giving me a pain in the neck I protect my neck by tightening my neck muscles, which gives me the pain in the neck you are.*[26]

The interaction of individuals thus provides an additional layer of interpretation and complexity. The cue that we may attend to, the expectation we may have, the assumptions we may make, the response pattern that occurs, leave more scope for errors and distortions. We are not only perceiving the stimulus (i.e. the other person), but also processing their reactions to us at the same time that they are processing our reactions to them. Thus interpersonal perception differs from the perception of objects because it is a continually dynamic and changing process, and the perceiver is a part of this process who will influence and be influenced by the other people in the situation (*see* Figure 6.12).[27]

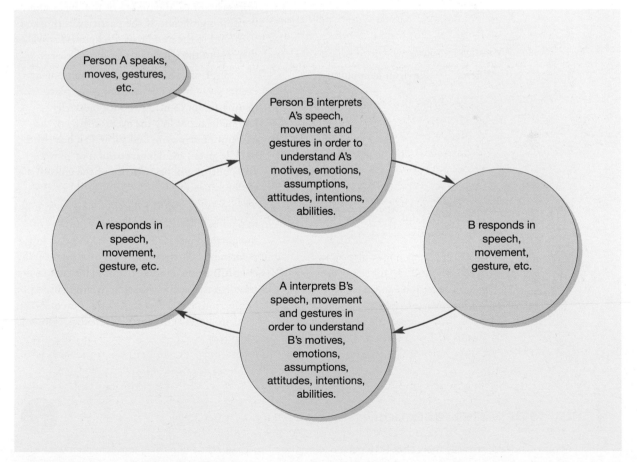

Figure 6.12 Cycle of perception and behaviour

Source: From Guirdham, M. *Interactive Behaviour at Work,* third edition, Financial Times Prentice Hall (2002), p. 162. Reproduced with permission from Pearson Education Ltd.

Setting and environment

Interpersonal perception will also be affected by the setting, and the environment may play a critical part in establishing rapport. For example, next time you are involved in a formal meeting such as attending an in-house development centre, consider the following factors that will all influence the perceptual process:

Why?	Purpose of and motives for meeting	Likely to be an important event for the participant, may be a catalyst for promotion and may signal new and relevant development opportunities. Chance to be visible and demonstrate skills and abilities. Opportunity to network with other managers. Thus high emotional cost to participant
Who?	Status/role/age/gender/ethnic group/appearance/personality/interests/attitudes	How participant prepares for the event will be influenced by factors listed opposite and previous history and encounters of all parties
When?	Time, date of meeting	The timing of the event might be particularly affected by events outside of the workplace. So if the participant has dependants or responsibilities, the timing of this event may become significant. If the participant is asked to attend in the middle of a religious festival, then again the relevance of time is critical
Where?	Environment/culture	Organisations will often stage development events away from the 'normal' workplace in an attempt to bring about objectivity and neutrality. How the event is staged, the amount of structure and formality, how feedback is given, the demonstration of power and control will be evidence of the culture of the organisation
How?	Past experience/rapport	The experience of the development event will in part be influenced by the expectations of the participant. If this is the second development centre, then experiences of the first will colour the perceptions; if this is the first centre, then the participant may be influenced by previous experiences of similar events (selection event) or by stories from previous attendees

Critical review and reflection

Most people do not consciously think about the person with whom they are interacting. They translate their view of the world around them from their own perceptions and assume that others are working from the same view.

To what extent are YOU able to challenge this assertion? How well do you think YOU relate to, and interact with, other people?

The importance of language and communication

Our language plays an important role in the way we perceive and communicate with the world. Language not only labels and distinguishes the environment for us, but also structures and guides our thinking patterns.

Marrs points out that every profession has its own language. For example, accountants and marketing executives are experts at bamboozlement and mysterious acronyms but perhaps the IT profession has the worst reputation.

> *Managers need to get straight answers from their IT professionals at several key points in the business cycle . . . If the IT department can't communicate without using jargon or acronyms . . . then you have got a solution looking for a problem rather than the other way round . . . Senior managers have to pick the people to run their IT departments. They need those who have technical skills – but who are also able to communicate IT considerations simply to the rest of the business.*[28]

Language as part of culture

Our language is part of the culture we experience and learn to take for granted. Culture differences are relevant because they emphasise the impact of social learning on the perception of people and their surroundings. Language not only reflects our experiences, but also shapes whether and what we experience. It influences our relationships with others and with the environment.

Consider a situation where a student is using a library in a UK university for the first time. The student is from South Asia, where the word 'please' is incorporated in the verb and in intonation; a separate word is not used. When the student requests help, the assistant may consider the student rude because they did not use the word 'please'. By causing offence the student has quite innocently affected the library assistant's perceptions.

Much is also communicated in how words are said and in the silences between words. In the UK, speech is suggestive and idiomatic speech is common: 'Make no bones about it' (means get straight to the point), 'Sent to Coventry' (means to be socially isolated). And action is implied rather than always stated: 'I hope you won't mind if I' (means 'I am going to'), 'I'm afraid I really can't see my way to . . . ' (means 'no').

Conversational pitfalls

A well-known quotation, attributed to George Bernard Shaw, is:

> *England and America are two countries divided by a common language.*

From frequent visits to America, the author can give numerous personal testimonies to this, including these actual words: 'I am just going to the trunk (boot of the car) to get my purse (handbag), fanny bag (bum bag) and money wallet (purse).'

McCrum gives some examples of conversational pitfalls[29] (many of which the present author can attest to from personal experience).

Australia	Talking disparagingly about Aboriginal people
China	Human rights; Tibet, Taiwan; sex; religion; bureaucracy
Far East	Confusing Japanese, Chinese or Korean
Greece/S. Cyprus	Asking for Turkish coffee
India	Poverty; sex; dowry deaths
Ireland	Referring to Great Britain as the 'mainland'; talking about 'the British Isles' to include Ireland; asking why they use euros rather than pounds sterling

Latin America	Talking about 'Americans' to mean just North America
Mexico	Nepotism
The Netherlands	Calling the country 'Holland' (inaccurate and offensive to people not from the Holland provinces)
New Zealand	Using the term 'mainland' for either North or South Island; mispronouncing Maori place-names
Northern Ireland	Asking people whether they are Catholic or Protestant
Russia	Corruption, contract killings, etc.
South Africa	Banging on about apartheid (it ended some time ago)
Spain	Criticism of bullfighting
US South	The Confederate flag

Source: McCrum, M. *Going Dutch in Beijing*, Profile Books (2007), pp. 44–5. Reproduced with permission from Profile Books Ltd.

Non-verbal communication and body language

We have referred previously to the significance of non-verbal communication and body language. This includes inferences drawn from posture, gestures, touch, the use of personal space (proxemics), extent of eye contact, tone of voice or facial expressions. People are the only animals that speak, laugh and weep. Actions are more cogent than speech and humans rely heavily on body language to convey their true feelings and meanings.[30]

As *'Pease and Pease'* point out:

> *All things are not what they seem. The ability to work out what is really happening with a person is simple – not easy, but simple. It's about matching what you see and hear to the environment in which it all happens and drawing possible conclusions. Most people, however, only see the things they think they are seeing.*[31]

According to *Mehrabian*, in our face-to-face communication with other people as much as 93 per cent of the messages about our feelings and attitudes come from non-verbal channels:

7 per cent from the words we use;
38 per cent from our voice; and
55 per cent from body language, including facial expressions.

Significantly, when body language such as gestures and tone of voice conflicts with the words, greater emphasis is likely to be placed on the non-verbal message.[32]

Although actual percentages may vary, there appears to be general support for this contention. According to *Pivcevic*, 'It is commonly agreed that 80 per cent of communication is non-verbal; it is carried in your posture and gestures, and in the tone, pace and energy behind what you say.'[33]

McGuire suggests that when verbal and non-verbal messages are in conflict, 'Accepted wisdom from the experts is that the non-verbal signals should be the ones to rely on, and that what is not said is frequently louder than what is said, revealing attitudes and feelings in a way words can't express.'[34]

According to *James*, in a sense we are all experts on body language already and this is part of the survival instinct:

> *Even in a 'safe' environment like an office or meeting room you will feel a pull on your gaze each time someone new enters the room. And whether you want to or not, you will start to form opinions about a person in as little as three seconds. You can try to be fair and objective in your evaluation, but you will have little choice. This is an area where the subconscious*

mind bullies the conscious into submission. Like, dislike, trust, love or lust can all be promoted in as long as it takes to clear your throat. In fact most of these responses will be based on your perception of how the person looks.[35]

In our perceptions and judgement of others it is important therefore to observe and take careful note of their non-verbal communication. Managers should also be aware of the sub-conscious message that their own body language conveys to members of staff. For example, *Kennett* points out that we take signals from our leaders, and if managers are exhibiting signs of anxiety their body language and critical talk will amplify employees' susceptibility to stress.[36] However, although body language may be a guide to personality, errors can easily arise if too much is inferred from a single message rather than a related cluster of actions.

Consider the simple action of a handshake and the extent to which this can provide a meaningful insight into personality. Does a firm handshake by itself necessarily indicate friendship and confidence? And is a limp handshake a sign of shyness or lack of engagement with the other person? The reality is that body language is not a precise science. One gesture can be interpreted in several ways. It may give a possible indication of a particular meaning but by itself cannot be interpreted with any certainty. Crossing the arms is often taken as a sign of defensiveness but could equally mean that the person is feeling cold or finds this a comfortable position.[37] Despite these limitations, it is essential that managers have an understanding of non-verbal communication and body language and are fully cognisant of the possible messages they are giving out.

Cultural differences

There are many cultural variations in non-verbal communications, the extent of physical contact and differences in the way body language is perceived and interpreted. Italians and South Americans tend to show their feelings through intense body language, while the Japanese tend to hide their feelings and have largely eliminated overt body language from interpersonal communication. When talking to another person, the British tend to look away spasmodically, but Norwegians typically look people steadily in the eye without altering their gaze. In South Korea, women refrain from shaking hands. The Japanese often have a weak handshake, whereas in the UK a firm handshake is encouraged. When the Dutch point a forefinger at their temples this is likely to be a sign of congratulations for a good idea, but with other cultures the gesture has a less complimentary implication. In many European countries it is customary to greet people with three or four kisses on the cheek and pulling the head away may be taken as a sign of impoliteness.

All cultures have specific values related to proxemics, that is the use of personal space and 'comfort zone'. Arabs tend to stand very close when speaking to another person, but most Americans when introduced to a new person will, after shaking hands, move backwards a couple of steps to place a comfortable space between themselves and the person they have just met. One reason why Americans tend to speak loudly is that their sense of personal space is twice that of the British.[38] (**See also discussion on violation of territory in Chapter 3.**) A concept map of interacting and networking with other people is set out in Figure 6.13.

Critical review and reflection

There are so many forms of non-verbal communication cues, either intentional or unintentional, that can be interpreted in different ways. There are also wide cultural variations in the context and essential meaning of the cues. Attempting to make valid inferences from body language is of little real value and its use should be discouraged.

How would YOU argue against this assertion? How well can YOU read body language and non-verbal communication?

INTERACTING & NETWORKING WITH PEOPLE

* DEFINITION
* FACTORS CONTRIBUTING TO RAPPORT

FACTORS
* Proxemics
* Orientation
* Environmental characteristics
* Non-verbal signs
* Other spoken communication
* Dominance roles & rituals

DEFINITION
* An interview is a conversation with a purpose usually 1:1
  Tx – THE TRANSMITTER OF THE COMMUNICATION
  Rx – THE RECEIVER OF THE COMMUNICATION (there may be many Rxs)
  Including touching the Rx

'PURPOSE-LESS CONVERSATION'
– a form of 'social grooming' e.g. about the weather
– often with casual or unknown contacts 'Good morning, how are you?'
– ritualisation of everyday contact prior to important communications (not to do this in the UK is often considered impolite)

PROXEMICS
The closeness of the Tx to the Rx(s)
* Consider closeness but be aware of cultural differences & taboos, especially between strangers
* With closeness note mirroring of body movements

ORIENTATION
Relative positions
– Side-by-side can imply friendliness, intimacy, helpfulness, etc.
– Face-to-face can imply competition, confrontation, etc.
– Territorially – on whose ground will the interview/meeting take place? (theirs/yours/neutral?)

NETWORKING
An increasingly important way in which workers in emerging organisations:
– exchange information
– give and receive support
– make personal performance comparisons
Some networks are formal (through, for example professional body membership), and some based on interests outside work (sports, the arts, voluntary organisation)

ENVIRONMENTAL CHARACTERISTICS
– In a large space, Rxs group … to hear better?
– In a small space, Rxs separate … to maintain personal space?
– Furniture, e.g. tables … could form psychological barriers
– No furnishings … Rx feels exposed & vulnerable
– Ambient noise too high … may hinder communication flow
– Distances too great
– Atmospheric conditions (heating/lighting/ventilation)

GRAMMATICAL GIMMICKS
Superfluous & meaningless, e.g.
– 'you know'
– 'whatever'
– 'I mean'
– 'really'
– & also grunts, snorts, etc.

DOMINANCE ROLES & RITUALS
Rituals of greetings & farewells
– handshake, kiss, hug, bow, salute, curtsy, raised hat, etc.

NON-VERBAL SIGNALS
GAZE   direct mutual gaze implies intimacy
          emotions perceived from eyes, e.g. anger, pleasure, surprise

MOUTHS   a smile encourages and reassures
          – communicates emotional state
          – controlled or uncontrolled

EYEBROWS raised rapidly – greeting, flirting, etc.
          furrowed – puzzled, angry, etc.

TONE   soft/friendly or loud/assertive (of voice)
          pitch, stress and timing imply mood and emphasis

POSTURE   lean forward – confidentiality, intimacy, etc.
          lean back – relaxed, easy, less concerned, etc.

GESTURES position of fingers/hands/arms
          the same gesture may have different meanings across cultures

TOUCH   hands – fingers open, closed, fist formed
          fingers – relaxed, pointed …
          limbs – open or closed
          hands – moving or positioned

CLOTHES   indicate something of a person's values, status and authority, or just bodily adornment

HEAD   nods, shakes
MOVEMENTS & tilts
          indicative of emotional states or moods

BETWEEN SEXES
– strokes, holds, pats … friendly
– hits … less friendly
– handshake – ritual touching for reassurance

may imply …
– aggressive intent
– defensive reaction
– submissive attitude etc.

Figure 6.13 Interacting and networking with people

Source: Copyright © 2009 The Virtual Learning Materials Workshop. Reproduced with permission.

Interpersonal communications

It is difficult to consider the process of interpersonal perception without commenting on how people communicate. Communication and perception are inextricably bound. How we communicate to our colleagues, boss, subordinates, friends and partners will depend on our perception of them, on our 'history' with them, on their emotional state.

Fitzherbert draws an interesting comparison between magic, perception and communication.

> *Magicians are acutely aware that the moment people see, hear, feel, taste or smell anything it automatically triggers a range of expectations and perceptions in their minds. In effect, it opens up a 'file' in their brain that tells them what they already know about the subject and rejects anything that doesn't fit. Magicians build their communication and effects around the expectations and perceptions they trigger.*

Clarity and impact aside, communication will be effective only if you can convince the audience about what you are telling them or showing them. Fitzherbert sets out twenty rules of perception and communication, shown in Figure 6.14.[39]

ENGAGEMENT	ATTENTION	IMPACT	CONVICTION
1 The framework for any communication is determined by the **expectations and perceptions** that you **trigger**	**5** Concentrated attention requires a **single point of focus**	**12** The senses offer **five different ways** into the brain	**17** To be convincing you, yourself, must **be convinced**
2 Expectations and perceptions can be reinforced or diminished by **prestige, atmosphere and environment** and **desire**	**6** Attention **tracks from left to right**, then settles at the left	**13** Firsts and lasts are remembered	**18** Doubts are reduced by **openness**, but may be increased by **over-stressing**
3 Communication can only register effectively when it builds on **what the audience already knows**	**7** The audience will look where you **look**, where you **point**, where you **tell them** to look	**14 Negatives impede** communication as they need unscrambling before the meaning can be interpreted	**19** People put more reliance on something they have **worked out for themselves**
4 The brain filters out most information it receives, leaving only what it considers important	**8 Curiosity, movement, sound, contrast** and **anything that is new or different** are friends *and* foes. Each has the potential to seize attention	**15 Over-familiarity** leads to 'invisibility'	**20** People's reactions are influenced by those of their **peers**
	9 The **wider environment** can often add to or detract from your message	**16** Sustained impact depends on transferring information **to long-term memory**	
	10 Every element of your **content** will either **add to or detract** from your message		
	11 Attention is sustained by variation, which **shortens mental time**		

Figure 6.14 Twenty rules of perception and communication
Source: Nick Fitzherbert, www.fitzherbert.co.uk. Reproduced with permission.

Getting your message across

Baguley points out that workplace communication can have a variety of aims and objectives, and if it is going to be successful there must be a two-way process. Channels of communication are proliferating but many people still struggle to get their message across effectively. It is important to use the right medium for your message: 'I'm appalled by incidents like, for example, sacking employees by text message'. To be a good communicator, Baguley suggests you need the following skills and understanding:

- Listen actively, rather than passively.
- 'Wear the other person's shoes' and understand the why and how of where that other person is coming from.
- Empathise with what is being said and felt by the other person.
- Be aware of and carefully observe body language.
- Plan your communication to take into account your objectives, the needs and abilities of the other person, the social and physical environment of the communication and the nature of the message.[40]

Importance of feedback

Feedback is a vital ingredient of the communication process. We may misjudge the receiver and regard our communication as unsuccessful, but unless we have some feedback from the other party we may never know whether what we have said or done was received in the way it was intended. The feedback may reaffirm our perceptions of the person or it may force us to review our perceptions. In our dealings with more senior staff the process of communication can be of special significance, including non-verbal communication, posture and tone.[41]

Two major approaches to, and ways of explaining, interpersonal communications are neuro-linguistic programming and transactional analysis.

Neuro-linguistic programming

Neuro-linguistic programming (NLP) emerged in the early 1970s as an offshoot of psychotherapy, psychology and hypnotherapy. It represents a collection of ideas and appears to offer lots of different things to different people. A popular definition of NLP is in terms of a model of interpersonal communication concerned with the relationship between successful patterns of behaviour and subjective experiences that underlie them. *John Grinder* and *Richard Bandler,* the co-founders of NLP, saw it as a means of helping to provide people with better, fuller and richer lives.[42] It is an approach that aims to enhance the effectiveness of interpersonal communications and facilitate learning and personal development. The name originates from the three disciplines that all have a part to play when people are communicating with others: neurology, linguistics and programming.

- **Neurology** – the nervous system, and processes linking body and mind.
- **Linguistics** – the study of words and how these are understood and communicated.
- **Programming** – refers to behaviours and strategies used by individuals.

The application of NLP shifted from therapy situations to work organisations, with clear messages for communicating and managing others. NLP emphasises the significance of the perceptual process and the way in which information is subjectively filtered and interpreted.

These interpretations are influenced by others and the world in which we live. Gradually, individuals learn to respond and their reactions and strategies become programmed, locked in, automatic.

Awareness and change

At its heart, NLP concerns awareness and change. Initially knowing and monitoring one's own behaviour and being able consciously to choose different reactions are fundamental to the process. Selecting from a range of verbal and non-verbal behaviours ensures control happens and changes 'automatic' reactions into consciously chosen programmes. Many different approaches and techniques are incorporated into NLP. Some concern mirroring and matching the micro-skills of communication in terms of body movements, breathing patterns or voice tempo. Others concern the positive thinking required in goal-setting 'outcome thinking' and the personal resources required in its achievement.

Another feature of NLP is 'anchors' that we all have. Anchors are 'triggers' that help keep habits in place and put us in a certain state of mind.[43]

> Anchors can be visual, like people, clothes and cars. They can be auditory, like a particular piece of music, an advertising jingle or the voice of a dear friend. They can be kinaesthetic, like the feel of your favourite clothes, sitting in your armchair or the warmth of a hot bath. They can be olfactory or gustatory, like the smell of a hospital (why do they all smell the same?) or the taste of coffee or chocolate (Lindt!). Words can be anchors because they evoke ideas; your name is a powerful anchor for your identity. Anchors evoke emotional states and most of the time we do not notice the anchors, only the states. Some anchors are neutral. Some put us into good states. Others put us into bad states.[44]

Agness suggests that in a tough market NLP can be applied to the main challenges faced by today's leaders, and identifies three main skills of NLP that help to get on customers' wavelength:

* **Sensory acuity** – developing an acute sense of awareness of what is going on around you moment to moment, and changes in your customer's physiology.
* **Rapport building** – developing fast a strong connection with your customers.
* **Improving sensory awareness** – intuitively picking up non-verbal signals in others. Increasing sensory acuity will improve communication with others.[45]

NLP and coaching

NLP has attracted considerable interest in recent years and there are a number of passionate devotees. There are numerous courses and seminars intended to demonstrate to participants how they can learn the skills to change themselves for improved personal or professional effectiveness and a greater enjoyment from life. It is also a popular approach to coaching (**discussed in Chapter 5**). Paul McKenna, the well-known television hypnotist, is a registered NLP practitioner and makes use of NLP principles in his courses on life training, including for example helping people to lose weight.

Paxton-Doggett reports on the use of NLP as part of executive coaching in business to aid freer and more open thinking in employees, and to achieve better results professionally and personally.

> Underlying much modern coaching practice is 'Neuro-linguistic programming' or NLP. Rather than simply moving a person towards new goals, NLP works on a more fundamental level by exploring the interaction of thoughts (Neuro), verbal and non-verbal communication (Linguistic) and patterns of behaviour and emotional responses (Programming). By using the methodology and techniques of NLP in coaching, thinking and behaviour are changed and different results produced.[46]

Critical review and reflection

Although much is written about the value of neuro-linguistic programming (NLP) it is really no more than an assembly of different ideas. It is a difficult concept to grasp and too abstract and theoretic to have meaningful applications for the practical manager.

What do YOU think? If YOU were a manager how might YOU apply NLP in a meaningful manner?

Transactional analysis

Transactional analysis (TA) is one of the most popular ways of explaining the dynamics of interpersonal communication. Originally developed by *Eric Berne,* it is a model of people and relationships that encompasses personality, perception and communication.[47] Although Berne used it initially as a method of psychotherapy, it has been convincingly used by organisations as a training and development programme.

TA has two basic underlying assumptions:

- All the events and feelings that we have ever experienced are stored within us and can be replayed, so we can re-experience the events and the feelings of all our past years.
- Personality is made up of three ego states that are revealed in distinct ways of behaving. The ego states manifest themselves in gesture, tone of voice and action, almost as if they are different people within us, and they converse with each other in 'transactions', either overtly or covertly.

Berne identified and labelled the ego states as follows, each with their own system of communication and language:

- **Adult ego state** – behaviour that concerns our thought processes and the processing of facts and information. In this state we may be objective, rational, reasonable – seeking information and receiving facts.
- **Parent ego state** – behaviour that concerns the attitudes, feelings and behaviour incorporated from external sources, primarily our parents. This state refers to feelings about right and wrong and how to care for other people.
- **Child ego state** – behaviour that demonstrates the feelings we remember as a child. This state may be associated with having fun, playing, impulsiveness, rebelliousness, spontaneous behaviour and emotional responses.

Berne believed that these transactions, which take place in face-to-face exchanges and verbal communication, form the core of human relationships. He claimed that the three ego states exist simultaneously within each individual, although at any particular time any one state may dominate the other two. All people are said to behave in each of these states at different times. We may be unaware which ego state we are operating in and may shift from one to another.

Preferred ego state

We all have a preferred ego state which we may revert to: some individuals may continually advise and criticise others (the constant Parents); some may analyse, live only with facts and distrust feelings (the constant Adult); some operate with strong feelings all the time, consumed with anger or constantly clowning (the constant Child). Berne emphasised that the states should not be judged as superior or inferior but as different. Analysis of ego states may reveal why communication breaks down or why individuals may feel manipulated or used.

Berne insists that it is possible to identify the ego state from the words, voice, gestures and attitude of the person communicating. For example, it would be possible to discern the ego state of a manager if they said the following:

'Pass me the file on the latest sales figures.'
'How do you think we could improve our safety record?'
(Adult ego state)
'Let me help you with that – I can see you are struggling.'
'Look, this is the way it should be done; how many more times do I have to tell you?'
(Parent ego state)
'Great, it's Friday. Who's coming to the pub for a quick half?'
'That's a terrific idea – let's go for it!'
(Child ego state)

Understanding human behaviour

Knowledge of TA can be of benefit to employees who are dealing with potentially difficult situations. In the majority of work situations the Adult–Adult transactions are likely to be the norm. Where work colleagues perceive and respond by adopting the Adult ego state, such a transaction is more likely to encourage a rational, problem-solving approach and reduce the possibility of emotional conflict.

Given the incidence of stress in the workplace, analysis of communication may be one way of understanding such conflict. By focusing on the interactions occurring within the workplace, TA can aid the understanding of human behaviour. It can help to improve communication skills by assisting in interpreting a person's ego state and which form of state is likely to produce the most appropriate response. This should lead to an improvement in both customer relations and management–subordinate relations. Therefore TA can be seen as a valuable tool to aid our understanding of social situations and the games that people play, both in and outside work organisations.[48]

Attribution theory

Part of the process of perceiving other people is to attribute characteristics to them. We judge their behaviour and intentions on past knowledge and in comparison with other people we know. It is our way of making sense of their behaviour. This is known as **attribution theory**. Attribution is the process by which people interpret the perceived causes of behaviour. The initiator of attribution theory is generally recognised as *Heider,* who suggests that behaviour is determined by a combination of **perceived** internal forces and external forces.[49] **Internal forces** relate to personal attributes such as ability, skill, amount of effort or fatigue. **External forces** relate to environmental factors such as organisational rules and policies, the manner of superiors, or the weather. Behaviour at work may be explained by the locus of control, that is whether each individual perceives outcomes as controlled by themselves or by external factors. Judgements made about other people will also be influenced strongly by whether the cause is seen as internal or external.

Basic criteria in making attributions

In making attributions and determining whether an internal or external attribution is chosen, *Kelley* suggests three basic criteria: distinctiveness, consensus and consistency.

- **Distinctiveness** – How distinctive or different was the behaviour or action in this particular task or situation compared with behaviour or action in other tasks or situations?
- **Consensus** – Is the behaviour or action different from, or in keeping with, that displayed by most other people in the same situation?

- **Consistency** – Is the behaviour or action associated with an enduring personality or motivational characteristic over time, or an unusual one-off situation caused by external factors?

Kelley hypothesised that people attribute behaviour to internal forces or personal factors when they perceive **low distinctiveness, low consensus** and **high consistency.** Behaviour is attributed to external forces or environmental factors when people perceive **high distinctiveness, high consensus** and **low consistency.**[50]

Implications of attribution theory

Employees with an internal control orientation are more likely to believe that they can influence their level of performance through their own abilities, skills or efforts. Employees with an external control orientation are more likely to believe that their level of performance is determined by external factors beyond their influence.

People with a high-achievement motivation may perceive that successful performance is caused by their own internal forces and their ability and effort rather than by the nature of the task or by luck. If members of staff fail to perform well on their tasks they may believe that external factors are the cause and as a result may reduce the level of future effort. However, if staff perform well but the manager perceives this as due to an easy task or to luck, the appropriate recognition and reward may not be given. If staff perceive that good performance was due to ability and/or effort, the lack of recognition and reward may well have a demotivating effect. (**Achievement motivation is discussed in Chapter 7.**)

Perceptual distortions and errors

We have seen that our perception results in different people seeing different things and attaching different meanings to the same stimuli. Every person sees things in their own way and as perceptions become a person's reality this can lead to misunderstandings. The accuracy of interpersonal perception and the judgements made about other people are influenced by:

- the nature of the relationship between the perceiver and the other person;
- the amount of information available to the perceiver and the order in which information is received;
- the nature and extent of interaction between the two people.

There are five main features that can create particular difficulties and give rise to perceptual problems, bias or distortions in our dealings with other people. These are:

- stereotyping
- the halo effect
- perceptual defence
- projection
- self-fulfilling prophecy.

To which could be added a sixth:

- unconscious bias.

See Figure 6.15.

These difficulties with people perception arise because of selectivity that exists in the perceptual process. We do not enjoy living in a world where uncertainty abounds and our perceptual system works to minimise energy consumption. We do not have to start every day afresh – we have our store of memories and experiences to guide us. The paradox is that this process is also our downfall.

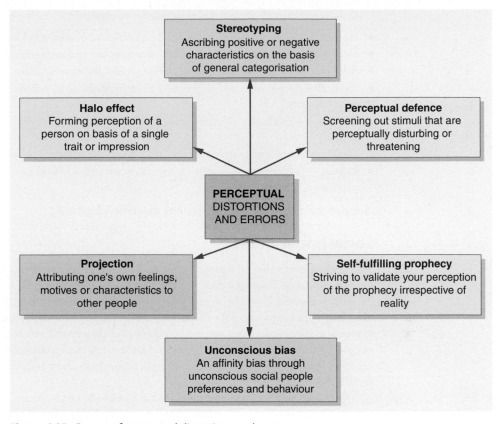

Figure 6.15 Causes of perceptual distortions and errors

Critical review and reflection

Bias and prejudice are inherent features of interpersonal perception and communication. Although exhortations can be made for us to become more aware of our own biases and to take more time in making judgements, we are working against our normal quick-fire perceptual system.

Do YOU believe this is fair comment? To what extent are YOU aware of YOUR own bias and prejudice?

Stereotyping

This is the tendency to ascribe positive or negative characteristics to a person on the basis of a general categorisation and perceived similarities. The perception of that person may be based more on certain expected characteristics than on the recognition of that person as an individual. It is a form of typecasting. **Stereotyping** is a means of simplifying the process of perception, making sense of the world and making judgements of other people instead of dealing with a range of complex and alternative stimuli. When a person is judged on the basis of the group to which it is perceived that the person belongs and as having the same characteristics, we are stereotyping. Pre-judgements are therefore made about an individual without ever really knowing whether such judgements are accurate; they may be wildly wrong.

Common stereotyping may be based on, for example:

- **Nationality** – Germans are orderly and industrious; Australians like cricket.
- **Occupation** – accountants are boring; librarians are serious and undemonstrative.
- **Age** – young people are unreliable; old people do not want to learn new ideas.
- **Physical** – people with red hair have a fiery temperament; people with visible tattoos are exhibitionists.
- **Education** – graduates are intelligent; graduates from Oxford or Cambridge are especially bright.
- **Social** – unemployed people are lazy; immigrants do not want to learn English.
- **Politics** – Labour voters favour strong trade unions; Conservative voters support private enterprise.

(See also the discussion of social identity theory in Chapter 8.)

Social implications

Stereotyping infers that all people within a particular perceived category are assumed to share the same traits or characteristics. A significant social implication of stereotyping is therefore the perception held about particular groups of people based on, for example, ethnicity, gender, disability, appearance, sexual orientation, age or religious belief. Stereotyping condenses the amount of information that we need to know and thus enables us to cope with a vast information flow. However, the consequences of attributing incorrect characteristics are extremely negative. Stereotyping can lead to misinterpretation, bias and a failure to try and really understand other people.[51]

A major danger of stereotyping is that it can block out accurate perception of the individual or individual situation. Stereotyping may lead to potential situations of prejudice or discrimination. An example might be the perception of people with HIV or AIDS.[52] Stereotyping may work either negatively or favourably for a particular group of people. For example, a sizeable number of employers still appear to maintain negative and inaccurate stereotypes about the capabilities and training of older workers. However, some firms, such as B&Q, the home improvement chain, have a policy of staffing certain stores with people over 50 years of age. (See the case study at the end of Chapter 4.)

The halo effect

The **halo effect** is the process by which the perception of a person is formulated on the basis of a single (or single series of) favourable or unfavourable trait or impression. The halo effect tends to shut out other relevant characteristics of that person. Some examples might be as follows:

- A candidate for employment who arrives punctually, is smart in appearance and friendly may well influence the perception of the selectors, who then place less emphasis on the candidate's technical ability, qualifications or experience for the job.
- A new member of staff who performs well in a first major assignment may be perceived as a likely person for promotion, even though that assignment is not typical of the usual duties the member of staff is expected to undertake.
- A single trait, such as good attendance and timekeeping, may become the main emphasis for judgement of overall competence and performance rather than other considerations such as the quantity, quality and accuracy of work.

A particular danger with the halo effect is that where quick judgements are made on the basis of readily available stimuli, the perceiver may become 'perceptually blind' to subsequent stimuli at variance with the original perception and (often subconsciously) notice only those characteristics that support the original judgement. (See also the self-fulfilling prophecy, discussed below.)

The rusty halo effect

The process may also work in reverse: the **rusty halo effect**. This is where general judgements about a person are formulated from the perception of a negative characteristic. For example, a candidate is seen arriving late for an interview. There may be a very good reason for this and it may be completely out of character. But on the basis of that one particular event the person may be perceived as a poor timekeeper and unreliable. Another example may be a new member of staff who performs poorly in a first major assignment. This may have been due to an unusual set of circumstances and not typical behaviour, but the person may still be perceived as a bad appointment.

Perceptual defence

Perceptual defence is the tendency to avoid or screen out certain stimuli that conflict with strongly held values and are perceptually disturbing or threatening. People may tend to select information that is supportive of their point of view and choose not to acknowledge contrary information. For example, a manager who has refused steadfastly to support promotion for a member of staff against the advice of other colleagues may select only unfavourable information which supports that decision and ignore favourable information which questions that decision.

Projection

Attributing, or projecting, one's own feelings, motives or characteristics to other people is a further distortion that can occur in the perception of other people. Judgements of other people may be more favourable when they have characteristics largely in common with, and easily recognised by, the perceiver. **Projection** may also result in people exaggerating undesirable traits in others that they fail to recognise in themselves.

Perception is distorted by feelings and emotions. Projection may be used as a means of attempting to externalise difficult or uncomfortable feelings. For example, a manager who is concerned about possible redundancy may perceive other managers to be even more concerned. People have a tendency to perceive others less favourably by projecting certain of their own feelings or characteristics onto them. As another example, supervisors may complain that their manager did not work hard enough to secure additional resources for the department when in fact the supervisors failed to provide the manager with all the relevant information and statistics. However, projection may also be used to externalise positive feelings onto other members of staff by attempting to create an overstated and unrealistic level of expectations and performance. (**Perception of 'self' and how people see and think of themselves, and evaluate themselves, are discussed in Chapter 8.**)

Self-fulfilling prophecy

A common feature of social interaction is the concept of the **self-fulfilling prophecy** (sometimes known as the Pygmalion effect), a term that is usually attributed to *Merton*.[53] The essence of the prophecy is that simply because it has been made, this will cause it to happen. People strive to validate their perceptions irrespective of the actual reality. People's beliefs or expectations influence their actions and behaviour in such a way as to make the beliefs or expectations more likely to come true. If staff believe a rumour (prophecy) that there will be no promotions or bonuses for the foreseeable future, they are likely to behave in such a way that their performance would not justify promotion or bonuses (even if the rumour was not true).

The expectation of managers has a powerful influence on the behaviour and performance of staff. (**See McGregor's Theory X and Theory Y assumptions in Chapter 10.**) If a manager expects only minimal performance from staff, they are not likely to perform to the best of their abilities. Therefore, managers need to establish an organisational framework and supportive culture that reinforces positive performance expectations at all levels of the organisation. Staff should also be encouraged to have high self-expectations of performance through working towards common goals.

Unconscious bias

Dan Robertson, Diversity and Inclusion Director of Employers Network for Equality and Inclusion, in conversation with *Davies,* draws attention to our 'preferred people preferences' that affect our unconscious social preferences. This type of **unconscious bias** may be demonstrated in 'micro-behaviours'.

> *For example, we may exhibit an affinity bias, where we respond positively to people who are similar to us or with whom we have something in common. We might give that person more airtime in a meeting, or agree more often with what they say. In contrast, we might cut short those with whom we do not have an affinity or disregard their viewpoints.*

These are subtle, unconscious behaviours and different from overt and discriminatory behaviour. Robertson maintains that such unconscious biases are hard-wired into us. We cannot eliminate them altogether so it is important to be aware of them and to change the way we work.[54]

Understanding the organisational process

The process of perception has been outlined as selective and subjective: we perceive the world in our own terms and expect the world to 'fit' into our constructs. Throughout our development we learn to distinguish what is important and significant (figure) from information that is additional and contextual (ground). This process is repeated when we join new organisations or take a new job within the same organisation. Fitting into the organisation involves selecting information that is necessary from that which is less significant. At times, the process can be distorted and we can also be 'tricked' into seeing the world in particular ways.

Although some organisations may discriminate, stereotyped perceptions are not always calculated: they are often made automatically and without conscious thought – in much the same way as we may be tricked by visual illusions. In fact, perceptual illusions are a very appropriate way of understanding the organisational setting.

For any organisation to be effective it is imperative that the staff are competent to undertake their work and satisfy the 'psychological contract' (**discussed in Chapter 1**). Part of the role of managers is to select and train individuals whom they predict will perform successfully on the job, and then to monitor and assess their competence for promotion. Accordingly, it is clearly important for managers to be aware of their own prejudices and assumptions. By opening channels and encouraging and developing all staff, trust might be fed back into the system from which equality and inclusion could flourish.

Critical review and reflection

It is not unreasonable to argue that there is no such thing as reality – only the individual's perception or interpretation of reality. Yet, managers require an understanding of perception in order to help interpret the behaviour and intentions of other people.

How can this conundrum be overcome? If YOU were a manager how would YOU hope to avoid organisational problems that result from perceptual differences?

Ten key points to remember

1 Perception is the root of all management and organisational behaviour and any situation can be analysed in terms of its perceptual connotations.

2 We all have our unique image of how we interpret the 'reality' of the world around us. A situation may be the same but individual interpretations may differ vastly.

3 The process of perception is based on both internal factors related to the individual's sensory limits or thresholds and external factors related to the nature and characteristics of the stimuli.

4 Perception gives rise to individual behavioural responses in given situations. It is important to be aware of potential perceptual illusions and impression management.

5 Managers must take care with how they organise and make judgements about their perceptions of other people, including both positive and negative messages.

6 There are many potential difficulties when perceiving other people. The manager's perception will influence the style of behaviour and relationship with other staff.

7 It is important to recognise the importance of the use of language and communication including cultural differences, and non-verbal communication and body language.

8 Perception and interpersonal communication are inextricably bound. Two major approaches to interpersonal communications are neuro-linguistic programming (NLP) and transactional analysis (TA).

9 Part of the process of perception is to attribute characteristics to other people. Attribution is the process by which people interpret the perceived causes of behaviour.

10 Perception results in different people attaching different meanings to the same stimulus. This gives rise to a number of potential perceptual distortions and errors.

Review and discussion questions

1 Explain fully why an understanding of perception is important in the study of management and organisational behaviour.

2 Discuss, with your own examples, both internal and external factors that affect selection and attention in the process of perception.

3 Debate the significance of impression management, including your own views on the importance of dress codes.

4 Identify clearly the most significant factors that you believe influence the judgement of other people. Provide your own example of each of these factors.

5 Discuss fully the importance of language and communication in the process of perception. Give your own examples of conversational pitfalls.

6 Discuss critically the amount of attention that you believe should be given to non-verbal communications and body language.

7 Justify what you see as the practical benefits of (i) neuro-linguistic programming (NLP) and (ii) transactional analysis (TA) as approaches to interpersonal communications.

8   Explain the principles of attribution theory and its importance to, and implications for, management. Apply the principles to your own working life.

9   Give your own examples of what you believe are the main causes and implications of perceptual distortions and errors.

10 Explain fully, with supporting examples, the importance of understanding cultural differences as an integral part of the perceptual process.

Assignment

Work in small groups, and share and discuss your responses with colleagues.

1. Think back to Figures 6.2, 6.5 and 6.7 in the text. For each of these figures:
    a. What image did you see first and how quickly?
    b. How difficult was it to see alternative images, including those suggested by your colleagues?
2. The text refers to the influence on perception from external stimuli such as:
    a. bright
    b. strong contrast to their background.
    Give your own example of how these stimuli feature in any two different advertisements, in any format, that have particularly caught your attention – in either a positive or negative manner. Can you think of any additional external stimuli that influence perception?
3. What did you learn from this assignment about the nature of perception?

Personal skills and employability exercise

Objectives

Completing this exercise should help you to enhance the following skills:

- Reflect on your understanding of, and behaviour towards, other people.
- Review your personal experiences of the process of perception.
- Learn and understand more about your inner self.

Part 1

Look back at the different reactions from five managers to the situation referred to at the start of this chapter. What do you think might be the underlying reasons for the individual responses and how might these responses relate to the perceptual process?

Part 2 – Exercise

You are required to work in small self-selecting groups with colleagues you trust and feel comfortable with, and with whom confidences are assured.

Relate honestly and fully:
a. your bias and prejudices about other people; and
b. bias and prejudices you perceive in other people.

Examples when you have been guilty of:

c. making a pre-judgment about an individual without really knowing the true circumstances. To what extent did you then filter stimuli to receive only that which supported your initial reactions? How did you eventually resolve or reconcile this pre-judgment?

d. impression management.

e. perceptual errors or misjudgements arising from cultural differences. What action did you take subsequently and to what extent was the 'error' resolved?

Discussion

- What were your colleagues' reactions to your revelations? Did anything surprise you? Or them?
- To what extent has undertaking this exercise made you more aware of yourself?
- What have you learnt from this exercise and what conclusions do you draw?

Case study
Behavioural economics

So, you have an assignment due tomorrow, 2,500 words, deadline 16:00. Have you written it yet? Maybe a paragraph or two? But you have got lots of notes, a heap of books from the library, a few articles downloaded from Google Scholar and some ideas, but you just have not quite got them down on paper yet. And you have known about this deadline for, what, two weeks? A month? More . . . ? Still, no worries; twenty-four hours to go. But first you need some more coffee – and, drat! The milk has run out so a quick trip to the corner store. And perhaps you can just have a quick glance at Facebook. And then you can get on with it. Honestly.

If you are 'human', the chances are you may recognise at least part of this scenario. The good news is that almost everybody else does. The less good news is that you will probably do it again. It is painful, it is frustrating, but it is true. Luckily, a few recent and highly readable studies by behavioural economists can give you an insight into why, and how it can be avoided.

Reason and irrationality

The basis for these ideas is the link between perception, thought and behaviour, and particularly our behaviour in terms of the economic decisions and choices people make in their everyday life. Many of these choices are personal: how much to pay for a coffee at Waterloo train station, where to rent or buy a house, how much to put into a pension plan or why you should be the first to order your food when you go out to dinner with a group of friends.[55] However, the principles shed light on the perception – thought – behaviour process, which

Behavioural economics explores the links between perception, thought and behaviour, particularly in terms of the economic choices people make in their everyday lives.
Source: David Samuel Robbins/Getty Images

is equally important in organisational contexts. Some choices and decisions are specifically related to management and organisational behaviour: matters of pay, reward, performance, honesty and discrimination. In the cases discussed, the decisions people make appear to be both irrational and entirely understandable. This was the starting point for Dan Ariely, who explains that behavioural economics is a relatively new field that links economics and psychology; it focuses on judgement and decision-making and seeks to identify the causes of 'irrational' behaviour. Moreover, he considers that:

we are not only irrational, but predictably irrational – that our irrationality happens in the same way, again and again. Whether we are acting as consumers, businesspeople or policy makers . . . Moreover, these irrational behaviors of ours are neither random nor senseless. They are systematic, and since we repeat them again and again, predictable.[56]

Social and market norms

Much of Ariely's research has been experimental, and one set of experiments offers an insight into the nature of the effort–reward bargain. Do we work harder when we are paid? Not necessarily. The experiment that revealed this involved three groups of participants who were asked to carry out a simple repetitive task of clicking and dragging circles across a computer screen using a mouse. The system counted how many circles were moved in the five minutes given for the task. Some groups were paid well for participating, others paid less well and yet others asked to take part as a favour. As anticipated, the well-paid worked harder than the poorly paid (by about 50 per cent), but the unpaid outperformed both. Why? Ariely's conclusion was that different norms had been applied – social ones rather than market ones – and that in many circumstances social norms are more effective motivators.

Does this mean organisations can use social norms as well as market norms to encourage effort? A group of lawyers was shown to be content to offer *free* legal advice to needy retired clients, but not at all likely to offer the same service for a reduced fee. Here social norms were powerful whereas market norms actually had a deterrent effect. Indeed, further experiments showed that even the mention of money could drive out social norms and change behaviour. The psychological technique of 'priming' (the creation of a certain set of expectations, indirectly, prior to some kind of activity) was used to introduce the *idea* of market norms to some people but not others, although nobody was actually going to be paid for taking part this time. Some participants were primed to think about money via a sentence unscrambling task before attempting a difficult visual puzzle (the sentences they were given used words like salary), and others were given neutral sentences. The behaviour of the primed participants during the puzzle element was notably different:

> *They were more selfish and self-reliant; they wanted to spend more time alone; they were more likely to select tasks that required individual input rather than teamwork; . . . Indeed, just thinking about money makes us behave as most economists believe we behave – and less like the social animals we are in our daily lives.*[57]

Moreover, it seems that once we have switched over from social to market norms in our thinking, it is very difficult for us to switch back. The social relationship may have been irretrievably ruined.[58]

Obviously, the vast majority of work organisations rely on market norms to a significant extent, and rarely more so than when people are paid for performance. The link between pay and performance seems logical, and much managerial work involves performance measurement and judgement with the aim of improving performance. For instance, when salaries were replaced by piecework in a car windscreen repair business (workers were paid per windscreen refit, and required to correct any mistakes they made without extra pay), productivity improved and errors were reduced.[59] However, the problem for advocates of this type of incentive scheme is that performance in most jobs is not as easily measured as it is in the windscreen repair business, and workers will generally adjust their behaviour to achieve the measured targets, regardless of the overall result.

> *It's simply too difficult for managers to work out the details of what should be done, and to judge whether what should be done is being done. The frustrations of working life are a direct result of that struggle.*[60]

All you need is nudge

An example of the application of behavioural economics shows how people can be encouraged, rather than forced, to behave in ways that are seen to be beneficial (to themselves, to their communities, the environment, etc.) and deals with the age-old problem of why we cannot seem to do things that we know are good for us or 'right'. We lack self-control, especially when costs are felt immediately but the pay-off does not arrive for some time. This is why dieting is hard but chatting on Facebook is easy. We tend to defer changes to our behaviour and are over-optimistic about our future behaviour; our diets always start tomorrow and will be spectacularly effective. But it seems that we can be 'nudged' to change our *future* behaviour in a way that makes it stick. For instance, *Thaler and Sunstein* report on the success of the 'Save More Tomorrow' plan as a means of encouraging people to contribute more sensibly to pension schemes. Instead of requiring people to contribute more of their pay today, they were asked to commit to increasing their savings in the future. The savings plan deducted the money from their salaries, and the increased deductions were timed to coincide with pay raises.

> *By synchronising pay raises and savings increases, participants never see their take-home amounts go down, and they don't view their increased retirement contributions as losses.*[61]

The scheme enlisted the power of four key behavioural responses to perceived factors. The 'painful' part was deferred; there was never a perception of 'loss', in this case of spending power; the system was easy and the default contributions were the increasing ones; and the power of inertia meant that opting out of the increases was more effort than staying in. The combined effects meant that the 'nudge' was effective, even though there was no obligation to continue with the increases.

Now, about that essay

A further practical example of this is the website created by Yale Economics Professor Dean Karlan called **'StickK.com'** which is described as a 'commitment store', and which is based on two key principles of behavioural economics:

1. People do not always do what they claim they want to do.
2. Incentives get people to do things.

The process is described by Thaler and Sunstein:

An individual puts up money and agrees to accomplish a goal by a certain date. He also specifies how to verify that he has met his goal. For example he might agree to a weigh-in at a doctor's office . . . (if the goal is to lose weight). If the person reaches his goal, he gets his money back. If he fails, the money goes to charity.[62]

A review in 2014 suggests that the most effective 'stick-Kers' are those who publish their goals via the site to a group of friends, family or colleagues who can monitor their progress and cheer them on – effectively using social norms to reinforce behaviour.[63]

So, back to that essay. Only twenty hours to go and still only 426 words. If only you had written 250 words a day for the last ten days, you would be polishing off the references and making it look nice by now! So, next time you get an assignment, how about you and your mates visit **StickK.com?**

Tasks

1 Discuss and plan an experiment like the 'circle dragging' one carried out by Ariely, which you could use to see if you find the same differences in motivation resulting from the use of 'social' and 'market' norms.

2 To what extent should managers appeal to 'social' norms when planning the work of their staff? What are the benefits and what are the dangers?

3 Consider the idea of 'priming'. Explain how this might fit into the cycle of perception and behaviour illustrated in Figure 6.12. How might a manager, either consciously or unconsciously, 'prime' others to receive their communications in different ways?

4 What can we learn from the ideas behind the 'Save More Tomorrow' scheme or **'StickK.com'** about how to help people to change both their perceptions and behaviour at work in such a way as to improve personal effectiveness?

Notes and references

1. Bartlett, F. C. *Remembering Cambridge*, Cambridge University Press (1932).
2. Kohler, I. 'The Formation and Transformation of the Visual World', *Psychological Issues*, vol. 3, 1964, pp. 28–46, 116–33.
3. Myers, I. B. *Introduction to Type*, Oxford Psychologists Press (1987).
4. Schein, E. H. *Organizational Culture and Leadership*, Jossey-Bass (1992), p. 9.
5. Ling, C. and Masako, I. 'Intercultural Communication and Cultural Learning: The Experience of Visiting Japanese Students in the US', *The Howard Journal of Communications*, vol. 14, 2003, pp. 75–96.
6. McCrum, M. *Going Dutch in Beijing*, Profile Books (2007), p. vii.
7. Stewart-Allen, A. L. 'Changing the Mindset about Americans', *Professional Manager*, vol. 15, no. 5, 2006, p. 37.
8. Block, J. R. and Yuker, H. E. *Can You Believe Your Eyes?*, Robson Books (2002).
9. Morgan, C. T. and King, R. A. *Introduction to Psychology*, third edition, McGraw-Hill (1966), p. 343.

10. Stroop, J. R. 'Studies of Interference in Serial Verbal Reactions', *Journal of Experimental Psychology,* vol. 4, no. 18, 1935, pp. 643–62; and Penrose, L. S. and Penrose, R. 'Impossible Objects: A Special Type of Illusion', *British Journal of Psychology,* part 1, February 1958.

11. Goffman, E. *The Presentation of Self in Everyday Life*, Penguin (1971).

12. Kendon, A. 'Some Functions of Gaze Direction in Social Interaction', *Acta Psychologica,* vol. 26, 1967, pp. 22–63.

13. Mehrabian, A. *Nonverbal Communication,* Aldine Atherton (1972).

14. Lucas, E. 'Check the label', *Professional Manager,* November 2009, pp. 22–5.

15. Rigby, R. 'What's Holding Him Back?', *Management Today,* December 2009, pp. 54–6.

16. Everett, L. 'First impressions', *Governance + Compliance,* November 2012, p. 54.

17. Willis, J. and Todorov, A. 'First Impressions: Making Up Your Mind After a 100-Ms Exposure to a Face', *Psychological Science,* vol. 17, no. 7, 2006, pp. 592–8.

18. Schneider, S. C. and Barsoux, J. *Managing Across Cultures,* second edition, Financial Times Prentice Hall (2003), p. 29.

19. Ziolo, K. 'A stitch in time', *Professional Manager,* July/August 2011, pp. 31–3.

20. Cohen, A. *The Tall Book: A Celebration of Life from on High,* Bloomsbury (2009).

21. See, for example, Leitch, L. 'The Big Problem that Short Men Face', *The Times,* 24 June 2009.

22. Dib, F. 'The Anatomy of a Leader', *Professional Manager,* September/October 2012, pp. 34–8.

23. Mintzberg, H. *Managing,* Financial Times Prentice Hall (2009).

24. Guirdham, M. *Interactive Behaviour at Work,* third edition, Financial Times Prentice Hall (2002), p. 161.

25. Wexley, K. N., Yukl, G. A., Kovacs, S. Z. and Sanders, R. E. 'Importance of Contrast Effects in Employment Interviews', *Journal of Applied Psychology,* vol. 56, 1972, pp. 45–8.

26. Laing, R. D. *Knots,* Penguin (1971), p. 30.

27. Guirdham, M. *Interactive Behaviour at Work,* third edition, Financial Times Prentice Hall (2002).

28. Marrs, C. ' It's all **geek** to me', *Professional Manager,* Winter 2012, pp. 32–5.

29. McCrum, M. *Going Dutch in Beijing,* Profile Books (2007), pp. 44–5.

30. See, for example, Torrington, D. *Face-to-Face in Management,* Prentice Hall (1982).

31. Pease, A. and Pease, B. *The Definitive Book of Body Language,* Orion (2005), p. 2.

32. Mehrabian, A. *Tactics of Social Influence,* Prentice Hall (1970).

33. Pivcevic, P. 'Taming the Boss', *Management Today,* March 1999, p. 70.

34. McGuire, T. 'Don't Just Listen', *Chartered Secretary,* September 1998, p. 24.

35. James, J. *Body Talk at Work,* Piatkus (2001), p. 3.

36. Kennett, M. 'First-Class Coach', *Management Today,* May 2008, p. 68.

37. See, for example, James, J. *The Body Language Bible,* Vermilion (2008).

38. For other examples of cultural differences, see French, R. *Cross-Cultural Management in Work Organisations,* second edition, Chartered Institute of Personnel and Development (2010).

39. 'Nick Fitzherbert Applies the Rules of Magic to Coaching People in Communication Skills', **www.fitzherbert.co.uk**; see also Fitzherbert, N. 'Magic Tricks in Communication', *Professional Manager,* vol. 14, no. 5, 2005, pp. 32–3.

40. Baguley, P. 'Putting Your Message Across', *Professional Manager,* September 2009, pp. 33–5.

41. See, for example, Pivcevic, P. 'Taming the Boss', *Management Today,* March 1999, pp. 68–72.

42. Bandler, R., Grinder, J., Dilts, R. and Delozier, J. Neuro *Linguistic Programming Volume I: The Study of the Structure of Subject Experience*, Meta Publications (1980).

43. Shapiro, M. 'Getting Your Brain in Gear', *Professional Manager,* vol. 16, no. 5, 2007, pp. 26–9.

44. O'Connor, J. and Lages, A. *Coaching with NLP,* Element (2004), pp 114–15.

45. Agness, L. 'Using NLP to get on your customers' wavelength', *Manager, The British Journal of Administrative Management,* Summer 2011, pp. 22–3.

46. Paxton-Doggett, K. 'Unlocking the Inner Genius', *Governance + Compliance,* September 2013, pp. 52–3.

47. Berne, E. *Games People Play,* Penguin (1966).

48. For a summary of NLP, TA and other thoughts on business psychology, see Butcher, D. 'Buyer's Guide to Business Psychology', *Management Today,* May 2005, pp. 54–7.

49. Heider, F. *The Psychology of Interpersonal Relations,* Wiley (1958).

50. Kelley, H. H. 'The Process of Causal Attribution', *American Psychologist,* February 1973, pp. 107–28.

51. See, for example, Stewart-Allen, A. L. 'Changing the Mindset about Americans', *Professional Manager,* vol. 15, no. 5, 2006, p. 37.

52. Goss, D. and Adam-Smith, D. *Organizing AIDS,* Taylor & Francis (1995).

53. Merton, R. K. *Social Theory and Social Structure,* Free Press (1957).

54. Davies, C. M. 'You are blind to your bias', *Professional Manager,* September/October 2012, p. 53.

55. Ariely, D. *Predictably Irrational: The Hidden Forces that Shape our Decisions*, Harper Collins (2008), see ch. 13.
56. Ibid., p. xx.
57. Ibid., p. 75
58. The first of the 2009 Reith Lectures by Professor Michael Sandel 'Markets and Morals' makes similar points; available as a podcast and transcript from the BBC website **http://www.bbc.co.uk/programmes/b00729d9**
59. Harford, T. *The Logic of Life*, Little, Brown (2008).
60. Ibid., p. 102.
61. Thaler, R. and Sunstein, C. *Nudge; Improving Decisions about Health, Wealth and Happiness*, Yale University Press (2008), p. 11.3
62. Ibid., p. 231.
63. Blanding, M. 'The Business of Behavioural Economics', Harvard Business School Working Knowledge, 11 August 2014, **http://hbswk.hbs.edu/item/7588.html** (accessed 16 February 2015).

CHAPTER 7
Work motivation and job satisfaction

Effective organisational performance is dependent upon human activity and the efforts of members of staff. The structure of the work organisation, styles of leadership and the design and content of jobs can have a significant effect on the attitude, motivation and satisfaction of staff. The manager needs to know how best to elicit the co-operation and motivation of staff, and direct their efforts to achieving the goals and objectives of the organisation.

Learning outcomes

After completing this chapter you should have enhanced your ability to:

- explain the significance and underlying concept of motivation;
- detail the various needs and expectations of people at work;
- examine content theories of motivations and the work of leading writers;
- review process theories of motivation and relevance to particular work situations;
- assess broader approaches to work motivation and satisfaction;
- explore the nature and dimensions of job satisfaction, frustration-induced behaviour and alienation;
- evaluate the relationships between work motivation, satisfaction and performance.

Critical review and reflection

Some writers argue that people do not lack inherent motivation, only the right triggers to evoke their efforts. Some claim that motivation can only come from within and attempts from other people to motivate you have little lasting influence.
  What are YOUR views? In YOUR own words, what motivates YOU most and to what extent are YOU influenced by other people?

The significance of motivation

The relationship between the organisation and its members is influenced by what motivates them to work and the rewards and fulfilment they derive from it. The more highly engaged and motivated the workforce, the more likely the success of the organisation in achieving its goals and objectives. Motivation is at the basis of all organisational activity.

The study of **motivation** is concerned, basically, with why people behave in a certain way. The basic underlying question is 'Why do people do what they do?' In general terms, motivation can be described as the direction and persistence of action. It is concerned with why people choose a particular course of action in preference to others, and why they continue with a chosen action, often over a long period and in the face of difficulties and problems.[1]

From a review of motivation theory, *Mitchell* identifies four common characteristics that underlie the definition of motivation:

- Motivation is typified as an individual phenomenon. Every person is unique, and major theories of motivation allow for this uniqueness to be demonstrated in one way or another.
- Motivation is described, usually, as intentional. Motivation is assumed to be under the worker's control, and behaviours that are influenced by motivation, such as effort expended, are seen as choices of action.
- Motivation is multifaceted. The two factors of greatest importance are: (i) what gets people activated (arousal); and (ii) the force of an individual to engage in desired behaviour (direction or choice of behaviour).
- The purpose of motivational theories is to predict behaviour. Motivation is not the behaviour itself and it is not performance. Motivation concerns action and the internal and external forces that influence a person's choice of action.

On the basis of these characteristics, Mitchell defines motivation as 'the degree to which an individual wants and chooses to engage in certain specified behaviours'.[2]

A fuller definition from the Chartered Management Institute is:

Motivation is the creation of incentives and working environments that enable people to perform to the best of their ability. The aim of motivation is to engage people with the work they are doing in order to achieve the best possible outcomes for individuals and the organisation as a whole.[3]

Underlying concept of motivation

The underlying concept of motivation is some driving force within individuals by which they attempt to achieve some goal in order to fulfil some need or expectation. This concept gives rise to the basic motivational model, illustrated in Figure 7.1.

People's behaviour is determined by what motivates them. Their performance is a product of both ability level and motivation:

$$\text{Performance} = \text{function (ability} \times \text{motivation)}$$

Kreitner et al. suggest that although motivation is a necessary contributor for job performance, it is not the only one. Along with ability, motivation is also a combination of level of skill, knowledge about how to complete the task, feelings and emotions, and facilitating and inhibiting conditions not under the individual's control.[4] However, what is clearly evident is that if the manager is to improve the work of the organisation, attention must be given to the level of motivation of its members. The manager must also encourage staff to direct their efforts (their driving force) towards the successful attainment of the goals and objectives of the organisation.

Figure 7.1 A simplified illustration of the basic motivational model

Needs and expectations at work

But what is this driving force and what do people really want from work? What are people's needs and expectations and how do they influence behaviour and performance at work? Motivation is a complex subject, it is a very personal thing and it is influenced by many variables. For example, *Farren* reminds us of the twelve human needs that have been around since the beginning of recorded history: family, health and well-being, work/career, economic, learning, home/shelter, social relationships, spirituality, community, leisure, mobility and environment/safety: 'Work and private life in the new millennium will continue to revolve around the 12 human needs.'[5]

Early writers, such as F. W. Taylor, believed in economic needs motivation. Workers would be motivated by obtaining the highest possible wages through working in the most efficient and productive way. Performance was limited by physiological fatigue. For Taylor, motivation was a comparatively simple issue – what the workers wanted from their employers more than anything else was high wages. The ideas of F. W. Taylor and his **rational–economic concept of motivation** (discussed in **Chapter 3**) and subsequent approaches to motivation at work have fuelled the continuing debate about financial rewards as a motivator and their influence on productivity.

Money as a motivator

Where there is little pleasure in the work itself or the job offers little opportunity for career advancement, personal challenge or growth, many people may appear to be motivated primarily, if not exclusively, by money. *Weaver* suggests that for many hourly workers in the hospitality industry, such as dishwashing, waiting or housekeeping staff, the work does not change much among different companies and there is little attachment to a particular company. For such staff, Weaver proposes a 'Theory M' programme of motivation based on direct cash rewards for above-average performance. A percentage base is calculated from the average performance of workers on the staff.[6]

Different generations in the workforce (**discussed in Chapter 3**) are also likely to have contrasting sets of motivations. For example, baby-boomers may well be concerned primarily about security, paying their large mortgages or funding their retirement. Generation X may be concerned about the changing nature of the work organisation, their financial future and continuing job security for the rest of their working life. On the other hand, Generation Y may be more footloose, have less interest in or doubts about affording to buy their own home and be less concerned about security or a long-term career.

For the vast majority of people, money is clearly important and a motivator at work *but* to what extent and *how* important depends upon personal circumstances and other satisfactions they derive from work. Although pay may still make people tick, there are now a number of other important influences on motivation. For many people, the feeling of being recognised and valued appears more important than money in motivating them to stay in a particular job. Note also that money may seem important as symbolising successful task performance and goal achievement. (**See achievement motivation below; see also the ultimatum game below.**)

As *Chamorro-Premuzic and Fagan* point out, few management topics have attracted as much discussion as the relationship between money and motivation. It seems that money is not a great motivator at work, and under certain circumstances may even demotivate. Extrinsic incentives such as financial rewards may extinguish or crowd out intrinsic rewards such as engagement and job satisfaction. This finding has important implications for managers.

> *It suggests that before incentivising their employees with external rewards – money, promotions or titles – they must first work out to what degree the job or task is meaningful or interesting for employees. And just as money can compensate for drearier jobs, it may also dilute employees' passion and joy in doing something that they love – like the artist whom is offended by questions about the price of his work.*

The authors also report on evidence that suggests that people are far more sensitive to the loss of money than the gaining of money. A pay rise may not necessarily make people happy, but a pay cut will be sure to make them miserable.[7]

Critical review and reflection

It is all very well talking about a contented workforce, praise and recognition, but at times of recession, rapid change or uncertainty, a secure job and high income are the true motivators. In the real world, money is the most potent need and strongest motivator.

Can YOU argue convincingly against this contention? To what extent are YOU motivated by money?

Extrinsic and intrinsic motivation

The various needs and expectations at work can be categorised in a number of ways – for example, the simple divisions into physiological and social motives or into extrinsic and intrinsic motivation.

- **Extrinsic motivation** is related to 'tangible' rewards such as salary and fringe benefits, security, promotion, contract of service, the work environment and conditions of work. Such tangible rewards are often determined at the organisation level and may be largely outside the control of individual managers.

- **Intrinsic motivation** is related to 'psychological' rewards such as the opportunity to use one's ability, a sense of challenge and achievement, receiving appreciation, positive recognition and being treated in a caring and considerate manner. The psychological rewards are those that can usually be determined by the actions and behaviour of individual managers.[8]

According to *Sauermann and Cohen,* overall intrinsic motives, particularly the desire for intellectual challenge, appear to benefit innovation more than extrinsic motives such as pay: 'However, management also need to recognise that appealing to individuals' motives can occasionally detract from organizational goals. For example, there are cases where individuals pursued research projects out of their own interest, against explicit policies of management.'[9]

Broader intrinsic motivation

Popular press reports appear to indicate that many people are increasingly motivated by broader concerns such as their work/life balance (**discussed in Chapter 3**), opportunities for flexible working, career advancement and personal development and growth and a feeling of identification with the values of the organisation. The motivation to work is also influenced by the changing nature of the work environment and the concept of the 'psychological contract' (**discussed in Chapter 1**).

However, according to *Gratton,* finding intrinsically motivating tasks is not easy.

> *Finding tasks and experiences that are intrinsically motivating sounds relatively straight forward but in fact it requires a heightened awareness of who we are. Without this emotional self-awareness we have no capacity to judge whether the tasks available to us could be intrinsically motivating . . . Finding intrinsically motivating tasks also requires the companies of which we are members to communicate the tasks available and to encourage volunteering.*[10]

Waller refers to the importance today of identity, and that work inevitably plays a key role in shaping identity. Waller questions how much of ourselves we put into our job. He points out that, not long ago, a job was something you did to put bread on the table, but nowadays (global financial situation apart) people in a cushy job with a decent salary, paid holiday, pension, healthcare and a well-stocked sandwich trolley will jack it all in, saying 'It's not really me.' If people are getting absorbed by their work-life, they expect their job to help them to discover and develop themselves.[11]

According to *Kets de Vries,* the best-performing companies possess a set of values that creates the right conditions for high performance. In addition to the motivational needs system for physiological needs, sensual and enjoyment needs and the need to respond to threatening situations, companies that get the best out of their people are characterised by a system based on a higher set of motivational needs:

- **attachment/affiliation** – concerning the need for engagement and sharing, a feeling of community and a sense of belonging to the company; and
- **exploration/assertion** – concerning the ability to play and work, a sense of fun and enjoyment, the need for self-assertion and the ability to choose.[12]

Developing a passion for work

Blanchard has identified eight critical employee needs that should be in place if organisations are to develop a passion for work and get the best out of their people and have them thrive:

- **Meaningful work** – People need to know that their work is worthwhile at both the individual and organisation levels and this is arguably the most important need.
- **Collaboration** – Working in a culture and environment that is encouraging, collaborative and co-operative.
- **Fairness** – People expect to be treated with respect, ethically, fairly and justly.
- **Autonomy** – To have influence and input over how tasks are performed, and freedom to make personal decisions about their work.
- **Recognition** – The feeling they are making a positive contribution through praise and appreciation or other recognition for their achievements.
- **Growth** – The opportunities to learn, grow and develop skills that lead to advancement in a chosen career.

- **Connectedness with leaders** – People need leaders they can trust and who share information and build rapport with them.
- **Connectedness with colleagues** – Solid relationships with colleagues and co-workers in order to provide willingness to apply discretionary effort.[13]

Threefold classification

Given the complex and variable nature of needs and expectations, the following is a simplistic but useful, broad, threefold classification as a starting point for reviewing the motivation to work (*see* Figure 7.2):

- **Economic rewards** – such as pay, fringe benefits, pension rights, material goods and security. This is an instrumental orientation to work and concerned with 'other things'.
- **Intrinsic satisfaction** – derived from the nature of the work itself, interest in the job and personal growth and development. This is a personal orientation to work and concerned with 'oneself'.
- **Social relationships** – such as friendships, group working and the desire for affiliation, status and dependency. This is a relational orientation to work and concerned with 'other people'.

A person's motivation, job satisfaction and work performance will be determined by the comparative strength of these sets of needs and expectations and the extent to which they are fulfilled. For example, some people may make a deliberate choice to forgo intrinsic satisfaction and social relationships in return for high economic rewards and/or job security. For other people, psychological well-being or social relationships would appear to be an important feature. For people working in caring organisations or the hospitality industry, where pay is often not very high, the interactions with other people and importance of supportive working relationships and good teamwork can be strong motivators at work.[14]

However the needs and expectations at work are categorised, a central motivational issue is the underlying importance for management to foster a genuine sense of engagement so that employees have a feeling of connection with the organisation and their jobs. (**Employee engagement is discussed in Chapter 16.**)

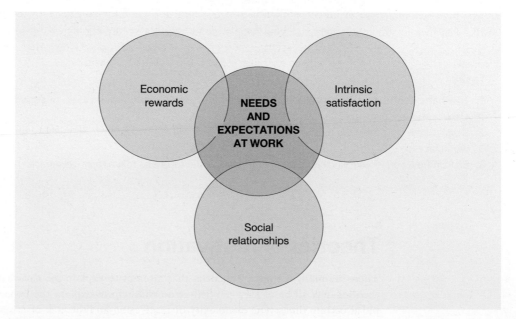

Figure 7.2 Needs and expectations of people at work

Critical review and reflection

Given the large number of identified critical employee needs and expectations at work, the threefold classification of economic rewards, intrinsic satisfaction and social relationships is far too simplistic as a meaningful focus of analysis.
What is YOUR view? What manageable and useful framework of analysis would YOU propose?

Management and organisational behaviour in action case study
Happy and productive workplace

Henry Stewart of the training company Happy draws attention to the positive correlation between staff engagement and profitability. Employee contentment is an underlying key to maximising growth and performance. Key factors to a happy workplace include a no-blame culture, a good work/life balance, transparency and a genuine commitment to the wider community. Applying the ten guiding principles of the Happy Manifesto across many organisations has created happier and more productive workplaces.[15]

Ten steps to a happy workplace

1. Trust your team. Step out of approval. Instead, pre-approve and focus on supporting your people.
2. Make your people feel good. Make this the focus of management.
3. Give freedom within clear guidelines. People want to know what is expected of them. But they want freedom to find the best way to achieve their goals.
4. Be open and transparent. More information means more people can take responsibility.
5. Recruit for attitude, train for skill. Instead of qualifications and experience, recruit on attitude and potential ability.
6. Celebrate mistakes. Create a truly no-blame culture.
7. Community: create mutual benefit. Have a positive impact on the world and build your organisation too.
8. Love work, get a life. The world, and your job, needs you well rested, well nourished and well supported.
9. Select managers who are good at managing. Make sure your people are supported by somebody who is good at doing that, and find other routes for those whose strengths lie elsewhere. Even better, allow people to choose their own managers.
10. Play to your strengths – make sure your people spend most of their time doing what they are best at.

Source: Stewart, H. *The Happy Manifesto: Make Your Organisation a Great Workplace – Now!* Happy (2012), p. 121. Reproduced with permission.

Tasks

1. To what extent do you accept the contention that employee commitment is an underlying key to maximising growth and performance?
2. Discuss how you view the relationship between a genuine commitment to the wider community and a happy workplace.
3. Explain how *you* would place in order of importance the ten steps to a happy workplace.

Theories of motivation

There are many competing theories that attempt to explain the nature of motivation. These theories may all be at least partially true and help to explain the behaviour of certain people at certain times. The complexity of motivation and the lack of a ready-made solution or single answer for motivating people at work is what makes the different theories important to the manager. They show there are many motives that influence people's behaviour and

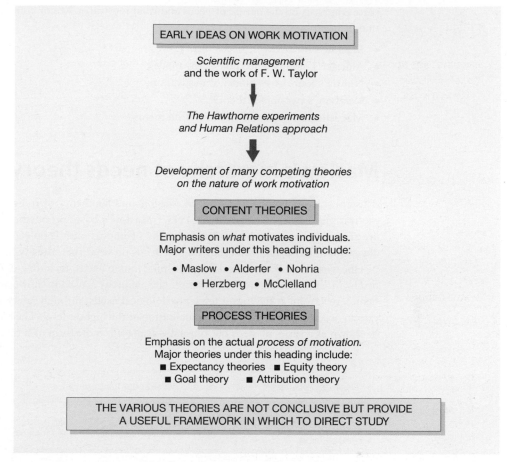

Figure 7.3 An overview of the main theories of work motivation

performance. Collectively, the different theories provide a framework within which to direct attention to the problem of how best to motivate staff to work willingly and effectively.

The usual approach to the study of motivation is through an understanding of internal cognitive processes – that is, what people feel and how they think. This understanding should help the manager to predict likely behaviour of staff in given situations. These different cognitive theories of motivation are usually divided into two contrasting approaches: content theories and process theories.

It is important to emphasise, however, that these various theories are not conclusive. They all have their critics (this is particularly true of the content theories of motivation) or have been subject to alternative findings. Many of these theories were not intended initially to have the significance that some writers have subsequently placed upon them. It is always easy to quote an example that appears to contradict any generalised observation on what motivates people to work. Despite these reservations, the different theories provide a basis for study and discussion, and for review of the most effective motivational style (*see* Figure 7.3). The manager must judge the relevance of these different theories, how best to draw upon them and how they might effectively be applied in particular work situations.

Content theories of motivation

Content theories of motivation attempt to explain those specific things that actually motivate the individual at work. These theories are concerned with identifying people's needs and their relative strengths, and the goals they pursue in order to satisfy these needs. Content theories place emphasis on the nature of needs and what motivates. Major content theories of motivation include:

- Maslow's hierarchy of needs theory;
- Alderfer's modified need hierarchy model;
- Nohria's four-drives model of motivation;
- Herzberg's two-factor theory;
- McClelland's achievement motivation theory.

Maslow's hierarchy of needs theory

A useful starting point is the work of *Maslow* and his theory of individual development and motivation, published originally in 1943.[16] Maslow's basic proposition is that human needs are arranged in a series of levels, a hierarchy of importance. People are wanting beings, they always want more, and what they want depends on what they already have.

Huczynski and Buchanan refer to the nine innate needs, including drives and goals, identified by Maslow (*see* Figure 7.4). However, the hierarchy is usually shown as ranging through five main levels from, at the lowest level, physiological needs, through safety needs, love needs and esteem needs, to the need for self-actualisation at the highest level. The **hierarchy of needs** may be shown as a series of steps but is usually displayed in the form of a pyramid (*see* Figure 7.5).

Figure 7.4 Abraham Maslow's needs hierarchy

Source: reproduced with permission from Andrzej A. Huczynski and David A. Buchanan, Organizational Behaviour, Pearson Education, 8th ed., p.293

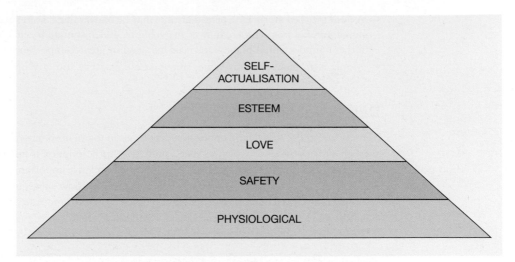

Figure 7.5 Maslow's hierarchy of needs model

This is an appropriate form of illustration as it implies a thinning out of needs as people progress up the hierarchy:

- **Physiological needs** – include homeostasis (the body's automatic efforts to retain normal functioning), such as satisfaction of hunger and thirst, the need for oxygen and to maintain temperature regulation, and also sleep, sensory pleasures, activity, maternal behaviour and, arguably, sexual desire.
- **Safety needs** – include safety and security, freedom from pain or threat of physical attack, protection from danger or deprivation, and the need for predictability and orderliness.
- **Love needs** (often referred to as social needs) – include affection, sense of belonging, social activities, friendships and both the giving and receiving of love.
- **Esteem needs** (sometimes referred to as ego needs) – include both self-respect and the esteem of others. Self-respect involves the desire for confidence, strength, independence and freedom, and achievement. Esteem of others involves reputation or prestige, status, recognition, attention and appreciation.
- **Self-actualisation needs** – once a lower need has been satisfied, it no longer acts as a strong motivator. The needs of the next higher level in the hierarchy demand satisfaction and become the motivating influence. Only unsatisfied needs motivate a person. Thus Maslow asserts that '*a satisfied need is no longer a motivator*'. Maslow claims the hierarchy is relatively universal among different cultures, but recognises there are differences in an individual's motivational content in a particular culture.

Not necessarily a fixed order

Although Maslow suggests that most people have these basic needs in about the order indicated, he makes clear that the hierarchy is not necessarily a fixed order. For some people there will be a reversal of the hierarchy, for example:

- Self-esteem may seem to be more important than love to some people. This is the most common reversal of the hierarchy. People who seek love may try to put on a show of aggressive, confident behaviour. They are not really seeking self-esteem as an end in itself but for the sake of love needs.
- For some innately creative people the drive for creativity and self-actualisation may arise despite lack of satisfaction of more basic needs.
- Higher-level needs may be lost in some people who will continue to be satisfied at lower levels only, for example a person who has experienced chronic unemployment.
- Some people who have been deprived of love in early childhood may experience the permanent loss of love needs.

- A need satisfied over a long period of time may be undervalued. For example, people who have never suffered from chronic hunger may tend to underestimate its effects, and regard food as rather unimportant. A higher-level need may assume greater importance than more basic needs.
- People with high ideals or values may become martyrs and give up everything else for the sake of their beliefs.

Degrees of satisfaction

Maslow points out that a false impression may be given that a need must be satisfied fully before a subsequent need arises. He suggests that a more realistic description is in terms of decreasing percentages of satisfaction along levels of the hierarchy. The relative importance of these needs changes during the psychological development of the individual. Maslow subsequently modified his views by noting that satisfaction of self-actualisation needs by growth-motivated individuals can actually enhance these needs rather than reduce them. Furthermore, he accepted that some higher-level needs may still emerge after long deprivation of lower-level needs, rather than only after their satisfaction.

Applications to the work situation

Based on Maslow's theory, once lower-level needs have been satisfied, giving more of the same does not provide motivation. Individuals advance up the hierarchy as each lower-level need becomes satisfied. Therefore, to provide motivation for a change in behaviour, the manager must direct attention to the next higher level of needs that seek satisfaction. However, there are a number of difficulties in relating Maslow's theory to the work situation. These include the following:

- People do not necessarily satisfy their needs, especially higher-level needs, just through the work situation but through other areas of their life as well. The manager would need a complete understanding of people's private and social lives, not just their behaviour at work.
- Individual differences mean that people place different values on the same need. For example, some people prefer what they see as the comparative safety of working in a bureaucratic organisation to a more highly paid and higher-status position, but with less job security, in a different organisation.
- Some rewards or outcomes at work satisfy more than one need. Higher salary or promotion, for example, can be applied to all levels of the hierarchy. Even for people within the same level of the hierarchy, the motivating factors will not be the same. There are many different ways in which people may seek satisfaction of, for example, their esteem needs.
- Maslow viewed satisfaction as the main motivational outcome of behaviour. But job satisfaction does not necessarily lead to improved work performance.

Useful basis for evaluation

Although Maslow did not originally intend that the need hierarchy should be applied to the work situation, it remains popular as a theory of motivation. Despite criticisms and doubts about its limitations, the theory has had a significant impact on management approaches to motivation and the design of organisations to meet individual needs. It is a convenient framework for viewing the different needs and expectations that people have, where they are in the hierarchy and the different motivators that might be applied to people at different levels. The need hierarchy model provides a useful base for the evaluation of motivation at work. For example, *Steers and Porter* suggest a list of general rewards and organisational factors used to satisfy different needs.[17]

Saunders contends that, despite the time that has elapsed, Maslow's theory remains watertight.

> *When prehistoric man first took shelter in a cave and lit a fire, he was satisfying his lowest – physiological and safety – needs. When a Buddhist achieves a state of nirvana, she is satisfying the fifth and highest – self-actualisation . . . The cave these days might be a three-bedroom semi with garden and off-street parking, but the fact remains that once we've got enough to feed, clothe and house our families money is a low-level motivator for most people. The dash for cash is soon replaced by the desire for recognition, status and ultimately (although Maslow reckoned that a lot of us never get this far) the need to express yourself through your work.[18]*

Critical review and reflection

Adair points out that presenting Maslow's hierarchy as a pyramid model gives the impression that the greatest needs are in the lower levels. Adair suggests that the pyramid should be inverted as physiological needs, for example, are limited but there are fewer limitations the further up you go.[19]

How would YOU best explain and present Maslow's hierarchy of human needs?

Alderfer's modified need hierarchy model

A modified need hierarchy model has been presented by *Alderfer*.[20] This model condenses Maslow's five levels of need into only three levels, based on the core needs of existence, relatedness and growth (ERG theory):

- **Existence needs** are concerned with sustaining human existence and survival and cover physiological and safety needs of a material nature.
- **Relatedness needs** are concerned with relationships to the social environment and cover love or belonging, affiliation and meaningful interpersonal relationships of a safety or esteem nature.
- **Growth needs** are concerned with the development of potential and cover self-esteem and self-actualisation.

A continuum of needs

Alderfer suggests that individuals progress through existence needs to relatedness needs to growth needs as the lower-level needs become satisfied. However, these needs are more a continuum than hierarchical levels. More than one need may be activated at the same time. Individuals may also progress down the hierarchy. There is a frustration–regression process. For example, if an individual is continually frustrated in attempting to satisfy growth needs, relatedness needs may reassume most importance. The lower-level needs become the main focus of the individual's efforts.

Unlike Maslow's theory, the results of Alderfer's work suggest that lower-level needs do not have to be satisfied before a higher-level need emerges as a motivating influence. The results, however, do support the idea that lower-level needs decrease in strength as they become satisfied. ERG theory states that an individual is motivated to satisfy one or more basic sets of needs. Therefore, if a person's needs at a particular level are blocked, attention should be focused on the satisfaction of needs at the other levels. For example, if a subordinate's growth needs are blocked because the job does not allow sufficient opportunity for personal development, the manager should attempt to provide greater opportunities for the subordinate to satisfy existence and relatedness needs.

Nohria's four-drives model of motivation

Another theory similar to Maslow's is that by *Nohria et al*. Based on a survey of a wide range of Fortune 500 and other companies, they formulated a model to increase work motivation based on four basic innate drives:

- The drive to **acquire** – scarce goods and intangibles such as social status.
- The drive to **bond** – connections with individuals and groups.
- The drive to **comprehend** – satisfy curiosity and master the world around us.
- The drive to **defend** – against external threats and to promote justice.

For each of these drives there is a primary organisational lever that front-line managers can use in order to best meet these deep needs and drives. Reward systems that value good performance fulfil the drive to acquire. A collaborative and open culture fulfils the drive to bond. Meaningful and challenging jobs fulfil the need to comprehend. Transparent performance management systems fulfil the drive to defend. All four levers are important, and failure to fulfil any one drive adequately will impact on the satisfaction of other drives. However, using all four levers simultaneously can lead to a noticeable increase in motivation.[21]

Herzberg's two-factor theory

The link between motivation, job design and satisfaction was established by *Herzberg et al.*, who used a critical incident method in interviews with 203 accountants and engineers from different industries in the Pittsburgh area of the USA. Subjects were asked to describe times when they felt exceptionally good or exceptionally bad about their present job or any previous job. Responses to the interviews were generally consistent and revealed that there were two different sets of factors affecting motivation and work. **This led to the two-factor theory of motivation and job satisfaction.**[22]

Hygiene and motivating factors

One set of factors is those that, if absent, cause dissatisfaction. These factors are related to job context; they are concerned with job environment and are extrinsic to the job itself. They are the **hygiene or maintenance factors** ('hygiene' being used as analogous to the medical term meaning preventive and environmental). The other set of factors is those that serve to motivate the individual to superior effort and performance. These factors are related to job content of the work itself. They are the **motivators or growth factors**. The strength of these factors will affect feelings of satisfaction or no satisfaction, but not dissatisfaction. **The opposite of dissatisfaction is not satisfaction but, simply, no dissatisfaction** (*see* Figure 7.6).

Herzberg emphasises that hygiene factors are not a 'second-class citizen system'. They are as important as the motivators, but for different reasons. Hygiene factors are necessary to avoid unpleasantness at work and to deny unfair treatment: 'Management should never deny people proper treatment at work.' To motivate workers to give of their best, the manager must give proper attention to the motivators or growth factors. The motivators relate to what people are allowed to do and the quality of human experience at work. They are the variables that actually motivate people.

Evaluation of Herzberg's work

Herzberg's theory is a source of frequent debate. There are two common general criticisms of his theory. One is that the theory has only limited application to people in largely unskilled jobs or whose work is uninteresting, repetitive and monotonous, and limited in scope. Yet these are the people who often present management with the biggest problem of motivation. Some workers do not seem greatly interested in the job content of their work or with the motivators or growth factors. A second, general criticism concerns the critical incident methodology. People are more likely to attribute satisfying incidents at work, that is, the motivators, as a favourable reflection on their own performance. The dissatisfying incidents, the hygiene factors, are more likely to be attributed to external influences and the efforts of other people.

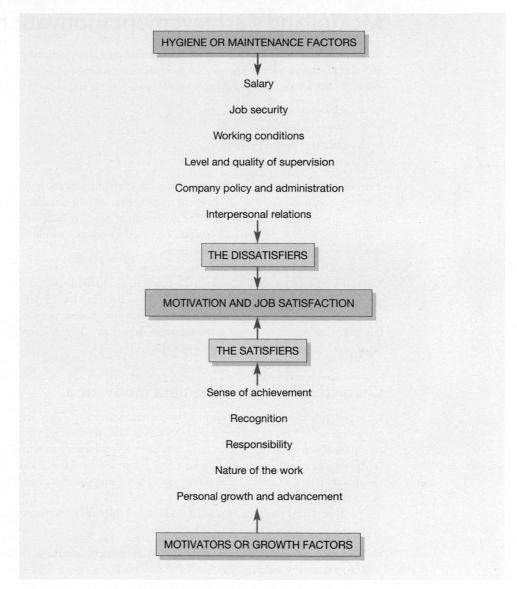

Figure 7.6 Representation of Herzberg's two-factor theory

Despite such criticisms, there is still evidence of support for the continuing relevance of the theory. For example, according to *Crainer and Dearlove:*

> *Herzberg's work has had a considerable effect on the rewards and remuneration packages offered by corporations. Increasingly, there is a trend towards 'cafeteria' benefits in which people can choose from a range of options. In effect, they can select the elements they recognise as providing their own motivation to work. Similarly, the current emphasis on self-development, career management and self-managed learning can be seen as having evolved from Herzberg's insights.*[23]

Whatever the validity of the two-factor theory, much of the criticism is with the benefit of hindsight, and Herzberg did at least attempt an empirical approach to the study of motivation at work and job satisfaction. Furthermore, his work has drawn attention to the importance of job design in the 'quality of work-life'. The work of Herzberg indicates it is more likely that good performance leads to job satisfaction rather than the reverse.

McClelland's achievement motivation theory

McClelland's work originated from investigations into the relationship between hunger needs and the extent to which imagery of food dominated thought processes. From subsequent research McClelland identified four main arousal-based, and socially developed, motives:

- the **achievement** motive;
- the **power** motive;
- the **affiliative** motive;
- the **avoidance** motive.[24]

The relative intensity of these motives varies between individuals. It also tends to vary between different occupations. Managers appear to be higher in achievement motivation than in affiliation motivation. McClelland saw the achievement need (n-Ach) as the most critical for the country's economic growth and success. The need to achieve is linked to entrepreneurial spirit and the development of available resources.

Research studies by McClelland use a series of projective 'tests' – Thematic Apperception Tests (TATs) – to gauge an individual's motivation. Individuals are shown a number of pictures in which some activity is depicted. They are asked to look briefly (10–15 seconds) at the pictures and then describe what they think is happening, what people in the picture are thinking and what events have led to the situation depicted.[25] The descriptions are used as a basis for analysing the strength of the individual's motives.

Characteristics of achievement motivation

Some individuals rate very highly in achievement motivation. They are challenged by opportunities and work hard to achieve a goal. Money is not an incentive but may serve as a means of giving feedback on performance. High achievers seem unlikely to remain long with an organisation that does not pay them well for good performance. Money may seem to be important to high achievers, but they value it more as symbolising successful task performance and goal achievement.

From empirical research McClelland identified four characteristics of people with a strong achievement need (n-Ach):

- **Moderate task difficulty and goals as an achievement incentive.** If the task is too difficult or too risky, it would reduce chances of success and gaining need satisfaction. If the course of action is too easy or too safe, there is little challenge in accomplishing the task and little satisfaction from success.
- **Personal responsibility for performance.** They like to attain success through the focus of their own abilities and efforts rather than by teamwork or chance factors outside their control. Personal satisfaction is derived from the accomplishment of the task and recognition need not come from other people.
- **Need for clear and unambiguous feedback on how well they are performing.** A knowledge of results within a reasonable time is necessary for self-evaluation. Feedback enables them to determine success or failure in the accomplishment of their goals and to derive satisfaction from their activities.
- **More innovative.** As they always seek moderately challenging tasks, they tend always to be moving on to something a little more challenging. In seeking shortcuts they are more likely to cheat. There is a constant search for variety and for information to find new ways of doing things. They are more restless, avoid routine and also tend to travel more.

McClelland and Burnham have also suggested that as effective managers need to be successful leaders and to influence other people, they should possess a high need for power.[26]

However, the effective manager also scores high on inhibition. Power is directed more towards the organisation and concern for group goals and is exercised on behalf of other people. This is 'socialised' power. It is distinguished from 'personalised' power, which is characterised by satisfaction from exercising dominance over other people, and personal aggrandisement.

Critical review and reflection

The difficulty with the theory of achievement motivation is that far too few organisations provide the culture or opportunities for individuals to satisfy the characteristics of high achievement needs.

To what extent do YOU believe this is fair comment? How would YOU describe the extent of YOUR own need for achievement?

Process theories of motivation

Process theories of motivation, or extrinsic theories, attempt to identify the relationships among the dynamic variables that make up motivation and the actions required to influence behaviour and actions. These theories are concerned more with the actual process of motivation and how behaviour is initiated, directed and sustained. Many of the theories cannot be linked to a single writer, but major approaches and leading writers under this heading include:

- expectancy-based models – Vroom, and Porter and Lawler;
- equity theory – Adams;
- goal theory – Locke;
- attribution theory – Heider and Kelley (**discussed in Chapter 6**).

Expectancy theories of motivation

The underlying basis of **expectancy theory** is that people are influenced by the expected results of their actions. Motivation is a function of the relationship between:

1. effort expended and perceived level of performance; and

2. the expectation that rewards (desired outcomes) will be related to performance.

   There must also be:

3. the expectation that rewards (desired outcomes) are available.

These relationships determine the strength of the 'motivational link' (*see* Figure 7.7). Performance depends upon the perceived expectation regarding effort expended and achieving the desired outcome. For example, the desire for promotion will result in high performance only if the person believes there is a strong possibility this will lead to promotion. If, however, the person believes promotion to be based solely on age and length of service, there is no motivation to achieve high performance. A person's behaviour reflects a conscious choice between the comparative evaluation of alternative behaviours. **The choice of behaviour is based on the expectancy of the most favourable consequences.**

   More recent approaches to expectancy theory have been associated with the work of Vroom and of Porter and Lawler.

MOTIVATION – a function of the **perceived** relationship between

Figure 7.7 Expectancy theory: the motivational link

Vroom's expectancy theory

Vroom was the first person to propose an expectancy theory aimed specifically at work motivation.[27] His model is based on three key variables: **valence, instrumentality** and **expectancy** (VIE theory or expectancy/valence theory). The theory is founded on the idea that people prefer certain outcomes from their behaviour over others. They anticipate feelings of satisfaction should the preferred outcome be achieved.

- **Valence** – the term used for the feeling about specific outcomes. **This is the attractiveness of, or preference for, a particular outcome to the individual.** It is the anticipated satisfaction from an outcome. The valences of certain outcomes may be derived in their own right, but more usually are derived from other outcomes to which they are expected to lead. An obvious example is money. Some people may see money as having an intrinsic worth and derive satisfaction from the actual accumulation of wealth. Most people, however, see money in terms of the many satisfying outcomes to which it can lead.

- **Instrumentality** – from which the valences of outcomes are derived. This leads to a distinction between first-level outcomes and second-level outcomes. **The first-level outcomes are performance related.** Some people may seek to perform well as part of their work ethic and without thinking about the expected consequences of their actions. Usually, however, performance outcomes acquire valence because of the expectation that they will lead to other outcomes as an anticipated source of satisfaction – second-level outcomes. **The second-level outcomes are need related.** Many need-related outcomes are dependent upon actual performance rather than effort expended. People generally receive rewards for what they have achieved rather than for effort alone or through trying hard. On the basis of Vroom's expectancy theory it is possible to depict a general model of behaviour (*see* Figure 7.8).

- **Expectancy** – when a person chooses between alternative behaviours that have uncertain outcomes, the choice is affected not only by the preference for a particular outcome but also by the probability that the outcome will be achieved. This is expectancy. People develop a perception of the degree of probability that the choice of a particular action will actually lead to the desired outcome. Expectancy relates effort expended to the achievement of first-level outcomes. Its value ranges between 0, indicating zero probability, and 1, indicating certainty that an action will result in the outcome.

Motivational force

The combination of valence and expectancy determines the person's motivation for a given form of behaviour. This is the **motivational force**. Expressed as an equation, motivation (*M*) is the sum of the products of the valences of all outcomes (*V*) times the strength of expectancies

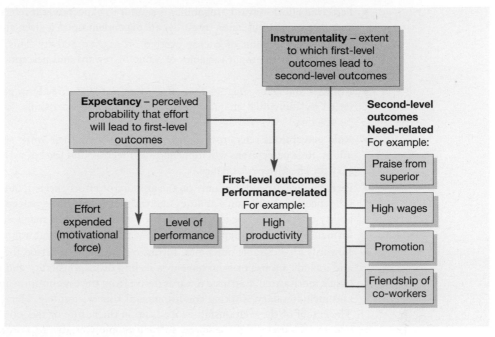

Figure 7.8 Basic model of expectancy theory

that action will result in achieving these outcomes (E). Therefore, if either, or both, valence or expectancy is zero, then motivation is zero. The choice between alternative behaviours is indicated by the highest attractiveness score.

$$M = \sum_n E \cdot V$$

There are likely to be a number of outcomes expected for a given action. Therefore, the measure of $E \cdot V$ is summed across the total number of possible outcomes to arrive at a single figure indicating the attractiveness for the contemplated choice of behaviour.

The Porter and Lawler expectancy model

Vroom's expectancy/valence theory has been developed and expanded by *Porter and Lawler*.[28] Their model goes beyond motivational force and considers performance as a whole. They point out that effort expended (motivational force) does not lead directly to performance. It is mediated by individual abilities and traits, and by the person's role perceptions. Porter and Lawler also introduce both intrinsic rewards and extrinsic rewards as intervening influences with feedback to perceived effort–reward probability. Perceived equitable rewards is also an influence on the level of satisfaction.

Explanation of relationships

Porter and Lawler see motivation, satisfaction and performance as separate variables and attempt to explain the complex relationships among them. In contrast to the human relations approach, which tended to assume that job satisfaction leads to improved performance, Porter and Lawler suggest that satisfaction is an effect rather than a cause of performance. It is performance that leads to job satisfaction.

- **Value of reward** is similar to valence in Vroom's model. People desire various outcomes (rewards), which they hope to achieve from work. The value placed on a reward depends on the strength of its desirability.

- **Perceived effort–reward probability** is similar to expectancy. It refers to a person's expectation that certain outcomes (rewards) are dependent upon a given amount of effort.

- **Effort** is the amount of energy exerted on a given activity. This is dependent upon the interaction of the input variables of value of reward and perception of the effort–reward relationship.

- **Abilities and traits** suggests that effort does not lead directly to performance but is influenced by individual characteristics such as intelligence, skills, knowledge, training and personality.

- **Role perceptions** refers to the way individuals view their work and the role they should adopt. Role perceptions will influence the direction and level of action believed to be necessary for effective performance.

- **Performance** depends not only on the amount of effort exerted, but also on the intervening influences of the person's abilities and traits, and their role perceptions. Lack of the right ability or an inaccurate role perception of what is required may result in a low level of performance or task accomplishment, despite exertion of a large amount of energy.

- **Rewards** are desirable outcomes. Intrinsic rewards derive from the individuals themselves and include a sense of achievement, a feeling of responsibility and recognition (e.g. Herzberg's motivators). Extrinsic rewards derive from the organisation and the actions of others and include salary, working conditions and supervision (e.g. Herzberg's hygiene factors). The extent of the relationship depends upon the nature of the job and the extent to which it permits variety and challenge, so that people feel able to reward themselves for good performance.

- **Perceived equitable rewards** – most people have an implicit perception about the level of rewards they should receive commensurate with the requirements and demands of the job. Self-rating of performance links directly with the perceived equitable reward variable.

- **Satisfaction** is not the same as motivation. It is an attitude, an individual's internal state. Satisfaction is determined by both actual rewards received and perceived level of rewards from the organisation for a given standard of performance. The experience of satisfaction derives from actual rewards that meet or exceed the perceived equitable rewards.

Lawler's revised expectancy model

Following the original Porter and Lawler model, further work was undertaken by *Lawler* (*see* Figure 7.9).[29] He suggests that in deciding the attractiveness of alternative behaviours, there are two types of expectancies to be considered: effort–performance expectancies ($E \rightarrow P$) and performance–outcome expectancies ($P \rightarrow O$).

The **first expectancy** ($E \rightarrow P$) is the person's perception of the probability that a given amount of effort will result in achieving an intended level of performance. It is measured on a scale between 0 and 1. The closer the perceived relationship between effort and performance, the higher the $E \rightarrow P$ expectancy score.

The **second expectancy** ($P \rightarrow O$) is the person's perception of the probability that a given level of performance will actually lead to particular need-related outcomes. This is measured also on a scale between 0 and 1. The closer the perceived relationship between performance and outcome, the higher the $P \rightarrow O$ expectancy score.

Motivational force to perform

The multiplicative combination of the two types of expectancies, $E \rightarrow P$ and the sum of the products $P \rightarrow O$, determines expectancy. The motivational force to perform (effort expended) is determined by multiplying $E \rightarrow P$ and $P \rightarrow O$ by the strength of outcome valence (V):

$$E(\text{Effort}) = (E \rightarrow P) \times \sum [(P \rightarrow O)V]$$

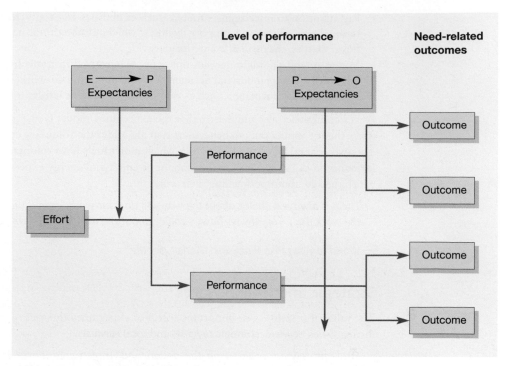

Figure 7.9 An illustration of the Lawler expectancy model

The distinction between the two types of expectancies arises because they are determined by different conditions. E → P expectancy is determined in part by the person's ability and self-confidence, past experience and the difficulty of the task. P → O expectancy is determined by the attractiveness of the outcomes and the belief about who controls the outcomes – the actual person or other people.

Implications of expectancy theories

There are a number of versions of expectancy theory. The main elements tend to be very similar, however, and this suggests the development of a generally accepted approach. Expectancy models are not always easy to understand, or to apply. There are many variables that affect behaviour at work. A problem can arise in attempting to include a large number of variables or in identifying those variables that are most appropriate in particular situations.

Expectancy theory does, however, draw attention to the complexities of work motivation. It provides further information in helping to explain the nature of behaviour and motivation in the work situation, and helps to identify problems in performance. Expectancy theory indicates that managers should give attention to a number of factors, including the following:

- Use rewards appropriate in terms of individual performance. Outcomes with high valence should be used as an incentive for improved performance.
- Attempt to establish clear relationships between effort–performance and rewards, as perceived by the individual.
- Establish clear procedures for the evaluation of individual levels of performance.

- Pay attention to intervening variables such as abilities and traits, role perceptions, organisational procedures and support facilities, which, although not necessarily direct motivational factors, may still affect performance.
- Minimise undesirable outcomes that may be perceived to result from a high level of performance, such as industrial accidents or sanctions from co-workers, or to result despite a high level of performance, such as short-time working or layoffs.

Porter and Lawler also emphasise that the expectancy model is just a model and that expectancy theory applies only to behaviours that are under the voluntary control of the individual. The two general types of choices over which individuals have voluntary control of work performance in organisations are the amount of effort and energy expended, and the manner in which they go about performing their work.

> *There is always a choice about the way you do your work, even if there is not a choice about the work itself. You always have a choice about the attitude you bring to the job.*
>
> World famous Pike Place Fish Market, Seattle[30]

Strategic and total rewards

The value of rewards is an important aspect of expectancy theories of motivation. The CIPD distinguishes between **strategic rewards** and **total rewards.**

> *Strategic reward is based on the design and implementation of long-term policies and practices to closely support and advance business or organisational objectives as well as employee aspirations. The concept of **total reward** encompasses all aspects of work that are valued by employees, including elements such as learning and development opportunities and/or an attractive working environment, in addition to the wider pay and benefits package.*[31]

The need to maintain the motivation, development and performance of employees has resulted in many organisations giving greater attention to a more comprehensive approach of total rewards, including attention to both extrinsic and intrinsic rewards (**discussed above**).

Critical review and reflection

Expectancy theories of motivation may make for interesting discussion in the classroom but are unlikely to have much appeal to the practical manager in modern work organisations.
    What do YOU think? How would YOU justify the potential benefits of expectancy theory to a sceptical manager?

Equity theory of motivation

One of the major variables of satisfaction in the Porter and Lawler expectancy model is perceived equitable rewards. This leads to consideration of another process theory of motivation – **equity theory.** Applied to the work situation, equity theory is usually associated with the work of *Adams.*[32]

Equity theory focuses on people's feelings of how fairly they have been treated in comparison with the treatment received by others. It is based on social exchange theory (**discussed in Chapter 1**). Social relationships involve an exchange process. For example, a person may expect promotion as an outcome of a high level of contribution (input) in helping to achieve an important organisational objective. People also compare their own position with that of others. They determine the perceived equity of their own position. Most exchanges involve a number of inputs and outcomes. According to equity theory, people place a weighting on these various inputs and outcomes according to how they perceive their importance. When there is an unequal comparison of ratios the person experiences a sense of inequity.

Behaviour as a consequence of inequity

A feeling of inequity causes tension, which is an unpleasant experience. The presence of inequity therefore motivates the person to remove or to reduce the level of tension and the perceived inequity. The magnitude of perceived inequity determines the level of tension and strength of motivation. Adams identifies six broad types of possible behaviour as consequences of inequity (*see* Figure 7.10):

- **Changes to inputs** – Increasing or decreasing level of inputs, for example through the amount or quality of work, absenteeism, or working additional hours without pay.
- **Changes to outcomes** – Attempting to change outcomes such as pay, working conditions, status and recognition, without changes to inputs.
- **Cognitive distortion** – Distorting, cognitively, inputs or outcomes to achieve the same results. Attempting to distort the utility of facts, for example the belief about how hard they are really working, the relevance of a particular qualification, or what they can or cannot obtain with a given level of pay.
- **Leaving the field** – Trying to find a new situation with a more favourable balance, for example by absenteeism, request for a transfer, resigning from a job or from the organisation altogether.

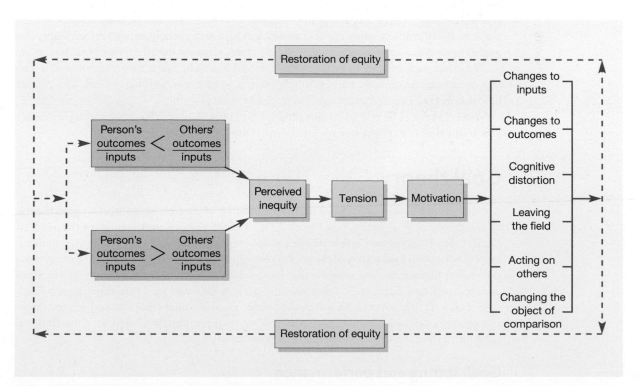

Figure 7.10 An illustration of Adams' equity theory of motivation

- **Acting on others** – Attempting to bring about changes in others, for example to lower their inputs or accept greater outcomes. The person may cognitively distort the inputs and outcomes of others, or alternatively try to force others to leave the field.
- **Changing the object of comparison** – Changing the reference group with whom comparison is made. For example, where another person with a previously similar ratio of outcomes–inputs receives greater outcomes without any apparent increase in contribution, that other person may be perceived as now belonging to a different level in the organisation structure.

Under the control of the manager

The manager may seek to remove or reduce tension and perceived inequity among staff by influencing these types of behaviour – for example, by attempting to change a person's inputs or encouraging a different object of comparison. People measure and compare their total inputs and outcomes, so, for example, a working parent may prefer greater flexibility in working hours in return for lower monetary rewards. However, there are likely to be only two courses of action under the direct control of the manager. Outcomes can be changed by, for example, increased pay, additional perks or improved working conditions; or by instigating a person leaving the field through transfer, resignation or, as an extreme measure, dismissal. It is important to remember that equity theory is about the **perceived** ratio of inputs to outcomes and these perceptions may not reflect the reality of the situation.

The ultimatum game

The **ultimatum game** is an economic behavioural game that can arguably be related to the concept of equity theory.[33] Two participants, A and B, are given the opportunity to split a given sum of money between them. The game is played anonymously and once only. One person (A) has to decide to make a one-time, take-it-or-leave-it offer (ultimatum) to the other person (B). If person B agrees to the division, both A and B keep their share of the money. However, if the offer is rejected then neither person receives anything. Experiments indicate that if A offers around 50 per cent of the money then B will accept the offer. But if A offers a noticeably lesser amount than 50 per cent, B will typically refuse the offer in which case neither participant receives anything. One might expect B to accept because even a lesser amount, whatever the offer, is better than nothing.

The conclusion appears to be that people do not like to be taken advantage of, and in certain circumstances at work, fairness in treatment is more important than money. Can you see how this might be related to perceptions of equity theory?

Viewers of the ITV1 television quiz programme *Divided*, in which contestants have to agree how to divide a cash prize, may see a similarity with the ultimatum game.

Goal theory

Another theory usually considered under the heading of motivation to work is **goal theory**, or the theory of goal-setting (*see* Figure 7.11). This theory is based mainly on the work of *Locke*.[34] The basic premise is that people's goals or intentions play an important part in determining behaviour. Locke accepts the importance of perceived value, as indicated in expectancy theories of motivation, and suggests that these values give rise to the experience of emotions and desires. Goals direct work behaviour and performance and lead to certain consequences or feedback. People strive to achieve goals in order to satisfy their emotions and desires. *Locke* subsequently pointed out that 'goal-setting is more appropriately viewed as a motivational technique rather than as a formal theory of motivation'.[35]

Goal-setting and performance

The combination of **goal difficulty** – the extent to which it is challenging and demanding – and the **extent of the person's commitment** regulates the level of effort expended. People with specific quantitative goals, such as a defined level of performance or a given deadline for

Figure 7.11 An illustration of Locke's theory of goal-setting

completion of a task, will perform better than people with no set goal or only a vague goal such as 'do the best you can'. People who have difficult goals will perform better than people with easier goals.

Gratton refers to 'stretch goals', which are ambitious, highly targeted opportunities for breakthrough improvements in performance. These goals should stem from critical success indicators and come from deep discussions within the company, and from collaboration within and across task forces, and lead to the development of activities and tactics to achieve the goals.[36] People lacking positive motivation at work may also help gain improved results and a better sense of achievement by setting themselves specific goals and identifying tasks directly related to their work and measurable targets of time and performance.

Practical implications for the manager

Goal theory has a number of practical implications for the manager:

- Individuals lacking in motivation often do not have clear goals. Specific performance goals should systematically be identified and set in order to direct behaviour and maintain motivation.
- Goals should be set at a challenging but realistic level. Difficult goals lead to higher performance. However, if goals are set at too high a level or are regarded as impossible to achieve, this can lead to stress and performance will suffer, especially over a longer period.
- Complete, accurate and timely feedback and knowledge of results is usually associated with high performance. Feedback provides a means of checking progress on goal attainment and forms the basis for any revision of goals.
- Goals can be determined either by a superior or by individuals themselves. Goals set by other people are more likely to be accepted when there is participation. Employee participation in the setting of goals may lead to higher performance.

However it is viewed, the theory of goal-setting provides a useful approach to work motivation and performance. And *Hannagan* goes so far as to suggest: 'At present goal-setting is one of the most influential theories of work motivation applicable to all cultures.'[37]

A concept map of motivation and work is set out in Figure 7.12.

Critical review and reflection

The underlying essence of motivating employees to improved performance is easy. An emphasis on clear, stretching but attainable targets; constructive feedback; and an equitable system of extrinsic and intrinsic rewards.

What is YOUR critical view of this assertion? How would YOU explain the underlying essence of work motivation?

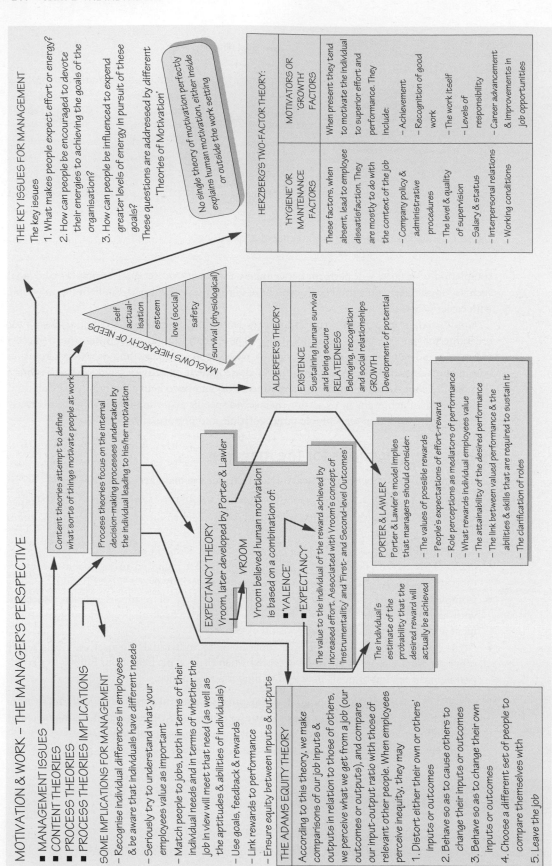

Figure 7.12 Motivation and work – the manager's perspective

Source: Copyright © 2011 The Virtual Learning Materials Workshop. Reproduced with permission.

Attribution theory

A more recent approach to the study of motivation is attribution theory. Attribution is the process by which people interpret the perceived causes of behaviour. **Attribution theory was discussed in detail in Chapter 6.**

Relevance today

Given that most major theories of motivation date back many years, it is inevitable that questions are raised about their relevance today. The Chartered Management Institute suggests that looking at both theories and real-life examples of motivation should stimulate your thoughts, and give you some 'starter' ideas on how to motivate your own people.[38]

Whatever the relevance of the different theories of motivation, to what extent do individuals have control over their own level of motivation or how much is dependent upon the leadership they encounter? *Adair* reassesses the theories of Maslow and Herzberg in terms of action-centred leadership (**discussed in Chapter 9**). Adair also argues that the extent to which you can motivate anyone else is limited and refers to the fifty–fifty rule of motivation, that is:

> *Fifty percent of motivation comes from within a person and 50% from his or her environment, especially from the leadership encountered there. The fifty-fifty rule in motivation does not claim to identify the different proportions in the equation exactly. It is more like a rough and ready rule of thumb. In effect it says no more than a substantial part of motivation lies with a person while a substantial part lies, so to speak, outside and beyond control.*[39]

Cross-cultural dimensions of motivation

Whatever the popularity of different theories of motivation, doubts are raised about their universality on the ground that they have not adequately addressed the factor of culture.[40] Are theories of motivation universally applicable or are there meaningful differences in motivation at work, or in life more generally, in different societies? A number of writers have questioned whether motivational theories and models originating in one culture are amenable to transference to other parts of the world. For example, *Francesco and Gold* devote a substantial proportion of a discussion of motivation to examining the extent to which American motivation theories are applicable outside the USA.[41]

One criticism of content theories of motivation centres on its relative applicability in different circumstances, and the suggestion that there may be variations across cultures falls within this line of reasoning. However, perhaps less obviously, process theories of motivation have also been criticised for being culture-bound. As they focus on process rather than content, such theories may appear to be more applicable in diverse cultural contexts. Nonetheless it has been suggested that process theories of motivation contain certain inbuilt assumptions that are themselves culturally derived.

Adler reminds us that expectancy models of motivation assume that individuals believe that they can, to some extent, control their environment and influence their fate. If, as in the cases of more fatalistic cultures such as China, people do not have the same sense of internal attribution, the expectancy model may have less force and therefore less applicability. When Adams' equity theory is applied across the world, differences in interpretation have been recorded.[42]

Organisational behaviour modification

Another possible approach to motivation is that of **organisational behaviour modification (OBMod).** This is the application of learning principles to influence organisational behaviour. In particular it can be seen as a form of Skinner's operant conditioning, or reinforcement theory (**discussed in Chapter 5**). Reinforcement is a feature of the behaviourism approach and is shaped by environmental influences. The reward for a particular form of behaviour is likely to result in the reinforcement of that behaviour. A negative outcome or lack of acknowledgement for the behaviour is likely to mean that the behaviour will stop. *Luthans and Kreitner* suggest that OBMod 'represents a merging of behavioral learning theory on the one hand and organizational behavior theory on the other'.[43]

According to Luthans and Kreitner, a major premise of OBMod is that positive consequence management is much more effective than negative consequence management. Organisations that encourage the members to learn and undertake desired behaviours and not to undertake undesired behaviours follow five main steps:

1. **Identify** the observable, objective and measurable behaviours relevant to the desired organisational performance.

2. **Measure** the frequency with which those behaviours actually occur under normal conditions. Provide baseline performance data as a point of reference to compare with changes in step 5.

3. **Determine** the antecedents of the behaviours, the reinforcements to encourage patterns of behaviour and the consequences that follow from those behaviours.

4. **Develop** an intervention strategy for change in order to strengthen desirable behaviours and weaken undesirable behaviours, through the use of operant conditioning and reinforcement theory including punishment if necessary.

5. **Measure and evaluate** systematically (using the same measure as in step 2) the extent to which the frequencies of desired behaviours and undesired behaviours have changed, and improvements in organisational performance.

Applications of OBMod

To what extent can OBMod be applied effectively to improve motivation and performance in work organisations? OBMod works best for behaviours that are specific, objective and countable. There have been a number of studies in the USA that indicate positive results in behaviours that improved performance in reducing errors, attendance and punctuality, health and safety and customer service.[44]

In a study of a Russian textile factory, following the OBMod approach, workers were subjected to two forms of intervention – extrinsic rewards and social rewards. The extrinsic rewards provided valued American products, such as clothing, music tapes and hard-to-get foods, for improved performance. Social rewards such as attention, recognition and praise from supervisors were for performing specified actions such as checking looms, undertaking repairs and helping others.

Both the extrinsic and social interventions led to highly significant increases in performance. This contrasted with a previous participative job design approach that involved asking workers for ideas for improving performance and enriching their jobs that did not work. The researchers suggest cultural issues and the workers' past experiences may explain the failure of the participative intervention strategy, and that the OBMod approach has wider application.[45]

Although there appear to be a number of supporters in the USA, in the UK it is a controversial concept. Critics claim that OBMod is not an accepted theory of motivation and that there are too many individual differences for people to be treated as subjects of operant conditioning. OBMod is concerned only with shaping. There is the added criticism of a 'Big Brother' approach with excessive management manipulation and control over employees, more in line with scientific management (**recall the discussion in Chapter 2**). This in turn could also have the added disadvantage of discouraging individual initiative and adaptability to change circumstances. Workers subject to OBMod programmes may tend to ignore those aspects of voluntary behaviours, such as social support or assistance to colleagues, that are not subject to direct reward and reinforcement.

Motivation of knowledge workers

Recent advantages in telecommunications and in scientific and technological knowledge have led to greater emphasis on the knowledge and expertise of staff and the importance of creativity. *Tampoe* suggests that at the core of the new industrial trend are the 'knowledge workers' – those employees who apply their theoretical and practical understanding of a specific area of knowledge to produce outcomes of a commercial, social or personal value. The performance of knowledge workers should be judged on both the cleverness of ideas and the utility and commercial value of their applied knowledge. Creativity is necessary and needs to be encouraged, but should be bounded by commercial realism. This presents management with a new challenge of how to motivate the knowledge workers.[46]

Tampoe suggests that the personal motivation of knowledge workers is based on the value they place on the rewards they expect to earn at work. In addition to the individual's own motivation, the performance of knowledge workers is dependent upon four key characteristics (*see* Figure 7.13):

- task competence;
- peer and management support;
- task and role clarity; and
- corporate awareness.

The challenge to management is to ensure the effectiveness of the four key variables and to recognise the need for staff to supervise and manage themselves and the wider rewards expected by knowledge workers.

Climate of creativity

Whitmore suggests that in order to create a climate for creativity among employees, recognition must be given to the importance of two human needs that rise above all others and exist independent of race, creed and culture: the need for self-belief and the development of emotional intelligence; and the ever-present need that every human being has for a sense of meaning and purpose in their lives.

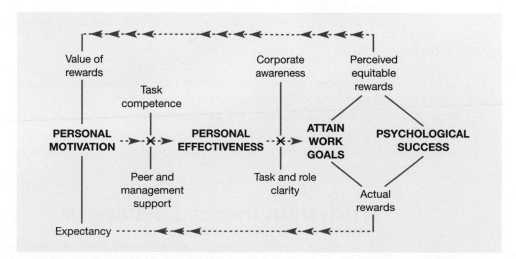

Figure 7.13 Motivating knowledge workers

Source: Tampoe, M. 'Knowledge Workers: The New Management Challenge', *Professional Manager*, Institute of Management, November 1994, p. 13. Reproduced with permission from Chartered Management Institute.

Self-belief and meaningful work are the fundamental bedrocks that underlie business performance. Of course, pay and conditions are important too, but we know that. It is these two others that are barely recognised . . . but business leaders ignore them at their peril.[47]

Matson and Prusak of management consultants McKinsey & Company report that despite the high stakes in knowledge workers, there is a lack of understanding of what it takes to bolster their productivity. This lack of clarity is partly because knowledge work involves more diverse and amorphous tasks than do production or clerical positions, and partly because performance metrics are hard to come by in knowledge work. Knowledge workers spend half their time on interactions and, in order to improve their productivity, companies should explore the barriers that impede these interactions:

- **Physical and technical** – including geographical distance, different time zones or lack of effective tools.
- **Social or cultural** – including rigid hierarchies or ineffective incentives.
- **Contextual** – the sharing of and translating knowledge from colleagues in different fields.
- **Time** – or rather the perceived lack of time.[48]

Goffee and Jones suggest that future prosperity rests with organisations that make their living from the knowledge they themselves are able to develop. Clever people are highly talented individuals with the potential to create disproportionate amounts of value from the resources that the organisation makes available to them. Keeping and leading the clever people who inhabit these organisations becomes a critical challenge.

Exceptionally sharp and creative executives often come with characteristics that make them hard to handle. They can be egotistical, disdainful of hierarchies and prone to asking awkward questions . . . Yet research has repeatedly demonstrated that creativity and innovation are inextricably linked to energy, edge and fun, which organisational attrition is in danger of crushing.

Clever people do not like to be led or told what to do and are at their most productive when faced with really hard questions. Tell them something is not possible and they will be highly motivated to prove you wrong. They must be given enough space to try out new things and given recognition for their work. Goffee and Jones suggest that clever people can be difficult to lead and have developed new rules to help guide their leaders.[49]

Critical review and reflection

The motivation of so-called knowledge workers is no different from motivating any other worker – that is, recognition of their individual value to achieving the objectives of the organisation.

What do YOU think? How far do YOU agree with the characteristics of clever people? Do you see YOURSELF as a potential knowledge worker?

Frustration-induced behaviour

What happens if a person's motivational driving force is blocked and they are unable to satisfy their needs and expectations, and what is the likely effect on their work performance? There are two possible sets of outcomes: constructive behaviour or frustration (*see* Figure 7.14). **Constructive behaviour** is a positive reaction to the blockage of a desired goal and can take two main forms: problem-solving or restructuring.

Figure 7.14 A basic model of frustration

- **Problem-solving** is the removal of the barrier – for example, finding an alternative means of undertaking a task, repairing a damaged machine or bypassing a non co-operative superior.
- **Restructuring,** or compromise, is the substitution of an alternative goal, although such a goal may be of a lower or different order – for example, taking an additional part-time job because of failure to be promoted to a higher grade, or reassessing the work/life balance.

Frustration (negative responses)

Frustration is a negative response to the blockage of a desired goal and results in a defensive form of behaviour. There are many possible reactions to frustration caused by the failure to achieve a desired goal. These can be summarised under four broad headings: aggression, regression, fixation and withdrawal.[50] However, these categories are not mutually exclusive. Most forms of frustration-induced behaviour at work are a combination of aggression, regression and fixation.

Aggression is a physical or verbal attack on some person or object, for example striking a supervisor, rage or abusive language, destruction of equipment or documents, or malicious gossip about a superior. Where a direct attack cannot be made against the actual barrier or blocking agent, because for example the source of frustration is not clear or specific, or where the source is feared, as with a powerful superior, aggression may be displaced towards some other person or object. With **displaced aggression** the person may find a scapegoat for the outlet of frustration – for example, picking arguments or being short-tempered with colleagues or slamming the filing cabinet. A more constructive form of displaced aggression is working off frustrated feelings through demanding physical work or sport, or perhaps by shouting/cursing when alone or in the company of an understanding colleague.

Regression is reverting to a childish or more primitive form of behaviour – for example, sulking, crying, tantrums or kicking a broken machine or piece of equipment.

Fixation is persisting in a form of behaviour that has no adaptive value and continuing to repeat actions that have no positive results – for example, the inability to accept change or new ideas, repeatedly trying a door that is clearly locked or a machine that clearly will not work, or insisting on applying for promotion even though not qualified for the job.

Withdrawal is apathy, giving up or resignation – for example, arriving at work late and leaving early, sickness and absenteeism, refusal to accept responsibility, avoiding decision-making, passing work over to colleagues or leaving the job altogether.

Factors influencing frustration

Among the factors that determine an individual's reaction to frustration are the:

- strength of motivation;
- level and potency of need (see, for example, Maslow's theory of motivation);
- degree of attachment to the desired goal;
- perceived nature of the barrier or blocking agent; and
- personality characteristics of the individual.

It is important that managers attempt to reduce potential frustration-induced behaviour through, for example:

- effective recruitment, selection and socialisation;
- training and development;
- job design and work organisation;
- equitable HRM policies;
- recognition and rewards;
- effective communications;
- participative styles of management; and
- attempting to understand the individual's perception of the situation.

Critical review and reflection

Motivation at work is very subjective and affected by many variables including personality, cultural influences, unknown circumstances and relationships outside of work. Generalised theories cannot meet all individual circumstances and are therefore a complete waste of your study time.

To what extent do YOU agree? What practical value do YOU place on the various theories of motivation?

Job satisfaction

Attempting to understand the nature of job satisfaction, its relationship with motivation and its effects on work performance is not easy. Job satisfaction is a complex and multifaceted concept, which can mean different things to different people. Although the level of job satisfaction may well affect strength of work motivation, this is not always the case. Satisfaction is not the same as motivation. **Job satisfaction** is more of an attitude, an internal state. It could, for example, be associated with a personal feeling of achievement, either quantitative or qualitative.

The relationship between job satisfaction and work performance is an issue of continuing debate and controversy. One view, associated with the early human relations approach, is that satisfaction leads to performance. An alternative view is that performance leads to satisfaction. Recall, for example, the Porter and Lawler expectancy model (**discussed above**).

Reeves draws attention to the relationship between accomplishment at work and the need to 'work harder':

> *All this busy-ness and stress is creating more heat than light. It is a sign not of work being too hard but too shallow. Human nature is driven by a desire to accomplish things, and so the fewer opportunities for accomplishment a job contains, the more likely we are to fill the void by tearing around in a frenzy in an effort to persuade ourselves and others that our work has a purpose, that it is important.[51]*

Dimensions of job satisfaction

There is doubt whether job satisfaction consists of a single dimension or a number of separate dimensions. Some workers may be satisfied with certain aspects of their work and dissatisfied with other aspects. The level of job satisfaction is affected by a wide range of variables relating to individual, social, cultural, organisational and environmental factors:

- **Individual factors** include personality, education and qualifications, intelligence and abilities, age, marital status, orientation to work.
- **Social factors** include relationships with co-workers, group working and norms, opportunities for interaction, informal organisation.
- **Cultural factors** include ethnicity, underlying attitudes, beliefs and values.
- **Organisational factors** include nature and size, formal structure, HR policies and procedures, nature of the work, technology and work organisation, styles of leadership, management systems, working conditions.
- **Environmental factors** include economic, social, technical and governmental influences.

These different factors all affect the job satisfaction of certain individuals in a given set of circumstances but not necessarily in others. For example, in times of economic depression and fears of high unemployment, job security is likely to be a prominent concern. A survey by the Chartered Management Institute found that organisational culture and values emerged as very strong motivational drivers, and managers' relationship with their line manager had a powerful impact on job satisfaction and related measures.[52] The FreshMinds survey (**discussed in Chapter 3**), suggests that when it comes to job satisfaction it pays to be older. Apparently 100 per cent of older baby-boomers (born between 1946 and 1963) are satisfied with their job, but only 66 per cent of Generation Y (typified by travel first, then a career) feel the same way. And Generation Y want more at work, such as gym membership and sabbaticals.[53]

According to *De Vita,* well-being at work pays because employees who are happy and healthy take fewer days off sick, are more productive and more likely to stay with their organisation. The starting point to supporting and promoting well-being in the workplace has to be good people management and effective work organisation. Good line management is the most important of the characteristics of a high-quality workplace that has high levels of commitment and low absence rates.[54]

An increasingly important issue affecting job satisfaction and efficiency is the nature of the work environment and workplace facilities (**discussed in Chapter 11**).

> *Over the years, a number of different surveys suggest good interpersonal relationships with colleagues is more important to enjoying your work than a high salary. In 2014, a Cabinet Office survey of life satisfaction of 274 different occupations found members of the clergy, farmers, fitness instructors, school secretaries, dental nurses and farm workers among those with modest salaries but high personal job satisfaction.[55]*

Alienation at work

One main approach to job satisfaction is in terms of frustration and alienation at work. Job satisfaction can be seen as the obverse of frustration at work (**discussed above**). **Alienation** refers to the detachment of the person from their work role. The concept of alienation at work is associated originally with the views of *Marx*.[56] He saw the division of labour in pursuit of profit, and exploitation by employers, as a denial of the workers' need for self-expression. Workers become estranged from the product of their work. Work no longer provides a satisfying experience in itself, but represents a means of satisfying other external demands.

The concept of alienation has been extended by *Blauner*.[57] He describes alienation in terms of four dimensions: powerlessness, meaninglessness, isolation and self-estrangement.

- **Powerlessness** denotes the workers' lack of control over management policy, immediate work processes, or conditions of employment.
- **Meaninglessness** stems from standardisation and division of labour. It denotes the inability to see the purpose of work done or to identify with the total production process or finished product.
- **Isolation** is not belonging to an integrated work group or to the social work organisation and not being guided by group norms of behaviour.
- **Self-estrangement** is the failure to see work as an end in itself or as a central life issue. Workers experience a depersonalised detachment and work is seen solely as a means to an end.

In recent years attention to job satisfaction has also become more closely associated with broader approaches to improved job design and work organisation (**discussed in Chapter 11**), and the quality of working life movement, and with stress and the work/life balance (**discussed in Chapter 3**).

Comprehensive model of job enrichment

Attempts to improve intrinsic motivation must not only include considerations of job characteristics, but also take account of individual differences and attributes, and people's orientation to work. A popular and comprehensive model of job enrichment has been developed by *Hackman and Oldham* (*see* Figure 7.15).[58] The model views job enrichment in terms of increasing five core job dimensions: skill variety, task identity, task significance, autonomy and feedback from the job.

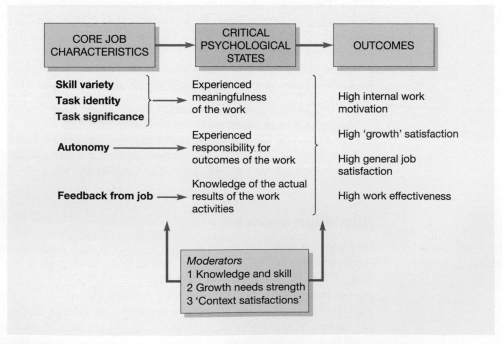

Figure 7.15 A job characteristics model of work motivation

Source: Hackman, J. R. and Oldham, G. R. *Work Redesign*, 1st ed., © 1980, Addison-Wesley Publishing Company, Inc. (1980), Figure 4.6, p. 90. Reprinted and electronically reproduced by permission of Pearson Education, Inc, New York.

Five core dimensions

The five core job dimensions can be summarised as follows:

- **skill variety** – the extent to which a job entails different activities and involves a range of skills and talents;
- **task identity** – the extent to which a job involves completion of a whole piece of work with a visible outcome;
- **task significance** – the extent to which a job has a meaningful impact on other people, either inside or outside the organisation;
- **autonomy** – the extent to which a job provides freedom, independence and discretion in planning the work and determining how to undertake it;
- **feedback** – the extent to which work activities result in direct and clear information on the effectiveness of job performance.

The extent of these core job dimensions create three critical psychological states based on the individual's perception of:

- experienced value and meaningfulness of the work;
- experienced personal responsibility for the outcomes of the work; and
- clear knowledge of actual results of work activities and level of performance.

An example of a job with little enrichment could be that of a production assembly line worker or a kitchen porter, where all five core characteristics are likely to score low. An example of an enriched job could be that of a parish priest who draws upon a wide range of social skills and talents, who can usually identify with the whole task and whose job has clear and important meaning and significance. There is a very high level of autonomy and likely to be direct and clear feedback.

Motivating potential score

From these five core job dimensions, Hackman and Oldham have developed an equation that gives a single index of a person's job profile. By answering a questionnaire – the Job Diagnostic Survey (JDS) – and by giving a score (between 1 and 7) to each job dimension, the person can calculate an overall measure of job enrichment, called the motivating potential score (MPS).

Examples of questions from the JDS are:

- How much variety is there in your job?
- To what extent does your job involve doing a whole and identifiable piece of work?
- In general, how significant or important is your job?
- How much autonomy is there in your job?
- To what extent does doing the job itself provide you with information about your work performance?

$$\text{MPS} = \frac{\{\text{Skill variety} + \text{Task identity} + \text{Task significance}\}}{3} \times \text{Autonomy} \times \text{Feedback}$$

The first three job dimensions of skill variety, task identity and task significance are averaged, since it is the combination of these dimensions that contributes to experienced meaningfulness of work. The remaining two job dimensions, autonomy and feedback, stand on their own. Since scores for skill variety, task identity and task significance are additive, this means that the absence of one dimension can be partially offset by the presence of the other dimensions. However, if either autonomy or feedback is absent then, because of the multiplicative relationship, the MPS would be zero. The job would offer no potential to motivate the person.

From their studies, Hackman and Oldham claim that people with enriched jobs and high score levels on the JDS experienced more satisfaction and internal motivation. The core job dimensions of skill variety, task identity and task significance combined to predict the level of experienced meaningfulness of the work. The core dimensions of autonomy and feedback did not relate so clearly to experienced responsibility and knowledge of results

Based on integrating Hackman and Oldham's job characteristics model with Maslow's hierarchy of needs, *Roe et al.* propose a general model of work motivation, tested with Bulgarian, Hungarian and Dutch workers. The model indicates that situational characteristics lead to critical psychological factors, inducing two main motivational factors – job involvement and organisational commitment – which in turn lead to two proximal outcomes of work motivation – effort and job satisfaction – which affect performance, stress and tendency to leave the organisation. Although there were some differences that draw attention to cultural variables, there was also a large degree of similarity in results across the three countries.[59]

Critical review and reflection

Individuals have a variety of changing, and often conflicting, needs and expectations, which they attempt to satisfy in a number of ways at different times.

What are the most powerful influences on YOUR own potential work motivation and job satisfaction? How do YOU think these are likely to change in five years' time?

Ten key points to remember

1 The relationship between the organisation and its members is influenced by what motivates them to work, and the rewards and fulfilment derived from it.

2 Individuals have a variety of changing, and often competing, needs and expectations at work, which they attempt to satisfy in a number of ways.

3 A person's work motivation, satisfaction and performance are determined by the comparative strength of economic rewards, intrinsic satisfaction and social relationships.

4 There are many competing theories that attempt to explain motivation at work. They show there are many motives that influence people's behaviour and performance.

5 Content theories place emphasis on what actually motivates the individual at work. Main theories include those of Maslow, Alderfer, Nohria, Herzberg and McClelland.

6 Process theories are concerned with the dynamic variables that make up motivation. Major approaches include expectancy-based models, equity theory, goal theory and attribution theory.

7 Another possible approach to motivation is organisational behaviour modification and the application of learning principles to behaviour at work.

8 Understanding the nature of job satisfaction and links with work performance is not easy. Job satisfaction may affect motivation but this is not always the case.

9 Satisfaction is an internal state associated with a feeling of personal achievement. One approach is in terms of frustration and alienation at work.

10 Attention has also been given to a comprehensive model of job enrichment based on skill variety, task identity, task significance, autonomy and feedback.

Review and discussion questions

1   Explain fully what you understand by the underlying concept of motivation.

2   How would you attempt to summarise the main needs and expectations to be taken into account in considering the motivation of people at work?

3   Assess critically the practical value of Maslow's hierarchy of needs model. Give examples of the extent to which the theory could meaningfully be applied to university students and/or staff in your own organisation.

4   Explain your understanding of expectancy-based theories of motivation. Use a simple diagram to illustrate an expectancy theory of your choice. What implications do expectancy theories of motivation have for the manager?

5   Give detailed practical examples of situations in which each of the following theories of motivation might be appropriate: (i) achievement motivation; (ii) equity theory; (iii) goal theory.

6   To what extent do you see yourself as a knowledge worker? And to what extent are you motivated by a climate of creativity?

7   What do you understand by frustration-induced behaviour? Give a practical example, preferably from your experience, of each of the main forms of this behaviour.

8   Debate critically the validity of the contention that the motivation to work well depends on more than a high salary and good working conditions.

9   What exactly do you understand by job satisfaction and what are the main dimensions? Relate specific examples of situations that have influenced your own job satisfaction.

10   Evaluate critically how you see the relationship between motivation, job satisfaction and effective work performance. Give reasons in support of your views.

Assignment

Work with two partners chosen by your tutor.

a. In private, you each number **in rank order** the following 20 factors in terms of the extent to which they are likely to motivate you in *preferring* to work for a particular organisation.

	YOU	PARTNER 1	PARTNER 2
Contributory pension scheme			
Long-term job security			
Safe working environment			
Harmonious working relationships			
Personal development and career progression			
Attractive benefits package (and perks)			
Leisure and sports facilities			
Size of the organisation			
Location			
Average age of working colleagues			
Group or team working			
Flexible working hours			

	YOU	PARTNER 1	PARTNER 2
High basic salary			
Perceived status of the organisation and/or its work			
Wide diversity of members of staff			
Extent to which work involves high level of ICT			
Voluntary paid overtime			
Challenging work with a sense of achievement			
Autonomy on manner of undertaking tasks			
Employee share ownership scheme			

a. Record all three lists, and together compare and discuss your rankings.
b. Do any of the rankings surprise you or your colleagues?
c. To what extent do you think you would enjoy working together?

Personal skills and employability exercise

Objectives

Completing this exercise should help you to enhance the following skills:

- Review the nature of, and influences on, motivation to work.
- Take account of individual needs and expectations at work.
- Reflect upon your perceptions about the motives of other people.

Exercise – working in conjunction with a partner

1 FIRST, you each list, as far as possible in rank order, the specific needs and expectations that are most important to you as an individual. (Do *not* include basic physiological needs such as to satisfy thirst or hunger, or a *minimal* standard of accommodation.) Explain, briefly, to what extent these needs and expectations were met currently by any work experience that you have had – even a short-term or part-time job – and/or to what extent you anticipate they will be met by your future career ambitions. Exchange accounts with your partner before proceeding further.
2 NOW, you each describe fully two recent situations in which you felt:
   (i) highly motivated, enthusiastic; and
   (ii) when you lacked enthusiasm, felt half-hearted and found it difficult to put in much effort.
   Both you and your partner attempt to interpret the events of both situations with possible reasons for the other person's behaviour, needs and motivation.
3 NEXT, refer back to Blanchard's eight critical employee needs described in the text of this chapter: meaningful work, collaboration, fairness, autonomy, recognition, growth, connectedness with leaders and connectedness with colleagues. Attempt to place in rank order the importance of each of these needs. Discuss with your partner, with supporting reasons where possible.
4 THEN, discuss together what conclusions you draw from this exercise, and what you have each learnt about work motivation.

Discussion

- How difficult was it to avoid generalisations about what motivates other people?
- In your discussions, how far were you able to distance your own motivations?
- To what extent can you relate responses to underlying theories of motivation?

Case study
Managers and motivation

Most people who work in an organisational setting find that, apart from their immediate colleagues, their line manager is perhaps the most significant influence on their life at work. Relationships with the immediate boss can affect individuals' performance, motivation and engagement with organisational aims and objectives, and because these managers usually work in close proximity with their staff, their strengths and limitations are often very visible. Almost everyone will have an opinion about their boss, who is likely to be somewhere in the middle between the team with its day-to-day tasks and those senior managers who make the big, strategic decisions. What exactly does it feel like to be a middle manager, and what are the challenges and rewards for those who put themselves in the managerial front line?

Middle managers: telling it like it is

In 2006 *Management Today* published the results of a survey into the experiences of middle managers.[60] Part of its purpose was to match a similar survey of top business leaders, which had taken place six months earlier, and to discover more about the role and nature of mid-ranking managers, many of whom might not have the ambition to become chief executives or captains of industry, but upon whom most organisations depend for the regular delivery of core activities. Over 1,000 managers took part in the survey, representing both public- and private-sector organisations, and a good 40 per cent of respondents were women. Some of the headline figures demonstrated a strong sense of job satisfaction, and in answer to a question about whether, if they had their time again, they would choose to become a manager, 92 per cent of respondents answered that they had not regretted their choice. A small majority, 54 per cent, were not actively seeking promotion and a significant majority, almost 69 per cent, did not want to step into their own boss's job. Clearly the picture here was one of broad satisfaction with the work and the nature of their managerial role. However, 43 per cent felt that they were not valued.

The survey seemed to highlight a number of common reasons why managers enjoyed their work. Chief among these were the following:

- Influence and achievement – the ability to see themselves making positive contributions to the organisation and the way it worked. A significant 88 per cent of those surveyed said that this was one of the strongest motivating factors for them.

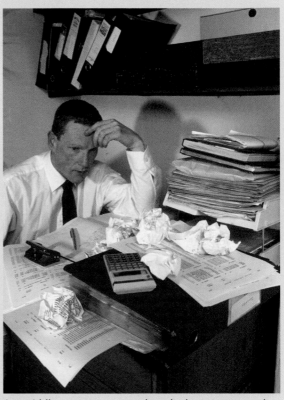

Are middle managers stressed out by bureaucracy and organisational politics, or inspired by their role and prospects?
Source: © Paul Ridsdale/Photofusion Picture Library

- Autonomy – 79 per cent considered that a relative degree of autonomy was also a source of satisfaction. The managers who were happiest in their work were those whose own bosses were able to allow them a relatively free rein.
- Developing people – again, almost 80 per cent of the managers considered that their role in developing others, helping people to achieve better levels of performance and encouraging newer or younger workers to be a major source of work-related pleasure.

Things that managers reported as being de-motivating and that frustrated them in their jobs were the following:

- Bureaucracy – 48 per cent cited excessive and bureaucratic systems as being what they disliked most about their work.
- Pressure to do more with less – this was often what stressed managers most. As customers and clients

become more demanding, the lack of resources, coupled with increasing spans of control, were clearly putting managers under significant strain.

- Politics – 45 per cent of the survey respondents believed that office politics was damaging to their organisations.

There were some marked differences of opinion about how the question of organisational politics should be approached; one manager who was interviewed in detail for the *Management Today* report considered it was something that had to be understood and handled, but others were very critical of the sort of behaviour that caused different units or departments of (mostly larger) organisations to become close-knit and focused on protecting their own interests, often at the expense of overall organisational success. This problem surfaced again in 2007 when another CMI survey reported that 44 per cent of senior managers felt they were diverted from work by internal politics.[61]

Leading isn't easy

Becoming a manager means, for many, a significant change in role and perspective, and the transition causes a number of common problems for those who find themselves in 'the middle'. One aspect of their managerial work that many reported as problematic was the need to learn effective delegation, and to become a leader rather than a 'doer'. One respondent from Hewlett Packard illustrated this point:

When I first became a manager, I tried to do everything myself, my old job plus my new responsibilities, but I soon realised this was a mistake.

She also noted that being judged on the success of her team, rather than on her individual performance, was difficult to get used to. This related to another problem – the difficulty of identifying and dealing with underperforming staff. While workers might believe their colleagues to be lazy, they also clearly felt that managers were not doing enough to tackle matters of poor performance.[62]

As Ruth Spellman, Chief Executive of IIP, observed in her commentary on the findings:

It is clear from the findings that UK managers are aware that dead wood is a problem that can damage their organisation – but are failing to do anything about it. However, left unchecked . . . [it] . . . can breed resentment amongst colleagues and cripple an organisation's productivity.[63]

On the other hand, if this is set against the complaints of micro-management that many employees voiced, it becomes clear that the delicate balance between effective monitoring and interference is a difficult one to achieve.

Another common theme running through the *Management Today* and the CMI surveys was that of middle-manager stress. This arises partly from the causes highlighted above, but also from the ambiguity that often surrounds the role. Middle managers might be pivotal to the actual running of the day-to-day activities of the organisation, but while they are accountable to senior people who are often the strategic decision-makers, they are also embroiled in the minutiae of daily work. This results in two very different sets of demands from two different directions. A 2010 study by the mental health charity Mind found that the level of stress-related absence among middle managers was reportedly double that of company directors, with 29 per cent of those surveyed saying that they had lost their temper with colleagues, and 25 per cent reporting that they had cried at work. A contributory factor was certainly the amount of unpaid overtime, which seems to be the lot of the middle manager, and issues of work/life balance are problematic for them:[64]

middle managers are least satisfied with their work–life balance, most likely to say they are under excessive pressure every day, and also most likely to be looking for a new job. They also have least job security, with nearly one in three thinking it likely they could lose their job as a result of the economic downturn.[65]

In some cases, managers felt not only that the additional stresses of taking on a managerial workload removed them from the work they enjoyed as specialists, but also that the additional pay was scarcely adequate to compensate for the added pressure. One respondent noted that:

There's only £2k difference in a managerial role pay and an analyst below, but the workload increases by 45%.[66]

Similarly, while middle managers are the key players in organisational change and development, they report that they often find themselves driving through initiatives that have been developed and determined by those above them in the organisation, who are sometimes those who lack recent knowledge of the realities of life on the front line.

But what does the team think?

Finally, what do staff think about their managers? In its winter 2014–15 'Employee Outlook' survey, which focused on managers,[67] the Chartered Institute of Personnel and Development (CIPD) noted that, on the whole, employees are quite positive about their immediate managers, with 67 per cent of respondents reporting satisfactory relationships with their line manager. In particular, employees were happy that they were treated fairly (69 per cent), received support when they had problems (65 per cent), that their suggestions were listened to (64 per cent) and were clear about what was expected of them (61 per cent). They were less content with discussion of training and development (only 36 per cent of respondents reported that line managers talked with them about training needs) and even fewer (30 per cent) reported that they received coaching on the job.

The quality of the relationship with line managers can also be seen to underpin levels of employee commitment and engagement.

Both positive line manager behaviours and satisfaction with the relationship with the supervisor are positively associated with employees being motivated by their organisation's core purpose.[68]

This echoes findings by *Purcell* and others, who discovered that the line manager's ability to consult staff, then communicate and explain decisions in a way that treats them respectfully, is an important factor in creating the sense of fairness that, in turn, supported engagement.[69]

So, however managers are feeling about their own work, one thing is clear: they continue to have a major influence on the way in which employees think about their jobs and the motivation and commitment they show towards the organisation where they work. And perhaps that is the most important finding of all.

Tasks

1 Using *either* the achievement motivation theory of McClelland *or* Porter and Lawler's expectancy model as the basis for your analysis, explain what might motivate someone to take on a line manager or supervisory role in an organisation for which they have worked for some time as a team member.

2 What are the main elements of job satisfaction that managers appear to experience? Which are most important, and why? What are the major frustrations, and how do you think a manager should deal with them?

3 To what extent do the results of the CIPD employee survey of winter 2014–15 indicate the motivational effect of job enrichment?

4 What lessons could managers take from the Hackman and Oldham model (Figure 7.15) of job enrichment, and how could a line manager use these ideas to improve employee commitment and engagement at work?

Notes and references

1. Krech, D., Crutchfield, R. S. and Ballachey, E. L. *Individual in Society,* McGraw-Hill (1962).

2. Mitchell, T. R. 'Motivation: New Directions for Theory, Research, and Practice', *Academy of Management Review,* vol. 7, no. 1, 1982, pp. 80–8.

3. 'Motivating Your Employees in a Time of Change', Checklist 068, Chartered Management Institute, August 2012.

4. Kreitner, R., Kinicki, A. and Buelens, M. *Organizational Behaviour,* first European edition, McGraw-Hill (1999).

5. Farren, C. 'Mastery: The Critical Advantage', in Chowdhury, S. (ed.) *Management 21C,* Financial Times Prentice Hall (2000), p. 95.

6. Weaver, T. 'Theory M: Motivating with Money', *Cornell HRA Quarterly,* vol. 29, no. 3, 1988, pp. 40–5.

7. Chamorro-Premuzic, T. and Fagan, P. 'Money Talks, But Do People Still Listen?', *Management Today,* November 2014, pp. 50–3.

8. See, for example, Rudolph, P. A. and Kleiner, B. H. 'The Art of Motivating Employees', *Journal of Managerial Psychology,* vol. 4, no. 5, 1989, pp. i–iv.

9. Sauermann, H. and Cohen, W. M. 'What Makes Them Tick? Employee Motives and Firm Innovation', Working Paper 1443, National Bureau of Economic Research. © 2008 Henry Sauermann and Wesley M. Cohen.

10. Gratton, L. *Hot Spots,* Financial Times Prentice Hall (2007), p. 133; Blanchard, K. 'Do you get passionate at work?', *Manager, The British Journal of Administrative Management,* Autumn 2011, p. 26.

11. Waller, D. 'Are You What You Do?', *Management Today,* October 2008, pp. 42–6.

12. Kets de Vries, M. 'Beyond Sloan: Trust is at the core of corporate values', in Pickford, J. (ed.) *Financial Times Mastering Management 2.0,* Financial Times Prentice Hall (2001), pp. 267–70.

13. Blanchard, K. 'Do you get passionate at work?', *Manager, The British Journal of Administrative Management,* Autumn 2011, p. 26.

14. For a fuller discussion, see Mullins, L. J. and Dossor, P. *Hospitality Management and Organisational Behaviour,* fifth edition, Pearson Education (2013).

15. Stewart, H. *The Happy Manifesto: Make Your Organisation a Great Place to Work – Now,* Happy (2012); see also Stewart, H. 'How to have a happy and productive office', *Management Today,* February 2012, pp. 38–41.

16. Maslow, A. H. 'A Theory of Human Motivation', *Psychological Review,* 50, July 1943, pp. 370–96; and Maslow, A. H. *Motivation and Personality,* third edition, Harper and Row (1987).

17. Steers, R. M. and Porter, L. W. *Motivation and Work Behaviour,* fifth edition, McGraw-Hill (1991).

18. Saunders, A. 'Keep Staff Sweet', *Management Today,* June 2003, p. 75.

19. Adair, J. *Leadership and Motivation,* Kogan Page (2006).

20. Alderfer, C. P. *Existence, Relatedness and Growth,* Collier Macmillan (1972).

21. Nohria, N., Groysberg, B. and Lee, L.-E. 'Employee Motivation: A Powerful New Model', *Harvard Business Review,* vol. 86, July 2008, pp. 78–84.

22. Herzberg, F., Mausner, B. and Snyderman, B. B. *The Motivation to Work,* second edition, Chapman and Hall (1959).

23. Crainer, S. and Dearlove, D. (eds) *Financial Times Handbook of Management,* second edition, Financial Times Prentice Hall (2001), p. 361.

24. McClelland, D. C. *Human Motivation,* Cambridge University Press (1988).

25. For examples of pictures, see Osland, J. S., Kolb, D. A. and Rubin, I. M. *Organizational Behaviour: An Experimental Approach,* seventh edition, Prentice Hall (2001).

26. McClelland, D. C. and Burnham, D. H. 'Power Is the Great Motivation', *Harvard Business Review,* vol. 54, March–April 1976, pp. 100–10.

27. Vroom, V. H. *Work and Motivation,* Wiley (1964); also published by Krieger (1982).

28. Porter, L. W. and Lawler, E. E. *Managerial Attitudes and Performance,* Irwin (1968).

29. Lawler, E. E. *Motivation in Work Organizations,* Brooks/Cole (1973).

30. Lundin, S., Paul, H. and Christensen, J. *Fish: A Remarkable Way to Boost Morale and Improve Results,* Hyperion Press (2001), p. 37.

31. CIPD 'Strategic reward and total reward', CIPD Factsheet, Chartered Institute of Personnel and Development, March 2014.

32. Adams, J. S. 'Injustice in Social Exchange', in Berkowitz, L. (ed.) *Advances in Experimental and Social Psychology,* Academic Press (1965); also abridged in Steers, R. M.

and Porter, L. W. *Motivation and Work Behavior,* second edition, McGraw-Hill (1979), pp. 107–24.

33. Werner, G., Schmittberger, R. and Schwarze, B. 'An Experimental Analysis of Ultimatum Bargaining', *Journal of Economic Behavior and Organization,* vol. 3, no. 4, 1982, pp. 367–88.

34. Locke, E. A. 'Towards a Theory of Task Motivation and Incentives', *Organizational Behavior and Human Performance,* vol. 3, 1968, pp. 157–89.

35. Locke, E. A. 'Personal Attitudes and Motivation', *Annual Review of Psychology,* vol. 26, 1975, pp. 457–80.

36. Gratton, L. Living Strategy: Putting People at the Heart of Corporate Purpose, Financial Times Prentice Hall (2000), p. 193.

37. Hannagan, T. *Management,* fourth edition, Financial Times Prentice Hall (2005), p. 363.

38. 'Motivating Your Staff in a Time of Change', Management Checklist 068, Chartered Management Institute, August 2012.

39. Adair, J. *Leadership and Motivation,* Kogan Page (2006), p. 38.

40. See, for example, Cheng, T., Sculli, D. and Chan, F. S. 'Relationship Dominance – Rethinking Management Theories from the Perspective of Methodological Relationalism', *Journal of Managerial Psychology,* vol. 16, no. 2, 2001, pp. 97–105.

41. Francesco, A. M. and Gold, B. A. *International Organizational Behavior,* second edition, Pearson Prentice Hall (2005), p. 126.

42. Adler, N. J. *International Aspects of Organizational Behaviour,* third edition, South Western College Publishing (1997).

43. Luthans, F. and Kreitner, R. *Organisational Behavior Modification and Beyond,* second edition, Scott Foresman (1985), p. 36.

44. Stajkovic, A. D. and Luthans, F. 'Differential Effects of Incentive Motivators on Work Performance', *Academy of Management Journal,* vol. 44, no. 3, 2001, pp. 580–90.

45. Luthans, F., Stajkovic, A., Luthans, B. C. and Luthans, K. W. 'Applying Behavioral Management in Eastern Europe', *European Management Journal,* vol. 16, no. 4, 1998, pp. 466–74.

46. Tampoe, M. 'Knowledge Workers – The New Management Challenge', *Professional Manager,* November 1994, pp. 12–13.

47. Whitmore, Sir J. 'Breaking Down the Barriers to Management Creativity', *Manager, The British Journal of Administrative Management,* May/June 2002, pp. 24–6.

48. Matson, E. and Prusak, L. 'Boosting the productivity of knowledge workers', *Management Services,* vol. 57, no. 2, 2013, pp. 14–15.

49. Goffee, R. and Jones, G. 'How to harness the special talents of Clever People', *Management Today,* September 2009, pp. 56–60.

50. See, for example, Brown, J. A. C. *The Social Psychology of Industry*, Penguin (1954 and 1986).

51. Reeves, R. 'Reality Bites', *Management Today*, May 2003, p. 37.

52. Worrall, L. and Cooper, C. 'The Quality of Working Life 2007', Chartered Management Institute, October 2007.

53. Stern, S. 'My Generation', *Management Today*, March 2008, pp. 40–6.

54. De Vita, E. 'Best Fit,' *Management Today*, September 2008, pp. 54–8.

55. For the full list see **www.dailymail.co.uk/happiest_jobs** (accessed 22 March 2014).

56. Marx, K. 'The Notion of Alienation', in Coser, L. A. and Rosenburg, B. *Sociological Theory*, Collier Macmillan (1969), pp. 505–10.

57. Blauner, R. *Alienation and Freedom*, University of Chicago Press (1964).

58. Hackman, J. R. and Oldham, G. R. *Work Redesign*, Addison-Wesley (1980).

59. Roe, R. A., Zinovieva, I. L., Dienes, E. and Ten Horn, L. A. 'A Comparison of Work Motivation in Bulgaria, Hungary and the Netherlands: Test of a Model', *Applied Psychology: An International Review*, vol. 49, 2000, pp. 658–87.

60. Kennett, M. 'View from the Middle', *Management Today*, March 2006.

61. Peacock, L. 'Senior executives struggling to manage their workloads', *Personnel Today*, 2 November 2007.

62. BBC News, 19 August 2006, 'Staff brand colleagues as "lazy"', **http://news.bbc.co.uk** (accessed 23 February 2015).

63. IIP Press Release, 19 August 2005.

64. Waller, D. 'Stress hits middle managers the hardest', *Management Today*, 21 December 2010.

65. CIPD, *Employee Outlook Winter 2011–12*, p. 17, **www.cipd.co.uk** (accessed 23 February 2015).

66. Kennett, M. 'View from the Middle', op. cit., pp. 35–42.

67. CIPD, *Employee Outlook Winter 2014–15*, **www.cipd.co.uk** (accessed 23 February 2015).

68. Ibid., p. 4.

69. Purcell, J. 'Time to focus on employee voice as a prime antecedent of engagement: Rediscovering the black box', *The Future of Engagement Thought Piece Collection*, Institute for Employment Studies (2014).

Academic viewpoint

Below you will find the title and abstract of a recent article in an academic journal that explores a topic relevant to the chapters in Part 2.

Timming, A. R. 'Visible tattoos in the service sector: A new challenge to recruitment and selection', *Work, Employment and Society*, vol. 29, no. 1, 2015, pp. 60–78. doi: 10.1177/0950017014528402

Abstract

Drawing on 25 in-depth interviews with hiring managers and visibly tattooed respondents, this article explores the nature of prejudice surrounding body art in the service sector. It focuses on the impact of visible tattoos on employment chances. The study reveals a predominantly negative effect on selection, but the extent of employer prejudice is mitigated by: where the tattoo is located on the body; the organization or industry type; proximity of the role to customers; and the genre of the tattoo. Employer prejudice against tattoos is also driven largely by hiring managers' perceptions of consumer expectations regarding body art in the workplace.

Commentary

Andrew Timming notes that body art such as tattoos and piercings are becoming an increasingly popular and therefore common means of self-adornment among young people in Western societies. In particular he is concerned to investigate the degree to which visible tattoos – those on the face, arms or hands, for instance – have an impact on the way in which workers in the service sector are viewed by colleagues, managers and customers. This in turn is likely to affect their job prospects and relationships in the workplace. He explains that while anthropological studies of tattoos and body art are common, it is rare as a subject of employment-related research, and that attitudes to body art in the workplace, especially when they are hostile, could be examined as a form of prejudice and discrimination. The stigma arises from the perceived relationship between tattooing and anti-social behaviour. The study is based on a small number of case histories and examines managerial attitudes to the tattooed subjects. It analyses the attitudes of hiring managers in relation to their personal views, their views about the expectation of customers and the way that these two might act together to disadvantage the prospects of a visibly tattooed job applicant.

The article might prompt you to consider some of the following questions

- Should recruiting managers take into account visible tattoos and other forms of body art when hiring people for customer-facing jobs?

- Is such body art likely to be more acceptable in certain industries and organisations than others, and does the nature of the tattoo itself make a difference? The article contrasts attitudes towards images of butterflies or flowers and those of politically loaded symbols such as swastikas.
- Should those with visible tattoos be included as a legally protected category with regard to workplace discrimination?
- Are you likely to be more favourably disposed to someone with a tattoo if you have one yourself?

Part 2 Case study
Philanthropy: the resurgence of personal social responsibility?

Something rather spectacular happened on 26 June 2006: Warren Buffett, then the world's second wealthiest man, announced that he intended to give 85 per cent of his fortune to the Bill and Melinda Gates Foundation. There, it will join the billions that Bill Gates, the world's wealthiest man, has already pledged, to make an enormous sum of money to support good works around the world. A few months earlier, Anita Roddick, who founded and built up Body Shop International, had announced her intention to give away half of her fortune. Philanthropy has long been a noble and admirable part of the capitalist tradition and seemed to be back in the news.

Why is this sort of philanthropy of interest to students of organisational behaviour? Several reasons can be suggested:

- Firstly, of course, the wealth that is given away is often the result of setting up and running an organisation that successfully fulfils its purpose over a long period: the profits that flow to the owner result from customers choosing and paying for its output.
- Also, the generosity of wealthy individuals makes an interesting contrast with the more familiar concept of 'corporate social responsibility', which sometimes involves donations of company, rather than personal, money.
- The charitable foundations, together with their external relationships, are of interest in their own right

The word 'philanthropy' is derived from the Greek and is defined as 'love of humankind; the disposition or effort to promote the happiness of and well-being of one's fellow-people'.[1] The practice of philanthropy was well established before that of capitalism of course, but the early stages of the growth of the US economy saw a significant surge in the social custom of philanthropy. Although it may have been no part of their aim, the names of some of the USA's most significant philanthropists are as well known for their giving as for the business careers that made the money. Two celebrated examples from the same era provide a view of the way a philanthropic life can be lived.

From Carnegie and Rockefeller to Bill and Melinda Gates

Andrew Carnegie (1835–1919) was born in Dunfermline, Scotland. He was the son of a weaver and the family emigrated to the USA in 1848. Like many at that time, Carnegie started work at the age of 13 doing a number of jobs until 1865, when he started his own business. This was to become the foundation of the steel industry in Pittsburgh and the origin of Carnegie's fortune. At the turn of the new century, Carnegie sold the business for $480 million and spent the rest of his life devoted to his philanthropic interests. These were diverse, but centred around the theme of the provision of public libraries and education.[2] Over his life, Carnegie gave away more than $350 million (multiply by about twenty for today's values). Some of the quotes attributed to him[3] show the combination of hard-nosed business acumen and the strong sense of social duty that characterises this type of philanthropist:

And while the law of competition may be sometimes hard for the individual, it is best for the race, because it ensures the survival of the fittest in every department.

Bill Gates and his wife set up the Bill and Melinda Gates Foundation with part of the personal fortune he had earned from the success of Microsoft
Source: Adrian Wyld/AP/Press Association Images

> *Surplus wealth is a sacred trust which its possessor is bound to administer in his lifetime for the good of the community.*
>
> *I would as soon leave my son a curse as the almighty dollar.*

As will be seen, similar sentiments and values continue to motivate today's philanthropists.

John D. Rockefeller (1839–1937) was born in the USA to a farming family. In his business career, he founded and developed the Standard Oil Company, which became the leading force in the fast-growing oil industry. At the age of 57, Rockefeller decided that he should step aside from the day-to-day leadership of Standard Oil and devote himself to philanthropy. This had been important to him from his early life, but also because of his religious convictions and his approach to finance:

> *I believe it is every man's religious duty to get all he can honestly and to give all he can.*

Like Carnegie, his philanthropic interests centred on education, with substantial donations to found and develop universities and research institutes, as well as the establishment of trusts and foundations for the improvement of education at all levels. Over his life,

he gave away some $550 million.[4] Again, some of the quotes attributed to the man[5] show a mixture of hard-headedness and generosity that is far from sentimental:

> *Charity is injurious unless it helps the recipient to become independent of it.*
>
> *I believe that every right implies a responsibility; every opportunity, an obligation; every possession, a duty.*

Both Carnegie and Rockefeller were members of the group of very powerful US business giants in the late 1800s known by some as 'robber barons'. John Kampfner's 2014 book[6] about the super-rich through history finds familiar themes in their behaviour, including their notable involvement in philanthropy later in their lives. For him, the educational foundations, art galleries and concert galleries are as much about 'reputation laundering' as philanthropy, something that has characterised the behaviour of the super-rich over the ages. In his view:

> *Wealth rarely buys peace of mind. The super-rich are consumed by what happens next. They fear for their legacies and for their children. Will the money they have made be safe in their hands? Will the standing they have acquired in society be frittered away? Will statues be cast in their image?*
>
> *They want to be remembered for more than making a fortune. What matters to them most is reputation.*
>
> (Kampfner 2014, Prologue)

Not everyone would share this level of cynicism about the motives of the givers, of course, but there is often a tension between the means through which fortunes are amassed and the great works that are funded by the philanthropy.

The emerging philanthropists of the twenty-first century have often made their money through businesses that were not even heard of in the lifetimes of Carnegie and Rockefeller. Bill Gates, for example, is one of the founders of the enormously successful Microsoft Corporation, whose information products are about as far from steel and oil as can be imagined. This case is mainly concerned with the Bill and Melinda Gates Foundation (BMGF), which was established in 1997 with an initial gift from the two founders.[7] It grew rapidly from 1999: in a list published in 2014[8] it was by a significant margin the largest foundation in the USA, in terms of both value of assets (about $37 billion at the end of 2012) and total giving (about $3 billion in year ending 2012). By 2014, total grants from the BMGF since its inception had grown to almost $33 billion and the organisation employed more than 1,200 people in eight locations

→

(Seattle, Washington DC, Delhi, Beijing and London, together with three offices in Africa: Addis Ababa, Abuja and Johannesburg).[9]

The organisation is organised around its four main priorities, which are: global development; global health; global policy and advocacy; and US programmes. In a letter published on the BMGF website,[10] Bill and Melinda Gates explain their aims in respect of global health, pointing out that health is fundamental to economic development:

> Our friend and co-trustee Warren Buffett once gave us some great advice about philanthropy: 'Don't just go for safe projects,' he said. 'Take on the really tough problems.'
>
> We couldn't agree more. Our foundation is teaming up with partners around the world to take on some tough problems: extreme poverty and poor health in developing countries, the failures of America's education system. We focus on only a few issues because we think that's the best way to have great impact, and we focus on these issues in particular because we think they are the biggest barriers that prevent people from making the most of their lives.
>
> For each issue we work on, we fund innovative ideas that could help remove these barriers: new techniques to help farmers in developing countries grow more food and earn more money; new tools to prevent and treat deadly diseases; new methods to help students and teachers in the classroom. Some of the projects we fund will fail. We not only accept that, we expect it – because we think an essential role of philanthropy is to make bets on promising solutions that governments and businesses can't afford to make. As we learn which bets pay off, we have to adjust our strategies and share the results so everyone can benefit.
>
> We're both optimists. We believe by doing these things – focusing on a few big goals and working with our partners on innovative solutions – we can help every person get the chance to live a healthy, productive life.

In the world of business, as opposed to philanthropic foundations, there has been growing interest in recent years in the subject of corporate governance: what the business is aiming to do and how it can be sure that its actions are consistent with those aims. It has been common for wealthy individuals to adopt a corporate format in making good works happen, often by setting up and then directing a dedicated foundation to look after both the strategic and operational aspects of the task. This seems to acknowledge the benefits of the corporate approach in terms of efficiency and the ability

to recruit and apply specialist skills, while still retaining control by the founder or the founding family. It is also easy to appreciate how focused and effective such an organisation can be in pursuing the goals of the founder, and to acknowledge the possibility that an effective philanthropic foundation may be at least as effective as, say, a government or international agency.

As will already be clear, some of the world's philanthropic foundations have multinational corporation-sized (even government-sized) budgets, meaning that the issue of governance is rightly of some concern to the society within which these organisations operate. One does not need to be a fan of James Bond movies to appreciate that very rich individuals using their wealth to pursue their private aims is not in itself guaranteed to be in the general interest.

In fact, foundations often go to some lengths to communicate their values and aims publicly. For example, the BMGF website sets out some key principles in the section 'Who We Are', whose subheadings are as follows:[11]

- We seek to unlock the possibility inside every individual.
- We are focused on the areas of greatest need, on the ways in which we can do the most good.
- We are focused on results. Those that can be measured. And those measured in ways beyond numbers.
- We seek to drive change on a global scale.
- We are impatient optimists.

Warren Buffett and Anita Roddick

Warren Buffett's fortune was made through the Berkshire Hathaway organisation, which for many years has been very successful in providing investment management services for its clients. Buffett himself is famously moderate in his lifestyle, with a liking for a diet of burgers and Cherry Coke. His extraordinary wealth was recently augmented by his firm decision not to get involved in the late 1990s dotcom boom and subsequent bust: his policy has always been to concentrate on business fundamentals and to invest for the long term. He also has a long-standing reputation for pithy quotes and one attributed remark seemed to sum up the chaos caused by the collapse of rapid stock market growth and the series of corporate scandals that followed:

> It's only when the tide goes out that you can see who's been swimming without their trunks on.

From remarks made by Buffett since the announcement of his association with the BMGF,[12] it seems clear that he had been thinking about an involvement in philanthropy for some time. Some of his motivation is bound up with the American tradition of philanthropy by wealthy individuals, including the notion that there is something problematic about the idea that huge wealth should result from accidents of birth. As he has suggested, children should be left wealthy enough to do anything, but not enough to do nothing. He had also become very impressed by the approach taken by the BMGF and by Bill and Melinda themselves; the announcement coincided with that of the succession plans for Gates's leadership of Microsoft, which allowed Gates to devote more time to the BMGF. Buffett has become a trustee of the BMGF and jokingly promised at the launch not to assess Gates's efforts more than once a day. At the same meeting, both men acknowledged the inspirational value that the news of the donation could have: one questioner suggested that the success of organisations like the BMGF could do much to improve public confidence in charitable donation in general and perhaps increase the willingness of a far wider spectrum of people to give. Since 2010, Gates and Buffett have also turned their attention to persuading other very rich people to give their wealth away through their Giving Pledge campaign.[13] One notable feature of the annual Forbes Magazine list of the world's dollar billionaires[14] has been the arrival of more and more very wealthy people from the fast-emerging BRIC economies (e.g. the 2014 list showed three Brazilians in the top 100, along with six Russians, five Indians and nine from China/Hong Kong). It will be interesting to see how the practice of philanthropy develops in these and other emerging economies, where cultural traditions may differ from the West and where the local needs are often urgent.

The decision by the late UK entrepreneur Anita Roddick to join the ranks of business-based philanthropists adds some interesting features to the discussion. Roddick was something of a business celebrity for much of her career, having founded and built up the very successful Body Shop International, a business whose market appeal was always strongly centred on the values of its founder. Its campaigns against animal testing of cosmetics and in favour of fair trade, for example, became prominent during the 1990s. Explaining that she did not want to die rich, Roddick announced at the end of 2005[15] that she intended to give away half her £100 million fortune, much of which resulted from the sale of her business to L'Oreal. Sadly, she died suddenly aged just 64 in September 2007, but the Roddick Foundation survives her.[16]

In her lifetime, Anita Roddick was often sharply critical of some aspects of business life in the UK, especially where attitudes seemed to her to be selfish and

The world's most generous man? In 2006 Warren Buffet, the world's second wealthiest man, promised to give 85 per cent of his fortune to support good works around the world
Source: Seth Wenig/AP/Press Association Images

short-termist. But, in her view, the rich had to look after the poor, and:

> *I don't think in our society we have any understanding of that.*

A BBC article[17] commented at the time that personal philanthropy was less prominent in the UK than in the USA, possibly because people in the UK regard it as a government responsibility to look after the poor, with projects financed from general taxation and with additional contributions from companies under the heading of 'corporate social responsibility'. This is not to suggest that government programmes and corporate donations are by any means unimportant in the USA, but rather to emphasise how unusual personal philanthropy has been in the UK. However, one recent initiative in the UK made its appeal to people on ordinary incomes, rather than the world's billionaires. The organisation Giving What We Can[18] seeks pledgers to donate 10 per cent of personal incomes and offers guidance on the most cost-effective charities. As it points out, significant impacts can be made by donations at this level over the long term.

Corporate versus personal philanthropy

Many large businesses in the UK have made significant donations to charity from corporate funds, which may be partly motivated by a desire for approval from some stakeholder groups. As such, corporate philanthropy – and corporate social responsibility in general – has come in for criticism from some quarters, on the basis that it amounts to acts of generosity using other people's money (specifically, that of the shareholders, who own the company). The economist Milton Friedman forcefully suggested for some decades that business should get on with the business of business: making money for its owners through successfully marketing products and services within the law. From this point of view, donations to charity by individuals making choices about their own funds are more desirable than acts of corporate generosity using other people's funds. In reality, public opinion seems to be sympathetic towards the idea of corporate donations to charity, whatever scepticism may sometimes be expressed about motives. However, from any reasonable point of view, there remains an important difference between giving personally and approving corporate gifts: the difference perhaps, between signing your own, rather than a company, cheque.

At the BMGF conference mentioned above, Bill Gates alluded to the celebrated work of Adam Smith, the Scottish economist who first explained the general benefits of free markets in identifying and providing for needs effectively and efficiently. From these ideas have come the modern economies that provided the context in which organisations such as Microsoft, Berkshire Hathaway and Body Shop International can generate large amounts of wealth, mainly through providing products and services that are attractive enough to cause people to choose to spend their own money on them. In short, this is the main reason why recent generations have in most cases been richer than their predecessors. The tradition of philanthropy on the part of wealthy individuals is by no means contrary to the desirability of free and fierce competition; rather, wealth generation and philanthropy can only go hand in hand.

What is generally less well known about Adam Smith is his significant contribution to moral philosophy. Perhaps the way to bring this discussion to a close is with a quote from the beginning of Adam Smith's *Theory of*

Anita Roddick, founder of the Body Shop, who built a business based on caring values, gave half of her wealth away.
Source: Jean/Empics Entertainment/Press Association Images

Moral Sentiments, which was highlighted by Bill Gates in explaining the basic importance of philanthropy.

> *How selfish soever man may be supposed, there are evidently some principles in his nature which interest him in the fortune of others and render their happiness necessary to him though he derives nothing from it except the pleasure of seeing it.*

Philanthropic foundations are organisations that are interesting in their own right, in respect of the origin of their funds, in their interaction with other types of organisation and, of course, in the effects they have on the societies within which they operate.

Tasks

1 Not all successful business leaders become renowned philanthropists like Gates, Roddick and others. Using concepts from Chapter 4 as the basis for your analysis, suggest which aspects of individual personality might explain why some do and others do not.
2 Philanthropic foundations have often been created to transfer knowledge and skills from their countries of origin to people living in parts of the developing world. What challenges might those who work for such organisations face in achieving this task, and how could theories of learning help them?
3 To some extent, philanthropic foundations are engaged in the same types of social projects as government agencies. How might approaches to employee motivation differ between the two types of organisation? What could either type of organisation usefully learn from the other?

Notes and references

1 *New Shorter Oxford English Dictionary* (1993).

2 http://www.carnegie.org/sub/about/biography.html (accessed 23 February 2015).

3 http://www.brainyquote.com/quotes/authors/a/andrew_carnegie.html (accessed 23 February 2015).

4 http://www.notablebiographies.com/Pu-Ro/Rockefeller-John-D.html (accessed 23 February 2015).

5 http://www.brainyquote.com/quotes/authors/j/john_d_rockefeller.html (accessed 23 February 2015).

6 Kampfner, J. *The Rich – From Slaves to Super-Yachts: A 2000-Year History*, Little Brown (2014).

7 http://www.gatesfoundation.org/about/Pages/foundation-timeline.aspx (accessed 23 February 2015).

8 http://foundationcenter.org/findfunders/topfunders/top100assets.html (accessed 23 February 2015).

9 http://www.gatesfoundation.org/about/Pages/foundation-fact-sheet.aspx (accessed 23 February 2015).

10 www.gatesfoundation.org/Who-We-Are/General-Information/Letter-from-Bill-and-Melinda-Gates (accessed 23 February 2015).

11 http://www.gatesfoundation.org/who-we-are (accessed 23 February 2015).

12 http://www.nytimes.com/2006/06/27/business/27friends.html?_r=1& (accessed 23 February 2015).

13 http://givingpledge.org/ (accessed 23 February 2015).

14 http://www.forbes.com/billionaires/list/#tab:overall (accessed 23 February 2015).

15 http://news.bbc.co.uk/1/hi/business/4524046.stm (accessed 23 February 2015).

16 http://www.theroddickfoundation.org/ (accessed 23 February 2015).

17 http://news.bbc.co.uk/1/hi/business/4524046.stm (accessed 23 February 2015).

18 http://www.givingwhatwecan.org/ (accessed 23 February 2015).

PART 3
Groups, leadership and management

CHAPTER 8
Working in groups and teams

Work is a group-based activity and if the organisation is to function effectively it requires collaboration and co-operation among its members. Most activities of the organisation require at least some degree of co-ordination through groups and teamwork. Understanding the nature, operation and impact of groups and teams is vital if the manager is to influence the behaviour and performance of people in the work situation.

Learning outcomes

After completing this chapter you should have enhanced your ability to:

- explain the nature and significance of work groups and teams;
- relate the nature of informal groups and importance of group values and norms;
- examine factors that influence group cohesiveness and performance;
- identify characteristics of an effective work group and virtual teams;
- explain role structure of the organisation and individual role relationships;
- evaluate individual compared with group or team performance;
- review the importance and characteristics of successful groups or teams.

Critical review and reflection

Self-interest and opportunism are natural features of human behaviour and will always take preference over the demands and best interests of the group or teamwork.

To what extent can YOU present a counter point of view? How far are YOU prepared to put the interests of a work group or team before YOUR own interests?

The importance and significance of groups

Groups are a characteristic of all social situations. Individuals seldom work in isolation from others. The work organisation and its sub-units are made up of groups of people. **Groups** are an essential feature of any organisation and almost every member of staff will belong to one or more groups. Although there is no single accepted definition, most people will readily understand what constitutes a group. The essential feature is that its members regard themselves as belonging to the group. A popular definition defines the group in psychological terms as:

> any number of people who (1) interact with one another; (2) are psychologically aware of one another; and (3) perceive themselves to be a group.[1]

Another useful way of defining a work group is a collection of people who share most, if not all, of the following characteristics:

- a definable membership;
- group consciousness;
- a sense of shared purpose;
- interdependence;
- interaction;
- ability to act in a unitary manner.[2]

Members of a group must co-operate in order for work to be carried out, and managers themselves will work within these groups. The working of groups and the influence they exert over their membership is an essential feature of management and organisational behaviour. People in groups influence each other in many ways and groups develop their own hierarchies and leaders. Group pressures can have a major influence over the behaviour of individual members and their work performance.

Peterson and colleagues discuss the importance of morale as an indicator of group well-being. The attention of positive psychology to promote good life (**discussed in Chapter** 1) should include not only individuals but also groups within which individuals live, work, love and play. Groups should be a primary focus of research into health and well-being.[3]

Groups and teams

The use of the word 'teams' has become increasingly fashionable in recent years. In common usage and literature, including in this book, there is a tendency for the terms 'groups' and 'teams' to be used interchangeably and based on personal preference. It is not easy to distinguish clearly between a group and a team. According to ACAS:

> Teams have been around for as long as anyone can remember and there can be few organisations that have not used the term in one sense or another. It is common to hear of management teams, production teams, service teams or even whole organisations referred to as teams . . . The term 'team' is used loosely to describe many different groupings and a variety of labels are given to the types of teams . . . It is doubtful whether any definition of types of teams would be universally acceptable.[4]

Holpp poses the question 'Why do you want teams?' While many people are still paying homage to teams, teamwork, empowerment and self-management, others have become disillusioned.

> If teams are just a convenient way to group under one manager a lot of people who used to work for several downsized supervisors, don't bother. But if teams can truly take ownership of work areas and provide the kind of up-close knowledge that's unavailable elsewhere, then full speed ahead.[5]

Cane suggests that organisations are sometimes unsure whether they have teams or simply groups of people working together.

> *It is certainly true to say that any group of people who do not know they are a team cannot be one. To become a team, a group of individuals needs to have a strong common purpose and to work towards that purpose rather than individually. They need also to believe that they will achieve more by co-operation than working individually.*[6]

Teamwork as a fashionable term

Belbin points out that to the extent that teamwork was becoming a fashionable term, it began to replace the more usual reference to groups and every activity was now being described as 'teamwork'. He questions whether it matters whether one is talking about groups or teams and maintains that the confusion in vocabulary should be addressed if the principles of good teamwork are to be retained. Belbin suggests there are several factors that characterise the difference between groups and teams (*see* Figure 8.1). The best differentiator is size: groups can comprise any number of people but teams are smaller with a membership between (ideally) four and six. The quintessential feature of a small, well-balanced team is that leadership is shared or rotates, whereas large groups typically throw up solo leaders.[7]

While acknowledging the work of Belbin, it appears that the term 'group' is often used in a more general sense and 'team' in a more specific context. We continue to refer to 'group' or 'team' according to the particular focus of attention and the vocabulary of the quoted authors. **Whereas all teams are, by definition, groups, it does not necessarily follow that all groups are teams.** The Chartered Management Institute maintains that a team is more than just a group of people who happen to work together.

> *It is a group of people working towards common goals and objectives and sharing responsibility for the outcomes. Team building is the process of selecting and grouping team members effectively and developing good working relationships and practices enabling the team to steer and develop the work and reach their goals. Increasingly, a team may be composed of people drawn from different functions, departments and disciplines whom have been brought together for a specific project.*[8]

	Team	Group
Size	Limited	Medium or large
Selection	Crucial	Immaterial
Leadership	Shared or rotating	Solo
Perception	Mutual knowledge understanding	Focus on leader
Style	Role-spread co-ordination	Convergence conformism
Spirit	Dynamic interaction	Togetherness persecution of opponents

Figure 8.1 Differences between a team and a group

Source: Belbin, R. M. *Beyond the Team*, Butterworth–Heinemann (2000). Copyright © 2000. Reproduced with permission from Belbin, www.belbin.com.

Whatever the debate on 'groups' or 'teams', what is clear is the increasing popularity of teamworking and the importance to organisations of effective group working or teamworking.

Critical review and reflection

It is almost impossible to distinguish clearly or in any meaningful way between work groups and teams. Attempting to do so is a vain, and pointless, quest. It is a waste of study time.

What is YOUR reaction to this assertion? How do YOU distinguish between a work group and team?

Formal and informal groups

Groups are formed as a consequence of the pattern of organisation structure and arrangements for the division of work, for example the grouping together of common activities into divisions or sections. **Formal groups** are created to achieve specific organisational objectives and are concerned with the **co-ordination of work activities.** People are brought together on the basis of defined roles within the structure of the organisation. The nature of the tasks to be undertaken is a predominant feature of the formal group. Goals are identified by management, and certain rules, relationships and norms of behaviour established.

Groups may result from the nature of technology employed and the way in which work is carried out, for example bringing together a number of people to carry out a sequence of operations on an assembly line. Groups may also develop when a number of people of the same level or status within the organisation see themselves as a group, for example departmental heads of an industrial organisation or chief officers of a local authority. Formal groups tend to be relatively permanent, although there may be changes in actual membership. However, temporary formal groups may also be created by management, as with, for example, the use of project teams in a matrix organisation. (**See also matrix organisation in Chapter 11.**)

Informal groups

The formal structure of the organisation, and system of role relationships, rules and procedures, will be augmented by interpretation and development at the informal level. Groups will also arise from social processes and the informal organisation (**discussed in Chapter 3**).

Informal groups are based more on personal relationships and agreement of group members than on defined role relationships. They serve to satisfy psychological and social needs not related necessarily to the tasks to be undertaken. Informal groups may devise ways of attempting to satisfy members' affiliation and other social motivations lacking in the work situation. Membership can cut across the formal structure. These groups may comprise individuals from different parts of the organisation and/or from different levels of the organisation, both vertically and diagonally, as well as from the same horizontal level. An informal group could also be the same as the formal group, or it might comprise a part only of the formal group (*see* Figure 8.2).

Members of an informal group may appoint their own leader who exercises authority by consent of the members themselves. The informal leader may be chosen as the person who reflects the attitudes and values of the members, helps to resolve conflict, leads the group in satisfying its goals, or liaises with management or other people outside the group. The informal leader may change according to the particular situation facing the group. Although not usually the case, it is possible for the informal leader to be the same person as the formal leader appointed officially by management.

Figure 8.2 Examples of informal groups within the formal structure of an organisation

Major functions of informal groups

Lysons suggests four main reasons for informal groups:

- **Perpetuation of the informal group 'culture'.** Culture in this context means a set of values, norms and beliefs that form a guide to group acceptance and group behaviour. Unless you broadly subscribe to the group culture, you will not belong and will be an 'outsider' or 'isolate'.
- **Maintenance of a communication system.** Groups want all the information that affects their welfare, either negatively or positively. If groups are not apprised of policies and motives behind actions, they will seek to tap into formal communication channels and spread information among group members.
- **Implementation of social control.** Conformity to group culture is enforced by such techniques as ridicule, ostracism and violence. This is illustrated, for example, by the enforcement of group norms in the bank wiring room discussed in the next section.
- **Provision of interest and fun in work-life.** Many jobs are monotonous and fail to hold workers' attention. Work may also offer few prospects. Workers may try to compensate by interpersonal relations provided by the group and in such activities as time wasting by talking, gambling, practical joking and drinking.[9]

As *Law* reminds us:

We humans are a gregarious lot. We like to gather together and establish our own social networks, which are often the real key to creativity and innovation in organisations . . . But many managers are unaware that seemingly pointless social networking does in fact play a crucial part in the way people interact with each other and get work done.[10]

Group values and norms

The classical approach to organisation and management tended to ignore the importance of groups and the social factors at work. The human relations approach, however (**discussed in Chapter 2**), gave recognition to the work organisation as a social organisation and to the importance of the group, and group values and norms, in influencing behaviour at work.

In the Hawthorne studies, one experiment involved the observation of a group of fourteen men working in the bank wiring room who formed their own sub-groups or cliques, with natural leaders emerging with the consent of the members. Despite a financial incentive scheme for the more work they did, the group decided on a level of output well below what they were capable of achieving. Group pressures on individual workers were stronger than financial incentives offered by management.

Informal social relations

The group developed its own pattern of informal social relations and codes and practices ('norms') of what constituted proper group behaviour.

- **Not to be a 'rate buster'** – Not to produce at too high a rate of output compared with other members or to exceed the production restriction of the group.
- **Not to be a 'chiseller'** – Not to shirk production or to produce at too low a rate of output compared with other members of the group.
- **Not to be a 'squealer'** – Not to say anything to the supervisor or management that might be harmful to other members of the group.
- **Not to be 'officious'** – People with authority over members of the group, for example inspectors, should not take advantage of their seniority or maintain a social distance from the group.

The group had its own system of sanctions including sarcasm, damaging completed work, hiding tools, playing tricks on the inspectors and ostracising those members who did not conform to the **group norms**. Threats of physical violence were also made and the group developed a system of punishing offenders by 'binging', which involved striking someone a fairly hard blow on the upper part of the arm. This process of binging also became a recognised method of controlling conflict within the group.

Importance of social norms

According to *Riches,* one way to improve team performance is to establish agreed norms or rules for how the team is to operate and rigorously stick to them. Norms could address the obligations of individual members to the team, how it will assess its performance, how it will work together, what motivation systems will be used, how it will relate to customers, and the mechanisms to facilitate an honest exchange about the team norms and behaviour.[11]

A study by the Economic & Social Research Council draws attention to the importance of social norms among employees and questions whether employees are guided not only by monetary incentives, but also by peer pressure towards social efficiency for the workers as a group: 'Intuitively, social norms among workers must be important if they work in teams where bonuses are dependent on group rather than individual effort.'[12] (You may see some similarity here with the bank wiring room experiment, discussed above.)

A concept map of group norms is set out in Figure 8.3.

Reasons for formation of groups or teams

Individuals have varying expectations of the benefits from group membership, both formal and informal, relating to both work performance and social processes.

- **Certain tasks can be performed only through the combined efforts of a number of individuals working together.** The variety of experience, knowledge and expertise among members provides a synergetic effect that can be applied to the increasingly complex problems of modern organisations.
- **Collusion between members** in order to modify formal working arrangements more to their liking – for example, by sharing or rotating unpopular tasks. Membership therefore provides the individual with opportunities for initiative and creativity.

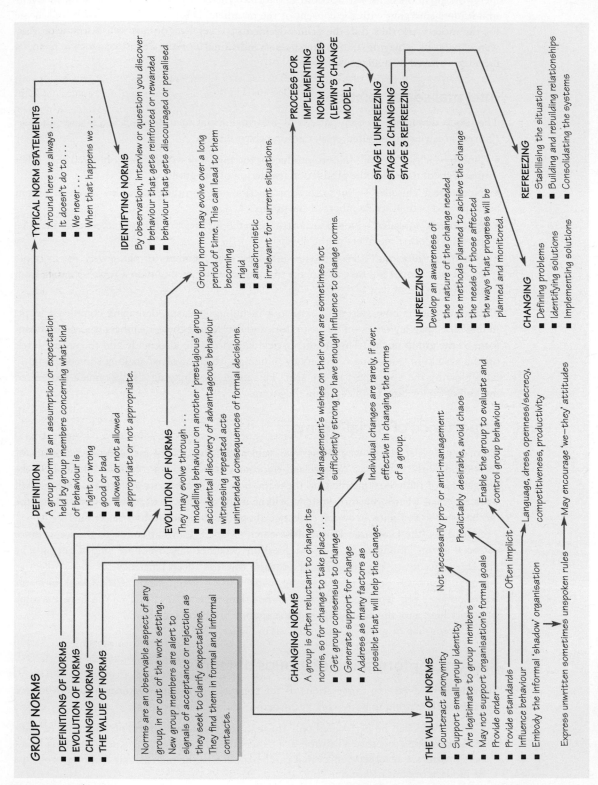

Figure 8.3 Concept map of group norms

Source: Copyright © 2008 The Virtual Learning Materials Workshop. Reproduced with permission.

- **Companionship and a source of mutual understanding and support from colleagues.** This can help in solving work problems and also to militate against stressful or demanding working conditions.
- **Membership provides the individual with a sense of belonging.** It provides a feeling of identity and the chance to acquire role recognition and status within the group or team. (**See the discussion on social identity theory below.**)
- **Guidelines on generally acceptable behaviour.** These help to clarify ambiguous situations, such as the extent to which official rules and regulations are expected to be adhered to in practice, the rules of the game and what is seen as the correct actual behaviour. Allegiance to the group or team can serve as a means of control over individual behaviour and individuals who contravene the norms may be disciplined.
- **Protection for its membership.** Group or team members collaborate to protect their interests from outside pressures or threats.

Critical review and reflection

Given the importance of social interactions and interpersonal relationships for morale, job satisfaction and work performance, the main focus of your studies should be on the operations and management of the informal organisation.

Can YOU present a counterargument to this contention? How much have YOU learned about the importance and influence of the informal organisation?

Group cohesiveness and performance

Social interaction is a natural feature of human behaviour and work organisation but ensuring harmonious working relationships and effective teamwork is not an easy task. Co-operation is likely to be greater in a united, cohesive group. Membership can be a rewarding experience for the individual, contribute to the promotion of morale and aid release of creativity and energy. Members of a high-morale group are more likely to think of themselves as a group and work together effectively. Strong and cohesive work groups can, therefore, have beneficial effects for the organisation. There are many factors that affect group cohesiveness and performance, which can be summarised under four broad headings, as shown in Figure 8.4.

Membership

Size of the group

As a group increases in size, problems arise with communications and co-ordination. Large groups are more difficult to handle and require a higher level of supervision. Absenteeism also tends to be higher. When a group becomes too large it may split into smaller units and friction may develop between the sub-groups. It is difficult to put a precise figure on the ideal size of a work group. Much will depend upon other variables, but it seems to be generally accepted that cohesiveness becomes more difficult to achieve when a group exceeds ten to twelve members.[13] Beyond this size the group tends to split into sub-groups. A figure of between five and seven is often quoted as an apparent optimum size for full participation within the group.

Cane asks the question: 'How many people should be in a team?'

The answers from different organisations as to what is the perfect number vary from between four and fifteen depending on a whole range of variables. Fifteen is about the maximum

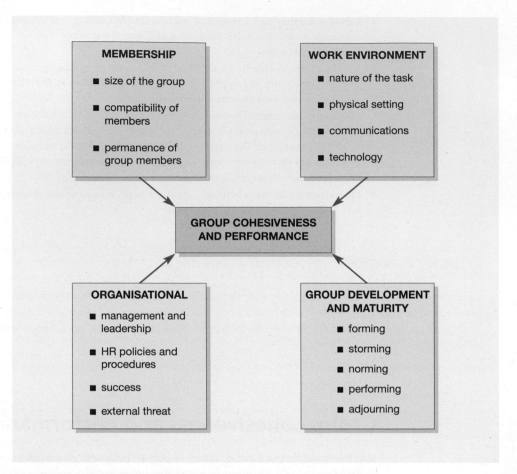

Figure 8.4 Factors contributing to group cohesiveness and performance

*number of people anyone can communicate with without having to raise their voice signifi-
cantly and any less than four has a restriction in the amount of creativity and variety that
can be produced. It is interesting to note that these figures range between the maximum and
minimum numbers of sports teams – perhaps less of a coincidence than it seems.*[14]

Compatibility of members

The more homogeneous the group in terms of such features as shared backgrounds, interests,
attitudes and values of its members, the easier it is usually to promote cohesiveness. Variations
in other individual differences, such as personality or skills of members, may serve to complement each other and help make for a cohesive group. However, such differences may be the
cause of disruption and conflict. Conflict can also arise in a homogeneous group where members are in competition with each other. Individual incentive payment schemes, for example,
may be a source of conflict.

Permanence of group members

Group spirit and relationships take time to develop. Cohesiveness is more likely when members of a group are together for a reasonable length of time and changes occur only slowly. A
frequent turnover of members is likely to have an adverse effect on morale and on the cohesiveness of the group.

Work environment

Nature of the task

Where workers are involved in similar work, share a common task or face the same problems, this may assist cohesiveness. The nature of the task may serve to bring people together when it is necessary to communicate and interact regularly – for example, members of a research and development team. Even if members of a group normally work at different locations they may still experience a feeling of cohesiveness if the nature of the task requires frequent communication and interaction – for example, security guards patrolling separate areas who need to check with each other on a regular basis.

Physical setting

Where members of a group work in the same location or in close physical proximity to each other this may generally help cohesiveness. However, this is not always the case. For example, in large open-plan offices staff often tend to segregate themselves from colleagues and create barriers through the strategic siting of such items as filing cabinets, bookcases or indoor plants. The size of the office and the number of staff in it are, of course, important considerations in this case. Isolation from other groups of workers will also tend to build cohesiveness. This often applies to a smaller number of workers on a night shift.

Communications

The more easily members can communicate freely with each other, the greater the likelihood of group cohesiveness. Communications are affected by the work environment, by nature of the task and technology. For example, difficulties in communication can arise with production systems where workers are stationed continuously at a particular point with limited freedom of movement. Even when opportunities exist for interaction with colleagues, physical conditions may limit effective communication. For example, the technological layout and high level of noise with some assembly line work can limit contact between workers. Changes in the nature of work, including increasing demand for flexible working arrangements, may restrict opportunities for social interaction and hamper internal group unity.[15]

Technology

Technology is clearly a major influence on patterns of group operation and behaviour. ACAS draws attention to technological advances and how new technology enables production to be tailored quickly to customer requirements, often on an individual basis.

> *Mass production techniques, where jobs are broken down into simple tasks, are not suitable for the new customer focused manufacturing nor the expectations of an educated workforce. Organisations need workers to be more flexible, to co-operate with other workers, supervisors and managers throughout the organisation, to operate sophisticated technology and to be more adaptable. In addition, the sheer complexity of operations in industry, commerce and the services places them beyond the expertise and control of any one individual. In these circumstances some form of teamwork becomes not just desirable but essential.[16]*

The impact of IT demands new patterns of work organisation and affects the formation and structure of groups. Improvements in telecommunications mean that support staff need no longer be located within the main production unit. Individuals may work more on their own, from their homes, shared offices or hotels, or work more with machines than with other people.

Organisational

Management and leadership

Teams tend to be a mirror image of their leaders. The form of management and style of leadership adopted are major determinants of group cohesiveness. In general terms, cohesiveness will be affected by such things as the manner in which the manager gives support, guidance and encouragement to the group, provides opportunities for participation, attempts to resolve conflicts and gives attention to both employee relations and task problems.

McKenna and Maister draw attention to the importance of the group leader establishing a level of trust among the group by helping its members understand the behaviours that build trust: 'The job of the group leader is to encourage people to earn the trust of others in their group and then show them how it can translate into greater commitment, greater creativity, greater professional satisfaction, and better performance.'[17] *Farrell* makes the point that managers are ultimately responsible for creating a balance in the workplace and should take the lead in setting standards of behaviour in teams.[18]

HR policies and procedures

Harmony and cohesiveness within the group are more likely to be achieved if HR policies and procedures are well developed and perceived to be equitable, with fair treatment for all members. Attention should be given to the effects that appraisal systems, discipline, promotion and rewards and opportunities for personal development have on members of the group.

Success

Success is usually a strong motivational influence on cohesiveness and level of work performance. Success or reward as a positive motivator can be perceived by group members in a number of ways – for example, the satisfactory completion of a task through co-operative action, praise from management, a feeling of high status, achievement in competition with other groups or benefits gained, such as high wage payments from a group bonus incentive scheme.

External threat

Cohesiveness may be enhanced by members co-operating with one another when faced with a common external threat, such as changes in their method of work or the appointment of a new manager. Even if the threat is subsequently removed, the group may continue to have a greater degree of cohesiveness than before the threat arose. Conflict between groups will also tend to increase the cohesiveness of each group and the boundaries of the group become drawn more clearly.

Group development and maturity

The degree of cohesiveness is affected also by the manner in which groups progress through the various stages of development and maturity before getting down to the real tasks in hand. This process can take time and is often traumatic for the members. A popular model by *Tuckman* identifies five main successive stages of group development and relationships: **forming, storming, norming, performing** and **adjourning**.[19]

- **Stage 1 – forming.** This concerns initial formation of the group and bringing together individuals who identify, tentatively, the purpose of the group, its composition and terms of reference. Consideration is given to the hierarchical structure of the group, pattern of leadership, individual roles and responsibilities and codes of conduct. There is likely to be considerable anxiety as members attempt to create an impression, test each other and establish their personal identity within the group.

- **Stage 2 – storming.** As members of the group get to know each other better they will put forward their views more openly and forcefully. Disagreements will be expressed and challenges offered on the nature of the task and arrangements made in the earlier stage of development. This may lead to conflict and hostility. The storming stage is important because, if successful, there will be discussions on reforming arrangements for the working and operation of the group, and agreement on more meaningful structures and procedures.

- **Stage 3 – norming.** As conflict and hostility start to be controlled, members of the group will establish guidelines and standards and develop their own norms of acceptable behaviour. The norming stage is important in establishing the need for members to co-operate in order to plan, agree standards of performance and fulfil the purpose of the group.

- **Stage 4 – performing.** When the group has progressed successfully through the three earlier stages of development it will have created structure and cohesiveness to work effectively as a team. At this stage the group can concentrate on the attainment of its purpose and performance of the common task is likely to be at its most effective.

- **Stage 5 – adjourning.** This refers to the adjourning or disbanding of the group because of, for example, completion of the task, members leaving the organisation or moving on to other tasks. Some members may feel a compelling sense of loss at the end of a major or lengthy group project and their return to independence is characterised by sadness and anxiety. Managers may need to prepare for future group tasks and engendering team effort.

Another writer suggests that new groups go through the following five stages:

- the polite stage;
- the why are we here, what are we doing stage;
- the power stage, which dominant person will emerge;
- the constructive stage when sharing begins; and
- the unity stage – this often takes weeks, eating together, talking together.[20]

Critical review and reflection

Modern systems of communication, such as email and the increasing use of social media, restrict personal interaction and have only a negative effect on group development, cohesiveness and performance.

To what extent do YOU believe this fair comment? How has email or social media affected YOUR experience of group membership?

Creative leadership and group development

In an examination of creative leadership and team effectiveness, *Rickards and Moger* propose a modification to the Tuckman model and suggest a two-barrier model of group development. From their empirical studies of small groups and project teams, Rickards and Moger put forward two challenges to the prevailing model of team development:

1. Weak teams posed the question 'What is happening if a team fails to develop beyond the storm stage?'.

2. The exceptional teams posed the question 'What happens if a team breaks out of the performance norms developed?'.

The suggestion is that teams are differentiated by two barriers to performance. The weak barrier is behavioural and defeated a minority of teams; the strong barrier was a block to creativity or innovation, and defeated the majority of those teams who passed through the weak barrier. The two-barrier model provides a starting point for exploring the impact and influence of a team leader on the performance of teams. Rickards and Moger identified seven factors through which a leader might influence effective team development:

- building a platform of understanding;
- creating a shared vision;
- providing a creative climate;
- showing a commitment to idea ownership;
- resilience to setbacks;
- developing networking skills;
- learning from experience.[21]

Social identity theory

Within work organisations there will be a number of different but overlapping groups representing a variety of functions, departments, occupations, technologies, project teams, locations or hierarchical levels. Organisational effectiveness will be dependent upon the extent to which these groups co-operate, but often the different groupings are part of a network of complex relationships resulting in competitiveness and conflict. A feature of the importance and significance of group membership is the concept of social identity theory. *Tajfel and Turner* originally developed the idea of **social identity theory** as a means of understanding the psychological basis of inter-group discrimination.[22] Individuals are perceived as having not just one 'personal self' but a number of 'selves' derived from different social contexts and membership of groups.

Because of the need for a clear sense of personal identity, the groups or social categories with which we associate are an integral part of our self-concept (social identity). A natural process of human interaction is social categorisation, by which we classify both ourselves and other people through reference to our own social identity. For example, membership of high-status groups can increase a person's perceived self-esteem. According to *Guirdham*, 'self-categorisation is the process that transforms a number of individuals into a group'.[23] *See* Figure 8.5.

Haslam refers to the relationship between individuals and groups in an understanding of organisational behaviour, and argues that:

> in order to understand perception and interaction in organizational contexts we must do more than just study the psychology of individuals as individuals. Instead, we need to understand how social interaction is bound up with individuals' social identities – their definition of themselves in terms of group memberships.[24]

Identification with social groupings

We identify ourselves in terms of membership of certain social groupings and differentiate ourselves from other social groupings. This leads to minimising differences between members of our own groupings (in-groups) and maximising differences from other groupings (out-groups). Over time the sense of shared identity with the in-group increases a feeling of what is right and proper and highlights differences from the out-groups.[25] As a result, this reinforces both social identity with our own category and the projection of negative perceptions and stereotypes towards out-groups.

Stereotyping can lead to shared attitudes to out-groups and to increased conflict among work groups. The examples of group stereotyping (**discussed in Chapter 6**) are associated with social identity theory. Tajfel and Turner suggest that the mere act of individuals categorising themselves as group members leads them to exhibit in-group favouritism. *Hewstone et al.*

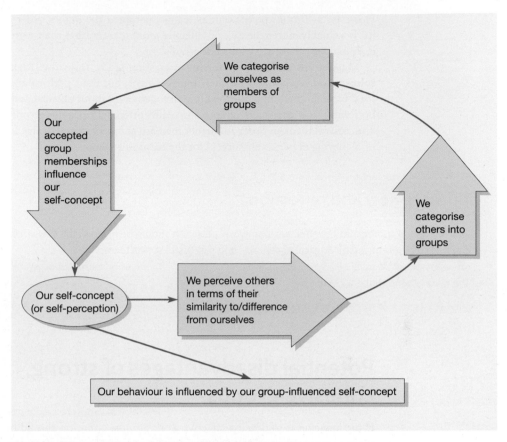

Figure 8.5 Processes of social and self-categorisation
Source: Guirdham, M. *Interactive Behaviour at Work*, third edition, Financial Times Prentice Hall (2002), p. 119. Reproduced with permission of Pearson Education Ltd.

suggest that, even without realising it, we tend usually to favour the groupings we belong to more than denigrate out-groups. Successful inter-group bias enhances self-esteem.[26] (**See also the discussion on social exchange theory in Chapter 1 and possible effects on group membership, norms and control.**)

Characteristics of an effective work group

The characteristics of an effective work group are not always easy to isolate clearly. The underlying feature is a spirit of co-operation in which members work well together as a united team and with harmonious and supportive relationships. This may be evidenced when members of a group exhibit:

- belief in shared aims and objectives;
- sense of commitment to the group;
- acceptance of group values and norms;
- feeling of mutual trust and dependency;
- full participation by all members and decision-making by consensus;
- free flow of information and communications;
- open expression of feelings and disagreements;
- resolution of conflict by the members themselves;
- lower level of staff turnover, absenteeism, accidents, errors and complaints.

However, as *Brooks* points out, as teams operate at the higher order of group dynamics this list is arguably more reflective of 'effective *work teams* rather than work groups and this is how it should be – these are teams not groups'.[27]

Musical ensembles make for an interesting study. Individual members may be brilliant soloists and often noted for their temperament, but their performance is as much about the total blend and working noticeably well together as about musical ability. By comparison, it is noticeable how managers of sporting teams often deliberately introduce new players, even to a successful team, in order to further increase competition or rivalry for places, with the hope of achieving even greater success for the team as a whole.

Critical review and reflection

To gain a greater appreciation of effective teamwork, attention should be given in the classroom to the management and functioning of successful musical ensembles and successful sports teams.

To what extent do YOU believe an understanding of musical ensembles or sports teams relates in a meaningful way to the work organisation?

Potential disadvantages of strong, cohesive groups

If the manager is to develop effective work groups, attention should be given to those factors that influence the creation of group identity and cohesiveness. This may result in greater inter-action between members, mutual help and social satisfaction, lower turnover and absenteeism, and often higher production.[28] However, strong and cohesive groups also present potential disadvantages for management. Working in groups may result in members spending too much time talking among themselves. Cohesive groups do not necessarily produce a higher level of output. It may be remembered that in the bank wiring room experiment of the Hawthorne studies the level of output was restricted to a standard acceptable as a norm by the group.

Once a group has become fully developed, created cohesiveness and established its own culture, it is more difficult for the manager successfully to change attitudes and behaviour of the group. It is important that the manager attempts to influence the group during the norming stage, when members are establishing their own guidelines and standards and their own norms of acceptable behaviour.

Inter-group conflict

Strong, cohesive groups may develop a critical or even hostile attitude towards people outside the group or members of other groups. Groups may also compete against each other in a non-productive manner. This can be the case, for example, when group cohesiveness is based on common status, qualifications, technical expertise or professional standing. As a result, resentment and inter-group conflict may arise to the detriment of the organisation as a whole. (**Recall the discussion on social identity theory, above.**) In order to help prevent, or overcome, unconstructive inter-group conflict, the manager should attempt to stimulate a high level of communication and interaction between groups.

Yet, inter-group rivalry may be deliberately encouraged as a means of building stronger within-group cohesiveness. The idea is that a competitive element may help to promote unity within a group. However, inter-group rivalry and competition need to be handled carefully to avoid development of 'win–lose' situations. Emphasis should be placed on overall objectives of the organisation and superordinate goals. These are goals over and above the issues at conflict and which, if they are to be achieved, require the co-operation of the competing groups.

Virtual teams

The combination of increasing globalisation, competition and widespread developments in ICT has given greater emphasis to the opportunities for, and need of, **virtual teams.** Instead of involving face-to-face proximity, virtual teams are a collection of people who are geographically separated but still need to work together closely. The primary interaction among members is by some electronic information and communication process. This enables organisations to function away from traditional working hours and the physical availability of staff. Computer-based information systems and increased wireless connectivity further the opportunities for virtual working. By their very nature, virtual teams are likely to be largely self-managed.

According to *Hall*, the virtual team is a potential future compromise between fully fledged teams and well-managed groups.

> I am watching the rise of this idea with interest but am sceptical that it will actually create a 'third way'. Real teams can only be forged in the crucible of personal interaction: videoconferences and Net communications are still poor substitutes for this. Of course, once a team has formed it can use these media, as members will know each other well, but that's not the important bit. It's the forming, norming and storming that make a team.[29]

Virtual teams may lead to an increase in productivity through a reduction in commute time and greater personal flexibility. Organisations are able to establish a greater worldwide presence. Virtual teams can comprise people with different types of knowledge, help to reduce discrimination and provide wider employment opportunities. A potential difficulty is maintaining effective communications, bearing in mind the lack of body language and non-verbal communication (**discussed in Chapter 6**). Virtual teams demand good leadership and management, including competence in ICT. Virtual working is not always to the initial liking of all people and it is important to have a remote working strategy.

Some people seem clearly to welcome virtual working with its feeling of autonomy, freedom from distractions and interruptions and less time and stress on commuting. However, despite the increase in remote working, it does not appeal to everyone. Not everyone enjoys working on their own and they miss group membership, social structure, contact and interaction. They may feel ignored by the organisation and experience an increasing feeling of isolation. For some people, trust is difficult when they cannot see the other person. Without direct personal interaction some people find it difficult to motivate themselves. A sense of discipline and self-motivation is important for effective remote working.

Leadership and motivation

Symons considers that one advantage of virtual teamworking is the clarity and richness of contributions when respondents are removed from the urgency of immediate interaction, and that this can be particularly relevant in cross-cultural groups. However, as the leader cannot influence by physical presence, and as hierarchies fade online, managing dispersed teams requires a range of subtly different leadership skills. It is important to develop mutual trust and a democratic approach of shared control and decision-making, and adopt the role and style of a coach: 'The leader has to establish and maintain "credit" with the group, as "position power" has little or no currency in virtual working.'[30]

Garrett maintains that collaborating with other people in different cities or countries is not always a successful arrangement and lists the following suggestions for helping to organise the virtual team:

- **Say hello** – The most successful teams spend time during their formation period face to face, getting to know each other.
- **Build trust** – This holds the team together so that you can depend on other team members and feel comfortable opening up to them.
- **Recruit with care** – People who can communicate in the right way at the right time are more likely to be successful in virtual teams.
- **Do not rely on email** – The written word is easily misunderstood so supplement its use with other forms of communication.
- **Encourage dissent** – Without face-to-face meetings people become reluctant to speak out, but a healthy organisation needs people to speak out and challenge leaders and each other.
- **Use technology thoughtfully** – Used badly, sophisticated tools can be a disaster, and people need to be trained to use the technology, not simply have it imposed on them.
- **Measure outcomes** – Focus on the outcomes rather than time management, find a personal way to appraise performance, rather than email, and hold regular chats with members.
- **Do say** – 'By proactively creating virtual teams we can go where talent is, extend our reach and work more efficiently.'
- **Do not say** – 'We call them a virtual team because they're not quite the real thing.'[31]

Cultural diversity

One reason for the growth in virtual teams is increasing globalisation and team members working and living in different countries. This gives rise to potential difficulties of cultural diversity. As *Francesco and Gold* point out:

> *The more culturally diverse the members, the more difficult it is to manage a virtual team. Cultural diversity, which will be increasingly common, adds to the complexity of managing virtual teams because different values, customs, and traditions require more leadership under conditions that reduce the ability to use direct leadership.*[32]

And, according to *Murray,* although virtual working presents some unexpected benefits, if managing diversity in the workplace is a tough task for business leaders, the challenges of keeping executives from different backgrounds working together in various parts of the world is even more difficult. Virtual working does not eradicate the sort of cultural misunderstandings that can arise in a face-to-face situation.

> *Cultural or behavioural differences that can manifest themselves in face-to-face working situations can be exacerbated in virtual team working, particularly when the group has members from different backgrounds.*[33]

Hazlehurst points out that the rise of the virtual organisation is not a universal development.

> *In emerging economies, the office is still a novelty and young people are clamouring to work in them. It may seem hard to understand to westerners with generations of travel-weary commuters in their family tree, but if you are the first person in your family to move from a village to a city, an office job is alive with exciting possibilities, as well as being a potent symbol of personal success.*[34]

Critical review and reflection

With continuing globalisation and advances in ICT, the days of people spending most of their time working together in physical contact with colleagues are gone. Global virtual teams are the way forward.

How far do YOU agree? What difficulties and problems do YOU foresee? Are YOU concerned about the prospect of virtual teamworking?

Management and organisational behaviour in action case study
Remote teamworking

Joanne Mooney, Customer Journey and Online Experience Manager, British Gas, based in Stockport, and her boss, **Lucy Shadholt,** Head of Channel Development for British Gas New Energy, based in Staines

In the two years she's been working remotely for British Gas, Joanne Mooney has enjoyed the flexibility and greater access to her young family, and feels she mostly gets the balance right.

You have to know when to switch off. At home, define your space, define your roles in the house, be disciplined in your working day, when it starts and stops. It's not always fair to the family – they know mummy's working, so they have to talk in hushed tones and that seems restrictive to them in their own home.

She had managed a call centre of 150 people and sometimes misses the banter: 'When I started, I was 100% working from home. I prefer the mix of the new role, where I'm getting out and meeting people. It's easier to build the relationship over the phone if you've met the person.'

Lucy Shadbolt is Mooney's boss. Since taking on the role in October she has built a team of ten, all of whom work at least part of the time remotely, including herself. 'It suits me; I get so much more done. The whole team love it,' she says. Shadbolt runs weekly meetings from the Staines office and is in regular contact with each team member. 'Some things are not suitable for conference calls. If I have to have a difficult conversation it needs to be face to face.' She's confident she's getting good performance from each of them:

You have to trust them. I make it clear with new team members that working from home is a privilege. If you give clear objectives it's easy to monitor output. People don't work 9 to 5, they work longer. It's not unusual to send an email at 10 pm. Work is where your laptop is.

Shadbolt acknowledges some aspects of her own career development are more difficult to achieve at arm's length – such as getting the ear of the boss. 'When I go into the office, where we hot-desk, I have to make an effort to position myself near my boss. You need to consciously build relationships when you don't have those water-cooler moments naturally occurring.'

Source: 'Remote control - how to manage homeworkers - Take-home lessons: Tips from remote workers and their bosses', *Management Today,* March 2011, p. 49 (www.managementtoday.com). Reproduced with permission.

Tasks

1. What particular problems do you envisage with remote teamworking?
2. Explain how would you attempt to establish mutual trust when you cannot see the other person.
3. Discuss fully the extent to which you would be happy as a remote teamworker.

Role structure of the organisation

In order for the organisation to achieve its goals and objectives, the work of individual members must be linked into coherent patterns of activities and relationships. This is achieved through the 'role structure' of the organisation.

A **role** is the expected pattern of behaviours associated with members occupying a particular position within the structure of the organisation. It also describes how a person perceives their own situation. The concept of role differentiation helps to clarify structure and define the pattern of complex relationships within the group.

The role, or roles, that the individual plays within the group is influenced by a combination of:

- **situational factors** such as the requirements of the task, nature of technology employed, time scales, style of leadership, position in the communication network; and
- **personal factors** such as values, culture, attitudes, motivation, ability and personality.

However, everyone within a group is expected to behave in a particular manner and to fulfil certain role expectations. The formal organisational relationships (line, functional, staff or lateral) – **discussed in Chapter 11** – can be seen as forms of role relationships that determine the pattern of interaction with other roles.

A person's role set

In addition to the role relationships with members of their own group – peers, superiors, subordinates – the individual will have a number of role-related relationships with outsiders, for example members of other work groups, trade union officials, suppliers, consumers. This is a person's **role set**. The role set comprises the range of associations or contacts with whom the individual has meaningful interactions in connection with the performance of the role (*see* Figure 8.6).

Role incongruence

An important feature of role relationship is the concept of **role incongruence**. This arises when a member of staff is perceived as having a high and responsible position in one respect but a low standing in another respect. Difficulties with role incongruence can arise from the nature of groupings and formal relationships within the structure of the organisation. There are a number of work-related relationships, such as doctor and nurse, chef and waiter, senior manager and personal assistant, which can give rise to a potential imbalance of authority and responsibility.

Difficulties with role incongruence can also arise in line-staff relationships: for instance, a relatively junior member of the HR department informing a senior departmental manager that a certain proposed action is contrary to the policies of the organisation. Another example with staff relationships is where a person establishes themselves in the role of 'gatekeeper' to the boss[35] – for instance, where a comparatively junior personal assistant passes on the manager's instructions to one of the manager's more senior subordinates.

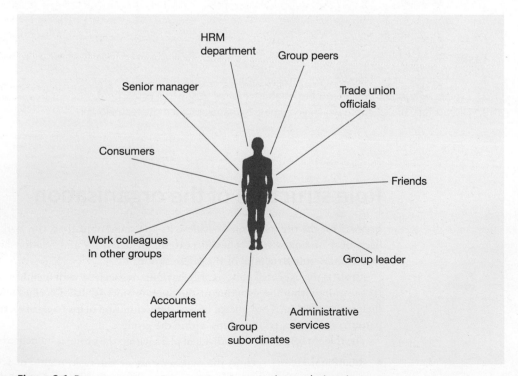

Figure 8.6 Representation of a possible role set in the work situation

Role expectations

Many **role expectations** are prescribed formally and indicate what the person is expected to do, their duties and obligations, and provide guidelines for expected behaviours. Examples are written contracts of employment, rules and regulations, standing orders, policy decisions, job descriptions, or directives from superiors. Formal role expectations may also be derived clearly from the nature of the task. They may, in part at least, be defined legally: for example, under Health and Safety at Work legislation; obligations of a company secretary under the Companies Acts; or responsibilities of a district auditor under the Local Government Acts.

Not all role expectations are prescribed formally, however. There will be certain patterns of behaviour which, although not specified formally, will nonetheless be expected of members. These informal role expectations may be imposed by the group itself, or at least communicated to a person by other members of the group. Examples include general conduct, mutual support to co-members, attitudes towards superiors, means of communicating, dress and appearance. Members may not always be consciously aware of these informal expectations, yet they still serve as important determinants of behaviour. Under this heading could be included the concept of a psychological contract (**discussed in Chapter 1**).

Self-established roles

Some members may have the opportunity to determine largely their own role expectations, where, for example, formal expectations are specified loosely or only in very general terms. Opportunities for **self-established roles** are more likely in senior positions, but also occur within certain professional, technical or scientific groups, for example senior research staff, or where there is a demand for creativity or artistic flair, for example head chefs. Such opportunities may be greater within an 'organic' organisation and will also be influenced by the style of leadership adopted – for example, where a laissez-faire approach is adopted.

Critical review and reflection

Despite apparent advantages of group working, the reality is that most people prefer the freedom of working on their own. Individuals have varying and often conflicting expectations of the benefits from group membership and this distracts from effective work performance.

To what extent do YOU feel this is a valid contention? Would YOU really prefer working on your own?

Role conflict

Patterns of behaviour result from both the person's role and personality. The concept of role focuses attention on aspects of behaviour existing independently of an individual's personality. **Role conflict** arises from inadequate or inappropriate role definition and needs to be distinguished from personality clashes. These arise from incompatibility between two or more people as individuals, even though their roles may be defined clearly and understood fully. In practice, the manner in which a person actually behaves may not be consistent with their expected pattern of behaviours. This inconsistency may be a result of role conflict. Role conflict as a generic term can include:

- role incompatibility
- role ambiguity
- role overload
- role underload.

These are all problem areas associated with the creation of role expectations (*see* Figure 8.7).

- **Role incompatibility** arises when a person faces a situation in which simultaneous different or contradictory expectations create conflict or inconsistency. Compliance with one set of expectations makes it difficult or impossible to comply with other expectations. A typical example concerns the person 'in the middle', such as the supervisor or section head, who faces opposing expectations from workers and from management. Another example might be the situation of a manager who believes in a relaxed, participative style of behaviour but whose superior expects a more formal and directive style of behaviour.

- **Role ambiguity** occurs when there is lack of insufficient information or clarity as to the precise requirements of the role and the person is unsure what to do. The person's perception of their role may differ from the expectations of others. It is likely to arise in large, diverse groups or at times of constant change. Uncertainty often relates to such matters as method of performing tasks, extent of the person's authority and responsibility, standards of work, time for completion, and evaluation and appraisal of performance.

- **Role overload** is when a person faces too many separate roles or too great a variety of expectations. The person is unable to meet satisfactorily all expectations and some must be neglected in order to satisfy others. This leads to a conflict of priority and potential stress. Some writers distinguish between role overload and work overload. Role overload is seen in terms of the total

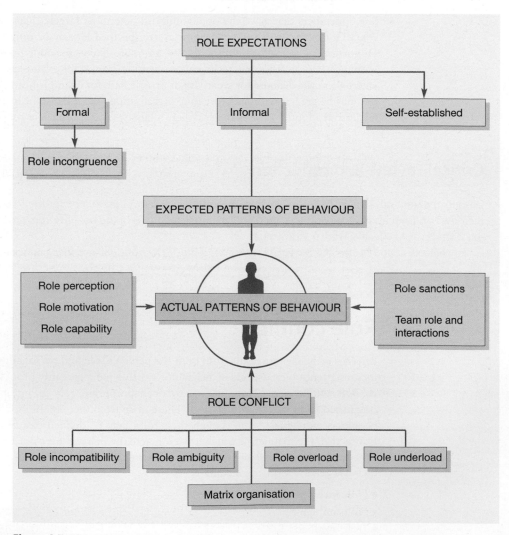

Figure 8.7 Role relationships and conflicts
Source: based on Miner, J. B. *Management Theory*, Macmillan (1971), p. 47.

role set and implies that the person has too many separate roles to handle. Where there are too many expectations of a single role – that is, a problem of quantity – this is work overload.

- **Role underload** can arise when the prescribed role expectations fall short of the person's perception of their role. The person may feel their role is not demanding enough and that they have the capacity to undertake a larger or more varied role, or an increased number of roles. Role underload may arise, for example, when a new member of staff is first appointed or from the initial effects of empowerment.

Role conflict and matrix organisation

Problems of role conflict can often arise from the matrix form of organisation (**discussed in Chapter 11**) and, for example, from the use of flexible project teams. Where staff are assigned temporarily, and perhaps on a part-time basis, from other groups this creates a two-way flow of authority and responsibility.

Unless role differentiations are defined clearly, this can result in conflicting expectations from the manager of the person's own functional grouping and from the manager of the project team (role incompatibility). It can also lead to uncertainty about the exact requirements of the part the person is expected to play as a member of the project team (role ambiguity). The combinations of expectations from both managers may also result in role overload.

Other influences on behaviour

Even if there is an absence of role conflict and role stress, a person's actual behaviour may still be inconsistent with their expected pattern of behaviours. *Miner* gives three reasons that may account for this disparity:

- The person does not perceive their job in the way the role prescriptions specify. This is a form of role ambiguity but may arise not because the role prescriptions themselves are unclear, but because the person misunderstands or distorts them.
- Motivation is lacking and the person does not want to behave in the way prescribed.
- The person does not have the capabilities – knowledge, mental ability or physical skills – required to behave in the way the role prescriptions specify.[36]

Application of sanctions

Organisations apply a number of both positive and negative sanctions as inducements for members to contribute and behave in accordance with their prescribed roles. Typical examples are: an increase in salary or wages; promotion; upgrading to the latest equipment or technology; a sideways or downwards move in the organisation structure; and the threat of dismissal. There are also a number of less direct sanctions that may be adopted. These include the size of office or work area, the allocation of unpopular tasks, giving opportunities for paid overtime work, priority for holiday rotas, level of supervision or empowerment, the amount of information given or the extent of consultation and granting or withholding privileges. Role sanctions may also be applied through the operation of the informal organisation. Members of the group may impose their own sanctions and discipline individuals who contravene the norms of the group or expected standards of behaviour.

Interactions among members

Whatever an individual's role within the structure of an organisation, if groups are to be successful and perform effectively, there must be a spirit of unity and co-operation. As Crainer reminds us, in most teams people will contribute individual skills, many of which will be different. However, referring to the work of *Obeng*,[37] *Crainer* points out that it is not enough to have a rag-bag collection of individual skills.

The various behaviours of the team members must mesh together in order to achieve objectives. For people to work successfully in teams, you need people to behave in certain ways. You need some people to concentrate on the task at hand (doers). You need some people to provide specialist knowledge (knowers) and some to solve problems as they arise (solvers). You need some people to make sure that it is going as well as it can and that the whole team is contributing fully (checkers). And you need some people to make sure that the team is operating as a cohesive social unit (carers).[38]

Individual team roles

One of the most popular analyses of individual roles within a work group or team is that developed by *Belbin,* who concludes that groups composed entirely of clever people, or of people with similar personalities, display a number of negative results and lack creativity. The most consistently successful groups comprise a range of roles undertaken by various members. The constitution of the group itself is an important variable in its success.[39]

A **team role** is a pattern of behaviour, characteristic of the way in which one team member interacts with another whose performance serves to facilitate the progress of the team as a whole.[40] Strength of contribution in any one role is commonly associated with particular weaknesses. These are called allowable weaknesses. Members are seldom strong in all nine team roles. A description of the evolved nine team roles is given in Table 8.1.

Table 8.1 Belbin's evolved nine team roles

Roles and descriptions – team-role contribution		Allowable weaknesses
Plant	Creative, imaginative, free-thinking. Generates ideas and solves difficult problems	Ignores incidentals. Too preoccupied to communicate effectively
Resource investigator	Outgoing, enthusiastic, communicative. Explores opportunities and develops contacts	Over-optimistic. Loses interest once initial enthusiasm has passed
Co-ordinator	Mature, confident, identifies talent. Clarifies goals. Delegates effectively	Can be seen as manipulative. Offloads own share of the work
Shaper	Challenging, dynamic, thrives on pressure. Has the drive and courage to overcome obstacles	Prone to provocation. Offends people's feelings
Monitor–evaluator	Sober, strategic and discerning. Sees all options and judges accurately	Lacks drive and ability to inspire others. Can be overly critical
Teamworker	Co-operative, perceptive and diplomatic. Listens and averts friction	Indecisive in crunch situations. Avoids confrontation
Implementer	Practical, reliable, efficient. Turns ideas into actions and organises work that needs to be done	Somewhat inflexible. Slow to respond to new possibilities
Completer–finisher	Painstaking, conscientious, anxious. Searches out errors. Polishes and perfects	Inclined to worry unduly. Reluctant to delegate
Specialist	Single-minded, self-sharing, dedicated. Provides knowledge and skills in rare supply	Contributes on only a narrow front. Dwells on technicalities

Source: Belbin © 2015, www.belbin.com.

An extensive study by *Aritzeta et al.* points to a number of critical assessments of Belbin's work, such as:

- concerns about the theoretical basis of the inventory;
- questions concerning the relationship between the role of personality and team roles;
- lack of clear differentiation among the nine team roles;
- insufficient account of the type of task undertaken by the group;
- influence of organisational factors such as strategy, resources, structure, leadership and management style;
- a dominant psychological approach to understanding teamwork that needs to be complemented by socio-technical considerations

However, despite negative criticisms the authors do not think it justifiable to suggest the team-role theory is flawed. While evidence is mixed they conclude, on balance, that the model and accompanying inventory have adequate convergent validity.[41]

Critical review and reflection

The study of evolved team roles has little practical value. Behaviour does not fit into neat categories and most people do not acknowledge allowable weaknesses. The two most important roles for effective teamwork are a competent, decisive and fair leader, and a humourist to make people laugh and reduce tension.

What is YOUR honest opinion of this contention? How would YOU explain your role as a team member?

Analysis of individual behaviour

In order to understand and to influence the functioning and operation of a group or team, it is necessary to study patterns of interaction and the parts played by individual members. Not all skilled and capable individuals are necessarily good team players and, for example, it may sometimes be an advantage to have someone with a more sceptical attitude and open to change. The basic assumption behind the analysis of individual behaviour in groups is from the viewpoint of its function.

A popular classification of member roles in the study of group behaviour is that devised originally by *Benne and Sheats*.[42] The description of member roles performed in well-functioning groups is classified into three broad headings: group task roles, group building and maintenance roles, and individual roles.

- **Group task roles** – These assume that the task of the group is to select, define and solve common problems. For example, initiator–contributor, opinion seeker, co-ordinator, evaluator, recorder.
- **Group building and maintenance roles** – The analysis of member functions is orientated towards activities that build group-centred attitudes or maintain group-centred behaviour. For example, encourager, gatekeeper, standard setter, group commentator.
- **Individual roles** – These are directed towards the satisfaction of personal needs. Their purpose is not related either to group task or to the group functioning. For example, aggressor, blocker, dominator, help-seeker.

Sociometry

Originally developed by *Moreno* in 1953, **sociometry** is a method of indicating the feelings of acceptance or rejection among members of a group.[43] The basis of sociometry is usually 'buddy rating' or 'peer rating'. Each member is asked to nominate or to rate, privately, other members in terms of some given context or characteristic – for example, with whom they communicate, or how influential or how likeable they are. Questions may relate to either work or social activities. For example:

- Who would you most prefer or least prefer to work with closely?
- Who would make a good leader?
- With whom would you choose and not choose to have a drink in the pub or to go on holiday?

Positive and negative choices may be recorded for each person, although sometimes positive choices only are required. Sometimes individuals may be asked to rank their choices.

A sociogram is a diagrammatical illustration of the pattern of interpersonal relationships derived from sociometry and depicts choices, preferences, likes or dislikes and interactions between individual members. An advantage of a diagrammatical illustration is that it can also display a visual description of the structure of the group. It can indicate cliques and sub-groups, compatibility, and members who are popular, isolated or who act as links. Figure 8.8 gives a simple illustration of an actual sociogram for a group of fifteen members with single, positive choices only.

1. G and M are popular (the stars) and most often chosen by members.
2. M is the link between two overlapping cliques, KML and MNO.
3. H and P are unpopular (isolated) and chosen least by members.
4. JKMO is a chain.
5. ABCD is a sub-group and separated from the rest of the members.

There are several methods of compiling and drawing sociograms, and a number of potential criticisms and limitations. Problems also arise over how to draw the sociogram and how to interpret the roles of individual members. However, if handled sensitively it can serve to encourage meaningful discussions on patterns of social interactions, group behaviour and the perceptions of individual members towards each other. This can serve as a useful basis for the development of both employability and wider social skills.

Self-insight and the Johari window

A simple framework for looking at self-insight is the **Johari window**[44] (*see* Figure 8.9). This classifies behaviour in matrix form between what is known–unknown to self and what is known–unknown to others in order to encourage a reduction of the individual's 'hidden' behaviour through self-disclosure and of the 'blind' behaviour through feedback from others.

- **Hidden behaviour** is that which the individual wishes to conceal from, or not to communicate to, other group members. It is part of the private self. An important role of the group is to establish whether members conceal too much, or too little, about themselves from other members.

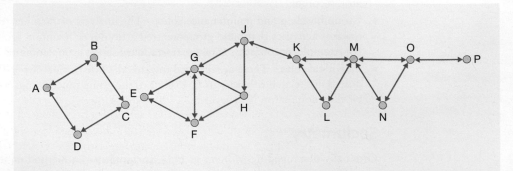

Figure 8.8 A simple illustration of a sociogram

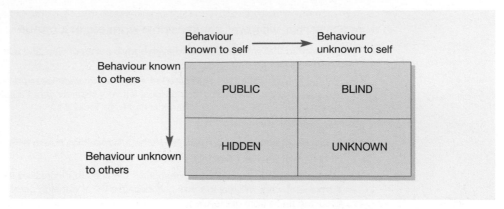

Figure 8.9 The Johari window

- **The blind area** (i.e. behaviour known to others but unknown to self) includes mannerisms, gestures and tone of voice, and represents behaviour of the impact on others of which the individual is unaware. This is sometimes referred to as the 'bad breath' area.

Members must establish an atmosphere of openness and trust in order that hidden and blind behaviours are reduced and the public behaviour enhanced. (**Recall also the comment in Chapter 4 on making public people's private attitudes.**)

Balance between team and individual

Group performance and the satisfaction derived by individuals are influenced by the interactions among members of the group. Individuals in groups interact extensively with each other and with other groups in the organisation. Although everyone operates fundamentally as a loner at work, *James* draws attention to the need in most jobs for teamworking.

> *Effective teams need equilibrium, no matter how uneasy. The perfect team will have balance, with each member aware of their role and happy to add that value to the task. The natural leaders for any given job will be in charge and their leadership will be cherished by mutual consent. Being a perfect team member means commitment to the task and overrides personal ambition and glory. Unfortunately this is rarely achieved in the workplace.*[45]

Working in a group is likely to be both a psychologically rewarding and a potentially demanding experience for the individual. As an example of this, Figure 8.10 gives an unsolicited commentary from five final-year business studies degree students after completing a group-based assignment.

Friendships and relationships at work

Increasing attention has been given to the possible effects of friendships and relationships at work, and potential conflict between personal freedom and team performance. While work may be one of the best sources of friends as well as the most desirable place to have them, the trouble is that friendships at work are full of ambiguities. For friendships, the trouble with work is that you are there to be useful: to do something for a client, team or boss. Professional friendships will always be influenced and possibly determined by the utility factor.[46] Romance in the workplace presents managers with an interesting problem: 'On the one hand, you seek to shape a team with close bonds; a degree of flirtation may well accompany, even promote this. On the other; an ill-starred liaison that jeopardises harmony and risks litigation is emphatically to be avoided'.[47]

WHAT WE FEEL WE HAVE LEARNED FROM WORKING IN A GROUP

1 'We learned that we has to listen to everybody's points of view and take these into consideration.'

2 'We found that we had to be prepared to make certain sacrifices and adopted a democratic decision process. However, if an individual felt very strongly about a specific point and persisted with a valid argument then this had to be included.'

3 'We often felt frustrated.'

4 'It was time-consuming and difficult to schedule meetings due to differences in timetables and preferences in working hours.'

5 'We learned that it is good to pool resources because this increased the overall standard of the piece of work. We feel this was only because we all set high personal standards and expected these from our fellow group members. We learned that it is possible to work in other less productive groups where individual levels of achievement may decrease.'

6 'We learned that it is better to work in a smaller and not a larger group, as there is a tendency for individual ideas to be diluted.'

7 'Groups formed on the basis of friendship are not as effective as groups formed with work as the major influence. The former tend to be unproductive.'

8 'We found that it was good to get positive response, encouragement and fedback from team members. Likewise, it was demotivating to receive a negative response.'

9 'We learned a lot about our individual personalities.'

10 'We benefited from sharing peresonal experiences from our industrial placements.'

11 'It is important to separate work and personal relationships.'

Figure 8.10 Unsolicited commentary from students after completing a group-based assignment

Critical review and reflection

Students would learn much about themselves and how they are perceived by others through regular participation in a sociometry exercise with members of their classmates. Possible difficulties are outweighed by potential benefits. *To what extent do YOU agree? How specifically would YOU expect to benefit from sociometry exercises?*

Individual compared with group or team performance

Despite apparent advantages of group working, it is difficult to draw any firm conclusions from a comparison between individual and group or team performance. Group decision-making can be frustrating and stressful as well as costly and time consuming. According to *Hall*, there is a danger of elevating teams into a 'silver bullet' – a magic solution to all business problems.

> *It is not that I don't think teams work. They clearly do and it would be difficult to run an organisation of any size if you couldn't create and manage a team . . . The truth is that teams are not always the right answer to a problem. Often a well-briefed and well-managed group of individuals will do a task fine . . . A further point is that some very skilled individuals are not good team players.*[48]

However, the general feeling appears to be that the collective power of a group outshines individual performance.[49] 'Even though individuals working on their own are capable of phenomenal ingenuity, working together as a team can produce astounding results and a better decision.'[50] *Guirdham* believes that: 'Compared with individuals, groups can make objectively better decisions to which people feel more commitment, while teams can perform functions and carry out projects better and more efficiently. This can only happen, however, if the people have the special skills and abilities needed.'[51]

One might expect, therefore, a higher standard of decision-making to result from group discussion. There are, however, particular features of individual versus team performance, including:

- social loafing
- risky-shift phenomenon
- groupthink
- brainstorming.

Social loafing

The concept of **social loafing (or the Ringelmann effect)** is the tendency for individual members of a group to expend less effort than if they were working on their own. A German psychologist, Maximilien Ringelmann, compared results of individual and group performance on a rope-pulling task. Workers were asked to pull as hard as they could on a rope, performing the task first individually and then with others in groups of varying size. A meter measured the strength of each pull. Although the total amount of force did increase with the size of the work group, the effort expended by each individual member decreased with the result that the total group effort was less than the expected sum of the individual contributions.[52] Replications of the Ringelmann effect have generally been supportive of the original findings.[53]

The risky-shift phenomenon

This suggests that instead of the group taking fewer risks and making safer or more conservative decisions, the reverse is often the case. Pressures for conformity mean there is a tendency for groups to make more risky decisions than would individual members of the group on their own. People are arguably less averse to risk when there is an emotional bond with others in the group. Studies suggest that people working in groups generally advocate more risky alternatives than if they were making an individual decision on the same problem.[54] Presumably, this is because members do not feel the same sense of responsibility for group decisions or their outcomes: 'A decision which is everyone's is the responsibility of no one.'

Other explanations offered for the **risky-shift** phenomenon include the following:

- People inclined to take risks are more influential in group discussions than more conservative people.
- Risk-taking is regarded as a desirable cultural characteristic that is more likely to be expressed in a social situation such as group working.[55]

However, groups do appear to work well in the evaluation of ideas and to be more effective than individuals for problem-solving tasks requiring a range of knowledge and expertise. From a review of the research, *Shaw* suggests that evidence supports the view that groups produce more solutions and better solutions to problems than do individuals.[56]

'Groupthink'

The effectiveness of group behaviour and performance can be adversely affected by the idea of **groupthink**. From an examination of some well-known government policy-making groups, *Janis* concluded that decisions can be characterised by groupthink, which he defines as 'a deterioration of mental efficiency, reality testing, and moral judgment that results from in-group pressures'.[57] Groupthink results in the propensity for the group just to drift along. It is a generalised feature and can be apparent in any organisational situation where groups are relied upon to make important decisions.

Janis identifies a number of specific symptoms of groupthink, including: an illusion of invulnerability; discrediting of negative feedback that contradicts group consensus; an unquestioned belief in the inherent morality of the group; negative stereotyping of opponents or people outside the group, or to the acceptance of change; and pressure on individual members to conform and reach consensus so that minority or unpopular ideas may be suppressed.

Brainstorming

A **brainstorming** approach (sometimes referred to as **thought showers** or 'cloud bursting' in order not to offend people with conditions such as epilepsy) involves a group of between six and ten members adopting a 'freewheeling' attitude and generating as many ideas as possible, the more wild or apparently far-fetched, the better.[58]As an illustrative exercise a group may be asked to generate as many and varied possible uses as they can for, for example, a man or woman's leather belt. Brainstorming is based on encouraging members to suspend judgement, the assumption that creative thinking is achieved best by encouraging the natural inclinations of group members, and free association of ideas. The quantity of ideas will lead to quality of ideas.

There are a number of basic procedures for brainstorming:

- Maximum freedom of expression with a totally relaxed and informal approach. Members are encouraged to elaborate or build on ideas expressed by others and to bounce suggestions off one another.
- Initial emphasis is on the quantity of ideas generated, not the quality of ideas. No individual ideas are criticised or rejected at this stage, however wild or fanciful they may appear.
- Need for good reporting of all the ideas either in writing and/or by tape or video recording.

An interesting and popular exercise to help illustrate the suspension of initial perceived barriers and the encouragement of creative thinking is given in Figure 8.11. This exercise may also be used to compare individual and group/team-based performance. Your tutor will provide an answer. There may be others that the author is unaware of!

One might reasonably expect that members of a brainstorming group would produce more creative problem-solving ideas than if the same members worked alone as individuals. Availability of time is an important factor. Over a longer period of time the group may produce more ideas through brainstorming than individuals could. Perhaps surprisingly, there appears to be doubt about the effectiveness of brainstorming groups over an individual working under the same conditions. However, any procedure that aids the process of creativity (**discussed in Chapter 5**) should be welcomed, and there are a number of potential positive achievements in terms of related structural techniques for stimulating innovation.

The task is to see if it is possible to touch each of the nine spots using only four straight, interconnected lines.

Figure 8.11 An example of creative thinking

Building effective teams

Whatever the debate about individual and group or team performance, effective teamworking is of increasing importance in modern organisations. The Chartered Management Institute points out that teams can play a key role in organisational success, but the development of good working relationships is vital to team performance.

> *A team is more than just a group of people who happen to work together. It is a group of people working towards common goals and objectives and sharing responsibility for the outcomes. Team building is the process of selecting and grouping team members effectively and developing good working relationships and practices enabling the team to steer and develop the work and reach their goals. Increasingly, a team may be composed of people drawn from different functions, departments and disciplines who have been brought together for a specific project.[59]*

Yukl refers to the purpose of team building as being to increase cohesiveness, mutual co-operation, and identification with the group. Based on research, theory and practice, Yukl identifies eight team-building procedures:

- **Emphasise common interests and values** – collective identification is stronger when members agree about objectives, values, priorities, strategies and the need for co-operation.
- **Use ceremonies and rituals** – to increase identification with the group and make membership appear special. The use of rituals for initiation and retirement, and ceremonies for special occasions or events.
- **Use symbols to develop identification with the group** – such as team name, logo, insignia, emblem or particular colour to help create a special identity for the team.
- **Encourage and facilitate social interaction** – development of a cohesive group is more likely when members get to know each other on a personal basis and find social interactions satisfying.
- **Tell people about group activities and achievements** – keeping members informed about the plans, activities and achievements and how their work contributes to the success of the mission.
- **Conduct process analysis sessions** – frank and open discussions of interpersonal relationships and group processes, including suggestions on how to improve effectiveness.
- **Conduct alignment sessions** – to increase mutual understanding among team members and to overcome negative stereotypes and attributions.
- **Increase incentives for mutual co-operation** – incentives based not individually but on group performance to encourage co-operation, such as bonus based on team performance.[60]

'Away days'

Another approach to team building is the use of activity-based exercises undertaken as part of corporate bonding, usually referred to as **away days.** The main objective is often the building of team spirit and working relationships involving formal team dynamics and assessment, although this may also be linked with a social purpose, for example to develop interactions with colleagues, improve motivation or to thank and reward staff. The idea of away days is subject to frequent criticism and even ridicule. Individuals may feel pressurised into participating for fear of not appearing to support management initiative or their group colleagues.

Baroness Kingsmill suggests that of course there is a case to be made for getting away from day-to-day routines and pressures and spending time with colleagues: 'Fostering relationships, encouraging creativity and innovative thinking and promoting better communication are all desirable goals. It is just that it is usually done so badly and is often a waste of time and resource. Companies spend millions on away-days every year but rarely do they make much difference to the way the business is run.' A successful away day should be small, with perhaps no more than twenty participants, provide an opportunity for wide-ranging and out-of-the-box thinking and conversation, be accompanied by some social activity to foster relationships and, if it involves sleeping away from home, have comfort-able surroundings.[61]

Critical review and reflection

The nature of the hierarchical structure and inevitable role conflicts, power struggles, politics and personality clashes mean that individuals working on their own will usually complete a task more quickly and effectively than a group or team.

To what extent do YOU think this is fair comment? What has been YOUR own experience? Do YOU prefer to work on YOUR own or as a member of a group/team?

Skills of successful teamwork

How people behave and perform as members of a group is as important as their behaviour or performance as individuals. Harmonious working relationships and good teamwork help make for a high level of staff morale and work performance. Teamwork is important in any organisation but may be especially significant in emergency and caring industries or ser-vice industries such as hospitality organisations, where there is a direct effect on customer satisfaction.[62]

According to *Guirdham*, the growth of teamwork has led to the increased interest in inter-face skills at work.

> *More and more tasks of contemporary organisations, particularly those in high technology and service businesses, require teamwork. Taskforces, project teams and committees are key elements in the modern workplace. Teamwork depends not just on technical competence of the individuals composing the team, but on their ability to 'gel'. To work well together, the team members must have more than just team spirit. They also need collaborative skills – they must be able to support one another and to handle conflict in such a way that it becomes constructive rather than destructive.[63]*

Peeling maintains that to build good teams you need a wide pool of staff with different talents to draw upon.

> *Good managers should delight in the diversity and excellence of their staff and know that one of their main jobs is to manage the problems that come with any diverse group of talented people. In any group of talented people you will naturally get interpersonal ten-sions. It is important that you show you respect all the different skills and personalities in your team.[64]*

Autonomous working groups

An important development in work redesign and job enrichment is a form of work organisa-tion based on autonomous work groups (or self-managed work groups) who are encouraged to manage their own work and working practices. The group operates without direct supervi-sion and decides for itself how work should be distributed and carried out. Members of the group assume greater autonomy and responsibility for the effective performance of the work.

With greater empowerment the belief is that members will feel more committed to the objectives and operations of the group.

Key features of the self-managed work group include the following:

- Specific goals are set for the group but members decide the best means by which these goals are to be achieved and have greater freedom and wider discretion over the planning, execution and control of their work.
- Collectively members of the group have the necessary variety of expertise and skills to undertake the tasks of the group successfully.
- The level of external supervision is reduced and the role of supervisor becomes more one of giving advice and support to the group. Feedback and evaluation are related to the performance of the group as a whole.

ACAS strongly supports autonomous work groups for both increased competitiveness and for the quality of working life.

> *The concept of autonomous teams may be misleading as teams will always be answerable to management and rely on the provision of resources and other support. Nevertheless, one of the best ways to ensure that teams continue to develop is to move towards self-regulation – an important way of monitoring the progress of teams is to assess the level of dependence on management. It is for management to encourage progress by helping the teams develop greater independence. Reorganising the workforce into teams is not easy but when successfully developed, team working has been shown to be a way of improving competitiveness and at the same time enhancing the quality of working life for employees.*[65]

Autonomous working groups are not free of potential difficulties. With greater independence there may be a resistance to change and the acceptance of new ideas or responsibilities. With less management control internal battles over authority may develop within the group. A self-managed group is more likely to establish its own values and norms, including the pace of work, that may be at variance with those of the organisation. Developments in ICT and the growth of remote teamworking enable individuals to work collaboratively despite physical distance.

Skills to build self-managed teams

Cloke and Goldsmith refer to the special skills required for successful teamwork and list ten skills team members can develop in order to build innovative self-managing teams. All of these skills are interrelated, mutually reinforcing and dependent upon each of the others.[66]

- **Skill of self-management** – Overcoming obstacles together, and building a sense of ownership, responsibility, commitment and efficiency within each team member.
- **Skill of communication** – Collaboratively developing skills in becoming better listeners, communicating honestly about things that really matter.
- **Skill of leadership** – Creating opportunities for each member to be skilled in order to serve as leader.
- **Skill of responsibility** – Personal responsibility not only for their own work but for the work of every other member of the team in order to become self-managing.
- **Skill of supportive diversity** – Allowing team members to overcome prejudices and biases and not create winners and losers, reject outsiders or mistrust people who are different.
- **Skills of feedback and evaluation** – Essential to improving learning, team communication and the quality of products, processes and relationships.
- **Skill of strategic planning** – Identifying challenges and opportunities collaboratively. Think long term, be proactive and focus on solutions rather than problems.
- **Skill of shaping successful meetings** – Team meetings can be streamlined and made shorter, more satisfying and more productive, and result in expanded consensus.

- **Skill of resolving conflicts** – Encouraging members to improve skills in problem-solving, collaborative negotiation, responding to difficult behaviour and conflict resolution.
- **Skill of enjoyment** – Most team members enjoy working together to accomplish difficult tasks, meeting high-performance challenges and producing results that benefit themselves and their teams, organisations and communities.

The Margerison 'Team Wheel'

From work with teams in major oil companies, Charles Margerison concluded that they lacked a common teamwork language to deal with team issues or for learning and development. After further work with Dick McCann in a range of other organisations, *Margerison* identified nine major skills necessary in every business and team that can improve work contribution. The key to the system is the 'Team Wheel' (*see* Figure 8.12).

The nine key factors cover all aspects of teamwork in every organisation. Linking is the all-encompassing area of co-ordination, and organisation success depends on how effectively members of the team link to achieve objectives:

- **Advising** – Gathering and reporting information.
- **Innovating** – Creating and experimenting with ideas.
- **Promoting** – Exploring and presenting opportunities.
- **Developing** – Assessing and planning applications.
- **Organising** – Organising staff and resources.
- **Producing** – Concluding and delivering output.
- **Inspecting** – Controlling and auditing contracts and procedures.
- **Maintaining** – Upholding and safeguarding standards and values.
- **Linking** – Co-ordinating and integrating the work of others.

The 'Team Wheel' can also be used as a focus for reviewing both internal links between each member of the team and external linking with other teams and key stakeholders such as clients.[67]

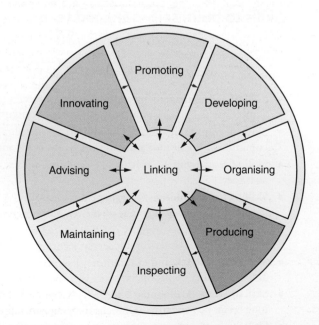

Figure 8.12 Margerison 'Team Wheel'
Source: Charles J Margerison, *Team Leadership: A guide to success with Team Management Systems*, Thomson (2002), p. 8.

The role of team leader

Building successful teams requires effective leadership with an emphasis on trust, clear communications, full participation and self-management: 'The influence and usefulness of team leaders comes, not from their delivery of traditional supervisory and control methods, but from their ability to lead from the front and in training, coaching and counselling their team members to high standards of performance.'[68]

In her discussion of the 'democratic enterprise' (organisations that can flourish economically and can also be places of excitement and stimulation, fulfilment and tranquillity), *Gratton* maintains that it is the leaders of the teams across the organisation who make the company vision a reality on a day-to-day basis. The team leaders are the creators of space in which choice and freedom can be exercised; they delineate the obligations and accountabilities contained within the business goals; they become role models for how members should behave; and they bring the philosophy of autonomy and personal development to realisation by the manner in which they act as mentors and coaches.[69]

According to *Powell*, if you want to see the efficacy of a leader and his or her leadership style, then you need to look no further than the team he or she leads.

> *A team rarely demonstrates more passion or behaves more positively than its leader. Similarly, cynical leaders produce, and therefore deserve, cynical teams. Innovative, creative and developmental leaders help to produce creative, innovative and developed followers. A team that is enthusiastic, energetic and innovative will have at its heart a leader who is correspondingly so.*[70]

With the football business as an example, *Brady* refers to the importance for any organisation, especially with a people business, of bringing staff with you, building a team around you and how team ethic leads to success.

> *The reason it works is because of the respect we have for each other. We all know each other's strengths and weaknesses and we work around them. We don't step into each other's territories. We leave each one to each role, but we support them instead.*[71]

Continuous improvement and innovation

The requirement for continual development and improvement is a necessary part of effective teamwork. The ACAS advisory booklet concludes that although self-regulation is necessary if the potential of teamworking is to be realised, teams will always need some degree of management direction. The task of management is to oversee the development of teams and provide the necessary support and training. Even when in place, teams will need constant monitoring and development. Teamworking is not a finite project but a process of continuous improvement and innovation.

> *The introduction of team working is a major step for an organisation to take. It is important that management, trade unions and employees ensure they know how team working will contribute to their business strategy and that it is likely to involve a long-term transformation . . . The early challenge and excitement of establishing teams may fade and it is easy for organisations to accept a level of performance which is short of optimum . . . In order to achieve high performance, teams require regular changes and challenges. These may include: changes to team personnel; new tasks; re-examining the contribution the team makes to the overall business aims; and ensuring that the team has regular dealings with other teams.*[72]

Critical review and reflection

Discussion about building successful teams sounds fine in the classroom. But it ignores the reality of the work environment, for example managing groups of people in a restaurant kitchen, a production assembly line, a gay pub, an orchestra, or professionals such as lecturers.
What do YOU think? Give YOUR own examples of the reality of teamworking in a specific environment.

Ten key points to remember

1 Groups are characteristic of all social situations. Individuals seldom work in isolation, and groups and teams are a major feature of the work organisation.

2 The terms 'groups' and 'teams' are to be used interchangeably. Whereas all teams are groups, it does not necessarily follow that all groups are teams.

3 Formal groups are concerned with co-ordination of work activities. Within the formal structure informal groups develop to satisfy psychological and social needs.

4 The manager's main concern is that members work together as a united, cohesive team with supportive relationships and to prevent unconstructive inter-group conflict.

5 Continuing globalisation and developments in ICT have given emphasis to the virtual teams. Members are geographically separated but still need to work together closely.

6 The role structure of the organisation, interactions among members and individual team roles are important to an understanding of group processes and behaviour.

7 In order to understand and influence the working of groups it is necessary to understand patterns of interactions and parts played by individual members.

8 Working in groups would appear to offer advantages to performance but it is difficult to draw any firm conclusion from comparison with individual performance.

9 The growth of teamwork has led to increased interest in attention to social skills, competencies and leadership in order to build and develop effective teams.

10 How to behave and perform as members of a group is as important as their actions as individuals. Continual development and improvement is a necessary part of effective teamwork.

Review and discussion questions

1 How would you distinguish between a 'group' and a 'team'? To what extent do you believe the distinction has practical significance for managers?

2 Distinguish between formal and informal groups. Explain the importance and influence of group values and norms and give practical examples from within your own university and/or organisation.

3 Explain fully the extent to which you prefer working on your own or as part of a group. What benefits would you expect both to give up and to receive from group membership?

4 Identify different stages in group development and maturity. What other factors influence the cohesiveness of work groups? Give examples by reference to a work group to which you belong.

5 Set out in detail the advantages and potential difficulties of virtual teams. Explain how you believe virtual teamworking is likely to develop in the future.

6 What is meant by the role structure of an organisation? Construct a diagram that shows your own role set within your university or any work situation. Give examples of informal role expectations to which you are, or have been, a party.

7   Discuss critically what you believe could be learnt in the classroom from a study of successful music ensembles *and* sporting teams.

8   Explain fully your understanding of (a) groupthink; (b) the risky-shift phenomenon; and (c) brainstorming. Assess critically the likely standard of individual performance compared with group or team performance.

9   Discuss potential benefits and limitations of team-building exercises including 'away days'. Where possible relate to your own experiences.

10   Detail fully what you believe are the essential characteristics of a successful work group or team. As a manager, explain how you would attempt to develop effective group/team relationships and performance.

Assignment

Working in small self-selecting teams, you are required to design and present an 'ice-breaker' exercise as a fun way to help groups of new students (or other new members or delegates) to get to know and interact with each other. The exercise should be **simple, easy to understand and undertake, entertaining, something to which all members of the team/group can contribute, and that can be completed within thirty minutes.**

Your tutor will be asked to decide which team has come up with the most novel, engaging and appropriate exercise.

*   If possible, attempt to employ the chosen exercise in a real-life situation. How successful was the exercise?

Personal skills and employability exercise

Objectives

Completing this exercise should help you to enhance the following skills:

*   Evaluate the role(s) you play within the team and the contribution you make.
*   Explore your relationships with other members of the team.
*   Receive and give honest feedback about strengths and personal weaknesses.

In order to work well with other people you need to know and understand yourself and be prepared to receive honest feedback from your colleagues. The effectiveness of a team can be enhanced by a genuine openness among its members.

Exercise

For this exercise, work in pairs with another team member – if possible from a different ethnicity, culture, gender or age group. You should both agree to honour confidentiality and to conduct the exercise as a means of providing constructive feedback.

Part 1

Refer to Belbin's nine team roles (Table 8.1 in the text of this chapter) and ask the following question of each other:

1   For what role do you think I am most suited – and why?

Next refer to the Margerison 'Team Wheel' (Figure 8.12 in the text) and ask the following question of each other:

2   In what ways can I contribute more to the work of the team?

Part 2

Now ask the follow-up questions, below, of each other:

1 Which member of the team do you believe I am most close to and which member most distant from?
2 What do you see as my major strengths and personal weaknesses as a member of the team?
3 What is it about me that you find most annoying?
4 In what ways could we help each other in our work?
5 How can I be a better all-round member of the team?

Discussion

After you have both completed these questions, consider carefully and honestly:

● What have you learned about yourself from this activity?
● What response from your colleague surprised you the most?
● To what extent has this exercise helped you to understand how well you work as a team member? Put this in writing as an aid to discipline and for your personal reflection.

Case study
The Red Arrows

In the spring of 2014 the Queen celebrated her 88th birthday in the year that also marked the 50th anniversary of the D-Day Normandy landings during the Second World War. As part of this event one of the most spectacular examples of teams at work was seen – and heard – in the skies above London. The nine pilots of the Royal Air Force Aerobatic Team, better known as the Red Arrows, combine extraordinarily high levels of individual skill with strongly disciplined teamwork to mount displays that can be breathtaking, in terms of both the expertise on show and the balletic quality of the patterns and images that they paint in the air.

Source: Graham Taylor/Shutterstock.com

The full display team comprises nine pilots, and many of the manoeuvres that are part of the Red Arrows display involve all of them. However, some of the formations require smaller configurations, and the nine are divided into two sub-teams: a team of five (Reds 1–5) called 'Enid' (named after the Enid Blyton characters the Famous Five), who fly at the front of the characteristic V-formation; and a further team of four (Reds 6–9) called, for reasons lost in the mists of time, 'Gypo', who fly at the rear.[73] Two members of team Gypo (Reds 6 and 7) also fly as the 'Synchro Pair', undertaking specific 'opposition' manoeuvres such as describing patterns of loops or hearts in the air using the aircrafts' smoke trails.

The nine pilots of the Hawk T1 jet aircraft are the mere tip of the Red Arrows iceberg. Each pilot is accompanied to and from displays by their personal flight engineer, whose job is to service the aircraft and to ensure peak performance during flights. These flight engineers (who are known collectively as the 'Circus') work with their specified pilots and aircraft throughout the summer display season. The full technical support team on the ground numbers over 100 and is distinguishable by its blue overalls, contrasting with the pilots' red ones. Among the support team's number is another specialist group, the 'Dye Team' – six personnel who have the specific responsibility for replenishing the diesel and dye mix that the pilots use to create the dramatic red, white and blue vapour trails that enhance the displays. These trails also serve a technical safety purpose, as they help Red 1 to judge wind speed and direction, thereby ensuring that the display team can adjust to variations on the day.

In 2009, Flight Lieutenant Kirsty Moore made history when she became the first female pilot to join the Red Arrows. The selection criteria are very demanding: no pilots can even be shortlisted until they have been assessed as above average during their flying career, have a minimum of 1,500 flying hours' experience and have completed at least one operational tour. But individual excellence and celebrity cannot be allowed to get in the way of teamwork; as the then Red 1, Wing Commander Jas Hawker, pointed out during an interview in 2009:

> there's zero place in the Red Arrows for an egoist even though we do get associated with pop-star lifestyle. I think if there were big egos around they'd be stamped out by the team.[74]

Building the team

Many of the team's set pieces look scarily dangerous and many an amateur photographer has caught what he or she believed to be a near miss on film. The choreography often requires the Hawk jets to be very close in aeronautical terms and certainly the visual effect of two jets apparently hurtling towards each other on collision course at 400 mph (640 km/h) can be breathtaking. The key to this is, of course, a rigorous and continuous training programme, the start of which coincides with the selection of the next year's new pilots at the end of the display season. Three new recruits will take the places of three pilots whose time with the squad is finished; and only Red 1 will continue to fly in the same position, meaning that all the pilots need to learn new roles in an updated formation.

During the period from the end of the display season (September/October) to the following February, squad members fly three times a day from their HQ at RAF Scampton, wearing the normal green flying suits of any RAF pilot. They work individually, then in smaller groups of three or four, with intensive review using video footage and other debriefing methods to ensure that mistakes and errors are corrected. After both practice sessions and actual displays, the pilots watch recordings of their performance to identify flaws or moments when the formation was not as precisely aligned as the leader would like. In order to remove the personal aspects of criticism that might get in the way of focused analysis, the team adopts the simple psychological technique of referring to each other as numbers rather than by name when reviewing the performance of the members.[75] By March the nine are ready to begin flying as an entire team (starting with their classic formation, the 'Diamond Nine') and the more complex display work can be developed.

On the ground

During the months while the nine are consolidating their skill in the air, the aircraft themselves also have to be thoroughly overhauled. Maintenance and technical work is carried out in shifts, starting at 6.30 in the morning and continuing through to the early hours so that enough aircraft are ready for the first training flight of the day. Finally, in March, the whole operation moves to the RAF base of Akrotiri in Cyprus and the team puts the final touches to its programme. When judged sufficiently safe and professional in their performance, the nine are given formal permission to display by the Commander-in-Chief (Public Display Authority). Only then can they wear the characteristic red and blue overalls in recognition of this annual milestone, and as the next set of applicants begin their tests, the core team embarks on the summer display programme.

In addition to the flight and engineering co-ordination, the logistics of both training sessions and displays demand high levels of organisation and teamwork. During the summer the public display schedule dictates the life of the Circus. Technical staff, equipment, fuel and other resources must be available as necessary, wherever in the world the team is likely to be based for displays. This task is carried out by the Display Co-ordination and Administration Group and regularly briefed to all staff through a detailed schedule called WHAM (What's Happening According to the Manager). The image of the squadron has to be managed as well, not only to satisfy public interest in the team, but also to ensure that it retains popular support in an era of environmental concern and government austerity. A small group of RAF personnel handles enquiries from the public and press, runs the official website and organises publicity around the Reds' appearances. They are sometimes involved in charity events and challenges, such as their 'Jet Pull' in aid of the Soldiers, Sailors, Airmen and Families Association (SSAFA), when teams and individuals from the Circus compete to pull a Hawk T1 50 metres (Joe Tiley, one of the Blues, achieved this feat in 1 minute and 12 seconds in 2013).

Nevertheless, despite the rigorous and thorough training and close team co-ordination, very occasionally something goes terribly wrong. Fatalities are rare – only ten since the team was founded in 1965 – but 2011 was a tragic year. Two pilots, Jon Egging and Sean Cunningham, died in separate accidents, both of which were away from the crowds and neither of which was the result of a display manoeuvre.[76] In March 2010 there was an incident during pre-season training when Reds 6 and 7, the 'Synchro Pair', struck each other during a practice flight. Red 7 was able to land safely, but the pilot of Red 6 had to eject from his plane, sustaining significant injuries to shoulder and knees that put him out of action for the 2010 display season. His aircraft was also seriously damaged; flight training was suspended until an accident investigation had been completed and the squad cleared to fly again. The immediate result for the team was the need, once the all-clear had been given, to integrate a new member since the majority of the Red Arrows' stunts require all nine aircraft. In this highly structured organisational environment the choice of replacement meant the recall of a previous Red 6.

In February 2015 Red 1 – David Montenegro – unveiled a new livery for the squadron's tailfins, and explained something of the philosophy behind the Arrows' work:

> we aim to inspire young people by giving a tangible demonstration of what professionalism, hard work and teamwork can achieve – not just in the Armed Forces but in whatever career they choose for their future.[77]

A Red Arrows display is, for many, a blend of sights and sounds that is not easily forgotten, and a powerful reminder of the possibilities opened up by effective teamwork.

Tasks

1 Explain the importance of group cohesiveness to the Red Arrows. How can cohesiveness be achieved when team members are so physically isolated as they train and perform?

2 Analyse the Red Arrows' yearly programme using Tuckman's model of group development and relationships. Explain how far the schedule reflects the model, and identify key transition points between the five stages.

3 Examine the whole team (including the pilots as well as the engineers and administration staff of the 'Circus') using Belbin's model of team roles. Where would you expect to find people with each of the characteristics Belbin identifies?

4 What do you think are the particular challenges facing Red 1 as leader of the display team? How might concepts outlined in the chapter help the leader understand and manage such challenges?

Notes and references

1. Schein, E. H. *Organizational Psychology*, third edition, Prentice Hall (1988), p. 145.

2. Adair, J. *Effective Teambuilding*, Gower (1986).

3. Peterson, C., Park, N and Sweeney, P. J. 'Group Well-Being: Morale from a Positive Psychology Perspective', *Applied Psychology: An International Review*, vol. 57, 2008, pp. 19–36.

4. ACAS *Teamwork: Success Through People*, advisory booklet, ACAS (2007), p. 24.

5. Holpp, L. 'Teams: It's All in the Planning', *Training & Development*, vol. 51, no. 4, 1997, pp. 44–7.

6. Cane, S. *Kaizen Strategies for Winning Through People*, Pitman (1996), p. 116.

7. Belbin, R. M. *Beyond the Team*, Butterworth–Heinemann (2000).

8. 'Steps in Successful Team Building', Checklist 088, Chartered Management Institute, June 2011.

9. Lysons, K. 'Organisational Analysis', *Supplement to The British Journal of Administrative Management*, no. 18, March/April 1997.

10. Law, S. 'Beyond the Water Cooler', *Professional Manager*, January 2005, pp. 26–8.

11. Riches, A. 'Emotionally Intelligent Teams', Organisational Change & Leadership Development, **www.anneriches.com.au** (accessed 5 March 2009).

12. Huck, S., Kubler, D. and Weibull, J. 'Social Norms and Economic Incentives in Firms', Economic & Social Research Council, 5 March 2003.

13. See, for example, Jay, A. *Corporation Man*, Penguin (1975). In an amusing historical account of the development of different forms of groups, Jay suggests that ten is the basic size of human grouping.

14. Cane, S. *Kaizen Strategies for Winning Through People*, Pitman (1996), p. 131.

15. Hazlehurst, J. 'The Way We Work Now', *Management Today*, June 2013, pp. 46–9.

16. ACAS *Teamwork: Success Through People*, advisory booklet, ACAS (2007), p. 8.

17. McKenna, P. J. and Maister, D. H. 'Building Team Trust', *Consulting to Management*, vol. 13, no. 4, 2002, pp. 51–3.

18. Farrell, E. 'Take the Lead in Setting Standards of Behaviour in Your Team', *Professional Manager,* vol. 19, no. 1, 2009, p. 14.

19. Tuckman, B. W. 'Development Sequence in Small Groups', *Psychological Bulletin,* vol. 63, 1965, pp. 384–99; and Tuckman, B. W. and Jensen, M. C. 'Stages of Small Group Development Revised', *Group and Organizational Studies,* vol. 2, no. 3, 1977, pp. 419–27.

20. Cited in Green, J. 'Are Your Teams and Groups at Work Successful?', *Administrator,* December 1993, p. 12.

21. Rickards, T. and Moger, S. T. 'Creative Leadership and Team Effectiveness: Empirical Evidence for a Two Barrier Model of Team Development', Working paper presented at the Advanced Seminar Series, University of Uppsala, Sweden, 3 March 2009; see also Rickards, T. and Moger, S. 'Creative Leadership Processes in Project Team Development: An Alternative to Tuckman's Stage Model?', *British Journal of Management,* Part 4, 2000, pp. 273–83.

22. Tajfel, H. and Turner, J. C. 'The Social Identity Theory of Intergroup Behavior', in Worchel, S. and Austin, L. W. (eds) *Psychology of Intergroup Relations,* Nelson-Hall (1986), pp. 7–24.

23. Guirdham, M. *Interactive Behaviour at Work,* third edition, Financial Times Prentice Hall (2002), p. 118.

24. Haslam, S. A. *Psychology in Organizations: The Social Identity Approach,* second edition, Sage (2004), p. 17.

25. See, for example, Flynn, F. J., Chatman, J. A. and Spataro, S. E. 'Getting to Know You: The Influence of Personality on Impressions and Performance of Demographically Different People in Organizations', *Administrative Science Quarterly,* vol. 46, 2001, pp. 414–42.

26. Hewstone, M., Ruibin, M. and Willis, H. 'Intergroup Bias', *Annual Review of Psychology,* vol. 53, 2002, pp. 575–604.

27. Brooks, I. *Organisational Behaviour: Individuals, Groups and Organisation,* fourth edition, Financial Times Prentice Hall (2009), p. 132.

28. Argyle, M. *The Social Psychology of Work,* second edition, Penguin (1989).

29. Hall, P. 'Team Solutions Need Not Be the Organisational Norm', *Professional Manager,* July 2001, p. 45

30. Symons, J. 'Taking Virtual Team Control', *Professional Manager,* vol. 12, no. 2, March 2003, p. 37.

31. Garrett, A. 'Crash Course in Managing a Virtual Team', *Management Today,* September 2007, p. 20.

32. Francesco, A. M. and Gold, B. A. *International Organizational Behavior,* second edition, Pearson Prentice Hall (2005), p. 118.

33. Murray, S. 'Virtual Teams: Global Harmony Is Their Dream', *Financial Times,* 11 May 2005.

34. Hazlehurst, J. 'The Way We Work Now', *Management Today,* June 2013, pp. 46–9.

35. See, for example, Lerner, P. M. 'Beware the Gatekeeper', *Amtrak Express,* July/August 1994, pp. 14–17.

36. Miner, J. B. *Management Theory,* Macmillan (1971).

37. Obeng, E. *All Change,* Pitman (1994).

38. Crainer, S. *Key Management Ideas: Thinkers That Changed the Management World,* third edition, Financial Times Prentice Hall (1998), p. 238.

39. Belbin, R. M. *Management Teams: Why They Succeed or Fail,* Butterworth–Heinemann (1981).

40. Belbin, R. M. *Team Roles at Work,* Butterworth–Heinemann (1993); see also Belbin, M. *The Belbin Guide to Succeeding at Work,* A & C Black (2009).

41. Aritzeta, A., Swailes, S, and Senior, B. 'Belbin's Team Role Model: Development, Validity and Applications for Team Building', *Journal of Management Studies,* vol. 44, no. 1, 2007, pp. 96–118.

42. Benne, K. D. and Sheats, P. 'Functional Roles of Group Members', *Journal of Social Issues,* vol. 4, 1948, pp. 41–9.

43. Moreno, J. L. *Who Shall Survive?* Beacon House (1953). See also Moreno, J. L. and Jennings, H. H. *The Sociometry Reader,* Free Press of Glencoe (1960).

44. Luft, J. *Group Processes: An Introduction to Group Dynamics,* second edition, National Press (1970). (The term 'Johari window' was derived from a combination of the first names of the original authors, Joseph Luft and Harry Ingham.)

45. James, J. *Body Talk at Work,* Piatkus (2001), p. 212.

46. Vernon, M. 'Office Friends: Who needs them?', *Management Today,* September 2005, pp. 59–61.

47. Newman, R. 'Love Games', *Professional Manager,* September/October 2011, pp. 19–23

48. Hall, P. 'Team Solutions Need Not Be the Organisational Norm', *Professional Manager,* July 2001, p. 45.

49. See, for example, Blanchard, K. and Bowles, S. *High Five: None of Us Is As Smart As All of Us,* HarperCollins Business (2001).

50. Stanley, T. J. 'The Challenge of Managing a High-Performance Team', *SuperVision,* vol. 63, no. 7, 2002, pp. 10–12.

51. Guirdham, M. *Interactive Behaviour at Work,* third edition, Financial Times Prentice Hall (2002), p. 498.

52. Kravitz, D. A. and Martin, B. 'Ringelmann Rediscovered: The Original Article', *Journal of Personality and Social Psychology,* May 1986, pp. 936–41.

53. See, for example, Karau, S. J. and Williams, K. D. 'Social Loafing: A Meta-Analysis Review and Theoretical Integration', *Journal of Personality and Social Psychology,* October 1993, pp. 681–706; and Liden, R. C., Wayne, S. J., Jaworkski, R.A. and Bennett, N. 'Social loafing: a field investigation', *Journal of Management,* vol. 30, no. 2, 2004, pp. 285–304.

54. Kogan, N. and Wallach, M. A. 'Risk-Taking as a Function of the Situation, the Person and the Group', in Newcomb, T. M. (ed.) *New Directions in Psychology III,* Holt, Rinehart and Winston (1967).

55. For a comprehensive review of the 'risky-shift' phenomenon, see, for example, Clarke, R. D. 'Group Induced Shift Towards Risk: A Critical Appraisal', *Psychological Bulletin,* vol. 76, 1971, pp. 251–70; see also Vecchio, R. P. *Organizational Behavior,* third edition, Harcourt Brace (1995).

56. Shaw, M. E. *Group Dynamics,* McGraw-Hill (1976).

57. Janis, J. L. *Victims of Groupthink,* Houghton Mifflin (1972); and Janis, J. L. *Groupthink,* second edition, Houghton Mifflin (1982).

58. Osborn, A. F. *Applied Imagination: Principles and Procedures of Creative Thinking,* Scribner's (1963).

59. 'Steps in Successful Team Building', Checklist 088, Chartered Management Institute, June 2011.

60. Yukl, G. *Leadership in Organizations,* seventh edition, Pearson Prentice Hall (2010), pp. 374–7.

61. Baroness Kingsmill, 'Survive awayday season', *Management Today,* January 2010, p. 24.

62. See, for example, Mullins, L. J. and Dossor, P. *Hospitality Management and Organisational Behaviour,* fifth edition, Pearson Education (2013).

63. Guirdham, M. *Interactive Behaviour at Work*, third edition, Financial Times Prentice Hall (2002), p. 12.

64. Peeling, N. *Brilliant Manager: What the Best Managers Know, Do and Say,* Pearson Prentice Hall (2005), pp. 129–30.

65. ACAS *Teamwork: Success Through People,* advisory booklet, ACAS (2007), p. 30.

66. Cloke, K. and Goldsmith, J. *The End of Management and the Rise of Organizational Democracy*, Jossey-Bass (2002).

67. Margerison, C. J. *Team Leadership: A Guide to Success with Team Management Systems,* Thomson (2002).

68. ACAS *Teamwork: Success Through People,* advisory booklet, ACAS (2007), p. 31.

69. Gratton, L. *The Democratic Enterprise,* Financial Times Prentice Hall (2004).

70. Powell, N. 'Teams Are a Mirror Image of Their Leaders', *Professional Manager,* vol. 16, no. 5, 2007, p. 41.

71. Brady, K. in conversation with Webber, M. 'Team Focus', *Manager,* Spring 2013, pp. 36–8.

72. ACAS *Teamwork: Success Through People,* advisory booklet, ACAS (2007), p. 34.

73. The Red Arrows, **http://www.raf.mod.uk/reds** (accessed 2 March 2015).

74. Brown, I. 'The Red Arrows: aerial acrobats', *Telegraph,* 1September 2009.

75. BBC, *Inside the Bubble,* documentary broadcast by BBC2 on 27 July 2014.

76. Lowbridge, C. 'How dangerous is life as a Red Arrow?', BBC News, 2014, **http://www.bbc.co.uk/news/uk-england-lincolnshire-25763663** (accessed 2 March 2015).

77. The Red Arrows, **http://www.raf.mod.uk/reds/news/** (accessed 2 March 2015).

CHAPTER 9
Leadership in organisations

An essential element of management and organisational behaviour is co-ordinating the activities of people and guiding their efforts towards the goals and objectives of the organisation. This involves the process of leadership and the choice of an appropriate form of behaviour and action. The manager needs to understand the nature and influence of leadership and factors that determine the effectiveness of the leadership relationship.

Learning outcomes

After completing this chapter you should have enhanced your ability to:

- explain the meaning and significance of leadership in work organisations;
- contrast main approaches to, and studies of, leadership;
- explore different styles and forms of leadership;
- detail situational forces and variables in the style of leadership adopted;
- explain the leadership relationship, and power and leadership influence;
- examine the variables affecting effective leadership;
- review the nature and importance of leadership development.

Critical review and reflection

Leadership is one of the holy grails of management and organisational behaviour. However complex or nebulous the subject area may appear, an understanding of leadership is an essential part of your studies.
What benefits do YOU expect to achieve from YOUR study of leadership?

The significance of leadership

The changing nature of work organisations involves moving away from an emphasis on command and getting results by the close control of the workforce and towards an environment of teamwork coaching, support and empowerment. This places an ever-growing importance on leadership. The leader–follower relationship is reciprocal, and effective leadership is a two-way process that influences both individual and organisational performance. Leadership is related to motivation and interpersonal behaviour.[1] A CBI report makes the point that: 'Effective leaders, who can inspire their people to realise their personal and collective potential, are often the deciding factor between a company being good at what it does and achieving greatness.'[2]

Leadership and management

What is the relationship between leadership and management? Although the two terms are often used interchangeably, management may be viewed as relating to people working within a structured organisation and with prescribed roles, in order to achieve stated organisational objectives (**see Chapter 10**). The emphasis of leadership is on interpersonal behaviour in a broader context. It is often associated with the willing and enthusiastic behaviour of followers.

Arguably there are differences between leadership and management. For example, *Zaleznik* explores difference in attitudes towards goals, conceptions of work, relations with others, self-perception and development:

- Managers tend to adopt impersonal or passive attitudes towards goals. Leaders adopt a more personal and active attitude towards goals.
- In order to get people to accept solutions, the manager needs continually to co-ordinate and balance in order to compromise conflicting values. The leader creates excitement in work and develops choices that give substance to images that excite people.
- In their relationships with other people, managers maintain a low level of emotional involvement. Leaders have empathy with other people and give attention to what events and actions mean.
- Managers see themselves more as conservators and regulators of the existing order of affairs with which they identify and from which they gain rewards. Leaders work in, but do not belong to, the organisation. Their sense of identity does not depend upon membership or work roles and they search out opportunities for change.[3]

Summarising the views of scholars who have attempted to differentiate between leading and managing, *Kent* draws attention to the following characteristics:

- managers do things right; leaders do the right things;
- managing is an authority relationship; leading is an influence relationship; and
- managing creates stability; leading creates change.

Kent suggests that although the ideas are provocative and stimulating, they provide a basis for a deeper understanding of the dynamics behind the two processes.[4]

Leadership role not defined

The key point about leadership is that it does not necessarily take place within the hierarchical structure of the organisation. It can occur at different levels and be manifested in different ways. Many people operate as leaders without their role ever being clearly established or defined.

For example, *Belbin* suggests that:

> there is a clear implication that leadership is not part of the job but a quality that can be brought to a job . . . The work that leadership encompasses in the context clearly is not assigned but comes about spontaneously.[5]

Radcliffe maintains that leadership is not mysterious, it is completely natural. Leadership is plain and simple. The only qualification to be a leader is the desire to grow. It absolutely does not matter where you are in an organisation.

> *This 'leadership stuff' really needn't be complicated. I believe that leading is a natural, human activity that is part of all of us. You don't need a certain IQ or job title to be a leader.*

There are only three aspects to leading: Future, Engage, Deliver.

- First, leading always starts in the Future.
- Second, if you want the help of others to create that Future, you need to Engage them.
- Third, in Deliver, you make things happen.[6]

Different perspectives

Despite continuing debate on differences between management and leadership, there is a close relationship and it is not easy to separate them as distinct activities. There appears to be an increasing tendency to emphasise the interrelationship between management and leadership and to see them more as synonymous. Many methods of management training can also be used as a means of measuring leadership style. For example, the Leadership Grid® (**discussed in Chapter 10**) was until recently known as the Managerial Grid®.

Mintzberg does not accept a distinction between the manager or the leader and poses the questions: 'How would you like to be managed by someone who doesn't lead; or why would you want to be led by someone who doesn't manage?'

> *Frankly, I don't understand what this distinction means in the everyday life of organizations. Sure, we can separate leading and managing conceptually. But can we separate them in practice? Or, more to the point, should we even try?*[7]

Moorcroft suggests two perspectives on the debate between leadership and management:

> *The debate between Leadership and Management is well rehearsed, and usually produces shades of two perspectives, presented here as extremes: A hierarchical relationship with Leadership at the top; Leadership and Management equal in status, but at opposite ends of a continuum. Frankly, there is little evidence to support one view over the other. But there is overwhelming evidence that people like the idea of being a 'leader'. Indeed this may be the reason why the debate still rages, as it fulfils a need for differentiation.*[8]

Critical review and reflection

In universities, many lecturers inspire students and are viewed usually as leaders not managers. In sport, we hear frequent talk about great leaders who are not managers of the team. There appears to be a clear and accepted distinction between leadership and management.

Why do YOU think this distinction does not appear to apply in the same way within business organisations? How do YOU distinguish between leadership and management?

Approaches to leadership

There are many ways of looking at **leadership** and interpretations of its meaning. Leadership might be interpreted in simple terms, such as 'getting others to follow' or 'getting people to do things willingly', or interpreted more specifically, for example as 'the use of authority in decision-making'. It may be exercised as an attribute of position or because of personal knowledge or wisdom. Leadership might be based on a function of personality or it can be seen as a behavioural category. It may also be viewed in terms of the role of the leaders and their ability to achieve effective performance from others. Leadership can also be discussed in terms of a form of persuasion or power relationship. It is difficult, therefore, to generalise about leadership, but essentially it is a **relationship through which one person influences the behaviour or actions of other people.** This means that the process of leadership cannot be separated from the activities of groups and effective team building.

Due to its complex and variable nature, there are many alternative ways of analysing leadership. It is helpful, therefore, to have some framework in which to consider different approaches to study of the subject.

One way is to examine managerial leadership in terms of:

- a qualities or traits approach;
- a functional or group approach, including action-centred leadership;
- styles of leadership;
- contingency theories;
- transitional or transformational leadership;
- inspirational or visionary leadership; and
- servant leadership. (*See* Figure 9.1.)

Qualities or traits approach

This approach assumes that leaders are born and not made. Leadership consists of certain inherited characteristics, or personality traits, which distinguish leaders from their followers. The **qualities (traits) approach** focuses attention on the man or woman in the job and not on the job itself. It suggests that attention is given to the selection of leaders rather than to training for leadership.

Drucker (writing originally in 1955) makes the point that:

> *Leadership is of utmost importance. Indeed there is no substitute for it. But leadership cannot be created or promoted. It cannot be taught or learned.*[9]

However, attempts at identifying common personality, or physical and mental, characteristics of different 'good' or 'successful' leaders have met with little success.[10] Investigations have identified lists of traits that tend to be overlapping, contradictory or with little correlation for most features. It is noticeable that 'individuality' or 'originality' usually features in the list. This suggests there is little in common between specific personality traits of different leaders. It is perhaps possible therefore to identify general characteristics of leadership ability, such as self-confidence, initiative, intelligence and belief in one's actions, but research into this area has revealed little more than this.

Limitations of the traits approach

There are three further limitations with this approach:

- There is bound to be some subjective judgement in determining who is regarded as a 'good' or 'successful' leader. (This can make for an interesting class discussion.)
- The lists of possible traits tend to be very long and there is not always agreement on the most important.
- It ignores the situational factors.

Even if it were possible to identify an agreed list of more specific qualities, this would provide little explanation of the nature of leadership or the development and training of future leaders. The qualities or traits approach gives rise to the questions of whether leaders are born or made and whether leadership is an art or a science. The important point, however, is that **these**

QUALITIES OR TRAITS APPROACH

Assumes leaders are born and not made. Leadership consists of certain inherited characteristics or personality traits. Focuses attention on the person in the job and not on the job itself.

THE FUNCTIONAL OR GROUP APPROACH

Attention is focused on the functions and responsibilities of leadership, what the leader actually does and the nature of the group. Assumes leadership skills can be learned and developed.

STYLES OF LEADERSHIP

The way in which the functions of leadership are carried out and the behaviour adopted by managers towards subordinate staff. Concerned with the effects of leadership on those being led.

SITUATIONAL APPROACH AND CONTINGENCY MODELS

The importance of the situation. Interactions between the variables involved in the leadership situation and patterns of behaviour. Belief that there is no single style of leadership appropriate to all situations.

TRANSFORMATIONAL LEADERSHIP

A process of engendering motivation and commitment, creating a vision for transforming the performance of the organisation, and appealing to the higher ideals and values of followers.

INSPIRATIONAL LEADERSHIP

Based on the personal qualities or charisma of the leader and the manner in which the leadership influence is exercised.

SERVANT LEADERSHIP

More a philosophy based on an ethical responsibility of leaders. A spiritual understanding of people; and empowering people through honesty, respect, nurturing and trust.

ALTERNATIVE VIEWS OF LEADERSHIP

Broader approaches to the study of leadership, including shared and distributed leadership, and responsible leadership.

Figure 9.1 Framework for study of managerial leadership

are not mutually exclusive alternatives. Even if there are certain inborn qualities that make for a good leader, these natural talents need encouragement and development. Even if leadership is something of an art, it still requires the application of special skills and techniques. Although there is still limited interest in the qualities or traits approach, attention has been directed more to other approaches to leadership.

Functional (or group) approach

This approach to leadership focuses attention not on the personality of the leader, nor on the man or woman in the job, per se, but on the contents or **functions of leadership.** Leadership is always present in any group engaged in a task. The functional approach views leadership in terms of how the leader's behaviour affects, and is affected by, the group of followers. This approach concentrates on the nature of the group, the followers or subordinates.

The functional approach believes the skills of leadership can be learned, developed and perfected. In contrast to the view of Drucker (referred to above), *Kotter* makes the point that successful companies do not wait for leaders to come along: 'They actively seek out people with leadership potential and expose them to career experiences designed to develop that potential. Indeed, with careful selection, nurturing and encouragement, dozens of people can play important leadership roles in a business organisation.'[11] A similar point is made by *Whitehead:*

> *There has been a dramatic change in how management thinkers regard leadership today. Leaders are not born, they say, but made. And the good news is everyone can do it. You don't have to be promoted to a management position. You can be a leader whatever job you do. You don't have to be the boss to be a leader.*[12]

Critical review and reflection

Leadership is all about determination, personality and innate ability at the right time for a particular competitive situation. Many effective business leaders have no formal academic qualifications and each has their own individual leadership style.

Does this suggest to YOU that successful leaders are more likely born rather than trained? Do YOU believe YOU would make a successful leader?

Action-centred leadership

A general theory on the functional approach is associated with the work of *John Adair* and his ideas on **action-centred leadership,** which focuses on what leaders actually *do.*[13] The effectiveness of the leader is dependent upon meeting three areas of need: the need to achieve the common **task;** the need for **team maintenance;** and the **individual needs** of group members – symbolised by three overlapping circles (*see* Figure 9.2).

- **Task needs** involve achieving objectives and defining group tasks, organising the work, duties and responsibilities and controlling quality and performance.
- **Team maintenance needs** involve maintaining morale and team spirit, maintaining standards and discipline, and training and communication within the group.
- **Individual needs** involve meeting needs of individual members and attending to personal problems, giving praise and status, and reconciling conflicts between group needs and needs of the individual.

Action by the leader in any one area of need will affect one or both of the other areas. The ideal position is where complete integration of the three areas of need is achieved.

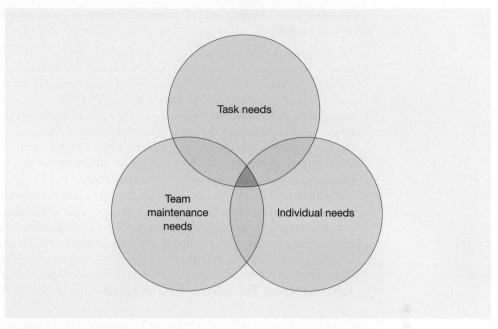

Figure 9.2 Interaction of needs within the group
Source: Adair, J. *Action-Centred Leadership*, Gower Press (1979), p. 10. Reproduced with permission from John Adair.

Are leaders born or made?

There are times when leadership comes out of all of us. A few years ago, some of my team and I were caught up in the terrorist attack on the Taj Hotel in Mumbai. We were stuck inside, debris was falling and people were screaming. But a young member of staff rose to the situation and took care of us. This 22 year-old woman guided us through the hotel and led us to safety. Nothing in her training had ever taught her how to respond in a situation like that, but she was calm, composed and unflappable. The way she exerted her authority was amazing. She showed me a lesson in leadership – you can lead in a moment, with your heart.

Source: Leena Nair, 'Debate: The Changing Face of the Leader', *Management Today*, 3 June 2013, p. 53.

Styles of leadership

In the work situation it has become increasingly clear that managers can no longer rely solely on the use of their position in the hierarchical structure. To get the best results from subordinates the manager must also have regard for the need to encourage high morale, a spirit of involvement and co-operation, and a willingness to work. This gives rise to consideration of the style of leadership and provides another heading under which to analyse leadership behaviour.

Leadership style is the way in which the functions of leadership are carried out, the way in which the manager typically behaves towards members of the group. There are many possible ways of describing leadership style, such as abdicatorial, benevolent, bureaucratic, charismatic, consultative, dictatorial, inspirational, participative, servant or unitary. With so many potential descriptions of leadership styles it is useful to have a broad framework in which to focus attention and study. The style of managerial leadership towards subordinate staff and the focus of power can therefore be considered within a simplified three-fold heading:

- **Authoritarian (autocratic) style**, where the focus of power is with the manager and interactions within the group move towards the manager. The manager alone exercises decision-making and authority for determining policy, procedures for achieving goals, work tasks and relationships and control of rewards or punishments.
- **Democratic style**, where the focus of power is more with the group as a whole and there is greater interaction within the group. The leadership functions are shared with members of the group and the manager is more part of a team. Group members have a greater say in decision-making, determination of policy and implementation of systems and procedures.
- **Laissez-faire (genuine) style**, where the manager observes members of the group are working well on their own. The manager consciously makes a decision to pass the focus of power to members, allow them freedom of action 'to do as they think best', not to interfere but to be readily available if help is needed. There is often confusion over this style of leadership. The word 'genuine' is emphasised because this is to be contrasted with the manager who could not care, who deliberately keeps away from the trouble spots and does not want to get involved. Members are then left to face decisions that rightly belong with the manager. This is more a non-style of leadership, or it could perhaps be labelled as abdication.

Continuum of leadership behaviour

One of the best-known works on leadership style is that by *Tannenbaum and Schmidt (see Figure 9.3)*.[14] Originally written in 1958 and updated in 1973, their work suggests a continuum of possible leadership behaviour available to a manager. The continuum presents a range of action related to the degree of authority used by the manager and to the area of freedom available to non-managers in arriving at decisions.

Four main styles of leadership

Moving along the continuum, the manager may be characterised according to the degree of control that is maintained. Neither extreme of the continuum is absolute as there is always some limitation on authority and on freedom. This approach can be seen as identifying four main styles of leadership by the manager: tells, sells, consults, joins.

- **Tells** – The manager identifies a problem, makes a decision and announces this to subordinates, expecting them to implement it without an opportunity for participation.
- **Sells** – The manager still makes a decision but recognises the possibility of some resistance from those faced with the decision and attempts to persuade subordinates to accept it.
- **Consults** – The manager identifies the problem but does not make a decision until the problem is presented to the group, and the manager has listened to the advice and solutions suggested by subordinates.
- **Joins** – The manager defines the problem and the limits within which the decision must be made and then passes to the group, with the manager as a member, the right to make decisions.

Three main forces

Tannenbaum and Schmidt suggest that there are three factors, or forces, of particular importance in deciding what types of leadership are practicable and desirable. These are: forces in the manager, forces in the subordinate and forces in the situation.

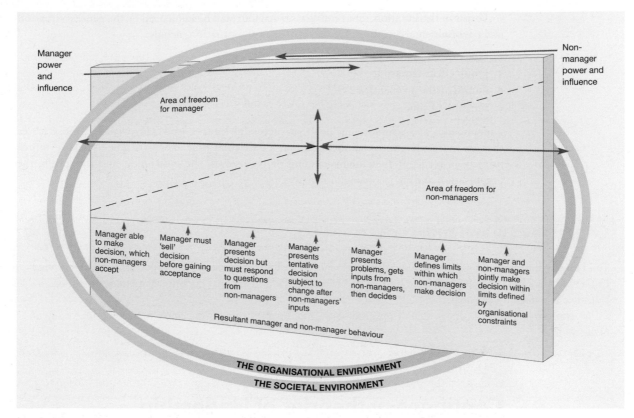

Figure 9.3 Continuum of manager–non-manager behaviour

Source: From Tannenbaum, R. and Schmidt, W. H. 'How to Choose a Leadership Pattern', *Harvard Business Review*, May/June 1973, p. 167. Copyright © 1973 by Harvard Business School Publishing Corporation; all rights reserved.

Forces in the manager. The manager's behaviour will be influenced by his or her personality, background, knowledge and experiences. These internal forces will include:

- value-systems;
- confidence in subordinates;
- leadership inclinations;
- feelings of security in an uncertain situation.

Forces in the subordinate. Subordinates are influenced by many personality variables and their individual set of expectations about their relationship with the manager. Characteristics of the subordinate are:

- strength of the need for independence;
- readiness to assume responsibility for decision-making;
- degree of tolerance for ambiguity;
- interest in the problem and feelings as to its importance;
- understanding and identification with the goals of the organisation;
- necessary knowledge and experience to deal with the problem;
- extent of learning to expect to share in decision-making.

The greater the positive response to these characteristics, the greater freedom of action can be allowed by the manager.

Forces in the situation. The manager's behaviour will be influenced by the general situation and environmental pressures. Characteristics in the situation include:

- type of organisation;
- group effectiveness;
- nature of the problem;
- pressure of time.

Tannenbaum and Schmidt conclude that successful leaders are keenly aware of those forces that are most relevant to their behaviour at a particular time. They are able to behave appropriately in terms of their understanding of themselves, the individuals and the group, the organisation and environmental influences.

Critical review and reflection

The Tannenbaum and Schmidt continuum is the single most relevant study of leadership. Successful managers need to be consistent in both personality and behaviour, yet adaptable to forces that continually influence their leadership style and decision-making.

To what extent can YOU argue against this assertion? What do YOU think is the single most important study of leadership?

Contingency theories of leadership

The continuum of leadership behaviour draws attention to forces in the situation as one of the main forces influencing the nature of managerial behaviour. The **contingency or situational approach** emphasises the situation as the dominant feature in considering the characteristics of effective leadership. There are, however, limitations to this approach. There are people who possess the appropriate knowledge and skills and appear to be the most suitable leaders in a given situation, but who do not emerge as effective leaders. Also, in the work organisation, it is not usually practicable to allow the situation continually to determine who should act as the leader.

Despite limitations of the contingency approach, situational factors are important in considering the characteristics of leadership. Contingency models focus on the interactions between the variables involved in a leadership situation and patterns of leadership behaviour. Major contingency models of leadership include:

- Favourability of leadership situation – Fiedler
- Quality and acceptance of leader's decision – Vroom and Yetton
- **Path–goal theory** – House, and House and Dessler
- Readiness level of followers – Hersey and Blanchard.

Fiedler's contingency model

One of the first leader–situation models was developed by *Fiedler* in his contingency theory of leadership effectiveness.[15] In order to measure the attitudes of the leader, Fiedler developed a 'least preferred co-worker' (LPC) scale. This measures the rating given by leaders about the person with whom they could work least well. The questionnaire contains up to twenty items. Examples of items in the LPC scale are pleasant/unpleasant, friendly/unfriendly, helpful/frustrating, distant/close, co-operative/unco-operative, boring/interesting, self-assured/hesitant, open/guarded.

Each item is given a single ranking of between 1 and 8 points, with 8 points indicating the most favourable rating. For example:

Pleasant	:	:	:	:	:	:	:	:	Unpleasant
	8	7	6	5	4	3	2	1	

The LPC score is the sum of the numerical ratings on all the items for the 'least preferred co-worker'. The original interpretation of the LPC scale was that the leader with a high LPC score derived most satisfaction from interpersonal relationships. The leader with a low LPC score derived most satisfaction from performance of the task and achieving objectives. However, the interpretation of LPC has changed a number of times and there is still uncertainty about its actual meaning.

Favourability of the leadership situation

Fiedler suggests that leadership behaviour is dependent upon the favourability of the leadership situation. There are three major variables that determine the favourability of the situation and that affect the leader's role and influence:

- **Leader–member relations** – degree to which the leader is trusted and liked by group members, and their willingness to follow the leader's guidance.
- **The task structure** – degree to which the task is clearly defined for the group and the extent to which it can be carried out by detailed instructions or standard procedures.
- **Position power** – power of the leader by virtue of position in the organisation, and the degree to which the leader can exercise authority to influence (for example) rewards and punishments, or promotions and demotions.

From these three variables, Fiedler constructed eight combinations of group–task situations through which to relate leadership style (*see* Figure 9.4).

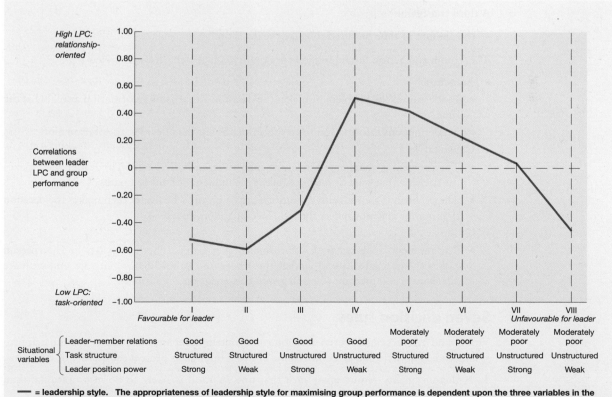

Figure 9.4 Correlations between leader's LPC scores and group effectiveness

Source: Adapted from Fiedler, F. E. A *Theory of Leadership Effectiveness*, McGraw-Hill (1967), p. 146. Reproduced with permission from Fred E. Fiedler.

When the situation is **very favourable** (good leader–member relations, structured task, strong position power) or **very unfavourable** (poor leader–member relations, unstructured task, weak position power), then a **task-oriented leader** (low LPC score) with a directive, controlling style will be more effective.

When the situation is **moderately favourable** and the variables are mixed, then the leader with an **interpersonal relationship orientation** (high LPC score) and a participative approach will be more effective.

Fiedler argues that leadership effectiveness may be improved by changing the leadership situation. Position power, task structure and leader–member relations can be changed to make the situation more compatible with the characteristics of the leader.

Fiedler's work has been subject to much debate and criticism but it does provide a further dimension to the study of leadership.[16] It brings into consideration the organisational variables that affect leadership effectiveness and suggests that in given situations a task-oriented, or structured, style of leadership is most appropriate. The 'best' styles of leadership will be dependent upon the variable factors in the leadership situation.

Vroom and Yetton contingency model

Vroom and Yetton base their analysis on two main aspects of a leader's decision: its quality and its acceptance.[17]

- **Decision quality, or rationality,** is the effect that the decision has on group performance.
- **Decision acceptance** refers to the motivation and commitment of group members in implementing the decision.

A third consideration is:

- **the amount of time** required to make the decision.

The Vroom and Yetton model suggests five main management decision styles:

- Autocratic
  - Leader solves the problem or makes the decision alone using information available at the time.
  - Leader obtains information from subordinates but then decides on solution alone.
- Consultative
  - The problem is shared with relevant subordinates, individually. The leader then makes the decision that may or may not reflect the influence of subordinates.
  - The problem is shared with subordinates as a group. The leader then makes the decision that may or may not reflect the influence of subordinates.
- Group
  - The problem is shared with subordinates as a group. The leader acts as chairperson rather than an advocate. Together the leader and subordinates generate and evaluate alternatives and attempt to reach group consensus on a solution.

Seven decision rules

Vroom and Yetton suggest seven decision rules to help the manager discover the most appropriate leadership style in a given situation. The first three rules protect the **quality of decisions**.

1. Is there a quality requirement such that one solution is likely to be more rational than another?
2. Is there sufficient information to make a high-quality decision?
3. Is the problem structured?

The last four rules protect the **acceptance of decisions.**

1. Is acceptance of the decision by subordinates critical to effective implementation?
2. If you were to make the decision yourself, is it reasonably certain that it would be accepted by subordinates?
3. Do subordinates share the organisational goals to be obtained in solving the problem?
4. Is conflict among subordinates likely in preferred solutions?

These rules indicate decision styles that the manager should **avoid** in a given situation and indicate the use of others. Decision-tree charts can be produced to help in the application of the rules and to relate the situation to the appropriate leadership style.

Path-goal theory

A third contingency model of leadership is the **path-goal theory,** the main work on which has been undertaken by *House*[18] and by *House and Dessler.*[19] The model is based on the belief that the individual's motivation is dependent upon expectations that increased effort to achieve an improved level of performance will be successful, and expectations that improved performance will be instrumental in obtaining positive rewards and avoiding negative outcomes. This is the 'expectancy' theory of motivation (**discussed in Chapter 7**).

Path–goal theory of leadership suggests that the performance of subordinates is affected by the extent to which the manager satisfies their expectations. Subordinates see leadership behaviour as a motivating influence to the extent that it means:

- satisfaction of their needs is dependent upon effective performance; and
- the necessary direction, guidance, training and support, which would otherwise be lacking, are provided.

Main types of leadership behaviour

House identifies four main types of leadership behaviour:

- **Directive leadership** – letting subordinates know exactly what is expected of them and giving specific directions. Subordinates are expected to follow rules and regulations. This type of behaviour is similar to 'initiating structure' in the Ohio State Leadership Studies.
- **Supportive leadership** – having a friendly and approachable manner and displaying concern for the needs and welfare of subordinates. This type of behaviour is similar to 'consideration' in the Ohio State Leadership Studies.
- **Participative leadership** – consulting with subordinates and the evaluation of their opinions and suggestions before the manager makes the decision.
- **Achievement-oriented leadership** – setting challenging goals for subordinates, seeking improvement in their performance and showing confidence in subordinates' ability to perform well.

Path–goal theory suggests that the different types of behaviour can be practised by the same person at different times in varying situations. By using one of the four styles of leadership behaviour the manager attempts to influence subordinates' perceptions and motivation, and smooth the path to their goals (*see* Figure 9.5).

Two main situational factors

Leadership behaviour is determined by two main situational factors: personal characteristics of subordinates and nature of the task.

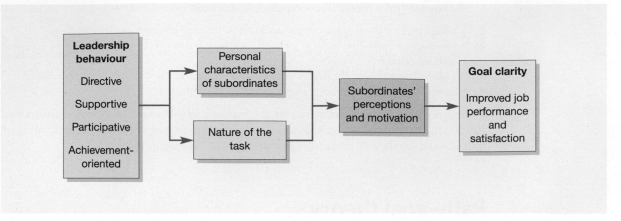

Figure 9.5 Representation of the path–goal theory of leadership

- **Personal characteristics of subordinates** determine how they will react to the manager's behaviour and the extent to which they see such behaviour as an immediate or potential source of need satisfaction.
- **Nature of the task** relates to the extent that it is routine and structured or non-routine and unstructured.

Effective leadership behaviour is based, therefore, on both the willingness of the manager to help subordinates and the needs of subordinates for help. Leadership behaviour will be motivational to the extent that it provides necessary direction, guidance and support, helps clarify path–goal relationships and removes any obstacles that hinder attainment of goals. For example, when a task is highly structured, the goals readily apparent and subordinates are confident, attempts to further explain the job or to give directions are likely to be viewed as unacceptable behaviour. However, when a task is highly unstructured, the nature of the goals is not clear and subordinates lack experience, a more directive style of leadership behaviour is likely to be welcomed by subordinates.

Critical review and reflection

Common sense suggests that situational factors are clearly a major determinant of the most appropriate leadership style. But, realistically, contingency models appeal only to teachers rather than practitioners of management.
    What do YOU think? Can YOU relate any practical example of the apparent application of a contingency model of leadership?

Readiness of the followers or group

A major variable in the style of leadership adopted by the manager is the nature of subordinate staff. This view is developed by *Hersey and Blanchard*, who present a form of situational leadership based on the 'readiness' level of the people the leader is attempting to influence. Readiness is the extent to which followers have the ability and willingness to accomplish a specific task. It is not a personal characteristic of the individual but how ready the individual is to perform a particular task.[20]

    Readiness (R) is divided into a continuum of four levels: R1 (low), R2 and R3 (moderate) and R4 (high):

- **R1 – low follower readiness** – refers to followers who are both *unable and unwilling* and who lack commitment and motivation, or who are *unable and insecure*.
- **R2 – low to moderate follower readiness** – refers to followers who are *unable but willing* and who lack ability but are motivated to make an effort, or who are *unable but confident*.
- **R3 – moderate to high follower readiness** – refers to followers who are *able but unwilling*, and who have the ability to perform but are unwilling to apply their ability, or who are *able but insecure*.
- **R4 – high follower readiness** – refers to followers who are both *able and willing* and who have the ability and commitment to perform, or who are *able and confident*.

Task behaviour and relationship behaviour

For each of the four levels of maturity, the appropriate style of leadership is a combination of task behaviour and relationship behaviour:

- **Task behaviour** is the extent to which the leader provides directions for the actions of followers, sets goals for them and defines their roles and how to undertake them.
- **Relationship behaviour** is the extent to which the leader engages in two-way communication with followers, listens to them and provides support and encouragement.

From the combination of task behaviour and relationship behaviour four leadership styles (S) are derived: telling (S1), selling (S2), participating (S3) and delegating (S4). The appropriate leadership style corresponds with the readiness of the followers (*see* Figure 9.6).

- **S1 – telling** – emphasises high amounts of guidance (task behaviour) but limited supportive (relationship) behaviour. This style is most appropriate for *low follower readiness* (R1).
- **S2 – selling** – emphasises high amounts of both directive (task) and relationship behaviours. This style is most appropriate for *low to moderate follower readiness* (R2).
- **S3 – participating** – emphasises a high amount of two-way communication and supportive (relationship) behaviour but low amounts of guidance (task behaviour). This style is most appropriate for *moderate to high follower readiness* (R3).
- **S4 – delegating** – emphasises little direction or support with low levels of both task and relationship behaviours. This style is most appropriate for *high follower readiness* (R4).

Development of subordinates

Hersey and Blanchard suggest the key to using situational leadership is that any leader behaviour may be more or less effective according to the readiness of the person the leader is attempting to influence. The model draws attention to the importance of developing the

S1 – TELLING – emphasises high amounts of guidance (task behaviour) but limited supportive (relationship) behaviour. This style is most appropriate for ***low follower readiness* (R1)**.
Leadership behaviour based on detailed instructions and close supervision

S2 – SELLING – emphasises high amounts of both directive (task) and relationalship behaviours. This style is most appropriate for ***low to moderate follower readiness* (R2)**.
Leadership behaviour based on explanation and discussion of decision

S3 – PARTICIPATING – emphasises high amounts of two-way communication and supportive (relationship) behaviour but low amounts of guidance (task behaviour). This style is most appropriate for ***moderate to high follower readiness* (R3)**.
Leadership behaviour based on sharing ideas and facilitating decision-making

S4 – DELEGATING – emphasises little direction or support with low levels of both task and relationship behaviour. This style is most appropriate for ***high follower readiness* (R4)**.
Leadership behaviour based on delegation of responsibility for decisions

Figure 9.6 Hersey and Blanchard's four leadership styles ability, confidence and commitment of subordinates. The manager should help subordinates to develop in readiness to the extent that they are able and willing to go. This development should take place by adjusting leadership behaviour through the four styles of telling, selling, participating and delegating.

Transformational leadership

Increasing business competitiveness and need for the most effective use of human resources have resulted in writers on management focusing attention on how leaders revitalise or transform organisations. Based on the work of writers such as *Burns*, this has given rise to a distinction between two fundamental forms of leadership: transactional leadership and transformational (or creative) leadership.[21]

- **Transactional leadership** is based on legitimate authority within the bureaucratic structure of the organisation. The emphasis is on the clarification of goals and objectives, work task and outcomes, and organisational rewards and punishments. Transactional leadership appeals to the self-interest of followers. It is based on a relationship of mutual dependence and an exchange process of 'I will give you this, if you do that.'
- **Transformational (or creative) leadership,** by contrast, is a process of engendering higher levels of motivation and commitment among followers. The emphasis is on generating a vision for the organisation and the leader's ability to appeal to higher ideals and values of followers, and creating a feeling of justice, loyalty and trust. In the organisational sense, transformational leadership is about transforming the performance or fortunes of a business.

Components of transformational leadership

Applying the ideas of Burns to organisational management, *Bass* proposed a theory of transformational leadership that argues that the leader transforms and motivates followers by:

1. Generating greater awareness of the importance of the purpose of the organisation and task outcomes.
2. Inducing them to transcend their own self-interests for the sake of the organisation or team.
3. Activating their higher-level needs.[22]

Transformational leadership comprises four basic components:

- **idealised influence** – the charisma of the leader, and the respect and admiration of the followers;
- **inspirational motivation** – the behaviour of the leader, which provides meaning and challenge to the work of the followers;
- **intellectual stimulation** – leaders who solicit new and novel approaches for the performance of work and creative problem solutions from followers; and
- **individualised consideration** – leaders who listen and give special concern to the growth and developmental needs of the followers.[23]

Set of guidelines

Yukl provides a set of guidelines for transformational leadership:

- **Articulate a clear and appealing vision** of what the organisation could accomplish or become to help people understand the purpose, objectives and priorities of the organisation, and to help guide the actions and decisions of members.
- **Explain how the vision can be attained** and establish a clear link between the vision and a credible conventional yet straightforward strategy for attaining it.
- **Act confident and optimistic** about likely success, demonstrate self-confidence and conviction and emphasise positive aspects of the vision rather than the obstacles and dangers.

- **Express confidence in followers** and their ability to carry out the strategy for accomplishing the vision, especially when the task is difficult or dangerous, or when members lack confidence in themselves.
- **Use dramatic, symbolic actions** to emphasise key values and demonstrate leadership behaviour through dramatic, highly visible actions including risking personal loss, self-sacrifice or acting unconventionally.
- **Lead by example** by recognising actions speak louder than words, through exemplary behaviour in day-to-day interactions with subordinates and by demonstrating consistency in daily behaviour.[24]

Critical review and reflection

Transactional and transformational leadership should not be seen as alternatives. Any effective leader will clearly use a balance of both legitimate authority and attention to higher ideals and values of followers.

To what extent do YOU agree? How difficult do YOU think it is to apply this balance in practice? What would be the most likely problem areas?

Inspirational or visionary leadership

Many writers see transformational leadership as the same thing as charismatic, visionary or inspirational leadership. *Kreitner et al.* refer to charismatic leadership as transforming employees to pursue organisational goals over self-interests:

> Charismatic leaders transform followers by creating changes in their goals, values, needs, beliefs, and aspirations. They accomplish this transformation by appealing to followers' self-concepts – namely, their values and personal identity.[25]

Successful transformational leaders are usually identified in terms of providing a strong vision and sense of mission, arousing strong emotions in followers and a sense of identification with the leader. Leadership today is increasingly associated with the concept of creating a vision with which others can identify, getting along with other people and the concept of inspiration. This might be considered as part of transformational leadership or arguably it has given rise to a new approach to leadership – that of **inspirational or visionary leadership.** Inspirational leadership is not concerned so much with the theory of leadership but more with the skills of motivating and inspiring people.

In her discussion of the creation of the democratic enterprise (organisations that can flourish economically and can also be places of excitement and stimulation, fulfilment and tranquillity), *Gratton* maintains that it is the creation of a shared purpose and the role of the leadership team that are most vital. The role of the leader as visionary is fundamental to creating the broad philosophical context of democracy and as the architect of shared purpose.[26]

Goffee and Jones point out that the need for visionary leadership is becoming increasingly important. Traditional business hierarchies gave managers and workers a sense of their own position and what was expected of them. Now, as these hierarchies break down, it is leaders themselves who must fill the void, helping subordinates to understand their place and purpose. Personal leadership is beginning to replace organisation structure.[27]

Personal qualities or charisma

Leadership may be based on the personal qualities, or charisma, of the leader and the manner in which influence is exercised. The concept of charismatic or inspirational leadership is not new and has been applied in the organisational context by writers such as Max Weber

(1864–1920).[28] The importance of charisma for effective leadership today is emphasised by *Conger*, who also believes that many of the traits that make a successful leader can be taught, including charisma.

> Now the big question is whether you are born with charisma or whether you can develop it. I believe you can develop elements of it. For example, you can take courses to improve your speaking skills. You can learn to stage events that send powerful messages. You can learn to think more critically about the status quo and its shortcomings. You can do more on a daily basis to motivate your team. What you simply cannot learn is how to be passionate about what you do. You have to discover that for yourself, and passion is a big part of what drives a charismatic leader. It is also what motivates and inspires those who work for the charismatic leader.[29]

However, the extent to which charismatic or inspirational leadership helps bring about improvement in organisational performance is open to debate. Conger also draws attention to the danger that the leader's vision, dynamism and inspirational nature are highly attractive to followers, which leads to a natural dependence. Staff see this extraordinary figure as a model to be emulated and the leader's abilities become the yardstick by which they measure their own performance. This is a potential source of leadership derailment. Dependence makes the followers more susceptible to deception.[30]

Leadership not about the leader

Adair argues that to be a truly inspirational leader one must understand the spirit within. All people have the potential for greatness. The inspirational leader connects with the led, appreciates the capabilities of others and through trust will unlock the powers in others. Adair refers to 'the inspired moment' – a recognition and seizure of a brief window of opportunity that can act as a powerful catalyst that inspires both the leader and the led.[31]

> Leadership is not about the leader, it is about how he or she builds the confidence of everyone else. Leaders are responsible for both the big structures that serve as the cornerstone of confidence, and for the human touches that shape a positive emotional climate to inspire and motivate people . . . Leaders deliver confidence by espousing high standards in their messages, exemplifying these standards in the conduct they model and establishing formal mechanisms to provide a structure for acting on those standards.[32]

Kingsmill suggests that the belief that real change and transformation will come from a charismatic visionary may have an immediate appeal to some but all too often this can prove to be a shallow myth rather than a reality.

> Frequently, boards of companies that are in trouble look for a corporate saviour from outside rather than choose the internal candidate who may have a better understanding of the problems and how to solve them. Grand strategies that never come to fruition, demoralised people whose voices are not heard and innovations that are stifled are all too often the real result of this preoccupation with the hero leader.[33]

Critical review and reflection

Charisma and the ability to inspire and move loyal followers in the desired direction are among the most controversial leadership qualities. Despite the apparent attraction of charisma by itself, it is unlikely to lead to a noticeable improvement in organisational performance.

To what extent do YOU believe in the organisational benefits of charismatic leadership? To what extent do YOU possess, or would you like to possess, charisma?

Servant leadership

In recent years renewed attention has been given to the idea of **servant leadership**, originally proposed in 1970 by *Robert Greenleaf*.[34, 35]

> *The servant-leader is servant first . . . It begins with the natural feeling that one wants to serve, to serve first. Then conscious choice brings one to aspire to lead. That person is sharply different from one who is leader first, perhaps because of the need to assuage power drive or to acquire material possessions . . . The difference manifests itself in the care taken by the servant-first to make sure that other people's highest priority needs are being served.*[36]

Rather than the use of position power, servant leadership is more a philosophy based on an ethical responsibility of leaders, a spiritual understanding of people and empowering people through honesty, respect, nurturing and trust. A servant leader gives attention to the needs of people and the promotion of their personal development. The focus of leadership is on a supportive and participative style of management. A test of servant leadership is the extent to which the followers, that is those served, benefit. It might therefore be particularly appropriate in service organisations such as in the hospitality industry.[37] Servant leadership can be associated with the idea of positive psychology with an emphasis on human strengths, how things go right and how to enhance people's satisfaction and well-being (**discussed in Chapter 1**).

Critical characteristics

A set of ten critical characteristics central to servant leadership has been identified by *Spears*:

- Good communication skills and the motivation to **listen actively**
- Understanding and **empathy** with others
- Ability to **heal** oneself and others
- **Self-awareness** and to view situations from a holistic position
- Rely on **persuasion** as opposed to the use of power or status
- Able to **conceptualise** and think beyond day-to-day realities and focus on long-term goals
- **Foreseeing** likely outcomes, learning from the past and identifying consequences of future decisions
- **Stewardship** of their organisations for the greater good of society
- Commitment to the personal, professional and **spiritual growth** of people
- Building a strong organisational **community**.[38]

According to *Yukl*, the values emphasised in servant leadership are primarily about helping people and fostering a relationship of trust and cooperation. Yukl lists seven key values and examples of how these might be expressed in a leader's behaviour:

- **Integrity** – open and honest communications, keeps promises and commitments, accepts responsibility for mistakes.
- **Altruism** – helps others and puts their need before your own, willing to takes risks and make sacrifices to benefit others.
- **Humility** – treats others with respect, avoids status symbols and privileges, modest about achievements, emphasises contributions of others.
- **Empathy and healing** – helps others cope with emotional distress, acts as mediator, encourages reconciliation.
- **Personal growth** – encourages development of individual confidence and ability, provides learning opportunities and mentoring and coaching.
- **Fairness and justice** – encourages and supports fair treatment, speaks out against unfair and unjust practices or policies.
- **Empowerment**– consults with others about decisions that affect them, provides autonomy and discretion, encourages expression of dissenting views.[39]

The focus of servant leadership

According to *Wong*, the focus of leadership needs to shift from process and outcome to people and the future. Servant leadership represents a radical approach – it is humanistic and spiritual rather than rational and mechanistic. Command and control leadership no longer works because leaders must earn people's respect and trust. New types of leaders are needed to create new futures, and the challenge for management and leadership education is to:

- develop workers and unleash their creative potential;
- create a positive workplace that will attract and retain knowledge workers; and
- reinforce innovations and risk-taking to adapt to an uncertain future.

However, Wong acknowledges common criticism of servant leadership including that it is too restrictive, too unrealistic and impractical and would not work in situations such as military operations or prison systems. It is too idealistic and naive, too closely related to Christian spirituality and too foreign to a preferred alternative leadership style.[40]

A summary of leadership and management is set out in the concept map in Figure 9.7.

Power and leadership influence

Leadership influence is a social process and may be seen in terms of the type of power that the leader can exercise over the behaviour and actions of others. An early view of social power upon which the influence of the leader is based has been presented by *French and Raven*, who identify five main sources: reward power, coercive power, legitimate power, referent power and expert power.[41] We shall consider these in terms of the manager (as a leader) and subordinate relationship. It is important to note that these sources of power are based on the subordinates' perception of the influence of the leader, whether it is real or not.

- **Reward power** is based on the subordinate's *perception* that the leader has the ability and resources to obtain rewards for those who comply with directives – for example, pay, promotion, praise, recognition, increased responsibilities, allocation and arrangement of work and granting of privileges.
- **Coercive power** is based on fear and the subordinate's *perception* that the leader has the ability to punish or to bring about undesirable outcomes for those who do not comply with directives – for example, withholding pay rises, promotion or privileges, allocation of undesirable duties or responsibilities, withdrawal of friendship or support and formal reprimands or possibly dismissal. This is in effect the opposite of reward power.
- **Legitimate power** is based on the subordinate's *perception* that the leader has a right to exercise influence because of the leader's role or position in the organisation. Legitimate power is based on authority – for example, that of managers and supervisors within the hierarchical structure of an organisation. Legitimate power is therefore 'position' power because it is based on the role of the leader in the organisation, and not on the nature of the personal relationship with others.
- **Referent power** is based on the subordinate's *identification* with the leader. The leader exercises influence because of perceived attractiveness, personal characteristics, reputation or what is called 'charisma'. For example, a particular manager may not be in a position to reward or punish certain subordinates, but may still exercise power over the subordinates because the manager commands their respect or esteem.
- **Expert power** is based on the subordinate's *perception* of the leader as someone who is competent and who has some special knowledge or expertise in a given area. Expert power is based on credibility and clear evidence of knowledge or expertise, including 'functional' specialists such as the management accountant or systems analyst.

French and Raven point out that the five sources of power are interrelated and the use of one type of power (e.g. coercive) may affect the ability to use another type of power (e.g. referent).

LEADERSHIP AND MANAGEMENT

Managers have to ensure their subordinates collectively or separately reach their goals

- MANAGEMENT
- LEADERSHIP

Leadership by function
Leadership by personality

Charisma ⟷ Technocrat

LEADERSHIP
– the ability to ensure subordinates perform their tasks and duties up to the standards required, by inspiration or inducement

Leaders cannot achieve the goals by themselves
Subordinates require direction to obtain the goals

Therefore co-operation or coercion required
– Leaders are those individuals who are perceived most frequently to perform those roles and functions which initiate or control behaviour of others towards the achievement of group goals or sub goals (Gibb)

No single trait or group of characteristics has been isolated which sets off the leader from members of groups (Jenkins)

FOUR VARIABLES
1 Characteristics/traits of the leader
2 Attitudes of the followers
3 Organisation purpose, technology, ethos, values, structure
4 Social economic and political milieu (McGregor) between countries between cultures

MANAGERS have the authority to direct work and behaviour
LEADERS have influence through example, persuading, motivating, teaching

- Group tasks usually complex
- Organisations require stability not continuous change in leader

- Situational Theory Leadership is specific to the situation under investigation, i.e. a leader emerges in response to the problem or challenge

- Personnel with highly technical skills possessing wide sapiential (knowledge) gives authority/ leadership

Leadership may be situationally governed
– arising due to a set of circumstances
Some managers are more suitable to operate in one set of situations than others

LEADERSHIP TRAITS
- Intelligence
- Self-confidence
- Initiative taking
- Empathy
- Self-awareness
- Objectivity (human relationships)

THE ESSENTIALS OF LEADERSHIP
– Social skills
– Ability to communicate
– Flexibility/judgement as to which management style to adopt

ACTION-CENTRED LEADERSHIP (ADAIR)

INDIVIDUAL NEEDS
– Concern for the individual
- fairness and consistency in disciplinary matters
- help with training, career prospects with … preparation for retirement recognition of performance
- good or adequate with …
- commendation or helpful criticism
– Job enrichment
– Giving status

GROUP NEEDS
Defence of the group needs
– laterally and vertically
Building up teamwork, recognising informal groups
Protection of interests which may lead to disruption e.g. relocation to another site; uneven work loads; accommodation; pay differentials

TASK NEEDS
Task definition
Planning
Allocating work and resources
Controlling quality, pace of work
Monitoring
Amending the plans
Co-ordinating with other groups
Obtaining resources required

Group Needs
Task Needs
Individual Needs

Use of authority by manager | Area of freedom by subordinate

tell | sell | consult | share | delegate | abdicate
1 | 2 | 3 | 4 | 5 | 6 | 7

1 Tell them
2 Tell them and sell it to them
3 Tell them and talk about it
4 Tentative decision and talk
5 Problem – talk and manager decides
6 Manager gives limits; all discuss, group decides
7 Manager gives limits; group discusses and decides

- Organisational leadership
- Personal leadership … contribution by the individual in the post showing – charisma/energy/vision

Authoritarian ⟷ Democratic

KINDS OF LEADERSHIP
Formal
– appointed in the hierarchy by the management
Informal
– exercises influence but is not in formal position; can initiate or block actions; can be in conflict with the formal leader; can set the group norms

Figure 9.7 Concept map of leadership and management

Furthermore, the same person may exercise different types of power, in particular circumstances and at different times.

Yukl suggests that a further relevant source of power is **control over information**.[42]

The leadership relationship

Whatever the perceived approach to leadership, an underlying feature of leadership is *the manner* in which the leader influences the behaviour and actions of other people. Leadership is a dynamic form of behaviour and there are a number of variables that affect the leadership relationship. For example, *Bass* reviews leadership influence in terms of persuasion, a power relation, an instrument of goal achievement, an emerging effect of interaction and the initiation of structure.[43] Four major variables are identified by *McGregor* as:

- the characteristics of the leader;
- the attitude, needs and other personal characteristics of the followers;
- the nature of the organisation, such as its purpose, its structure and the tasks to be performed; and
- the social, economic and political environment.

McGregor concludes that 'leadership is not a property of the individual, but a complex relationship among these variables'.[44]

According to *Kouzes and Posner*, 'credibility is the foundation of leadership'. From extensive research in over thirty countries and response to the question of what people 'look for and admire in a leader, in a person whose direction they would willingly follow', people have consistently replied that they want:

> *leaders who exemplify four qualities: they want them to be honest, forward-looking, inspiring and competent. In our research our respondents strongly agree that they want leaders with integrity and trustworthiness, with vision and a sense of direction, with enthusiasm and passion, and with expertise and a track record for getting things done.*[45]

Fullan refers to the importance of relationship building as a basic component of the change process and effective leadership: 'Leaders must be consummate relationship builders with diverse people and groups – especially with people different from themselves. Effective leaders constantly foster purposeful interaction and problem solving, and are wary of easy consensus.'[46]

Roddick makes the point that:

> *You have to look at leadership through the eyes of the followers and you have to live the message. What I have learned is that people become motivated when you guide them to the source of their own power and when you make heroes out of employees who personify what you want to see in the organisation.*[47]

Power, responsibility and wisdom

Lloyd suggests that the way we think about leadership is a contributory factor to the leadership crisis. Leadership has traditionally been associated with those who have power and there is a need to re-examine the core relationship between power and responsibility. Rather than gaining and keeping power for ourselves, more emphasis should be given to unifying consideration of the two concepts together with greater attention to the subject of wisdom.

> *The new agenda moves us from that narrow focus to a much broader concept of leadership that is more concerned with how power is used, i.e. in whose interest power is used. This explicitly recognises that the use of power is deeply values driven . . . We need to give much greater attention to the values agenda by exploring wisdom, then seeing that emphasis reflected as wise leadership.*[48]

Critical review and reflection

Whatever the debate on leadership relationship and ideas such as servant leadership, the harsh reality is that influence exercised by a leader depends on the amount of power and authority the leader can exert over other people.
  Can YOU present a strong argument against this assertion? What form of leadership influence best describes YOUR relationship with tutors or senior administrative staff?

Culture as a contingent factor?

The contribution of contingency approaches to understanding leadership suggests that contrasting types and styles of leadership may be more or less appropriate in different situations. A consistent view expressed within the literature is that a major variable influencing choice of leadership style may be national culture. We should be wary of stereotyping the behaviour of leaders or subordinates, and many myths appear to have grown around notions of 'orderly' German, 'undisciplined' Italian and even 'obstructive' British workers. However, there are reasons to suggest that there may indeed be national cultural differences that are relevant to an understanding of leadership.

Global Leadership and Organizational Behavior Effectiveness (GLOBE)

Project GLOBE was a large-scale research project that sought to identify those leader behaviours and attributes that would be accepted and therefore effective in all societies and, contrastingly, those that would only be accepted and effective in some cultural contexts. This study was conducted by an international team of researchers led by *Robert House* and encompassed sixty-two countries across the world, including some that had not always featured in cross-cultural study – for example, newly capitalist states in Eastern Europe. The GLOBE study commenced in 1991 and led to a series of publications in the early twenty-first century.[49]

The results, according to the GLOBE researchers, are some significant variations in leadership style, attributes and behaviour. Charismatic and team-orientated leaders were shown to be globally endorsed – and hence universally effective. Leaders who displayed high levels of trust, integrity and vision were supported by subordinates in all societies. It was also found that there were so-called universal impediments to success: for example, *self-protective* leaders characterised by malevolence and 'face-saving' were viewed negatively by subordinates in all cultures.

There were some aspects of leadership that varied between societies. In common with Hofstede (**see Chapter 1**), the GLOBE study identifies clusters of societies with important points of commonality. To take one example, in a situation that might imply a directive style of leadership, subordinates in the 'Anglo' cluster of societies (in effect, the main English-speaking countries) would prefer some degree of informality on the part of the leader and as much of a participative style as the situation allowed.

The GLOBE study recognises that strategic organisational contingencies such as the sector an organisation operates in will affect leadership style and behaviour. However, the GLOBE researchers concluded that such factors would be moderated by the national cultural context. Leader effectiveness will be influenced by the interaction between leaders and subordinates, which is dependent on the nature of power relations within the particular culture, and organisational contingencies applying in all societies.[50]

Differences or shared values?

According to *Walker*, too much focus in recent decades has been on Western approaches to leadership and that a study of alternative methods can help inspire leaders – wherever they are. In the Far East, for example, face-to-face contact and relationship building are prized more highly than here. Walker suggests that new thinking sees Asian business culture not as a challenge to be overcome but as a source of leadership inspiration.[51]

However, in response to the question of whether different business cultures affect how we view good leadership, *Murray* refers to the importance of shared company values overriding any cultural differences.

> *A shared set of company values is the glue that binds people, builds trust and enables an organisation to function across cultural barriers . . . While expectations on leaders might not be the same everywhere, and may have cultural variations, there is no doubt employees have a general desire to be respected, valued and involved. This is a trend that transcends geographical and cultural barriers. Leaders must respond to this demand, wherever they are.[52]*

Leadership effectiveness

Attention to style of leadership has come about because of a greater understanding of the needs and expectations of people at work. It has also been influenced by such factors as: broader standards of education and training and advances in scientific and technical knowledge; pressure for a greater social responsibility towards employees, for example through schemes of participation in decision-making and work/life balance; legislation, for example in the areas of employment protection; and influence of the European Union.

These factors have combined to create resistance against purely autocratic styles of leadership. There is an assumption that subordinates are more likely to work effectively for managers who adopt a certain style of leadership than for managers who adopt alternative styles.

Goleman reports that the most effective executives use a collection of distinct leadership styles, each in the right measure, at just the right time. Although the authoritative style of leadership can be occasionally overbearing, it was found to be most effective and can motivate and inspire commitment to the goals of the organisation. The affiliative style has potential to create harmony within teams and can be used in conjunction with the authoritative style. The democratic approach was seen as positive, and encourages input from staff and helps build consensus through participation. The coaching style, although the least frequently used, can help staff identify their strengths and encourage long-term development goals. The study concludes that the most effective leaders rely on more than one leadership style and were able to master a mixture of authoritative, democratic, affiliative and coaching styles. Leaders with the best results use most of the styles in a given week – seamlessly and in different measure – depending on the business situation.[53]

The shadow of leadership

Leadership is clearly a major feature of effective teamwork. Good leaders surround themselves with talented and capable members of staff, and their behaviour and actions serve as a role model. *McCabe* suggests that leaders who want to transform their performance and the effectiveness of the team should look at how their own shadow could be getting in the way. Leaders focus on what they see as important and they are typically quite unconscious of the unintended but massive impact they are having on their colleagues, teams and clients. All leaders cast a shadow, and whatever a particular leadership style, the shadow will affect others and can compromise people's engagement at work and business effectiveness. Leaders need to be fully aware of the shadow they cast and the impact they have on others.

> *To be successful, leaders today have to find ways to engage people's ideas, energy and inspiration and this means they will have to build much stronger relationships – and what will prevent such relationships from occurring is their shadow.[54]*

Authority without arrogance

In his discussion on the skills of clear leadership, and sustaining collaboration and partnership at work, *Bushe* draws attention to the importance of authority. Collaborative work systems may flatten hierarchies and reduce command and control but do not decrease or eliminate authority.

Authority and hierarchy are two separate things. In collaborative organisations authority is widely spread and more people are authorised to make decisions and take actions. Authority is the power to make and enforce decisions. This is one reason why these organisations need people using the skills of clear leadership: self-awareness, descriptiveness, curiosity and appreciation.[55]

The turbulent and uncertain economic situation of recent times has resulted in many commentators drawing attention to the expectations for clear, decisive and authoritative leadership. For example, *Masson* refers to the leadership attribute of self-assurance, being authentic and comfortable with whom you are. What leaders need is an acute self-awareness and to avoid arrogance.

> *That self-assurance needs to come with an honest assessment of oneself. The whole idea of perfection in leadership is outdated and unhelpful, and leaders who don't open themselves to feedback, and don't reflect on their own behavior, come across as arrogant. Part of being 'authentic' is being open to vulnerability and admitting to one's mistakes.*[56]

Reeves and Knell suggest that being a successful leader is less about who you are or what you do than about what you know. This includes four pieces of knowledge: where the organisation is heading; what is going on; who they are; and how to build a strong team. Leaders in the most successful organisations are authoritative but their secret is that they use their authority without arrogance. Successful leaders:

- build a 'culture of discipline' and are about getting things done, controlling costs and marshalling resources;
- keep in touch with how people are feeling – they do not waste time worrying if everyone is happy but understand the emotional temperament of the organisation and emotional responses from people;
- know where they are strong but also know their weaknesses and display a fierce humility;
- are motivated by what they build, such as great teams and talented people, rather than what they get;
- have a clear sense of where the organisation is going, but very often this is the result of collective decision-making in a talent team.[57]

No one best form of leadership

We have seen that there are many alternative forms and styles of managerial leadership. Within an organisation different individuals may fulfil the functions of leadership and there are many different styles of leadership. A potential danger with the contingency approach is that the manager may appear to lack consistency in leadership style. However, although subordinates may reasonably expect some degree of consistency from the manager in approaching the same type of problem with the same style, this is not to say that different types of problems should be approached in the same manner. Subordinates would ordinarily expect a different style of managerial leadership according to the contingencies of the situation.

Variables affecting leadership effectiveness

Clearly, there is no one 'best' form of leadership that will result in the maintenance of morale among group members and high work performance. Three main aspects to be considered in determining the most appropriate style of leadership are the manager, the group and the work environment. However, there are many variables that underlie the effectiveness of leadership in work organisations. More specifically, these include the following:

- **characteristics of the manager** – personality, attitudes, abilities, value-system and personal credibility;
- **type of power of the manager** and basis of the leadership relationship;
- **characteristics of the followers** – diversity, needs and expectations, attitudes, knowledge, confidence and experience, and motivation and commitment;
- type and nature of the organisation, organisation culture and structure;
- nature of the tasks to be achieved and time scales;

- technology, systems of communication and methods of work organisation;
- **informal organisation,** and the psychological contract;
- nature and influence of the external environment and national culture.

In addition there is an argument that physical attributes, such as height, can be associated with good leadership (**discussed in Chapter 6**).

Right style for the right situation

An effective manager will clearly recognise that different styles of leadership are called for in different situations. As an extreme example, emergency situations demand an assertive, directive style of action. (Recall the actual example of the Mumbai hotel attack given above.) As *Rajan* also points out: 'Of course, different leadership styles are needed to cope with different situations: for example, the autocratic style makes sense when an organisation is in deep trouble and needs to achieve a rapid turn-around. That style would be counter-productive when the organisation is in a growth situation.'[58]

And *Stern* maintains that although in more carefree times business gurus exalted leaders who admitted to frailty, this is not so any more. The task of sustaining growth in a sluggish market calls for driven, leather-skinned bosses. Instead of touchy-feely management the quality of 'mental toughness' is needed to help elite performers to prevail.[59]

Different types of leadership may also be most appropriate at different stages in the development of a business organisation. Leadership can also vary between public and private sectors and depend upon the size of the organisation. A primary challenge for organisational leaders in promoting innovation is to:

> *Recognise and develop appropriate leadership for the different stages of the innovation process. How leaders are selected, supported, evaluated, motivated and developed is likely to differ depending upon the stage of the innovation process they are responsible for. For instance, transformational leadership skills may be more useful in early-stage innovation activity, such as R & D and product development, but transactional leadership skills are also essential to the smooth functioning of commercialisation.*[60]

Critical review and reflection

There is much commentary on the need for less hierarchical structures and a changed culture of leadership based on skills and competencies throughout the organisation as a whole.

How realistic do YOU think this is? How do YOU believe leadership potential can best be developed? And what do YOU see as the future of leadership?

Alternative views of leadership

In recent years the changing nature of the work organisation, referred to at the start of this chapter, has drawn attention to different, broader approaches to the study of leadership, including shared and distributed leadership and responsible leadership.

Shared and distributed leadership

As with servant leadership, discussed earlier, the original idea of distributed leadership can be traced back many years. For example, *Mary Parker Follet,* writing in 1941, envisioned management responsibility not just concentrated at the top of the hierarchy, but diffused throughout the organisation from the depersonalising of orders and obeying the law of the situation.[61, 62]

Rather than a traditional view of a single, all-powerful and visionary appointed leader, the underlying concept of **shared and distributed leadership** is of multiple leaders throughout the organisation. As opposed to hierarchical leadership, distributed leadership gives recognition to the sharing of the leadership function, power and decision-making among staff at all levels and positions including the role of the informal organisation (**discussed in Chapter 3**). *Day et al.* suggest that collective leadership from many different members of the organisation is of more importance than the actions of any individual leader.[63]

With the continuing pace of change, developments in ICT and uncertain economic environment, leadership functions will evolve and leadership roles change according to the situation. With increasing emphasis on teamwork, attention has been focused on the significance of the leadership function for team performance. Greater awareness of the benefits from a more diverse workforce has also encouraged distributed leadership. *Hewlett et al.* draw attention to the wider community leadership roles of ethnic minority staff who may hold only junior positions in the organisation.[64]

Responsible leadership

The term **responsible leadership** has emerged as an organisation's approach to governance, social responsibilities and business ethics. According to Business In The Community, the challenge for business leaders is to ensure the wider responsibilities of business are understood within their organisation and in society to demonstrate how a responsible approach to business will create value.

> *Business leaders must be seen to act and demonstrate their commitment to creating a fairer society and a more sustainable future by fostering a culture that will encourage innovation, reward the right behaviours and regain trust. In short, leaders must write a new contract with society into their own business.[65]*

However, as the *Financial Times* points out:

> *Responsible Leadership, as a business school subject area, is less about ethical theory and more about ethical practice based on case studies. The practice has a particular focus on an individual's values system and the pragmatic application of an individual's values in the real-life challenging dilemmas of business.[66]*

Corporate responsibility and ethics are the subject of Chapter 14.

Management and organisational behaviour in action case study
The Post Office – Women in Leadership Programme

The Post Office is a commercial organisation with a social purpose. Its network of around 11,800 branches delivers over 170 products and services, serves 18 million customers per week and has 7,845 employees. Facing a specific challenge of declining female representation (March 2013: 61.4 per cent of frontline positions/43.8 per cent of first-line management/35.5 per cent of senior management/22.2 per cent of senior leadership), and a quarter of roles were part-time (90 per cent filled by women), it needed to increase females in senior teams. Initiatives included:

The Women in Leadership Programme
Senior Leadership Endorsement – the female chair and chief executive both acted as figure-heads. Sponsored by the Chief Executive, Paula Vennells, who attended each event to provide an introduction and undertake a question and answer session.

Transparent Diversity Targets – For 2013–14 the business set a target of appointing women into 40 per cent of its senior leadership and senior management roles, a 7 per cent increase on the 2012–13 out-turn.

Line Manager Support – workshops for seventy senior managers were run to explain the target and what people could do to support it. Sessions focused on the business case and unconscious bias.

Each event brings together eighty of the organisation's high-potential women identified through existing performance and potential data. The events take place every three months with the objectives of:

1. Profiling female role models (internal and external).
2. Working on real business problems (a recent event focused on our female SME customer proposition).
3. Networking (our full Executive is invited to the events so our aspiring female leaders can meet them informally).

Regular Follow-Up Communication – Bi-annual Women in Leadership events where high-potential women met role models, networked and worked on real business problems. Launch of a communications campaign called '3 minutes with' featuring an interview with someone in the Post Office with a diverse perspective. Feedback for the event has been very positive with an average rating of 9.5 out of 10. The outcome resulted in 45.7 per cent of women appointed into senior management roles. The senior leadership team is now 28.3 per cent female.

This activity is supporting the business to achieve a greater level of customer excellence and business engagement. The employee survey saw a 2 per cent increase in the level of customer understanding. The senior management talent programme identified 40 per cent female members, over 4 per cent above the wider female representation at that level and a female engagement index of 58 per cent– currently 7 per cent above the organisational norm.

Source: Aidan Alston, Talent and Diversity Manager, Post Office Ltd. Reproduced with permission.

Tasks

1. Give your views on the Women in Leadership Programme. What in particular do you think has contributed to the success of the programme?
2. Explain why you think there has been an under-representation of women in senior leadership positions.
3. Comment critically on the representation, and actual responsibilities, of women in senior leadership positions in your own university and/or other organisation with which you are familiar.

Leadership development

Education and training in management needs to emphasise not only interpersonal skills, but also a flexibility of approach, diagnostic ability and realisation that the most effective form of leadership behaviour is a product of the total leadership situation. *Melville-Ross* refers to the importance of developing leadership skills in everyone, not just those at the top.[67] Even people in the most junior positions can play a leadership role. It is about the dissemination of ideas, taking the initiative and encouraging others to see it that way. For this to happen, there has to be an open leadership culture that runs right through the organisation. People are encouraged to take personal responsibility and are not afraid to speak up with ideas or take risks.

The leadership jigsaw

Cutler has designed a 'jigsaw' of best practice. There are six interlinking pieces: vision, example, relationships, motivation, empowerment and communications as a guide to the measurement and development of leadership skills. Cutler believes that leadership is not such a difficult role if condensed to these essential elements and has devised a set of questions to help aspiring leaders to find out if they have all the necessary pieces of the jigsaw (*see* Figure 9.8).[68]

VISION – Do you:
1 Work hard at communicating your vision for the organisation to all staff at all levels?
2 Understand that your vision must appeal to your staff at both an emotional and practical level if they are to join you on your journey?
3 Understand the culture and values of your organisation and their impact on its future development?
4 Recognise blind alleys?

MOTIVATION – Do you:
1 Understand that every member has a different set of motivational stimuli?
2 Explain your decisions in terms of their benefit to the organisation and its members?
3 Celebrate and reward individual and team achievements?
4 Prefer to offer carrots, rather than wield sticks?

EXAMPLE – Do you:
1 Match your words with your actions?
2 Take full responsibility for organisational problems, even if you were not directly responsible?
3 Occasionally muck in when your staff are under pressure at work?
4 Regularly consider what you see in the bathroom mirror?

EMPOWERMENT – Do you:
1 Believe that people generally respond well when given greater responsibility for their own performance?
2 Allocate sufficient resources to training and development?
3 Get a buzz when staff set and achieve their own goals?
4 Realise that the organisation would still function if you were not there?

RELATIONSHIPS – Do you:
1 Work hard at countering a 'them and us' culture within your organisation?
2 Set clear codes of acceptable conduct and take action against breaches of them?
3 Stress that everyone contributes to the success of the team(s) they belong to?
4 Admit when you make a mistake?

COMMUNICATIONS – Do you:
1 Use your influence to encourage two-way communications at all levels in your organisation?
2 Encourage personal contact rather than written, mechanical or technological alternatives?
3 Encourage a diversity of opinion and constructive criticism?
4 Walk the talk?

Figure 9.8 The leadership 'jigsaw'
Source: Cutler, A. 'A Good Fit Is Essential', *Professional Manager*, vol. 15, no. 3, May 2005, p. 38. Reproduced with permission from Chartered Management Institute and Alan Cutler.

Seven principles for developing leaders

Referring to his action-centred leadership model (discussed earlier in this chapter), *Adair* identifies seven key principles of leadership development that can be applied successfully in different kinds of organisations in both the public and private sectors.

- **Development of a strategy for leadership development** for each of the three levels of leadership – operational, strategic and team.
- **Selection** of those with high potential for becoming effective leaders.
- **Training for leadership** that implies instruction with a specific end in view. Identify your business training needs in the leadership context and assign them priorities.
- **Career development** through giving a person the right job at the right time. People grow as leaders through the actual practice of leading.

- **Line managers as leadership developers** by developing the individual's potential and sharing their knowledge of leadership.
- **Corporate culture** that is valued at all levels and should encourage a climate of self-development in leadership.
- **The chief executive** who should be leading from the front and who owns the problem of growing leaders.

The seven principles are complementary and are likely to have a synergetic effect if applied as a whole. Although a simple framework, Adair maintains the seven principles form the first coherent and effective approach for growing leaders.[69]

> *We are not born as leaders, but we are born with the potential to become a leader. This potential has to be worked on and we have to go through a learning experience to equip us to become leaders. Sometimes the potential is realised and sometimes it is not. Opportunities play a part in this; the best organisations seem to grow their own leaders. The best, the very good and the excellent do give priority to developing leaders.*[70]

Intuitive intelligence in leadership

According to *Bacon*, a critical factor in leadership development is the intuitive intelligence of leaders, especially when it comes to decision-making. We use our instinct and intuition in many facets of our personal lives, but Bacon questions if we underutilise one of the most powerful leadership tools at work. Much credence is given to emotional intelligence (**discussed in Chapter 4**) but perhaps the greatest weapon for business decision-making is intuitive intelligence.

> *Many people feel that intuition has little or no place in business, that decisions should be based on empirical evidence rather than on trusting your gut feeling. But there is increasing evidence that intuition is more than merely a feeling. Many scientists now believe that it is, in fact, the result of our brains piecing together information and experiences to come to different, and less obvious conclusions.*

Bacon maintains that intuitive intelligence can be trained, and the best leaders have learned not only to just trust their instincts but to obey them by listening to one's own internal voice. Situations in which leaders rely most consistently on their intuitive intelligence include:

- **in a crisis** when rapid response is required;
- **high-speed change** when situations are changing rapidly without warning;
- **in a messy situation** when a problem or challenge is poorly constructed;
- **in an ambiguous situation** when there are contradictory factors to consider.[71]

Importance of self-awareness

An underlying feature of effective leadership is self-awareness: understanding who you are, and what you are thinking and feeling. *Benjamin* sees a leader simply as someone who takes the lead and whom other people are inclined to follow willingly. The sense of who you are is so important because leadership is, at heart, about leading people.

> *Approaching leadership with a clear sense of self will give you the strength to work with others respectfully but also the confidence to challenge another's opinion or authority because you know what you stand for, and what your principles and beliefs are.*[72]

Blanchard believes that all good leadership starts with a shared vision. The best and most respected leaders share not just their visions for the future of their organisations with their people, but also their personal beliefs about how and why they lead as they do. Blanchard suggests clarifying and sharing your leadership point of view means answering seven questions:

1. Who are the people who have influenced you in your life?
2. What is your life purpose?

3. What core values will guide your behaviour as you live your life 'on purpose'?

4. What are your beliefs about leading and motivating people?

5. What can people expect of you?

6. What do you expect from your people?

7. How will you set an example?[73]

In his discussion on the future of management, *Hamel* argues the point that in any constitutional democracy success does not depend upon brilliant leadership. If democracies are more resilient than large companies it is not because they are better led. In a democracy, the pace of change depends only tangentially on the vision and moral courage of those in power: 'The real challenge, then, isn't to hire or grow great leaders, but to build companies that can thrive with less-than-perfect leaders.'[74]

Critical review and reflection

Despite vast amounts of writing on the subject, it is extremely difficult to give a precise and agreed meaning of leadership. Nor is there agreement on one best model or style of leadership, or how leadership potential can best be developed.

Do YOU find this confusing and a hindrance to your studies? What do YOU believe are the essential and distinctive characteristics that make for an effective leader?

Ten key points to remember

1 There are many ways of looking at leadership but essentially it is a relationship through which one person influences the behaviour or actions of other people.

2 There is arguably a close relationship between leadership and management. However, it does not follow that every leader is a manager.

3 Due to its complex and variable nature, there are many alternative ways of analysing leadership and different approaches to study of the subject area.

4 A simple threefold heading of leadership behaviour is authoritarian, democratic or laissez-faire. Four main styles of leadership are tells, sells, consults and joins.

5 Contingency theories draw attention to major variables and forces in the situation as one of the main forces influencing the nature of managerial behaviour.

6 Attention has been focused on charisma, leaders creating a vision with which others can identify, and inspiring followers to improve organisational performance.

7 Leadership is a dynamic form of behaviour. The leadership relationship is a social process dependent upon the type of power and influence exercised over other people.

8 Attention needs to be given to the criteria for leadership effectiveness and sets of skills to work within less hierarchical-based systems of command and control.

9 There is no one 'best' form or style of leadership. There are many variables that underlie the effectiveness of leadership, including national culture.

10 Leadership development needs to emphasise interpersonal skills and recognise that successful leadership behaviour is a product of the total leadership situation.

Review and discussion questions

1   Explain clearly what you understand by the meaning of leadership and give your own definition. To what extent do you believe leadership differs from management?

2   Distinguish between different approaches to the study of leadership and discuss critically what you see as the relevance today of each of these approaches.

3   Using the Tannenbaum and Schmidt continuum, identify, with reasons, what would be your preferred style of leadership.

4   Assess the practical value to the manager of: (i) Fiedler's contingency model of leadership effectiveness; and (ii) Hersey and Blanchard's readiness of the followers or group situational model.

5   Discuss critically the contention that in times of uncertainty or economic depression a confident, authoritarian style of leadership is likely to be the most effective.

6   Explain clearly the nature and main features of transformational leadership. Give your own examples of people you would regard as transformational leaders. Discuss critically the relevance of personality and charisma for effective leadership.

7   Discuss the main sources of power and leadership influence. Give a practical example of each of these main sources of power and influence within your own university or organisation.

8   Explain why self-awareness is increasingly highlighted as an important feature of leadership. To what extent are you aware of who you are, and what you are thinking and feeling?

9   If you were a consultant on leadership, what areas of needs would you include in designing a leadership development programme for managers in a large work organisation? Justify your ideas.

10   Discuss the main situational forces and variables likely to influence the most appropriate form of managerial leadership. Give an example of when a particular style of leadership is likely to be most effective.

Assignment

Prepare to lead a seminar discussion in which you:

a.   Explain fully a situation from university and/or any work experience where you have been inspired by a person through their charisma and natural leadership authority.
b.   Identify clearly the specific personal qualities exhibited by the person.
c.   Describe how the experience has influenced your views on the nature of leadership.
d.   Debate the extent to which it is possible to learn charisma and the ability to inspire other people.
e.   Write a short paper in which you summarise conclusions from the discussion.

Personal skills and employability exercise

Objectives
Completing this exercise should help you to enhance the following skills:

•   Recognise your self-awareness and understanding of who you are.
•   Explore attributes associated with leadership.
•   Evaluate your readiness for a leadership role.

Exercise

Self-knowledge about who you are, and what you are thinking and feeling, is crucial if you are to be an effective and inspiring leader. Work together in small groups.

To gain maximum benefit from this exercise it is important to be completely honest with yourself.

First, for each of the following twenty-five items, consider honestly and fully the extent to which you:

1 Have a strong work ethic
2 Are adaptable to changes in the work situation
3 Place emphasis on service to others over self-interest
4 Stretch yourself to meet objectives
5 Take time in connecting with group members
6 Set yourself clear goals and criteria for success
7 Believe in doing things right the first time
8 Have strong moral values
9 Think leadership is simple if you have the right personality
10 Find it easy to compliment fellow colleagues
11 Are competitive and take pride in winning
12 Communicate easily your ideas, thoughts or concerns to others
13 Tolerate genuine mistakes by others that affect your work
14 Believe respect for superiors is more important than popularity
15 Enjoy others relying on you or coming to you for help
16 Respect hierarchical authority and chain of command
17 Believe leadership depends on confidence and courage
18 Are prepared to place trust in your fellow colleagues
19 Believe everyone is responsible for their own actions and behaviour
20 Get upset by disagreements or confrontation with your peers
21 Simplify and explain complex situations to others
22 Tend naturally to take the initiative in group situations
23 Encourage challenging debate and dialogue
24 Do not put off for tomorrow what can be done now
25 Believe you would make an effective leader

There are no right or wrong answers, but score and record each item from 1 to 10 with 10 as the highest. Second, share and discuss fully and openly your scoring among other members of the group.

Discussion

- How difficult was it for you to complete this exercise? How well do you think you know yourself?
- To what extent do colleagues agree with your own scoring, including an honest evaluation of your perceived readiness for a leadership role?
- What benefits have you gained from this exercise and what have you learned about yourself as a potential leader?

Case study
A change of leadership at Barclays Bank

On 4 July 2012, Bob Diamond, the former Group Chief Executive (GCE) of Barclays, who had resigned a few days earlier, was asked by Labour MP John Mann at a Treasury Select Committee hearing whether he could name the three Quaker values that had inspired the founders of Barclays. He could not, prompting this retort from Mann:

Honesty. Integrity. Plain dealing. That's the ethos of the bank you've just spent two hours telling us is doing so well – in fact so well that I wonder why you've not received an extra bonus rather than the sack.[75]

Diamond's replacement was Antony Jenkins, who was appointed in August 2012. The appointment was hailed

Source: Tupungato/Shutterstock.com

as a new chapter for the beleaguered bank, with press reports highlighting Jenkins' career experience at Barclays and Citibank,[76] his distinctly unflashy image and his solid track record of effectiveness, most recently at Barclaycard.[77]

Barclays under Diamond

The events that led to this remarkable transition can be briefly summarised. Bob Diamond had joined Barclays in 1996 and rose to head Barclays Capital, its investment banking[78] arm. An American by birth, his earlier career in the banking industry with Morgan Stanley and CS First Boston was in investment banking. Investment banking is mainly concerned with assisting individuals, businesses and governments to raise capital. These operations are important for the creation and growth of businesses, and although they are relatively risky, they can generate very high rewards. Retail or 'personal' banking, by contrast, involves providing banking services such as current and savings accounts, mortgages, loans, credit card operations, etc., directly to individual or business customers. Risks are lower, but so are potential profits. Barclays was a straightforward retail bank until the 1980s when changes to banking regulations gave it the opportunity to move into investment banking, which it did with some limited success.

When Diamond became CEO his priorities reflected his career background; his ambition for the company was to grow Barclays Capital into an operation that could rival the global banks of Wall Street. Following the financial crash of 2008, Barclays acquired the remains of Lehman Brothers' US operations for what looked (at the time) like a bargain price. In 2011, he was appointed GCE of Barclays, and in the same year delivered the BBC inaugural Today Business Lecture in which he argued for the importance of investment banking to the growth and development of businesses and

economies.[79] However, Diamond's style at Barclays was not universally popular and he was criticised for his very high pay levels and his apparent lack of humility; however, those criticisms became more focused as a series of scandals emerged in the banking industry. Many of these scandals – for example, the mis-selling of Payment Protection Insurance – involved a wide range of banks, but the UK's Financial Services Authority's report into the manipulation of the key interest rate known as LIBOR[80] was particularly critical of the behaviour of Barclays employees. By the summer of 2012, in the face of pressure from both the Bank of England and the Financial Services Authority,[81] the Barclays board bowed to the inevitable and Diamond resigned. In his evidence to the Select Committee, he remained adamant that he had not known about much of the malpractice, which led John Mann to suggest that:

> He was either in there doing it or deliberately turned a blind eye, or he was so useless that he couldn't see fiddling on his own trading floor [. . .] I think he must have known what was going on.[82]

Barclays under Jenkins

It is probably fair to say that the job of a bank CEO in the wake of such scandal is not only difficult, but also carried out under fairly hostile public scrutiny. Leading a successful organisation might be a tough job, but what are the leadership challenges faced by those attempting to restore damaged and unpopular organisations, and what qualities and behaviours are needed in such circumstances?

When Antony Jenkins became CEO in 2012 there were reports that the bank had struggled to find a successor, and that two of the most credible candidates had already turned down the job before Jenkins was approached. Unusually for a bank CEO, he is not an investment banker; he ran Barclays credit card operations and had also managed the retail arm of the business. The contrast with Diamond was clear:

> In Jenkins you've got the archetypal English CEO who is seen as rather safe, compared with the typically aggressive US investment banker that was Bob Diamond. His appointment signals that the bank is not going to be as brazen as it has been in the past.[83]

He has been described as the 'nice guy' of banking, a calm, softly spoken and mild-mannered individual who, nevertheless, could be 'scary'. He explains this by saying:

> What that means is you don't have to raise your voice or thump the table to get your point across. When you have a very measured style, you don't need to shout.

You just need to make your point a little more directly and people notice.[84]

In an early move to signal his views about the bank's road ahead, Jenkins circulated a letter to all 140,000 staff emphasising his commitment to restoring its integrity and reputation by a return to five 'core' values: respect, integrity, service, excellence and stewardship. He warned that:

There might be some who don't feel they can fully buy into an approach which so squarely links performance to the upholding of our values. My message to those people is simply: Barclays is not the place for you. The rules have changed. You won't feel comfortable at Barclays and, to be frank, we won't feel comfortable with you as colleagues.[85]

The strategy is known as the 'TRANSFORM'[86] programme, which aims to reinvigorate the bank not only morally but also commercially. To that end he has said that he would not indulge underperforming parts of the company, essentially the investment bank for which Diamond had such great ambitions. In 2014 Jenkins announced a three-year programme of job cuts that would see Barclays Capital lose 7,000 staff – a quarter of its workforce – as part of a general restructuring and simplification programme.

In the future, Barclays will be leaner, stronger, much better balanced and well positioned to deliver lower volatility, higher returns, and growth.[87]

In 2015 he continued to assert that he would not be 'patient' with poor returns from any part of the bank; again it was Barclays Capital that was underperforming and that seemed most under threat, and its relatively poor performance will clearly not be allowed to drag the bank down either in shareholder value or in reputation.[88]

Another contrast with the Diamond years was Jenkins' decision not to take the usual banker's bonus for his first two years in post. Whereas Diamond famously received £17 million total reward in 2011,[89] the jazz-loving Jenkins took the relatively modest sum of £5.4 million for his third year as CEO, including a £1.1 million bonus payment. Even so, some commentators considered that he had not yet fully earned this perk as the group's overall performance remained weak, particularly that of Barclays Capital. Additionally profits have been undermined by the need to set aside significant sums to cover the cost of litigation and potential regulatory fines as yet more scandals from earlier years come to light.[90]

Jenkins is seen as the 'clean-up guy' at Barclays. He has made a number of painful and important changes but the company is not yet out of the woods. It is still one of the most complained-about banks in the UK, the investment arm remains under serious threat and the shadows of its past misbehaviour still loom large. The challenge for Barclays continues, and it remains to be seen whether Jenkins' leadership can restore its good name and commercial fortunes.*

Tasks

1 To what extent could it be argued that Diamond was a leader but Jenkins is a manager? Explain your view with reference to concepts from the chapter.

2 Examine the tasks facing each of the two CEOs of Barclays at different points in the company's history. How did the business environment affect the requirements of leadership? Use one of the contingency models outlined in the chapter to explain your view.

3 Discuss the proposition that although Jenkins has adopted a strategy of transformation at Barclays, he is in fact a transactional, not a transformational, leader.

4 How many of the characteristics and behaviours of servant leadership (as identified by Spears and Yukl) can be identified in Jenkins' approach at Barclays? Explain which you think are present, and which are missing.

5 How far do you think cultural difference between the American and British approaches to banking and business contributed to the problems encountered by Diamond?

* The Barclays story continues to get more interesting, and you might like to catch up with the events of July 2015 when Jenkins was fired by the new Chairman, John McFarlane (see, for instance, the summary by Kamal Ahmed, Business Editor for the BBC, on 8 July 2015, **http://www.bbc.co.uk/news/business-33438914**).

Notes and references

1. See, for example, Adair, J. *Leadership and Motivation*, Kogan Page (2006).

2. *CBI The Path to Leadership: Developing a Sustainable Model within Organisations*, Caspian Publishing (2005), p. 4.

3. Zaleznik, A. 'Managers and Leaders: Are They Different?', *Harvard Business Review*, May–June 1977, pp. 67–78.

4. Kent, T. W. 'Leading and Managing: It Takes Two to Tango', *Management Decision*, vol. 43, no. 7/8, 2005, pp. 1010–17.

5. Belbin, R. M. *Changing the Way We Work*, Butterworth–Heinemann (1997), p. 98.

6. Radcliffe, S. *Leadership: Plain and Simple*, Financial Times Prentice Hall (2010).

7. Mintzberg, H. *Managing*, Financial Times Prentice Hall (2009), p.8.

8. Moorcroft, R. 'To Lead or to Manage? That Is the Question', *Manager, The British Journal of Administrative Management*, November 2005, p. 4.

9. Drucker, P. F. *The Practice of Management*, Heinemann Professional (1989), p. 156.

10. See, for example, Bryman, A. 'Leadership in Organisations', in Clegg, S. Hardy, C. and Nord, W. (eds) *Managing Organsations: Current Issues*, Sage (1999), pp. 26–62.

11. Kotter, J. P. 'What Leaders Really Do', *Harvard Business Review*, May–June 1990, p. 103.

12. Whitehead, M. 'Everyone's a Leader Now', *Supply Management*, 25 April 2002, pp. 22–4.

13. Adair, J. *Action-Centred Leadership*, Gower (1979); see also Adair, J. *The Skills of Leadership*, Gower (1984).

14. Tannenbaum, R. and Schmidt, W. H. 'How to Choose a Leadership Pattern', *Harvard Business Review*, May–June 1973, pp. 162–75, 178–80.

15. Fiedler, F. E. *A Theory of Leadership Effectiveness*, McGraw-Hill (1967).

16. See, for example, Yukl, G. *Leadership in Organizations*, fifth edition, Prentice Hall (2002).

17. Vroom, V. H. and Yetton, P. W. *Leadership and Decision-Making*, University of Pittsburgh Press (1973).

18. House, R. J. 'A Path–Goal Theory of Leadership Effectiveness', *Administrative Science Quarterly*, vol. 16, September 1971, pp. 321–38.

19. House, R. J. and Dessler, G. 'The Path–Goal Theory of Leadership', in Hunt, J. G. and Larson, L. L. (eds) *Contingency Approaches to Leadership*, Southern Illinois University Press (1974).

20. Hersey, P. and Blanchard, K. H. *Management of Organizational Behavior: Utilizing Human Resources*, sixth edition, Prentice Hall (1993).

21. Burns, J. M. *Leadership*, Harper & Row (1978).

22. Bass, B. M. *Leadership and Performance Beyond Expectations*, Free Press (1985).

23. Bass, B. M. and Avolio, B. J. *Improving Organizational Performance Through Transformational Leadership*, Sage (1994).

24. Yukl, G. *Leadership in Organizations*, sixth edition, Pearson (2006).

25. Kreitner, R., Kinicki, A. and Buelens, M. *Organizational Behaviour*, First European edition, McGraw-Hill (1999), p. 487.

26. Gratton, L. *The Democratic Enterprise*, Financial Times Prentice Hall (2004).

27. Goffee, R. and Jones, G. *Why Should Anyone Be Led By You?*, Harvard Business School Press (2006).

28. Weber, M. *The Theory of Social and Economic Organization*, Oxford University Press (1947).

29. Conger, J. 'Charisma and How to Grow It', *Management Today*, December 1999, pp. 78–81.

30. Conger, J. 'The Danger of Delusion', *Financial Times*, 29 November 2002.

31. Adair, J. *The Inspirational Leader: How to Motivate, Encourage and Achieve Success*, Kogan Page (2003).

32. Kanter, R. M. *Confidence: Leadership and the Psychology of Turnarounds*, Random House (2004), pp. 325–6.

33. Kingsmill, D. ' Leaders who can recruit and reward teams for their unique skills will always achieve the best results', *Management Today*, September 2014, p. 20.

34. Greenleaf, R. K., *Servant Leadership: A Journey into the Nature of Legitimate Power and Greatness*, Paulist Press (1977); see also, for example, Spears, L. C. and Lawrence, M. (eds.) *Practicing servant leadership: Succeeding through trust, bravery and forgiveness*, Jossey-Bass (2004).

35. See also, for example, Smith, B. N., Montagno, R. V. and Kuzmenko, T. N. 'Transformational and servant leadership: Content and contextual comparisons', *Journal of Leadership & Organizational Studies*, vol. 10, no. 4, 2004, pp. 80–91.

36. 'What is Servant Leadership?', Greenleaf Centre for Servant Leadership, www.Greenleaf.org (accessed 2 September 2011).

37. See, for example, Brownell, J. 'Leadership in the Service of Hospitality', *Cornell Hospitality Quarterly*, vol. 51, no. 3, 2010, pp. 363–78.

38. Spears, L. C. (ed.) *Reflections on Leadership*, Wiley (1997).

39. Yukl, G. *Leadership in Organizations*, seventh edition, Pearson (2010).

40. Wong, P. T. P. 'Best Practices in Servant Leadership', *School of Global Leadership & Entrepreneurship*, Regent University, July 2007, pp. 1–15.

41. French, J. R. P. and Raven, B. 'The Bases of Social Power', in Cartwright, D. and Zander, A. F. (eds) *Group Dynamics: Research and Theory,* third edition, Harper & Row (1968).

42. Yukl, G. *Leadership in Organizations,* sixth edition, Pearson Prentice Hall (2006).

43. Bass, B. M. *Handbook of Leadership: Theory, Research and Managerial Applications*, third edition, Free Press (1990), p. 11.

44. McGregor, D. *The Human Side of Enterprise,* Penguin (1987), p. 182.

45. Kouzes, J. M. and Posner, B. Z. 'The Janusian Leader', in Chowdhury, S. (ed.) *Management 21C,* Financial Times Prentice Hall (2000), p. 18.

46. Fullan, M. *Leading in a Culture of Change,* Jossey-Bass (2001), p. 5.

47. Roddick, A. *Body and Soul,* Ebury Press (1991), p. 214.

48. Lloyd, B. 'Balancing Power with Responsibility and Wisdom', *Professional Manager,* vol. 17, no. 3, 2008, p. 37.

49. House, R. J., Hanges, P. J., Javidan, M., Dorfman, P. J. and Gupta, V. (eds) *Culture, Leadership, and Organizations: The GLOBE Study of 62 Societies,* Sage (2004).

50. For a fuller account of Project GLOBE see French, R. *Cross-Cultural Management,* second edition, Chartered Institute of Personnel and Development (2010).

51. Walker, B. 'Feast On The East', *Professional Manager,* Spring 2014, pp. 46–9.

52. Murray, K. in conversation with Benner, V. 'Is good leadership the same around the world?', *Professional Manager,* September/October 2012, p. 24.

53. Goleman, D. 'Leadership That Gets Results', *Harvard Business Review,* vol. 78, no. 2, March–April 2000, pp. 78–90.

54. McCabe, B. 'The Disabling Shadow of Leadership', *Manager, The British Journal of Administrative Management,* April/May 2005, pp. 16–17.

55. Bushe, G. R. *Clear Leadership,* Davies-Black (2009). For a short extract, see *Manager, The British Journal of Administrative Management,* Summer 2009, pp. 26–7.

56. Masson, L. 'Leading through Turbulent Times', *Chartered Secretary,* June 2008, p. 16.

57. Reeves, R. and Knell, J. 'Your Mini MBA', *Management Today,* March 2009, pp. 60–4.

58. Rajan, A. 'Meaning of Leadership in 2002', *Professional Manager,* March 2002, p. 33.

59. Stern, S. 'If You Think You're Hard Enough', *Management Today,* March 2003, pp. 46–51.

60. 'Leadership for Innovation', Advanced Institute of Management Research, March 2005.

61. Metcalfe, H and Urwick, L (eds), *Dynamic Adnministration – The collected papers of Mary Parker Follett,* Harper (1941).

62. See also Semler, R. 'Managing without managers', *Harvard Business Review,* September–October 1989, pp. 76–84.

63. Day, D. V., Gronn, P. and Salas, E., 'Leadership capacity in teams', *Leadership Quarterly,* vol. 15, 2004, pp. 857–80.

64. Hewlett, S.A., Luce, C. B. and West, C., 'Leadership in your midst: Tapping the hidden strengths of minority executives', *Harvard Business Review,* vol. 83, 2005, pp. 74–82.

65. 'Responsible leadership', Business In The Community, **www.bitc.org.uk/issues/responsibleleadership** (accessed 3 October 2014).

66. 'Responsible leadership', *Financial Times,* **http://lexicon. ft.com/=responsible-leadership** (accessed 4 October 2014).

67. Melville-Ross, T. 'A Leadership Culture has to Run Right Through an Organisation', *Professional Manager,* vol. 16, no. 1, 2007, pp. 18-21.

68. Cutler, A. 'A Good Fit Is Essential', *Professional Manager,* vol. 14, no. 3, 2005, p. 38.

69. Adair, J. *How to Grow Leaders,* Kogan Page (2005).

70. 'A Conversation with John Adair', *Manager,* April/May 2007, p. 20.

71. Bacon, B. 'Intuitive intelligence in leadership', *Governance + Compliance,* September 2013, pp. 24–5.

72. Benjamin, D. 'In my opinion', *Management Today,* May 2011, p. 58.

73. Blanchard, K 'Developing your leadership point of view', *Manager, The British Journal of Administrative Management,* Spring 2010, p. 15.

74. Hamel, G. with Breen, B. *The Future of Management,* Harvard Business School Press (2007), p. 169.

75. Transcript available at **http://www.parliament.uk/ documents/commons-committees/treasury/Treasury-Committee-04-July-12-Bob-Diamond.pdf** (accessed 4 March 2015).

76. **http://m.bbc.co.uk/news/business-19421534** (accessed 4 March 2015).

77. **http://www.bloomberg.com/bw/articles/2012-09-06/ barclays-gets-a-quiet-leader-for-a-change** (accessed 4 March 2015)

78. Investment banking is defined at **http://www. investopedia.com/terms/i/investment-banking.asp** It is usually defined in contrast to 'retail' banking, which provides the more familiar services such as bank account management, lending, savings products and taking deposits.

79. BBC Today Business Lecture 2011, **http://news.bbc. co.uk/today/hi/today/newsid_9630000/9630673.stm** (accessed 5 March 2015).

80. LIBOR, or the London Interbank Offer Rate, determines the rate of interest at which banks lend money to each other on the open market. A number of banks had been colluding in what was essentially a price-fixing exercise, and Barclays was the first to be investigated and fined by the then Financial Services Authority.

81. http://m.bbc.co.uk/news/business-18690102 (accessed 4 March 2015).

82. The Telegraph online, **http://www.telegraph.co.uk/ finance/newsbysector/banksandfinance/9374516/Bob-Diamond-questioned-by-MPs-on-Barclays-Libor-scandal-as-it-happened.html** (accessed 5 March 2015).

83. **http://www.bloomberg.com/bw/articles/2012-09-06/ barclays-gets-a-quiet-leader-for-a-change** (accessed 4 March 2015).

84. **http://www.telegraph.co.uk/finance/6591628/Nice-guy-of-banking-Antony-Jenkins-is-the-big-winner-at-Barclays.html** (accessed 5 March 2015).

85. Moore, J. 'Can Antony Jenkins get rid of Bob Diamond's legacy at Barclays?', *Independent*, 17 January 2013, **http://www.independent.co.uk/news/business/ analysis-and-features/can-antony-jenkins-get-rid-of-bob-diamonds-legacy-at-barclays-8456614.html** (accessed 5 March 2015).

86. Turnaround, Return Acceptable Numbers, Sustain FORward Momentum.

87. **http://www.telegraph.co.uk/finance/newsbysector/ banksandfinance/10815350/Barclays-cuts-7000-investment-bank-jobs-in-overhaul.html** (accessed 5 March 2015).

88. **http://www.telegraph.co.uk/finance/newsbysector/ banksandfinance/11445210/Barclays-sets-aside-another-750m-for-FX-rigging-fines.html** (accessed 5 March 2015).

89. **http://www.theguardian.com/business/2012/mar/ 09/barclays-chief-bob-diamond-pay** (accessed 5 March 2015).

90. Guthrie, J. 'Barclays: Antony Jenkins's L'Oréal moment', Ft.com, **http://www.ft.com/cms/s/0/48dc4866-c184-11e4-8b74-00144feab7de.html#axzz3TWh45dva** (accessed 5 March 2015).

CHAPTER 10
Understanding management

Management is fundamental to the effective operation of work organisations. It is by the process of management and execution of work that the activities of the organisation are carried out. Management is essentially an integrating activity that permeates every facet of the operations of an organisation. Attention must be given to the manner in which management is exercised and forms of managerial behaviour.

Learning outcomes

After completing this chapter you should have enhanced your ability to:

- explain the main activities and processes of management;
- analyse the essential nature of managerial work;
- contrast management in private-enterprise and public-sector organisations;
- outline empirical studies on the nature of managerial work;
- examine styles of managerial behaviour;
- debate suggested philosophies for managing with and through people;
- review the importance and future of management.

Critical review and reflection

Managers do not really have much influence. They follow where the organisation appears to be going, and avoid upsetting other people or making serious errors. People regarded as good managers are usually those who are remembered as not being bad managers.

How far do YOU agree with this assertion? What is YOUR experience of a good manager?

The importance of management

Organisations can only achieve their goals and objectives through the co-ordinated efforts of their members. It is by the process of management and execution of work that the activities of the organisation are carried out. Effective management is clearly essential for organisational success.

In certain respects everyone can be regarded as a manager. We all manage our own time and everyone has some choice whether or not to do something, and some control, however slight, over the planning and organisation of their work. However, we are concerned with management as involving people looking beyond themselves and exercising formal authority over the activities and performance of other people.

Even within a work organisation one cannot necessarily identify a manager by what a person is called or by their job title. In some organisations there is a liberal use of the title 'manager' in an apparent attempt to enhance the status and morale of staff. As a result there are a number of people whose job title includes the term 'manager' but who, in reality, are not performing the full activities of a manager. Yet there are many people whose job title does not include the term 'manager' but who, in terms of the activities they undertake and the authority and responsibility they exercise, may be very much a manager.

Management as making things happen

For our purposes, therefore, we can regard **management** as:

- taking place within a structured organisational setting with prescribed roles;
- directed towards the attainment of aims and objectives;
- achieved through the efforts of other people; and
- using systems and procedures.

At its most basic, management may be viewed as 'making things happen'. Recall also the discussion on the nature of leadership (**see Chapter 9**). Whereas leaders are not necessarily managers, it could be argued that all managers should be leaders.

It is the responsibility of management to manage. But organisations can achieve their aims and objectives only through the co-ordinated efforts of their members. This involves good people management.

A heavy responsibility is placed on managers and the activity of management – on the processes, systems and styles of management. Attention must be given to the work environment and appropriate systems of motivation, job satisfaction and rewards. It is important to remember that improvement in organisational performance will come about only through the people who are the organisation. It is also important to bear in mind that the activity of management takes place within the broader context of the organisational setting and subject to the organisational environment and culture. There are also variations in systems and styles of management and in the choice of managerial behaviour. Figure 10.1 shows a basic five-stage framework of study.

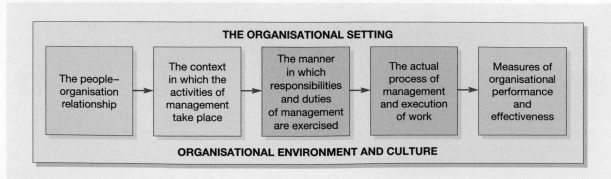

Figure 10.1 A basic framework of study

But what *is* management?

Management is a generic term and subject to many interpretations. A number of contrasting ideas are attributed to the meaning of management and to the work of a manager.[1] There are also different ways of viewing the study and knowledge of management. *Drucker* sees management as denoting a function as well as the people who discharge it, a social position and authority, and also a discipline and field of study: 'Management is tasks. Management is a discipline. But management is also people. Every achievement of management is the achievement of a manager. Every failure is a failure of a manager.'[2]

Significance of cultural influences

Schneider and Barsoux contend that trying to define the meaning of management shows up differences in beliefs and values. Cultural influences are a significant feature of management. Managers in some countries might have more concern for the 'spiritual' aspects of management, while in others there would be greater concern for the business sense. Developing people through work could be seen as an intrusion of privacy, and others may perceive empowerment as another name for manipulation.[3] According to *Francesco and Gold,* if international managers are to perform successfully in the global economy they need to understand the effects of different cultures on organisational behaviour. Reliance on theories developed in one culture is not sufficient.[4]

Managers born or made? Management an art or science?

There is frequent debate about whether managers are born or made or whether management is an art or a science. Briefly, the important point is that neither of these is a mutually exclusive alternative. Even if there are certain innate qualities that make for a potentially good manager, these natural talents must be encouraged and developed through proper guidance, education and training, and planned experience. Clearly, management must always be something of an art, especially in so far as it involves practice, personal judgement and dealing with people. However, it still requires knowledge of the fundamentals of management, and competence in the application of specific skills and techniques – as illustrated, for example, with developments in IT.

> *The trouble is that, for all the techniques at their disposal, managers generally act at a very intuitive level. Managers may have absorbed the latest thinking on core competencies, but are more likely to base a decision on prejudice or personal opinion rather than a neat theory.*[5]

The discussion of management as an art or a science is developed by *Watson,* who suggests that in order to make sense of the complex and highly ambiguous situations in which managers find themselves, management can be viewed not only as both art and science, but also as magic and politics (*see* Figure 10.2).[6]

Two views on management as a science

Dib provides an account of hearing contrasting views on management as a science. One view is *yes* – there is clearly science in management although a purely scientific approach omits human beings as the most important factor. Management is about the application of knowledge: 'The most successful managers are those who use scientific models, theories and concepts, and then apply them using their own style, experience and personality.' The other view is *no* – both management and science apply and extend our knowledge, but management needs more than just observations and experiments and needs to be based on practice, reflection and action. Management is too eclectic to be a science in itself: 'The very nature of management means that without applying and reflecting upon the practice of management we will be more inclined to measure than to take action'.[7]

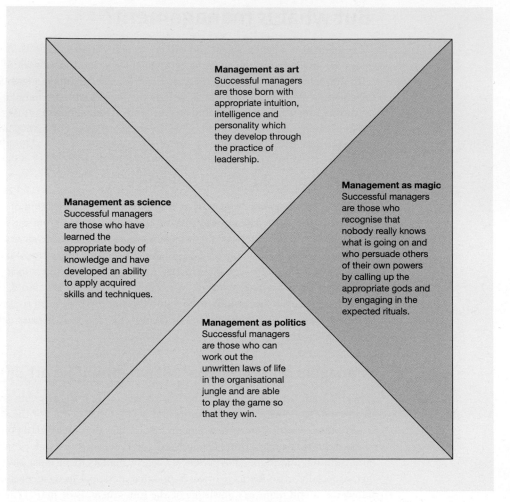

Figure 10.2 Management as art, science, magic and politics

Source: From Watson, T. J. *Management, Organisation and Employment Strategy*, Routledge & Kegan Paul (1986), p. 29. Reproduced by permission of the publishers, Routledge, a division of Taylor & Francis, Ltd.

Thinking about management at university level

Foppen questions the relationship between management practice and education, and whether management has not always been illusory. However, Foppen emphasises the importance of management performance.

> *Management is of pivotal importance for modern society. It is for this reason that, no matter what, thinking about management, certainly at university level, is of great relevance to management practice. So apart from the question of whether management's claim that it is indispensable is really valid or not, the fact that practically everyone believes it is, is what counts.[8]*

Critical review and reflection

According to Foppen, management is of pivotal importance for modern society and thinking about management at university level is of great relevance to management practice.

To what extent is YOUR course of study encouraging YOU to think about management? How do YOU see the relationship between management practice and management education?

The process of management

The nature of management is variable. It is not a separate, discrete function but relates to all activities of the organisation. It cannot be departmentalised or centralised. With the possible exception of the board of directors, or similar, an organisation cannot have a department of management in the same way as it can have a department for other functions, such as research and development, production, marketing or finance. Management is seen best, therefore, as a process common to all other functions carried out within the organisation. Through the execution of work, the central focus of management is on achieving the goals and objectives of the organisation, and satisfying the needs and expectations of its members. **As mentioned earlier (Chapter 1), management is essentially an integrating activity** (*see* Figure 10.3).

But what does the process of management actually involve and what activities does it encompass? Management is a complex and discursive subject. Moreover, 'management' is not homogeneous. It takes place in different ways and at different levels of the organisation. One approach, especially favoured by classical writers, is to analyse the nature of management and to search for common activities (or functions, or elements) applicable to managers in all organisations.

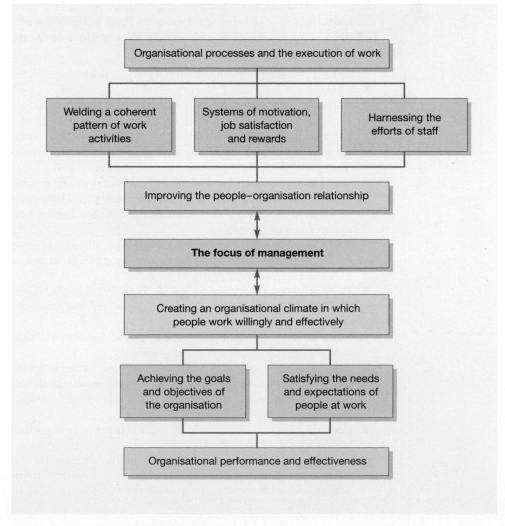

Figure 10.3 The central focus of management

Common activities of management

One of the first, and most widely quoted, analyses is that given by *Henri Fayol* (1841–1925), who divided the managerial activity into five elements of management, defined as: 'to forecast and plan, to organise, to command, to co-ordinate and to control':[9]

- **Forecasting and planning** – examining the future, deciding what needs to be achieved and developing a plan of action.
- **Organising** – providing the material and human resources and building the structure to carry out the activities of the organisation.
- **Commanding** – maintaining activity among personnel, getting the optimum return from all employees in the interests of the whole organisation.
- **Co-ordinating** – unifying and harmonising all activities and efforts of the organisation to facilitate its working and success.
- **Controlling** – verifying that everything occurs in accordance with plans, instructions, established principles and expressed commands.

Principles of management

Fayol also suggests that a set of well-established principles would help concentrate general discussion on management theory. He emphasises, however, that these principles must be flexible and adaptable to changing circumstances. Fayol recognised that there was no limit to the principles of management but in his writing advocated fourteen of them:

1. **Division of work.** The object is to produce more and better work from the same effort, and the advantages of specialisation. However, there are limits to division of work, which experience and a sense of proportion tell us should not be exceeded.

2. **Authority and responsibility.** Responsibility is the corollary of authority. Wherever authority is exercised, responsibility arises. The application of sanctions is essential to good management, and is needed to encourage useful actions and to discourage their opposite. The best safeguard against abuse of authority is the personal integrity of the manager.

3. **Discipline** is essential for the efficient operation of the organisation. Discipline is, in essence, the outward mark of respect for agreements between the organisation and its members. The manager must decide on the most appropriate form of sanction in cases of offences against discipline.

4. **Unity of command.** In any action an employee should receive orders from one superior only; if not, authority is undermined and discipline, order and stability threatened. Dual command is a perpetual source of conflicts.

5. **Unity of direction.** In order to provide for unity of action, co-ordination and focusing of effort, there should be one head and one plan for any group of activities with the same objective.

6. **Subordination of individual interest to general interest.** The interest of the organisation should dominate individual or group interests.

7. **Remuneration of personnel.** Remuneration should as far as possible satisfy both employee and employer. Methods of payment can influence organisational performance and the method should be fair and should encourage keenness by rewarding well-directed effort, but not lead to overpayment.

8. **Centralisation** is always present to some extent in any organisation. The degree of centralisation is a question of proportion and will vary in particular organisations.

9. **Scalar chain** – the chain of superiors from the ultimate authority to the lowest ranks. Respect for line authority must be reconciled with activities that require urgent action, and with the need to provide for some measure of initiative at all levels of authority.

10. **Order.** This includes material order and social order. The object of material order is avoidance of loss. There should be an appointed place for each thing, and each thing in its appointed place. Social order involves an appointed place for each employee, and each employee in their appointed place. Social order requires good organisation and good selection.

11. **Equity.** The desire for equity and for equality of treatment are aspirations to be taken into account in dealing with employees throughout all levels of the scalar chain.

12. **Stability of tenure of personnel.** Generally, prosperous organisations have stable managerial personnel, but changes of personnel are inevitable and stability of tenure is a question of proportion.

13. **Initiative.** This represents a source of strength for the organisation and should be encouraged and developed. Tact and integrity are required to promote initiative and to retain respect for authority and discipline.

14. **Esprit de corps** should be fostered, as harmony and unity among members of the organisation are a great strength in the organisation. The principle of unity of command should be observed. It is necessary to avoid the dangers of divide and rule of one's own team, and the abuse of written communication. Wherever possible, verbal contacts should be used.

A number of these principles relate directly to, or are influenced by, the organisation structure in which the process of management takes place.

Relevance today

Inevitably there are doubts about the relevance of these activities and principles today, but it is hard to argue against their continuing, underlying importance. What is perhaps debatable is the manner of their interpretation and implementation. *McLean* maintains that although proposed almost a hundred years ago, Fayol's definition of management remains one of the most cited of modern times. Fayol has left an indelible mark on management history, and forged an inextricable link between the manager and the organisation.[10]

Hamel suggests that there would be little argument from modern-day executives about Fayol's description of the work of a manager, but puts forward his own synthesis of what the *practice* of management entails:

- Setting and programming *objective*
- Motivating and aligning *effort*
- Co-ordinating and controlling *activities*
- Developing and assigning *talent*
- Accumulating and applying *knowledge*
- Amassing and allocating *resources*
- Building and nurturing *relationships*
- Balancing and meeting *stakeholder demands*.[11]

Critical review and reflection

Despite criticisms of the prescriptive nature of activities and principles of management, they do provide important guidelines for establishing a framework within which the work of an organisation is carried out.

What is YOUR opinion? To what extent do activities and principles of management appear relevant to the execution of work in YOUR university or organisation?

Responsibility for the work of other people

Yet another approach to describing management is given by *Drucker*, who identifies three tasks, equally important but essentially different, that have to be performed:

1. Fulfilling the specific purpose and mission of the institution, whether business enterprise, hospital or university.
2. Making work productive and the worker achieving.
3. Managing social impacts and social responsibilities.[12]

Drucker also argued that the traditional definition of management based on the responsibility for the work of other people is unsatisfactory and too narrow, and emphasises a secondary rather than a primary characteristic. There are people, often in responsible positions, who are clearly 'management' but who do not have responsibility for the work of other people. A person's function and contribution may be unaffected by the number of subordinate staff. A 'manager' is someone who performs the tasks of management whether or not they have power over others.

> Who is a manager can be defined only by that person's function and by the contribution he or she is expected to make. And the function that distinguishes the manager above all others is the function no one but the manager can perform. The one contribution a manager is uniquely expected to make is to give others vision and ability to perform. It is vision and moral responsibility that, in the last analysis, define the manager.[13]

Drucker was, according to *Stern*, a visionary predicting future trends ahead of the rest and dealing with big ideas but in a practical and down-to-earth way. His work and insights have lasted. Drucker was arguably the foremost thinker on management and business of the twentieth century and we need him as much as ever.[14]

Essential nature of managerial work

Despite the view expressed by Drucker (in 1977) on the tasks and contribution of a manager, one of the most popular ways of defining management today is that it involves getting work done second-hand – that is, through the efforts of other people. Managers are judged, ultimately, not just on their own performance but on the results achieved by subordinate staff. If we look at how people at work actually spend their time, we should be able to distinguish between those whose main occupation is the carrying out of discrete tasks and the actual doing of work themselves, and those who spend proportionally more of their time in determining the nature of work to be undertaken by other people, the planning and organising of their work, providing directions and advice and guidance, and checking on their performance.

'Managing' and 'doing'

By distinguishing 'managing' from 'doing' in this way, we can see management as clarifying objectives and the planning of work, organising the distribution of activities and tasks to other people, direction of subordinate staff and controlling the performance of other people's work. **This provides us with a convenient description and summary of managerial work as the clarification of objectives, planning, organising, directing and controlling** (*see* Figure 10.4). The degree of emphasis given to these different activities may vary widely, however, from one manager to another. Some managers are likely to spend more time on certain activities than

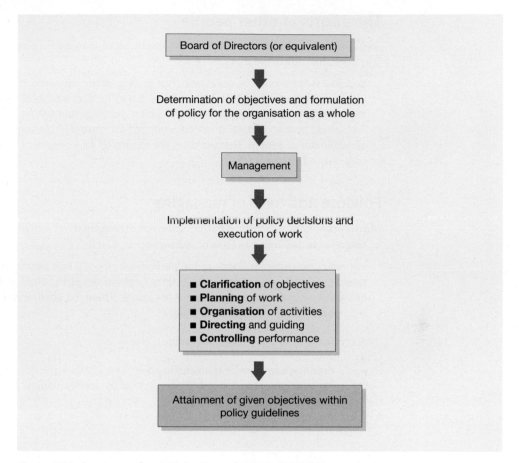

Figure 10.4 Summary of essential nature of managerial work

other managers. The application of these activities reflects a wide range of organisational situations, management practice and managerial style.

Direction, motivation or leadership?

It is tempting to use the term 'motivating' or 'leading', as preferred by some other writers, instead of 'directing' as is shown in our definition of the activities of management above. Motivation and leadership are perhaps less emotive words, but is either an adequate description? It is certainly part of the manager's job to motivate staff, but it also involves development and guidance. Staff need **to perform well in the right areas,** and to be effective as well as efficient. Leadership is clearly important but the efforts of staff need to be **directed** towards the achievement of given objectives in accordance with stated policy. This involves the process of control. It is acknowledged that control is another emotive word and some writers prefer alternatives such as monitoring, inspecting or checking – although, whatever the wording, the functions that it embraces are usually very similar. The real importance is not the particular term itself but what it is intended to achieve and the manner in which 'control' is exercised (**see Chapter 13**). For example, according to *Sir Alex Ferguson:*

> *Management is all about control. Success gives you control and control gives you longevity as a manager. In football very few managers achieve a position of complete control over their teams.*[15]

The efforts of other people

Stewart attempts to integrate the various definitions of management and summarises the manager's job, broadly defined as:

> deciding what should be done and then getting other people to do it. A longer definition would be concerned with how these tasks are to be accomplished. The first task comprises setting objectives, planning (including decision-making), and setting up formal organization. The second consists of motivation, communication, control (including measurement), and the development of people. The two tasks are separated for convenient analysis, but in practice they may often overlap.[16]

Folklore and facts of managing

Mintzberg suggests that the basic processes of managing do not change much over time. But he refers to the folklore and facts of managing.

> We have this common image of the manager, especially in a senior job, as a reflective, systematic planner 'sitting at a desk, thinking grand thoughts, making great decisions, and, above all, systematically planning out the future.' There is a good deal of evidence about this, but not a shred of it supports this image.
>
> Facts: Study after study has shown that
>
> (a) managers work at an unrelenting pace;
> (b) their activities are typically characterized by brevity, variety, fragmentation, and discontinuity; and
> (c) they are strongly oriented to action.[17]

Critical review and reflection

The idea of 'getting work done through the efforts of other people' may not satisfy all possible criteria for the role of the manager. It does, however, have the advantage of simplicity and focuses on what in reality is at the heart of effective management.

What do YOU think? Do YOU agree with Drucker that this definition is unsatisfactory? How would YOU define the true meaning of management?

Management in private-enterprise and public-sector organisations

The general movement of major organisations away from direct governmental control to greater responsibility for managing their own affairs has led to blurring of the traditional distinction between the private and public sectors (**see discussion in Chapter 3**). There are, however, still perceived differences between management in the private and public sectors. These differences arise from particular features of public-sector organisations. For example:

* aims concerned with providing a service for, and for the well-being of, the community rather than just of a commercial nature;
* the scale, variety and complexity of their operations;
* the tendency for them to be subject more to press reports on their activities;

- the political environment in which they operate, and in the case of local government, for example, the relationship between elected members and permanent officers;
- high levels of statutory regulations, legislation and ministerial guidance;
- the generally high level of trade union involvement;
- difficulties in measuring standards of performance of services provided compared with profitability;
- demand for uniformity of treatment and public accountability for their operations;
- tendency towards more rigid HR policies – for example, specific limitations on levels of authority and responsibility, fixed salary grades based on general pay scales, long-term career structures and set promotion procedures.

A number of these features frequently combine to result in increased bureaucracy within public-sector organisations.

Same general problems of management

Both private-enterprise and public-sector organisations, however, face the same general problems of management. Both are concerned with, for example:

- the clarification of aims and objectives;
- the design of a suitable structure;
- carrying out essential administrative functions; and
- the efficiency and effectiveness of their operations.

Basic principles of management apply in any series of activities in any organisation. Although actual methods and procedures will of necessity differ, the common activities and concerns of management apply to a greater or lesser extent in both private-enterprise and public-sector organisations. However, as *Walker* points out:

> *Despite the talent in all three sectors of the economy, cultural differences, alien practices and even mutual suspicion mean moving between the private, public and voluntary sectors can be a bumpy ride.*

Beyond differences in management styles, a key factor is that in the private sector there is more of a strategic focus, while in the public sector it is much more about here and now. Nine out of ten private-sector employers would be unlikely to take employees offloaded from the public sector.[18]

Richard Vince is the Governor of HMP Manchester, the only UK prison to be run by the prison service under a government contract

I don't have to make a profit. I don't pay dividends. And I don't have shareholders or owners in the strictest sense of the word. I am less exposed to the market and less exposed to financial pressures brought to bear externally. You could argue that this could lead to financial indiscipline. But I would argue that it enables me to spend what I need to spend to deliver the service required. And if there is an excess, I give it back. To say the private sector is always cheaper is a very broad and sweeping statement, particularly if you consider it in the context of PFI (Private Finance Initiative) arrangements. You have to look at the whole life cycle of a contract if you are to evaluate it properly.

I don't doubt that as markets mature, new providers will develop the necessary expertise, but when you are dealing with public safety, public protection and reoffending you need a proven and trusted supplier. That's what the public sector offers.

→

Public service shouldn't be dirty words. Public servants work on behalf of the public and are proud of that. Businesses are there to make a profit – that's an absolute truth. But freed up from those constraints, I'm here to deliver a public service – and there is a clear distinction between those two priorities. They can be conflicting at worst; at a minimum they can create tension.

Any organisation, whether public or private, needs to be showing best value for money against the highest standard of delivery. So my position here has been to deliver public services while applying commercial disciplines in the way that we operate – ensuring we always get the best provider of services, whether internal or external, and that contracts are hard negotiated and hard applied. We view public money not as a right, but something to be managed with great prudence and on which to maximise return. What we mustn't lose sight of is the fact that what we are providing is public services. How that is delivered is really not the issue. It's about the quality of the service and the price.

Source: Management Today, March 2012, p. 53. Reproduced with permission.

Importance of skills and behaviour

A report from the CIPD points out that although public services are not homogeneous and specific issues facing managers will differ between sectors and localities, there is a shared agenda in improving people management in the public-sector workplaces. It is important to recognise that without more effective people management, there is no chance of introducing positive and lasting change. Management need to support and empower front-line staff. The report makes clear that:

> an improvement in the quality of people management, particularly among line managers and supervisors, is central to more effective delivery of public services and greater local accountability. Inadequate people management skills are also often at the heart of catastrophic service failure.[19]

Sir Howard Bernstein refers to the challenging economic climate that has focused the public sector on the need for radical reform to tackle the cost pressures on it and the development of the skills to deliver public-sector reform. Significant long-term culture change is required across a range of partners to overcome professional, organisational and technical barriers. All levels of managers and leaders have a vital role in delivering community services in a more integrated way.

> This type of reform will require different skills and behaviours across all levels of management. Some of the key leadership and management skills necessary for public service reform include the ability to adapt; to lead across organisational boundaries; to exert influence outside traditional hierarchies; to demonstrate political intelligence; and the ability to engage with the community.[20]

Critical review and reflection

The basis of ownership and finance, public accountability, demand for uniformity of treatment and the political environment in which they work mean the nature of management in the public sector is fundamentally different from that in the private sector.

To what extent are YOU able to challenge this assertion? Do YOU think there are more similarities or differences between management in the two sectors?

Management and organisational behaviour in action case study

Putting the customer first in a service organisation: cultural change at Fareham Borough Council

Faced with continual economic pressure, how does a thriving borough council change the culture of the organisation in a way that results in improved customer service and delivers efficiency savings? Fareham Borough Council is located along the south coast of Hampshire with a growing population, currently 112,800. The biennial Residents' Survey shows existing high levels of customer satisfaction; the 2013 survey identified that over 90 per cent of residents were happy with the way that Fareham Borough Council runs things. With such a high level of satisfaction, the need for further improvement or the possibility of doing so might be questioned; however, the purpose of the work being undertaken is to drive out complacency and ensure that satisfaction does not decline in the future and customers receive the best service possible.

Cultural change is difficult to achieve, but Fareham Borough Council is using a unique approach to achieving cultural transformation by putting the customer at the core of its work. Services are being redesigned to drive out waste and focus on working with an understanding of what matters to the customer. Driven from the top by the Leader of the Council and the Chief Executive, the Council is using the Vanguard Method.

Service is different to manufacturing. In simple terms there is inherently greater variety in customer demand, hence the need to design to absorb that variety. The Vanguard Method transfers expertise to people (managers and staff) in the organisation and helps change from command and control to a systems approach to the design and management of work. Emphasis is placed on the customer and measurement of success as opposed to targets of expected performance. Rather than concern with individual functions or activities, the organisation is viewed as an integrated system. The focus of attention is predominately on the flow of the needs of the customer throughout the system. Vanguard uses guides, people who are experts in both intervention theory (how to make a change) and systems theory (how to analyse and design work). **(See also discussion in Chapter 2.)**

The results

Unlike its traditional application, which is focused on a single service area, Fareham Borough Council has implemented a programme that will see all services reviewed across the whole organisation. Each of the interventions is being led by a Head of Service to provide support to the employees involved and ensure buy-in at all levels of the organisation. Analysing a service from a customer's perspective has revealed dramatic ways to change the way services are delivered. The points below indicate the services being reviewed and key improvements identified so far:

- **Housing repairs** – The average time to complete a day-to-day repair on a council property has fallen from 89 days to less than 8 days. This length of time is from when the customer reports the repair, up to when the repair is complete and stays fixed. Tradespeople are able to access a customer's property on the first visit in over 97 per cent of cases. This demonstrates the success of customers advising the council when it is convenient to them for tradespeople to attend. Changes in the approach to electrical testing are expected to deliver savings of approximately £88,000 per annum (50 per cent of the original cost); savings of approximately £30,000 are also anticipated following changes to the testing of emergency lighting.
- **Planning applications** – Average time taken to process applications has dropped from 56 days to 36.
- **Benefits** – The time taken to process new benefit claims has fallen from approximately 20 days to 6 days. Customers now deal with a single employee as handoffs are virtually non-existent.
- **Parking enforcement** – The number of Informal Challenges to Penalty Charge Notices (PCNs) has dropped from 45 per week to 23. This demonstrates how the Parking Enforcement Officers are making better decisions when issuing a PCN.

Conclusion

By engaging with every employee and understanding what matters to customers, the Council has been able to affect a cultural change at all levels of the organisation. In the first year of the programme, the Council is already seeing significant improvements in customer service and has been able to capture savings of £381,000 per annum.

Source: Thanks to Christopher Cotmore, Corporate Policy Officer, Fareham Borough Council. Reproduced with permission.

Tasks

1. What do you think are the main reasons for the key improvements identified by Fareham Borough Council?
2. Discuss critically how you view the idea of culture change with management based on the flow of customer needs rather than individual functions or activities.
3. To what extent do you think managing through putting the customer first could, or should, be applied meaningfully to your university or organisation?

The work of a manager

Despite similarities in the general activities of management, the jobs of individual managers will differ widely. In practice, it will be influenced by such factors as:

- the nature of the organisation, its culture, philosophy, objectives and size;
- the type of structure;
- activities and tasks involved;
- technology and methods of performing work;
- the nature of people employed; and
- the level in the organisation at which the manager is working.

These differences do not just exist between organisations in the private and public sectors; they are often more a matter of degree. For example, many large business organisations may have more in common in their management and operations with public-sector organisations than with small private firms.

The environmental setting

A major determinant of the work of the manager is the nature of the environment, both internal and external, in which the manager is working. Managers have to perform their jobs in the situation in which they find themselves (*see* Figure 10.5).

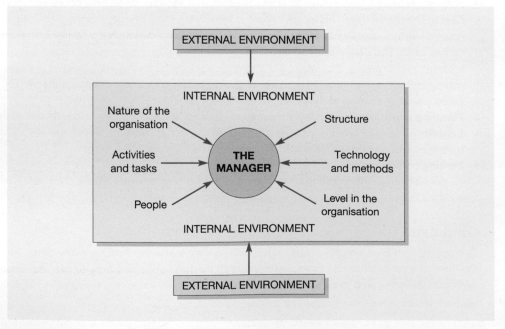

Figure 10.5 The work of a manager: the environmental setting

The **internal environment** relates to the culture and climate of the organisation – 'how things are done around here' – and to the prevailing atmosphere surrounding the organisation. (**Organisational culture and climate are discussed in Chapter 15.**) The **external environment** relates to the organisation as an open system (**discussed in Chapter 3**). Managers must be responsive to the changing opportunities and challenges, and risks and limitations, facing the organisation. External environmental factors are largely outside the control of management.

The diversity of management

Studies on the nature of management have been based on wider observation and research, and have concentrated on the diversity of management and differences in the jobs of managers. Among the best-known empirical studies on the nature of managers' jobs, and how managers actually spend their time, are those by *Henry Mintzberg, John Kotter* and *Rosemary Stewart*.[21]

Managerial roles

Based on the study of the work of five chief executives of medium-sized to large organisations, Mintzberg classifies the activities that constitute the essential functions of a top manager's job.[22] What managers do cannot be related to the classical view of the activities of management. The manager's job can be described more meaningfully in terms of various 'roles' or organised sets of behaviour associated with a position.[23] Mintzberg recognises that people who 'manage' have formal authority over the unit they command and this leads to a special position of status in the organisation.

As a result of this formal authority and status, managerial activities can be seen as a set of ten **managerial roles**, which may be divided into three groups:

- interpersonal roles;
- informational roles; and
- decisional roles.

Interpersonal roles

The **interpersonal roles** are relations with other people arising from the manager's status and authority:

1. **Figurehead role** is the most basic and simple of managerial roles. The manager is a symbol and represents the organisation in matters of formality, participation as a social necessity and being available for people who insist on access to the 'top'.
2. **Leader role** is among the most significant of roles and permeates all activities of a manager. By virtue of the authority vested in the manager, there is a responsibility for staffing, and for the motivation and guidance of subordinates.
3. **Liaison role** involves the manager in horizontal relationships with individuals and groups outside the manager's own unit or the organisation. An important part of the manager's job is the linking between the organisation and the environment.

Informational roles

The **informational roles** relate to the sources and communication of information arising from the manager's interpersonal roles:

1. **Monitor role** identifies the manager in seeking and receiving information to develop an understanding of the working of the organisation and its environment. Information may be received from internal or external sources, and may be formal or informal.

2. **Disseminator role** involves the manager in transmitting external information through the liaison role into the organisation, and internal information through the leader role between the subordinates. The information may be largely factual or may contain value judgements.

3. **Spokesperson role** involves the manager as formal authority in transmitting information to people outside the unit and the general public such as suppliers, customers, government departments and the press.

Decisional roles

The **decisional roles** involve the making of strategic organisational decisions on the basis of the manager's status and authority, and access to information:

1. **Entrepreneurial role** is the manager's function to initiate and plan controlled change through exploiting opportunities or solving problems, and taking action to improve the existing situation.

2. **Disturbance handler role** involves the manager in reacting to involuntary situations and unpredictable events. When an unexpected disturbance occurs the manager must take action to correct the situation.

3. **Resource allocator role** involves the manager in using formal authority to decide where effort will be expended, and making choices on the allocation of resources such as money, time, materials and staff.

4. **Negotiator role** is participation in negotiation activity with other individuals or organisations. Because of the manager's authority, credibility, access to information and responsibility for resource allocation, negotiation is an important part of the job.

Mintzberg emphasises that this set of ten roles is a somewhat arbitrary division of the manager's activities. It presents one of many possible ways of categorising the view of managerial roles. The ten roles are not easily isolated in practice but form an integrated whole. If any role is removed, this affects the effectiveness of the manager's overall performance.

Why organisations need managers

As a result of describing the nature of managerial work in terms of a set of ten roles, Mintzberg suggests six basic purposes of the manager, or reasons why organisations need managers:

- to ensure the organisation serves its basic purpose – the efficient production of goods or services;
- to design and maintain the stability of the operations of the organisation;
- to take charge of strategy-making and adapt the organisation in a controlled way to changes in its environment;
- to ensure the organisation serves the ends of those people who control it;
- to serve as the key informational link between the organisation and the environment; and
- as formal authority to operate the organisation's status system.

Agenda-setting and network-building

From a detailed study of fifteen successful American general managers involved in a broad range of industries, *Kotter* found that although their jobs differed and the managers undertook their jobs in a different manner, they all had two significant activities in common: **agenda-setting** and **network-building**.[24]

- **Agenda-setting** is a constant activity of managers. This is a set of items, or series of agendas, involving aims and objectives, plans, strategies, ideas, decisions to be made and priorities of action in order to bring about desired end results. This requires individual managers responsible for achieving targets to have a continual and changing series of agendas to help bring intentions into reality.

- **Network-building** involves the managers interacting with other people and establishing a network of co-operative relations outside the formal structure. The network often includes a large number of people, many in addition to their boss or direct subordinates, and individuals and groups outside the organisation. Meetings provide exchanges of information over a wide range of topics in a short period of time. A major feature of network-building is to establish and maintain contacts that can assist in the successful achievement of agenda items.

Demands, constraints and choices

Based on earlier studies of managerial jobs, *Stewart* has developed a model for understanding managerial work and behaviour. The model directs attention to the generalisations that can be made about managerial work, and differences that exist among managerial jobs. It acknowledges the wide variety, found from previous studies, among different managers in similar jobs in terms of how they view their jobs and the work they do.[25]

The three main categories of the model are **demands, constraints** and **choices**. These identify the flexibility in a managerial job.

- **Demands** are what anyone in the job has to do. They are not what the manager ought to do, but only what must be done: for example, meeting minimum criteria of performance, work that requires personal involvement, complying with bureaucratic procedures that cannot be avoided, meetings that must be attended.
- **Constraints** are internal or external factors that limit what the manager can do: for example, resource limitations, legal or trade union constraints, the nature of technology, physical location, organisational constraints, attitudes of other people.
- **Choices** are the activities that the manager is free to do, but does not have to do. They are opportunities for one job-holder to undertake different work from another, or to do the work in a different way: for example, what work is done within a defined area, to change the area of work, the sharing of work, participation in organisational or public activities.

Stewart suggests that the model provides a framework for thinking about the nature of managerial jobs, and about the manner in which managers undertake them. To understand what managerial jobs are really like it is necessary to understand the nature of their flexibility. Account should be taken of variations in behaviour and differences in jobs before attempting to generalise about managerial work.

An overview of management is set out in the concept map of Figure 10.6.

Critical review and reflection

The work of a manager is not easy to describe as aspects that are common in many applications escape us in others and all managers have their individual way of working. Understanding the nature of management can therefore be no more than a compromise between the ideas of the more lucid writers on the subject.

To what extent do YOU accept this view of the study of management? How would YOU explain the essential nature of managerial work and the role of the manager?

Importance of managerial style

There appears to be a growing recognition that managers can no longer rely solely on their perceived formal authority as a result of a hierarchical position in the structure of the organisation. More than ever an essential ingredient of any successful manager is the ability to handle people successfully. This changing relationship places a heavy responsibility on managers, and on the systems and styles of management adopted.

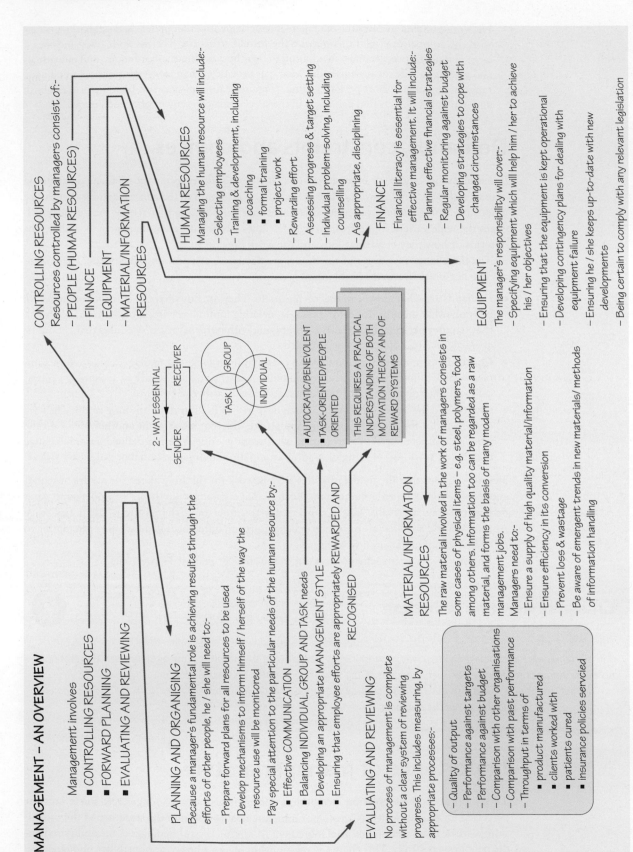

Figure 10.6 Management – an overview

It is, however, interesting to note the views of *Watson* who, while acknowledging that to create the goods, services and quality of life that people look for in the modern world, rather complex patterns of co-operative behaviour have to be orchestrated and 'managed', identifies three major problems in thinking about organising and managing work in terms of 'managing people':

- *Firstly,* in a modern democratic society, is it realistic even to contemplate the possibility of managing people and that there are people willing to be managed?
- *Secondly,* can it be argued that a manager has no moral right to direct, manage or boss any individual?
- *Thirdly,* does the focus on people management tend to blur the part played by structures, systems, cultures, processes and the rest?[26]

Good people management

Whatever the veracity of these problems or the importance attached to the management of systems, the organising and management of work depends ultimately on the people who make up the organisation. Without people, systems and procedures and indeed organisations themselves are meaningless. And people need to be managed. But, of course, of increasing importance are:

- how the process of management is actually carried out;
- the style of managerial behaviour; and
- its effectiveness for *both* organisational performance and the satisfaction of its members.

With the general movement towards flatter organisation structures, flexible working and greater employee empowerment, there is more emphasis on an integrating rather than a traditional controlling style of management. Management style and behaviour can be as important as management competence.

Style and context

Mintzberg draws attention to the relationship between managerial style and the importance of context, and questions how much personal style has an influence on what managers do. People do not usually find themselves in managerial jobs by chance to shape as they wish. What you do as a manager is mostly determined by what you face as a manager.

> Personal style is important, no question. But that seems to be more about how managers do things, including the decisions they make and the strategies they shape, than what they do as managers. In this regard, the literature, practitioner and academic alike, may be vastly overrating the importance of personal style. Style matters and context matters, but mostly they matter together, in a symbiotic relationship.[27]

Theory X and Theory Y management

The way in which managers approach the performance of their jobs and the behaviour they display towards subordinate staff are likely to be conditioned by underlying predispositions about people, and human nature and work. Drawing on Maslow's hierarchy of needs model (**discussed in Chapter 7**), *McGregor,* in 1960, put forward two suppositions about human nature and behaviour at work. He argued that the style of management adopted is a function of the manager's attitudes towards people and assumptions about human nature and behaviour. The two suppositions are called Theory X and Theory Y and are based on polar assumptions about people and work.[28]

Theory X assumptions

Theory X represents the carrot-and-stick assumptions on which traditional organisations are based. Its assumptions are that:

- the average person is lazy and has an inherent dislike of work;
- most people must be coerced, controlled, directed and threatened with punishment if the organisation is to achieve its objectives;
- the average person avoids responsibility, prefers to be directed, lacks ambition and values security most of all; and
- motivation occurs only at the physiological and security levels.

The central principle of Theory X is direction and control through a centralised system of organisation and the exercise of authority. McGregor questioned whether the Theory X approach to human nature is correct and the relevance of management practices that are based upon it. Assumptions based on a Theory X approach, and the traditional use of rewards and sanctions exercised by the nature of the manager's position and authority, are likely to result in an exploitative or authoritarian style of management.

Theory Y assumptions

At the other extreme to Theory X is **Theory Y**, which represents the assumptions consistent with current research knowledge. **The central principle of Theory Y is the integration of individual and organisational goals.** Its assumptions are:

- for most people, work is as natural as play or rest;
- people will exercise self-direction and self-control in the service of objectives to which they are committed;
- commitment to objectives is a function of rewards associated with their achievement;
- given the right conditions, the average worker can learn to accept and to seek responsibility;
- the capacity for creativity in solving organisational problems is distributed widely in the population;
- the intellectual potential of the average person is only partially utilised; and
- motivation occurs at the affiliation, esteem and self-actualisation levels as well as at the physiological and security levels.

The Theory Y approach is not a 'soft' option. In practice it is often difficult to achieve successfully. It can be frustrating and time consuming, and mistakes will occur. For example, as *Townsend* reports:

> Since 1952 I've been stumbling around buildings and running primitive Theory Y departments, divisions, and finally one whole Theory Y company: Avis. In 1962, after thirteen years, Avis had never made a profit (except one year when they jiggled their depreciation rates). Three years later the company had grown internationally (not by acquisitions) from $30 million in sales to $75 million in sales, and had made successive annual profits of $1 million, $3 million, and $5 million. If I had anything to do with this, I ascribe it all to my application of Theory Y. And a faltering, stumbling, groping, mistake-ridden application it was.[29]

Demands of the situation

The two views of Theory X and Theory Y tend to represent extremes of the natural inclination of managers towards a particular style of behaviour. In practice, however, the actual style of management behaviour adopted will be influenced by the demands of the situation.[30] Where the job offers a high degree of intrinsic satisfaction or involves a variety of tasks, an element of problem-solving and the exercise of initiative, or where output is difficult to measure in quantitative terms, then an informal, participative approach would seem to be more effective. In many cases this would apply to work of a scientific, technical or professional nature. Where commitment to the goals of the organisation is almost a prerequisite of membership, such as in certain voluntary or charity organisations, for example, then a Theory Y approach would clearly seem to be most appropriate.

However, even if a manager has a basic belief in Theory Y assumptions, there may be occasions when it is necessary, or more appropriate, to adopt a Theory X approach. This approach may be indicated in emergency situations, or where shortage of time or other overriding factors demand the use of authority in directing actions to the tasks in hand. For example, in the hustle, heat and noise of a busy hotel kitchen preparing fresh meals for a large banquet, with many tasks to be co-ordinated over very short time scales, it seems to be recognised that a Theory X style of management is most appropriate. In such circumstances this style of management appears often to be accepted by the kitchen staff.

Critical review and reflection

Although published in 1960, the underlying concepts of McGregor's Theory X and Theory Y are still some of the most significant and meaningful insights into our understanding of managerial behaviour.

What do YOU think? What experiences have YOU had of Theory X or Y management? What would be YOUR preferred natural style of managerial behaviour, and why?

The Managerial/Leadership Grid®

One means of describing and evaluating different styles of management is the *Blake and Mouton* **Managerial Grid®** (*see* Figure 10.7). First published as the Managerial Grid in 1964, restated in 1978 and 1985[31] and republished in 1991 as the **Leadership Grid®**,[32] the Grid provides a basis for comparison of managerial styles in terms of two principal dimensions: concern for production and concern for people.

- **Concern for production** is the amount of emphasis that the manager places on accomplishing the tasks in hand, achieving a high level of production and getting results or profits. This is represented along the horizontal axis of the Grid.
- **Concern for people** is the amount of emphasis that the manager gives to subordinates and colleagues as individuals and to their needs and expectations. This is represented along the vertical axis of the Grid.

Five basic combinations

The four corners and the centre of the Grid provide five basic combinations of degree of concern for production coupled with degree of concern for people (*see* Figure 10.7a):

1. **Managers with a 1,1 rating,** the impoverished manager, tend to be remote from their subordinates and believe in the minimum movement from their present position.
2. **Managers with a 9,1 rating,** the authority–compliance manager, are autocratic. They tend to rely on a centralised system and the use of authority.
3. **The 1,9 rating managers,** country club managers, believe that a contented staff will undertake what is required of them and achieve a reasonable level of output.
4. **The 5,5 rating,** middle-of-the-road managers, have the approach of 'live and let live' and a tendency to avoid the real issues.
5. **Managers with a 9,9 rating, the team manager,** believe in the integrating of task needs and concern for people.

These five styles of management represent the extremes of the Grid. With a 9-point scale on each axis there is a total of 81 different 'mixtures' of concern for production and concern for people. Most people would come up with a score somewhere in an intermediary position on the Grid.

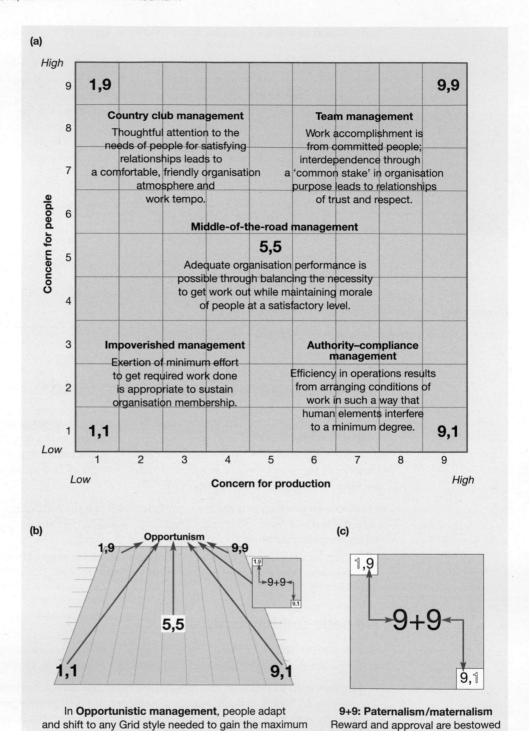

Figure 10.7 The Leadership Grid®

Source: Blake, R. R. and McCanse, A. A. *Leadership Dilemmas – Grid Solutions*, Gulf Publishing (1991), Grid Figure, p. 29, Paternalism Figure, p. 30, Opportunism Figure, p. 31. Reproduced by permission from Elsevier Ltd.

Two additional grid styles

The 1991 edition of the Grid covers two additional styles, opportunism and 9 + 9 paternalism/maternalism, which take account of the reaction of subordinates. In opportunistic management, organisational performance occurs according to a system of exchanges, whereby effort is given only for an equivalent measure of the same. People adapt to the situation to gain maximum advantage of it (see Figure 10.7b).

In 9 + 9 paternalistic/maternalistic management, reward and approval are granted to people in return for loyalty and obedience, and punishment is threatened for failure to comply (see Figure 10.7c).

A summary of the seven basic combinations of the Grid is given in Table 10.1.

Table 10.1 Leadership Grid style definitions

9,1 Authority–compliance management	Managers in this position have great concern for production and little concern for people. People are seen as 'tools' for production. They demand tight, unilateral control in order to complete tasks efficiently. They consider creativity and human relations to be unnecessary
1,9 Country club management	Managers in this position have great concern for people and little concern for production. They try to avoid conflicts and concentrate on being liked, even at the expense of production. To them the task is less important than good interpersonal relations. Their goal is to keep people happy. (This is a soft Theory X and not a sound human relations approach)
1,1 Impoverished management	This style is often referred to as laissez-faire. Leaders in this position have little concern for people or productivity. They avoid taking sides and stay out of conflicts. They do just enough to maintain group membership
5,5 Middle-of-the-road management	Leaders in this position have medium concern for both people and production. They rely on tried and true techniques and avoid taking untested risks. They attempt to balance their concern for both people and production, but are not committed strongly to either. Conflict is dealt with by avoiding extremes and seeking compromise rather than sound resolution
9 + 9 Paternalistic 'father knows best' management	This leader takes the high 9 level of concern from 9,1 and 1,9 to create a combined style of controlling paternalism. The paternalist strives for high results (high 9 from 9,1) and uses reward and punishment to gain compliance (high 9 from 1,9). The paternalist uses a high level of concern for people to reward for compliance or punish for rejection
Opportunistic 'what's in it for me?' management	The opportunists use whatever Grid style is needed to obtain selfish interest and self-promotion. They adapt to situations to gain the maximum advantage. They may use 9,1 to push their own goals with one person, and 1,9 to gain trust and confidence with another. Performance occurs according to a system of exchanges. Effort is given only for an equivalent measure of the same
9,9 Team management	These managers demonstrate high concern for both people and production. They work to motivate employees to reach their highest levels of accomplishment. They explore alternatives openly and aggressively. They are flexible and responsive to change. This style is considered ideal

Source: Blake, R. R. and McCanse, A. A. *Leadership Dilemmas – Grid Solutions*, Gulf Publishing Company (1991), p. 29. Reproduced with permission from Elsevier Ltd.

Relevance today

According to *Newborough,* 'an organisation's structure, plan and concept are crucial to its effectiveness. Yet beyond these, the most significant single factor is the behaviour of the management team. Its members must act as leaders. They must accomplish their objectives through their ability to guide, motivate and integrate the efforts of others'. The ultimate purpose of studies of managerial style is to aid in the training and development of those who wish to become better leaders. Grid organisation development identifies and applies relevant aspects of behavioural science, and Newborough maintains that the Grid is as relevant today as when it was first launched.[33] And according to *Crainer and Dearlove,* 'Crude as it is, the Grid helps people who are not conversant with psychology to see themselves and those they work with more clearly, to understand their interactions, and identify the sources of resistance and conflicts.'[34]

Critical review and reflection

Whatever the talk about a more consultative style of managerial behaviour, the main complaint from disgruntled members of staff is usually about lack of clear direction and strong decisive management.

To what extent would YOU challenge this contention? What has been YOUR personal experience? How does this relate to YOUR own views on managerial behaviour?

Management systems

Work by McGregor, and by Blake and Mouton, suggests that an organisation is more likely to harness its staffing resources effectively if there is a participative style of management. This view is supported by the work of *Likert,* writing in the 1960s and 1970s. On the basis of a questionnaire to managers in over 200 organisations and research into the performance characteristics of different types of organisations, Likert identifies a fourfold model of management systems.[35] These systems are designated by number:

- System 1 – Exploitive authoritative. Decisions are imposed on subordinates, motivation is based on threats, there is very little teamwork or communication; responsibility is centred at the top of the organisational hierarchy.
- System 2 – Benevolent authoritative. A condescending form of leadership, motivation is based on a system of rewards, there is only limited teamwork or communication; responsibility is at managerial levels but not at lower levels of the organisational hierarchy.
- System 3 – Consultative. Leadership involves some trust in subordinates, motivation is based on rewards but also some involvement, there is a fair degree of teamwork, and communication takes place vertically and horizontally; responsibility for achieving the goals of the organisation is spread more widely throughout the hierarchy.
- System 4 – Participative. Leadership involves trust and confidence in subordinates, motivation is based on rewards for achievement of agreed goals, there is participation and a high degree of teamwork and communication; responsibility for achieving the goals of the organisation is widespread throughout all levels of the hierarchy.

Supportive relationships

The nearer the behavioural characteristics of an organisation approach System 4, the more likely this will lead to long-term improvement in staff turnover and high productivity, low scrap, low costs and high earnings. Likert sets out three fundamental concepts of System 4 management. These are the use of:

- the principle of supportive relationships among members of the organisation and in particular between superior and subordinate;
- group decision-making and group methods of organisation and supervision; and high-performance aspirations for all members of the organisation.

In considering high-performance aspirations, Likert refers to studies that suggest that employees generally want stable employment and job security, opportunities for promotion and satisfactory compensation. They want, also, to feel proud of their organisation and its performance and accomplishments. In System 4 management, superiors should therefore have high-performance aspirations, but so also should every member of the organisation. To be effective, these high-performance goals should not be imposed but set by a participative mechanism involving group decision-making and a multiple overlapping group structure. The mechanism should enable employees to be involved in setting high-performance goals that help to satisfy their needs.

Managing with and through people

Although there are many aspects to management, one essential ingredient of any successful manager is the ability to handle people effectively. Recall, for example, the previous discussion (**Chapter 1**) on people and organisational behaviour. A genuine concern for people and for their welfare goes a long way in encouraging them to perform well. A positive policy of investment in people and an interpersonal relationship approach to management are, in the longer term, worth the effort. For example, the UK government-sponsored initiative Investors in People is based on a commitment to the benefits that organisations can gain through their people and on the vital role of managers.

It is possible to put forward a number of underlying philosophies that arguably are likely to make for the successful management of people, and lead to both improved work performance and more contented staff (*see* Figure 10.8). **These philosophies are not intended to be prescriptive but to encourage discussion on the extent to which you agree with the points of view.**

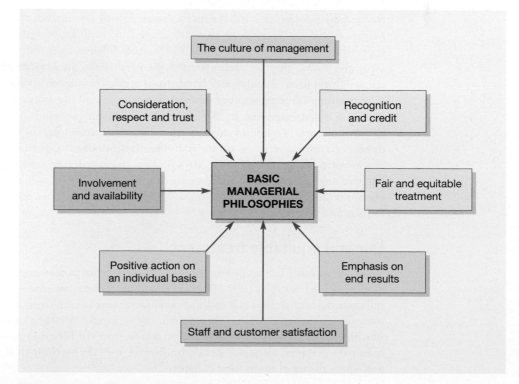

Figure 10.8 The effective management of people

Consideration, respect and trust

People generally respond according to the way they are treated. If you give a little, you will invariably get a lot back. Make people feel important and give them a sense of personal worth. The majority of staff will respond constructively if treated with consideration and respect, and as responsible individuals who wish to serve the organisation well.

However, how can members of staff show that they can be trusted unless trust is first placed in them? **The initiative must come from management:** 'Lack of trust is probably one of the greatest time and resource wasters in the workplace. Managers who do not trust their employees are probably wasting hours every week checking up on them at every turn and failing to utilise the resources at their disposal.'[36]

Research from the CIPD shows that employee attitudes to senior management across the public sector are generally more negative than their private-sector counterparts. Public-sector employees are less likely to feel they are treated with respect by senior managers, and they have less trust and confidence in them.[37]

Recognition and credit

People can be praised to success. Give genuine recognition and credit when it is due and let people know you appreciate them. Too often managers appear unresponsive to good performance, taking this for granted. But they are quick to criticise on the occasions when performance falls below expectations. **It should not be assumed that staff would necessarily take a lack of response as a sign of positive recognition rather than just the absence of criticism.** So often you hear the comment 'Well nobody has complained so I suppose everything is all right.' What a poor indictment of management style! Positive feedback on good performance is a strong motivator and staff are then more likely to accept and respond to constructive criticism.

Involvement and availability

Involve yourself with the work of the staff and make sure you fully understand the difficulties and distastes of their job. Ensure an open flow of communications and encourage participation and feedback. Take an active interest in the work of staff but without excessive supervision or inhibiting their freedom of action. Wherever possible be available to staff as a priority, rather than to administration. Remember the importance of giving time to listen genuinely to the feelings and problems of staff. This means giving staff your full attention including adopting appropriate body language (**recall the discussion in Chapter 6**). The approach of 'Management By Walking About' (MBWA), together with effective communication processes, is often heralded as a positive management practice. However, there is the danger of arousing mistrust among staff, the suspicion of management snooping and doubts about 'what are you doing here?'. MBWA is not just wandering aimlessly. It is unlikely to be effective unless perceived by staff as part of a genuine belief by management in the continuing importance of keeping staff informed and giving time to listen to, and understand, their feelings and problems.

Fair and equitable treatment

Treat people fairly but according to merit. Ensure justice in treatment, equitable systems of motivation and rewards, clear HR policies and procedures, avoidance of discrimination and full observance of all laws and codes of conduct relating to employment. People expect certain outcomes in exchange for certain contributions or inputs. A feeling of inequality causes tension and motivates the person to indulge in certain forms of behaviour in order to remove or to reduce the perceived inequity.[38] **Recall the discussion on the psychological contract (Chapter 1) and equity theory of motivation (Chapter 7).**

Positive action on an individual basis

Deal with individual situations on an individual basis and avoid the 'blanket' approach. For example, it has come to a manager's attention that a couple of members of staff have failed to provide some urgently requested information on time. The manager's reaction is to send a circular email to *all* members of the department reminding them of the need for, and importance of, meeting deadlines. This may appear to be an easy way out to the manager. But what are the likely reactions of staff? The two members concerned might shield behind the generality of the email and persuade themselves that it does not apply particularly to them. They might even choose to believe that the manager must be referring to other members of staff, perhaps in a different section, and take little notice of the circular. In contrast, the majority of staff in the department who do have a good record of providing requested information on time may well be annoyed or upset by the circular.

There could be staff who, despite pressing difficulties, have taken great pride in their work and made a special effort to maintain an excellent record of co-operation – quite possibly without any previous positive recognition from management. **It would be understandable if the reaction of these staff was one of resentment and disillusionment, and with a possible adverse effect on their future attitude to work.**

Emphasis on end results

Place emphasis on end results and levels of actual performance and achievement rather than on compliance with detailed instructions, rules or regulations. Where set attendance times are *clearly* seen as a necessary requirement of the job, it is right that managers should ensure that timekeeping is adhered to and enforced as appropriate. But in many cases rigid times of attendance are not an essential requirement for effective performance. The increasing movement to work/life balance, flexible working patterns and teleworking coupled with demands to boost productivity are placing growing emphasis on what staff actually achieve rather than the time spent at work. The important criteria are the level and quality of performance.

Staff and customer satisfaction

The starting point for customer, or consumer, satisfaction is good manager–subordinate relationships. Supportive and harmonious working relationships are more likely to create a working environment that results in high levels of both staff *and* consumer satisfaction. Managers need to adopt a positive attitude towards staff and to develop a spirit of mutual co-operation. Staff should feel that they are working *with* the manager rather than *for* the manager.

Critical review and reflection

The idea of basic philosophies such as managing by consideration, respect and trust may seem enlightened but is naive and idealistic. Given the natural scepticism of staff, such philosophies are difficult to implement in practice and subject to abuse.

What are YOUR views? To what extent would YOU feel confident in managing by respect and trust?

A looser approach to management

It is not suggested that managers should give up the right to manage: it is a question of *how* they manage and how they use their authority. For example, a Theory X style with emphasis on direction and control, and the use of rewards and sanctions exercised by nature of the manager's position and authority; or a Theory Y style in which individuals may satisfy their motivational needs through integration with meeting the goals of the organisation.

Management may also be based on 'organisational power' derived from status or position within the hierarchical structure, and the use of formal authority; or 'personal power' derived from competence and expertise, identification with subordinates, commanding respect, and urging and encouraging people in the performance of their tasks.[39]

Thomas suggests the need for a loose approach to business, in which tight controls are replaced with a more relaxed management style. As a result of employee and customer expectations, and social and technological change, the modern workforce expects to play a greater role in service delivery and not be hampered by strict rules and inflexible regulations: 'For a business to survive in these changing times, it needs to adopt a far looser approach in which specific rules are replaced with broad business principles . . . You have to build a culture of trust where people want to behave in a way that is best for the organisation.' However, Thomas believes the biggest obstacle is middle managers who fear they do not have authority to make big decisions and rely on management by the rule book, their process, templates and rigid structures.[40]

The importance of emotions and mood

We have mentioned previously that people are not homogeneous and human behaviour is capricious. People bring to work their own perceptions, feelings and attitudes. The importance of human foibles and emotions should not be forgotten. *Robbins*, for example, points out that employees bring an emotional component with them to work every day.

> *Emotions are part of our lives. That is, we not only think, we feel! But the field of management has been guilty for a long time of treating employees as if they're nonemotional. All work behavior is assumed to be fully rational. While this makes for simpler analysis of workplace behavior, it also creates highly unrealistic and inaccurate assessments.*[41]

Bolchover draws attention to the importance of mood as crucial to job performance in areas such as decision-making, creativity, teamwork, negotiation and leadership. Leaders' moods are highly contagious and what makes moods even more potentially beneficial or destructive is their infectiousness. Bolchover suggests that this 'emotional contagion' lies at the root of what we call corporate morale. Managers must appreciate that their own attitudes are contagious, profoundly affecting those who work for them: 'Pretty much everything that determines an employee's fundamental attitude at work is under the control of the manager.'[42]

Guidance on good management

GOV.UK has produced a 'Guidance to Good Management' (published 27 October 2014).

Managers play a central role in any organisation. They connect people to the purpose of their work and help them understand why their work is important. They set tasks and track performance, and they recognise the contribution of each individual in achieving the organisation's goals. They also play a leading role in helping their team to identify the areas they need to develop.

What makes a good manager?

What all inspirational managers have in common is they have taken the time to demonstrate one or more of the following positive behaviours that people look for in a good manager:

- they understand how to model leadership behaviours, inspire a shared vision and enable and support others to act;
- they champion learning and development for themselves and their teams and create an environment where the giving and receiving of feedback is the norm;
- they know and listen to their team and encourage open discussion and constructive challenge.

I am valued and recognised by BIS for the time and effort I put in to people management. BIS provides the tools and training I need and is intolerant of poor practice.

I take my **responsibility** as a line manager seriously.
- I am generous with my time. Supporting my team is a priority.
- I recognise that I am a role model. I lead by example.
- I get the basics right. Appraisals are done well and on time.

I know the people I manage, their abilities, aspirations, frustrations and motivations. I am also self aware, and open about my own strengths and weaknesses.

I create a safe environment for open discussion and construtive challenge by:
- Being **visible** and accessible
- Openly **inviting the views** of others
- **Listening** and acting

I give honest, timely, objective **feedback.**
- I give recognition when people have done well.
- I take prompt action to address under-performance.

I champion **learning and development** including for myself.

I work with my team to **manage workloads,** find **smarter** ways of working and clearly **define our roles.**

I **delegate** responsibilities not tasks. I **coach** more than I direct.
- I understand the fine line between empowerment and abandonment.

I value diversity and promote equality. I show this by being **inclusive** and welcoming the contributions and views of all.

I am supported by staff who live the BIS values, take responsibility for their own development and give me feedback on how I am doing.

Figure 10.9 BIS Manager's Charter
Source: https://www.gov.uk/government/publications/improving-civil-service-skills-good-management, (accessed 19 September 2014)

As part of the Good Management campaign there is a Department of Business, Innovation and Skills (BIS) Manager's Charter (*see* Figure 10.9).

The qualities of a manager and managerial effectiveness are also discussed later (**see Chapter 16**).

The future of management

According to *Owen*, the death of modern management is nigh and the old world of simplistic formulae for strategy, finance and leadership no longer work. After the first wave of management with tradition carefully handed down from master to apprentice, and the second wave of modern management following the Industrial Revolution, we are now embarking on the third wave of management. Organisations are moving from command and control to co-operation and commitment. To manage in an increasingly uncertain world risks must be turned into opportunity and challenges into success.

The job of the manager is changing out of all recognition. Managers are still the glue that holds the organisation together. But it is no longer about connecting the top and bottom of the organisation. It is about connecting a network of power and influence to make things happen through other people. This requires a changed set of skills . . . The job is just not command and control. The job is about orchestrating the skills of the network, helping the organisation discover and deliver the best solution. The job has changed from instructing to enabling. This makes the manager's job harder but more rewarding.[43]

A manager-less workplace?

With the demise of the hierarchy and a future that is flat, *Howes* questions if managers can survive in the workplace. Austerity measures in the UK have resulted in public-sector organisations making several structural changes including a reduction in senior management. However, Howes points out that those making flatter structural changes in the public or private sectors are smaller organisations with fewer employees. In a leadership environment one person dominates naturally. The group must show willingness and consensual agreement to an unofficial manager lurking within the group.

> *Leadership environments are a good starting point, but ultimately, someone will step up or things won't get done.[44]*

But what is actually 'new'?

There is much written today about changes in the workforce and new approaches to management. It is interesting to note, however, the ideas on the nature of managerial behaviour put forward many years ago by eminent writers such as Mary Parker Follett and Peter Drucker.

Over seventy years ago, *Follett's* thinking was based on concern for social, evolutionary progress, and the organisation and management of people for effective performance and a fuller life. Follett envisioned the successful operation of groups, and management responsibility diffused through the organisation and not just concentrated at the top of the hierarchy.[45]

Drucker suggested that one of the essential principles of management is that it is about human beings.

> *Management is about human beings. Its task is to make people capable of joint performance, to make their strengths effective and their weaknesses irrelevant. This is what organization is all about, and it is the reason that management is the critical, determining factor . . . We depend on management for our livelihoods and our ability to contribute and achieve.[46]*

> *The fact is that management ultimately depends on an understanding of human nature. I suggest it goes much further than that. In the first place, good management depends on the acceptance of certain basic values. It cannot be achieved without honesty and integrity, or without consideration for the interests of others. Secondly, it is the understanding of human foibles that we all share, such as jealousy, envy, status, prejudice, perception, temperament, motivation and talent, which provides the greatest challenge to managers.*

> *HRH The Duke of Edinburgh[47]*

Critical review and reflection

A number of writers have drawn attention to the changing nature of management and the work of the manager. Yet reading the ideas of eminent writers such as Mary Parker Follett (1942) and Peter Drucker (1954) it appears little is really new, and the underlying role of management remains unchanged.

What are YOUR views? What specifically do YOU see as the likely role of the manager in ten years' time?

Ten key points to remember

1 Management is fundamental to the effective operation of work organisations. It is essentially an integrating activity that permeates every facet of the organisation.

2 Management is directed towards attainment of aims and objectives, within a structured organisation and achieved through the efforts of other people.

3 One approach to the process of management is attention to common activities and principles of management. These are not prescriptive but guidelines for action.

4 A popular way of describing the essential nature of managerial work is getting work done second-hand and responsibility for the work and efforts of other people.

5 There is debate about the extent to which there are general common features of management in both private-enterprise and public-sector organisations.

6 The jobs of individual managers differ widely and are influenced by a number of factors. There are a number of significant empirical studies into the work of a manager.

7 The way in which managers carry out their responsibilities is important. Increasing attention is given to managerial style and the ability to handle people successfully.

8 Managerial behaviour is likely to be influenced by attitudes towards people and assumptions about human nature and behaviour at work – called Theory X and Theory Y.

9 As a basis for discussion, it is possible to suggest a number of underlying philosophies that arguably make for success in managing with and through people.

10 Much is written today about changes in the workplace and the future of management. However, one can reasonably question how much is actually new.

Review and discussion questions

1 How would you summarise the essential nature of managerial work? In what ways does the job of a manager differ from any other job in a work organisation?

2 Give detailed reasons for whether you believe: (i) managers are born or made; *and* (ii) management is an art or a science.

3 To what extent is it possible to establish rules or principles of good management? Assess critically the practical applications of these rules or principles.

4 Contrast critically the nature of management in private-enterprise and public-sector organisations.

5 Why do organisations need managers? Suggest which *one* writer has in your opinion made the greatest contribution to our understanding of the nature of management. Justify your answer.

6 Give your own views on the importance of managerial style.

7 Contrast sets of attitudes and assumptions about people at work that might be held by managers. Suggest how these attitudes and assumptions might influence actual managerial behaviour.

8 Discuss critically the suggestion that management is a much more human activity than is commonly suggested in management textbooks. Support your discussion with practical examples.

9 Give your own critical views on the practical implementation of basic underlying philosophies for managing with and through people.

10 Explain fully, with supporting reasons, how you see the future of management in work organisations.

Assignment

Complete the 'Your management style questionnaire'. Move quickly and do not think too deeply about each question but give your first immediate response.

Your management style questionnaire

There are ten pairs of statements. Assign a weight from 0 to 10 to each statement to show the relative strength of your belief in the statements in each pair. The points assigned for each pair must total 10 in each case. Be as honest with yourself as you can and resist the natural tendency to respond as you would 'like to think things are'. This instrument is not a test. There are no right or wrong answers. It is designed to be a stimulus for personal reflection and discussion.

1. It's only human nature for people to do as little work as they can get away with. _____ (A)

    When people avoid work, it's usually because their work has been deprived of its meaning. _____ (B)

    10

2. If employees have access to any information they want, they tend to have better attitudes and behave more responsibly. _____ (C)

    If employees have access to more information than they need to do their immediate tasks, they will usually misuse it. _____ (D)

    10

3. One problem in asking for employees' ideas is that their perspective is too limited for their suggestions to be of much value. _____ (E)

    Asking employees for their ideas broadens their perspective and results in the development of useful suggestions. _____ (F)

    10

4. If people don't use much imagination and ingenuity on the job, it's probably because relatively few people have much of either. _____ (G)

    Most people are imaginative and creative but may not show it because of limitations imposed by supervision and the job. _____ (H)

    10

5. People tend to raise their stakes if they are accountable for their own behaviour and for correcting their own mistakes. _____ (I)

    People tend to lower their stakes if they are not punished for their misbehaviour and mistakes. _____ (J)

    10

6. It's better to give people both good and bad news because most employees want the whole story, no matter how painful. _____ (K)

    It's better to withhold unfavourable news about business because most employees really want to hear only the good news. _____ (L)

    10

7. Because a supervisor is entitled to more respect than those below him or her in the organisation, it weakens the supervisor's prestige to admit that a subordinate was right and he or she was wrong. _____ (M)

    Because people at all levels are entitled to equal respect, a supervisor's prestige is increased when he or she supports this principle by admitting that a subordinate was right and he or she was wrong. _____ (N)

    10

8. If you give people enough money, they are less likely to be concerned with such intangibles as responsibility and recognition. _____ (O)

 If you give people interesting and challenging work, they are less likely to complain about such things as pay and supplemental benefits. _____ (P)

 10

9. If people are to set their own goals and standards of performance, they tend to set them higher than the boss would. _____ (Q)

 If people are allowed to set their own goals and standards of performance, they tend to set them lower than the boss would. _____ (R)

 10

10. The more knowledge and freedom people have regarding their jobs, the more controls are needed to keep them in line. _____ (S)

 The more knowledge and freedom people have regarding their jobs, the fewer controls are needed to ensure satisfactory job performance. _____ (T)

 10

Source: Adapted from Myers, M. S. *Every Employee a Manager*, McGraw-Hill (1970).

Personal skills and employability exercise

Objectives

Completing this exercise should help you to enhance the following skills:

- Act in the role of the manager to handle a number of real-life situations.
- Conduct management–staff interviews and discussions.
- Review critically your ability to deal with emotionally difficult situations.

Exercise

Given below are a number of real-life situations. You are required to:

a. Think through each one and explain how you as the manager might best handle the discussion with your member of staff.
b. Record how you would approach each discussion/interview.
c. Consider what specific questions might you be likely to ask, and why?
d. Share and compare your responses with colleagues in a small-group situation.

Situation 1

One of your employees, who is hard-working and conscientious with tasks, continually arrives late for work. This is the sixth time this has happened. The person's excuse is that they have to take their child to nursery because they are getting divorced and their spouse refuses to do this task.

Situation 2

You receive a complaint from one of your female employees who claims to have accidently found a pornographic image on the PC of another employee and finds this offensive.

Situation 3

One of your permanent employees has been accused of assaulting another member of staff who works in the same organisation but as an independent contractor.

Situation 4

You overhear a member of your department comment of you that 'he/she has no idea of the technical complexity of my work . . . I don't know how he/she can manage a department like this!'

Situation 5

A key client calls you to complain about sarcastic and impatient comments made by one of your more experienced technicians. Comments like 'Your people must be really thick if they think that's how it works' have proved less than helpful. You know this person has been working long hours, achieving excellent results and is clearly committed to their job and the department. In fact, you have recently promoted the technician for these very reasons.

Situation 6

In a recent management meeting, a relatively new colleague repeatedly contradicted you and appeared to be 'scoring points' at your expense. Although the colleague had made some valid, even perceptive comments, it is not exactly helping your relationship get off to an encouraging start. Furthermore, this has happened on a previous occasion.

Discussion with colleagues

- How would you summarise the essential nature of the manager–subordinate relationship?
- Using your own examples, explain the importance of using appropriate approaches when dealing with potentially difficult situations.
- What have you learned about your potential skills of effective people management?

Case study
Is everybody happy?

Is happiness an important component of a well-managed organisation? It might seem intuitively correct to believe that people work better when they are relaxed and enjoying their work, and much research has gone into the examination of the links between job satisfaction, work motivation and overall organisational efficiency as demonstrated earlier **(Chapter 7).** But does human happiness per se (as separate from the enjoyment of the work itself) make any difference to performance? Experimental data reported by a team of researchers at Warwick University seem to suggest that it does.[48]

The experiments were similar to those described in the earlier case study on behavioural economics **(Chapter 6).** The 'work' was a simple but uninteresting mathematical task designed to simulate a piece-rate 'white-collar' (non-managerial) type of job. The 'work' could be evaluated for both quantity (how many calculations were performed during a specified time) and quality (how many of them were correct) and participants were paid according to output.

Individuals are asked to add sequences of five 2-digit numbers under timed conditions. This task is simple but is taxing under pressure. We think of it as representing – in a stylized way – an iconic white-collar job: both intellectual ability and effort are rewarded.[49]

Participants' mathematical ability was tested and matched, and payment was offered according to the number of correct results achieved in the timed sessions, which happened over several weeks. The experimental groups were shown a short series of popular comedy sketches before attempting the task. At the end of every session, all groups were asked to complete a questionnaire to gauge both their general levels of happiness and (importantly) any increase in happiness experienced by members of the control group after watching the film. The result? A consistent and significant rise in productivity – up 12 per cent – for the experimental groups compared with the control groups. As the authors conclude:

if well-being boosts human performance, that raises the possibility of self-reinforcing spirals from productivity-to-well-being-to-productivity.[50]

Bad apples

Contrast this with work done back in 2006 that examines an opposing effect: the influence of negativity displayed by a member on group performance.[51] The so-called 'bad apples' who spoil the whole barrel were defined as exhibiting behaviours such as withholding of effort, being affectively negative and violating important interpersonal norms, but not behaving in an illegal way or such as would incur disciplinary sanctions. It was noted that consistent negative behaviour by even one member had a disproportionately severe negative impact on overall group performance. In other words, 'unhappy' members could have a depressing effect on colleagues' output by causing them to withdraw, react against the negativity or to seek distractions.

> Almost all of us have either had the personal experience of working with someone who displayed bad apple behaviours . . . When this process starts to unfold at work, it consumes inordinate amounts of time, psychological resources, and emotional energy.[52]

It would seem, therefore, that general workplace happiness – quite distinctly from job satisfaction – is valuable, and unhappiness can be damaging or lead to 'emotional contagion'. So what are the implications for management? One example of a company that seems to take the happiness of its workforce very seriously is media company UKRD.

William Rogers, CEO of UKRD
Source: UKRD Group Limited

Open, honest, fun, fair, professional and unconventional

UKRD owns and operates seventeen commercial radio stations throughout the UK, from Pirate FM in Cornwall to Star Radio in County Durham. It was awarded top place in the *Sunday Times* 100 Best Companies to Work For[53] in 2011 for the first time, and in 2014 it received the same accolade for the fourth year in a row. The award is based on the views of employees – and in 2014 the Chief Executive Officer William Rogers was also named Best Leader in the survey's mid-sized company category – for the third time. In a press release, the Company Chairman explained that:

> William epitomises the approach to management that we have at all levels in the company and his recognition in the Sunday Times in this way highlights the quality, not only of his leadership, but of the whole UKRD leadership team.[54]

Rogers, who became CEO of the organisation in 2002, has focused his management team's style around six core values:

- **Open** – Being open-minded to new ways of thinking, being open to criticism constructively delivered from wheresoever it may come and the welcoming of new ideas and opportunities. A requirement not just to hear, but to listen.
- **Honest** – The reflection of views and opinions delivered in a considered but clear and frank way. Expressing your real opinion, upward or downward, and an obligation to deal ethically and with integrity with colleagues and customers.
- **Fair** – A requirement to consider fairness in the broadest sense of the word. Fairness to the business, to colleagues, to customers and, on occasion, to all in balance. What appears to be fair at first sight may be less fair after due consideration.
- **Fun** – Enjoy work. Whether it be spontaneous or organised, delivering an environment in which a smile hits the faces of you and your colleagues on a regular basis is the responsibility of all.
- **Professional** – The highest standards of commitment and delivery across all areas of responsibility for which an individual, at any level, may have.

Delivering on commitments, honouring obligations and respecting those things that make a difference to the reputation of the company and those that work for it.

- **Unconventional** – Be different, try different things and challenge the norm. It may be 'done that way', but should it be? Innovate, take risks and be prepared to fail.[55]

He explains that the values are intended to have a direct effect on the way staff behave towards each other, even to change employees' lives for the better; he believes that if people are happy at work then they are generally happy in life too. In the *Sunday Times* survey, 94 per cent of the workforce reported that they loved their jobs, and the company was ranked particularly highly for giving employees a sense of well-being as well as offering opportunities for personal growth. Rogers sees both of these qualities as being vital to unlock the 'discretionary dividend' of individual performance that makes a big difference to the bottom line.

Spread a little happiness

His personal style of management, and that which he insists on for the whole management team, is about approachability and openness. He does not have a personal assistant to gate-keep his diary and allocate his time, and he spends most of his working week out and about visiting the stations. He makes sure he speaks directly to everyone on the team, and takes time to say a proper farewell:

If I or any of our senior team are visiting one of the 17 stations that we have around the country – and the meeting is scheduled to go from 10am until 12.30pm, we don't put a 12.30 departure in our diary: it's 12.45 so we build in time to say goodbye to everyone before we leave.[56]

Rogers also recognises that living the core values, especially for managers, can be a challenge:

People have left our business because they didn't get it . . . Two senior managers were removed from our organisation because they couldn't deliver management in a style that reflected those values. Great sales people have been removed or have left because they couldn't operate within those values.[57]

Nevertheless, management commitment to the values is crucial, and recognised as one of the company's key strengths by the *Sunday Times* adjudicators:

'The reason the vision and values work is because they're demonstrated from the top,' says Eagle's managing director Paul Marcus. '[Rogers is] a fabulous person to work for, a joy.' Staff agree: they have a great deal of faith in him (95%, first), and find him inspiring (94%, also first).[58]

Of course, any organisation could be a nice place to work without actually being efficient. However, if one of the key indicators of organisational performance is return on investment for shareholders, UKRD seems to be on the button. In the summer of 2014 it announced two dividend payments to shareholders based on strong growth and increased revenue across the group. Commenting on the company's performance, Rogers himself made it clear that the true drivers of the business and its profitability, even in difficult times, were the local staff and managers.

The local focus is truly paying off and we are seeing the clearest evidence yet that when you deliver truly local radio to an audience that is keen to be served by the kind of committed teams we have in all our stations, the results feed through.[59]

So maybe real life bears out the findings of the Warwick research team: there is indeed a lot to be said for spreading a little happiness at work.

Tasks

1 What sort of management style does William Rogers exhibit? Base your answer on one of the models in the first part of the chapter. What risks might be associated with this style?

2 Compare and contrast the six core values of UKRD with the eight basic managerial philosophies (*see* Figure 10.8). How far do they overlap, and where do they differ?

3 If, as the evidence suggests, happiness can improve performance, what are the implications for a manager's or team leader's own behaviour towards his or her staff?

4 Consider the concept of 'emotional contagion' described in the chapter and the case. What steps could a manager take to improve a situation where negativity of a member is harming the team's effectiveness?

Notes and references

1. See, for example, Margretta, J. *What Management Is: How it Works and Why it's Everyone's Business*, HarperCollins (2002).
2. Drucker, P. F. *Management*, Pan Books (1979), p. 14.
3. Schneider, S. C. and Barsoux, J. *Managing Across Cultures*, second edition, Financial Times Prentice Hall (2003).
4. Francesco, A. M. and Gold, B. A. *International Organizational Behavior*, second edition, Prentice Hall (2005).
5. Crainer, S. 'The Rise of Guru Scepticism', *Management Today*, March 1996, p. 51.
6. Watson, T. J. *Management, Organisation and Employment Strategy*, Routledge & Kegan Paul (1986).
7. Dib, F. 'Is management a science?', *Professional Manager*, Autumn 2014, pp. 38–9.
8. Foppen, J. W. 'Knowledge Leadership', in Chowdbury, S (ed.) *Management 21C*, Financial Times Prentice Hall (2000), pp. 160–1.
9. Fayol, H. *General and Industrial Management*, Pitman (1949).
10. McLean, J. 'Fayol – standing the test of time', *Manager, The British Institute of Administrative Management*, Spring 2011, pp. 32–3.
11. Hamel, G. with Breen, B. *The Future of Management*, Harvard Business School Press (2007), p. 20.
12. Drucker, P. F. *People and Performance*, Heinemann (1977), p. 28.
13. Ibid., p. 59.
14. Stern, S. 'Peter the Great', *Management Today*, December 2011, pp. 56–7.
15. Ferguson, (Sir) A. in Gwyther, M. and Saunders, A. 'United They Stand?', *Management Today*, April 2005, p. 41.
16. Stewart, R. *The Reality of Management*, third edition, Butterworth–Heinemann (1999), p. 6.
17. Mintzberg, H. *Managing*, Financial Times Prentice Hall (2009), p. 19.
18. Walker, B. 'How to switch sides', *Professional Manager*, Spring 2013, pp. 4–7.
19. 'Building productive public sector workplaces: Part One, Improving People Management', CIPD, January 2010.
20. Bernstein, Sir Howard, 'In My Opinion', *Management Today*, February 2012, p. 62.
21. For a useful summary of the work of the manager, see, for example, Birchall, D. W. 'What Managers Do', in Crainer, S. and Dearlove, D. (eds) *Financial Times Handbook of Management*, second edition, Financial Times Prentice Hall (2001), pp. 110–31.
22. Mintzberg, H. *The Nature of Managerial Work*, Harper and Row (1973).
23. Mintzberg, H. 'The Manager's Job: Folklore and Fact', *Harvard Business Review Classic*, March–April 1990, pp. 163–76.
24. Kotter, J. P. *The General Managers*, Free Press (1982).
25. Stewart, R. *Contrasts in Management*, McGraw-Hill (1976).
26. Watson, T. *Organising and Managing Work*, second edition, Financial Times Prentice Hall (2006).
27. Mintzberg, H. *Managing*, Financial Times Prentice Hall (2009), p. 130.
28. McGregor, D. *The Human Side of Enterprise*, Penguin (1987).
29. Townsend, R. *Further Up the Organisation*, Coronet Books (1985), pp. 168–9.
30. See, for example, Mullins, L. J. 'Management and Managerial Behaviour', *International Journal of Hospitality Management*, vol. 4, no. 1, 1985, pp. 39–41.
31. Blake, R. R. and Mouton, J. S. *The Managerial Grid III*, Gulf Publishing (1985).
32. Blake, R. R. and McCanse, A. A. *Leadership Dilemmas – Grid Solutions*, Gulf Publishing (1991).
33. Newborough, G. 'People vs Production', *British Journal of Administrative Management*, May/June 1999, pp. 13–14.
34. Crainer, S. and Dearlove, D. (eds) *Financial Times Handbook of Management*, second edition, Financial Times Prentice Hall (2001), p. 364.
35. Likert, R. *New Patterns of Management*, McGraw-Hill (1961).
36. Mann, S. 'Give a Little Gain a Lot', *Professional Manager*, March 1999, p. 32.
37. 'Building productive public sector workplaces: Part Three, Developing positive employee relations', CIPD, August 2010, p. 5.
38. Adams, J. S. 'Injustice in Social Exchange', abridged in Steers, R. M. and Porter, L. W. *Motivation and Work Behavior*, second edition, McGraw-Hill (1979), pp. 107–24.
39. See, for example, Beggs, A. 'The Real Meaning of Empowerment', *Financial Times Mastering Management Review*, September 1997, pp. 14–15.
40. Thomas, M. cited in Smith, P. 'Why it's time to break the rules', *Professional Manager*, vol. 20, no. 2, 2011, pp. 33–5; see also Thomas, M. *Loose: The Future of Business is Letting Go*, Headline Publishing (2011).
41. Robbins, S. P. *The Truth About Managing People*, second edition, Pearson Education (2008), p. 202.
42. Bolchover, D. 'Why Mood Matters', *Management Today*, November 2008, pp. 46–50.

43. Owen, J. *The Death of Modern Management: How to lead in the new world disorder*, Wiley (2009), pp. 241–2.

44. Howes, L. 'Life In A Managerless World', *Professional Manager,* Autumn 2013, pp. 42–5.

45. Metcalfe, H. and Urwick, L. (eds) *Dynamic Administration – The Collected Papers of Mary Parker Follett*, Harper (1941).

46. Drucker, P. F. *Classic Drucker,* Harvard Business School Press (2006), p. 194.

47. 'In Celebration of the Feel-Good Factor', *Professional Manager,* March 1998, p. 6.

48. Oswald, A.J., Proto, E. and Sgroi, D., 'Happiness and Productivity', Warwick University (2012), http://www.andrewoswald.com/docs/6MayOsProtoSgroi2012.pdf (accessed 20 February 2015).

49. Ibid., p. 9.

50. Ibid., p. 23.

51. Felps, W., Mitchell, T. and Byington, E. 'How, When, and Why Bad Apples Spoil the Barrel: Negative Group Members and Dysfunctional Groups', *Research in Organizational Behavior,* vol. 27, 2006, pp. 175–222. doi:10.1016/S0191-3085(06)27005-9.

52. Ibid., p. 213.

53. The Sunday Times online, http://features.thesundaytimes.co.uk/public/best100companies/live/template (accessed 20 February 2015).

54. http://www.ukrd.com/news/latest-ukrd-news/629214/double-2012-sunday-times-success-for-ukrd-group/

55. Rogers, W. 'Values: Sound advice', *People Management,* August 2012, pp. 40–3.

56. Ibid.

57. Ibid.

58. The Sunday Times online, http://features.thesundaytimes.co.uk/public/best100companies/live/template (accessed 20 February 2015).

59. Radio Today online, http://radiotoday.co.uk/2015/01/ukrd-celebrating-sixth-sunday-times-award/ (accessed 20 February 2015).

Academic viewpoint

Below you will find the title and abstract of a recent article in an academic journal that explores a topic relevant to the chapters in Part 3.

Marinova, S., Van Dyne, L. and Moon, H. 'Are Good Citizens Good Transformational Leaders as Well? An Employee-Centric Perspective on Transformational Leadership', *Group & Organization Management*, vol. 40, no. 1, 2015, pp. 62–87. doi: 10.1177/1059601114561257

Abstract

Research has demonstrated robust positive relationships between transformational leadership and employee attitudes and behaviors. To date, the preponderance of the literature has been leader-centric and focused on individuals who are already in leader roles. In this article, we adopt an employee-centric perspective and focus on behaviors of professionals who are not in formal leader roles. Specifically, we apply evolutionary theory as a theoretical lens for proposing that those who perform organizational citizenship behaviors (OCBs) will be seen as transformational leaders. We hypothesize linkages between four types of OCBs and four dimensions of transformational leadership. Multi-source field sample results based on more than 1,000 participants provide general support for the predictions. We discuss theoretical and practical implications.

Commentary

The authors have researched their hypothesis that not all people who show leadership are in formal leader or management roles within organisations. In professional organisations where people often put in a lot of 'discretionary effort' (going to great lengths to get jobs done) it seems possible that those who behave in the same way as transformational leaders can affect their colleagues in ways that encourage them to be loyal and put in extra effort on behalf of the organisation (organisational citizenship behaviours or OCBs). Individuals who seem to put the good of the organisation above their own personal interests are often well regarded by their colleagues and become role models. They indicate four ways in which OCB can be demonstrated (being a 'change agent' who tries to improve things, being a 'good Samaritan' who takes care of people, being a 'good soldier' who ensures things go to plan, and being a 'good sportsman' who acts as a stabilizing influence when there is conflict) and the circumstances under which each type of OCB is effective. They conclude that organisations could benefit from this understanding to develop training programmes to encourage transformational leadership and thereby increased organisational effectiveness.

The article might prompt you to consider some of the following questions

- To what extent does your own experience, either at work or in a social or sporting context, bear out the hypothesis that not all those who show leadership are in formal leader roles?

- Do you think it is better for organisations to identify and promote individuals who encourage OCBs or to leave them in non-leadership roles, and why?
- To what extent might managers feel threatened by informal types of transformational leadership in their team?
- Does the nature and structure of an organisation affect the likely emergence of transformational leaders who are *not* formal leaders? Would you expect to find similar results in different types of organisations such as manufacturing plants, large retail businesses or service organisations?

Part 3 Case study
The Eden Project

If a single word can be used to sum up the achievements of Tim Smit, that word might be 'regeneration'. To turn one derelict, neglected corner of southwest England into a successful tourist business attracting millions of visitors is a remarkable achievement, but to do it twice is simply astonishing. Yet this is precisely what Smit has done, and in the Eden Project we can see the nature of this achievement through a blend of visionary and innovative leadership combined with a strong sense of the value of teamwork.

Before Eden

Cornwall is one of several parts of the UK that suffered economic decline during the later twentieth century. Its industrial heritage has all but disappeared in the wake of globalisation and the shifting nature of the industrial world landscape. The last tin mine closed in 1998, and the ruined mine towers are witness to what was once the largest tin mining industry in the world. The production of china clay remains one of Cornwall's oldest current industries, but that too is in decline and a European Union report of 2014 noted that Cornwall was possibly the poorest region in the UK.[1] The fishing business is contracting, and traditional agricultural and horticultural production, mainly vegetables and flower bulbs, is being challenged by similar, year-round levels of production in developing countries. Cornwall as a county has, for some years, been in receipt of European Union Objective One funding destined to assist with economic regeneration in Europe's poorest regions. This level of relative poverty is probably something that many of the tourists who visit Cornwall's beautiful landscapes,

The Eden Project is the realisation of one man's extraordinary vision through powerful teamwork and global co-operation.
Source: Tamsyn Williams/The Eden Project

historic properties and wild coastland do not generally see; indeed tourism has become one of the largest single income-generating business sectors in the area. While there are some strong indications that the Cornish economy might be revitalised by the arrival of new, knowledge-based industries that are supported by technological developments, tourism remains at the heart of the county's economy.[2]

In 1990, in a project that would contribute substantially to Cornwall's reputation as a tourist destination, John Willis, Tim Smit and John Nelson began to restore the long-derelict gardens surrounding the stately home and seat of the Tremayne family at Heligan, near Mevagissey. The story of this garden, its dereliction after the start of the Great War of 1914, its rediscovery following

→

a storm in 1990 and its restoration, in part as a memorial to the gardeners who would have died in the war, is one of enormous poignancy and beauty.[3] For Smit, an archaeology and anthropology graduate who had also developed a love of gardens, it was a project that enabled him to use many of his professional skills, and the garden itself has become one of England's most loved,[4] and a major attraction for Cornwall.

However, while Heligan is horticultural archaeology, and the gardens today are, in essence, a living museum of nineteenth-century estate gardening, the Eden Project was a very different type of restoration, and one that drew upon Smit's additional skills as a rock music producer and showman. What Smit was restoring in his second major project was land, and the vision and purpose behind the Eden Project looks to the future rather than the past.

Ten things to do with a disused clay pit. . .

Photographs of what was to become the Eden Project prior to the arrival of Tim and his team reveal the extent of the transformation. In the mid-1990s the worked-out Bodelva china clay pit near St Austell looked very much like what many believed it to be: a derelict, polluted and worthless piece of land stripped of fertile soil – essentially a 34-acre puddle. The statistics behind its transformation into one of the most spectacular tourist attractions in the country are mind-boggling. The first task, in 1998 when the project began, was to landscape the site and shift 1.8 million tons of earth to reduce the pit-side gradients, a task that took twelve dumper trucks and eight bulldozers six months. During the first few months of work, it rained almost continuously, which resulted in 43 million gallons of water draining into the clay-lined pit.[5] This was both a problem and an opportunity: the problem was to design a drainage system that would prevent the whole site turning into a soggy bog during the average English summer; but the opportunity was to demonstrate one of the founding principles of sustainability, and use the run-off water to service the site. The system designed to meet this purpose collects, on average, 22 litres a second, and about two-thirds of the water needed to run the project (including plant watering, a 22-metre waterfall in the tropical biome and the numerous toilets!) is 'grey' water, in other words that which can be harvested from the site itself. Over 85,000 tonnes of soil, made from waste products and other organic material, were needed to turn the clay-lined puddle into the fertile ground in which over 1,000,000 plants of more than 5,000 species could grow, to create a series of global gardens.

The two original 'biomes', spectacular greenhouses that recreate a humid tropical environment and warm temperate climate respectively, are perhaps what most visitors remember about the project, although more than half the site is actually open air. The Humid Tropics biome is the largest conservatory in the world at 240 metres by 100 metres by 55 metres high, enclosing 15,590 square metres. It houses 'the biggest jungle in captivity' and contains plants native to the tropical areas of the world including Malaysia, West Africa and South America as well as islands like the Seychelles. The Warm Temperate biome covers 6,540 square metres, and replicates a Mediterranean climate housing plants that represent those that grow between 30°–40° north and south of the equator. The 'Core' is the project's education centre, the roof of which is constructed on the same mathematical principle (the Fibonacci sequence of interwoven spirals) that appears in nature in many plant formations, and which is also the way in which some plants pack the maximum number of seeds, spines or leaves into the smallest possible area.[6] And since summer 2012 you can fly over the entire site on a 740-metre-long zipwire – if you have a head for heights!

If you build it, they will come

The Eden Project is a wholly owned subsidiary of the Eden Trust, a registered charity, and initially cost £120 million to build. The money was raised from a variety of sources including grant funding, such as that from the UK government's Millennium Project Fund. Together with commercial loans, the grant money is used for capital investment on the site and educational or conservation projects in other parts of the world. Revenue comes from both the commercial activities of the project and gifts or donations.[7] The money is used to run the operation, maintain the asset base and service the commercial loans; so although as a charity it does not make a profit, it does have to run at commercially successful levels. Visitors provide the major source of revenue, and Eden has regularly attracted over a million a year since it opened in 2001 – although the recession combined with a very wet year saw them drop below that number for the first time during 2012–13. Nevertheless, Eden won the British Travel Awards accolade as Best UK Leisure Attraction for the third year running in November 2013.[8] So what exactly do people come to see?

Tim Smit's vision for Eden is far from being that of just another garden. He is, as we have noted, not a horticulturalist, but an archaeologist, anthropologist and former rock-show organiser. The purpose of Eden is essentially to educate people about the environment and the human relationship with the plant world, but to do so in such a way as to set a conservation and sustainability example that is, above all things, spectacular fun. The 2012–13 Annual Sustainability Report explains how:

> The Eden Project tells the story of people's dependence on the natural world, of regeneration and what people can achieve when they work together and with nature. It is designed to give our visitors a great day out while demonstrating, in a serious yet playful way, how indispensable plants and people are to each other; how we all can adapt together to this challenging new world; and how even the most barren, worked-out China clay pit can be transformed into a place of beauty. This same message underpins all of our educational and outreach projects which explore new ways of living in the 21st century. Eden is also a social enterprise, demonstrating that doing business while improving the environment and livelihoods and building stronger communities can work hand in hand.[9]

The Eden Project identifies three essential elements in its approach to this task:

- Educational programmes – This includes the design of the site, and all the events that happen there, many of which are connected with schools and colleges or seek to convey important social messages.[10] Recent activities include an 'Empty Classrooms Day' in July, a national event to encourage schools to make the most of outdoor spaces and use them to animate lessons, and, in collaboration with Anglia Ruskin University, the launch of a masters-level programme, the 'MSc Sustainability: Working for Positive Change', some of which is delivered at the Eden site.
- Operational practice – Eden believes the way it runs the site should be an inspiration and example to both commercial corporations and public bodies; this is part of its aim to develop the notion and currency of social enterprises. As well as its 'waste-neutral' ambitions, the project has partnered with EGS Energy to build a geothermal electricity plant that will not only power the project, but contribute to the national grid.
- Spreading Eden's mission through outreach activities and acting as an agency for change – This aspect involves using the Eden venue to host both major events that facilitate dialogue about significant environmental matters and smaller courses and

programmes to teach horticultural techniques. There are business development programmes, team-building workshops and corporate away days, and courses to help teachers integrate outdoor activities into the school curriculum.

The educational purpose that underlies the Eden Project shows that this is, indeed, far more than just another garden. The achievement of these objectives requires both focused and decisive leadership, but also powerful teamwork.

Taking a lead

The television series *Gardeners of Eden*[11], which presented a year in the life of the Eden Project, gives some insight into both the nature of Tim Smit's leadership style and the range of activities undertaken by the different teams required to run the project. It also shows some of the very human problems associated with such an enterprise, including conflicts of interest between the project's main purpose and some of the professional teams whose tasks are to contribute to that objective.

Smit generally dresses casually and has the slightly scruffy air of someone who is not accustomed to spending much of his working day in an office or behind a desk. In a *Guardian* article prior to a major lecture at the Royal Society of Arts (RSA), the interviewer noted some of Smit's key qualities:

> Smit's secret, if there is one, seems to be that he can bring people of very different disciplines and skills together, get them to brainstorm and collaborate, and come up with the extraordinary. The Eden Project, he says, has attracted locals by the score, but also high-flying artists, businessmen, architects, scientists, engineers, educationalists, horticulturalists and ecologists from all over Britain. 'It feels like a renaissance organisation,' says one woman who left a senior management job to work there as a director and has been amazed both at what gets done and the way it works. 'It's attracted a critical mass of people, and there's this passionate belief, right through the project, that it belongs to everyone who works there, that it's a team thing. I guess it demonstrates that you can have an organisation that is highly effective financially, environmentally and socially. It's a kind of experiment to show that you can work in different ways.' A local woman who has been with Eden since the start is more succinct: 'It's the most equal place I've known,' she says.
>
> 'This is a stage for change,' says Smit, who admits that Eden can seem like a sect to outsiders. 'Many people have made life choices to come here. Most could earn

five times as much elsewhere. But I'm aware that if you want to effect real change, and we do, that you must not own it. You have got to make sure that it's owned by more than one person.'[12]

Smit is described as optimistic and positive, with a mission to make people think differently. He is concerned to challenge dogma from all sides and is happy to question the views of committed environmentalists like José Bové, as well as those of traditionalists. Although educational, he is convinced that the Eden Project need not be stuffy or seek to preach; above all, fun, excitement and spectacle are integral to the educational process. This lays him open to the accusation that it is no more than a 'green theme park'; indeed his desire to make the project a centre for spectacle and display brings him into conflict with the horticulturalists on the site. In the year of filming, it is clear that the two managers of the biomes deeply resent the disturbance and damage done to their plants by teams of electricians hired to lay lighting cables in and around the buildings to support some of the spectacles and events that are planned. A third curator-in-waiting is frustrated that the project to build the dry tropics biome, which is planned to house his extensive cactus and succulent collection, has been put back by several years, leapfrogged by the project to build the 'Core' education centre.

Smit is also very 'hands-on' in the sense that he is both integral to many of the special events and equally prepared to help with selling tickets and guiding visitors on the peak season 'tricky days' – peak visitor days on which staff who do not normally work with visitors are encouraged to follow his example and pitch in to help keep the operation moving.[13]

Working in paradise

By 2014, the Eden Project had grown to be a major local employer with almost 500 staff on the payroll, and some 400 or more additional volunteer workers who are drafted in to help with peak seasonal activities such as horticulture and visitor operations. A regular internship programme brings in new graduates, helping them build their CVs and network with professionals in their field while developing practical skills in the workplace. The workforce is focused into a number of 'Eden Teams', the main one being the **Destination Team.** This team includes the **Green Team** of horticultural curators and other experts who manage the biomes and the planting, but in addition the people who run events and exhibitions as well as the retail and catering operations. This team is very much the 'front of house', as the gardeners work in the public eye during the day. However, as the programme shows, they also work

outside opening hours, often at night, to carry out certain potentially hazardous activities, such as lopping unstable branches from trees in the rainforest. It is also clear from the series that there can be significant differences of opinion and interest between the Green Team and Smit. This came to the fore when Smit planned the first major winter event, the 'Time of Gifts' festival. This was partly an attempt to increase winter visitor numbers to the site, but required special construction (of an ice rink) and lighting in order to accommodate a variety of story-telling activities in the biomes, as well as 'light-and-magic' processions and shows. The whole event clearly opened something of a rift between members of the Green Team and Smit, since many felt that their values were being compromised and the whole project was becoming a sort of Disneyland. One curator told the BBC crew that the events not only did physical damage, but also damaged the morale of staff. Not only were curators upset, but the catering and housekeeping staff were also very concerned by the heavy demands (not least of which was having to learn to skate!) that would be made, and Smit is seen running a fairly fraught staff meeting with Destination Team personnel in an attempt to encourage them and gain extra commitment. When the event was successful, the staff were thrown a celebratory party, but nevertheless some of the Green Team were absent in protest. Smit explains his view about this conflict of interests:

I'm not into horticulture; my role isn't horticulture. My job is to fizz people into getting excited about horticulture, which is a very very different activity. And actually, the certainties that horticulturalists want are exactly the sort of thing I want to shake up.[14]

While the Destination Team is clearly the face of the Eden Project, other teams include the **Foundation Team,** which works with supporters of the project and also looks outwards to develop education and other scientific and technological projects; the **Marketing Team** and the **Communications Team,** which run an in-house publishing company as well as more traditional communications activities including the website; the **Development Team,** which is involved with major projects such as building and includes people from partner organisations such as architects and construction companies; the **Finance Team,** which ensures the project is economically viable and fully accountable to its various stakeholders; the **Creative Team,** which develops and produces events, including the regular concerts, many of which feature major pop and rock artists (Elton John played to 6,000 people there in June 2015); and the **Organisational Development Team,** which 'looks after our people' and is essentially concerned to link the processes and operations and build the Eden culture. Eden also includes the public as its **Visiting Team,** in other words the paying customers whose interaction with the project is vital to its continuation.

Between them, Tim Smit (who was awarded an honorary knighthood in 2011) and the Eden Project teams have been tremendously successful in both business and educational terms. Not only has a vision been realised in terms of the physical development of the site, but it has created well over 400 jobs, and the majority of staff were recruited locally. But above all, it has provided millions of people with a memorable and exciting experience, which almost all would recommend to others.

Tasks

1. In the television programme, Smit explains part of his management philosophy thus:

    It is essential for me to like everybody I work with, which is not a very professional thing if you were doing an MBA; you employ people on their merits and their CVs. Bugger that for a game of darts! If I'm going to get out of bed in the morning to do something like this, I want to walk through that door really looking forward to seeing everybody that's there. And you know what? I have the tremendous privilege of that being so.

    Using frameworks and concepts from the chapter on work groups and teams, critically review this approach to the creation of work teams and organisations. What are the strengths and the risks of taking such a view about the people who work for you?

2. Analyse Tim Smit's leadership style in the light of appropriate theories. Does it help or hinder his leadership that, as chief executive of a project about plants, he is 'not a horticulturalist'?

3. During 2013, and as a result of a downturn in its business, Eden had to restructure its business and make a number of people redundant (see the Eden Project's Annual Sustainability Report 2012–13, page 16, available on its website for details). How might the organisation's leaders help minimise the effects on staff motivation of this change? Explain whether you think its status as a social enterprise makes the task more or less difficult.

4. Tim Smit now lectures to all sorts of both commercial and non-commercial organisational leaders about management. Analyse the extent to which his approach might be transferable to both profit-making organisations and public-sector ones, whose stakeholder groups are very different from those at Eden.

Notes and references

1 Demianyk, G. 'Cornwall economy slips back in fight with Europe's poorest', *Western Morning News*, 7 May 2014, **http://www.westernmorningnews.co.uk/Cornwall-economy-slips-fight-Europe-s-poorest/story-21063726-detail/story.html** (accessed 16 February 2015).
2 **Smale, W. 'How Cornwall's economy is fighting back', BBC News, 2006, http://news.bbc.co.uk** (accessed 16 February 2015).
3 Smit, T. *The Lost Gardens of Heligan*, Orion Books (2000; first published 1997).
4 Visit the Lost Gardens of Heligan website at **www.heligan.com** to get a feel for this glorious garden.
5 The Eden Project Guide 2004–5.
6 For instance, pine cones, sunflower heads, pineapples and many cacti show this pattern.
7 Eden Project, Annual Sustainability Report 2012–13, **www.edenproject.com** (accessed 16 February 2015).
8 Eden Project Annual Report 2013–14, p. 33.
9 Eden Project, Annual Sustainability Report 2012–13, p. 1.
10 Eden, for instance, ran an 'Africa Calling' concert during the 2005 'Live8' day which featured a host of bands and internationally known artists from many parts of Africa.
11 The BBC DVD, *The Eden Project: The Gardeners of Eden*, BBC (2005), covers part of the years 2004–5.
12 Vidal, J. 'Shaping the Future', *Guardian*, 6 October 2004.
13 BBC DVD 2005, op. cit.
14 BBC DVD 2005, op. cit.

PART 4
Structure, strategy and effectiveness

CHAPTER 11
Organisation structure and design

It is by means of structure that the work of the organisation is carried out. Structure provides the framework of an organisation and its pattern of management. Some structure is necessary to make possible the effective performance of key activities and to support the efforts of staff. The manager needs to understand the importance and effects of structure, and the variables that influence the most appropriate structure for a particular organisation.

Learning outcomes

After completing this chapter you should have enhanced your ability to:

- detail the purpose and importance of good structure and consequences of a deficient structure;
- explore the underlying dimensions and design features of organisation structure;
- explain formal organisational relationships that exist between individuals;
- explore situational variables influencing patterns of structure;
- review the nature of the contingency approach and main contingency models;
- assess the changing nature of the workplace and demand for flexibility;
- debate realities of structure and organisational behaviour.

Critical review and reflection

Structure is the defining feature of a work organisation. However good the goals and objectives, systems of management or quality of its members, an organisation will not achieve optimum performance without a sound and appropriate structure.

Give YOUR critical view of this assertion. What do YOU expect to learn from YOUR study of organisation structure?

The purpose and importance of structure

The purpose of structure is the division of work among members of the organisation and the co-ordination of their activities so they are directed towards the goals and objectives of the organisation. Structure makes possible the application of the process of management and creates a framework of order and command through which the activities of the organisation can be planned, organised, directed and controlled. The structure defines tasks and responsibilities, work roles and relationships, and channels of communication.

Underlying the effective management of people is the requirement for a clear understanding of the nature of the business in which the organisation is engaged. If the organisation is to be successful then its structure must be related to its objectives and to its strategy. Structure must be designed to be appropriate to environmental influences, the continued development of the business and the management of opportunities and risks. There is obviously a close relationship between organisation structure and corporate strategy (**discussed in Chapter 14**). It is by means of the organisation's structure that its goals and objectives are attained.

Structure is clearly important for any organisation, whatever its size. However, in the smaller organisations there are likely to be fewer problems of structure. The distribution of tasks, the definition of authority and responsibility, and the relationship between members of the organisation can be established on a more personal and informal basis. With increasing size, however, there is greater need for a carefully designed and purposeful form of organisation. There is need for a formal **organisation structure**. There is also need for a continual review of structure to ensure that it is the most appropriate form for the particular organisation, and in keeping with its growth and development.

Structure provides the framework for the activities of the organisation and must harmonise with its goals and objectives. The purpose of structure may be summarised as to provide for:

- economic and efficient performance of the organisation and level of resource utilisation;
- monitoring activities of the organisation;
- accountability for areas of work undertaken by groups and individual members of the organisation;
- co-ordination of different parts of the organisation and different areas of work;
- flexibility in order to respond to future demands and developments, and to adapt to changing environmental influences; and
- social satisfaction of members working in the organisation.[1]

Structure, though, is not an end in itself but a means of improving organisational performance. According to *Drucker*, it is the correct design of structure that is of most significance in determining organisational performance.

> *Good organisation structure does not by itself produce good performance. But a poor organisation structure makes good performance impossible, no matter how good the individual managers may be. To improve organisation structure . . . will therefore always improve performance.*[2]

The importance of good structure is also emphasised by *Child:*

> *In the final resort, it is vital that we understand what organization is, what it does, and the grounds on which it can be justified because it is not just a means to achieving better economic performance but also exerts a profound influence on the societies in which we live . . . The form of organization we employ transports values back into society and carries a message about how to treat other people.*[3]

The human element

The functions of the formal structure, and the activities and defined relationships within it, exist independently of the members of the organisation who carry out the work. Structure should be designed, therefore, so as to encourage both the willing participation of members of the organisation and effective organisational performance. *Lord Forte,* for example, has drawn attention to the importance of the human element in organisation structure:

> *The human aspect in a business is vital: you can keep drawing squares and lines, but within these squares you must have people and they must be deeply involved with the business. If this does not happen, then the lines and squares and the diagrams mean nothing.*[4]

One of the strongest critics of the formal organisation is *Argyris.* He claims that the formal, bureaucratic organisation restricts individual growth and self-fulfilment and, in the psychologically healthy person, causes a feeling of failure, frustration and conflict. Argyris argues that the organisation should provide a more 'authentic' relationship for its members. Managers need to consider how structural design and methods of work organisation influence the behaviour and performance of members of the organisation.[5]

Lucas points out that rigid structures are all very well but they can and do inhibit free thinking, which is vital for creativity. Referring to the parallels between 'the stage' and working life, Lucas reports on the use of improvisation as a means of helping managers work together better in teams, release creativity and improve their presentation skills.[6]

Critical review and reflection

Personalities are an important part of the work organisation. Whatever its formal structure, in practice the actual operations of the organisation and success in meeting its objectives will depend upon the behaviour and actions of people within the structure.

To what extent do YOU think people give shape and personality to the formal structure of YOUR university or organisation?

Levels of organisation

Determination of policy and decision-making, the execution of work, and the exercise of authority and responsibility are carried out by different people at varying levels of seniority throughout the structure. In small organisations, these activities tend to be less distinct, but in the larger organisations it is possible to look at organisations in terms of three broad interrelated levels in the hierarchical structure: the **technical level**, the **managerial level** and the **community level.**[7] These last two levels are often referred to as middle management and senior management.

The **technical level** is concerned with specific operations and discrete tasks, with the actual job or tasks to be done, and with performance of the technical function. Examples are the physical production of goods in a manufacturing firm, administrative processes giving direct service to the public in government departments and the actual process of teaching in an educational establishment. The technical level interrelates with the **managerial** (or organisational) **level**, concerned with the co-ordination and integration of work at the technical level. Decisions at the managerial level relate to the resources necessary for performance of the technical function and to the beneficiaries of the products or services provided.

In turn, the managerial level interrelates with the **community** (or institutional) **level**, concerned with broad objectives and the work of the organisation as a whole. Decisions at the community level will be concerned with the selection of operations and the development of the organisation in relation to the wider social environment. Examples of the community level within organisations are the board of directors of joint-stock companies, governing bodies of educational establishments that include external representatives, and trustees of non-profit organisations. Such bodies provide a mediating link between the managerial organisation and co-ordination of work of the technical organisation and the wider community interests.

Divide between senior and middle management

Rawson draws attention to the increasing absence of mutuality between senior and middle managers in both the public and private sector.

> *Traditionally, senior managers have been concerned with setting the strategic direction and objectives for the organisation; middle managers with making it happen – resourcing and managing the changes. The corollary is that senior managers are concerned with results and middle managers with how these are achieved. The divide appears as middle levels complain that their seniors are solely concerned with short-term financial results and as seniors reply that the middle strata devote more effort to voicing problems than to finding solutions. In both sectors the delayering of organisations has dramatically reduced the resources available to middle managers. The divide deepens as each accuses the other of pursuing their own personal rather than organisational ends. Middle accuse senior of being concerned with their own career advancement: senior accuse middle of directing their efforts to protecting their positions.[8]*

Blurring of differentiation

In practice, there is no clear division between determination of policy and decision-making, co-ordination of activities and the actual execution of work. Most decisions are taken with reference to the execution of wider decisions, and most execution of work involves decision. Decisions taken at the institutional level determine objectives for the managerial level, and decisions at the managerial level set objectives for the technical level (*see* Figure 11.1). Movement towards more democratic organisations, empowerment, an increase in knowledge workers and technological advances have contributed to lack of a clear distinction between policy, management and the execution of work. Flatter structures, the dismantling

Figure 11.1 Interrelated levels of organisation

of hierarchies and virtual teams all contribute to a further blurring of differentiation. The three broad levels do, however, provide a basis for a critical analysis of the interrelated activities of the organisation.

Underlying dimensions of organisation structure

There are many variables that influence the most appropriate organisation structure and system of management. There is nevertheless an underlying need to establish a framework of order and system of command by which the work to be undertaken is accomplished successfully. **These principles and considerations are not prescriptive but present a series of initial important decision points for design of organisation structure, or in reviewing the effectiveness of an existing structure (*see* Figure 11.2).**

Figure 11.2 Considerations in design of organisation structure

Task and element functions

In order to produce some product, or provide some service, there are four essential functions that the organisation must perform:

1. The product or service must be developed.
2. Something of value must be created – the production or manufacture of a product or provision of a service.
3. The product or services must be marketed, and distributed or made available to those who are to use them.
4. Finance is needed in order to make available resources for the development, creation and distribution of the products or services provided.

These essential functions, what *Woodward* refers to as the **'task' functions,** are the basic activities of the organisation related to the actual completion of the productive process and directed towards specific and definable end results.[9] Other activities of the organisation not directed towards specific and definable ends are supportive of the task functions and an intrinsic part of the management process. These are referred to as **'element' functions** and include, for example, human resources, planning, management services, public relations, quality control and maintenance. In the majority of organisations, the HR function does not normally have any direct accountability for the performance of a specific end-task. In certain organisations, however, noticeably in service industries involving direct customer contact, HR management can arguably be seen as closely associated with a task function.[10]

Failure to distinguish between the two types of functions can lead to confusion in the planning of structure and in the relationship between members of the organisation. For example, in her study of the management organisation of firms in this country, Woodward comments on the bad relationships between accountants and other managers referred to during the study. One reason for this hostility was the bringing together of two quite separate financial functions essential to the efficient operation of a business.

> *People concerned with works accounting tended to assume responsibility for end results that was not properly theirs; they saw their role as a controlling and sanctioning one rather than as a servicing and supportive one. Line managers resented this attitude and retaliated by becoming aggressive and obstructive.*[11]

According to Woodward, activities concerned with raising funds for the business, keeping accounts and determination of financial policy are task functions. Management accounting, however, concerned with prediction and control of production administration, is an element function, and is primarily a servicing and supportive one. Relationships between the accountants and other managers seemed better when the two functions were organisationally separate.

Critical review and reflection

Many organisational conflicts arise through element functions, such as human resource management, overstepping responsibilities and failure to recognise the primary purpose as support to the essential task functions of the organisation.

How valid do YOU think the distinction is between task and element functions? To what extent can YOU see conflict between the two functions in YOUR university or organisation?

Division of work and grouping of people

Within the formal structure, work has to be divided among its members and different jobs related to each other. The division of work and the grouping together of people should, wherever possible, be organised by reference to some common characteristic that forms a logical link between the activities involved. Work can be divided, and activities linked together, in a variety of ways.

Major purpose or function

The most common basis for grouping activities is according to specialisation, the use of the same set of resources, or the shared expertise of members of staff. It is a matter for decision in each organisation as to which activities are important enough to be organised into separate functions, departments or sections. Work may be departmentalised and based, for example, on differentiation between task and element functions, discussed above (*see* Figure 11.3).

Product or service

Contributions of different specialists are integrated into separate, semi-autonomous units with collective responsibility for a major part of the business process or for a complete cycle of work. This form of grouping is more common in the larger diversified organisations and may be used as a means of sub-dividing departments into sections. An example is the bringing together of all activities concerned with a particular production line, product or service (*see* Figure 11.4). Another example is a hospital where medical and support staff are grouped together in different units dealing with particular treatments such as accidents and emergency, medical or surgery. With grouping by product or service there is a danger that the divisions may attempt to become too autonomous, presenting management with a problem of co-ordination and control.

Location

Different services are provided by area or geographical boundaries according to particular needs or demands, the convenience of consumers, or for ease of administration (*see* Figure 11.5). Examples are the provision of local authority services for people living in a particular locality, sales territories for business firms or the grouping of a number of retail shops under an area manager. Another example is provided by organisations with multi-site working and the grouping of a range of similar activities or functions located together on one site. Improvement

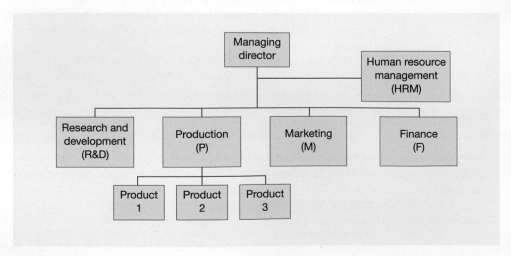

Figure 11.3 Division of work by major purpose or function

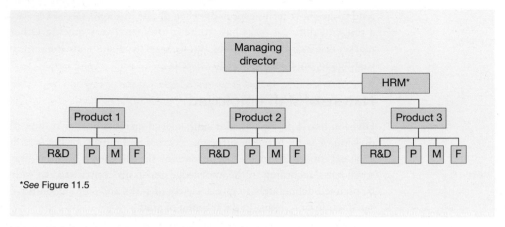

*See Figure 11.5

Figure 11.4 Division of work by product or service

*In the case of division of work by product or service, or by geographical location, it is possible that certain aspects of support services, such as human resource management, may also be assigned to individual units of the organisation. However, the main responsibility of the HRM manager, as a separate entity, is to provide a specialist advisory service to all unit managers and to ensure implementation of HRM policy throughout the organisation as a whole. Responsibility for the main aspects of the HRM function is likely to remain, therefore, in a direct line of authority from top management.

Figure 11.5 Division of work by location

in telecommunications tends, however, to reduce the importance of location. For example, administrative staff may no longer need to be located within the main production unit.

Nature of work performed

This is division according to the nature of work performed where there is some special common feature of the work, such as the need for speedy decisions, accuracy, confidentiality/security, or where local conditions require first-hand knowledge not immediately available elsewhere. Another example may be the grouping of equipment or machinery that is noisy or produces dust, fumes or unpleasant odours. When common processes are used in a range of different activities, this may also be used as the basis of division. This method of grouping includes, for example, the decision as to whether to establish a centralised resource centre for all departments of the organisation or to allow each department to have its own service.

Common time scales

Division according to time scales, for example shift working. In a further education college there may be separate departments or groupings to deal with the different needs of full-time day and part-time evening students. Another example is in a hotel. Activities in the kitchen tend to be short term, especially when guests in the restaurant are waiting to be served, and a range of different tasks have to be co-ordinated very quickly. Other activities, for example market research and forecasting future room occupancy, are longer-term decisions and subject to different organisational requirements.

Nature of staff employed

Division based on a particular skill, special qualification or responsibility – for example, the division of work between surgeons, doctors and nurses, or between barristers, solicitors and legal executives. In smaller organisations the allocation of work may be on an ad hoc, personal basis according to the knowledge and skills contributed by individuals. Work may also be planned deliberately to give a variety of tasks and responsibilities to provide improved job satisfaction or to assist in the training of staff.

Customers or clients to be served

Separate groups may be established to deal with different consumer requirements – for example, the division between trade and retail customers or between home and export sales. In hospitals there are different groupings dealing with, for example, patients in the gynaecology, geriatric and children's wards. In large clothes shops there may be separate departments for men's, women's and children's clothing. Government departments are often grouped by this method and work is divided according to whom the services are provided – for example, the unemployed, low-pay families, students, people or senior citizens. A further example is the provision of restaurant services according to type of customer or customer demand such as price, range or standard of meals and speed of service.

Centralisation and decentralisation

The balance between centralisation and decentralisation is one of the major debates in organisation structure. Most organisations necessarily involve a degree of **decentralisation** arising from such features as an increase in size, the geographical separation of different parts of the organisation, or the need to extend activities or services to remote areas. Our main concern is with decentralisation or devolution in terms of specific delegation or empowerment to sub-units or groups within the organisation such that they enjoy a measure of autonomy or independence.

Advantages often claimed for centralisation tend to relate to economic and administrative considerations. However, such advantages frequently are not realised fully and do not lead to an actual improvement in service. There are a number of contrary arguments against centralisation, including the criticism that it creates a more mechanistic structure and may result in lengthening the chain of command. There are also positive arguments, which tend to relate more to behavioural considerations, in favour of decentralisation (*see* Figure 11.6).

Extent of decentralisation

Growing emphasis on participation and empowerment suggests a focus of attention on the principles of decentralisation, yet senior management still need to maintain effective co-ordination and overall control of the activities of the organisation as a whole. The balance between centralisation and decentralisation will be affected by such factors as the importance of decision-making, the urgency of the situation and time scales, and also by technological developments, changes in structure, the prevailing organisational climate and the nature of staff employed. Decentralisation generally tends to be easier to implement in

Advantages of centralisation

■ the easier implementation of a common policy for the organisation as a whole;

■ provides a consistent strategy across the organisation;

■ prevents sub-units from becoming too independent;

■ makes for easier co-ordination and management control;

■ improved economies of scale and a reduction in overhead costs;

■ greater use of specialisation, including better facilities and equipment;

■ improved decision-making, which might otherwise be slower and a result of compromise because of diffused authority.

Advantages of decentralisation

■ enables decisions to be made closer to the operational level of work;

■ increased responsiveness to local circumstances;

■ improved level of personal customer service;

■ more in keeping with developments in flatter and more flexible structures;

■ support services, such as adminstration, are more likely to be effective if provided as close as possible to the activities they are intended to serve;

■ provides opportunities for training and development in management;

■ usually, it has an encouraging effect on the motivation and morale of staff.

Figure 11.6 Advantages of centralisation or decentralisation

private-sector organisations than in public-sector organisations, where there is a greater demand for the accountability of their operations, regularity of procedures and uniformity of treatment.

Critical review and reflection

Attention to basic principles and considerations in the design of structure, such as division of work, grouping of people and extent of decentralisation, is essential for effective management and organisational performance.

To what extent do YOU support this contention? How well are these design principles applied to the structure of YOUR university or organisation?

Principles of organisation

As mentioned earlier (**Chapter 2**), the classical writers placed emphasis on the requirements of the formal organisation and the search for a common set of principles applicable to all circumstances. The idea of common sets of principles on organisation and management has been subject to much criticism. Statements are expressed in non-operational terms and give little basis for specific managerial action, and tend to view people as a given rather than as a variable in the system. However, it is difficult to argue against the principles providing general guidance on the structuring of organisations. The basic concepts can be of value to the practical manager, **if modified to suit the demands of the particular situation,** including the nature of staffing in the organisation. The proper application of these principles is likely to help improve organisational performance. Three of the more specific principles of general interest in the structuring of organisations are: (i) the hierarchy; (ii) the span of control; and (iii) the chain of command.

Importance of the hierarchy

Early writers on management drew attention to the importance of the **hierarchy**. That is, clearly delineated levels of management authority as a means of co-ordination and control. However, the changing nature of work has led to discussion on the continuing role and importance role of the hierarchy and the extent to which managers can rely solely on their perceived formal authority within the structure of the organisation.

The importance of the hierarchy is emphasised strongly by *Drucker,* who asserts: 'One hears a great deal today about "the end of the hierarchy". This is blatant nonsense. In any institution there has to be a final authority, that is, a "boss" – someone who can make the final decisions and who can expect them to be obeyed.'[12]

However, contrary to the view of Drucker, *Cloke and Goldsmith* question whether we are accustomed to and have accepted the hierarchy, rules and managers as an essential part of organisational life. Have managers been seduced by the apparent power over others that a hierarchical organisation offers and by the disproportionate rewards it can provide to those at the top? If so, this is depriving individuals of the chance to develop themselves to their full potential and cluttering organisations with wasteful and counterproductive processes.[13]

Gratton has maintained that, more than at any other point in time, there is a chance to create the democratic enterprise.

> *Over the last decade it has become increasingly clear that through the forces of globalization, competition and more demanding customers, the structure of many companies has become flatter, less hierarchical, more fluid and virtual. The breakdown of hierarchies provides us with fertile ground on which to create a more democratic way of working.*[14]

Note, however, that *Child* maintains: 'despite the widespread disparagement of hierarchy, most companies find it very difficult to avoid it once they have grown beyond a very small size'.[15]

Span of control

Span of control refers to the number of subordinates who report directly to a given manager or supervisor. It does not refer to the total of subordinate operating staff, that is those who report first to another person. Hence the term 'span of responsibility' or 'span of supervision' is sometimes considered to be more appropriate. *Graicunas* developed a mathematical formula for the span of control.[16] The limitation of the number of subordinates who can effectively be supervised is based on the total of direct and cross-relationships

$$R = n\left\{\frac{2^n}{2} + n - 1\right\}$$

where *n* is the number of subordinates and *R* is the number of interrelationships. For example, with five subordinates the total number of interrelationships requiring the attention of the manager is 100; with six subordinates the number of interrelationships is 222.

If the span of control is *too wide,* it becomes difficult to supervise subordinates effectively and this places more stress on the manager. With larger groupings, informal leaders and subgroups or cliques are more likely to develop. If the span of control is *too narrow,* this may present a problem of co-ordination and consistency in decision-making and hinder effective communications. Morale and initiative of subordinates may suffer as a result of too close a level of supervision. Narrow spans of control can lead to additional levels of authority in the organisation, creating an unnecessarily long chain of command.

Chain of command

This refers to the number of different levels in the structure of the organisation. The **chain of command** establishes the vertical graduation of authority and responsibility, and the framework for superior–subordinate relationships in an unbroken line down from the top of the organisation. Every person should know their position within the structure of the organisation. Most organisation charts demonstrate that this principle is used widely as a basis for organisation design. A clear line of authority and responsibility is necessary for the effective operation of the organisation.

It seems generally accepted that for reasons of morale and to help decision-making and communications, there should be as few levels as possible in the chain of command. There is danger in adding to the structure in such a way that it results in increased hierarchical authority and control, and leads to the risk of empire building and the creation of unnecessary work in justification of the new position. However, if efforts are made to reduce the number of levels this may bring about an increase in the span of control.

Need for a balanced structure

The balance of span of control and chain of command determines the overall pyramid shape of the organisation and whether the hierarchical structure is 'flat' or 'tall' (*see* Figure 11.7). Broader spans of control and fewer levels of authority result in a **flat hierarchical structure** as tends to be found, for example, in universities. Narrower spans of control and more levels of authority result in a **tall hierarchical structure** as tends to be found, for example, in the civil service or the armed forces. There is no one, ideal combination of span of control and scalar chain. This depends upon the particular situation for each organisation, but it is important to provide an appropriate, balanced structure.

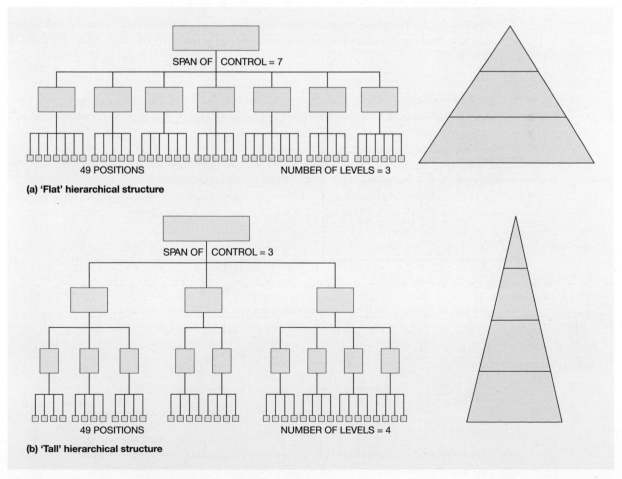

(a) 'Flat' hierarchical structure

SPAN OF CONTROL = 7
49 POSITIONS   NUMBER OF LEVELS = 3

(b) 'Tall' hierarchical structure

SPAN OF CONTROL = 3
49 POSITIONS   NUMBER OF LEVELS = 4

Figure 11.7 How span of control affects organisation structure

Critical review and reflection

Advancement through the hierarchy is seen as an indicator of career progression, recognition of merit and reward for achievement. Organisations are a form of social stratification. Removing the hierarchy will only cause lack of ambition and dissatisfaction.

To what extent do YOU think this statement has validity for modern work organisations? How do YOU feel about working in an organisation with little or no hierarchy?

Formal organisational relationships

In any organisation structure, certain formal relationships between individuals will arise from the defined pattern of responsibilities. There is often confusion over the meaning of different terms and their implications for organisation structure, but these **individual relationships** may be identified as:

- line;
- functional;
- staff; or
- lateral (*see* Figure 11.8).

The design of structure in terms of the principle of line, functional, staff or lateral determines the pattern of organisational role relationships and interactions with other roles (**discussed in Chapter 8**).

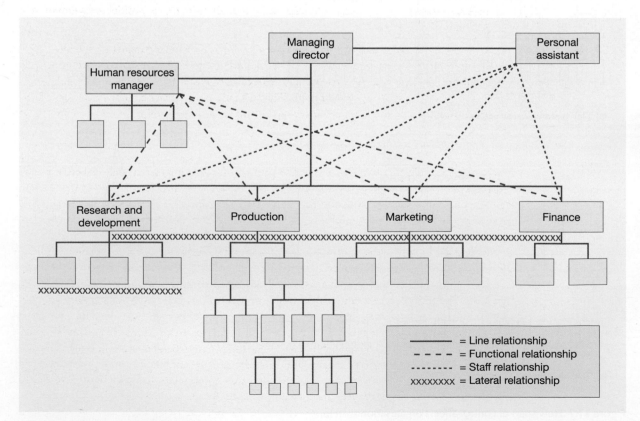

Figure 11.8 Illustration of formal organisational relationships

In **line relationships,** authority flows vertically down through the structure – the chain of command. There is a direct relationship between superior and subordinate, with each subordinate responsible to only one person. Line relationships are associated with functional or departmental division of work and organisational control. Line managers have authority and responsibility for all matters and activities within their own department.

Functional relationships apply to people in specialist or advisory positions, and line managers and their subordinates. The specialist offers a common service throughout all departments of the organisation, but has no direct authority over those who make use of the service. For example, the HR manager has no authority over staff in other departments – this is the responsibility of the line manager. However, as the position and role of the HR manager would have been sanctioned by top management, other staff might be expected to accept the advice that is given. The HR manager, however, could be assigned some direct, executive authority for certain specified responsibilities such as health and safety matters throughout the whole organisation.

Staff relationships arise from the appointment of personal assistants to senior members of staff. There is no formal relationship between the personal assistant and other staff except where delegated authority and responsibility have been given for some specific activity. They exercise only 'representative' authority and often act in a 'gatekeeper' role. In practice, however, personal assistants often have influence over other staff. This may be because of the close relationship between the personal assistant and the superior, the knowledge and experience of the assistant, or the strength of the assistant's personality.

> *In business and governmental agencies, from doctors' offices to licensing and regulatory boards, one may come face to face with people who have established themselves as gatekeeper to the boss. Gatekeepers aspire to and are rewarded with various titles, like administrative assistant, office manager or special assistant to such-and-such. But the essential role is usually that of secretary to the boss . . . Aspiring gatekeepers typically evoke polarised reactions among the office staff . . . Peers, unlike the boss, quickly recognise the individual's lack of integrity and willingness to step on all toes en route to the position of guardian and the gate.*[17]

Lateral relationships exist between individuals in different departments or sections, especially individuals on the same level. These lateral relationships are based on contact and consultation and are necessary to maintain co-ordination and effective organisational performance. Lateral relationships may be specified formally but in practice they depend upon the co-operation of staff and, in effect, are a type of informal relationship.

Line and functional organisation

As organisations develop in size and work becomes more complex, the range of activities and functions undertaken increases. People with specialist knowledge have to be integrated into the managerial structure. **Line and functional organisation** provides a means of making full use of specialists while maintaining the concept of line authority. It creates a type of informal matrix structure (*see* Figure 11.9).

The distinction between a line manager and a functional manager is not absolute. With the increasing complexity of organisations and the rise of specialist services it becomes harder to distinguish clearly between what is directly essential to the operation of the organisation and what might be regarded only as an auxiliary function. Functional managers may feel that their difficulties and work problems are not appreciated fully by the line managers. Functional managers often complain about resistance to their attempts to provide assistance and co-ordination, and the unnecessary demands for departmental independence by line managers. A major source of difficulty is to persuade line managers to accept, and act upon, the advice and recommendations that are offered. The line and functional relationship can also give rise to problems of 'role incongruence' (**discussed in Chapter 8**).

Keohane refers to the challenge of achieving the potential benefits of a more integrated approach.

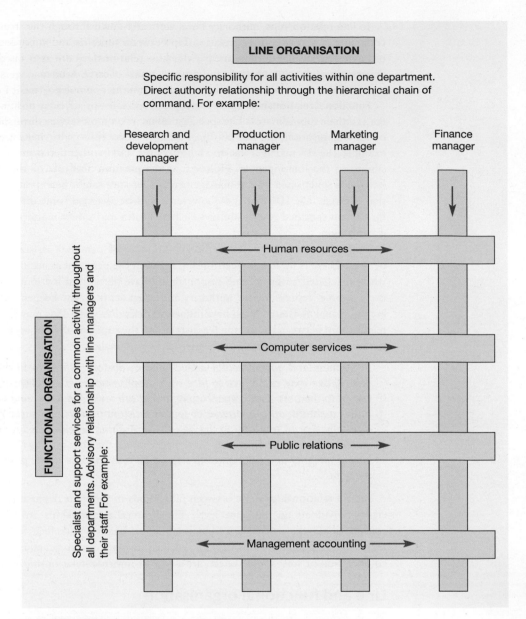

Figure 11.9 Representation of line and functional organisation

Why is that? It's because organisations, quite logically, shape themselves around specialist functional expertise. That's sensible, but it becomes less sensible when the agenda of the specialist function begins to overshadow that of the organisation. All too often the functional agenda elevates its own views, methods, systems and terminology at the expense of a more outcome-focused, clear and simple approach.[18]

Project teams and matrix organisation

The division of work and methods of grouping described earlier tend to be relatively permanent forms of structure. With growth of newer, complex and technologically advanced systems it has become necessary for organisations to provide greater integration of a wide range of functional activities. Although bureaucratic structures and hierarchies still exist in many organisations, increasing attention has been given to the creation of groupings based on project teams and matrix organisation. Members of staff from different departments or sections are assigned to the team for the duration of a particular project.

A **project team** may be set up as a separate unit on a temporary basis for the attainment of a particular task. When this task is completed the project team is disbanded or members of the unit are reassigned to a new task. Project teams may be used for people working together on a common task or to co-ordinate work on a specific project such as the design and development, production and testing of a new product; or the design and implementation of a new system or procedure. For example, project teams have been used in many military systems, aeronautics and space programmes.

The matrix structure

The matrix structure is a combination of:

- departments that provide a stable base for specialised activities and a permanent location for members of staff; and
- units that integrate various activities of different functions on a project team, product, programme, geographical or systems basis.

A **matrix structure** might be adopted in a university or college, for example, with grouping both by common subject specialism and by association with particular courses or programmes of study. The matrix organisation therefore establishes a grid, or matrix, with a two-way flow of authority and responsibility (*see* Figure 11.10). Within the functional departments authority and responsibility flow vertically down the line, but the authority and responsibility of the 'project' manager (or course programme manager) flow horizontally across the organisation structure.

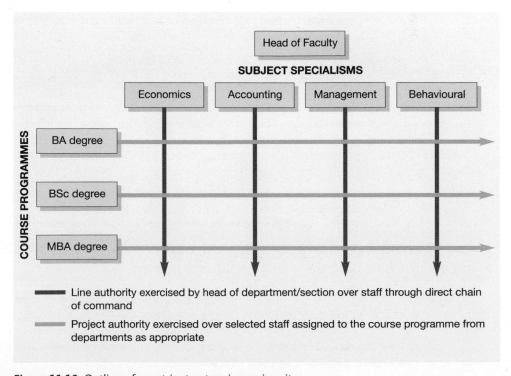

Figure 11.10 Outline of a matrix structure in a university

A matrix design might be adopted in the following circumstances:

1. **More than one critical orientation to the operations of the organisation.** For example, an insurance company has to respond simultaneously to both functional differentiation (such as life, fire, marine, motor) and different geographical areas.

2. **A need to process simultaneously large amounts of information.** For example, a local authority's social services department seeking help for an individual will need to know where to contact help from outside agencies (such as police, priest, community relations officer) and at the same time who to contact from internal resources within the organisation (such as the appropriate social worker, health visitor or housing officer).

3. **The need for sharing of resources.** This could be justified only on a total organisational basis, such as the occasional or part-time use by individual departments of specialist staff or services.

Developing an effective matrix organisation, however, takes time and a willingness to learn new roles and behaviour; this means that matrix structures are often difficult for management to implement effectively.[19]

Difficulties with matrix structures

The matrix structure offers the advantages of flexibility, greater security and control of project information, and opportunities for staff development. There are, however, a number of potential difficulties and problem areas. The matrix structure can result in a more complex structure. By using two methods of grouping it sacrifices the unity of command and can cause problems of co-ordination. An underlying difficulty with matrix structures is that of divided loyalties and role conflict, with individuals reporting simultaneously to two managers; this highlights the importance of effective teamwork. *Senior and Swailes* make the point that:

> *Matrix structures rely heavily on teamwork with managers needing high-level people management skills. The focus is on solving problems through team action. In a mature matrix structure, team members are managed simultaneously by two different managers – one is their functional line manager and the other the team or project leader. This type of organizational arrangement, therefore, requires a culture of co-operation, with supportive training programmes to help staff develop their team working and conflict-resolution skills.*[20]

Critical review and reflection

The idea of a matrix structure may appeal to those critical of a so-called prescriptive approach to organisation design. But in reality a matrix structure is an unnecessary complication. It is difficult to manage effectively, hard for people to shine and creates more potential problems than it answers.

What do YOU see as the benefits of a matrix structure? What is YOUR impression of organisation design in YOUR university? Would YOU be comfortable working in a matrix structure?

Management and organisational behaviour in action case study
Working structure: Geoplan Spatial Intelligence Limited

In 2000 Geoplan, a consultancy organisation in Yorkshire and Humberside, was in meltdown. As well as a growing number of market and technological challenges, the company was grappling with a structure that did not work and in which all roads led back to Managing Director John Taylor. Finance Director Sara McCartney explains: 'John would go out and win new business, which created a buzz of excitement. But this was quickly overtaken by a feeling of dread about how we were going to deliver on that promise.'

John and Sara realised that they had to find a better way of working. This meant finding a way of decentralising the business to get away from a line management structure that put John – and everyone else – under huge pressure. They also recognised that they needed to invest in developing their people if they were going to succeed.

Initially Geoplan used a facilitator to help John share his vision and mission for the company, something he found difficult: 'It felt like being in a padded cell, kicking it around until it all came out.' But, ultimately, Investors in People gave the team a 'Geoplan way of working'. Next, Geoplan used Investors in People to help them develop a new 'matrix' structure for the company. This meant that the business became increasingly self-managed and anyone – rather than just John – could lead a project. John credits the leadership and management criteria in the Investors in People framework with helping him to realise that everyone could be a leader at some point in their role. But now Geoplan's staff had to step up to that challenge. As Sara said: 'We've worked very hard to develop an Investors in People framework that helps people to understand their own competences. That knowledge has given them confidence that they know their stuff and can deliver to global businesses.'

Now people focus on outputs and the value they add to the business. Effective planning and organisation, teamwork and prioritisation have delivered a significant increase in performance.

In 2003, Geoplan was making a loss of nearly half a million pounds a year. In 2011, it made a profit of £400,000. The value of the average contract has risen from £20,000 to £150,000–£200,000, and productivity has gone up from £56,000 per head in 2002 to £93,000 per head in 2011. Geoplan puts its improved results down to the increased confidence and ability of its people, who now form project teams to win new business and work much more closely with clients. They win and retain more customers, and their improved performance has enabled them to move from 'data assembly' work to large, bespoke jobs where Geoplan can add value. This consultancy approach is also more profitable.

Involving all staff in management and strategy has also enabled Geoplan to cope with rapid technological change in its sector. This meant Geoplan had to change from being a desktop-based business used by specialists, to online systems used by a wide range of business customers and sectors. This change has also enabled it to expand from being a UK business to working with global clients such as TNT and KFC owners Yum! Brands. John says that Investors in People also helps Geoplan 'to explain to a billion-pound business why they should work with you rather than a big company'.

Source: For case study: Investors in People content provided by the UK Commission for Employment and Skills. **www.investorsinpeople.co.uk**

Tasks

1. Discuss potential problem areas in decentralising a business away from a line management structure.
2. What do you see as the advantages of a matrix structure with a business becoming more self-managed?
3. Discuss the implications for organisation structure with a change from desktop-based business to online systems.

Boundaryless organisation

The idea of boundaryless organisation originated with Jack Welch, former Chairman of General Electric, in the 1990s. Despite the enormous size of the organisation, the idea was to eliminate internal barriers: both vertical boundaries between different levels of the management hierarchy and horizontal boundaries between different departments; and external barriers between the company, suppliers and customers. The concept has been popularised by *Ashkenas* and colleagues.[21] A number of organisations have since attempted to follow this idea.

Francesco and Gold refer to the globalisation of the economy that has created new types of structures such as the 'boundaryless organization', which breaks the traditional demarcations of authority and task specialisation associated with bureaucracies and other structures: 'Features of a boundaryless organization include a widespread use of project teams, interfunctional teams, networks, and similar structural mechanisms, thus reducing boundaries that typically separate organizational functions and hierarchical levels.' A key management challenge is the socialisation and training of members of the organisation away from the effects of the bureaucratic mentality. Although there is still some form of authority structure, and task and political boundaries, such boundaries are flexible and unlike the rigid horizontal and vertical dimensions of traditional organisations.[22]

Advances in ICT and the growth of social networking together with the general movement towards less rigid chains of command and empowered teamwork have given impetus to the boundaryless organisation. However, as *Nicholson* points out:

> *Of course, no organisation can function without boundaries – they just sometimes become less visible. Neither might it be desirable – boundaries can actually foster freedom by making people safe.*[23]

Effects of a deficient organisation structure

It is not easy to describe, in a positive manner, what constitutes a 'good' or effective organisation structure, although the negative effects of a poorly designed structure can be identified more easily. In his discussion on the principles of organisation and co-ordination, *Urwick* (writing in 1947) suggests that 'lack of design is Illogical, Cruel, Wasteful and Inefficient'.

> *In short, a very large proportion of the friction and confusion in current society, with its manifest consequences in human suffering, may be traced back directly to faulty organisation in the structural sense.*[24]

Urwick's emphasis on the logical design of organisation structure rather than the development around personalities is typical of the classical approach to organisation and management. Despite this rather narrow view, more recent writers have drawn similar conclusions as to the consequences of badly designed structure. For example, *Child* points out the consequences of structure deficiencies:

> *Certain problems arise time and time again in struggling companies. Even at the best of times they can point to incipient dangers that have to be dealt with. Deficiencies in organisation can play a part in exacerbating each of these problems. High on the list are (1) low motivation and morale, (2) late and inappropriate decisions, (3) conflict and lack of co-ordination, (4) a generally poor response to new opportunities and external change, and (5) rising costs.*[25]

Organisation charts

The structure of an organisation may be depicted in the form of a chart that provides a pictorial representation of the overall shape and structural framework of the organisation. Some charts are very sketchy and give only a minimum amount of information. Other charts give varying amounts of additional detail, such as an indication of the broad nature of duties and responsibilities of the various units.

Charts are usually displayed in a traditional, vertical form such as those already depicted in Figures 11.5 and 11.6. They can, however, be displayed either horizontally with the information reading from left to right, or concentrically with top management at the centre. Organisation charts are useful in explaining the outline structure of an organisation. They may be used as a basis for the analysis and review of structure, and for formulating changes. The chart may indicate **apparent weaknesses** in structure such as, for example:

- too wide a span of control;
- overlapping areas of authority;
- too long a chain of command;
- unclear reporting relationships and/or lines of communication;
- unstaffed functions.

Probably the most immediate and accessible way to describe any formal organisation is to outline its structure. For the student of organisations, knowledge of its structure is indispensable as a first step to understanding the processes which occur within it. When asked to describe their organisation, managers will frequently sketch an organisation chart to show how their organisation 'works'.[26]

Limitations of organisation charts

There are, however, a number of limitations with traditional organisation charts. They depict only a static view of the organisation, and show how it looks and what the structure should be. Charts do not show the comparative authority and responsibility of positions on the same level, or lateral contacts and informal relations. Neither do charts show the extent of personal delegation from superior to subordinates, or the precise relationships between line and staff positions. Organisation charts can become out of date quickly and are often slow to be amended to reflect changes in the actual structure.

While acknowledging that organisation charts have some uses, *Townsend* likens them to 'rigor mortis' and advises that they should be drawn in pencil.

Never formalize, print and circulate them. Good organizations are living bodies that grow new muscles to meet challenges. A chart demoralizes people. Nobody thinks of himself as below other people. And in a good company he isn't. Yet on paper there it is . . . In the best organizations, people see themselves working in a circle as if around one table.[27]

Critical review and reflection

Although no longer common in many organisations, and despite their weaknesses, a chart portraying a clear representation of the overall shape and structure of an organisation with indication of broad duties and responsibilities of various units can serve many useful features.

Have YOU seen an organisation chart for YOUR own university or department? If so, how helpful was it? If not, in what ways would a chart be beneficial to YOU?

A summary of formal organisations and organisation charts is set out in the concept map in Figure 11.11.

Variables influencing organisation structure

Earlier approaches to organisation and management (**discussed in Chapter 2**) believed in one best form of structure and tended to concentrate on limited aspects of organisation. They also tended to study the organisation in isolation from its environment. According to *Bouchikhi and Kimberly,* a feature that differentiates the nineteenth-, twentieth- and twenty-first-century management paradigms is that as customers and shareholders have been more proactive, market-driven strategies and flexible organisations have developed as a consequence. The changing nature of the work environment, the increasing demands for flexibility and concerns with the contextual factors influencing structure have drawn attention to the contingency approach to organisation design.[28]

Contingency approach

The **contingency approach** can be seen as a development of the systems approach; it goes a stage further in relating the environment, and other variables, to specific structures of organisation. The contingency approach takes the view that there is no one best, universal structure.

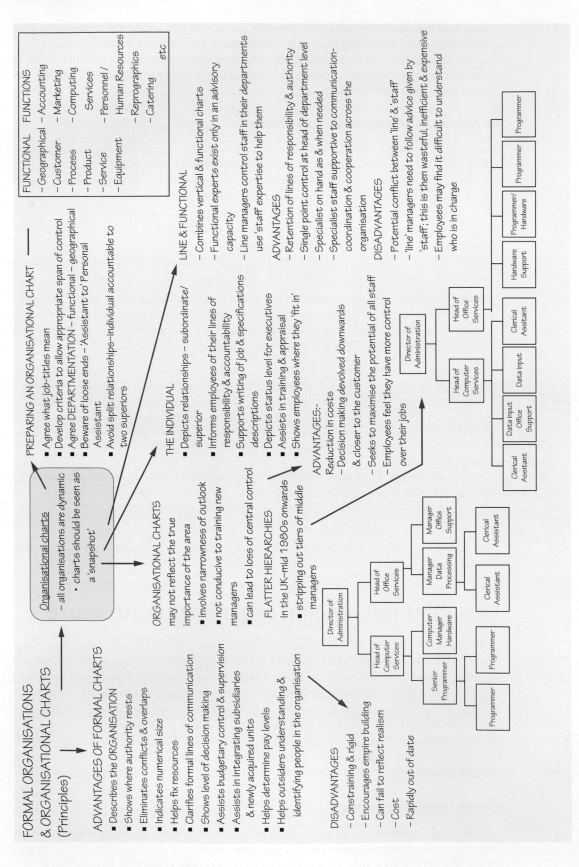

Figure 11.11 Formal organisations and organisation charts

Source: Copyright ©2012 The Virtual Learning Materials Workshop. Reproduced with permission.

There are a large number of variables, or situational factors, that influence organisation design and performance. The contingency approach emphasises the need for flexibility.

As *Vecchio* puts it: 'The goal of the contingency view is to explain how differences in the contextual and structural dimensions are related. As the term *contingency* implies, this approach does not seek universal principles that can be used for every situation, but instead seeks to explain how one attribute or characteristic depends upon another.'[29] The most appropriate structure is dependent, therefore, upon the contingencies of the situation for each individual organisation. These situational factors account for variations in the structure of different organisations.

Lynch points out that 'Every organisation is unique in size, products or services, people, leadership and culture' and provides helpful examples of some of the possible implications for organisation design (*see* Figure 11.12).[30]

Situational factors may be identified in a number of ways. Obvious bases for comparison include the type of organisation and its purpose, history, and the characteristics of the members of the organisation such as their abilities, skills and experience. Other important variables are **size, technology** and **environment.** A number of studies have been carried out into the extent to which these contingency factors influence organisation design and effectiveness.

Size of organisation

Size has clear implications for organisation structure. In the very small organisations there is little need for a formal structure. With increasing size, however, and associated problems of execution of work and management of staff, there are likely to be more formalised relationships and greater use of rules and standardised procedures. Size explains best many of the characteristics of organisation structure, for example bureaucracy and the importance

Purpose	Implications for organisation design
• 'Ideas factory' such as an advertising or promotions agency	• Loose, fluid structure with limited formalised relationships. As it grows in size, however, more formal structures are usually inevitable
• Multinational company in branded goods	• Major linkage and resource issues that need carefully co-ordinated structures, e.g. on common suppliers or common supermarket customers for separate product ranges
• Government civil service	• Strict controls on procedures and authorisations. Strong formal structures to handle major policy directions and legal issues
• Non-profit-making charity with a strong sense of mission	• Reliance on voluntary members and their voluntary contributions may require a flexible organisation with responsibility devolved to individuals
• Major service company such as a retail bank or electricity generating company	• Formal structures but supported by some flexibility so that variations in demand can be met quickly
• Small business attempting to survive and grow	• Informal, willingness to undertake several business functions such as selling or production, depending on the short-term circumstances
• Health service with strong professional service ethics, standards and quality	• Formalised structure that reflects the seniority and professional status of those involved while delivering the crucial complex service provisions
• Holding company with subsidiaries involved in diverse markets	• Small centralised headquarters acting largely as a banker, with the main strategic management being undertaken in individual companies

Figure 11.12 Examples of the connection between purpose and organisational design

Source: Lynch, R. *Strategic Management*, sixth edition, Pearson Education (2012), p. 464. Reprinted by permission of Pearson Education Ltd.

of standardisation through rules and procedures as a mechanism for co-ordination in larger organisations.

Size, however, is not a simple variable. It can be defined and measured in different ways, although a common indication is the number of persons employed. There is the problem of distinguishing the effects of size from other organisational variables. Furthermore, there is conflicting evidence on the relationship of size to the structure and operation of the organisation. There is a continuing debate about the comparative advantages of large and small organisations, or whether 'bigger is best' or 'small is beautiful'. The conclusion appears to be that complexity rather than size may be a more influential variable.[31]

Global companies and size

Birkinshaw draws attention to size as a particular feature of the structures of global companies: 'The reality is that global companies end up being perceived as complex, slow-moving and bureaucratic. The challenge for top managers lies in minimizing these liabilities, while retaining the benefits of size.' The pure matrix with equal stress on two lines of accountability does not work. Attention must be given to strong but informal horizontal relationships and country managers in developing markets. The organisation of a global company depends on a host of factors including number of businesses and countries in which it operates, the type of industry, location of major customers and its own heritage.[32]

Technology

Two major studies concerning technology are those by:

- Woodward – patterns of organisation, production technology and business success; and
- Perrow – main dimensions of technology and organisation structure.

Woodward – structure and production technology

A major study of the effects of technology on organisation structure was carried out by *Joan Woodward* in the 1950s.[33] Her pioneering work presents the results of empirical study of 100 manufacturing firms in southeast Essex and the relationships between the application of principles of organisation and business success. The main thesis was:

> *that industrial organisations which design their formal organisational structures to fit the type of production technology they employ are likely to be commercially successful.*[34]

Firms were divided into nine different types of production systems, from least to most technological complexity, with three main groupings of:

- unit and small-batch production;
- large-batch and mass production;
- process production.

The firms varied considerably in their organisation structure and many of the variations appeared to be linked closely with differences in manufacturing techniques.

Patterns of organisation and business success

There appeared to be no direct link between principles of organisation and business success. There was, however, a stronger relationship between organisation structure and success within each of the three main groupings of production systems. Organisational patterns were found

Production systems	Manufacturing cycle			Relationship between task functions
Unit and small batch	Marketing	Most critical function Development	Production	Day-to-day operational relationship
Large batch and mass	Development	Most critical function Production	Marketing	Normally exchange of information only
Process	Development	Most critical function Marketing	Production	Normally exchange of information only

Figure 11.13 Characteristics of production systems

Source: Woodward, J. *Industrial Organization: Theory and Practice,* second edition, Oxford University Press (1980), p. 128. Reproduced with permission from Oxford University Press.

to be related more to similarity of objectives and production techniques than to size, type of industry or the business success of the firm. Woodward acknowledges that technology is not the only variable that affects organisation, but is one that could be isolated more easily for study. She does, however, draw attention to the importance of technology, organisation and business success.

Another important finding of Woodward's study was the nature of the actual cycle of manufacturing and the relationship between three key 'task' functions of development, production and marketing. The most critical of these functions varied according to the type of production system (*see* Figure 11.13).

- **Unit and small batch.** Production was based on firm orders only, with marketing the first activity. Greater stress was laid on technical expertise, and the quality and efficiency of the product. Research and development were the second, and most critical, activities. The need for flexibility, close integration of functions and frequent personal contacts meant that an organic structure was required.

- **Large batch and mass.** Production schedules were not dependent directly on firm orders. The first phase of manufacturing was product development, followed by production, which was the most important function, and thirdly by marketing. The three functions were more independent and did not rely so much on close operational relationships among people responsible for development, production and sales.

- **Process.** The importance of securing a market meant that marketing was the central and critical activity. Products were either impossible or difficult to store, or capacity for storage was very limited. The flow of production was directly determined, therefore, by the market situation. The emphasis of technical knowledge was more on how products could be used than on how they could be made.

Perrow – major dimensions of technology

The work by Woodward was extended by *Perrow,* who drew attention to two major dimensions of technology:

- the extent to which the work task is predictable or variable; and
- the extent to which technology can be analysed.[35]

Variability refers to the number of exceptional or unpredictable cases and the extent to which problems are familiar. For example, a mass-production factory is likely to have only a few exceptions, but the manufacture of a designer range of clothing would have many exceptional and unpredictable cases. The **analysis of technology** refers to the extent to which the task functions are broken down and highly specified, and the extent to which problems can be solved in recognised ways or by the use of routine procedures. Combining the two dimensions provides a continuum of technology from routine to non-routine. With non-routine technology there are a large number of exceptional cases involving difficult and varied problem-solving.

Technology and structure

The classification of each type of technology relates to a particular organisation structure. Perrow suggests that by classifying organisations according to their technology and predictability of work tasks, we should be able to predict the most effective form of structure. Variables such as the discretion and power of sub-groups, the basis of co-ordination and the interdependence of groups result from the use of different technologies.

In the **routine type of organisation** there is minimum discretion at both the technical and supervisory levels, but the power of the middle management level is high, co-ordination is based on planning and there is likely to be low interdependence between the two groups. This arrangement approaches a bureaucratic structure. In the **non-routine type of organisation** there is a high level of discretion and power at both the technical and supervisory levels, co-ordination is through feedback and there is high group interdependence. This model resembles an organic structure.

Uncertain external environment

Two important studies that focused not just on technology but also on the effects of uncertainty and a changing external environment on the organisation, and its management and structure, are those by:

- Burns and Stalker – divergent systems of management practice, 'mechanistic' and 'organic'; and
- Lawrence and Lorsch – the organisation of specific departments, and the extent of 'differentiation' and 'integration'.

Burns and Stalker – mechanistic and organic structures

The study by *Burns and Stalker* was an analysis of twenty industrial firms in the UK and the effects of the external environment on their pattern of management and economic performance. The firms were drawn from a number of industries: a rayon manufacturer, a large engineering company, Scottish firms attempting to enter the electronics field and English firms operating in varying sectors of the electronics industry.[36]

From an examination of the settings in which the firms operated, Burns and Stalker distinguished five different kinds of environments ranging from 'stable' to 'least predictable'. They also identified two divergent systems of management practice and structure – the 'mechanistic' system and the 'organic' system.

The **mechanistic system** is a more rigid structure that is unable to deal adequately with rapid change; it is therefore more appropriate for stable environmental conditions. The characteristics of a mechanistic management system are similar to those of bureaucracy. An example might be a traditional high-class and expensive hotel operating along classical lines with an established reputation and type of customer. However, major fast food chains that tend to operate along the lines of scientific management (**discussed in Chapter 2**) also require a mechanistic structure.

The **organic system** is a more fluid structure appropriate to changing conditions. It appears to be required when new problems and unforeseen circumstances arise constantly and require actions outside defined roles in the hierarchical structure. A holiday or tourist hotel with an unpredictable demand, offering a range of functions and with many different types of customers, requires an organic structure.

A summary of the characteristics of mechanistic and organic organisations is provided by *Litterer* (*see* Table 11.1).[37]

Burns and Stalker point out that there are intermediate stages between the two extreme systems that represent not a dichotomy but a polarity. The relationship between the mechanistic and organic systems is not rigid. An organisation moving between a relatively stable and a relatively changing environment may also move between the two systems.

'Mixed' forms of organisation structure

Organisations *tend* towards mechanistic or organic, and many will be hybrid – that is, a mix of both mechanistic and organic structures – and often this is an uneasy mix that can lead to tension and conflict. For example, a group of people engaged on a set of broad functional activities might prefer, and perform best in, an organic structure, while another group tends to prefer a mechanistic structure and to work within established rules, systems and procedures. Different preferences for organisational styles and working methods present a particular challenge to management.

Table 11.1 Characteristics of mechanistic and organic organisations

Mechanistic		Organic
High, many and sharp differentiations	SPECIALISATION	Low, no hard boundaries, relatively few different jobs
High, methods spelled out	STANDARDISATION	Low, individuals decide own methods
Means	ORIENTATION OF MEMBERS	Goals
By superior	CONFLICT RESOLUTION	Interaction
Hierarchical, based on implied contractual relation	PATTERN OF AUTHORITY CONTROL AND COMMUNICATION	Wide net based upon common commitment
At top of organisation	LOCUS OF SUPERIOR COMPETENCE	Wherever there is skill and competence
Vertical	INTERACTION	Lateral
Directions, orders	COMMUNICATION CONTENT	Advice, information
To organisation	LOYALTY	To project and group
From organisational position	PRESTIGE	From personal contribution

Source: Litterer, J. A. *The Analysis of Organizations*, second edition, John Wiley & Sons (1973), p. 339. Reproduced with permission from the estate of Joseph A. Litterer.

A typical example of a hybrid organisation could be a university with differences in perception between academic staff and non-teaching staff. Academic staff may feel they can work effectively only within an organic structure, and tend to see non-teaching staff as bureaucratic and resistant to novel or different ideas. Non-teaching staff have an important function in helping to keep the organisation operational and working effectively, and may fail to understand why academics appear to find it difficult, or resent, working within prescribed administrative systems and procedures. Universities may also tend to be more mechanistic at top management level, with an apparent proliferation of committees and sub-committees, because of their dealings with, for example, government bodies and other external agencies.

Critical review and reflection

Students of organisational behaviour often express a strong preference for working within an organic organisation. But then many express concerns about possible lack of superior competence, clear direction and strong management.

Why do YOU think this is? In which type of structure would YOU prefer to work, and why?

Lawrence and Lorsch – differentiation and integration

Lawrence and Lorsch undertook a study of six firms in the plastics industry followed by a further study of two firms in the container industry and two firms in the consumer food industry. They extended the work of Burns and Stalker and examined not only the overall structure, but also the way in which specific departments were organised to meet different aspects of the firm's external environment. The internal structures of the firms were analysed in terms of 'differentiation' and 'integration'.[38]

Differentiation describes 'the difference in cognitive and emotional orientation among managers in different functional departments' with respect to goal orientation, time orientation, interpersonal relations and formality of structure.

Integration describes 'the quality of the state of collaboration that exists among departments that are required to achieve unity of effort by the demands of the environment'. It is the degree of co-ordination and co-operation between different departments with interdependent tasks. Lawrence and Lorsch's view of integration was not the minimising of differences between departments and the provision of a common outlook. It was the recognition that different departments could have their own distinctive form of structure according to the nature of their task, and the use of mediating devices to co-ordinate the different outlooks of departments.

This view of differentiation and integration was confirmed in the subsequent study of firms in the container and consumer food industries. It was concluded that the extent of differentiation and integration in effective organisations will vary according to the demands of the particular environment:

- The more diverse and dynamic the environment, the more the effective organisation will be differentiated and highly integrated.
- In more stable environments, less differentiation will be required but a high degree of integration is still required. Differences in the environment will require different methods of achieving integration.
- Given the possibility that different demands of the environment are characterised by different levels of uncertainty, it follows that individual departments may develop different structures.

Integrating mechanisms

Mechanisms used to achieve integration depend on the amount of integration required and the difficulty in achieving it. In mechanistic structures, integration may be attempted through the use of policies, rules and procedures. In organic structures, integration may be attempted through teamwork and mutual co-operation. As the requirements for the amount of integration increase, additional means may be adopted, such as formal lateral relations, committees and project teams. It is important, however, to achieve the right balance of integration. Too high a level of integration may involve costs that are likely to exceed possible benefits. Too low a level of integration is likely to result in departments 'doing their own thing', poorer-quality decisions and failure to make the best use of resources.[39]

Evaluation of contingency approach

The contingency approach draws attention to situational factors that influence variations in the structure of organisations. It is more concerned with differences among organisations than with similarities, and rejects assumptions of the classical and human relations approaches and the idea of one best form of structure. For its part, however, the contingency approach tends to assume that organisational performance is dependent upon the degree to which the structure of the organisation matches the prevailing contingencies.

Hunt explains the concept of contingency as follows:

> *The concept of contingency also implies that there is no one, absolute 'best' design; rather, there is a multitude of possibilities and the best or preferred choice will be contingent on the situation being analysed. Universal models designed to suit all situations are therefore rejected. This is consistent with the fact that most organizations are networks of a variety of bits of design rather than conforming, as one entity, to a particular model. So we might find units of bureaucracy, units of matrix structures, units with project teams, units with extremely loose, almost ad hoc structures – and all these within, say, the same oil company. In this sense, the contingency theorists merely reflected the findings of hundreds of researchers. There are common elements in the hierarchies of different organizations but there are also very many differences peculiar to the local situation.[40]*

Not every situation is unique

According to *Robey*, modern contingency theory defines variables ignored in earlier work, and directs attention of the manager to contingencies to be considered in the design of organisation structure. However, the contingency approach runs the risk of concluding that 'it all depends on everything', and the greatest danger is the over-emphasis on differences between organisations and the exclusion of similarities. If the contingency approach is to be useful in guiding organisation design it should not treat every situation as being unique: 'Rather it must strike a balance between universal prescriptions and the statement that all situations are different (which is really no theory at all). Thus, modern theory uses a limited number of contingencies to help explain structural differences between organizations.'[41]

Organisation structure and culture

The pervasive nature of culture in terms of both external influences and 'how things are done around here' and common values, beliefs and attitudes will have a significant effect on organisational processes including the design of structure.

Schneider and Barsoux suggest that while managers are ready to accept national culture as an influence on the way people relate to each other, they are less convinced of its real effect on the structure, systems and process of the organisation. However, the emerging approaches to management reflect different cultural assumptions, and models of management have diffused across countries at different rates in different ways. Historical and societal context needs to be considered to understand the adoption and diffusion of different forms of organisation across countries. Schneider and Barsoux discuss the multidimensional impact of culture on organisations and management and maintain that it would be a mistake to base a prediction regarding structure or process on a single cultural dimension.

> *Managers need to recognise that the relationships between cultural dimensions and structure (or processes) are not simple cause–effect links, but instead, are multidetermined. Similar approaches may exist for the same reason. Thus formalized rules and procedures or participative management approaches may have a different raison d'être on different sides of the national border.*[42]

Watson suggests that we must be careful not to treat structures or cultures as if they were solid 'things' existing separately from the processes and relationships that the two concepts are intended to help us make sense of. The structure of work organisations also involves the wider context of societal structures and cultures: 'Societal structures both contribute to and result from organisational structures.' Watson also refers to the closeness and overlap of structure and culture: 'Many of the processes and practices we observe in an organisation could as readily be said to be part of the structure of the organisation as part of its culture.'[43]

An interesting set of caricatures for organisation charts of different countries is given in Figure 11.14.

Critical review and reflection

According to the contingency approach, different situational variables may have some relevance for certain types of organisations at certain times given a particular set of circumstances. This *it all depends* approach is too vague to have any practical benefit for managers.

How would YOU attempt to defend the value of the contingency approach? To what extent have YOU seen applications of contingency theory in YOUR university or organisation?

The changing face of the workplace

Birchall refers to the changing world of organisations and its impact on management. Much of the work undertaken by middle management no longer requires the considerable layers of management. Tasks that used to take up a great deal of management time in hierarchical structures are now possible with minimal supervision or intervention. Much of the organisation's work is carried out in projects. Many managers will find themselves managing people who spend much of their time outside the office. There is a strong move towards the use of consultants. Managers will need to be familiar with electronic networks, the operation of dispersed teams and virtual organisations.[44]

A similar point is made by *Cloke and Goldsmith*, who maintain that management is an idea whose time is up and the days of military command structures are over.

> *Rather than building fixed structures with layers of middle management, many innovative organizations function as matrixed webs of association, networks, and fast-forming high-performance teams . . . The most significant trends we see in the theory and history of management are the decline of the hierarchical, bureaucratic, autocratic management and the expansion of collaborative self-management and organizational democracy.*[45]

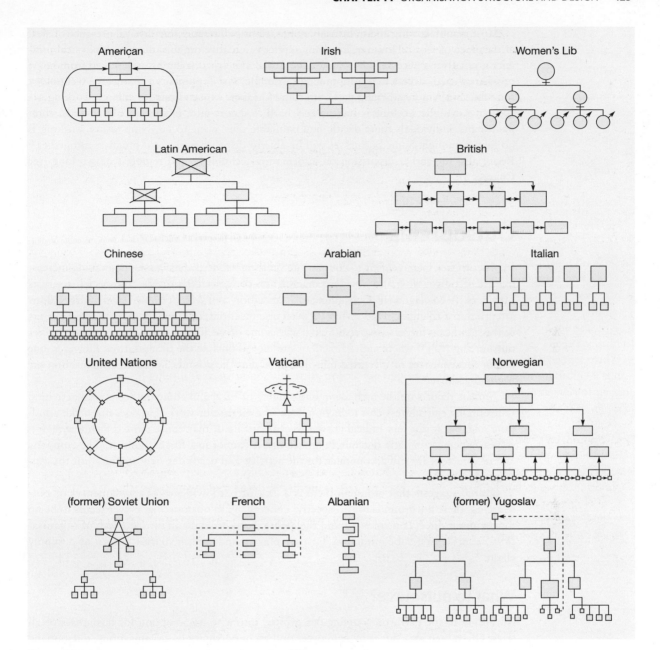

Figure 11.14 Caricatures of organisation charts for different countries
Source: Copyright © Reed Business Information, reprinted with permission.

Information technology

The impact of information technology has significant effects on the structure, management and functioning of most organisations. IT influences the need for restructuring the organisation and changes to lines of command and authority. Computer-based information and decision-support systems influence choices in design of production or service activities, hierarchical levels and organisation of support staffs. IT may influence the centralisation/decentralisation of decision-making and control systems. New technology has typically resulted in a 'flatter' organisational pyramid with fewer levels of management required. In the case of new office technology it allows the potential for staff at clerical/operator level to carry out a wider range of functions and to check their own work. The result is a change in the traditional supervisory function and a demand for fewer supervisors.

Most manufacturing and industrial organisations still require the physical presence of staff at the place of work. However, for many service or creative organisations such physical presence is not always necessary. For knowledge workers their work can be undertaken from home or where there is access to a computer. For example, *Fisher* points out that as the technology for achieving remote working gets better and cheaper, expectations for remote working are rocketing. Mobile working is increasingly hard to ignore and, facing global demands, companies and individuals must decide how available they want to be. Nine-to-five working is no longer enough. Some businesses will be able to dispense with fixed premises altogether.[46] **Recall also the earlier discussion on information technology and remote teamworking (see Chapter 8).**

Outsourcing

In order to free management to concentrate on core activities, businesses are making increasing use of outsourcing and a wider range of non-core services provided by specialist service providers. A Management Consultancies Association and *Management Today* survey drew attention to a changing relationship between organisations and individuals. The survey refers to the significant increase in outsourcing, with some of the highest growth in business process outsourcing (BPO) where entire functions are moved outside the organisation. However, one of the consequences of increased outsourcing is that the boundaries of the organisation are becoming blurred.[47]

Thomas reports on the increase in outsourcing of legal and company secretarial activities. Outsourcing can address cost reduction, lack of expertise or work that does not make a full-time role, but it is a very radical answer to cost cutting. It may cause more difficulties than it solves. When a company outsources an activity, it cannot just forget about it. The company and its directors are still accountable for the activity, and need to review and monitor the outsourced work.[48]

Overell suggests that although there is a lack of hard evidence of consequences of outsourcing, there are grounds for prospective concern. With outsourcing, power seems to be no longer about direct control but about the ability to co-ordinate an intricate web of organisations, contractors, subcontractors, bit-part players and intermediaries known as a supply chain.[49]

What to outsource?

According to the CMI, outsourcing has evolved into a strategic option for businesses of all sizes. Often seen as a threat by employees and an opportunity by organisations, outsourcing has nonetheless become standard practice in many businesses.

> On the surface, the benefits of outsourcing may seem both straightforward and considerable. However, in addition to cost-savings, there are many other factors that lead managers to consider outsourcing. These include access to skills and new technology, the desire to expand globally, and the need for flexibility both to deal with rises and falls in product development demand and to improve ways of delivering products or services . . . If you focus on identifying the core competencies of your organisation and on what differentiates the company and makes it unique, then those areas which make up the support, administration, routine and internal serving of the organisation will become potential areas for outsourcing.[50]

In the public sector there have been a number of recent high-profile problems associated with outsourcing of major government services. According to *Hazlehurst,* 'Outsourcing firms seem to stagger from one scandal to the next, with even their Government paymasters putting the boot in at times.' However, as Hazlehurst points out, outsourcing is not privatisation, and it is not going away.

Outsourcing makes sense . . . we don't expect local councils to design and build their own street-sweeping machines. They buy them from Volvo. So why shouldn't they buy services from experts too?[51]

Demand for flexibility

The nature of work is being redefined and this has created strong pressures for greater flexibility in patterns of work organisation and in the workforce. A report from ACAS examines the need for work/life balance and flexible working:

> *The hours and times people work have always been subject to change but the pace of this change is now more rapid than ever because: customers expect to have goods and services outside traditional working hours; organisations want to match their business needs with the way their employees work, individuals want to achieve a better balance between work and home life . . . Flexible patterns of work can help address these pressures by maximizing the available labour and improving customer service. Flexible working can also help to reduce absenteeism and increase productivity, employee commitment and loyalty.*[52]

Flexible working arrangements

Flexible working arrangements are a range of options designed to help employees balance work and home life and can describe the place of work or the contract of employment. There is a wide range of flexible working practices, which in many instances can be used in a wide variety of workplaces:

- part-time working;
- annual hours;
- staggered hours;
- job sharing;
- time off in lieu;
- flexitime;
- work at or from home;
- self-rostering;
- mobile working/teleworking.
- compressed working hours;
- shift swapping;
- term-time working;
- career breaks from work.

Telecommuting

Recent advances in computerisation and telecommunications have had a further significant effect on opportunities for flexible working. People can work from almost any geographic location: from head office, a satellite office, a shared access telecentre; or from their home, hotel room or car. An increasingly popular means of teleworking is **telecommuting**, where staff work from home with a computer network, telephone, etc.

Lucas reports on underlying resistance from organisations to flexible working. Despite the well-documented benefits, there are many organisations where it is just not happening on the front line. Workplace cultures make it too difficult for employees to ask and a 'can't do' attitude is the status quo. There is a different perspective between line managers and the HR department. The biggest hurdle is often concerns of line managers about the practicalities of a flexible working arrangement and worries over managing performance. However, objections often raised are not insurmountable. Managers need proper training on how to manage flexible working practices to make telecommuting a success in their team.[53]

Homeworking

A noticeable feature of the changing nature of the workplace is the growth in homeworking. Most commentators suggest that the benefits outweigh the drawbacks.[54] Figures from the ONS in June 2014 show homeworkers account for 14 per cent of the national workforce.[55] ACAS, however, points out that relatively few homeworkers, approximately 5 per cent of the workforce, carry out *all* or even *the majority* of their work at home. The greatest barrier to homeworking success is that of trust, and the traditional managerial attitude about employees needing to be seen to be considered productive.

> *If we accept as axiomatic the fact that not all job roles nor job holders will be suited to homeworking and that exclusive homeworking is not universally appropriate, the question that follows is what is the optimum balance between office and home? In one sense this is a futile question since any satisfactory answer will be specific to each organisation. But the question is helpful insofar as it reminds us that homeworking is an arrangement based on balance and not a binary practice, with staff being located either solely at home or entirely in an office.[56]*

Working from home does not appeal to everyone and it needs to be managed well, especially for full-time homeworkers. An increasing number of homeworkers report a feeling of detachment from the work situation and miss the interaction with colleagues. Homeworkers may struggle to escape the strains of domestic life and often report a feeling of exhaustion and increased conflict from demands of balancing work and family.

Critical review and reflection

Remote working, telecommuting and homeworking are clearly the way forward and should be the main feature of organisation design. Attention to traditional views on formal structure, and managerial authority and control, are no longer of significance.

How would YOU attempt to present a counterargument? To what extent would YOU be comfortable being employed by an organisation based largely on remote working and telecommuting?

Structure and organisational behaviour

It is clear, then, that it is essential to give full attention to the structure of an organisation. However, this is not always an easy task. Structuring an organisation involves balancing a series of trade-offs. In analysing the effectiveness of structure, consideration should be given to the formal and technological requirements, to principles of design and to social factors, and to the needs and demands of the human part of the organisation. Structure should be designed so as to maintain the balance of the socio-technical system and to encourage the willing participation of members and effective organisational performance.

> *An organisation can be separated into two parts or structures which can then be examined. One section is a definable structure that will be present in every company, the other is the structure caused by human intervention. The latter provides the company with its distinctive appearance, and may be regarded as the manager's particular response to the design requirements of organised behaviour. Essentially the effectiveness of an organisation depends on how accurately human design matches the structure of organised behaviour.[57]*

Trends towards flatter hierarchies, teamwork, empowerment and flexible working have reduced significantly the importance of formal structures. What really matters is that individuals know what is expected of them, work well with other people and perform their tasks successfully.

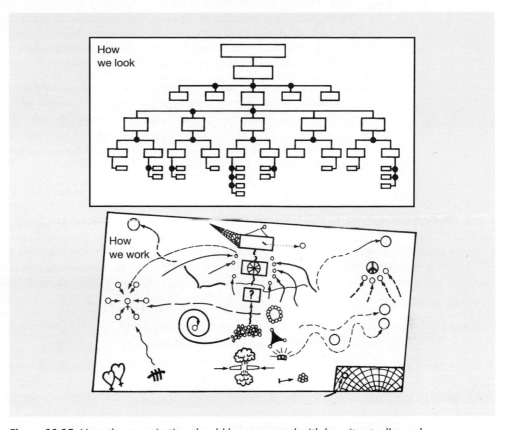

Figure 11.15 How the organisation should be, compared with how it actually works
Source: Gray, J. L. and Starke, F. A. *Organizational Behavior: Concepts and Applications*, fourth edition, © 1988. Reprinted and electronically reproduced by permission of Pearson Education, Inc., New York.

'Realities' of organisational behaviour

The structure or charts do not describe what really happens in work organisations. Individuals differ and people bring their own perceptions, feelings and attitudes towards the organisation, styles of management and their duties and responsibilities. The behaviour of people cannot be studied in isolation and we need to understand interrelationships with other variables that comprise the total organisation, including the social context of the work organisation and the importance of the informal organisation.

Gray and Starke provide a humorous but perhaps realistic illustration of how an organisation actually works (*see* Figure 11.15).[58] *Heller* also refers to 'the gap between the aims of big company organisations and what actually happens. Organisational form and organisational behaviour are not one and the same thing.'[59]

No perfect structure

As *Owen* points out, there is no such thing as the perfect organisation structure. Every structure is a trade-off between competing priorities. Building an effective organisation is becoming harder. With increasing size and complexity, challenges of co-ordination grow. Firms are becoming more complicated for two reasons: the rise of the global firm and re-engineering. The real problems of the cross-border team are about trust, power, belonging and identity. The structural revolution is more far-reaching and complicated than simply turning the pyramid on its head. The pyramid has been turned on its side and completely reconfigured.

> *The simplicity and certainty of the functional organisation has given way to the complexity of a multi-dimensional matrix in which processes count as much as functions . . . The challenge is to make the current style of organisation work. Many firms manage new style structures with old systems, then wonder why it does not work.*[60]

Whatever its structure, the various operations of the organisation have to be distributed among its members. It is necessary to plan, organise, direct and control their activities. The demand for flexibility and greater freedom and autonomy for individuals raises questions about the extent and nature of delegation and empowerment, the manager–subordinate relationship and the maintenance of management control within the formal structure of the organisation. (**This is discussed more fully in Chapter 13.**)

Critical review and reflection

> *We trained very hard, but it seemed every time we were beginning to form into teams we would be reorganised. I was to learn later in life that we tend to meet any new situation by reorganising and a wonderful method it can be for creating the illusion of progress while producing confusion, inefficiency and demoralisation.*
>
> (Gaius Petronius, AD 66)

To what extent do YOU think this is still true for a modern work organisation? Can YOU relate an example of reorganisation in YOUR university or organisation that has been clearly beneficial?

Ten key points to remember

1 The purpose of structure is the division of work among members of the organisation, and the means by which its goals and objectives are achieved.

2 Structure makes possible application of the process of management and creates a framework of order and system of command for the activities of the organisation.

3 Attention is focused on certain underlying dimensions in the design of organisation structure. These are not prescriptive but provide important decision points.

4 Critical decisions arise from division of work and grouping of activities, centralisation and decentralisation, role of the hierarchy and formal organisational relationships.

5 The need to integrate a wide range of activities has focused attention on more flexible forms of structure, such as line and functional, project teams and matrix organisation.

6 The contingency approach suggests there is no one best structure but a number of situational variables influencing organisation design and performance.

7 Situation variables may be identified in a number of ways, including size, technology and external environment, and arguably the influence of culture.

8 The changing nature of the workplace has drawn attention to influences such as information technology and demands for flexibility on organisation structure.

9 It is essential to give full attention to structuring an organisation but this is not an easy task. Consideration should be given to the realities of organisational behaviour.

10 There is no perfect structure. Organisation design involves balancing a series of trade-offs and attention to both the needs of staff and effective performance.

Review and discussion questions

1 Discuss the interrelationships between organisation structure and corporate strategy.

2 Give your views on the purpose and importance of structure. To what extent do you think there are clearly identified different levels in the structure of an organisation?

3 Explain the main determinants in design of an effective organisation structure. How effective do you think the structure is in your own university?

4 Discuss critically the continuing importance of the hierarchy.

5 Prepare your own diagrams to help explain: (i) line and functional organisation; and (ii) a matrix form of organisation structure. What are the reasons for adopting each of these forms of structure and what problem areas might arise?

6 Explain how the contingency approach differs from other approaches to organisation and management.

7 Contrast 'mechanistic' and 'organic' systems of management practice and structure. What is the significance of this distinction?

8 What are *your* views on the influence of advances in computerisation and telecommunications for patterns of structure and work organisation?

9 Discuss critically questions raised by increased demands for flexibility and greater freedom of choice for individuals at work.

10 To what extent would you agree with the contention that a logical structure for organisation is better for efficiency and morale than a structure allowed to develop around personalities? What are the likely consequences of a poorly designed structure?

Assignment

To cope with the changing nature of the workplace many writers are calling for more creative forms of organisation structure.

a. Explain how you believe the structure of your university, or other organisation with which you are familiar, affects your level of motivation and performance.
b. Detail fully, with supporting reasons, how you would design a more creative form of organisation structure.
c. Where appropriate, prepare a revised organisation chart.
d. Be prepared to lead a class discussion, including a question-and-answer session, to discuss your findings.

Personal skills and employability exercise

Objectives

Completing this exercise should help you to enhance the following skills:

• Diagnose specific features of structure within your university.
• Evaluate the significance and effects of structure on people within the university.
• Act as a senior manager.

Exercise

Remind yourself of key features in the text of this chapter relating to:

- centralisation and decentralisation;
- line and functional organisation;
- matrix structures; and
- mechanistic and organic structures of organisation.

1 Prepare a detailed report with specific examples on the manner in which these features are manifested in your university (and/or some other organisation well known to you).
2 Comment on how these features impact upon the apparent effectiveness of structure and influence various activities of the university, styles of management, the people employed and you as students.
3 Give examples of tensions and conflicts that arise from the implementation of these features, *for example* from a mix of mechanistic and organic structures.
4 As a senior manager, explain fully what changes you would recommend to organisation structure and actions to help overcome these tensions and conflicts.

Discussion

- To what extent does organisation structure influence the actions, behaviour and effectiveness of: (i) senior management; (ii) members of staff; and (iii) students?
- Who should realistically be involved in decision-making relating to structure?
- To what extent would you expect to see changes in the structure of your university in, say, the next five to ten years? And why?

Case study
John Lewis and Waitrose: distinctively successful

The John Lewis Partnership is a visionary and successful way of doing business, boldly putting the happiness of Partners at the centre of everything it does. It's the embodiment of an ideal, the outcome of nearly a century of endeavour to create a different sort of company, owned by Partners dedicated to serving customers with flair and fairness. All 90,000 permanent staff are Partners who own over 40 John Lewis shops across the UK, over 300 Waitrose supermarkets (www.waitrose.com), an online and catalogue business, johnlewis.com, a production unit and a farm. The business has annual gross sales of over £10bn. Partners share in the benefits and profits of a business that puts them first.[61]

John Lewis opened his Oxford Street department store for business in 1864. In its early days it was a traditional family-owned business, and his two sons followed him into the firm. John Spedan Lewis, later to found the John Lewis Partnership, became Director of a second store (Peter Jones' in Sloane Square) in 1905. When he inherited the whole enterprise in 1928, Spedan Lewis drew up the First Trust Settlement, which left him in control of the business but gave employees shares in its profits. Shortly before the Second World War the business acquired the Waite, Rose and Taylor grocery stores, and in 1950 the Second Trust Settlement created the John Lewis Partnership (JLP) as it is today, owned and run entirely by its employees. John Spedan Lewis died in 1963.

As a business, the John Lewis Partnership is therefore organisationally very different to its major rivals in the UK. It operates in a variety of highly competitive business environments: the UK food retail business is dominated by Tesco, Sainsbury's and Walmart (Asda); and John Lewis department stores compete not only with other department stores, but also with specialist high-street retailers of clothing, electrical goods, furniture and furnishings. Success in these markets requires very high standards of efficiency and effectiveness, and it is interesting to consider the extent to which JLP's distinctive organisation and culture explain its success.

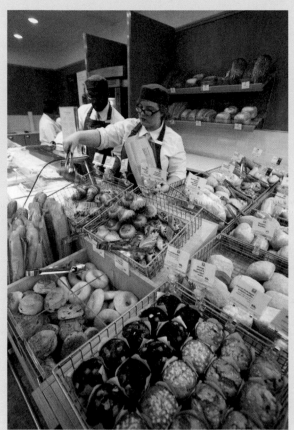

The John Lewis Partnership, including Waitrose, has a unique organisation structure, which has contributed to its business success
Source: Courtesy of Waitrose Ltd

How successful is it, and how is it successful?

The Constitution states that 'the happiness of its members' is the Partnership's ultimate purpose, recognising that such happiness depends on having a satisfying job in a successful business. It establishes a system of 'rights and responsibilities', which places on all Partners the obligation to work for the improvement of our business in the knowledge that we share the rewards of success.[62]

These words set an unusual objective for a business organisation. While many commercial organisations consider the happiness of the workforce as one among several key aims, few hold it to be an overriding one. JLP's structure is an example of representative democracy: all partners elect representatives to the governing Partnership Council; elected representatives account for 80 per cent of Council members, with the remaining 20 per cent appointed by the Chairman. The Chairman

and senior directors are required to give an annual account of their stewardship at a full Council meeting. Further means of communication and decision-making include branch forums and divisional councils, which reflect the various operating units including warehouses and factories as well as stores. Partners can therefore influence decisions and affect the company's activities; also, there is a direct pay-off in the shape of an annual bonus based on the company's profits. The Chairman and other directors must ensure the continuing solvency of the business as well as keeping funds available for growth, but, beyond whatever is necessary for these purposes, the annual profits are redistributed to members. All partners receive bonuses, which are calculated as a percentage of their base pay; in the financial year 2013–14 this resulted in £202.5 million of profit being redistributed at a rate of 15 per cent of salary.[63] In some years this has gone as high as 22 per cent, although a range of 9–15 per cent appears to be more usual. This direct form of 'industrial democracy' and high level of worker participation means that the management of the JLP does not recognise or negotiate with trade unions.

A further aspect of the objective of 'partner happiness' is the extensive range of benefits and services that the JLP provides to its workforce. There is a non-contributory final-salary pension scheme and many direct forms of assistance including a loans scheme. Holiday entitlements are generous, as are discounts on purchases, and the JLP owns social and sporting amenities as well as several estates that provide leisure activities and accommodation for Partners and their families.

Its commercial success, as we have noted, depends on performance in some very tough markets. How has the JLP maintained and grown its business?

Keeping the customer satisfied

Today, the John Lewis Partnership is the largest employee-owned business in the UK. Our Partnership model is admired across both the private and public sectors. Co-ownership gives us a distinctive culture – and a competitive advantage.[64]

In 2014 John Lewis was voted the UK's favourite overall retailer for the sixth time in seven years in a regular Verdict[65] survey of customer satisfaction, and Waitrose also topped the poll in the food and grocery category. Like most retail businesses, the JLP experienced a drop in operating profits during the economic downturn of 2008–9, although the company remained robust and rode the downturn better than many of its competitors.[66]

The introduction of its 'essential' range and the pledge to match Tesco on the prices of branded goods has helped drive up sales and keep customers during the recession. Part of its strength has to be the company's focus on quality and to offer value for money; John Spedan Lewis introduced the 'never knowingly undersold' principle in 1925.

Taking Waitrose as the main example, this has meant a defining principle of 'Quality food, honestly priced'. The effect can be seen in a number of ways, including a relatively early decision to integrate local products into its range (many major food retailers have preferred to stock only products that can be made available at all their stores nationally), thus anticipating a growing interest in localism and the environmental problems associated with long-distance haulage (food miles). In 2001 its television advertising campaign announced that it was selling only free-range eggs, and it has gone on to establish links with farmers whose meat and poultry are produced according to high standards of animal welfare. In 2014 all Waitrose fresh beef, pork, chicken, hens' eggs and milk were produced in the UK, and it works with feed companies to reduce farmers' reliance on overseas sources of animal feed. In recent years it has become an advocate for better standards of employment for migrant agricultural workers in the UK through links with the Gangmasters Licensing Authority and the charity Migrant Help.[67]

In 2005, and as part of a broader approach to corporate social responsibility, the JLP launched the Waitrose Foundation, which runs parallel to its commitment to fair trade. Operating in South Africa, Ghana and Kenya where the company has supply chain links, the Foundation supports local education, training and healthcare projects. This was followed, in 2010, by the creation of a similar organisation, The John Lewis Foundation, which has focused on projects to develop sustainable cotton farming in Gujarat. It aims to uphold the International Labour Organization standards within its supply chain, and JLP buyers are trained to ensure suppliers treat their workers fairly and uphold human rights and well-being.[68]

Getting the message across

These initiatives are supported by distinctive and superior advertising campaigns. The Waitrose advertisements generally focus on the provenance of the products and the lives and work of individual producers and suppliers in a way that emphasises the relationship between producer and consumer, and positions the company as a discreet intermediary between the two rather than a dominant brand. The John Lewis Christmas advertisements have become something of a national institution; the breakthrough came with the 2011 television advert 'The Long Wait', which featured a little boy waiting impatiently for the Big Day, with the final reveal that he was eager to give his parents their gift (rather than get his own presents). It went viral almost immediately, causing a media frenzy in which even hard-bitten journalists admitted that it had made them cry.[69] More recently the snowman searching for a scarf and hat for his snow-lady friend (2012) and Monty the Penguin's surprise present (2014) similarly tugged at middle-class heartstrings. Delia Smith and Heston Blumenthal – two very different types of celebrity chef – have also helped promote both ingredients and ready meals, further widening the brand's appeal.

And so?

Any company can start spending money on corporate social responsibility (CSR) ventures; all the main supermarkets do and many publicly announce a specific percentage of profits for the purpose. What appears to make the JLP different is the coherence and integration of a number of features, including:

- Structure, systems and culture (the Partnership, its consultative councils).
- Segmentation and positioning (its market is clearly identified as middle-class educated professionals in metropolitan and suburban areas).
- Product strategy and upstream relationships (high quality, locally sourced, Fairtrade).
- Customer service (universally appreciated in surveys and delivered by people who have every reason to care about the difference between adequate and very good).
- Specific CSR initiatives (the Waitrose and John Lewis Foundations, the 'model' estate farm at Leckford in Hampshire).
- Marketing communications (innovative, engaging, memorable, perfectly targeted and understated).

Twenty years ago, the JLP and Waitrose were admirable but not very exciting. Today, the brand is cool, with a seemingly effortless stylishness that makes some of the others look flatfooted, loud and desperate. It has formed a strong bond with a very profitable niche market of customers who love being treated that way. And it only works because the offering as a whole fits together and is utterly credible.

Tasks

1 Using the Litterer model summarised in Table 11.1 as the basis for analysis, identify the degree to which the John Lewis Partnership and Waitrose reflect mechanistic and organic structures of organisation.

2 Critically review the governing structure of the John Lewis Partnership. What are the strengths and weaknesses of such a structure in a fast-moving competitive environment?

3 Discuss and evaluate the possible impact of this democratic style of organisation on the role and behaviour of managers. How is it likely to differ from the role and behaviour of managers in a more traditional, shareholder-owned company?

4 The John Lewis Partnership is a UK-based organisation with a global supply chain. What cultural challenges might it face in attempting to ensure that its values are upheld by overseas suppliers? How might its structure influence its effectiveness in dealing with producers in, for instance, Africa and Asia?

Notes and references

1. Adapted from Knight, K. (ed.) *Matrix Management: A Cross-Functional Approach to Organization*, Gower (1977), pp. 114–15.

2. Drucker, P. F. *The Practice of Management*, Heinemann Professional (1989), p. 223.

3. Child, J. *Organization: Contemporary Principles and Practice*, Blackwell (2005), p. 399.

4. Forte, C. (Lord Forte) *Forte: The Autobiography of Charles Forte*, Sidgwick and Jackson (1986), p. 122.

5. Argyris, C. *Integrating the Individual and the Organization*, Wiley (1964).

6. Lucas, E. 'Work: Unlimited', *Professional Manager*, vol. 19, no. 4, 2010, pp. 22–55.

7. Parsons, T. 'Some Ingredients of a General Theory of Formal Organization', in Litterer, J. A. *Organizations: Structure and Behaviour*, third edition, Wiley (1980).

8. Rawson, M. 'Whose Side Are You On?', *Professional Manager*, November 1997, p. 3.

9. Woodward, J. *Industrial Organization: Theory and Practice*, second edition, Oxford University Press (1980).

10. See, for example, Mullins, L. J. and Dossor, P. *Hospitality Management and Organisational Behaviour*, fifth edition, Pearson Education (2013).

11. Woodward, J. *Industrial Organization: Theory and Practice*, second edition, Oxford University Press (1980), p. 113.

12. Drucker, P. F. *Management Challenges for the 21st Century*, Butterworth–Heinemann (1999), p. 11.

13. Cloke, K. and Goldsmith, J. *The End of Management and the Rise of Organizational Democracy*, Jossey-Bass (2002).

14. Gratton, L. *The Democratic Enterprise*, Financial Times Prentice Hall (2004), pp. xii–xiv.

15. Child, J. *Organization: Contemporary Principles and Practice*, Blackwell (2005), p. 76.

16. Graicunas, V. A. 'Relationship in Organization', in *Papers on the Science of Administration*, University of Columbia (1937).

17. Learner, P. M. 'Beware the Gatekeeper', *Amtrak Express*, July/August 1994, pp. 14–17.

18. Keohane, K. 'Get your brand and talent right', *Training Journal*, 1 May 2014, p. 29.

19. Adapted from Kolondy, H. F. 'Managing in a Matrix', *Business Horizons*, March/April 1981, pp. 17–24.

20. Senior, B. and Swailes, S. *Organizational Change*, fourth edition, Financial Times Prentice Hall (2010), p. 84.

21. Ashkenas, R., Ulrich, D., Jick, T. and Kerr, S. *The Boundaryless Organization: Breaking the Chains of Organizational Structure*, second edition, Jossey-Bass (2002).

22. Francesco, A. M. and Gold, B. A. *International Organizational Behavior*, second edition, Pearson Prentice Hall (2005), p. 246.

23. Nicholson, N. 'What's the big idea? Boundaryless organisation', *Management Today*, November 2010, p. 16.

24. Urwick, L. *The Elements of Administration*, second edition, Pitman (1947), pp. 38–9.

25. Child, J. *Organization: Contemporary Principles and Practice*, Blackwell (2005), p. 17.

26. Rosenfeld, R. H. and Wilson, D. C. *Managing Organizations: Text, Readings and Cases*, second edition, McGraw-Hill (1999), p. 255.

27. Townsend, R. *Further Up The Organisation*, Coronet Books (1985), p. 159.

28. Bouchikhi, H. and Kimberly, J. R. 'The Customised Workplace', in Chowdhury, S. (ed.) *Management 21C*, Financial Times Prentice Hall (2000), pp. 207–19.

29. Vecchio, R. P. *Organizational Behavior: Core Concepts,* fourth edition, Dryden Press (2000), p. 338.

30. Lynch, R. *Corporate Strategy,* fourth edition, Financial Times Prentice Hall (2006), p. 582.

31. See, for example, McKinley, W. 'Decreasing Organisational Size: To Untangle or Not to Untangle?', *Academy of Management Review,* January 1992, pp. 112–23; Shapiro, E. 'Power, Not Size Counts', *Management Review,* September 1996.

32. Birkinshaw, J. 'The Structures behind Global Companies', in Pickford, J. (ed.) *Mastering Management 2.0,* Financial Times Prentice Hall (2001), pp. 75–80.

33. Woodward, J. *Industrial Organization: Theory and Practice,* second edition, Oxford University Press (1980).

34. Dawson, S. and Wedderburn, D. 'Introduction' to Woodward, J. *Industrial Organization: Theory and Practice,* second edition, Oxford University Press (1980), p. xiii.

35. Perrow, C. *Organisational Analysis: A Sociological View,* Tavistock (1970).

36. Burns, T. and Stalker, G. M. *The Management of Innovation,* Tavistock (1966).

37. Litterer, J. A. *The Analysis of Organizations,* second edition, Wiley (1973).

38. Lawrence, P. R. and Lorsch, J. W. *Organisation and Environment,* Irwin (1969).

39. Boschken, H. L. 'Strategy and Structure: Reconceiving the Relationship', *Journal of Management,* vol. 16, no. 1, 1990, pp. 135–50.

40. Hunt, J. W. *Managing People at Work: A Manager's Guide to Behaviour in Organizations,* third edition, McGraw-Hill (1992), p. 170.

41. Robey, D. *Designing Organizations,* Irwin (1982), p. 59. See, for example, Fincham, R. and Rhodes, P. S. *The Individual, Work and Organization,* second edition, Weidenfeld & Nicolson (1992).

42. Schneider, S. C. and Barsoux, J. *Managing Across Cultures,* second edition, Financial Times Prentice Hall (2003), p. 101.

43. Watson, T. *Organising and Managing Work,* second edition, Financial Times Prentice Hall (2006), pp. 254–62.

44. Birchall, D. W. 'What Managers Do', in Crainer, S. and Dearlove, D. (eds) *Financial Times Handbook of Management,* second edition, Financial Times Prentice Hall (2001), pp. 110–31.

45. Cloke, K. and Goldsmith, J. *The End of Management and the Rise of Organizational Democracy,* Jossey-Bass (2002), p. 41.

46. Fisher, P. 'Truly Seamless Mobility', *Management Today,* May 2008, pp. 55–8.

47. Czerniawska, F. 'From Bottlenecks to Blackberries: How the Relationship between Organisations and Individuals is Changing', Management Consultancies Association (September 2005).

48. Thomas, A. 'At arm's length', *Chartered Secretary,* June 2010, pp. 28–9.

49. Overell, S. 'The Blurring of Control and Responsibility', ACAS, December 2012.

50. 'Deciding Whether to Outsource', Checklist 079, Chartered Management Institute, September 2014.

51. Hazlehurst, J. 'A New Deal for Public Services', *Management Today,* April 2014, pp. 42–5.

52. 'Flexible Working and Work-Life Balance', ACAS, September 2010.

53. Lucas, E. 'Underlying resistance to flexible working', *Professional Manager,* vol. 19, no. 6, 2010, pp. 26–8.

54. See, for example, Willis, B. 'Out Of Office', *Professional Manager,* Summer 2014, pp. 66–8.

55. 'Characteristic of Home Workers', Office for National Statistics, June 2014, **http://www.ons.gov.uk/ons/search/index.html?newquery=Characteristics+of+home+workers** (accessed 12 October 2014).

56. Sutherland, A. 'Agile but fragile: The changing face of UK homeworking – what works best for whom?', ACAS, July 2014.

57. Dunderdale, P. 'Analysing Effective Organisations', *Professional Manager,* September 1994, pp. 23–4.

58. Gray, J. L. and Starke, F. A. *Organizational Behavior: Concepts and Applications,* fourth edition, Merrill Publishing, an imprint of Macmillan (1988).

59. Heller, R. *In Search of European Excellence,* HarperCollins Business (1997), p. 4.

60. Owen, J. *The Death of Modern Management: How to lead in the new world disorder,* Wiley (2009), p. 175.

61. John Lewis Partnership, 'About Us', **http://www.johnlewispartnership.co.uk/** (accessed 20 February 2015).

62. The Constitution of the John Lewis Partnership, **http://www.johnlewispartnership.co.uk/about/our-constitution.html** (accessed 24 February 2015).

63. John Lewis Partnership Annual Report and Accounts 2014.

64. Ibid.

65. Verdict Retail, **http://www.verdictretail.com/john-lewis-retains-title-of-the-uks-best-retailer/** (accessed 20 February 2015).

66. John Lewis Partnership Annual Report and Accounts 2014.

67. John Lewis Partnership Sustainability Review, 2014.

68. Ibid.

69. BBC News, 22 November 2011, 'Ad breakdown: The John Lewis Christmas ad'. Recordings of all the John Lewis Christmas adverts can be found on the Marketing Magazine website, **http://www.marketingmagazine.co.uk/article/1320008/john-lewis-christmas-ads-2007-2014-humble-roots-national-event** (accessed 24 February 2015).

CHAPTER 12
Technology and organisations

Peter Scott

Technology is a very adaptable phenomenon and the use of technology is common in an increasing range of jobs. The way technology is actually used in organisations depends on decisions made by people and negotiations between people in particular social contexts. To get the best out of technology and the people that use it, managers need to understand the nature of technological change, its organisational and human resource dimensions and its circumstances of use.

Learning outcomes

After completing this chapter you should have enhanced your ability to:

- explain the role and increasing relevance of technology within organisations;
- recognise a number of different schools of thought on the way in which technology and social factors interact with each other;
- examine the nature and significance of the process whereby technology is brought into organisations;
- evaluate the involvement of non-technical specialists in technological change;
- explain the impact of technology on relationships with customers and users;
- evaluate different schools of thought on how technology interacts with the experience of work in organisations.

Critical review and reflection

The wider adoption of mobile devices, social networking, the Internet, artificial intelligence and robotics have the potential to create mass unemployment in the near future.

What are the main arguments FOR and AGAINST this proposition? What kinds of jobs do YOU think would be most at risk and what are the implications for management and organisational behaviour?

Why study technology?

Technology is found and used in all types of organisations. It is the source of new products, services, processes and ways of working that create new demands and improve productivity. Increasingly, technological change is accelerating and spreading out to parts of the economy and organisations previously little touched by it. Technical innovation is affecting the way in which workers interact with each other and, increasingly, with customers of the business too. Managers need to be aware of the nature of technology and technological change processes for four main reasons:

1. There is recurring evidence of technologies being introduced into organisations and subsequently failing. Research into technological innovation indicates that change programmes often neglect in practice to deliver the anticipated benefits, although the same observation could also be made of other types of change initiative.
2. Organisational change techniques (**discussed in Chapter 15**) are often underpinned by, and intertwined with, advances in IT.
3. Many of the insights from 'classic' studies of the introduction and use of technology remain valid. Today, for example, there is much debate on whether new forms of automation will herald a mass collapse of jobs; we can learn from previous such controversies in the 1960s and 1970s.
4. We are currently entering an era where the evolving design and use of information and communications technology (ICT), such as social media and social networking, are likely to be associated with further rapid major changes in the organisation of work and businesses alike.

Human dimensions of technical change

Available research suggests that neglect of the human dimension of change is often culpable in technological failure.[1] At the minimum, this might encompass failing to consider ergonomic concerns or training. More seriously, managers may fail to consider the applicability of designs to fulfil the intended purposes in conjunction with human operators or to consult with users.[2] Problems have bedevilled large, public-sector projects in particular. An independent review of failures in an electronic patient record system introduced by North Bristol NHS Trust in 2012 blamed, among several other factors, inadequate preparation and lack of staff training and engagement with the project.[3] Similarly, a 2012 National Audit Office evaluation of mobile technology in policing criticised the lack of consideration given to how officers would actually use mobile devices in practice and inability to maximise possible efficiencies through the use of such equipment.[4] At the extreme, lack of human understanding and oversight of incredibly complex ICT systems may lead to catastrophic failures, such as 'flash crashes' in the case of high-speed automated trading in the financial services sector.[5]

Features of technology

Technology is very wide ranging, encompassing innovations from ultra-small-scale nanotechnology incorporated in materials to computing. ICT is the technology that most people will be familiar with in both work and personal contexts, and it exemplifies many of the key features of technological development and how they affect organisations. ICTs are inherently flexible; they therefore allow a good deal of choice with regard to how and for which purposes, they are utilised in the organisation in terms of such matters as working practices, skill and control, and job design, as will be discussed below. Highlighted below are seven of ICT's important features:

1. **Compactness.** The space taken up by a given amount of computing power has shrunk enormously since the time of the earliest working computers, vastly increasing the processing power and storage capacity that can be utilised. Decreasing size makes feasible a number of the other features highlighted below.

2. **Increased portability,** because of ICT's shrinking size and weight. We see this advantage most obviously in the ubiquitous smartphone, which combines portability with a high level of computing power.

3. **Connectivity.** This is increasingly important and has a number of dimensions. The incorporation of radio frequency identification (RFID) tags into computing equipment enables signals to be sent from and received at any location that is within wireless range. The increasing use of **wireless connectivity** is most obvious in innovations such as the mobile phone, personal digital assistant and tablet computer. The ease with which many connected ICT devices can be transported increases significantly the locations in which everyday work tasks can take place. As computing power takes up ever less space, the possible range of applications that can be automated grows.

4. **Low energy use** and hence low running costs.

5. **Decreasing cost** in relation to **increasing processing power,** as mentioned above. Again, the increasingly favourable economics make technology potentially applicable to a much wider range of uses. It also makes more feasible the capture and analysis of large quantities of data about human behaviour; this is one aspect of the so-called 'big data' revolution.

6. **Software** that can be edited and reprogrammed, thus providing flexibility of application. Operating systems are becoming increasingly intuitive over time, as we see in the growing popularity of systems such as Android.

7. **Modularity,** by linking discrete types of computing equipment together, both in one location and across distance, using telecommunications to form dispersed **networks,** discussed below.

Main forms or applications

Technology's main forms or applications may be summarised as follows:

- Manufacturing, engineering and design technology, for the provision of goods. Nowadays, this is often interlinked and draws on common databases.

- Technology used for information capture, storage, transmission, analysis and retrieval. This covers many forms of computing and telecommunications equipment.

- Technology employed in the provision of services to customers, clients, patients, etc., in service-sector applications, such as in Internet banking or shopping.

- Technology as the product itself, or as a significant addition to the product, such as devices incorporating microprocessors or the addition of nanomaterials to existing products (enabling, for example, self-cleaning clothes or glass). Much ICT, such as laptops, notebook computers and mobile phones, is equally capable of being used for work or for leisure and social purposes. These are essentially a one-stop work and social centre, as they contain a keyboard and audio and video facilities, as well as Internet access.

Flexibility and networks

Development has been increasingly characterised by the integration of separate technologies, linked to form flexible, dispersed networks. Many now talk of the emergence of a new breed of electronically enabled 'network'-type organisations,[6] or even of 'virtual' organisations reliant on ICTs to conduct business, yet with few physical premises.[7] In particular, *Manuel Castells* is perhaps the foremost author to connect recent changes in technology to the development of 'network organisations' within what he terms a wider 'network society'.[8] For Castells, the 'new economy' is informational (dependent upon knowledge-based information), global (because of the impact of globalisation in extending the reach of capitalist markets) and networked (in the way in which business activity occurs through overlapping global networks). Enterprises become more decentralised and make more use of flexible workers hired for particular projects. These workers may also be parts of other networks. Castells has been criticised for seemingly attributing to networks a life of their own and for overstating the role of technology itself in restructuring organisations and society in some of his work.[9] However, his contribution to the significance of networks remains important.

Critical review and reflection

Technology is the tool that enables people to perform. Managers must have the understanding and skills of how to make the best use of technology, and knowledge of likely new technologies that could be introduced in the workplace.

What are YOUR views? How deep an understanding of the knowledge and skills of modern technology do YOU believe an effective manager really requires?

Approaches to technology and organisation

What do we actually mean by the nature of the relationship between 'technology' and organisation? The basic disagreement concerns where 'technology' begins and ends and the extent to which it can be separated from any surrounding social, political and organisational context in which it operates, for this decides the extent to which humans can hope to exercise influence over the development and use of technology.

Effectively, therefore, there is a debate about where, and whether, a boundary can be most appropriately drawn between two aspects to 'technology':

- **Firstly,** and least controversial, we could talk about the 'hard' aspects of machinery, software, equipment, processes, and so on, that are mainly subject to physical laws.
- **Secondly,** should we include the systems, procedures, work organisation and know-how that are subject to social organisation, but also necessary to convert raw material in whatever form to a transformed product or service?

To what extent are outcomes and consequences of technologies for humans set by inescapable physical requirements, or are people able to intervene during the system design or use phases to enable different outcomes with the same technologies? There is continuing debate about some of the classical views and their historical context, and implications of some of the different approaches to technical change in organisations. Figure 12.1 provides a general illustration of the theories discussed in this section. This is not meant to suggest that a simple division exists between 'technological' factors that influence society on the one hand and 'societal' factors that influence technology on the other; in fact, the construction of each is mutually shaped by the other.[10]

Technological determinism

Technological determinism, the idea that technology innately and inevitably causes certain consequences, has been attributed to several 'classic' studies of the impact of technologies within an industrial setting. Some influential research of the 1950s and 1960s identified associations between technology and a number of organisational phenomena, including *Woodward*'s studies of the structure of organisations[11] (**discussed in Chapter 11**), *Blauner*'s investigations of the degree of job satisfaction experienced by workers[12] (**discussed in Chapter 7**) and *Sayles*' work on the pattern and likelihood of industrial grievances.[13] For example, Blauner drew

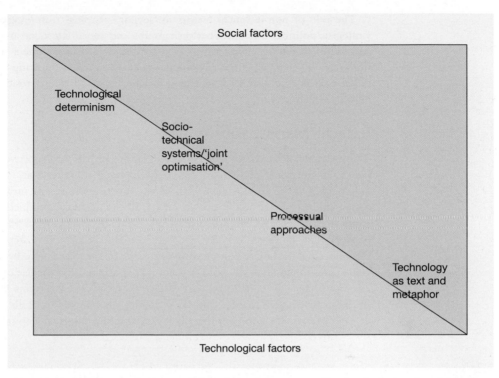

Figure 12.1 Differing explanations of the relative importance of technological and social factors

attention to the negative consequences for workers of 'Fordist' assembly-line technologies, visible in lack of job satisfaction, absenteeism and poor use of human skills. Many academics and others would argue that such a view of technology is now over-simplified, yet some commentaries on the current ICT revolution seem to suggest that technological change, of itself, will alter the structure of industries, commerce and jobs.[14]

Socio-technical systems

Even during early days in the study of technology, some writers argued that choices existed in the manner in which technical apparatus was used. (**The systems approach to the theorising and analysis of organisations is discussed in Chapter 3.**) Socio-technical approaches have a particular concern to find the 'best fit' in any given job/work design between the social 'sub-system' (such as people's psychological and social needs) and the technical 'sub-system' (such as the apparatus, its requirements, method of operation and physical location) of the overall organisational 'system'. This school of systems design anticipates that the 'best' overall socio-technical design is a compromise between what would constitute the ideal designs on either purely 'technical' or 'social' grounds alone. 'Joint optimisation' of the overall socio-technical system requires 'sub-optimisation' of its constituent technical and social sub-systems.

For socio-technical theorists such as *Trist* and his colleagues,[15] the eventual systems design is a matter for conscious organisational choice rather than any technical necessity (as a technical determinist would argue). Socio-technical analysts have put these views into practice in numerous workplace interventions, demonstrating improvements in productivity and social well-being by changing components of the overall socio-technical work system. However, *Kelly* argues that, in reality, socio-technical interventions have tended to modify social (work organisation) systems of the workplace more than they have redesigned technical systems.[16] Socio-technical systems largely approach the politics of choice in technology at the point at which technology is used rather than when it is designed.

The role of non-technical factors in 'socially shaping' technology,[17] such as managerial strategies, political differences between groups and prevailing social assumptions in the design and use of technology, is accorded even greater weight in a number of other approaches to this issue. All emphasise that technology is in fact a process allowing 'choices', although they differ in their relativism and the extent to which they allow any residual role for irreducibly 'technical' factors.

Radical/Marxist approach

This approach is based upon the so-called 'labour process' perspective, originating in *Braverman*'s seminal book, *Labor and Monopoly Capital*.[18] It argues that, in a capitalist society, the only parties to the employment relationship able to exercise any meaningful choice over the design and use of technology are the owners of the means of production. Braverman saw scientific management techniques (**discussed in Chapter 2**) as the main driver to simplify all forms of work. Having de-skilled workers, management's logical next step was to automate even these impoverished jobs. Thus, technology is one of the means used by managers to retain and extend control and de-skill work, a trend that continues into the use of IT for the monitoring and surveillance of work and employees, for example. The key point about the radical/Marxist perspective here is that it is not the technology per se that de-skills jobs (as a technological determinist would claim), but the way it is used in the hands of (capitalist) management.

Critical review and reflection

Technology in itself does not reduce the need for the exercise of human skill and decision-making. It is the way in which technology is actually applied within organisations that can cause this to happen.

To what extent do YOU agree with this assertion? How would YOU attempt to ensure that the use of technology is not at the expense of the demand for human skills?

Design and use of technology

Accepting that the creation, design and use of technology is an essentially social and political dialogue opens the door to further approaches to the subject developed mainly by sociologists of technology since the 1980s. These include the so-called 'processual' approach,[19] socio-economic shaping of technology (SST),[20] social construction of technology (SCT),[21] actor–network analysis (ANA)[22] and technology as text and metaphor (TTM).[23] It is not the purpose to discuss these sometimes quite complex approaches in depth, but it is relevant to draw attention to some of the main similarities and differences in these more sociological approaches. Each school agrees broadly that technological configurations are the outcome of interactions of, and negotiations between, various actors in the innovation process both inside and outside the organisation. For instance, processual approaches emphasise the interplay between three main elements that can be applied to technical change: what *Dawson* calls the substance of change (its actual technical content, its time frame and perceived centrality to the organisation); the context of change (both within the organisation and in the outside environment, including the activities of competitors); and the politics of change (the actions and attitudes of actors having influence over the change process).[24]

Different sociological theories

Among differences between these different sociological theories, three main distinctions are: their respective relativism; the extent to which they believe technologies become 'fixed'; and the influence attributed to social structures.

Firstly, the five approaches above differ in their degree of *relativism* regarding any essential manner in which 'technology' has a determining core. More than any of the other theories, the TTM approach goes furthest in the postmodern position that technology has no objective existence beyond the way we interpret it in our own subjective accounts and representations.

Secondly, TTM argues that 'technology' is continually being reinterpreted and redefined by social actors, therefore there is no point at which it *stabilises* at a fixed conjunction that can henceforth have impacts on other social phenomena. By contrast, the SCT approach argues that, although technological innovation is a multidimensional activity involving negotiations with many actors about the definition of technological problems and solutions, eventually the process will converge upon a particular design option. From that point on, search activity and debate is then closed, and the technology is 'stabilised' in a particular configuration. It becomes possible to talk about 'impacts' or 'effects' on the organisation in general, working practices, skill requirements, etc., although these impacts may be social as well as technical. As *McLoughlin et al.* summarise key differences:

> we can conceptualize technology as a stabilized set of meanings following a social process of closure [SCT]; as congealed social relations held together by a specific alignment of human and non-human actants [ANA]; and as a 'text' which is continually being (re-)written and (re-)read according to interpretative context.[25]

A **third** cleavage between these approaches lies in the extent to which they see prevailing social *structures* as important in influencing the path of technological development. On the one hand, approaches such as SST in particular stress the ways in which capitalist or gendered ideologies within society percolate into the assumptions of those designing, managing and commissioning technologies. On the other hand, relativist approaches such as TTM and ANA focus their main attention on the perceptions and activities of individual actors, while neither allocates much importance to wider social forces.

Decision-making processes

The above discussion suggests that different parties may be involved in decision-making on technologies and organisations. How do particular 'new' technologies come to be adopted in organisations for the first time and then used and operated in a particular way? Two issues relating to that process between them are likely to have far-reaching consequences for the eventual success and the acceptance of particular changes. Firstly, the different phases of the technical change process. In each of these stages, a range of decisions needs to be made by various interested parties, although the range of decisions is likely to get narrower and more detailed as the introduction process progresses. Secondly, which 'interested parties' get involved in the various 'design spaces' that are opened up at the various stages of the process? Our primary concern here is with the impact of decision-making on human behaviour in organisations. Therefore, we need to ask: is the decision-making process conceived as mainly the province of managers and technical 'experts', or do personnel specialists or users of the new technology become involved and, if so, to what extent?

Legal or collective stipulations

Decisions are not just a matter of individual organisational preference, but are, in certain circumstances, subject to legal or collective stipulations about how the process should be managed, and the extent to which various organisational actors should be permitted to influence the process. The prime example of this is the case of the introduction (and use) of remote teleworking in organisations within the European Union (EU), which is subject to the 2002 Framework Agreement on Telework between employers' organisations and trade unions. This affects numerous matters that organisations within Europe are required to take into account when making use of this form of work, recognises the rights of employees to be collectively consulted about the process, and requires employers and trade unions nationally to monitor the agreement.[26] In relation to decision-making processes on technology, the interesting issue is the different ways in which this agreement has been transposed to a national level in the different EU countries.

The various methods indicate that there is greater protection and opportunity for dialogue in some nations than others. Some countries, such as the Czech Republic and Portugal, incorporated the agreement's provisions into national labour law; countries such as France, Denmark and Sweden made national or sectoral collective agreements between their employers and trade unions; while in Ireland and the UK national employers' and trade union representatives agreed voluntary – and relatively weak – codes of conduct that are likely to allow workers or unions little influence at workplace level.[27] *Prosser* claims that such agreements can be more effectively implemented and monitored in countries with centralised and co-ordinated industrial relations systems – unlike the UK.[28]

Phases and stages of technology introduction

An important framework explaining the life cycle of the process whereby new technology comes into organisations has been developed by *Preece*, summarised below. It identifies two phases: new technology adoption; and introduction. Within these phases, it is possible to categorise seven separate stages (*see* Table 12.1 and Figure 12.2).[29] The **adoption phase** consists of four stages: initiation; progression/feasibility; investment decision; and planning and systems design. During this phase, no technology is yet on the site at which it is intended to be used. This happens during the **introduction phase**, consisting of installation, operationalisation and evaluation, where the project actually takes physical shape and becomes established as a technology in actual use. If problems occur at any stage, the process may loop back on itself and recommence from an earlier stage.

Table 12.1 Main elements of Preece's framework for the introduction of new technology into the firm

Phase	Stage	Details
Adoption	Initiation	The initial idea for introducing a particular technology, generated by persons either inside the firm (e.g. managers) or outside it (e.g. equipment suppliers), to satisfy particular organisational goals
	Progression/feasibility	Detailed follow-on work by managers to assess the feasibility of the initial idea (e.g. cost-effectiveness etc.), preparation of case for the technology, negotiations with potential objectors, etc.
	Investment decision	Putting the case to decision-makers, followed by approval of investment, revision of plans, or abandonment
	Planning and systems design	Detailed planning of system architecture, preparation of location, consideration about jobs and work design, training, etc.
Introduction	Installation	Bringing equipment on site and setting it up. Testing. Putting the system into operation in combination with those who will operate it. Debugging
	Operationalisation	Fine-tuning amendments by operators to optimise their everyday use of the system (with or without the knowledge of managers)
	Evaluation	Review of project in order to assess whether it has met the goals set for it

Source: Adapted from Preece, D. A. *Organizations and Technical Change: Strategy, Objectives and Involvement,* Routledge/ITBP (1995). Reproduced with permission.

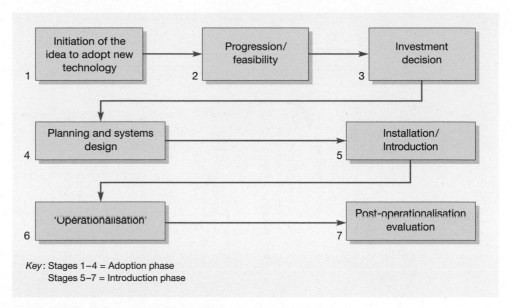

Figure 12.2 Stages in technology adoption and introduction

Source: Preece, D. A. *Organizations and Technical Change: Strategy, Objectives and Involvement*, Routledge/ITBP (1995), p. 7. Reprinted by permission of the publishers, Routledge, a division of Taylor & Francis, Ltd.

Initiation and operationalisation

The initiation and operationalisation stages, shown in Table 12.1 and Figure 12.2, are particularly important. In relation to the first of these stages, our earlier discussion argued that the very flexibility of modern technologies means that they can fulfil numerous goals. In initiating ideas to bring in new technologies, the sponsors may have various objectives and, indeed, different objectives may well be important to different players in the adoption process. *Child* has applied this to the new technology decision-making process in relation to his idea that managers have 'strategic choice' between different types of goal, and much of the argument over whether to introduce technology is likely to be over these kinds of issues.[30]

Objectives may be easily quantifiable financial measures, such as cost savings, or may be more abstract goals, such as the capability to manufacture more complex product designs. The latter type of benefit is less easily quantifiable according to traditional accounting techniques, but may be of longer-term value to the company. Different occupational specialisms may have conflicting concerns, motives and priorities in the introduction of new technology and are likely to pursue their objectives in the early stages of the new technology adoption process using particular arguments, which may jar with the views being put forward by other parties.[31]

Operationalisation is worthy of mention because it is here that the workforce will have a direct impact on the technology, even if the workforce was unable to do so previously in discussions about working practices, training and so on (see the next section). *Wilkinson* carried out an important study of this part of the introduction process, looking at the political behaviour associated with organisational and human resource (HR) issues arising out of technical change on the shop floor, especially as regards the skills and control that are exercisable. He demonstrated that a range of choices had been made, and were available, about work organisation, control and skill/de-skilling of jobs, and that the outcomes of technical change are partly dependent on the (sometimes covert) adjustments made by the users in order to optimise technological systems for everyday use.[32]

A concept map setting out the features of introduction of new technology is given in Figure 12.3.

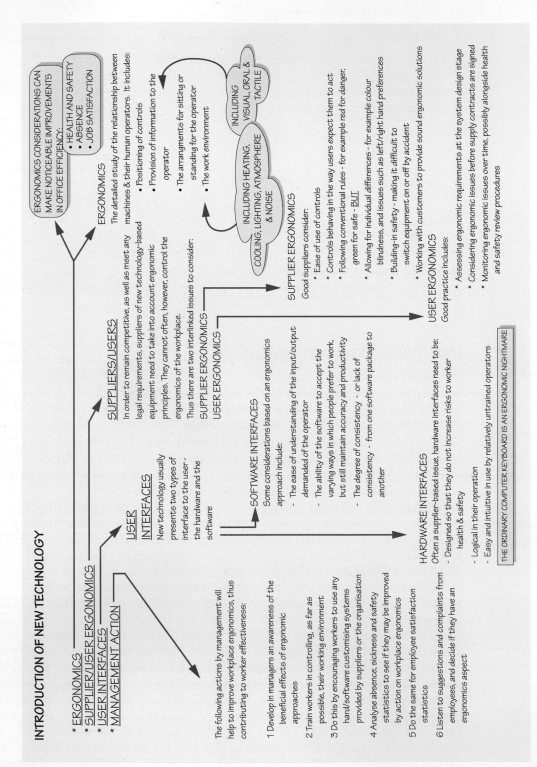

Figure 12.3 Introduction of new technology

Involvement of HR specialists and users of technology

As the previous discussion has indicated, one important issue in the above processes concerns whether, and at what stage, two groups of interested 'non-technical' stakeholders become involved. These groups are:

- those charged with management of HR matters within the enterprise; and
- the actual users of the technology.

The later they enter the process, the less far-reaching the influence they are likely to be able to have on it.

HR specialists

The role of HR specialists in the new technology adoption process shows how people with particular perspectives and expertise on aspects of organisational work can influence the process. They are the 'people specialists' in organisations and should be aware of issues such as alternative forms of job design and working practices, skill and de-skilling possibilities.

While some research suggests that personnel specialists' cross-organisational brief allows them to be technology 'change agents',[33] the balance of evidence argues that their involvement – if any – in technical change is more often belated and reactive.[34] *Legge* suggests that there are three main reasons for low levels of involvement:

1. Employees have been secondary to other considerations in the choice and implementation of new technology, and thus personnel specialists' peripheral and reactive involvement is only to be expected.
2. As employees typically welcome rather than resist new technology, personnel specialists' involvement did not take off at implementation either (e.g. they were rarely required to deal with tricky and complex issues relating to pay, gradings, employment, etc.).
3. Even on the odd occasion when resistance did occur, personnel's role was not seen as being crucial because of the weaknesses and divisions of the trade unions and employees more generally.[35]

Reference to HR specialists

A 2005 survey of its members by the Chartered Institute of Personnel and Development (CIPD) confirms this picture of low involvement. It reported that decisions to introduce new technology are taken with no reference to HR specialists in roughly half of the organisations surveyed. The reasons volunteered by the respondents mainly referred to such decisions being taken elsewhere in the organisation or suggested that they did not have enough specialist expertise to be able to contribute. A few respondents suggested that other departments were keen to preserve their autonomy and actively to keep HR out of the process.[36] An additional factor is that HR specialists are not directly present in the great majority of UK workplaces. For instance, the large-scale 2011 Sixth Workplace Employment Relations Survey classified only 22 per cent of its workplace-level management respondents as 'specialists' in employment relations issues, either by virtue of their job titles or because they spent more than half their time on such tasks.[37]

The CIPD survey referred to above indicated that, at whatever stage of the process they were involved, the most common roles for HR specialists were training, communication about the change process and the overall management of it. Clearly, those specialists whose expertise was sought at earlier stages of the decision-making process were more likely to be involved in strategic issues of the overall changes.[38]

Users of technology

Evidence also indicates that the users of technology are rarely involved in the process of technology adoption, although they are more likely to have input during the **operationalisation** stage, in terms of such aspects as working practices, tasks, decisions about methods, and tools and techniques. *Fröhlich et al.* conducted a survey of workplace involvement in technical change in twelve EU countries. Only 20 per cent of respondents reported consultation or negotiation between management and employees in the adoption stages of technological change, but this rose to 33 per cent in the implementation stages.[39]

Worker involvement was much more likely to occur in countries such as Germany and Denmark than in countries with fewer established mechanisms for involving workers, such as the UK. The study identified a number of costs and benefits of the involvement of workers in the decision-making process. Improved utilisation of skills and attending to different actors' concerns were seen as the greatest benefits, while extended time scales were the main costs. We must remember that user involvement is an inherently political process rather than simply 'good practice'. Managers are largely responsible for deciding on the extent, form and time scales of user involvement in technical change.[40]

Critical review and reflection

Nothing is to be gained by involving end-users in the adoption and introduction of technical change. They are not in a position to make any useful contribution and it is far simpler and quicker to tell them what will happen and what they will have to do.

To what extent do YOU agree? Would YOU be happy if the implementation of technology was entrusted solely to technology specialists? What is the situation in YOUR university?

Technology, work and organisational behaviour

In this section we review seven facets of the interaction between technology and the world of work. Some of these subjects have engendered lengthy academic debates and controversy, while others are emerging areas, particularly where they concern the implications of the most recent technological innovations.

- Technology influences the specific design of each member's pattern of work, affecting the skills exercisable and the overall quality of jobs.
- Technologies affect the degree of control that workers can exercise within their jobs. There is a fertile, unresolved debate over whether centralisation and closer control of workers or decentralisation and democratisation of technology in the workplace is the dominant trend.
- Technology changes the relationship between organisations and external customers or users in a number of ways that have implications for the structure and reputation of organisations, as well as the nature and experience of work within them.
- Technology affects where the 'workplace' is located.
- Technology affects the nature of social interactions between workers, particularly in cases where those working on a project are doing so from different places.
- Technology can influence the pace and intensity of work.
- Technology has an impact on job security and on the management of a workforce with varying levels of technical ability and awareness.

These factors are likely to affect the experience of work, and therefore ultimately the levels of job satisfaction that individuals are able to attain. We should also recognise that many of the seven factors are interlinked. For example, the setting-up of offshore telephone call centres represents a change in the location of work, but such moves are often also accompanied by the routinisation of the tasks in these establishments (a reduction in skill levels) and an expectation of faster throughput of calls (a change in the pace and intensity of work).

Skill, work design and job quality

The impact of technological change on the nature and variety of job activities performed, the skills that workers can exercise, and the amount of autonomy and control they have over their jobs have been among the most hotly contested areas in social science. In this section we concentrate particularly on skills and work organisation, and argue that different writers have associated technology with diametrically opposed types of effect on the skills that workers can exercise within their jobs: a reduction in skills, or the reverse trend, where automation is said to lead to increased levels of skill. If one looks at the workforce as a whole rather than trends within occupations, some writers find evidence of both processes simultaneously, and we consider this view in a later section below.

The influential work of *Braverman,* mentioned earlier in this chapter, questioned the assumption of contributors to the 'automation debates' of the 1960s, such as Blauner (**discussed above**), that technical change would lead, relatively unproblematically, to rising levels of job satisfaction and skills.[41] Instead, Braverman argued that automation, in the hands of managers, comprised the second stage of a strategy to de-skill and eliminate jobs that had started with the techniques of scientific management. The so-called 'labour process' debate that followed the publication of Braverman's work spawned numerous workplace studies producing evidence either to confirm or cast doubt on Braverman's original hypothesis.[42] An important insight was that the exact effects of technical change on skill levels depend on how managers organise job design and the patterns of work organisation more broadly. Research indicates that this varies considerably between workplaces and that it is even possible to identify differing patterns and preferences cross-nationally on how managers are likely to organise work.[43] In one example using case studies of similar technology matched across countries, *Gallie* showed how the jobs and skills of operatives varied between British and French oil refineries, with the French workers being able to exercise greater autonomy.[44]

Nevertheless, the idea of a **long-term** trend towards de-skilling through the application of new technology still holds some purchase,[45] despite the claims of those seeing a shift towards a 'knowledge' workforce (**discussed in Chapter 7**). Some argue that the concept of 'knowledge workers' is often used over-simplistically.[46] *Fleming et al.* argue, on the basis of a study of jobs in Australia that might be classified as 'knowledge work', that many such occupations involve merely relatively low-level information-processing skills, and thus it could be mistaken to anoint them as 'knowledge work'.[47] Other studies of the use of computing applications in different forms of clerical and professional work suggest that many of the 'skills' simply involve navigating standardised software interfaces, producing increasingly uniform work experiences.[48]

Technology and skills trajectories

The more widespread diffusion of more flexible forms of microprocessor-based automation since the 1980s has led other writers to adopt a contrary, but still controversial, view. Prior to current debates about 'knowledge workers', *Piore and Sabel* in the USA and *Kern and Schumann* in Germany claimed simultaneously that new categories of multiskilled workers capable of programming and overall system control were emerging in manufacturing industry.[49] *Zuboff*'s studies provided further evidence for why this might be the case. She argues that, whereas mechanisation had indeed tended simply to 'automate' human skill, the novel property of ICT was that it generates new streams of previously unavailable information about processes that require interpretation by human operators. To use her term, it 'informates' processes in ways that require new human skills to exploit successfully.[50] Technology's implications for skills within the workforce as a whole are potentially complex and will be discussed further in the section below on job security and the digital divide.

Critical review and reflection

Just because you are required to use IT equipment to do your job, it does not make you a 'knowledge worker'.
    What do YOU understand by the concept of a 'knowledge worker'? How useful is it as a way to encapsulate the nature of working in the present era?

Centralisation versus decentralisation of control

The debate about the effect of technology upon skills and work organisation necessarily raises the question of the consequences of technology for workers' autonomy and discretion. In other words, to what extent can it be an instrument of tighter monitoring and control or of greater liberation in the workplace? (**Organisational control and power is discussed in Chapter 13.**)

Surveillance

The advent of the ICT revolution has reinvigorated concern with the use of technology as a means of workplace control, particularly in relation to the information-gathering potential of ICTs and the use to which this could be put in technically monitoring or conducting surveillance on workers' performance and activity. Contributory factors include the sheer growth in the numbers and usage of technologies available to capture and store data generated within organisations,[51] coupled with higher pressures on staff to perform because of increased competition, financial constraints, or large firms' domination of integrated ICT networks in some sectors, such as retail.[52] The potential for surveillance encompasses technologies as established as closed circuit television[53] through to newer methods such as voice and image recognition software and RFID tags, which can be placed in goods and even people so as to enable tracking of their location and movement.[54] It is commonplace for RFID devices to be installed in delivery vans, for example.

    The origins of such concerns can be traced back to the writings about 'disciplinary power' of the French postmodernist *Foucault,* and particularly to his popularisation of Jeremy Bentham's proposed design for a prison that perfected the capability for surveillance of the prisoners' activities in their cells: a 'panopticon', the literal meaning of which is 'all-seeing eye'.[55] Some writers have expanded this metaphor to encompass the information-gathering potential of ICTs to produce the concept of the **electronic panopticon.** This literature draws attention to the insidious and not-so-insidious ways in which IT has been used by managers to monitor and record the work of employees, in some cases in such a way that they do not know exactly when they are being watched, but are aware that this could be at any time. For instance, the systems in telephone call centres typically permit managers to listen in randomly to the calls of selected operatives (a practice usually justified on the grounds of quality control). However, the operatives have no way of being aware of when managers may be monitoring their conversations with customers. Hence, it is argued, employees amend their behaviour to act as if they are under unseen surveillance all the time, just like the prisoners in Bentham's panopticon.[56]

McGovern et al. are among the few to employ survey evidence to try to uncover the extent of ICT-based monitoring of employees' work in the UK. Piecing together available surveys, they report that by the year 2000 approximately one-half of employees said that a computerised system logged the work they were doing and about one-quarter stated that their work was actually checked through the information thus collated. It can be reasonably assumed that these proportions are likely to have increased in the intervening years. There seemed to be little variation between different occupational categories in the likelihood of such remote checking.[57]

Caution and uncertainty

Mason et al. strike a note of caution, echoing previous debates on labour control: there is disagreement over whether the ability to collect such performance data necessarily means that managers always refer to, or act on, the data; whether technologies are actually capable of living up to their claimed surveillance potential; and to what extent employees can resist such techniques, rationalise their existence, or even turn them to their own advantage.[58] The conditional and partial nature of the potential for control within ICT is illustrated in a number of workplace studies, such as *Eriksson-Zetterquist et al.*'s work on the introduction of new technology into professional jobs and *Fisher*'s research into the introduction of ICTs and the restructuring of work within an agency of the UK civil service. Fisher, for example, shows how the complexity of the case work undertaken by the civil servants largely thwarted management attempts to de-skill the work technically and to exert more control over it, although managers were nevertheless able to use the new ICT systems to generate previously unavailable information about the work process that might assist future attempts to exert greater control.[59]

Further, in particular organisational contexts, some workers may also view surveillance as legitimate in proving their own levels of performance against allegedly less productive colleagues, as *Sewell et al.* find in a call centre,[60] or protecting their safety, as *Grampp et al.* find with the introduction of global positioning systems (GPS) for dispatch of taxi drivers in Dublin. GPS facilitated closer management control over the movements of drivers and limited their autonomy. Drivers were resigned to this rather than resistant: inasmuch as the system reduced the time that taxis were unoccupied, it also maximised driver income and, in many respects, the interests of company and drivers coincided. However, what really sold GPS to the drivers, and was emphasised by employer and equipment suppliers alike, was the potential to improve driver safety.[61] This study, and others like it, shows that we cannot conceive of organisational control as simple or unproblematic, and it is clearly mediated by other salient issues within the workplace.

Computer use and organisational policies

The generic nature of the software included on organisational networks and computing devices creates novel problems and dilemmas for managers about the control of employees' computer use in working hours. Access to the Internet, social networking sites and email is increasingly available within the workplace, and further applications similar to those already likely to be on employees' home computers and smartphones. This raises real problems about the boundaries between 'work' and 'personal' use of computers, what usage workers may legitimately make of the computing facilities available to them and how any restrictions should be devised, monitored and enforced. The extended hours that some employees spend at, or doing, work clearly exacerbate the likelihood that the employer's computing facilities may be the vehicle used for personal or social Internet traffic.[62]

A growing number of disciplinary, dismissal and Employment Tribunal (ET) cases have centred on the abuse of email, distribution of inappropriate images and negative posts by employees on social media.[63] ETs have ruled that employees were fairly dismissed even if the posts were not primarily work related, distribution was only to a small group of 'Facebook friends' or 'Twitter followers', or the employer was not mentioned by name. In cases where the employee won, ETs sometimes reduced compensation on the grounds that, by posting in a public forum, the employee contributed to the problem.[64] Even if used for work purposes, email can be used excessively or distributed to mailing lists beyond those who need to – or, in some cases, should – see the message concerned, thus contributing to information overload.

As both a legal defence and good HRM policy, organisations should therefore put in place clear and transparent guidelines to minimise the likelihood of abuse or misunderstandings about the nature and extent of computer use for reasons that may be considered unrelated to work. A number of such guidelines exist, including those produced by organisations such as ACAS and the CIPD.[65] These cover issues of access to computer systems, monitoring of employee usage, the degree to which personal use of computing facilities may be permissible in work time, data protection, use of disclaimers in emails to safeguard against legal action, the relative responsibilities of employers and employees, and so on.

Surveys of both UK and US employers by XpertHR find that most of the respondents do indeed have policies, some of which permit a certain level of non-work use of email and the Internet by staff for activities such as online shopping, but are less likely to permit online gambling, and all the policies surveyed prohibited accessing pornography.[66] Relatively minor transgressions by employees of such usage policies are also reported to be common. New technological developments, such as social networking, carry with them the need for organisational policies to be regularly updated if they are to remain relevant.

Critical review and reflection

The use of ICT as a means of increased managerial surveillance should be strictly limited by serious concerns for the social and ethical issues that arise from monitoring workers' activities and performance.

How far do YOU believe ICT can justifiably be used as a means of surveillance in the workplace? What social or ethical issues do YOU think are relevant?

Management and organisational behaviour in action case study
Negotiating the use of vehicle-tracking technology

The use of vehicle-tracking technology by managers of those who drive company vehicles as part of their job has resulted in a number of disputes between firms and trade unions about the monitoring of drivers. Among other things, drivers and their unions have been concerned about privacy and the possible use of such systems to monitor driver location and performance. For management's part, such workers have traditionally been very difficult to control, as they often work alone and cannot be readily supervised when off the company premises.

In 2009 British Telecom (BT) engineers in Southampton belonging to the Communication Workers' Union (CWU) organised a demonstration about the proposed installation of GPS vehicle-tracking systems in their vehicle cabs. In response to this disquiet, BT managers entered discussions with CWU representatives and the outcome was a jointly negotiated Memorandum of Understanding that stipulated how GPS equipment was to be used in the future. The agreement stated that the system would not be used as a means of engaging in surveillance of employees, nor would it be used as the sole basis for opening disciplinary proceedings against, or questioning the performance of, individuals. The agreement reached also gave guarantees about employees' reasonable expectations of privacy while out on the road and committed BT management and the CWU to consulting jointly in order to engage trust. As a result of the agreement, BT line managers were forbidden from accessing the GPS to view data in real time on tracked vehicle movements. This does not imply that they cannot access historical data.

As a result of this agreement, a potentially serious dispute was averted and relations between the company and the CWU appear to have been strengthened.

Source: The main source for this case study is Labour Research Department 'The Enemy Within: Negotiating on Monitoring and Surveillance', *Workplace Report*, no. 97, December 2011, pp. 15–16.

Tasks

1. Referring to the involvement of personnel specialists and users in the introduction of technological change, to what extent do you think it was possible to avoid this dispute?
2. How does this case illustrate the management dilemma of the extent to which employees should be *controlled* or *trusted?* What factors complicate this dilemma in the case of employees who mainly work off site?
3. To what extent do you think the case demonstrates the value of reaching joint agreement on technological change? What other possible approaches do you think could have been adopted and what would have been the likely outcome in each scenario you can identify?

Social networking

We have discussed the vertical control that employers can exercise over workers' tasks through ICT, and their ability to monitor the use that employees are making of the technologies that are made available to them. Social networking and other interactive technologies, such as Facebook, Twitter, virtual worlds (such as Second Life), weblogs (blogs), etc., permit the more lateral use of technologies to share information and digital content. Social networking sites such as Facebook have tens of millions of users, mostly in their teens and 20s, many of whom are currently part of the workforce and many more who soon will be.

Such developments create new problems for traditional authority relations and communications within organisations as these interactive technologies short-circuit existing organisational hierarchies.[67] Online social networking has increased rapidly, and at least some of this must be taking place in work time. One response is to clamp down. Fears that employees' productivity is declining through 'wasting' time on these kinds of allegedly unproductive activities have led a considerable number of employers to limit time spent on networking sites or to forbid such activities altogether.[68] Apart from social media's potential for new work-related misbehaviours, employers are also concerned about reputational damage. For example, cases exist of blogging employees being dismissed when the offending employer about whom they were blogging could be identified from details included in the posts.[69]

Others argue that organisations should come to terms with the new participatory opportunities offered by social media and should not 'kill the conversation'.[70] Social networking can be a positive phenomenon for recruitment, publicity, to build necessary business contacts and to expand sales and goodwill beyond organisational boundaries. ACAS argues it can be used to strengthen employee voice.[71] In relation to blogging, for example, *Ellis and Richards* dispute the common perception that it is solely a manifestation of covert resistance to the employer. Their research with bloggers finds that other motivations for blogging include using it as an outlet for workers' underemployed creativity, to build a virtual network of the like-minded and as a form of public relations for the job. This raises the worrying possibility that such employees are finding a form of autonomy and control in their blogs that they do not feel in their everyday jobs.[72]

Using networking sites for business communications and marketing purposes appears to be considered important in some firms, particularly those in creative industries and those whose business methods have traditionally relied heavily on more established forms of social networking.[73] While the more well-known sites such as Facebook tend to be used predominantly for social purposes, there exist other networks, such as LinkedIn, that are primarily intended for business use by professionals.[74] As with most electronic technologies, networking appears equally capable of being used for work and social purposes, thus one cannot draw blanket conclusions that such developments bode well or ill from a work perspective. *Bradwell and Reeves*[75] argue that any distinction between 'social' and 'professional' networking is becoming increasingly artificial, especially in relation to younger employees, and that the latter type of network is spreading its boundaries horizontally across organisations. Although they argue that such developments have considerable promise, dangers can be identified too.

Potential dangers and drawbacks

The development of individual workers' networks with those outside the organisation raises questions about the nature of commercial confidentiality, of loyalty, and also conceals dangers of iniquitous practices in hiring staff, awarding contracts, and suchlike. Others have indicated further drawbacks with networks, although some of these disadvantages accrue to different parties in the employment relationship. Firstly, one needs to question whether the forms of social interaction enabled by such sites are as rich in quality as traditional face-to-face networking,[76] considered further in the section on social interactions below.

Secondly, employees may easily forget that the electronic traces they leave on the Web and networking sites can be accessed by anyone who is able to track them down, including curious prospective future employers! Finally, employees may equally be able to use electronic networks against the interests of employers, as *Pliskin et al*. demonstrate in their study of how Israeli university lecturers created a successful email network to distribute information about, and maintain solidarity in, a pay dispute with their employers.[77] The uses of ICTs for organising protest are considered further in the next section.

Critical review and reflection

A manager who tries to ban the use of social media sites in the workplace is like King Canute trying to turn back the tides.

To what extent do YOU agree? What restrictions, if any, do YOU believe managers should put on the use of social media sites at work, and why?

Changing relations with customers and users

As the previous section suggested, current Internet developments blur the boundaries between the organisation and its external context in ways previously not experienced. This section considers three aspects of how such technologies impact on organisations' relations with their customers or service users. These are the implications for organisation structure and work of user-generated content and 'crowd-sourcing'; the use of technology to enable customer self-service; and organisations' increasing transparency and vulnerability to the views and opinions of external customers and service users.

Interactive technologies have increased the power of the user of products and services. One sees this, firstly, in user-generated content on Internet sites, such as in amateur reviews of products and services purchased. Organisations have little or no control over such content. Secondly, a more far-reaching development is the 'open-source' or 'crowd-sourcing' movement, where enthusiastic amateurs, often working unpaid, engage in dispersed 'mass collaboration' to author, develop and improve artefacts.[78]

Computer operating systems such as Linux, software ('freeware') such as Audacity and the online encyclopedia Wikipedia are among the better-known products of this movement. Torch-bearers for this movement, such as *Shirky,* consider it as 'organising without organisations'.[79] Pessimists interpret manifestations of crowd-sourcing such as Amazon's 'Mechanical Turk' as a further step on the road to casualised, insecure and poorly paid self-employment.[80] Such developments in mass co-operation have implications for traditional organisation structures, the distribution of power, the nature and value of professional expertise, and even the nature and value of paid work itself that are as yet in their infancy. The likely implications are as yet imperfectly understood and require further research.

A second trend enabled by increasingly interactive technologies is the transfer of what used to be paid work to the free labour of the customer or service user. Although a move from paid service to self-service has been visible for some time – think of the use of ATMs by banks over several decades – the Internet and user-friendly software have taken this to a new level. Self-service supermarket checkouts, online-only ordering (e.g. flight booking for certain budget airlines) and the development of so-called e-government services[81] provide examples of this. Such innovations change the relationship between the organisation and the customer/user.

Thirdly, interactive technologies have changed the dynamics of organisational power, not only internally within the organisation (as suggested in the previous section), but also in relation to interactions with customers, users and the wider public. This can happen in several ways. The perceived performance of workers in organisations can become more transparent to current and prospective customers. For instance, crowd-sourced taxi drivers for the smartphone-powered UberTaxi service are rated by customers according to the service they give. The visibility of drivers' ratings to potential customers acts as a powerful disciplinary force on the drivers concerned if they wish to continue receiving jobs.

The new social media provide further opportunities for reputational impacts on organisations and the organisation of protest and dissent. *Butler* argues that: 'Web technology has changed the relationship between authority, employee and citizen. In the past, it was relatively easy for public authorities to control the "authorised" version of events.'[82] Writers dispute the importance of the Internet and social media such as Facebook and Twitter as vehicles for activism. *Mason* argues that they have been significant, while *Gladwell* suggests that they are overrated, encouraging a relatively weak form of remote activism.[83] Nevertheless, such media have been used to co-ordinate campaigns against employment, environmental and other corporate policies of firms of all sizes, and the potential for reputational damage to organisations is clear.[84]

Critical review and reflection

Publicly available online reviews of organisational performance provide the only quick and effective way for prospective customers to judge the likely quality of that organisation's employees in serving the customer's needs.
On balance, how valid do YOU think such forms of feedback are? Put together YOUR list of possible arguments in favour of, and opposing, this statement.

Location of work

New technologies have facilitated the redistribution of where work is carried out in a number of ways, the full implications of which are not yet clear. Here we focus on two main developments. Firstly, the availability of ICTs has made the displacement of workers from the traditional individual location (desk or office) considerably easier. Thus workers may be working from home, on the move, or in some form of collective office space part or all of the time. Secondly, technology has made easier the move nationally or even internationally of certain forms of service sector activity that can be carried out over the telephone or via an Internet connection. This is one part of the phenomenon known as offshoring. In each of these cases, technology is certainly not the only factor in play, but it is an important one.

Remote and mobile working

The fragmentation of the 'workplace' is a multifaceted phenomenon, and some aspects are discussed elsewhere in this text (**see, for example, telecommuting in Chapter 11**). Here we concentrate more specifically on the trends towards working while on the move. Sociologists such as *Urry* have noted the simultaneous expansion in recent years of human travel and of the desire to maintain contact with other people at a distance through various communication technologies.[85] Such developments have expanded into the world of work in a variety of forms. Sixty-four per cent of the firms responding to a 2011 survey by Virgin Media Business claim to be equipping workers to work out of the office, a rapid growth that suggests that the relative positions of mobile and fixed desktop computing are gradually being reversed.[86]

Felstead et al. have conducted perhaps the most comprehensive study to date of workers whose jobs are located wholly or partly away from a conventional workplace. Felstead *et al.* detail the many ways in which traditional conceptions and routines of work are fragmented and displaced in such settings, but the most instructive lesson is that workers actively attempt to reconstruct for themselves some of the certainties of the traditional workplace, although sometimes in new ways. These include attempts to reconstruct 'personal' work space and a division between 'working' and 'non-working' time. Workers also invent new ways to circumvent the electronic supervision of their activities (as discussed above) and to alert their superiors to their 'presence' and productivity, by sending emails very early or late in the day, for example.[87]

Globalisation and offshoring

Certainly, we can say that economic factors are important too,[88] including the emergence as economic powers of new nations with skilled but relatively inexpensive workforces. This has created new options for organisations about where to locate the functions that need to be performed, but also numerous dilemmas concerned with co-ordination of the business and both political and customer reaction.

> The development of Information and Communication Technology (ICT) is, along with deregulation, the other key enabling factor for the changed nature of globalisation. It enables both a closer coordination of supply chain activities and more cost-efficient delivery across national borders. The other important implication of technological advances in ICT is that it has eroded some of the geographical limitations to the provision of services and opened up a wide range of service activities to international competition that were previously confined to national markets.[89]

As this quote suggests, it is clear that the development of broadband and the falling costs of computing and telephony are among the main reasons for the trend to export service jobs from the West to new parts of the world. ICTs are one of the main drivers of the globalisation of organisations and work, contributing to the wider fragmentation of organisational forms and structures in the process.[90]

Employment, social and organisational implications

Much of the debate about offshoring has been concerned with the employment, social and organisational implications of what the new technological possibilities unleash. The initial concern was with the impact on service sector work that is not – or can be reorganised so as not to be – performed face to face, especially in finance, insurance and other customer-service operations. Early public debate focused on the export from Western countries of such work and its concentration into telephone call centres in countries such as India, which have a highly qualified and plentiful supply of English-speaking labour and a developing technical infrastructure. Nevertheless, such workers are paid a fraction of the wages that comparable work in the UK would attract, although the wages in the recipient country may still seem high by its average standards and the relative 'wage gap' between the 'sender' and 'receiver' countries has declined over time. Research suggests that firms involved in offshored work tend to reorganise it along Taylorised lines, giving the workers limited discretion and subjecting them to a high degree of monitoring.[91] Similarly, Internet-based commercial activities can be based where the labour needed to run and maintain them is relatively cheap.

More recently, higher-value and professional activities have been considered candidates for offshoring, and a number of offshore service providers offer, for example, staff planning and other HR services, programming and software development, and so on. *Garner* classifies the types of service jobs that are economically attractive to move abroad as those that do not require the provider to be in physical contact with the recipient and are labour intensive, information based, codifiable (i.e. routinised) and highly transparent (involve dealing with easily measurable and verifiable information, such as the analysis of financial ratios).[92]

The future of offshoring

Indications are that offshoring is continuing to expand, despite a hiatus in the global recession. Despite its public profile and the predictions of offshoring's optimists,[93] a number of commentators have argued that its extent and impact has been exaggerated. Numerous international commentators[94] have argued that – with some exceptions – the proportion of jobs offshored from the developed West has been relatively low, although views differ about likely future changes.[95] Some have pointed to problems that have emerged, including a retreat from offshoring by some organisations due to political or customer pressure. Strains have emerged in the countries that have benefited disproportionately from offshoring, such as India. Some researchers have found that call-centre work is plagued by high levels of staff turnover. Also, the very success of countries such as India in attracting offshored work has led to a tightening of the labour market and wage inflation, which has given an incentive to relocate such work again to relatively cheaper regions or even to other countries.[96] For students of organisational behaviour, such events clearly demonstrate the often unintended consequences of the use of technical possibilities to restructure and relocate work processes within firms.

Critical review and reflection

ICTs have helped to enable the globalisation and 'offshoring' of certain types of work from the West to other parts of the world.

How important do YOU believe technology is compared with other possible causes? Do YOU think this kind of 'outsourcing' arguably causes more problems than benefits for organisations?

The nature of social interactions

Technology is likely to change the extent and manner in which managers and workers interact and workers interact with each other. It may affect the size and nature of work groups and the extent of physical mobility and of contacts with other people. These factors will certainly be magnified with ICTs, where people working on linked tasks may be at a variety of locations, including at home (**as discussed, for example, in the section on telecommuting in Chapter 11**), and individuals may work more on their own, from personal workstations, or work more with machines than with other people. There are clear dangers for organisations here that workers may become isolated from the workplace and that it becomes harder for the informal channels of information exchange on which organisations depend to flow freely.

Worse, information about developing problems can be more easily hidden when workers are not interacting face to face. A comment from a knowledge management worker participating in a research study of virtual working sums up the difficulty of creating high-quality social interactions when workers are communicating from different locations: 'We try to have what we call virtual coffee sessions, which were dreadful . . . all around the world we tried to get together and have a cup of coffee and sit down and look at each other, and you can't be spontaneous now, you can't do it, you can't force it.'[97]

Remote versus office-based workers

It is well established that remote workers face particular problems in being able to interact successfully with the organisation, and particular care is needed to integrate them and to assure that they face no detriment to their career development. Equally important, but subject to considerably less attention, is the quality and nature of interaction between staff who remain office based and their remote co-workers. The limited research that does exist suggests that office workers can resent their remote colleagues, both for the perceived advantages of the remote lifestyle and for the fact that their own presence in the office means they pick up tasks that the remote workers can avoid. *Golden* studied the job satisfaction and turnover intentions of office-based workers who have colleagues who telework.[98] He found that 'the prevalence of teleworkers in a work unit alters the flexibility and workload of non-teleworking colleagues, thereby impacting their satisfaction with co-workers and turnover intentions'.[99] Such negative findings for co-workers of teleworking are moderated the fewer the hours teleworked, the greater the opportunity for face-to-face interactions with teleworkers and the greater the degree of job autonomy experienced.

Fogarty et al. studied predominantly office-based workers in a publishing firm where some staff work remotely on an informal basis, alongside the existence of other employees on a formal teleworking scheme and yet others who always work in the office. Their findings question the practicalities of the 'virtual organisation'. They found that communications and social interactions between office-based and remote workers, as well as continuity of operations, can all be adversely affected by the uncertainties generated, especially by the practice of ad hoc informal off-site working.[100]

The pace and intensity of work

Considerable evidence now exists that modern work patterns are becoming more intensive and although organisational change more generally is one of the main causes of this, it is exacerbated by accompanying technical changes and the way in which technology is often utilised within organisations.[101] Technology can dictate the speed at which workers react and affect the pace and intensity of work, such as in the mechanical pacing of work on a mass-production assembly line or the manner in which electronic control devices can be programmed to demand a human response within a given time frame. If such demands are perceived as excessively frequent, persistent or intrusive, then this may result in the development of stress.

The introduction of ICT undoubtedly transforms, significantly, the nature of work and employment conditions for staff. The instantaneous connectivity of new technologies, notably email and instant messaging, has created a working climate in which there is a greater expectation of the immediacy of receipt and response, regardless of location or time, and this has added to the dangers of information overload. The ease of use only exacerbates the frequency of use. The lack of deliberation encouraged by this expectation of rapid response then generates further traffic to clarify previous communications. The danger is magnified by the ability to send a message to whole groups of people (whether warranted or not). *Symon* points out that the volume of information leads workers to develop strategies to ignore much of it, which is itself problematic if significant information is thus screened out.[102]

Views on ICT's contribution to workers' stress and impact on work/life balance are split into three broad categories. The more negative research finds that the ever-increasing use of ICT, and workers' propensity to check for messages repeatedly (with or without managerial expectations they will do so), are causes of rising stress levels in the workplace.[103] Conversely, others argue that fears of increasing user stress are exaggerated and that users – especially those who have grown up with ICT – can develop coping mechanisms to process and retrieve information without experiencing overload.[104] A third view, typified by *Madden and Jones'* PEW/Internet and American Life Project, suggests a more mixed, nuanced picture, where ICT's contribution to workers' productivity and flexibility is offset by difficulties in disengaging from an intensified work experience.[105]

We referred earlier to the increase in use of ICT for the purposes of monitoring workers, especially as uncovered by the longitudinal survey comparisons of *McGovern et al.*[106] These authors also demonstrate, as a relatively novel trend in the workplace, that ICT is associated with an observable increase in the levels of strain felt by workers, even when the technology is only used to record the work done. The degree of work strain tends to increase for administrative and semi-skilled employees when ICT is used as a means of checking work performance (but apparently not in the case of professional and managerial workers, although such use of ICT may well be less widespread here).[107]

A number of major European employers are now beginning to introduce organisational solutions to reduce the impact of ICT overload on staff. These include preventing the firm's servers from sending out email after the end of shifts, banning managers from contacting employees outside working hours and allowing staff to delete email sent to them while they are on leave.[108]

The 'digital divide' and job security

Finally, we consider the implications of technology, particularly ICTs, for exacerbating the divisions that exist, both within and outside of the organisation, between those with high levels of technical knowledge and skills and those without. This phenomenon of differing levels of technical literacy within the workforce and, indeed, within the population more widely, is often referred to as the 'digital divide'.

One of the most repetitive themes in debates about technology and organisations is automation's impact on jobs.[109] At the dawn of the microprocessor revolution in the late 1970s, *Jenkins and Sherman* famously predicted 'the collapse of work'.[110] In fact, new products, services and jobs arose to soak up any technological unemployment. In parallel to this, numerous researchers noted the growth of digital divides within and between countries, where those with the capacity to utilise new technologies fared better than the less technically skilled.[111] In the West, the latter group tended to stay in work if their jobs remained too cheap to be worth exporting or could not realistically be automated at all.[112]

Recently, however, writers such as *Brynjolfsson and McAfee* and *Frey and Osborne* have analysed the US labour market and again forecast the possibility of large-scale job losses. Frey and Osborne argue that 47 per cent of US jobs are at high risk from computerisation, 19 per cent at medium risk and the remaining third at low risk, under current conditions of low growth and high levels of inequality. As before, low-skilled jobs are at the greatest risk, but they suggest that the next generation of technologies, such as robotics, artificial intelligence, drones, etc., will also threaten more highly skilled and professional jobs.[113] It remains to be seen whether matters will turn out in the apocalyptic way predicted, although an increasing digital divide, with its divergent implications for skills, wages and job security, is a reasonable bet. However, our argument in this chapter is that developments depend strongly on the unpredictable processes by which technologies are introduced and used in organisations.

Implications for organisations and organisational behaviour

What are the implications for organisations and organisational behaviour? If this kind of polarisation is happening, it has obvious ramifications for skills, training and promotion, recruitment patterns and business strategies more generally. Clearly, there is an onus on managers to guide the process of technical change so that the more deleterious implications for job security and skills apparent in the scenario above are avoided, as far as possible. It is also important that managers do not stereotype the presumed abilities with ICTs of particular groups of workers, such as older employees. Nonetheless, it seems likely that those working in modern organisations might well have very different reactions to IT developments and use IT in different ways. For some, new systems and applications might be welcome as a means of becoming more effective; for others, perhaps those with less experience of IT, new systems might be viewed as threatening. While there might be fewer and fewer individuals in this latter category, their anxiety is likely to be very real as the ever-rising tide of technological possibilities washes over them.

For yet others, technological developments might be welcome, but their ability to make the most of what is on offer can be compromised by lack of time to learn about new systems or the lack of appropriate training. However, research suggests that there is also likely to be a fourth group, mostly younger workers, whose technological expertise is very sophisticated and who might find organisational systems archaic, frustrating and slow by comparison with those they encounter in their personal lives.[114]

Critical review and reflection

To make the best use of technology we must use it to support and develop the effectiveness of organisations, and not be tempted to adapt business activities to the technology. The tail must not be allowed to wag the dog.

Do YOU think technology is becoming too much our master rather than our servant? How would YOU go about making the best use of technology?

Ten key points to remember

1 Technology is increasingly pervasive and flexible in organisations. Human factors are important in successful technical change, and problems can result if they are underestimated or ignored.

2 There is continuing debate about different approaches to technology and organisations and the extent to which it consists of 'social' as well as 'purely' technical factors.

3 The introduction of technology into organisations involves a number of phases and stages. There can be considerable organisational choice over the use of technology.

4 Human factors tend to be considered at the later stages of the process. An important issue is the extent of early involvement of HR specialists and the extent to which the quality of decision-making is likely to be improved.

5 Considerable debate exists about the interactions between technology and organisational behaviour and the impact of technology change on workers' skill, work design and job quality.

6 Current technological innovations have increasing potential to gather data that can be used to control workers' behaviour and performance. Actual use depends on managerial policies and balance of power between managers and workers.

7 Collaborative networking, Internet and social media technologies present new opportunities and problems for organisations in their internal relations with workers and external relations with customers and users.

8 Technology is increasingly affecting where work is carried out and blurring the division between home, travel and work, and also between work and social life.

9 The above technological developments are contributing to an increased pace and intensity of work, yet workers seem willing to trade off such disadvantages in return for greater connectedness.

10 Research indicates a 'digital divide' between the unequal job opportunities and security available to workers with high levels of technical skill versus those without.

Review and discussion questions

1 Outline and comment upon ways in which users can participate in the adoption and introduction of new technology.

2 It is not unusual for the outcomes of technical change to fail to match up to expectations. What can cause this gap and how might it be prevented?

3 What objectives should managers set for the introduction of technological change? Draw upon case study research to support your answer.

4 To what extent do you agree with the contention that 'decision-making with respect to technical change is an inherently political process'?

5 'New technology has resolved the control question. Managers can now draw back from a Tayloristic approach to the supervision of employees.' Discuss.

6 Discuss the contention that a theoretical or practical perspective that sees technology as having independent effects upon people and organisations is misguided.

7 Compare the possible advantages and disadvantages of remote working from the perspectives of (a) mobile workers *and* (b) office-based workers.

8 In what ways can ICT lead to the intensification of work? To what extent do you think that such developments are inevitable?

9 How useful do you believe is Foucault's 'panopticon' metaphor for understanding the surveillance potential of ICTs?

10 Critically consider what, if any, *new* issues social media and social networking raise for the study of technology and organisational behaviour.

Assignment

For your university, or an organisation with which you are familiar, you are required to:

1 Detail fully an example of technical change that has taken place or is taking place, comparing the work processes involved and how they are carried out, both *before* and *after* the change
2 Analyse the origins and development of that change, drawing upon the technological and organisational change literatures discussed in this text.
3 Assess the main implications of that change for both the organisation and its employees. For example, what have been the effects on job numbers, the nature of the work required, skill levels, training requirements; has the change solved the problems it was intended to address, or has it thrown up new issues; what have been the main costs and benefits?

Personal skills and employability exercise

Objectives

Completing this exercise should help you to enhance the following skills:

● Understand better the impact of technology on an organisation and its members.
● Apply your theoretical knowledge to the analysis of organisational processes.
● Evaluate benefits and drawbacks resulting from technological change.

Exercise

Select and examine examples of two different jobs in your university, if possible, or in some other organisation with which you are familiar. Detail the main duties of the chosen jobs and both the technical skill and equipment necessary in undertaking each job.
Taking each job in turn, detail:

● Those aspects of the job that you think could, or should, be further automated, and why?
● Those aspects of the job that cannot, or should not, be further automated, and why?
● How the nature of the job would change if your suggestions were followed. What do you think would be the reaction of the occupant? Would the job become more or less fulfilling?
● To what extent do you think senior managers would come to the same conclusions as yourself, taking into account factors such as costs, product and service quality?

Discussion

● To what extent does theorising on the nature of technology help in analysing applications of technological change?
● On the basis of the jobs you have studied, does it suggest that further automation results in more positive or more negative implications for individuals in an organisation? Would you come to the same conclusion about further automation in general?
● Think back to the present occupants of each job. In what ways do you think there might be a different response depending upon the generation and age group of the occupants (**discussed in Chapter 3**) (e.g. Generation Y) and the technological sophistication of the occupants?

Case study
How many 'likes' do I get for my essay?

Few aspects of working life today remain untouched by technological change, and academia is no exception. The last ten years have seen rapid changes in the way that higher-education establishments operate, and student expectations are now conditioned by familiarity with social media technology (SMT) such as Facebook. This creates pressure for universities and colleges to adopt IT-based platforms for the management and delivery of study programmes; for instance, students expect many practical aspects of life – class and examination timetables, module choices, achievement records and so forth – to be online.

The adoption of proprietary web-based teaching tools or 'virtual learning environments' (VLEs) such as Blackboard and Moodle allow many teaching activities to be transferred to cyberspace, and have become almost universal accessories to taught programmes ('blended learning'). VLEs also support distance-learning courses: online materials, recorded lectures and real-time seminars (webinars) replicate traditional methods and can facilitate remote access to some of the best teaching in the world.

Assessment is another area where technology can support course delivery, and it is one that is proving somewhat contentious. Most universities have well-developed policies and procedures about assessment. These relate to the need for fairness, objectivity, speed and quality, yet student surveys have revealed that assessment and feedback on performance are areas where there is persistent dissatisfaction.[115] Why should this be the case? And can technology help? The experience of one UK institution can help us to understand the organisational benefits and people-related challenges associated with introducing a system for the electronic management of assessment (EMA).

Assessment and feedback

The assessment of student work and feedback on results is one of the most angst-ridden areas of academic life for students and teachers alike. To understand why, we need to separate out the components of this problem area.

There are two main types of assessment: formative and summative. Formative assessment has the main purpose of helping students to gauge their progress and identify mistakes or areas for improvement.[116] Summative

Source: Igor Normann/Shutterstock.com

assessment is intended to judge learning, and results in formal marks that will contribute to a student's individual grade. Feedback can mean simply the publication of results ('getting your mark back'), or it can mean receiving qualitative analysis of the assessed work and guidance for improvement. Arguably, qualitative feedback on *formative* assessment is less contentious and more valuable because it does not affect a formal grade. It is when handling *summative* assessment and feedback that things get tricky. Again, two distinct problems arise: the speed with which results arrive and the result itself. If you have worked hard on an essay or slogged through exams, you will want to know how you did as soon as possible. But you would also want to think that your work had been carefully and fairly marked, and that you can learn from any mistakes. You might also want to know that any of your peers who have cheated by copying or plagiarising have been duly detected and penalised. The tension between these two expectations – a quick response and high-quality marking and feedback – often causes problems for academic institutions. Teaching and administrative staff are faced with large peaks of work at submission and examination time that then has to be processed securely, fairly and accurately. EMA is designed to help, and a study at the University of Huddersfield shows the impact technology can make.[117]

The purpose of the study was to evaluate the introduction of a Turnitin-based electronic assessment management system[118] over six years between 2007 and 2012. During this time different cohorts of students were included in the project (starting with first-year

→

students in 2007–8) and different elements of electronic management were introduced stage by stage (removing the need for paper assignment submissions, adding new types of marking tool and enabling methods to store and handle cohort marks). Four main groups were affected by the project:

- students whose work was included;
- administrative staff who handle assessments and records;
- academics who mark and give feedback;
- managers who are concerned with costs and benefits of EMA.

Unsurprisingly, students were ultimately much happier with EMA than with traditional methods of submitting assignments:

> Amongst students, there is very strong evidence to suggest that not only is electronic assessment management their preference, but that those who come to appreciate its attendant benefits then begin to see . . . [it] . . . as their entitlement.[119]

This is not to say that there were no initial anxieties or that all students preferred electronic submission, but experience showed it to be easy, much like uploading a photo on Facebook. It was seen as removing the anxiety of printing close to submission deadlines, travelling to the administrative centre and queuing to hand in. There was also evidence that students had great confidence in the security of electronic submission, particularly as the system generated a timed receipt:

> it's that security of knowing that you've got something that says you've submitted it at this time so nobody can come back and say your work's missing, you can say I've got this proof.[120]

There was also general satisfaction with the electronic feedback and marker comments, not least of which being that they were legible!

Administrators were also generally content with a system that reduced mindless, repetitive tasks such as date-stamping and logging paperwork. There were time savings and an apparent increase in job satisfaction as they were able to devote more energy to helping students and academic colleagues.

Early adopters, healthy sceptics, reluctant users

As the study notes, the group most significantly affected by the use of EMA systems was that of academic staff and teachers. The research noted three distinct groups with respect to EMA:

> Amongst academic staff attitudes are split into three main groups: those who are innovators or early adopters and have migrated enthusiastically to eMarking, those who have approached it more cautiously and those who have done so reluctantly or have tried it and then moved back to paper marking.[121]

Early adopters were those who had generally chosen to use eMarking as soon as it became available and are seen as important for any future developments:

> while this is the group of staff that are the least likely to be disgruntled, it is vital that any EAM[122] system that is adopted allows them to continue working in the ways they prefer and ideal that it also be a system that rewards them for doing so.[123]

Healthy sceptics began by being neutral regarding the use of EMA. Not as enthusiastic as early adopters, they would not use a system that did not work better than the more traditional one.

> This group are characterised by not being prepared to tolerate interfaces with which or environments in which they were not comfortable or which felt unnecessarily difficult or cumbersome to use. They have, however, been persuaded to convert to eMarking either because of the benefits experienced by their colleagues, or because of other demonstrable benefits.[124]

Some of the benefits reported included better organisation of marking, not having to carry around mounds of paper that might get lost or muddled and easier detection of copying, plagiarism and other sorts of cheating that can be facilitated by EMA. The study notes that this group is particularly important as it can provide the critical mass that would enable an institution's managers to implement EMA successfully. The University of Huddersfield authors also suggest that the early adopters would be best placed to act as change agents and be more effective coaches to healthy sceptics in the use of eMarking than administrative or technology support staff.

Finally, the reluctant users are those for whom EMA is both problematic from a practical point of view and seems to challenge the values of personal interaction and 'old school' teaching.

Practical problems include the inability to mark assignments wherever they wanted to, for example on train journeys or in places without Internet connections. Additionally there was concern about the amount of time that would have to be spent in front of a computer screen reading and typing. Engaging reluctant users would thus be difficult. Two points on the topic in the Huddersfield report are worth noting:

One participant admitted to using his seniority to force more junior colleagues to use the tool, which suggests that this may be a relatively effective way of generating widespread take-up, especially across junior and part-time staff who have little option to refuse the directives of their more senior module leaders.[125]

and:

One participant reported that a colleague was forced into it by student complaints which were communicated at a student panel. He was the last academic staff member in his particular discipline area still marking on paper and this participant reported that the students demanded he start marking electronically.[126]

In any university or college the relationship between students, managers, administrators and academic staff is likely to be profoundly affected by the adoption of EMA systems. The experiences, attitudes and priorities of all four groups will be different, and managers of academic institutions are likely to be grappling with them even as you are reading this case; you could be shaping the future of higher education right now.

Tasks

1 Review this case in the light of the main phases and stages described in Preece's framework for the introduction of new technology (Table 12.1). To what extent does it follow the pattern suggested by the model?

2 What appear to be the social implications of the introduction of the EMA system? Use the list of seven points on page 446 as the basis for your analysis.

3 What evidence is there that some staff – and indeed some students – see the use of electronic forms of feedback as part of a surveillance system or an 'electronic panopticon'? What are the implications of this for the relationships between academic staff and university managers?

Notes and references

1. See, for example, the following report on the role of the human factor in accidents: Parliamentary Office of Science and Technology, 'Managing Human Error', *Postnote*, no. 156, Parliamentary Office of Science and Technology (2001), **http://www.parliament.uk/documents/post/pn156.pdf** (accessed 5 August 2015).

2. See notably Advisory Council on Science and Technology, People, Technology and Organisations: *The Application of Human Factors and Organisational Design*, HMSO (1993).

3. 'New Computer System Caused Hospital Chaos', *This is Bristol*, 17 July 2012, **http://www.thisisbristol.co.uk/New-caused-hospital-chaos/story-16547259-detail/story.html** (accessed 18 July 2012).

4. National Audit Office, *Mobile Technology in Policing*, NAO (2012).

5. See, for example, Tarafdar, M., Gupta, A. and Turel, O. 'Special issue on "Dark Side of Information Technology Use": An Introduction and a Framework for Research', *Information Systems Journal*, vol.25, no. 3, 2015. doi: 10.1111/isj.12070

6. Castells, M. *The Information Age: Economy, Society and Culture, Vol. 1: The Rise of the Network Society*, Wiley-Blackwell (2009).

7. Cooper, C. and Rousseau, D. (eds) *Trends in Organizational Behavior, Vol. 6: The Virtual Organization*, Wiley (1999).

8. Castells, op. cit.

9. For critiques of Castells, see for example Webster, F. *Theories of the Information Society*, Routledge (2000).

10. See, for example, the discussion in McLoughlin, I. and Badham, R. 'Political Process Perspectives on Organization and Technical Change', *Human Relations*, vol. 58, no. 7, 2005, esp. pp. 838–40.

11. Woodward, J. (ed.) *Industrial Organisation: Behaviour and Control*, Oxford University Press (1970); Woodward, J. *Industrial Organization: Theory and Practice*, second edition, Oxford University Press (1980).

12. Blauner, R. *Alienation and Freedom*, University of Chicago Press (1964).

13. Sayles, L. *Behavior of Industrial Workgroups: Prediction and Control*, Wiley (1958).

14. See optimistic views such as Cairncross, F. *The Death of Distance 2.0: How the Communications Revolution Will Change Our Lives,* Texere Publishing (2001); Leadbeater, C. Living on Thin Air: The New Economy, Viking (1999).

15. Trist, E. L., Higgin, G. W., Murray, H. and Pollack, A. B. *Organisational Choice,* Tavistock (1963).

16. Kelly, J. E. 'A Reappraisal of Socio-Technical Systems Theory', *Human Relations,* vol. 31, no. 12, 1978, pp. 1069–99.

17. MacKenzie, D. and Wajcman, J. (eds) *The Social Shaping of Technology,* second edition, Open University Press (1999).

18. Braverman, H. *Labor and Monopoly Capital: The Degradation of Work in the Twentieth Century,* Monthly Review Press (1974).

19. See, for example, Dawson, P. *Reshaping Change: A Processual Perspective,* Routledge (2003); Pettigrew, A. M. *The Politics of Organisational Decision-Making,* Tavistock (1973).

20. For an explanation of this perspective, see Mackenzie, D. and Wajcman, J. (eds) *The Social Shaping of Technology,* second edition, Open University Press (1999). Mosemghvhdlishvili, L. and Jansz, J. 'Negotiability of Technology and its Limitations', *Information, Communication and Society,* vol. 16, no. 10, 2013, pp. 1596–1618, apply the perspective to the increasingly democratized smartphone app development process.

21. See particularly Pinch, T. and Bijker, W. 'The Social Construction of Facts and Artefacts: Or How the Sociology of Science and the Sociology of Technology Might Benefit Each Other', in Bijker, W., Hughes, T. and Pinch, T. (eds) *The Social Construction of Technological Systems: New Directions in the Sociology of History and Technology,* MIT Press (1987).

22. Callon, M., Law, J. and Rip, A. (eds) *Mapping the Dynamics of Science and Technology in the Real World,* Macmillan (1986); Latour, B. *Science in Action: How to Follow Scientists and Engineers through Society,* Harvard University Press (1987).

23. Grint, K. and Woolgar, S. *The Machine at Work,* Polity Press (1997).

24. Dawson, P. *Reshaping Change: A Processual Perspective,* Routledge (2003), esp. ch. 2.

25. McLoughlin, I., Dawson, P. and Preece, D. 'Introduction: Theories, Concepts and Paradigms', in Preece, D., McLoughlin, I. and Dawson, P. (eds) *Technology, Organisations and Innovation: Critical Perspectives on Business and Management,* vol. II, Routledge (2000), p. ix.

26. Commission of the European Communities, *Framework Agreement on Telework,* European Commission (2002), **http://ec.europa.eu/employment_social/news/2002/ oct/teleworking_agreement_en.pdf** (accessed 18 March 2009); Welz, C. and Wolf, F. *Telework in the European Union,* Eurofound (2015).

27. Weiler, A. 'Diversity in Implementation of Telework Agreement across the EU', EIROnline, European Foundation (2006).

28. Prosser, T. 'Accounting for National Variance in the Implementation of European Social Partner "Soft Law": The Cases of the Implementation of the Telework and Work-related Stress Agreements', *British Journal of Industrial Relations,* vol. 53, no. 2, 2015, pp. 254–77.

29. Preece, D. A. *Organizations and Technical Change: Strategy, Objectives and Involvement,* Routledge (1995).

30. Child, J. 'Managerial Strategies, New Technology and the Labour Process', in Knights, D., Willmott, H. and Collinson, D. (eds) *Job Redesign: Critical Perspectives on the Labour Process,* Gower (1985), pp. 107–41.

31. Buchanan, D. and Boddy, D. *Organizations in the Computer Age,* Gower (1983).

32. Wilkinson, B. *The Shopfloor Politics of New Technology,* Heinemann (1983).

33. Preece, D. A. and Harrison, M. 'The Contribution of Personnel Specialists to Technology-Related Organisational Change', *Personnel Review,* vol. 17, no. 1, 1988, pp. 13–19.

34. See Daniel, W. W. and Millward, N. 'Findings from the Workplace Industrial Relations Surveys'; and Legge, K. 'The Role of Personnel Specialists: Centrality or Marginalization?', in Clark, J. (ed.) *Human Resource Management and Technical Change,* Sage (1993).

35. Legge, K. 'The Role of Personnel Specialists: Centrality or Marginalization?', in Clark, J. (ed.) *Human Resource Management and Technical Change,* Sage (1993).

36. Chartered Institute of Personnel and Development, *People Management and Technology: Progress and Potential,* CIPD (2007), p. 17.

37. Van Waanrooy, B., Bewley, H., Bryson, A., Forth, J., Freeth, S., Stokes, L. and Wood, S. *Employment Relations in the Shadow of the Recession: Findings from the 2011 Workplace Employment Relations Survey,* Palgrave Macmillan (2013), p. 51.

38. Chartered Institute of Personnel and Development, *People Management and Technology: Progress and Potential,* CIPD (2007), p. 17.

39. Fröhlich, D., Gill, C. and Krieger, H. *Workplace Involvement in Technological Innovation in the European Community* (2 vols), Office for Official Publications of the European Communities (1993).

40. Howcroft, D. and Wilson, M. 'Participation: "Bounded Freedom" or Hidden Constraints on User Involvement', *New Technology, Work and Employment,* vol. 18, no. 1, 2003, pp. 2–19.

41. Braverman, H. *Labor and Monopoly Capital: The Degradation of Work in the Twentieth Century*, Monthly Review Press (1974).

42. See Thompson, P. *The Nature of Work*, Macmillan (1989) for an overview of the main positions in the labour process debate.

43. Jones, B. *Forcing the Factory of the Future*, Cambridge University Press (1997).

44. Gallie, D. *In Search of the New Working Class*, Cambridge University Press (1978).

45. Armstrong, P. 'Labour and Monopoly Capital', in Hyman, R. and Streeck, W. (eds) *New Technology and Industrial Relations*, Blackwell (1988), pp. 143–59; Tinker, T. 'Spectres of Marx and Braverman in the Twilight of Postmodernist Labour Process Research', *Work, Employment and Society*, vol. 16, no. 2, 2002, pp. 251–81.

46. Darr, A. and Warhurst, C. 'Assumptions, Assertions and the Need for Evidence: Debugging Debates about Knowledge Workers', *Current Sociology*, vol. 56, no. 1, 2008, pp. 25–45; Thompson, P., Warhurst, C. and Callaghan, G. 'Ignorant Theory and Knowledgeable Workers: Interrogating the Connections between Knowledge, Skills and Services', *Journal of Management Studies*, vol. 38, no. 7, 2001, pp. 923–42.

47. Fleming, P., Harley, B. and Sewell, G. 'A Little Knowledge Is a Dangerous Thing: Getting Below the Surface of the Growth of "Knowledge Work" in Australia', *Work, Employment and Society*, vol. 18, no. 4, 2004, pp. 725–47.

48. Huws, U. 'The Making of a Cybertariat? Virtual Work in a Real World', in U. Huws (ed.) *The Making of a Cybertariat? Virtual Work in a Real World*, Merlin Press (2003), p. 166.

49. Piore, M. and Sabel, C. *The Second Industrial Divide: Possibilities for Prosperity*, Basic Books (1984); Kern, H. and Schumann, M. 'Limits of the Division of Labour: New Production and Employment Concepts in West German Industry', *Economic and Industrial Democracy*, vol. 8, no. 2, 1987, pp. 151–70.

50. Zuboff, S. *In the Age of the Smart Machine*, Harvard Business School Press (1988).

51. Blakemore, M. 'From Workplace Watch to Social Spy: Surveillance in (and by) the Workplace', Updated Briefing Paper for GMB, GMB Union (2011); Labour Research Department, *Social Media, Monitoring and Surveillance at Work*, Labour Research Department (2012).

52. See, for example, Newsome, K., Thompson, P. and Commander, J. '"You Manage Performance at Every Hour": Labour and the Management of Performance in the Supermarket Supply Chain', *New Technology, Work and Employment*, vol. 28, no. 1, 2013, pp. 1–15; De Vita, G. and Case, P. '"The Smell of the Place": Managerialist Culture in Contemporary UK Business Schools',

Culture and Organization, forthcoming, 2015, p. 8. doi: 10.1080/14759551.2014.971122

53. A 2015 survey of members by UK teachers' union NASUWT reports more extensive problems with the use of CCTV in schools to monitor teachers' performance than found in a parallel survey in 2014. See NASUWT 'Teachers subjected to professionally demeaning practices', NASUWT press release, April 2015, **http://www.nasuwt.org.uk/Whatsnew/NASUWTNews/PressReleases/NASUWT_013937** (accessed 6 May 2015).

54. See House of Lords Select Committee on the Constitution, *Surveillance: Citizens and the State: Report*, HL18-I, Second Report of Session 2008/9, Stationery Office (2009), p. 17.

55. Foucault, M. *Discipline and Punish – The Birth of the Prison*, Penguin (1977).

56. See, for example, Lyon, D. *The Electronic Eye: The Rise of the Surveillance Society*, Polity Press (1994); Sewell, G. 'The Discipline of Teams: The Control of Team-Based Industrial Work through Electronic and Peer Surveillance', *Administrative Science Quarterly*, vol. 43, no. 2, 1998, pp. 397–428.

57. McGovern, P., Hill, S., Mills, C. and White, M. *Market, Class and Employment*, Oxford University Press (2007), pp. 169–71.

58. Mason, D., Button, G., Lankshear, G. and Coates, S. 'Getting Real about Surveillance and Privacy at Work', in Woolgar, S. (ed.) *Virtual Society? Technology, Cyberbole, Reality*, Oxford University Press (2002), pp. 137–52.

59. Eriksson-Zetterquist, U., Lindberg, K. and Styhre, A. 'When the Good Times Are Over: Professionals Encountering New Technology', *Human Relations*, vol. 62, no. 8, 2009, pp. 1145–70; Fisher, M. 'The New Politics of Technology in the British Civil Service', *Economic and Industrial Democracy*, vol. 28, no. 4, 2007, pp. 523–51.

60. Sewell, G., Barker, J. and Nyberg, D. 'Working under Intense Surveillance: When Does "Measuring Everything that Moves" Become Intolerable?', *Human Relations*, vol. 65, no. 2, 2012, pp. 189–215.

61. Grampp, C., Houlihan, M. and McGrath, P. 'Who's Driving Now? GPS and the Restructuring of Taxi Work', in Bolton, S. and Houlihan, M. (eds) *Work Matters: Critical Reflections on Contemporary Work*, Palgrave (2009), pp. 232–49.

62. 'Shopping, gaming and gambling – how are your staff using company devices?', *HR Grapevine*, 21 November 2014, **http://www.hrgrapevine.com/markets/hr/article/2014-11-21-shopping-gaming-and-gambling-how-are-your-staff-using-company-devices?utm_source=eshot&utm_medium=email&utm_campaign=RR%20-%2021/11/2014** (accessed 21 November 2014).

63. See, for example, the case of three judges sacked for viewing Internet pornography through their work IT accounts: BBC News 'Judges sacked for watching porn', **www.bbc.co.uk**, 17 March 2015, **http://www.bbc.co.uk/ news/uk-31920906** (accessed 6 May 2015). Also see the first 'Twitter unfair dismissal' case: *Laws* v. *Game Retail Ltd.*: [2014] UKEAT_0188_14_0311.

64. See, for example, Labour Research Department, *Social Media, Monitoring and Surveillance at Work,* Labour Research Department (2012).

65. Advisory, Conciliation and Arbitration Service, *Advice leaflet – Internet and E-mail Policies,* ACAS (2006), **www .acas.org.uk/media/pdf/d/b/AL06_1.pdf** (accessed 4 August 2015); Chartered Institute of Personnel and Development, *Internet and Email Policies,* CIPD (2007).

66. For a 2013 survey in the USA see XpertHR 'Infographic: Social Media in the Workplace', **www.xperthr.com** (accessed 6 April 2015). For a 2007 UK survey see XpertHR 'Survey: Email, Internet and E-communications Policies 2007', **www.xperthr.co.uk** (accessed 26 September 2007).

67. Broughton, A., Higgins, T., Hicks, B. and Cox, A. 'Workplaces and Social Networking: The Implications for Employment Relations', ACAS Research Paper 11/11 (2011); Jennings, S., Blount, J. and Wetherly, M. 'Social Media – A Virtual Pandora's Box: Prevalence, Possible Legal Liabilities and Policies', *Business and Professional Communication Quarterly,* vol. 77, no. 1, 2014, pp. 96–113.

68. XpertHR 'Survey: Email, Internet and E-communications Policies 2007', **www.xperthr.co.uk** (accessed 26 September 2007).

69. Ellis, V. and Richards, J. 'Creating, Connecting and Correcting: Motivations and Meanings of Work-Blogging among Public Service Workers', in Bolton, S. and Houlihan, M. (eds) *Work Matters: Critical Reflections on Contemporary Work,* Palgrave (2009), pp. 253–4.

70. Stevens, M. 'Employers Are Urged not to "Kill the Conversation" on Social Media', *People Management,* 29 February 2012, **http://www.peoplemanagement.co.uk/ pm/articles/2012/02/employers-urged-not-to-kill-the-conversation-on-social-media.htm** (accessed 23 July 2012).

71. ACAS 'Does Social Media Strengthen or Dilute Employee Voice?', *ACAS Employment Relations,* Comment, August 2014.

72. Ellis, V. and Richards, J., op. cit., pp. 250–68.

73. Redford, K. 'Face the Future', **www.xperthr.co.uk** (accessed 26 September 2007).

74. Frost, V. 'Contact Sport', *Guardian,* Work section, 25 August 2007, pp. 1–2.

75. Bradwell, P. and Reeves, R. *Network Citizens: Power and Responsibility at Work,* Demos (2008).

76. Ibid.

77. Pliskin, N., Rom, C. and Markey, R. 'E-mail as a Weapon in an Industrial Dispute', *New Technology, Work and Employment,* vol. 12, no. 1, 1997, pp. 3–12.

78. See, for example, Surowiecki, C. *The Wisdom of Crowds,* Abacus (2005); Tapscott, D. and Williams, A. *Wikinomics,* Penguin (2007).

79. Shirky, C. *Here Comes Everybody: The Power of Organizing without Organizations,* Penguin (2009).

80. Bergvall-Kåreborn, B. and Howcroft, D. 'Amazon Mechanical Turk and the Commodification of Labour', *New Technology, Work and Employment,* vol. 29, no. 3, 2014, pp. 213–23.

81. Pollitt, C. 'Mainstreaming Technological Change in the Study of Public Management', *Public Policy and Administration,* vol. 26, no. 4, 2011, pp. 377–97.

82. Butler, P. 'The Power of the Secret Policeman's Blog', *Guardian,* Society section, 11 April 2007, p. 12.

83. Mason, P. *Why It's all Kicking off Everywhere: The New Global Revolutions,* Verso (2012); Gladwell, M. 'Small Change: Why the Revolution will not be Tweeted', *The New Yorker,* 4 October 2010, **http://www.newyorker. com/reporting/2010/10/04/101004fa_fact_gladwell** (accessed 23 July 2012).

84. For a small-scale instance organised through social media, see BBC News 'Breastfeeding mothers stage protest in a Bristol café', **http://www.bbc.co.uk/news/uk-england-bristol-18705583** (accessed 19 July 2012).

85. Urry, J. *Mobilities,* Polity Press (2007).

86. 'Mobile working – massive growth seen', **http://www .newbusiness.co.uk/news/mobile-working-massive-growth-seen**, Newbusiness.co.uk, 2011 (accessed 20 July 2012).

87. Felstead, A., Jewson, N. and Walters, S. *Changing Places of Work,* Palgrave (2005).

88. See, for example, Grimshaw, D., Cooke, F.-L., Grugulis, I. and Vincent, S. 'New Technology and Changing Organisational Forms: Implications for Managerial Control and Skills', *New Technology, Work and Employment,* vol. 17, no. 3, 2002, pp. 186–203.

89. European Foundation for the Improvement of Living and Working Conditions, *Global Competition and European Companies' Location Decisions. Background Paper,* European Foundation (2008), p. 2.

90. Garner, C. 'Offshoring in the Service Sector: Economic Impact and Policy Issues', *Federal Reserve Bank of Kansas City Economic Review,* Autumn 2004, pp. 12–15.

91. For research on the labour process and employment systems in Indian call centres, see Taylor, P. and Bain, P. '"India Calling to the Far Away Towns": The Call Centre

Labour Process and Globalization', *Work, Employment and Society,* vol. 19, no. 2, 2005, pp. 261–82.

92. Garner, op. cit., p. 17.

93. See, for instance, Venkatraman, N. V. 'Offshoring Without Guilt', *Sloan Management Review,* Spring 2004, pp. 14–16; Farrell, D. 'Offshoring: Value Creation Through Economic Change', *Journal of Management Studies,* vol. 42, no. 3, 2005, pp. 675–83.

94. For an international overview, see Bottini, N., Ernst, C. and Luebker, M. *Offshoring and the Labour Market: What Are the Issues?,* Economic and Labour Market Paper 2007/11, International Labour Organization (2007).

95. Nevertheless, there appears to be a general acceptance that those in the West whose jobs are displaced by offshoring are likely to have difficulty finding new jobs.

96. See, for example, Taylor, P. and Bain, P. 'Call Centre Offshoring to India: The Revenge of History?', *Labour and Industry,* vol. 14, no. 3, 2004, pp. 15–38; Taylor, P. and Bain, P. ' "India Calling to the Far Away Towns": The Call Centre Labour Process and Globalization', *Work, Employment and Society,* vol. 19, no. 2, 2005, pp. 261–82.

97. Cited in Jackson, P. (ed.) *Virtual Working: Social and Organisational Dynamics,* Routledge (1999), p. 53.

98. Golden, T. 'Co-workers Who Telework and the Impact on Those in the Office: Understanding the Implications of Virtual Work for Co-worker Satisfaction and Turnover Intentions', *Human Relations,* vol. 60, no. 11, 2007, pp. 1641–67.

99. Ibid., p. 1643.

100. Fogarty, H., Scott, P. and Williams, S. 'The Half-Empty Office: Dilemmas in Managing Locational Flexibility', *New Technology, Work and Employment,* vol. 26, no. 3, 2011, pp. 183–95.

101. On work intensification, and the contribution of technology, see the following *inter alia:* Beynon, H. *et al. Managing Employment Change: The New Realities of Work,* Oxford University Press (2002); Burchell, B. *et al.* (eds) *Job Insecurity and Work Intensification,* Routledge (2002); Green, F. 'It's Been a Hard Day's Night: The Concentration and Intensification of Work in Late Twentieth Century Britain', *British Journal of Industrial Relations,* vol. 39, no. 1, 2001, pp. 53–80; White, M., Hill, S., McGovern, P., Mills, C. and Smeaton, D. 'High Performance Management Practices, Working Hours and Work-Life Balance', *British Journal of Industrial Relations,* vol. 41, no. 2, 2003, pp. 197–214.

102. Symon, G. 'Information and Communication Technologies and the Network Organization: A Critical Analysis', *Journal of Occupational and Organizational Psychology,* vol. 73, 2000, p. 395.

103. Berkowsky, R. 'When you just cannot get away', *Information, Communication and Society,* vol. 16, no. 4, 2013, pp. 519–41. See also NASUWT's survey of the impact of email on teachers' work/life balance: NASUWT 'Home invasion on a grand and unacceptable scale', press release, 6 April 2015, http://www.nasuwt. org.uk/Whatsnew/NASUWTNews/PressReleases/ NASUWT_013939 (accessed 6 April 2015).

104. For example, Bittman, M., Brown, J. and Wajcmann, J. 'The Mobile Phone, Perpetual Contact and Time Pressure', *Work, Employment and Society,* vol. 23, no. 4, 2007, pp. 673–91; Bucher, E., Fieseler, C. and Suphan, A. 'The Stress Potential of Social Media in the Workplace', *Information, Communication and Society,* vol. 16, no. 10, 2013, pp. 1639–67.

105. Madden, M. and Jones, S. *Networked Workers,* PEW Research Center (2008), p. iii.

106. McGovern, P., Hill, S., Mills, C. and White, M. *Market, Class and Employment,* Oxford University Press (2007).

107. Ibid., pp. 180–3.

108. De Castella, T. 'The Big Ideas of 2014', *BBC News Magazine,* 1 January 2015, http://www.bbc.co.uk/ news/magazine-30576672 (accessed 6 May 2015).

109. Howcroft, D. and Taylor, P. '"Plus ça Change, Plus la Même Chose?" – Researching and Theorising the "New" New Technologies', *New Technology, Work and Employment,* vol. 29, no. 1, 2014, p. 1.

110. Jenkins, C. and Sherman, B. *The Collapse of Work,* Methuen (1979).

111. Goos, M. and Manning, A. 'Lousy Jobs and Lovely Jobs: The Growing Polarization of Work in Britain', *Review of Economics and Statistics,* vol. 89, no. 1, 2007, pp. 118–33; Dolphin, T. (ed) *Technology, Globalisation and the Future of Work in Europe,* Institute for Public Policy Research (2015).

112. Reich, R. *The Work of Nations,* Simon & Schuster (1991); Castells, M. *The Information Age: Economy, Society and Culture, Vol. 1: The Rise of the Network Society,* Wiley-Blackwell (2009).

113. Brynjolfsson, E. and McAfee, A. *The Second Machine Age: Work, Progress and Prosperity in a Time of Brilliant Technologies,* Norton (2014); Frey, C. and Osborne, M. 'The Future of Employment: How Susceptible Are Jobs to Computerisation?', Oxford University Working Paper (2013). See also Frey, C. and Osborne, M. *Technology at Work: The Future of Innovation and Employment,* Citi GPS (2015). Their analysis has been applied to the UK in Frey, C. and Osborne, M. *London Futures – Agiletown: The Relentless March of Technology and London's Response,* Deloitte LLP (2014).

114. For discussion of generational differences in use of technology, and disparities between work and personal use of technologies, see The Work Foundation, *Changing Relationships at Work,* The Work Foundation (2009).

115. Grove, J. 'National Student Survey 2014 results show record levels of satisfaction', Times Higher Education, 12 August 2014, **http://www.timeshighereducation.co.uk/ news/national-student-survey-2014-results-show-record-levels-of-satisfaction/2015108.article** (accessed 23 March 2015).

116. Mini-tests and 'quizzes' are popular ways of running formative assessment, and help to focus learning and teaching on problem areas.

117. Ellis, C. and Reynolds, C. 'EBEAM: Evaluating the Benefits of Electronic Assessment Management', Final Report, June 2013, **http://jiscdesignstudio.pbworks. com/w/file/fetch/66830875/EBEAM%20Project%20 report.pdf** (accessed 23 March 2015).

118. Referred to as EAM in this paper, although the term EMA is now more commonly used.

119. Ibid., p. 18.

120. Ibid., p. 58.

121. Ibid., p. 14.

122. See note 118 above.

123. Ibid., p. 15.

124. Ibid., p. 16.

125. Ibid., p. 91.

126. Ibid., p. 91.

CHAPTER 13
Organisational control and power

An underlying feature of organisational behaviour is the concept of control and power. Control systems exist in all spheres of the operations of the organisation and are a necessary part of the process of management. Work organisations are complex systems of social relationships, status and power, and attention should be given to the manager–subordinate relationships. The manager needs to understand the nature of power and control in order to improve work behaviour and organisational performance.

Learning outcomes

After completing this chapter you should have enhanced your ability to:

- explain the nature and importance of control in work organisations, and essential elements in a management control system;
- detail different forms of control and characteristics of an effective control system;
- explain perspectives of organisational power and pluralistic approaches to power;
- debate the nature and impact of financial and accounting systems of control;
- explore the concept of empowerment and the manager–subordinate relationship;
- examine the process of delegation, and the benefits and art of delegation;
- review the nature of organisational control and power, and influences on people's patterns of behaviour.

Critical review and reflection

Criticisms of control are totally misplaced. Although they may not always openly admit it, most members of staff want to know exactly what is expected of them, be given clear lines of direction and regular review and feedback on their performance. This is the essence of control.

How would YOU attempt to present a counterargument? To what extent do YOU welcome control over YOUR work performance?

The essence of control

In discussion on the nature of management (**Chapter 10**), reference was made to control as one of the essential features of managerial work. Traditional views of **control** placed emphasis on the need for conformity of activities with the organisation. *Tannenbaum*, for example, sees control as an inherent characteristic of the nature of organisations. The process of control is at the centre of the exchange between the benefits that the individual derives from membership of an organisation and the costs of such benefits.

> *Organization implies control. A social organization is an ordered arrangement of individual human interactions. Control processes help circumscribe idiosyncratic behaviors and keep them conformant to the rational plan of the organization. Organizations require a certain amount of conformity as well as the integration of diverse activities. It is the function of control to bring about conformance to organizational requirements and achievement of the ultimate purposes of the organization.*[1]

With both control and power, discussed later, it is important to remember they are the *perceived* influences over other people. It is the way in which people are seen rather than the actual control or power they are in a position to exercise.[2]

Feature of organisational behaviour

There is, however, far more to control than simply a means of restricting behaviour or the exercise of authority over others. Control is not only a function of the formal organisation and a hierarchical structure of authority, but also a feature of organisational behaviour and a function of interpersonal influence.[2] By their very nature, control systems are concerned with the regulation of behaviour. Unfortunately 'control' often has an emotive connotation and is interpreted in a negative manner to suggest direction or command by the giving of orders. People may be suspicious of control systems and see them as emphasising punishment, an indication of authoritarian management and a means of exerting pressure and maintaining discipline. Some writers seem to take this view, and even to suggest that organisational control is exploitation of employees.[3] Concern for the regulation of behaviour and improvement in performance raises questions as to the ethical nature of control. (**Ethical behaviour in business is discussed in Chapter 14.**)

Child suggests that although control is an essential process of management, it is strangely neglected by many writers on organisation. Among possible reasons for this is that:

> *control has a sinister ring to it, associated in people's minds with power and manipulation. As a result, there may be some reluctance among many business school writers to discuss control, in order to avoid embarrassment for their sponsors in positions of corporate power. The claim that it is a purely technical process, concerning feedback on accounting and operations, also amounts to a desensitizing of the subject.*[4]

Drummond, in a critical discussion about mechanistic thinking in organisations, makes the point: 'Common sense suggests that control is preferable to anarchy, and more control is preferable to less. While such assumptions are not necessarily wrong, they are not universally correct either.'[5]

Individual responses and behaviour

According to *Cloke and Goldsmith*, many employees have grown up in hierarchical organisations and become accustomed to external authority and the dead weight of organisational history.

Many employees actually prefer being told what to do by autocratic managers and are willing to accept being treated like children in exchange for irresponsibility and reduced stress. They are willing to blindly obey hierarchical authority and keep silent before their superiors in exchange for job security. It is easier by far to be an unthinking drone who obeys orders from above than a self-managing team member who is responsible for results.[6] (**You may wish to remind yourself of the discussion on Theory X and Theory Y management in Chapter 10.**)

However, as *Wilson* reminds us, individuals are not just passive objects of control: 'They may accept, deny, react, reshape, rethink, acquiesce, rebel, or conform and create themselves within constraints imposed on them.'[7]

Watson points out that although process-rational thinking recognises the aspiration of those 'in charge' of work organisations to achieve control over work behaviours, it also recognises two other things:

- Only partial control can ever be achieved. This is because organisations only exist through human relationships, and human relationships never allow the total control of some people over others. Power is rarely uncontested and, to a greater or less extent, attempts at control are typically resisted.

- Whatever control is achieved over work behaviour is brought about as much through processes of negotiation, persuasion, manipulation and so on, as through system 'devices' such as rules and official procedures.[8]

Most people show ambivalence towards control. While they may not wish to have it applied by other people to their own performance, they recognise the need for, and usefulness of, control systems. Individuals feel a sense of unease with what they perceive as lack of control over disruptive or anti-social actions or behaviour of work colleagues. Under certain conditions, individuals may actually desire greater control over their work performance. Whenever a person enquires 'I would like to know how well I am doing', this can arguably be seen as asking for control in the form of improved feedback. Members of staff want to know what is expected of them and how well they are progressing towards their objectives. Control can stand for reliability, order and stability. It is a basis for training needs, for the motivation to achieve standards and for the development of individuals.

Critical review and reflection

The controversial nature of control means that some writers avoid the word and use alternative terms such as 'monitoring' or 'evaluating'. But whatever wording is used, the process of maintaining good order is a necessary feature of management and organisational behaviour.

To what extent do YOU agree? What term would YOU favour for this process, and why?

Improvement in performance

Control completes the cycle of managerial activities. It involves the planning and organisation of work functions, and guiding and regulating the activities of staff. The whole underlying purpose of management control is improvement in performance at both the individual and organisational level (*see* Figure 13.1). According to *Zimmermann,* an organisation without control is impossible.

> *Every organization has control systems that co-ordinate the exercise of decision rights that are dispersed among individuals. Control systems also serve another important function in the organization. They measure how effectively decisions have been translated into results. This second feature of control systems relates to the goal achievement of the company. In this perspective, control systems are about influencing the behavior of individuals in the interest of the corporation. Both functions are closely interlinked.[9]*

Features of poor organisational performance can even lead to the collapse of a company.[10] A major international report undertaken by Proudfoot Consulting found that poor management

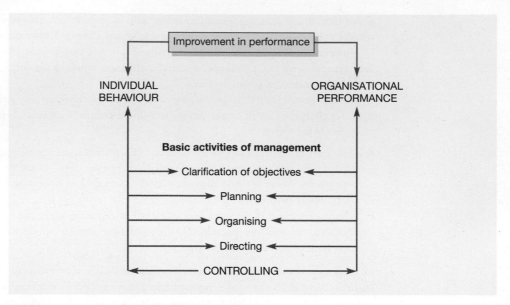

Figure 13.1 The nature of management control

in terms of inadequate planning and control and insufficient day-to-day supervision of work is still the largest single reason for lost productivity.[11]

Expression of managerial behaviour

The nature of management control is an organisational variable. Recall the discussion on the organisational environment (**Chapter 3**) and consider likely variations in the extent and form of control among a range of diverse organisations. While the need for some form of control is constant, the extent and manner of control is variable. The exercise of control is an expression of management systems and styles of behaviour. What is really important is what control is intended to achieve and the manner in which it is exercised.

More recent approaches question the extent to which **culture is a means of organisation control**. For example, *Ray* suggests that managers view organisational culture as an effective control tool[12] and *Egan* refers to culture as the largest organisational control system.[13] (**See the discussion on organisational culture in Chapter 15.**)

Elements of an organisational control system

Whatever the nature of control and whatever form it takes, there are five essential elements in an organisational control system (*see* Figure 13.2):

- planning objectives and targets;
- establishing standards of performance;
- monitoring actual performance;
- comparing actual achievement against the planned target; and
- rectifying and taking corrective action.

1. **Planning what is desired** involves clarification of the aims to be achieved. It is important that people understand exactly what is required of them. This requires that objectives and targets are specified clearly, particularly key activities. Planning provides the framework against which the process of control takes place.
2. Related to planning is the **establishment of defined standards of performance.** This requires realistic measurements by which achievement can be determined. Whenever possible these

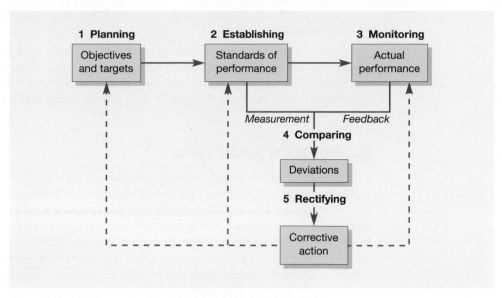

Figure 13.2 The five essential stages of organisational control

measurements are given some measurable attribute and stated in quantitative terms. Reasonable time scales should also be specified. Planning and measurement are prerequisites of control.

3. The third aspect of control is the need for a means of **monitoring actual performance.** This requires clear channels of communication and feedback, a system of reporting information that is accurate, relevant and timely. Feedback also provides the basis for decisions to adjust the control system, for example the need to revise the original plan.

4. Next, it is necessary **to compare actual performance against planned targets.** This requires a means of interpreting and evaluating information in order to give details of progress, reveal deviations and identify probable causes. This information should be communicated to those concerned to let them know how well they are getting on.

5. The final element is **taking corrective action to rectify** the situation that has led to any failure to achieve objectives or targets, or other forms of deviations identified. This requires authority to take appropriate action to correct the situation, review the operation of the control system and make any necessary adjustments to objectives and targets or to the standards of performance.

Forms of control

Control is far-reaching; it can serve a number of functions concerned with general results or specific actions and can be manifested in a number of forms. For example, controls can be concerned with:

- observance of legislation, standing orders and policies and procedures;
- day-to-day operational activities that call for more specific standards of performance and speedy corrective action;
- health and safety of all members of the organisation or people in contact with the organisation;
- the structure of the organisation and role relationships;
- type of production system and use of technology;
- measurement of inputs, outputs, processes or the behaviour of people;
- recruitment and selection, socialisation, training and development;
- performance of the organisation as a whole or with major parts of it. Total quality control, concerned with all areas of the organisation, can be seen as part of total quality management programmes (**discussed in Chapter 16**).

According to *McKenna,* organisational codes of conduct (**discussed in Chapter 14**) can constitute another form of control:

> *Developing and distributing a code of conduct is a form of control that sets out the rules of behaviour and values with which an organisation's senior managers expect their subordinates will conform. Such a code will only be accepted if subordinates observe that managers at all levels live this code in their actions, beliefs and involvement in collective learning.*[14]

Control in the public sector

Public-sector organisations have political purposes and are concerned with service to and the well-being of the community. At the same time, there has been increased government pressure to ensure cost-effectiveness, investment by private-sector involvement and efficiency and economy in their operations. The demand for uniformity of treatment and public accountability for their operations results in high levels of bureaucracy, statutory controls, legislation and ministerial guidance. In the case of local government, for example, there is the added consideration of the relationship between elected members and permanent officers.

Despite the apparent relaxation of authority and transfer of power from central government, there is evidence that public-sector managers are under increasing political pressure. The demand for strategic management in the public sector has resulted in a greater emphasis on performance output measures with indicators of both a qualitative and quantitative nature.

Technology and control systems

From a further analysis of the data collected from Woodward's South Essex study of 100 manufacturing firms (**discussed in Chapter 11**), clear links emerged between the original classification of technology and managerial control systems. Unit and small-batch production firms tended to have unitary and mainly personal controls. Process production firms tended to have unitary and mainly impersonal controls. In the case of large-batch and mass-production firms, those with predominantly personal controls had similar organisational characteristics to unit firms and those with predominantly mechanical controls had an organisation structure similar to process firms.

From the analysis, *Reeves and Woodward* suggest that control systems may be the underlying variable that links organisational behaviour and technology. The classification of control systems they propose might provide a better means of predicting certain facets of organisational behaviour than the classification of technology.[15]

Wilson points out that technology is not just about devices and machines but also about social relations that encourage some form of interaction. Technology is a human, political and social activity: 'The locus of control cannot always be moved from workers to managers during technical change nor from managers to workers. Control ultimately does lie with management, though workers may resist it.'[16]

Information and communications technology

In previous chapters we have referred to the impact of developments in ICT and these developments will also have a significant impact on management control systems. Processes of communication are increasingly linked to computer systems with the rapid transmission of more information to more people, including immediate access to other national or international offices. IT and office automation are changing the nature of the workplace and the way in which people work. For example, advances in telecommunications have resulted in a significant growth in telecommuting, with staff working from home with a computer network, telephone, etc. This has many potential advantages but also raises questions of self-motivation, security and systems of management control.

Another interesting situation arising from the increasing use of IT is the legal position on organisations monitoring staff emails and Internet usage. (**A more detailed discussion on technology, work and organisational behaviour is included in Chapter 12.**)

Critical review and reflection

Technology is the ultimate determinant of an effective control system, whether for mass-production systems, virtual teams or remote working, personal surveillance or working from home. There is not less control today, only different forms of control.

What are YOUR views? How do YOU believe technology is likely to influence the nature of control over YOUR behaviour at work?

Concertive control

Barker refers to a change from hierarchical, bureaucratic control to concertive control through the interaction of members in self-managing teams. **Concertive control** is not exerted by managers but by the value consensus of the team to a system of normative rules. Workers form their own cultural norms rather than bureaucratic rules and develop means for their own control.

> *I don't have to sit here and look for the boss to be around; and if the boss is not around, I can sit there and talk to my neighbor or do what I want. Now the whole team is around me and the whole team is observing what I'm doing.*[17]

However, *Wright and Barker* refer to the need for some form of functional self-control as an element of teamwork, though research has identified concertive control as a factor constraining teamwork. Teams can struggle with the collective manner in which teams control their own behaviours. Concertive peer-enforced control can create powerful constraining or oppressive systems. Negative implications can arise within a team when a concertive control system is either too constraining or too loose and that parallels disadvantages of external control systems.[18]

Strategies of control in organisations

Six significant strategies of control in organisations are explained by *Child* (*see* Figure 13.3):

1. personal centralised control;
2. bureaucratic control;
3. output control;
4. control through electronic surveillance;
5. HRM control; and
6. cultural control.[19]

Personal centralised controls

These are often found in small, owner-managed organisations and characterised by centralisation of decision-making and initiative around a leadership figure. Control consists largely of personal supervision and inspection. Once the organisation grows large enough to employ someone to undertake detailed supervision of everyday tasks, the locus of decision-making and close supervision will tend to become separated. The authority of the leader will usually rest upon the rights of ownership, special personal qualities (charisma) or technical expertise.

1 Personal centralised control

1.1 direct supervision of people's activities

1.2 centralised decision-taking

1.3 personal leadership: founded upon ownership rights, charisma, and/or technical expertise

1.4 reward and punishments reinforcing conformity to personal authority

2 Bureaucratic control

2.1 breaking down of task into easily definable elements

2.2 formally specified methods, procedures and rules applied to the conduct of tasks

2.3 budgetary and standard cost-variance accounting controls

2.4 technology designed to limit variation in conduct of tasks, with respect to pace, sequence and possibly physical methods*

2.5 routine decision-taking delegated within prescribed limits

2.6 reward and punishment systems reinforcing conformity to procedures and rules

3 Output control

3.1 jobs and units designed with responsibility for complete outputs

3.2 specification of output standards and targets

3.3 use of 'responsibility accounting' systems

3.4 delegation of decisions on operational matters: semi-autonomy

3.5 reward and punishment linked to attainment of output targets

4 Control through electronic surveillance

4.1 speed and quality of work recorded and assessed remotely via information and communication technology (ICT)

4.2 employee's performance assessed against that of other employees and trends

4.3 such monitoring of performance used to reward and discipline employees

5 HRM control

5.1 use of selection methods to ensure that new recruits 'fit' the profile of attitude, behaviour, and capabilities desired by management

5.2 training and development designed to reinforce this desired profile

5.3 assessment procedures and reward systems used to encourage conformity

6 Cultural control

6.1 development of employees' personal identification with management goals

6.2 strong emphasis on the collective and mutually supportive character of the organisation – e.g. analogy with the 'family'

6.3 employment characterised by security of tenure and progression within the organisation

6.4 semi-autonomous working: few formal controls

*Some authorities distinguish this as a separate control strategy. For example, Richard Edwards (1979), *Contested Terrain: The Transformation of the Workplace in the Twentieth Century*, New York, Basic Books.

Figure 13.3 Strategies of organisational control

Source: Child, J. *Organization: Contemporary Principles and Practice*, Blackwell Publishing (2005), p. 121. Reproduced with permission from Wiley-Blackwell.

Bureaucratic control

Familiar in public-sector organisations and many other types of large organisations, this form of control is based on the specification of how members should behave and carry out their work. There is an attempt to ensure predictability through formal job descriptions and procedures, and the specification of standard methods for the performance of tasks. Compliance can be rewarded by upgrading, improved status, favourable employment benefits and job security. Bureaucratic control will make use of accounting control systems such as budgetary control and standard cost variances. The bureaucratic strategy also permits delegation without loss of control. Managers can delegate routine decision-making within formally prescribed limits of discretion.

Output control

This relies upon the ability to identify specific tasks having a measurable output or criterion of overall achievement – for example, an end-product, a part manufactured to agreed standards, batch production or a sub-assembly. Rewards and sanctions can be related to performance levels expressed in output terms. Output control strategy is aimed at facilitating the delegation of operational decision-making without the need for bureaucratic controls or relying on close personal supervision. Output control may be difficult to apply to certain activities, such as the legal department of a business organisation.

Control through electronic surveillance

The essence of control is that the speed and quality of work is recorded and assessed remotely through the use of ICT without reliance on personal supervision. Monitoring of performance can be used readily as the basis for reward and discipline. Control through electronic surveillance is applied to many types and levels of activity. A common example is call centres, although customer-service representatives dislike the pressure from this form of control and the objectivity of relying on electronically produced statistics is subject to challenge.

HRM control

HRM procedures can be used both to develop people at work and to control their behaviour and performance. Systematic selection techniques are designed to ensure new recruits fit the profile and technical competencies required by management. Performance evaluation and appraisal provide feedback to both management and employees. Appraisals should provide the basis for reward and for an assessment of the need for further training or development.

Cultural control

This moves away from conventional forms of organisation and is based on maintaining control through internalised compliance rather than external constraint. The basis of cultural control is the acceptance and willing compliance with the requirements of management and belief of the organisation. A major example is the cultural control that tends to be exemplified by larger Japanese corporations, although this is subject to criticism of compulsory sociability. Cultural control, combined with personal autonomy, have long been associated with the professions. Despite criticisms of cultural control it is in tune with the increasing number of professional and knowledge workers, and is consistent with self-managing units or teams working with only limited formal controls.

Characteristics of an effective control system

Whatever the nature or form of control, there are a number of characteristic features of an effective control system. Control systems can have positive as well as negative effects. It is important therefore that they are designed and implemented in a constructive and rewarding way. An effective control system should:

- **Be understood by those involved in its operation.** The purpose of the control system and the information it provides must be fully comprehensible to those who have to act on the results.

- **Draw attention to the critical activities important to the success of the organisation.** Careful control must be maintained in key result areas and in those activities that are crucial to the success of the organisation.
- **Conform with the structure of the organisation and be related to decision centres responsible for performance.** Information should be supplied to those managers who have the responsibility for specified areas of activity and presented in a form that shows clearly when corrective action is necessary.
- **Be consistent with the objective of the activity to which it relates.** In addition to locating deviations from the planned standard of performance, the control system should be sophisticated enough to indicate ways in which performance can be improved. For example, in the field of social services it may not be sufficient just to know that expenditure has been kept within the budget. It would be more helpful to know in what areas expenditure has been incurred.
- **Report deviations from the desired standard of performance as quickly as possible.** Ideally, indications of likely deviations should be discovered before they actually occur. For example, information that the budget is likely to be overspent or underspent should arrive in sufficient time to enable those responsible to do something about it and avoid drastic last-minute action.
- **Be flexible** and yield information that is not influenced by other factors unconnected to the purpose of the control system. For example, a control system that specifies that reports to top management should be made whenever expenditure exceeds the same set amount means high-spending departments may be subject to excessive control and low-spending departments not monitored closely enough.
- **Be subject to a continual review** to ensure they are effective and appropriate in terms of the results they produce. They should not be too costly or elaborate, but should satisfy the characteristic features suggested above.

Critical review and reflection

Control systems would avoid all criticisms and negative reactions if the choice of strategy and essential characteristics were compatible with the nature and culture of the particular organisation.

Do YOU believe this to be fair comment? How well do YOU believe the strategy and operations of control in YOUR university are compatible with its nature and culture?

Power and management control

Work organisations are not only systems of hierarchical structure, but also systems of intricate social relationships, status and power. **Power** is a complex and dynamic concept and difficult to define easily. **At a broad level, power can be interpreted in terms of control or influence over the behaviour of other people with or without their consent.** Sometimes power is interpreted in terms of the *extent* of the influence that can actually be exercised over other people, and sometimes it is taken to include influence over objects or things as well as people. Like the meaning of control, power can have an emotive connotation.

However, power is an inherent feature of work organisations and is often the underlying reality behind the decision-making process. It is central to the framework of order and system of command through which the work and activities of the organisation are carried out, and the implementation of policies and procedures. Lack of power and influence, and office politics, are among the main sources of managerial stress within organisations.

Robbins and Judge suggest that as power may exist but not be used, it implies a potential that need not be actualised to be effective. Power is therefore a capacity or a potential. The most important aspect of power is probably dependency: 'A person can have power over you only if he or she controls something you desire.'[20]

Caulkin points out that, visible or not, power shapes everything. Hierarchy occurs everywhere in the natural order.

> *Yet for all the words devoted to 'official' topics such as strategy, leadership, shareholder value and customer focus, the truth is that the drive to win and keep power is the 'invisible hand' that yanks the strings which determine much of what happens in business.*[21]

The view of power as of functional importance is in keeping with a unitary approach to organisation. Management control is the predominant means by which the activities of staff are guided towards the achievement of organisational goals. The exercise of power is that which comes from a position of formal authority within the management structure of the organisation and that legitimises control over subordinate staff.

Types of authority and organisations

In one of the earliest studies of formal organisations, *Weber* distinguished three types of authority: **traditional, charismatic** and **legal–rational.**[22] These types of authority are based on the form of control regarded as legitimate by subordinates and their acceptance of the power of superiors. The three types of authority relate to different types of organisations.

- In **traditional organisations**, authority is legitimised by custom and a long-standing belief in the natural right to rule, or is possessed by traditional ('proper') procedure. Examples would be the authority of the pope, kings or queens or a paternalistic employer.
- In **charismatic organisations**, authority is legitimised by belief in the personal qualities of the leader; authority is based on the leader's strength of personality and inspiration. Winston Churchill might be quoted as an example. The practical need for some routine, for procedures and systems and for economic support means that if the movement is to continue it must become organised. On the impending demise of the charismatic leader, the movement might collapse unless a 'legitimate' heir is found. This process tends to transform a charismatic organisation into either a traditional organisation or a bureaucratic organisation.
- In **bureaucratic organisations**, authority is based on the acceptance of the law of formal rules and procedures, and on impersonal principles. There is a legal–rational authority that stems from hierarchical position in the organisation and not from personality. Examples are the armed forces and the authority of government ministers or a college principal.

The concept of legal–rational authority is of most interest to us because most business organisations, particularly large-scale ones, tend to be of the bureaucratic type of structure, although there are variations in degree. Bureaucracy, as applying to certain structural features of organisation, is the most dominant type of formal organisation. (**Bureaucracy as a form of structure is discussed in Chapter 2.**)

Power, involvement and compliance

From a comparative analysis of complex organisations, *Etzioni* provides a classification of organisational relationships based on structures of control and the use of power resources as a means of ensuring compliance among members.[23]

Power differs according to the means by which members of the organisation comply:

- **Coercive power** relies on the use of threats, or physical sanctions or force, for example controlling the need for food or comfort.
- **Remunerative power** involves the manipulation of material resources and rewards, for example through salaries and wages.
- **Normative power** relies on the allocation and the manipulation of symbolic rewards, for example esteem and prestige.

Involvement is the degree of commitment by members to the organisation:

- **Alienative involvement** occurs where members are involved against their wishes. There is a strong negative orientation towards the organisation.
- **Calculative involvement** occurs where attachment to the organisation is motivated by extrinsic rewards. There is either a negative orientation or a low positive orientation towards the organisation.
- **Moral involvement** is based on the individual's belief in, and value placed on, the goals of the organisation. There is high positive orientation towards the organisation.

When considered together, nine logical types of organisational relationships and compliance result from this typology (*see* Figure 13.4). Etzioni suggests that a particular kind of power usually goes with a particular kind of involvement:

- coercive power with alienative involvement – relationship 1 (typified, for example, by prisons);
- remunerative power with calculative involvement – relationship 5 (typified, for example, by business firms);
- normative power with moral involvement – relationship 9 (typified, for example, by churches).

The matching of these kinds of power and involvement is congruent with each other and represents the most common form of compliance in organisations. The other six types of organisational relationships are incongruent. Etzioni suggests that organisations with congruent compliance structures will be more effective than organisations with incongruent structures.

Critical review and reflection

Power is often associated with coercive and repressive features of social life but it is an inherent and necessary part of work organisations. What is important is the motivation for the use of power and manner in which it is exercised.

What are YOUR views? To what extent do YOU accept power as an essential feature of management and organisational behaviour?

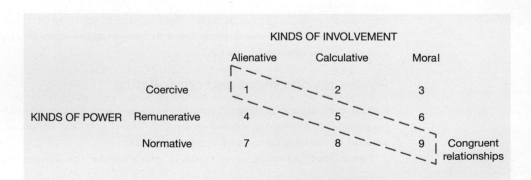

Figure 13.4 Organisational relationships and compliance

Source: Adapted with the permission of The Free Press, a Division of Simon & Schuster, Inc. from Etzioni, A. *A Comparative Analysis of Complex Organizations*, Revised and enlarged edition by Amitai Etzioni. Copyright © 1975 by Amitai Etzioni; copyright renewed © 2003 by Amitai Etzioni. All rights reserved.

Perspectives of organisational power

Watson suggests that power operates at three levels:

- The level of societies, where some people have a much greater capacity to influence others and gain a greater share of the 'good things' of that society.
- The level of organisation structures and cultures, where certain people are put into positions where they can shape what others do and take a greater share of the 'rewards' made available by the organisation.
- The interpersonal level, where some people get other people to do things they otherwise would not do and, as a result of this, typically 'do better' than these people in terms of the material and symbolic rewards available to people in the organisation.[24]

At the organisational level there are many potential sources of power that enable members of an organisation to further their own interests and that provide a means of resolving conflicts. Sources of organisational power include, for example, culture, structure, formal authority, rules and regulations, standing orders, control of the decision-making process, control of resources and technology, control of information or knowledge, trade unions and staff organisations, age coupled with experience, gender and the informal organisation.

Gender and power

You may recall the suggestion of the sex power differential as part of the evaluation of the Hawthorne experiments (**discussed in Chapter 2**). An example of gender and power is given by the Equality and Human Rights Commission, who report on a survey on women in positions of power and influence. The survey found noticeable examples of the lack of women in senior positions of power, including those in the senior civil service, top management, judiciary, health service, directors of FTSE companies, Members of Parliament and senior appointments in the armed forces and the police force.

> *Outdated working patterns and inflexible organisations continue to be the major barriers to women's participation in positions of authority. Company culture where long hours are the norm and the unequal division of domestic responsibilities limit women's potential to find the time and energy these top posts demand . . . As a nation, we cannot afford to waste the talent available to run our national institutions. As well as the moral argument for gender equality in positions of power and influence, women's equal participation in public, political and cultural institutions can play a pivotal role in the advancement of women . . . Where women do find positions of power and influence it is more likely to be in the public and voluntary sectors.*[25]

Social exchange theory

Social exchange theory (**discussed in Chapter 1**) can give rise to an imbalance of power among individual members of the organisation. Social exchanges are influenced by a web of power relationships and are not always equal. Individuals will seek to achieve a positive balance for themselves by maximising benefits and minimising costs of exchanges. Those with more power are likely to fare better in their dealings with others. As an example, part-time or casual staff often feel they have less power than their full-time colleagues. *Bloisi, et al.* suggest that one negative outcome is when ethnic minorities or women are confined to the low end of the power spectrum, caused in part by their fewer numbers and by token dynamics. Bloisi *et al.* also suggest that, in some cases, language is used as a power tactic to put down a minority or to be condescending.[26]

Pluralistic approaches to power

A classification by *French and Raven* of social power based on a broader perception of leadership influence was discussed earlier (**Chapter 9**).[27] French and Raven identified five main sources of power: reward power; coercive power; legitimate power; referent power; and expert power.

Power, however, arises not only from sources of structure or formal position within the organisation, but also from interpersonal sources such as the personality, experience, characteristics and talents of individual members of the organisation. For example, the discussion also covered charisma, or personal power, as a feature of transformational leadership. We can also distinguish between **legitimate (organisational) power,** which derives from a person's position within the formal structure of the organisation and the managerial hierarchy of command, and **personal (informal) power,** which derives from the individual and is in the eye of the beholders who believe that the person has the ability to influence other people or events and to make things happen.

The exercise of power is, then, a social process that derives from a multiplicity of sources and situations.[28] This suggests a more pluralistic approach and recognises power as a major organisational variable. Many different groups and individuals have the ability to influence the behaviour and actions of other people, and in a number of different ways. This is not a new concept, however. In the 1920s the renowned management writer Mary Parker Follett focused on a human-behaviour aspect, rejected the notion of domination and the exercise of power over other people, and argued for developing power with others in the organisation to make things happen. Effective control over work processes and social relationships would be achieved through group power and co-operative management. Follett advocated the replacement of personal power with the authority of task or function, and successful management based on the 'law of the situation'.[29]

Network of social relationships

Organisations function on the basis of networks of interdependent activities. Certain jobs or work relationships enable people to exercise a level of power in excess of their formal position within the structure of the organisation. A classic example is someone, perhaps a personal assistant or office manager, who fulfils the role of gatekeeper to the boss (**discussed in Chapter 11**). Another example is with IT problems where comparatively junior members of staff with particular technical expertise may have a way of ignoring the normal chain of command.

Many people within organisations also have the ability to grant or withhold 'favours' within the formal or the informal interpretation of their job role – for example, caretakers, security staff and telephonists. Staff may exercise negative power – that is, 'the capacity to stop things happening, to delay them, to distort or disrupt them'.[30] A common example could be the secretary who screens and intercepts messages to the boss, delays arranging appointments and filters mail. Negative power is not necessarily related proportionately to position and may often be exercised easily by people at lower levels of the hierarchical structure.

Realities of organisational life

A reality of organisational life is the vagaries of social relationships including power, office politics, and also the grapevine and gossip.

Misselhorn, for example, suggests that:

> Power is often seen as a dirty word. Yet it is a reality of human experience. We all use power in one way or another. We are also strongly influenced by our values. Then we draw on both our values and our power in what we believe to be our rational thinking about a problem situation. The difficulty we have is that 'power' and 'values' are mostly hidden forces which are at work from international politics to shop floor problem solving.[31]

Hazlehurst refers to the hoary old question of office politics:

> *We're all supposed to abhor it, but the truth is that power games are instinctive and most of us enjoy at least a modest level of politicking – either as players or amused spectators. And a recent study found that remote workers – with fewer opportunities to be seen to be in the right places and talk to the right people – get lower pay rises and fewer promotions than those who spend their days in the office, dripping honey into appropriate ears.*

Hazlehurst also refers to Sandberg, COO of Facebook, who 'retains that most traditional symbol of corporate power, a corner office'.[32]

Although a difficult topic to pin down, *Mann* refers to the key role that gossip plays in power relationships and knowledge production in organisations and maintains that: 'There is an undeniable relationship between knowledge and power which lies at the root of gossiping.'[33]

Motivational need for power and control

Power can be a positive source of motivation for some people (**see the discussion on achievement motivation in Chapter 7**). There is often a fine line between the motivation to achieve personal dominance and the use of social power. It has to be acknowledged, however, that there are some people who positively strive for and enjoy the exercise of power over other people. Some managers seek to maintain absolute control over subordinates and the activities of their department/section, and welcome the feeling of being indispensable. The possession of power is an ultimate ego satisfaction, and such managers do not seem unduly concerned if as a result they are unpopular with, or lack the respect of, their colleagues or subordinate staff.

Kirwan-Taylor discusses control freaks who exist in every office and are capable of making everyone's life a misery. Control freaks try to dominate the environment by establishing order on what they perceive as chaos and attempting to control how other people think and behave. At one end of the spectrum are motivated and organised employees and at the other end obsessional, temperamental bullies. Sometimes, however, being a control freak is considered a positive attribute and key to success. Although control freaks function to a high standard, few people can bear to work with them.[34]

Critical review and reflection

Lack of power and influence is a potential source of frustration and stress. In reality, most people in the work organisation actively seek power. It is a natural characteristic of human behaviour and will always be so.

Be honest – to what extent do YOU seek power, and for what reasons?

Financial and accounting systems of control

Management control systems are frequently thought of in terms of financial and accounting systems. The reasons for this are easy to understand:

- The stewardship of financial resources is of vital concern to the majority of organisations. In both private-enterprise and public-sector organisations there is an increasing need to demonstrate value for money expended. Organisational aims, objectives and targets are often expressed in financial terms and measured in terms of profitability. Results are measured and reported in financial terms.

- Money is quantifiable and a precise unit of measurement. It is easily understood, and often used as a common denominator and as a basis for comparison. Financial limits are easy to apply as a measure of control and easy to relate to. For example, the need for control is an integral part of the process of delegation or empowerment. This control may easily be applied where, for example, a manager gives a subordinate the authority, without prior reference, to incur expenditure on certain items up to a given financial cost limit.

Accounting systems and human behaviour

It is understandable, therefore, that so much attention is given to financial and accounting systems of measurement and control. However, accounting statements focus on only a limited area of activity. Management control embraces far more than just financial or accounting considerations. It is concerned with the whole process of management: with the extent to which organisational aims are achieved and with improvement in performance.

In their discussion of the role of accounting systems in organisational control, it is interesting to note the words of *Berry et al.*:

> *Accounting systems provide a fundamental way of handling high levels of complexity by the imposition of a set of standard operating procedures; this provides a major strength of accounting as a control system. However, weaknesses also stem from the imposition of standard systems in complex situations because inventive human minds find ways of reporting desired results through the manipulation of the system rather than by behaving in expected ways.*[35]

This wording appears to imply that the accounting system is the arbiter of correct behaviour and that people are to 'blame' for their failure to act in the way imposed by accounting systems (and presumably by the accountants who designed them).

Accounting control systems such as internal audit, management by exception and budgetary control tend to operate in a negative way and to report only on the unfavourable, or on favourable variances that may have adverse consequences – for example, less spent than budgeted. 'Success' for the accounting staff may be equated with the 'failure' of other staff. As a result there is no specific recognition from management. There is only a limited sense of achievement or self-esteem for favourable performance or where no corrective action is required. There is little, if any, positive motivation.

There is, of course, nothing wrong with the use of accounting systems of control such as internal auditing, management by exception and budgetary control. Control systems can have positive as well as negative effects. Financial and accounting control systems, as with other forms of control, should be designed and implemented in a constructive and rewarding way. To do this, they must take account of individual, social and organisational factors that determine people's patterns of behaviour.

Hilton suggests that the modern manager often lacks any feel for the unique culture of a business and therefore has an insufficient understanding or appreciation of the true drivers of its success. Unlike most developed countries, UK boardrooms are dominated by people with a financial background. The problem is that financial control is not enough. Conventional risk control systems can cover hard data, technical know-how, systems and strategies. What they do not do is handle softer issues such as management style, employee motivation, shared values and corporate culture.[36]

Influencing skills

Clearly power, in whatever form, is needed to get work done. As *Owen* points out, power skills are becoming more important because the nature of the manager's job is changing.

> *It is now normal for managers to find that their responsibilities exceed their authority. In the past, the art of management was getting things done through other people, whom the*

manager controlled. Now managers have to get things done through other people whom they do not control. The lack of control changes everything. New skills are required to make things happen when you lack formal authority. These skills include:

- Building networks of trust and influence
- Creating alliances to make things happen
- Dealing with conflict
- Shaping the organisation's agenda to meet your needs
- Dealing with organisational conflict and resistance
- Managing ambiguity and uncertainty
- Finding the right assignments and projects to work on
- Discovering the real rules of survival and success in your firm.[37]

Yukl suggests that rather than focusing exclusively on power as a source of potential influence, more attention is being given to specific types of behaviour used to exercise influence:

Rational Persuasion – the use of logical arguments and factual persuasion
Apprising – explaining the personal benefits or career advancement
Inspiration Appeals – to values and ideas or attempt to gain commitment
Consultation – seeking support and assistance by asking for assistance
Exchange – incentives or willingness to reciprocate
Collaboration – providing relevant resources and assistance in exchange for proposed change
Personal Appeals – based on friendship or personal favour
Ingratiation – use of praise or flattery
Legitimating Tactics – establishing legitimacy or verifying authority
Pressure – use of demands, threats, frequent checking
Coalition Tactics – seeking the aid or support of others.[38]

Balance between order and flexibility

Stewart refers to the classic dilemma that underlies the nature of control: finding the right balance for present conditions between order and flexibility. This involves the trade-off between trying to improve predictability of people's actions against the desirability of encouraging individual and local responsiveness to changing situations. The organisation may need a 'tight–loose' structure, with certain departments or areas of work closely controlled ('tight') while other departments or areas of work should be left fluid and flexible ('loose').[39]

According to Stewart, 'control can – and should – be exercised in different ways'. She identifies three main forms of control:

- **Direct control by orders, direct supervision and rules and regulations.** Direct controls may be necessary, and more readily acceptable, in a crisis situation and during training. But in organisations where people expect to participate in decision-making, such forms of control may be unacceptable. Rules and regulations that are not accepted as reasonable, or at least not unreasonable, will offer some people a challenge to use their ingenuity in finding ways round them.
- **Control through standardisation and specialisation.** This is achieved through clear definition of the inputs to a job, the methods to be used and the required outputs. Such bureaucratic control makes clear the parameters within which one can act and paradoxically makes decentralisation easier. Provided the parameters are not unduly restrictive they can increase the sense of freedom. For example, within clearly defined limits that ensure that one retail chain store looks like another, individual managers may have freedom to do the job as they wish.

- **Control through influencing the way that people think about what they should do.** This is often the most effective method of exercising control. It may be achieved through selective recruitment of people who seem likely to share a similar approach, through the training and socialisation of people into thinking the organisation's way and through peer pressure. Where an organisation has a very strong culture, people who do not fit in, or learn to adapt, are likely to be pushed out, even though they may appear to leave of their own volition.

Stewart also refers to a second, related dilemma of finding the appropriate balance between centralisation, as a means of exercising control, and decentralisation. (**Centralisation and decentralisation are discussed in Chapter 11.**)

Behavioural factors in control systems

Control systems can help fulfil people's needs at work and their presence may be welcomed by some members of staff. Often, however, control systems are perceived as a threat to the need satisfaction of the individual. Even when control systems are well designed and operated they may be viewed with a certain amount of suspicion and possible resentment by members of staff. Control often provokes an emotional response from those affected by it. Control over behaviour may be resented and provoke dislike of those responsible for its operation. **Control systems provide an interface between human behaviour and the process of management.** The manner in which control is exercised and the perception of staff will have a significant effect on the level of organisational performance.

There are a number of factors, discussed in other chapters, that can affect the successful implementation of management control systems, including the following:

- **Attitudes and response of staff.** That is, the way they perceive reasons for and methods of control. Consideration by management to the influences of diversity and inclusion. The extent to which control may help as a learning and development experience.
- **Motivation.** Motivation is a function of the relationship between effort expended and perceived level of performance. Recognition for a satisfactory level of attainment coupled with a suitable reward system, as integral parts of control, can do much to motivate staff and encourage improved performance.
- **Groups and the informal organisation.** Membership of a harmonious and effective work group can be a source of motivation and job satisfaction. Socialisation can help create a feeling of commitment to the group and reduce the need for formal management control. With the development of autonomous work groups, members have greater freedom and wider discretion over the planning, execution and control of their own work. Informal group 'norms' and peer pressure can be one of the most powerful forms of control.
- **Leadership style and systems of management.** The style of managerial leadership is a function of the manager's attitudes towards people, and assumptions about human nature and behaviour – for example, McGregor's Theory X and Theory Y. The character of control processes is one of the organisational variables identified in Likert's fourfold model of management systems. With System 4 (participative group), concern for performance of control functions is spread throughout the organisation, review and control functions are carried out at all levels, and the formal and informal organisation share the same goals.
- **Consultation and participation.** If staff are committed personally to particular objectives they are more likely to direct themselves and to exercise self-control over their level of performance.
- **Organisation structure.** Organisations with a mechanistic structure are more readily suited to the operation and implementation of traditional systems of control. In organic structures the effectiveness of control is more dependent upon individual involvement and commitment to the aims of the organisation. Increased flexible working arrangements and homeworking call for greater trust from managers.

Critical review and reflection

It is a poor manager who relies on the exercise of formal power and position within the hierarchical structure of control. Personal power is the only way to achieve effective leadership influence and control.
  What do YOU think? How well are YOU able to exercise personal power and influencing skills?

The concept of empowerment

Discussion on the balance between order and flexibility, and control versus autonomy, draws attention to the importance of empowerment. Despite a general movement towards less mechanistic structures and the role of managers as facilitators, there appears to be some reluctance, especially among top managers, to dilute or weaken hierarchical control.

Empowerment is generally explained in terms of allowing employees greater freedom, autonomy and self-control over their work, and responsibility for decision-making. However, there are differences in the meaning and interpretation of the term. The concept of empowerment also gives rise to a number of questions and doubts. For example, how does it differ in any meaningful way from other earlier forms of employee involvement? Is the primary concern of empowerment getting the most out of the workforce? Is empowerment just another somewhat more fanciful term for delegation? Some writers see the two as quite separate concepts while other writers suggest empowerment is a more proactive form of delegation.

According to *Mills and Friesen*, 'Empowerment can be succinctly defined as the authority of subordinates to decide and act.'

> It describes a management style. The term is often confused with delegation but, if strictly defined, empowerment goes much further in granting subordinates authority to decide and act. Indeed, within a context of broad limits defined by executives, empowered individuals may even become self-managing.[40]

Skill of empowerment and delegation

Delegation is not an easy task. Empowering other people is a matter of judgement. It involves the question of discretion. It involves behavioural as well as organisational and economic considerations, and it is subject to a number of possible abuses. Effective delegation is a social skill. It requires a clear understanding of people-perception, reliance on other people, confidence and trust, and courage. It is important that the manager knows what to delegate, when and to whom. Matters of policy and disciplinary power, for example, usually rest with the manager and cannot legitimately be delegated.

Attempting to distinguish clearly between empowerment and delegation is not always clear. However, empowerment is viewed generally as the more embracing term that describes a management style and granting of genuine additional power to other members of staff. Empowerment is viewed as the more embracing process. Arguably, it is the process of empowerment that gives rise to the act of delegation. According to *Tulgan,* for example: 'The key to empowerment is effective delegation; giving individual contributors ownership of tangible results.'[41]

At the individual (or personal) level, **delegation** is the process of entrusting authority and responsibility to others throughout the various levels of the organisation. It is the authorisation to undertake activities that would otherwise be carried out by someone in a more senior position. Downsizing and de-layering have arguably limited the opportunities for delegation, although this may be offset by demands for greater flexibility and empowerment. In any event, delegation is still an essential process of management.

Extreme forms of behaviour

The concept of delegation may appear to be straightforward. However, anyone with experience of a work situation is likely to be aware of the consequences of badly managed delegation. Successful delegation is a social skill. Where managers lack this skill, or do not have a sufficient awareness of people-perception, there are two extreme forms of behaviour that can result:

- At one extreme is the almost total lack of meaningful delegation. Subordinate staff are only permitted to operate within closely defined and often routine areas of work, with detailed supervision. Staff are treated as if they are incapable of thinking for themselves and given little or no opportunity to exercise initiative or responsibility.
- At the other extreme there can be an excessive zeal for so-called delegation when a manager leaves subordinates to their own resources, often with only minimal guidance or training, and expects them to take the consequences for their own actions or decisions. These 'super-delegators' misuse the practice of delegation and are often like the Artful Dodger, and somehow contrive not to be around when difficult situations arise. Such a form of behaviour is not delegation; it is an abdication of the manager's responsibility.

Either of these two extreme forms of behaviour can be frustrating and potentially stressful for subordinate staff, and unlikely to lead to improved organisational effectiveness. The nature of delegation can have a significant effect on the morale, motivation and work performance of staff. In all but the smallest organisation the only way to get work done effectively is through delegation, but even such an important practice can be misused or over-applied.

The manager–subordinate relationship

Delegation is not just the arbitrary shedding of work. It is not just the issuing and following of orders or carrying out of specified tasks in accordance with detailed instructions. Within the formal structure of the organisation, delegation creates a special manager–subordinate relationship. It is founded on the concept of:

- authority;
- responsibility; and
- accountability (ultimate responsibility).
- **Authority** is the right to take action or make decisions that the manager would otherwise have done. Authority legitimises the exercise of empowerment within the structure and rules of the organisation. It enables the subordinate to issue valid instructions for others to follow.
- **Responsibility** involves an obligation by the subordinate to perform certain duties or make certain decisions and having to accept possible reprimand from the manager for unsatisfactory performance. The meaning of the term 'responsibility' is, however, subject to possible confusion: although delegation embraces both authority and responsibility, effective delegation is not abdication of responsibility.
- **Accountability** is interpreted as meaning ultimate responsibility and cannot be delegated. Managers have to accept 'responsibility' for the control of their staff, for the performance of all duties allocated to their department/section within the structure of the organisation and for the standard of results achieved. That is, 'the buck stops here'.

The subordinate is responsible to the manager for doing the job, while the manager is responsible for seeing that the job gets done. The manager is accountable to a superior for the actions of subordinates.

Authority commensurate with responsibility

Delegation, therefore, embraces both authority and responsibility. It is not practical to delegate one without the other (*see* Figure 13.5). Responsibility must be supported by authority and by power to influence areas of performance for which the subordinate is held responsible.

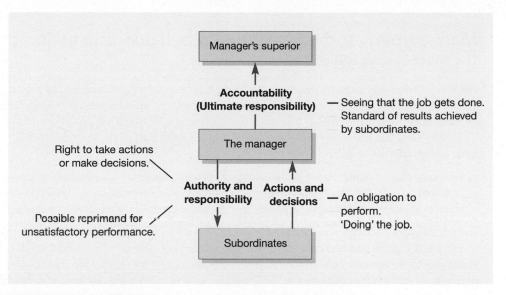

Figure 13.5 The basis of delegation

Authority can be delegated readily, but many problems of delegation stem from failure to delegate sufficient authority to enable subordinates to fulfil their responsibilities. For example, if a section head is held responsible to a departmental manager for the performance of junior staff but is not empowered (given authority) to influence their selection and appointment, their motivation, the allocation of their duties, their training and development, or their sanctions and rewards, then the section leader can hardly be held responsible for unsatisfactory performance of the junior staff. To hold subordinates responsible for certain areas of performance without also conferring on them the necessary authority within the limits of that responsibility is an abuse of delegation.

The manager should accept the blame as the person **accountable** for the performance of the department/section, and obligated to see that the task was completed satisfactorily. It is necessary to maintain the organisational hierarchy and structure of command. Managers should protect and support subordinate staff and accept, personally, any reprimand for unsatisfactory performance. It is then up to managers to sort out things in their own department/section, to counsel members of staff concerned and to review their system of delegation.

Bushe emphasises the continuing importance of authority.

> *Contrary to popular images and poorly thought through books on the subject, collaborative work systems do not decrease or eliminate authority even if they do flatten hierarchies and reduce command and control – quite the contrary. Authority and hierarchy are two separate things. Authority is the power to make and enforce decisions. Collaborative organizations create much more authority than command and control systems do because in collaborative organizations, authority is dispersed widely . . . But collaborative organizations still require hierarchy for focus and direction.*[42]

Critical review and reflection

The idea of empowerment and delegation is fine in theory. But if managers are still held accountable for performance of staff and any adverse consequences of their actions, it is only right that they should exercise close control and supervision over their behaviour.

What is YOUR point of view? How comfortable do YOU feel about empowerment and delegation?

Management and organisational behaviour in action case study
The police custody officer and empowerment

The Police Service has statutory responsibility for the treatment of persons detained by it (and other agencies, such as HMRC, that bring people into a police station). These people must be treated in accordance with the Police & Criminal Evidence Act 1984 (PACE) that was enacted in January 1986 and any code of practice issued under the Act.

Section 39 of PACE specifies that these duties should be the duty of the custody officer at a police station. The same section goes on to declare:

> where an officer of **higher** rank than the custody officer gives directions . . . which are at variance with any **decision** or **action** taken by the custody officer in the performance of a duty imposed on him under this Act the matter **shall** be referred at once to an officer of the rank of Superintendent or above who is responsible for that police station.

There is statutory backing for the decisions and actions taken by custody officers in the performance of their duties.

PACE sets out the provisions regarding the appointment of custody officers (Section 36). Custody officers are appointed to designated police stations, which are effectively police stations equipped to receive and house detained persons in the conditions that PACE requires. Subject to limited exceptions, all detained persons must go to a designated police station. Custody officers are appointed by the Chief Officer of Police for that area or by an officer directed by that Chief Officer of Police to do so. Importantly, no police officer may be appointed a custody officer unless at least the rank of sergeant, and significantly none of the functions of a custody officer shall be performed by an officer who is involved in the investigation of an offence for which the person is in detention (and there is case law that identifies what being involved in an investigation entails).

Most forces have adopted the sergeant rank as the best suited to the custody officer role (custody officers no longer have to be a police officer). On appointment, training is given in the role of sergeant and specifically custody-officer duties. Custody officers, though they work for the same organisation, have an element of impartiality through the statement that they must not be involved in the investigation of an offence for which that person is detained. This allows for their decision-making to be non-partisan. There is an argument, perhaps, that for the decision-making to be completely impartial, custody provisions should be independent of the police service, but in practice it is argued that custody officers value their impartiality and their decision-making is reflected in this.

The Act clearly defines the process for any challenge to custody officers' decision-making and that is by appeal to the station commander, a Superintendent. As well as providing support for custody officers in their decision-making it also affords protection for them from **rank pulling** in a hierarchically structured organisation such as the police.

Custody officers deal with people's liberty and determine whether they enter the legal process by charging them to appear at court. This is a serious business and in practical terms it is taken very seriously. Their decision-making in this process is subject to periodic review. In the first 24 hours of a person's detention that review is undertaken at the 6-, 15- and 24-hour stages. Any detention beyond 24 hours requires the authority of a Superintendent and any detention beyond 36 hours requires a warrant from a court. The custody officer's decision-making is subject to close scrutiny through the training process, accreditation process and local inspection processes. Most importantly, it is a legal requirement now that all designated custody centres are videotaped, which is perhaps the ultimate scrutiny. The arrival of video recording tapes in custody centres was welcomed by custody officers as it saw a corresponding fall in the number of complaints against them in the charge-room process.

In practical terms it is rare that decisions of a custody officer are challenged by a more senior officer (a Detective Chief Inspector). The fact that these occasions are so rarely reported is evidence of the seriousness and professionalism adopted by custody sergeants in their decision-making process. **A process that would only work with empowerment.**

Source: I am grateful to Sergeant Robert Collier of The Hampshire Constabulary for providing this information.

Tasks

1. Discuss critically the extent to which you believe this case illustrates the importance and potential benefits of empowerment.
2. How would you relate this case to the concept of authority commensurate with responsibility?
3. Explain the importance of protection from rank pulling in any other hierarchically structured organisations.

Reasons for lack of delegation

Properly handled, delegation offers many potential benefits to both managers and staff. Delegation should help make the best use of time, provide a means of training and development and lead to improved morale by increasing motivation and job satisfaction. Effective delegation results in optimum use of human resources and improved organisational performance.

With good reasons for delegation, why is it that managers often fail to delegate or do not delegate successfully? Delegation is influenced by the manager's perception of subordinate staff. It is also influenced by the subordinate's perception of the manager's reasons for delegation. Failure to delegate often results from the manager's fear:

- The manager may fear that the subordinate is not capable of doing a sufficiently good job. Also, the manager may fear being blamed for the subordinate's mistakes.
- Conversely, the manager may fear that the subordinate will do too good a job and show the manager in a bad light.
- The manager should, of course, remember that the task of management is to get work done through the efforts of other people. If the subordinate does a particularly good job this should reflect favourably on the manager. A reluctance to delegate might arise from the manager's belief in, and set of assumptions about, human nature and behaviour, Theory X and Theory Y (**discussed in Chapter 10**).

Ethical considerations

Moorcroft suggests that although delegation is a useful business tool it needs only occasional use and is one that demands strong ethical issues, for example:

- managers may be overwhelmed with work but it is what they get paid to do;
- some larger consultancy companies may 'sell' the consultancy through senior staff but then send junior staff;
- use of the argument of 'development of staff' to delegate tasks beyond the level of the subordinate with an unrealistic time scale hoping that the subordinate will fail and thus reinforcing the status of the manager.

When delegation does occur it is important to establish ethical rules relating to agreement on responsibility for outcomes, effective training and recognising credit for success.[43] Mistakes will inevitably happen and the subordinate will need to be supported by the manager, and protected against unwarranted criticism. The acceptance of ultimate responsibility highlights the educational aspect of the manager's job. The manager should view mistakes as part of the subordinate's training and learning experience and an opportunity for further development: 'Even if mistakes occur, good managers are judged as much by their ability to manage them as by their successes.'[44]

Trust and empowerment

Empowerment is also a matter of confidence and trust – in both subordinates and the manager's own performance and system of delegation. In allowing freedom of action to subordinates within agreed terms of reference and the limits of authority, managers must accept that subordinates may undertake delegated activities in a different manner from themselves. This is at the basis of the true nature of trust. However, learning to put trust in other people is one of the most difficult aspects of successful delegation for many managers, and some never learn it.

As *Stewart* points out, managers who think about what can be done only in terms of what they can do cannot be effective. Managing is not a solo activity.

> *Managers must learn to accept their dependence upon people. A key part of being a good manager is managing that dependence. Managers who say that they cannot delegate because they have poor staff may genuinely be unfortunate in the calibre of the staff that*

they have inherited or been given. More often this view is a criticism of themselves: a criticism either of their unwillingness to delegate when they could and should do so, or a criticism of their selection, training and development of their staff.[45]

The process of empowerment entails the removal of constraints and the granting of autonomy for independent actions. As part of her discussion on the democratic enterprise, *Gratton* refers to the importance of trust and power.

The re-appropriation of choice from senior members of the organization to individuals themselves implies trust on both parts, but particularly on the part of senior members. It is they who have to cede power to individual employees and to trust them to behave in an autonomous manner and make decisions and take action that serve their personal good and the good of the organization. Democracy implies the giving of authority to individuals to make choices within the context of obligations and accountabilities. Authority, obligations and accountability are deeply bound up with trust. Trust without accountability and obligation is likely to become one-sided, that is, to slide into dependence. Accountability without trust is impossible because it would mean the continual scrutiny of the motives and actions of individuals.[46]

The indispensability trap

Jolly comments on the 'curse of knowledge' – those individuals who have demonstrated technical expertise, worked hard and developed skills and competence. Your skill has become automatic, and when moving into management you are faced with supervising people who it's obvious don't know how to do what for you. If you have then managed to demonstrate your expertise and ability to supervise others, you are too good at your current job and risk getting stuck in it. You have become indispensable and too important to promote. To be an effective executive you need a strong desire and ability to control and this focus on control leads to 'I don't have time to delegate'. Delegation feels like losing control and takes valuable time. Hence the instinct to control can increasingly become a liability rather than an asset.

If managers are going to avoid the trap of indispensability, we have to stand back from our day-to-day tasks and think. We have to create an environment where others can grow and be held responsible. We have to fight our instincts to control.[47]

Critical review and reflection

Reasons for lack of effective delegation are easy to understand. It is faster and easier to do the work yourself and there is a reluctance to trust other people. The main problem is that few people are coached in the skills or art of delegation.

To what extent has YOUR course of study prepared YOU to be an effective delegator?

Systematic approach to empowerment and delegation

The manager must be on the lookout for subordinates who are more concerned with personal empire building than meeting stated organisational objectives and thus prevent a strong personality exceeding the limits of formal delegation. The manager must remain in control. We have said that delegation creates a special manager–subordinate relationship and this involves both the giving of trust and the retention of control. Control is, therefore, an integral part of the system of delegation. However, control should not be so close as to inhibit the effective operation or benefits of delegation. It is a question of balance.

In order to realise the full benefits of empowerment without loss of control, it is necessary to adopt a planned and systematic approach. Setting up a successful system of delegation involves examining five basic questions:

- How can I make better use of my time and expertise?
- What tasks could be performed better by other staff?
- What opportunities are there for staff to learn and develop by undertaking delegated tasks and responsibilities?
- How should increased responsibilities be implemented and to whom should they be given?
- What forms of monitoring control system would be most appropriate?

Delegation is not an irrevocable act and can always be withdrawn. In order to set up an effective system of delegation, subordinates should know exactly what is expected of them, what has to be achieved, the boundaries within which they have freedom of action and how far they can exercise independent decision-making. It is possible to identify six main stages in a planned and systematic approach to delegation (*see* Figure 13.6):

- **Clarification of objectives and suitable patterns of organisation.** Establish and define policies and procedures in order to provide a framework for the exercise of authority and acceptance of responsibility.
- **Agreement on terms of reference and acceptance of authority and responsibility.** Identify and agree role prescription and terms of reference, and areas of work in which responsible for achieving results. Emphasis should generally be placed on end results rather than a set of detailed instructions.
- **Guidance, support and training, and patterns of communication.** When subordinates have agreed and accepted the delegation, they should be properly briefed, given guidance and support and any necessary training. They should be advised where, and to whom, they could go for further advice or help.

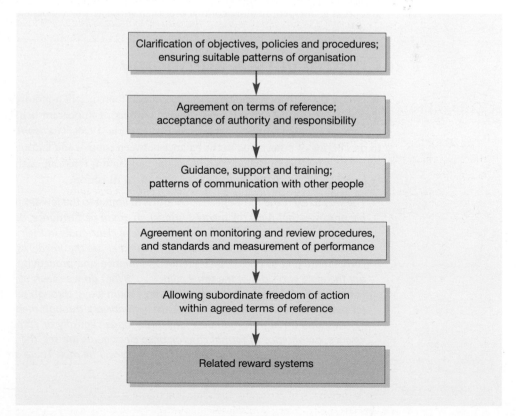

Figure 13.6 Main stages in the process of delegation

- **Effective monitoring and review procedures.** Agree time limits (such as a target date for completion of a specific task or a specified time period), level and nature of supervision, and establish a system to monitor progress and provide feedback.
- **Freedom of action within agreed terms of reference.** One of the most frustrating aspects of delegation is the manager who passes on authority but stays close behind keeping a constant watch over subordinates' actions. The true nature of successful delegation means that the subordinate is left alone to get on with the job and given freedom of action within the boundaries established and agreed in the previous stages.
- **Related reward system.** Wherever possible, the process of delegation should be related to some form of associated 'reward' system. Examples could include bonus payments, improved job satisfaction, reduction of work stress and enhanced opportunities for promotion or personal development, including further delegation.

A summary of delegation, authority, power and responsibility is given in the concept map set out in Figure 13.7.

Does empowerment deliver?

Effectively managed, empowerment can offer a number of potential benefits throughout all levels of the organisation. But does empowerment promote greater motivation and increase job satisfaction and work performance? Does empowerment deliver?

Wall and Wood suggest that although few manufacturing companies empower their staff, research shows that empowerment can be one of the most effective tools in raising both productivity and profit. Empowerment improves performance because of the opportunities it provides for staff to do their work more effectively. It develops individuals' knowledge so they take a broader and more proactive orientation towards their job and are more willing to suggest new ways of doing things and to engage in meaningful teamworking.[48]

Findings from a Whitehall II study of over 10,000 civil servants on work-related stress suggests that giving people more control over their jobs can greatly benefit their health.[49]

Control versus autonomy

Whatever the extent of employee empowerment, there is still a requirement for some form of management control and this gives rise to a number of important behavioural considerations. From their study of top-performing companies in the 1990s, *Goldsmith and Clutterbuck* refer to the sharing of power, and to the balance between control and autonomy. They question how companies manage to balance giving people maximum freedom against exerting controls to ensure the benefits of size and a common sense of direction.

> *The way to exert the most effective control is to limit it to the few simple, readily understandable processes that have the greatest impact on group performance, and to maximise the freedom that managers at all levels have to achieve clear goals in their own way. And the more rigidly those core controls are enforced, the greater are the freedoms people need in order to compensate and to release their creativity, initiative and proactivity. Control and autonomy are therefore two sides of the same coin . . . What do we mean by control and autonomy? Formal control seems to be exercised in three main ways: through setting or agreeing targets for performance (mainly but not exclusively financial); through measurement and reporting systems; and through certain decisions to be made centrally or corporately. Autonomy is, in essence, an absence of formal control: once clear goals are set, the individual manager has greater or lesser freedom to determine how they will be met. There are still controls in place, but they are much less obvious or intrusive.[50]*

DELEGATION, AUTHORITY, POWER & RESPONSIBILITY

"Delegation is part of a managerial function involving an element of risk"

Authority – the **right** to
Power – the **ability** to

AUTHORITY

- Given to the subordinate to do the manager's job (otherwise formal organisations cannot exist)
- Extent of delegated authority
- Anything the manager has the right to do (except where the manager is specifically prohibited from doing)
- Cannot totally delegate authority of performing the managerial functions viz: Planning
  Organising
  Motivating
  Communications

Measured in terms of
- Giving rewards
- Promising rewards
- Threat to withdraw current rewards
- Threaten punishment
- Punish

Influenced by
- Subjective factors – ethical, moral
  How much power should managers have?
  Power is the ability to influence another
- extent of power significantly determined by the person being controlled
- may be more important what person thinks the manager's power is, than what it actually is

■ EFFECTIVE DELEGATION
■ REASONS FOR INEFFECTIVE DELEGATION

INEFFECTIVE DELEGATION

■ Heavy work loads   of – Manager
■ Lack of appropriate staff   – Subordinates
■ Unfamiliarity with the task   Staff not trained
■ Personal characteristics   – Staff not in post
■ Fear of subordinate doing
  undesirable things   of – Manager
                                     – Subordinates

DELEGATION OF AUTHORITY & POWER

Authority & Power relationships
- A manager must posses both otherwise conflict occurs
- Subordinates must be provided with equal authority & power at all levels of an organisation = legitimate power or workable authority
- Managers have the right to require accounting for the authority delegated & tasks assigned to a subordinate
- Subordinates must answer to the managers concerning the stewardship of the authority granted to him or her by the manager

ALL RETAINED BY
MANAGEMENT

Management control
every detail

POWER

NONE RETAINED BY
MANAGEMENT

Management loses
control

Zone of
Instruction

Zone of
Delegation

Zone of
Empowerment

Zone of
Anarchy

EFFECTIVE
DELEGATION
■ Understanding the task

■ Identifying the correct person(s) to perform the task

■ Communicating the task
  Setting & discussing
  the objectives for the task

■ Monitoring progress
■ Evaluating feedback

Both by the delegate & the person(s) to inform the work is delegated

Based on
- Previous performance
- Special skills
- Special circumstances

Using appropriate communication methods
Verbal/written
Diagrammatic

Objectives require
- timescales
- quality of the results
- to be quantified

RESPONSIBILITY
The obligation to do something
■ The duty to perform the job or function in the organisation
■ An individual's obligation to him- or herself to perform the task
■ Responsibility cannot be delegated
■ Delegating authority can increase the manager's responsibility since there is an additional responsibility for the subordinate's tasks

BENEFITS OF EFFECTIVE DELEGATION
■ Efficient use of manager's & subordinate's time
■ Motivation of staff
■ Development of staff
■ Stress reduction in managers & subordinates

RESPONSIBILITY & ACCOUNTABILITY
– Accountability – a person is accountable to higher authorities
– Responsibility is created within a person when accepting a task & appropriate delegation of authority

Figure 13.7 Delegation, authority, power and responsibility

Source: Copyright © 2012 The Virtual Learning Materials Workshop. Reproduced with permission.

Critical review and reflection

Some form of hierarchical power and order is an essential feature of effective work performance, but the nature of modern organisations has noticeably diminished effective management control over the actions and behaviour of people at work.

What is YOUR considered opinion? Do YOU favour more or less control over your work activities?

Ten key points to remember

1 Control completes the cycle of managerial activities and its purpose is improvement in performance at both the individual and organisational level.

2 By its very nature, control is concerned with the regulation of behaviour. Control has an emotive connotation and most people show ambivalence towards control.

3 Control is an expression of managerial behaviour. There are important elements and characteristics of effective control systems, and of forms and strategies of control.

4 Work organisations are not just systems of hierarchical structure; they are complex systems of social relationships, status and power.

5 Power is real or perceived control or influence over other people. It differs according to how members of staff comply and operate at different levels.

6 Pluralistic approaches recognise power as a social process that derives from a multiplicity of interpersonal sources, social relationships and realities of organisational life.

7 Control systems are frequently thought of in terms of accounting or financial systems, but what also needs to be considered are social and behavioural factors.

8 Discussion on the balance between order and flexibility draws attention to the importance of empowerment and delegation and greater freedom for staff.

9 Delegation creates a special manager–subordinate relationship based on entrusting authority and responsibility to others, but accountability cannot be delegated.

10 Whatever the extent of employee empowerment, there is still need for some form of management control and there are a number of behavioural considerations.

Review and discussion questions

1 Give your own views on the controversial nature of management control. What do you see as the purpose and operation of control in work organisations?

2 Detail, with supporting examples, the essential elements of a management control system.

3 Explain fully the main factors that are likely to affect resistance to, and the successful implementation of, management control systems.

4 Discuss critically the use of technology as a determinant of an effective control system, including any legal or social considerations.

5 Debate the extent to which you believe too much attention is given to financial and accounting systems of control at the expense of behavioural considerations.

6 Explain fully the importance of the concept of power to management and organisational behaviour.

7 Discuss critically the nature of pluralistic approaches to power and give your own practical examples.

8 How would you explain the organisational and personal relationships between a manager and subordinate staff created by the process of empowerment?

9 As a departmental manager, explain fully how you would attempt to realise the full advantages of delegation without loss of control over subordinate staff.

10 Discuss critically what you see as the likely consequences of a manager exercising close personal supervision as a means of maintaining control and power over the work of subordinate staff.

Assignment *The empowerment questionnaire*

The following questionnaire consists of managerial behaviours that promote empowerment. Think of any work experience you have had – even a short-term, vacation or part-time job. How frequently did your manager do each of the following? Please mark the response that best describes the manager's behaviour.

My manager	Very infrequently	Infrequently	Sometimes	Frequently	Very frequently
1 Lets me do my job without interfering	❏	❏	❏	❏	❏
2 Makes an effort to locate and remove barriers that reduce efficiency	❏	❏	❏	❏	❏
3 Encourages all of us to work as a team	❏	❏	❏	❏	❏
4 Clearly defines what is expected of me	❏	❏	❏	❏	❏
5 Provides me with honest feedback on my performance	❏	❏	❏	❏	❏
6 Openly recognises work well done	❏	❏	❏	❏	❏
7 Keeps me focused on customer needs	❏	❏	❏	❏	❏
8 Encourages me to monitor my own efforts	❏	❏	❏	❏	❏
9 Makes sure I have the training I need to do my job	❏	❏	❏	❏	❏
10 Allows me to make decisions about my own work	❏	❏	❏	❏	❏

My manager	Very infrequently	Infrequently	Sometimes	Frequently	Very frequently
11 Listens to me before making decisions affecting my area	❏	❏	❏	❏	❏
12 Provides me with an environment conducive to teamwork	❏	❏	❏	❏	❏
13 Rewards me for meeting company goals	❏	❏	❏	❏	❏
14 Informs me regularly about the state of business	❏	❏	❏	❏	❏
15 Encourages me to make suggestions	❏	❏	❏	❏	❏
16 Makes sure I have all the information I need to do my work	❏	❏	❏	❏	❏
17 Behaves in ways that demonstrate respect for others	❏	❏	❏	❏	❏
18 Explains how my job fits into the company objectives	❏	❏	❏	❏	❏

Source: Osland, Joyce S., Kolb, David A. and Rubin, Irwin M. *Organizational Behaviour: An Experimental Approach*, seventh edition, Prentice Hall (2001). Copyright © 2001. Reproduced with permission from Pearson Education, Inc.

a. If this was *not* a permanent, full-time position, to what extent do you think this influenced your manager's behaviour towards you?

b. How did your experience compare with the manager's behaviour to other members of staff in the same department/section?

c. How would you describe the manager's general belief in, and approach to, empowerment? And what was your perception of the manager's overall effectiveness?

Personal skills and employability exercise

Objectives

Completing this exercise should help you to enhance the following skills:

- Review honestly and reflect upon features of your own personality.
- Assess the extent to which you are in danger of becoming a control freak.
- Sensitivity to your preferred managerial style.

Control in its many forms is an inherent and essential feature of management and organisational behaviour. However, the manner in which control is exercised is a variable dependent upon the extent to which a manager either prefers or believes it necessary to use positional power within the hierarchical structure of the organisation to maintain control. For some people, power can be a positive source of motivation.

Exercise

Working in small, self-selected groups, individually record honestly the extent to which you agree with the following ten questions. If necessary, think how you would be likely to behave in a given situation. Then compare and discuss responses with your colleagues.

1 I enjoy and strive for power over other people. It is a natural human characteristic.

2 I am generally happy to put my trust in others to get work done on time and to a good standard.

3 Charisma and personal power is the most effective source of management control.

4 I am happy to accept that other people often have better ideas than me.

5 It is only natural for managers to expect obedience based on their formal hierarchical authority.

6 Office politics, manipulation and the grapevine should be accepted as realities of organisational life.

7 I believe that I am right most of the time.

8 Control over members of staff through electronic surveillance is nothing more than an unwelcome invasion of privacy.

9 Financial and accounting systems are the most reliable and fairest forms of control.

10 The concept of empowerment sounds good in theory but far too often delegation is abused by managers for their own benefit.

Discussion

- Do you think you have controlling issues or can you exercise flexibility?
- How can you attempt to develop charisma and the use of personal power?
- To what extent has this exercise provoked further thoughts on your attitude towards organisational control and power?

Case study
Rogue traders

Over the last three decades rogue traders in the financial services sector have provided a dramatic illustration of the major risks that can result from poor organisational control. The term denotes an individual whose wayward and/or fraudulent activities at the trading desk have built up very high losses for the bank. Rogue traders usually find ways of hiding the escalating losses from sight, meaning that the collapse, when it finally comes, can be very damaging.

Perhaps because of the dizzying scale of the losses they create, rogue traders can become individually famous: Nick Leeson (Barings), Jerome Kerviel (Societé Générale) and Kweku Adoboli (UBS) are probably better known in the media than any of the senior managers in their institutions. The punishments handed down for their wrongdoing can be heavy: Leeson was sentenced to six and a half years in jail. Kerviel received a sentence of five years in prison (of which two were suspended); he was eventually released from prison in September 2014, having served about five months, and will wear an electronic tag for the rest of his sentence.[51] Adoboli was sentenced to seven years in prison in 2012.[52] One of the more remarkable characteristics of these traders is that they seem not to be seeking to embezzle money from their employer, or to cause deliberate damage to the

Nick Leeson returning to Singapore
Source: John MacDougall/AFP/Getty Images

bank.[53] They may well trade in the hope of large bonus payments in a good year – that is the culture in trading floors – but when they go rogue, it is more likely to be in a desperate effort to recover a large and embarrassing loss resulting from foolish trading or just plain bad luck.

Nick Leeson's story (back in 1995) has many features in common with more recent scandals in Japan, France and Switzerland, although today's greater complexity of financial products and the much more globalised nature of the market may well have increased the risk. Leeson was employed as a trader in the Singapore branch of

Barings Bank, a long-established London institution. As the son of a plasterer from a Watford council estate, his successful track record in the early 1990s must have looked at the time like a classic rags-to-riches story,[54] very much in line with the values of the recently liberalised City of London. In 1992, at the age of just 26, he was put in charge of a new Barings venture in futures trading – in effect, making money by correctly anticipating the movement of indices in key stock exchanges. He appeared to be highly successful in this role: in 1993, the £10 million profit from his operation represented 10 per cent of Barings' total profits.[55] Not surprisingly, his rewards from the bank grew rapidly, funding an extravagant lifestyle. The problems started when an inexperienced member of his team made a relatively modest loss as a result of a trading mistake, which Leeson decided to cover up by hiding it in a secret account. This was only possible because Leeson was in charge of both the front and back offices of his operation: in other words, he both carried out the trades and settled them, which turned out to be a key structural flaw in the controls applied by his employer. Once open, the secret account was available for hiding further losses, a habit that grew rapidly – by the end of 1994, the account contained losses of more than £200 million. As the unseen problem grew, Leeson requested further funds from his London headquarters, hoping to set up successful large trades that would wipe out the accumulated losses.[56] This desperate 'doubling up' of risk will be familiar to gamblers, but in this context the risk is magnified to catastrophic levels. Arguably, the edifice would have come crashing down sooner or later, but in this case the fatal damage was done on 17 January 1995 by the effects of the Kobe earthquake on the Japanese stock markets, on which Leeson had made a very large bet the day before. The rest of the story can be summarised quickly. The losses in the secret account quickly grew to more than £800 million and by the end of February 1995, some 233 years after its foundation, Barings was declared insolvent (the remains of the bank were taken over by the Dutch bank ING). Leeson disappeared, but was later found, arrested and sent back to Singapore, where he was tried and sentenced to jail.

Anyone can do it . . .

A number of writers have commented on the similarity between rogue trader episodes in different institutions. John Gapper[57] discusses research in psychology that shows how animals are more likely to gamble when under some form of stress: in more secure times, a low-risk choice is preferred. Human behaviour shows similar tendencies, together with a disproportionate inability to accept the discomfort of a loss. In a high-pressure environment like a trading floor, with the prospect of very high rewards for success and abrupt penalties for loss, it seems reasonable to speculate that the employing institution may – no doubt inadvertently – create a climate that can play a part in a rogue trader's headlong rush into disaster. A report by Aditya Chakrabortty in the *Guardian*[58] offered a guide to rogue trading, including the following suggestions:

- Anyone can do it – no special genius seems to be required.
- Come from the 'wrong' background – unlike high-fliers from the top universities, both Leeson and Kerviel came up through back-office experience, which later helped them to find and exploit weaknesses in control systems.
- Work on the newest (and so least well-understood) financial products.

A similar point is made by Gapper's quote from the advice given to its bank clients by a risk consultancy:[59]

Do you employ a likeable twenty-eight year old male index derivatives trader who has been promoted to the trading floor? Does he have a good understanding of your back- and middle-office systems, including where the weaknesses are? Does he have a decent finance- or business-related degree from a good (but not top end) university? If so, go and take a closer look at what he's doing.

Gapper also suggests that rogue traders seem to be much more likely to emerge in banks with a retail or commercial banking background that are relatively new to the world of investment banking/trading and are trying to make their mark in this new and unfamiliar world. As he suggested in his 2012 book, the major Wall Street investment banks have been largely unscathed by these problems over the last two decades.

However, in 2013 leading US bank JP Morgan was severely criticised by the US Senate in respect of large losses incurred following very large trades made in its London office,[60] not least because the problems appeared to be systemic, rather than exclusively to do with a rogue trader.[61] Any such impression might have been reinforced by the UK's Financial Conduct Authority (FCA) report in 2014 on the attempts by staff in six major banks to manipulate foreign exchange rates: the FCA report includes transcripts of crudely exultant messages between traders, sometimes even in collusion with traders in other institutions.

A similar point was made by the author of an article in the magazine *Rolling Stone*[62] in 2011, which criticised the use of the term 'rogue trader' by the industry and suggested that the problems are more deep-seated than just a few reckless young men:

> In the financial press you're called a 'rogue trader' if you're some overperspired 28 year-old newbie who bypasses internal audits and quality control to make a disastrous trade that could sink the company. But if you're a well-groomed 60 year-old CEO who uses his authority to ignore quality control and internal audits in order to make disastrous trades that could sink the company, you get a bailout, a bonus, and heroic treatment.

The employer's control systems are the key to minimising the risk of rogue trading, as regards both their design and their operation. Financial products are becoming more complex and systems more sophisticated, so that challenge grows in importance with each passing year. As the crisis of 2008 made chillingly clear, major global banks are strongly interlinked, to the extent that one bank's major embarrassment can easily become everyone's problem.

Tasks

1 Analyse the issue of rogue trading using Figure 13.2 on the stages of organisational control. Where do you think the failures occurred, and why?

2 Explain which of the six strategies of organisational control in Figure 13.3 appear to be used on the trading floors of investment banks.

3 Leeson and others were able to do the damage they did because they were both competent and trusted. To what extent do you think these are examples of a failure to delegate correctly? Explain your view with reference to the systematic approach outlined in the chapter (summarised in Figure 13.6).

Notes and references

1. Tannenbaum, A. S. *Control in Organizations,* McGraw-Hill (1968), p. 3.
2. Misselhorn, H. *Values, Power and Problem Solving,* MOD Associates, South Africa, 10 March 2014.
3. See, for example, Salaman, G. *Class and the Corporation,* Fontana (1981).
4. Child, J. *Organization: Contemporary Principles and Practice,* Blackwell (2005), p. 112.
5. Drummond, H. *Introduction to Organizational Behaviour,* Oxford University Press (2000), p. 25.
6. Cloke, K. and Goldsmith, J. *The End of Management and the Rise of Organizational Democracy,* Jossey-Bass (2002), p. 5.
7. Wilson, F. *Organizational Behaviour and Work: A Critical Introduction,* second edition, Oxford University Press (2004), p. 183.
8. Watson, T. J. *Organising and Managing Work,* second edition, Financial Times Prentice Hall (2006), pp. 55–6.
9. Zimmermann, J. 'The Different Centres of Control', *Mastering Management,* Financial Times/Pitman Publishing (1997), p. 21.
10. For examples, see Tibballs, G. *Business Blunders,* Robinson Publishing (1999).
11. 'Untapped Potential: The Barriers to Optimum Corporate Performance', Proudfoot Consulting, October 2002.
12. Ray, C.A. 'Corporate culture: The last frontier of control?', *Journal of Management Studies,* vol. 23, no. 3, 1986, pp. 287–97.
13. Egan, G. 'The Shadow Side', *Management Today,* September 1993, p. 37.
14. McKenna, R. *New Management,* Irwin/McGraw-Hill (1999), pp. 430–1.
15. Reeves, T. K. and Woodward, J. 'The Study of Managerial Control', in Woodward, J. (ed.) *Industrial Organization: Behaviour and Control,* Oxford University Press (1970).
16. Wilson, F. *Organizational Behaviour and Work: A Critical Introduction,* second edition, Oxford University Press (2004), p. 170.
17. Barker, J. R. 'Tightening the Iron Cage: Concertive Control in Self-Managing Teams', *Administrative Science Quarterly,* vol. 38, 1993, pp. 408–37.
18. Wright, B. M. and Barker, J. R. 'Assessing concertive control in the term environment', *Journal of Occupational and Organizational Psychology,* vol. 73, 2000, pp. 345–61.
19. Child, J. *Organization: Contemporary Principles and Practice,* Blackwell (2005).

20. Robbins, S. P. and Judge, T. A. *Organizational Behaviour,* thirteenth edition, Pearson Prentice Hall (2009), p. 485.

21. Caulkin, S. 'The Real Invisible Hand', *Management Today,* November 2011, pp. 40–4.

22. Weber, M. *The Theory of Social and Economic Organization,* Collier Macmillan (1964).

23. Etzioni, A. *A Comparative Analysis of Complex Organizations: On Power, Involvement and Their Correlates,* revised edition, Free Press (1975).

24. Watson, T. J. *Organising and Managing Work,* second edition, Financial Times Prentice Hall (2006), p. 201.

25. 'Sex and Power 2011', Equality and Human Rights Commission, August 2011.

26. Bloisi, W., Cook, C. W. and Hunsaker, P. L. *Management and Organisation Behaviour,* McGraw-Hill (2003).

27. French, J. P. and Raven, B. 'The Bases of Social Power', in Cartwright, D. and Zander, A. F. (eds) *Group Dynamics: Research and Theory,* third edition, Harper and Row (1968).

28. For an account of the use of power, see, for example, Guirdham, M. *Interactive Behaviour at Work,* third edition, Financial Times Prentice Hall (2002), ch. 9.

29. Parker, L. D. 'Shock of the New a Century On', *Professional Manager,* November 2005, pp. 34–5; and 'Mary Parker Follett, 'Prophet of Management', Thinkers Checklist No. 24, Chartered Management Institute, March 2002.

30. Handy, C. B. *Understanding Organizations,* fourth edition, Penguin (1993), p. 131.

31. Misselhorn, H. *Values, Power and Problem Solving,* MOD Associates, South Africa, 10 March 2014.

32. Hazlehurst, J. 'The Way We Work Now', *Management Today,* June 2013, pp. 47–9.

33. Mann, S. 'Oh I Heard It On the Grapevine', *Professional Manager,* July 1997, p. 33.

34. Kirwan-Taylor, H. 'People Who Can't Let Go', *Management Today,* March 2007, pp. 45–7.

35. Berry, A. J., Broadbent, J. and Otley, D. (eds) *Management Control: Theories, Issues and Practices,* Macmillan (1995), p. 77.

36. Hilton, A. 'People power', *Chartered Secretary,* September 2011, p. 14.

37. Owen, J. *The Death of Modern Management,* Wiley (2009), p. 230.

38. Yukl, G. *Leadership in Organizations,* seventh edition, Pearson (2010), p. 219.

39. Stewart, R. *Managing Today and Tomorrow,* Macmillan (1991).

40. Mills, D. Q. and Friesen, G. B. 'Empowerment', in Crainer, S. and Dearlove, D. (eds) *Financial Times Handbook of Management,* second edition, Financial Times Prentice Hall (2001), p. 323.

41. Tulgan, B. 'Winning the Talent Wars', in Crainer, S. and Dearlove, D. *Financial Times Handbook of Management,* second edition, Financial Times Prentice Hall (2001), p. 348.

42. Bushe, G. R. 'The Skills of Clear Leadership', *Manager, The British Journal of Administrative Management,* Summer 2009, p. 26. See also Bushe, G. R. *Clear Leadership: Sustaining real collaboration and partnership at work,* revised edition, Davies-Black (2010).

43. Moorcroft, R. 'Delegation, not relegation', *Manager, The British Journal of Administrative Management,* Autumn 2009, pp. 4–6.

44. Gracie, S. 'Delegate Don't Abdicate', *Management Today,* March 1999, p. 94.

45. Stewart, R. *The Reality of Management,* third edition, Butterworth–Heinemann (1999), p. 180.

46. Gratton, L. *The Democratic Enterprise,* Financial Times Prentice Hall (2004), pp. 188–9.

47. Jolly, R. 'The Indispensability Trap', *Management Today,* November 2012, pp. 48–52.

48. Wall, T. and Wood, S. 'Delegation's a Powerful Tool', *Professional Manager,* November 2002, p. 37.

49. Wheatley, R. 'Stress and Delegation', *Professional Manager,* vol. 12, no. 3, May 2003, p. 22 (The Whitehall II Study, HSE Contract Research, Report 422/2002).

50. Goldsmith, W. and Clutterbuck, D. *The Winning Streak Mark II,* Orion Business Books (1998), pp. 12–13.

51. http://m.bbc.co.uk/news/world-europe-29106135 (accessed 19 February 2015).

52. http://m.bbc.co.uk/news/uk-20338042 (accessed 19 February 2015).

53. http://www.ft.com/cms/s/2/cbff2b02-1bcc-11e1-8647-00144feabdc0.html#axzz23pNONkTP (accessed 19 February 2015).

54. http://news.bbc.co.uk/1/hi/business/the_economy/382707.stm (accessed 19 February 2015).

55. http://news.bbc.co.uk/1/hi/business/the_economy/382707.stm (accessed 19 February 2015).

56. http://news.bbc.co.uk/1/hi/business/the_economy/375259.stm (accessed 19 February 2015).

57. http://www.ft.com/cms/s/2/cbff2b02-1bcc-11e1-8647-00144feabdc0.html#axzz23pNONkTP (accessed 19 February 2015).

58. http://www.guardian.co.uk/commentisfree/2011/sep/19/brain-food-ubs-kweku-adoboli (accessed 19 February 2015).

59. Gapper, J. *How to be a Rogue Trader,* Penguin, Kindle edition, (2012), ch. 5.

60. http://www.ft.com/cms/s/0/ccb99df4-8d75-11e2-a0fd-00144feabdc0.html?siteedition=uk#axzz3SCMo0kcE (accessed 19 February 2015).

61. http://www.bloombergview.com/quicktake/the-london-whale (accessed 19 February 2015).

62. http://www.rollingstone.com/politics/blogs/taibblog/the-2-billion-ubs-incident-rogue-trader-my-ass-20110915 (accessed 19 February 2015).

CHAPTER 14
Strategy, corporate responsibility and ethics

The overall direction of an organisation is determined by the nature of its corporate strategy. Strategy links structure, the process of management and applications of organisational behaviour. Organisations play a major and increasingly important role in the lives of us all and have a responsibility to multiple stakeholders. The power and influence of a business organisation must be tempered by decisions relating to its broader social obligations and ethical responsibilities.

Learning outcomes

After completing this chapter you should have enhanced your ability to:

- explain the nature and importance of organisation strategy;
- assess the significance of organisational goals, objectives and policy;
- debate the significance of organisational ideologies, principles and values;
- review the concept and scope of corporate social responsibilities;
- detail approaches to the consideration of organisational values and ethics;
- evaluate the importance of ethics and corporate purpose and business ethics;
- review the nature and impact of codes of conduct or ethics.

Critical review and reflection

The most successful and enduring organisations are also those that give the greatest attention to the well-being of their staff and to their broader social and ethical responsibilities.

To what extent do YOU agree? What examples can YOU quote to support YOUR view? What would YOU say about YOUR university or organisation?

The importance of strategy

Underlying the effective management of people is the requirement for a clear understanding of the nature of the business that the organisation is engaged in and how best to provide customer or consumer satisfaction. We saw earlier (**Chapter 3**) that the context of the organisational setting is central to the application of organisational behaviour and the process of management. It is the interaction of people in order to achieve objectives that forms the basis of the particular organisation. An integral feature of the study of organisational behaviour is an understanding of the nature of corporate strategy for the formal organisation as a whole.

What is strategy?

Definitions of strategy vary. For example *Johnson et al.* view strategy in simple terms as about key issues for the future of organisations and the long-term direction of an organisation.[1] Some writers distinguish different terms and various levels of 'strategy', but **corporate strategy** is seen here as a generic term relating to the underlying purpose of the organisation and embracing links among structure, the process of management and applications of organisational behaviour. For some writers, such as *Andrews,* 'strategic management' is emerging as a more popular term than corporate strategy.

> *Strategic management is the pattern of major objectives, purposes or goals and essential policies or plans for achieving those goals, stated in such a way as to define what business the company is in or is to be in and the kind of company it is or is to be.*[2]

Strategy and structure

There is obviously a close relationship between strategy and organisation structure (**discussed in Chapter 11**). It is by means of the organisation's structure that its goals and objectives are attained. *Lynch* suggests that the nature of this relationship, and whether structure follows strategy or strategy follows structure, is not clear.

> *A major debate has been taking place over the last 30 years regarding the relationship between the strategy and the structure of the organisation. In the past, it was considered that the strategy was decided first and the organisation structure then followed . . . Recent research has questioned this approach and taken the view that strategy and structure are interrelated . . . Although it may not be possible to define which comes first, there is a need to ensure that strategy and structure are consistent with each other.*[3]

Strategy and people

Allen and Helms suggest that different types of reward practices may more closely complement different generic strategies and are significantly related to higher levels of perceived organisational performance.[4] According to *Stern,* it seems acceptable again to acknowledge the human factor in business: 'Niceness is back in vogue, at least for some of the time. People are talking about strategy not just in visionary terms but also in emotional ones.'[5] *Gratton* draws attention to people at the centre of business success and the importance of people-centred strategies.

> *Creating people-centred strategies is one of the means by which the organization balances the needs of the short term with those of the long term, as well as balancing financial capital with human potential. Creative and engaging people strategies have, at their core, an understanding of how the vision and business goals can be delivered through people, and of the specific actions which need to be taken in the short and longer term to bridge from reality to aspirations.*[6]

Strategy and culture

Schneider and Barsoux discuss the close link between culture and strategy and address such questions as: how does national culture affect strategy; how do different approaches to strategy reflect different underlying cultural assumptions; how do managers from different cultures respond to similar business environments; and in what ways does culture affect the content and process of decision-making? Among the examples quoted by Schneider and Barsoux are Japanese companies that challenge the Western view of strategic management and adopt a broader notion of strategy; managers from Nordic and Anglo countries who are less likely to see environments as uncertain; and managers from countries within Latin Europe or Asia who are likely to perceive greater uncertainty when faced with similar environments and perceive less control over what will happen.[7]

Critical review and reflection

Understandably, much attention is given to the importance of corporate strategy but not enough attention is normally given to the human factor or how the strategy impacts on people in the organisation.

To what extent can YOU identify with the strategy of YOUR university and/or organisation and how does it impact on YOUR actions or behaviour?

Organisational goals

The activities of the organisation are directed to the attainment of its goals. A goal is a future expectation, some desired future state, something the organisation is striving to accomplish. Goals are therefore an important feature of work organisations. **Organisational goals** are more specific than the function of an organisation. Goals will determine the nature of its inputs and outputs, the series of activities through which the outputs are achieved and interactions with its external environment. The extent to which an organisation is successful in attaining its goals is a basis for the evaluation of organisational performance and effectiveness.

To be effective, goals should be emphasised, stated clearly and communicated to all members of the organisation. At the individual level, the attainment of goals is the underlying influence on motivation. Movement towards greater delegation and empowerment through the hierarchy means that staff at all levels must be aware of their key tasks and actions, and exactly what is expected of them and their department/section. For example, goal-setting theory (**discussed in Chapter 7**) is widely recognised as a successful means of increasing work motivation and performance.[8]

According to *Reeves,* a few well-chosen aims in goal-setting can sharpen focus and boost productivity, but too many can lead to stress and even disaster. Clear objectives expressed as specific goals should improve performance, but measurement should not be confused with target-setting, and problems occur when there are too many targets and they are closely attached to individual performance.

> *The more freedom an individual has over the way their job is done, the higher the productivity and the bigger the rewards reaped by the firm for which they work. People need to know the objectives of their organisation and how their performance contributes to them. Employee engagement is much more likely to follow from autonomy than from a battery of management-dictated targets.[9]*

Objectives and policy

In addition to performing some function, all organisations have some incentive for their existence and for their operations. The goals of the organisation are translated into objectives and policy. Use of the two terms varies but objectives are seen here as the 'what' and policy as the 'how', 'where' and 'when' – the means that follow the objectives:

- **Objectives** set out more specifically the goals of the organisation, the aims to be achieved and the desired end results.
- **Policy** is developed within the framework of objectives. It provides the basis for decision-making and the course of action to follow in order to achieve objectives.

Choice of objectives is an essential part of corporate strategy and the decision-making process involving future courses of action. Objectives may be just implicit, but formal, explicit definition will assist communications and reduce misunderstandings, and provide more meaningful criteria for evaluating organisational performance. Clearly stated, good objectives can help provide unity of direction and aid employee engagement and commitment. However, objectives should not be stated in such a way that they detract from the recognition of possible new opportunities, potential danger areas, the initiative of staff or the need for innovation or change.

Policy is a guideline for organisational action and the implementation of goals and objectives. Policy is translated into rules, plans and procedures; it relates to all activities of the organisation and all levels of the organisation. Clearly stated, policy can help reinforce main functions of the organisation, make for consistency and reduce dependency on actions of individual managers. Policy clarifies roles and responsibilities of managers and other members of staff and provides guidelines for managerial behaviour. Some policy decisions are directly influenced by external factors – for example, government legislation on equal opportunities and diversity.

Corporate guidelines

Whatever the type of organisation, formulation of objectives and policy is a necessary function in every organisation and an integral part of the process of management. In terms of a systems approach, the objectives of an organisation are related to the input–conversion–output cycle. In order to achieve its objectives and satisfy its goals, the organisation takes inputs from the environment, through a series of activities transforms or converts these inputs into outputs and returns them to the environment as inputs to other systems. The organisation operates within a dynamic setting and success in achieving its goals will be influenced by a multiplicity of interactions with the environment (*see* Figure 14.1).

Together, objectives and policy provide corporate guidelines for the operations and management of the organisation. Clearly defined and agreed objectives are the first stage in the design of organisation structure and help facilitate systems of interaction and communication between different parts of the organisation. A commonly used mnemonic to summarise the characteristics of good objectives is 'SMART':

Specific – clear, detailed and understandable as to what is required
Measurable – to monitor and measure progress towards achievement of the objective
Achievable – challenging but obtainable by a competent person
Realistic – relevant to the goals of the organisation with a focus on outcomes of achievement
Timebound – outcomes to be achieved within an agreed time scale.

But note the observations from *Dryburgh:*

Figure 14.1 A systems view of organisational goals and objectives

Why SMART objectives are really DUMB

Alastair Dryburgh

We have all read about how objectives should be SMART – Specific, Measurable, Achievable, Realistic and Timed. This is well meaning but profoundly limiting. Let's take the points one by one and see where they lead us.

- **Specific.** Why is this a good thing, when it excludes objectives such as 'insanely great technology' (Apple), 'a totally new way of seeing' (Picasso) or 'customer service that gets customers raving about how good it is' (anyone? I wish someone would)?
- **Measurable.** Same problem as specific. Mediocrity is easy to measure, but greatness is harder – you know it when you see it.
- **Achievable and Realistic.** This is where the real problem occurs. I don't know, cannot know, how much I can achieve. If I want to set myself a goal that I know I can achieve, I have to set something that is much less than I could achieve. That's a recipe for mediocrity, at best. The worst thing that can happen with such a goal is that we do meet it, and we stop short of what we could have achieved. Consider instead the value of an impossible goal like 'be the world's greatest X'. It helps and inspires us. It sets a direction. We may never get there, but every day we know what to do to move closer.
- **Timed.** This creates the dangerous illusion that we make changes in order to arrive at a steady state at some defined point in the future. That's not how the world works – it keeps changing, and we need to keep changing with it.

SMART objectives are part of an obsolete management paradigm that assumes that we know what the future will look like (much like the present) and know how we will survive and thrive in that future. If Mother Nature had used SMART objectives instead of natural selection, we would still be no more than slightly improved monkeys.[10]

Organisational ideologies and principles

The goals of the organisation may be pursued in accordance with an underlying ideology, or philosophy, based on beliefs, values and attitudes. This **organisational ideology** determines the 'culture' of the organisation and provides a set of principles that govern the overall conduct of the organisation's operations, codes of behaviour, the management of people and dealings with other organisations.[11] These sets of principles may be recognised and implemented informally as 'accepted conventions' of the organisation or they may be stated formally in writing.

Forty years ago, *Brech* wrote about the ideology of an organisation related to the idea of both an ethical foundation and an organisational or operational foundation:

- **Ethical foundation** embodies the basic principles that govern the external and internal relations of the organisation. External relations concern standards of fair trading and relations with, for example, customers, suppliers and the general public. Internal relations are concerned with fair standards of employment and relations with members of the organisation, including authorised union representatives.
- **Organisational or operational foundation** is concerned with the structure, operation and conduct of the activities of the organisation. External aspects relate to, for example, methods of trading and channels of distribution. Internal aspects include methods of production, use of equipment and managerial practices relating to organisational performance, productivity and profitability.[12]

In recent years organisations have given growing attention to a set of stated corporate values displayed prominently for all to see. *Lucas* questions whether such grand statements of corporate principles really mean anything and concludes that they actually have a point and values can be used with success: 'A set of values is obviously a nice thing for an organisation to have; something to pin on the notice board. But for those organisations that have learned to walk the talk, deeply embedded values can attract the right people, underpin the business in times of crisis and provide direction for the future.'[13]

Cloke and Goldsmith contend that organisations can increase their integrity, coherence and integration, and improve their performance by reaching consensus on shared values. They can bolster value-based relationships by recognising and encouraging behaviours that uphold their values; communicate and publicise their values, and encourage individual and team responsibility for implementing them; and develop methods for monitoring compliance with values, providing feedback and identifying potential conflicts of interest. Most importantly, consensus on shared values means organisations can accomplish these goals without moralising, preaching, excusing or imposing their values on others.[14]

An organisation's 'signature' ideology

Certain aspects of an organisation's philosophy may be so dominant that they become the 'hallmark' of that organisation and place constraints on other areas or forms of activities. For example, the highest-quality hallmark of Rolls-Royce cars would presumably prevent entry into the cheaper mass-production market. With the Walt Disney Company, quality service is embedded deeply within its corporate culture.

Gratton refers to 'signature' processes of highly successful companies that are a direct embodiment of the history and values of the company and its top executive team, and their potential to create the energy to drive high performance. These signature processes, which differ significantly from general views of best practice, are acceptable within the companies in which they develop because of their association with the passion and value of the executive team, and are part of the fabric and ways of behaving.[15] A clear example of the point made by Gratton is Apple, with a signature that has survived the ultimate demise of its founder.

Critical review and reflection

Successful and enduring organisations may well have a clear ideology and idealistic motivation but members of staff are more likely to be committed to the goals and performance of the organisation by job security, high wages and good working conditions.

To what extent do YOU think core ideology and shared values are the hallmark of a successful organisation? Can YOU identify with the idea of a core ideology in YOUR university?

Vision and mission statements

It has become increasingly popular for an organisation to produce a **mission statement** and/or its 'vision' that sets out the purpose and general direction for the organisation. There is sometimes an apparent uncertainty over the distinction between the terms 'mission' and 'vision', which tend to be used interchangeably. It seems to be generally accepted that the vision provides the overall frame of reference of what the organisation would like to reach and how it will look. Within this vision the mission statement defines what the organisation aims to achieve, and its core business and activities.

Value of mission statements

The desire to identify with as many stakeholders as possible means that many mission statements are all-embracing with bland and abstract wording. The value of a mission statement is dependent, however, upon the extent to which it is understood and accepted throughout the organisation, and translated in meaningful terms to all members of staff including those at the operational level. A mission statement is only likely to be of any value if the organisation actually practises what it preaches. The purpose (strategy) and guiding principles of the John Lewis Partnership are set out below.

The John Lewis Partnership – defining principles

- **Purpose** – The Partnership's ultimate purpose is the happiness of all its members, through their worthwhile and satisfying employment in a successful business. Because the Partnership is owned in trust for its members, they share the responsibilities of ownership as well as its rewards of profit, knowledge and power.
- **Power** – Our Partners are able to influence their business at all levels of the Partnership through the democratic structure and the representative bodies which are defined in our **constitution**. Power in the Partnership is shared between three governing authorities: the **Partnership Council**, the **Partnership Board** and the **Chairman**.
- **Profit** – The Partnership aims to make sufficient profit from its trading operations to sustain its commercial vitality and finance its continued development, to enable it to undertake other activities consistent with its ultimate purpose and to distribute a share of those profits each year to its members. Our success relies on the collaboration and contribution of our Partners who receive a share of profits in the form of Partnership Bonus.
- **Knowledge** – We provide our Partners with the knowledge they need to carry out their responsibilities effectively as co-owners of the Partnership.
- **Members** – The Partnership aims to employ people of ability and integrity who are committed to working together and to supporting its Principles. Relationships are based on mutual respect and courtesy, with as much equality between its members as differences of responsibility permit. The Partnership aims to recognise their individual contributions and reward them fairly.
- **Customers** – The Partnership aims to deal honestly with its customers and secure their loyalty and trust by providing outstanding choice, value and service.
- **Business relationships** – The Partnership aims to conduct all its business relationships with integrity and courtesy and to honour scrupulously every business agreement.
- **The community** – The Partnership aims to obey the spirit as well as the letter of the law and to contribute to the wellbeing of the communities where it operates.

The profit objective – not a sufficient criterion

For business organisations, the objective of profit maximisation is undoubtedly of great importance but it is not, by itself, a sufficient criterion for effective management. There are many other considerations and motivations that influence assumptions underlying the economic theory of the firm. The meaning of 'profit maximisation' is not, by itself, very clear. Consideration has to be given to the range and quality of an organisation's products or services, and to environmental influences. Reducing attention to longer-term 'investments', such as quality and after-sales service, research and development, sales promotion, management development and employment conditions of staff, may increase profitability in the short term but is likely to jeopardise future growth and development, and possibly even the ultimate survival of the organisation.

This argument can be clarified to some extent by redefining the business goal as the maximisation of owner (shareholder) value, instead of 'profit'. The concept of value is defined as incorporating the short, medium and long term through the process of discounting (reducing the value of) future cash flows back to a present value. Thus managers seeking to maximise value have good reason to make investments in business activities that will yield profit in the future, even if the costs are immediate and the benefits are some years away.

A business organisation has to provide some commodity or service by which it contributes to the economic and/or social needs of the community. It also has broader social responsibilities to society (discussed later below). Profit can be seen as the incentive for an organisation to carry out its activities effectively. Profit does at least provide some broad measure of effectiveness and highlights the difficulty in evaluating the effectiveness of not-for-profit organisations, such as NHS hospitals, prisons or universities.

Fallacy of the single objective

The reality is that managers are usually faced with the challenge of several, often competing and/or conflicting objectives. *Drucker* has referred to the fallacy of the single objective of a business. The search for the one, right objective is not only unlikely to be productive, but also certain to harm and misdirect the business enterprise.

> *To emphasize only profit, for instance, misdirects managers to the point where they may endanger the survival of the business. To obtain profit today they tend to undermine the future . . . To manage a business is to balance a variety of needs and goals . . . the very nature of business enterprise requires multiple objectives which are needed in every area where performance and results directly and vitally affect the survival and prosperity of the business.*[16]

Drucker goes on to suggest eight key areas in which objectives should be set in terms of performance and results:

1. **Market standing** – for example, share of market standing; range of products and markets; distribution; pricing; customer loyalty and satisfaction.
2. **Innovation** – for example, innovations to reach marketing goals; developments arising from technological advancements; new processes and improvements in major areas of organisational activity.
3. **Productivity** – for example, optimum use of resources; use of techniques such as operational research to help decide alternative courses of action; the ratio of 'contributed value' to total revenue.
4. **Physical and financial resources** – such as plant, machines, offices and replacement of facilities; supply of capital and budgeting; planning for the money needed; provision of supplies.
5. **Profitability** – for example, profitability forecasts and anticipated time scales; capital investment policy; yardsticks for measurement of profitability.
6. **Manager performance and development** – for example, the direction of managers and setting up their jobs; the structure of management; the development of future managers.
7. **Worker performance and attitude** – for example, union relations; the organisation of work; employee relations.
8. **Public responsibility** – for example, demands made upon the organisation, such as by law or public opinion; responsibilities to society and the public interest.

Critical review and reflection

The single, most important objective for the business organisation is profit maximisation, ideally combined with high monetary rewards for members of staff. This is the bottom line and the only realistic criterion by which organisational effectiveness can be judged.

How would YOU attempt to challenge this assertion? How would YOU define the single, most important objective for a non-profit organisation such as YOUR university?

Organisational values and behaviour

Gidoomal maintains that we have taken it for granted that the ethical values and norms of society are there but they need to be spelled out.

> *It's almost a pity to say we need training in ethics. We should be brought up with it through the education system and the values taught at home and church. When you learn ethics and values as a kid you have learnt them for life. We have to be proud of our integrity and blow the whistle when things don't go right.*

Gidoomal also maintains that the ethical business dimension cannot be separated from the diversity issue (**discussed in Chapter 4**) and, while acknowledging that more and more companies now have diversity policies, wonders if they are just lying on a shelf gathering dust.[17]

The Institute of Chartered Secretaries and Administrators draws attention to the importance of creating a culture of integrity and raising awareness of the benefits of ethical behaviour within organisations.

> *Ethical behaviour touches every part of the organisation . . . in terms of a licence to operate such as Health and Safety, to control for example anti-bribery laws, and the most important piece – creating a culture with the expectation that you will do it right.[18]*

Ethical leadership

The importance of ethical behaviour, integrity and trust calls into question the extent to which managers should attempt to change the underlying values and beliefs of individual followers. (**See discussion on transformational leadership in Chapter 10.**) For example, *Yukl* discusses the controversy whereby some writers contend that this type of leader influence is clearly unethical even when intended to benefit followers as well as the organisation. A contrary view is that leaders have an important responsibility to implement major changes when necessary to ensure survival and effectiveness. Large-scale change would not be successful without some changes in member beliefs and perceptions.

> *The traditional perspective is that managers in business organizations are agents who represent the interest of the owners in achieving economic success for the organization. From this perspective, ethical leadership is satisfied by maximizing economic outcomes that benefit owners while not doing anything strictly prohibited by laws and moral standards . . . A very different perspective is that managers should serve multiple stakeholders inside and outside the organization.[19]*

According to a recent report from the Institute of Leadership and Management, despite the high level of public focus on ethics, managers are still placed under increased pressure from facing frequent ethical dilemmas at work. Although the majority of managers say their organisations have a statement of values, it is clear that they are not effective enough at influencing behaviour. Values need to be linked with strategy.

> *Building a set of values that do not link with targets is an ineffective way to influence behaviour. If values are contrary or irrelevant to the business goals, managers find themselves pulled in different directions trying to achieve both. But when values tie into the strategic objectives of an organisation, the way people are expected to behave and the goals they are required to achieve work in tandem.*[20]

The core values of Red Carnation Hotels are set out below.

Red Carnation Hotels – core values

Our core values reflect what is really important and matters to us as a company and group of individuals. They are the solid foundation and main principles of our company culture. By consistently working hard to maintain our values, we endeavour to preserve what makes Red Carnation Hotels so special – a sincere and deep commitment to each other, our guests whom we serve every day and the communities within which we work and live.

To give personalised, warm and consistently exceptional service We appreciate the myriad of choices and alternatives our customers have to choose from, and therefore set the bar high for ourselves, to provide the highest quality services and products we possibly can. We constantly challenge ourselves to update and enhance. Innovation, constant training and refurbishment help create an environment whereby our guests and our employees refer to our properties as their home from home.

To value, respect and support each other We believe that care comes from caring and so provide a level of care for our team members that inspires by example, generates trust, respect, open and honest communication and appreciation.

To create positive, memorable experiences for every guest We work hard to meet or exceed our customers' expectations on every visit or touch point they have with us. By delighting and satisfying our customers, we ensure the longevity of our business and employment for our team. By serving our customers with very personable, proficient, friendly, competent service, and listening to their needs we create memorable and distinctive experiences as well as loyal, returning guests.

To care about and give back to our local communities We recognize and appreciate our responsibility to be active participants in our local communities. We believe in trying to also give of our time to community and service organizations. We believe that it is important to give something back and make a difference. In a world of shrinking natural resources, we must endeavour to conserve, reuse and care about those around us.

All of our hotels make it an ongoing priority to support and contribute positively to a variety of charitable organizations within their respective communities. The charities we support in England include The Starlight Foundation, Great Ormond Street Children's Hospital, Action Against Hunger, the National Autistic Society and the Cystic Fibrosis Trust. In Geneva we have provided help for The Red Cross and in South Africa we support the Nelson Mandela Children's Fund, and our bath amenities are purchased from Charlotte Rhys, a Founding Member of the Proudly South African Organisation, dedicated to the support of disadvantaged women and men in South Africa. Recycling efforts continue to be reviewed and improved upon wherever possible.

Our guests, staff, and suppliers have been wonderfully sympathetic to our aims, assisting us with their wholehearted support, and we would like to send a sincere 'thank you' to every one of them. While we believe our collective contributions do make a difference we are not content to sit back, and constantly challenge ourselves to increase our involvement with the global community. We welcome ideas and input from our customers, staff and suppliers.

Jonathan Raggett
Managing Director, Red Carnation Hotels

Corporate social responsibilities

Organisations play a major and increasingly important role in the lives of us all, especially with the growth of large-scale business and expanding globalisation. The decisions and actions of management in organisations have an increasing impact on individuals, other organisations and the community. Organisations make a contribution to the quality of life and to the well-being of the community. The power and influence that many business organisations now exercise should be tempered, therefore, by an attitude of responsibility by management.

Organisational survival is dependent upon a series of continual interactions and exchanges between the organisation and its environment that give rise to a number of broader responsibilities to society in general. These broader responsibilities, which are both internal and external to the organisation, are usually referred to as **corporate social responsibility** (CSR).

Growing attention to social responsibilities

There has been growing attention given to the subject of CSR and an increasing amount of literature on the subject and on a new work ethic. According to The Chartered Management Institute, CSR is now an important and increasingly specialised aspect of strategy and management. Over recent decades, it has become a necessity rather than a choice, due to:

- legal changes that have made some aspects of CSR compulsory;
- increased public interest in environmental and ethical issues;
- a convincing business case linking CSR to better performance;
- shareholder pressure on businesses to show they operate ethically.

CSR is concerned with building integrity and fairness into corporate policies, strategies and decision-making. CSR policies can benefit an organisation by developing and enhancing relationships with customers and suppliers, help to attract and retain a strong workforce, and improve a business's reputation and standing. To be effective, it must be: embedded into everyone's thinking and behaviour, particularly that of leaders; integrated into organisational culture, policies and procedures; and built into organisational operations and activities at all levels.[21]

Pearce suggests that many companies were involved in CSR simply because it was the right thing to do, but the story now is very different.

The pure motives behind and areas of action in regard to corporate social responsibility have been blurred. There are now so many strands, aspects, viewpoints and stakeholders involved in CSR that it can be difficult for companies to get a grip on precisely what it is they are, or should, be doing. This is not something that can be shrugged off, or put on the back burner – those companies that fail to adequately address CSR issues could be putting themselves in the line of fire.[22]

Critical review and reflection

An NHS Trust chairperson was heavily criticised for maintaining that the primary loyalty of doctors was owed to their employers and that their duty to patients came third, after themselves.

What is YOUR reaction to this point of view? Do YOU believe owing first loyalty to YOUR organisation is such a bad thing?

Management and organisational behaviour in action case study
Corporate social responsibility: Graham McWilliam, BSkyB

CSR is good for brands

It always strikes me as surprising, when talking to my peers at other companies, how many of them talk about the substantial time they have to spend lobbying their colleagues to take CSR seriously.

Maybe one of the problems is the phrase itself – corporate social responsibility – which implies a commitment without a return; something you have to do, but from which you can derive little value. And why, in tough economic times, would companies prioritise something that doesn't help the bottom line? Why indeed.

At Sky, we look at things a little differently. We don't talk about CSR. Instead, we concentrate on long-term value creation, grounded in a focus on what really counts for customers. Looking at things from this angle, it makes perfect commercial sense to act responsibly day to day and to contribute broadly to the communities around you.

After all, like it or not, your brand isn't only created by what you say about yourself. It's built on what others say and think about you, which itself is built on their experience of what you do. For good or bad, that influences customer loyalty, employee engagement, investor sentiment and the regulatory and political climate.

This point is increasingly important in business. All those stakeholder groups now have fast and easy access to a wealth of information and commentary about your company, from news reports to social media conversations. Segmenting your audiences and controlling the message is becoming an impossible task. And, anyway, all the research shows people are more likely to trust what they hear through their informal networks than what they hear directly from you.

Don't just say it, do it

So, focus first on doing, rather than saying, the right things. Set it all in the context of long-term value creation, and you'll find it's no longer an unwanted responsibility to be discharged, but a positive opportunity to build trust, encourage reappraisal and open up new commercial avenues.

At Sky, we're proud of the positive contribution that our business makes to the communities around us, from bringing choice in TV to consumers, to the jobs that have been created for the 16,500 people who work at Sky.

But we want to do more, because we know it's what our customers and employees expect of us, and because we know that it drives positive reappraisal of our brand by those who haven't yet joined Sky.

So we've chosen three areas which we know our customers care about and where we think we can make the biggest difference: using our relationships with 10 million families across the UK and Ireland to inspire action on climate change, encourage participation in sport and open up the arts to more people.

How CSR creates opportunity

Our work in sport, for example, builds on our strong history and credibility in sports broadcasting to get more people active. Within this, our partnership with British Cycling takes a three-pronged approach: support for the GB cycling team, enabling our elite cyclists to be the very best they can be; the creation of Team Sky, the UK's only professional road racing team, to inspire a whole new generation of cyclists to get on their bikes; and Sky Ride, a series of mass summer cycling events across the UK, free to all and free of traffic, which more than 200,000 people took part in last year.

The long-term commercial benefits of such activity are clear to us at Sky, but are equally easy to see at a large and growing number of other successful UK companies. For such brands, CSR isn't about responsibility. It's about opportunity, creating sustainable value over the long term. And, if you want to be around for years to come, that's hard to argue with.

Source: Management Today, May 2011. p. 69. www.managementtoday.co.uk. Reproduced with permission.

Tasks

1. To what extent do you associate CSR as a commitment without a return?
2. Discuss Sky's approach of CSR as central to strategy and long-term value creation.
3. Give your own examples of how CSR can create opportunity and commercial benefits for an organisation.

Organisational stakeholders

Social responsibilities are often viewed in terms of **organisational stakeholders** – that is, those individuals or groups who have an interest in and/or are affected by the goals, operations or activities of the organisation or the behaviour of its members. Stakeholders include a wide variety of potential interests and may be considered under a number of headings. For example, drawing on the work of *Donaldson and Preston,*[23] *Rollinson* suggests a comprehensive view of stakeholders in terms of the potential harm and benefits approach.[24] See Figure 14.2.

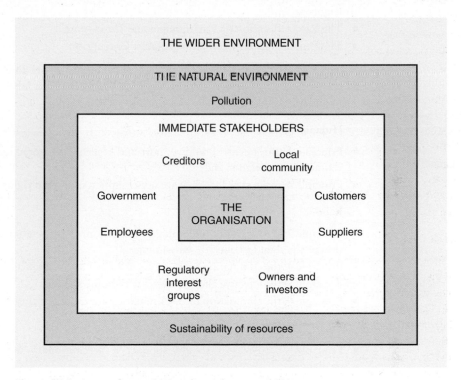

Figure 14.2 Areas of organisational social responsibilities

Source: Rollinson, D. *Organisational Behaviour and Analysis,* fourth edition, Financial Times Prentice Hall (2008), p. 56, Pearson Education Ltd.

A blurred distinction

Arguably, there is still something of blurred distinction between the exercise of a genuine social responsibility, on the one hand, and actions taken in pursuit of good business practice and the search for organisational efficiency on the other. One approach is that attention to social responsibilities arises out of a moral or ethical motivation and the dictates of conscience – that is, out of genuine philanthropic objectives. An alternative approach is that the motivation is through no more than enlightened self-interest and the belief that, in the long term, attention to social responsibilities is simply good business sense. In practice, it is a matter of degree and balance, of combining sound economic management with an appropriate concern for broader responsibilities to society.

The UN Global Compact

The United Nations Global Compact is a call to companies to align strategies and operations with universal principles on human rights, labour, environment and anti-corruption, and to take actions that advance societal goals. The UN Global Compact is a leadership platform for the development, implementation and disclosure of responsible corporate policies and practices. Launched in 2000, it is the world's largest voluntary corporate sustainability initiative, with over 12,000 signatories from business and key stakeholder groups based in 145 countries (**www.unglobalcompact.org**).

The UN Global Compact's ten principles in the areas of human rights, labour, the environment and anti-corruption enjoy universal consensus and are derived from:

- The Universal Declaration of Human Rights
- The International Labour Organization's Declaration on Fundamental Principles and Rights at Work
- The Rio Declaration on Environment and Development
- The United Nations Convention Against Corruption

The UN Global Compact asks companies to embrace, support and enact, within their sphere of influence, a set of core values in the areas of human rights, labour standards, the environment and anti-corruption:

Human rights

- **Principle 1:** Businesses should support and respect the protection of internationally proclaimed human rights; and
- **Principle 2:** make sure that they are not complicit in human rights abuses.

Labour

- **Principle 3:** Businesses should uphold the freedom of association and the effective recognition of the right to collective bargaining;
- **Principle 4:** the elimination of all forms of forced and compulsory labour;
- **Principle 5:** the effective abolition of child labour; and
- **Principle 6:** the elimination of discrimination in respect of employment and occupation.

Environment

- **Principle 7:** Businesses should support a precautionary approach to environmental challenges;
- **Principle 8:** undertake initiatives to promote greater environmental responsibility; and
- **Principle 9:** encourage the development and diffusion of environmentally friendly technologies.

Anti-corruption

- **Principle 10:** Businesses should work against corruption in all its forms, including extortion and bribery.[25]

Critical review and reflection

In George Bernard Shaw's play *Pygmalion* (which later became the basis for the very successful musical *My Fair Lady*), Eliza Doolittle's father complains that he is too poor to afford 'morals'.

In a similar vein, do YOU think that ideas of business ethics and corporate social responsibility can be argued to be mainly of relevance to larger corporations, because only they have the financial and other resources to behave in this way?

Values and ethics

The question of values and ethics in business has been thrown into sharp focus in the years following the financial crisis of 2007–8. Since the dramatic events of autumn 2008 that followed the collapse of prominent US investment bank Lehman Brothers, many of the major economies in the world have faced an extended period of low or negative growth, with rising unemployment and very low levels of business and consumer confidence, all of which made an early resumption of growth less likely. Some economists have published books suggesting that we must learn to accept, or even embrace, a future with much lower economic growth.[26]

Many governments have had to attempt to rein in public spending, with growing levels of resentment and disillusionment in some countries. In a number of parts of Europe, this has been linked with increased support for new political parties with populist agendas, whose manifestos often reflect a sense of unease at the effects of globalisation, together with a view that governments should intervene more, rather than less, to protect the interests of ordinary people. Unsurprisingly, given the origins of the 2008 crisis, bankers – or at least highly paid senior managers in global banks – were the initial focus of public opprobrium, but dissatisfaction with business and with capitalism has spread more broadly.

One consequence has been a growing focus in political discussions on inequality or, more specifically, on the way in which greatly increased rewards for the so-called 'super rich' have led to growing inequality in recent decades. An example of this was the remarkable sales success in 2014 of French economist Thomas Piketty's 700-page volume *Capital in the Twenty-First Century*, which led to lively discussions in the media about the causes and implications of these developments.[27] A similar sense of scepticism about the turn-of-the-century enthusiasm for lightly regulated business was reflected in Harvard philosopher Michael Sandel's 2012 book,[28] which warned of the risks of allowing markets – with their logic of buying and selling – to spread into areas beyond the commercial supply of goods and services.

A further trend in recent years has been the increasingly insistent demands that businesses – and particularly multinational businesses with global operations – should pay 'fair' levels of tax to the countries in which they sell products and services, rather than actively seeking to minimise the amounts due.

Moral compass

Opinions as to exactly *what* went wrong in 2008 varied widely – and still do. For many, the problem was one of inadequate regulation – rules that are insufficiently detailed and/or ineffectively applied. However, commentators across the political spectrum have sometimes also alluded to a lack of moral awareness in business and public affairs – the absence of an intuitive sense of right and wrong (sometimes referred to as a **moral compass**). These two aspects of ethical business will be discussed in greater detail later, but it should already be clear that these questions can be complex. In this section, we outline the influence of ethical considerations in terms of the actions taken by the organisation in pursuit of its strategic objectives, together with the ethical implications of interpersonal interaction, both inside the organisation and between individuals across organisational boundaries.

Ethics and business

Ethics is concerned with the study of morality: practices and activities that are considered to be importantly right or wrong, together with the rules that govern those activities and the values to which those activities relate.[29] It seeks to understand what makes good things good, for example, in ways that can be generalised to other similar cases. Business ethics can be seen as an example of applied ethics – just as medical ethics is about the application of general ethics to the human activity called medicine, business ethics seeks to explore the implications of general ethics for the conduct of business. This apparently obvious point is important: by taking this stance, one rejects the view that moral principles have no bearing on business, or that 'the business of business is business', as the common saying has it.

This is not to say that it is easy, or uncontroversial, to apply ethics to business; on the contrary, this fast-growing subject is characterised by a range of sharply contrasting views. Some of this controversy is inherent in ethics itself – as will be discussed below, there is no single clear view of how to judge good and bad, and this must impact on any application such as business ethics. This particular application of ethics, however, is also complicated by the fact that ethics mainly deals with good or bad conduct on the part of individuals, resulting in possible difficulties in applying these ideas to impersonal corporate entities like companies. Is it appropriate to regard companies as if they were individual people and, if not, what allowances should be made? Or, can the subject be satisfactorily seen as relating to the conduct of individuals as employees of businesses? Clearly, for very small businesses, the two views merge into one, but for larger, corporate entities, the position is more complex.

A discussion of ethics in business organisations has to take account of the purpose of the organisation, as well as its strategy: what it is trying to achieve, usually in competition with other similar businesses. These two factors are important because of their influence on what the organisation chooses to do and thus on the consequences for people inside and outside the organisation. A decision by an airline, for example, to pursue a low-cost strategy will have significant impacts on what is required of its staff and how well that business fares in the market. A successful implementation of such a strategy may mean fast growth, with attractive career development opportunities for some staff, but also more negative consequences for others. On the other hand, the failure of a strategy can lead to the end of the organisation as an independent entity, with more widespread adverse consequences for the organisation's people.

Critical review and reflection

Of course guidelines on values and business ethics are important, but in times of economic recession organisation survival and obligations to the workforce should take precedence. It is understandable if a blind eye is turned to bribery and corruption.

To what extent do YOU believe such a view can ever be justified?

Ethics and CSR

One illustration of the complexity of issues in business ethics is the diversity of opinion on the issue of CSR (discussed above). On one side of the debate are those who would share *Milton Friedman*'s view that the social responsibility of business is to make as much money as possible for the shareholders, within the law and the rules of the game (fair competition, no deception or fraud and so on).[30] This **shareholder-centred view** sees the directors of a company as agents of the owners, who are duty bound to act so as to maximise the interests of those owners, this being taken as the reason for owners having made the investment in the first place.

A more recent development of this general approach is that of *Sternberg* who proposes a teleological view of business ethics, based upon the pursuit of the business purpose – that of maximising long-term owner wealth by selling products and services.[31] Actions by a firm that are consistent with this aim and that satisfy the additional tests of common decency (e.g.

refraining from stealing, cheating, coercion and so on) and distributive justice (i.e. ensuring that rewards are proportional to contributions made) are ethical. Actions that fail any one of these three tests are, in this model, unethical.

At the other end of the spectrum are some forms of **stakeholder theory,** which emphasise a much broader set of social responsibilities for business. *Cannon* suggests that:

> *There exists an implicit or explicit contract between business and the community in which it operates. Business is expected to create wealth; supply markets; generate employment; inno- vate and produce a sufficient surplus to sustain its activities and improve its competitiveness while contributing to the maintenance of the community in which it operates. Society is expected to provide an environment in which business can develop and prosper, allowing investors to earn returns while ensuring that the stakeholders and their dependants can enjoy the benefits of their involvement without fear of arbitrary or unjust action. The interdepend- ence between society and business cannot be overstated.*[32]

Differing assumptions about a business

The two perspectives provide very different views of how a business should act, because of their differing assumptions concerning what a business is *for*. In the shareholder-centred view, a business is principally for the shareholders and its actions should mainly be judged on the criterion of maximising their interests. In the stakeholder view quoted above, a business is for its stakeholders (who are potentially a very large and diverse group) and its actions should be designed to balance stakeholder interests. From the point of view of business ethics – the study of good and bad conduct in business – this distinction is very important. The use of company resources to support a local community project, for example, might be seen as admirable in the stakeholder view but unethical in the shareholder-centred view, in that it would be a misap- plication of funds that belong to the owners (unless, of course, such an investment could be shown to be consistent with the shareholders' best interests).

'Goodness' of proposed action

Each of the two approaches adopts a different yardstick for judging the 'goodness' of a pro- posed action by a company. In the shareholder-centred view, the action has to be shown to be consistent with the duty of maximising owner wealth, which is conceptually relatively simple, but which necessarily involves assumptions concerning the likely effect of the proposed action (or, more precisely, the difference between taking the proposed action and not taking it). In the stakeholder view (or, at least in those versions of the stakeholder view that emphasise an accountability to stakeholders), the task of management is to balance stakeholder interests. However, managers seeking to do this – often in the face of loud opposing claims from the various interests – will very quickly encounter the practical problem of how that 'balance' should be defined and recognised.

Although difficult to reconcile in practice, the two approaches are not completely incom- patible: to a stakeholder theorist, shareholders count as one type of stakeholder, but not the only type to which duties are owed by the firm. Likewise, *Sternberg* acknowledges the impor- tance of understanding and remaining aware of the various stakeholder groups and of actively managing relationships between the company and these groups, because doing so is likely to be consistent with maximising owner wealth. As she points out, however, 'taking account' of something is importantly different from 'being accountable' to it.[33]

Intelligent self-interest

It is also worth emphasising that a company seeking to maximise its owners' long-term wealth may well do very good things for its 'stakeholders', not necessarily through any direct intent but in pursuit of its main duty. Providing customers with excellent products and ser- vices is the central example, of course, but this form of intelligent self-interest may also – for example – drive a firm to build strong, trusting relationships with its suppliers and distributors (because it will be better off as a result), or an attractive working environment for its employees (because it wishes to recruit and keep the best, in order to be able to compete more effectively).

Even beyond its immediate commercial relationships, an intelligently self-interested company may deliberately set out to build strong relationships with other stakeholders, or to take a principled stance on an issue such as the use of child labour, because to do so is to maximise owner value. The 'value' in question is not just next year's dividends, but refers to the value of the investment as a whole and thus obliges the management to think long term as well as short term and to consider the impact of company actions as broadly as possible.

Offshoring example

By way of an illustration of the two approaches, we could imagine how a UK-based company might think about an opportunity to 'offshore' part of its operation to a lower-cost Anglophone country. The shareholder-centred view would place emphasis on the unit cost savings to be achieved by moving the operation to a lower-cost area, provided that the required quality of service can be maintained. Other things being equal, lower unit costs obviously allow higher margins and improved rewards to shareholders. However, the assessment would also take into account the possibility of additional risks to be managed, such as security and quality control issues. Furthermore, this view would also consider the competitive implications of the decision: if other suppliers all outsource and reduce their prices to customers, a decision *not* to do the same could damage the company. On the other hand, being different could be a viable competitive stance for one or more competitors, particularly if some customers are concerned about reduced quality of service from offshoring; at one point, NatWest in the UK seemed to take this stance in its advertising.

A stakeholder-centred company would place more emphasis on the impacts of the decision on the various stakeholder groups, notably including UK employees in this case. Although the decision to offshore might still be seen as competitively necessary by such a company, it might feel impelled to make more generous arrangements for those whose jobs are to be replaced, both out of a sense of long-term obligation and to preserve its image in the UK labour market. The question as to whether the group defined as 'those that the company has not yet recruited in the offshore location' should also be considered to be a stakeholder group – with a legitimate claim for attention – is one of the numerous judgements to be made in this approach.

In the UK, the report of the RSA Inquiry 'Tomorrow's Company' referred to the concept of an imaginary 'operating licence' granted to a company by the public, which can be effectively suspended or withdrawn if a company appears to be behaving badly.[34] Doing business effectively and well relies upon hundreds, sometimes thousands, of transactions every day of the year. If some of these transactions become more difficult because trust has been squandered and co-operation has been withdrawn, then the firm will start to lose out to its better-behaved competitors and its owners' wealth will start to suffer.

Critical review and reflection

The stakeholder view of a business may appear ethically attractive but is too idealistic. The shareholder-centred view consistent with maximising owner wealth makes more sense. Without this wealth people would be reluctant to invest in a business and it would not be possible to satisfy fully the demands of the diverse group of stakeholders.

What do YOU see as the criticisms of this point of view? How would YOU prepare a counterargument?

Ethics and corporate purpose

How do these issues relate to the question of ethics and the corporate purpose? To return to the problems of the global financial services industry, events since 2008 have provided a stark example of a collapse in public trust of many formerly respected institutions.

There is much lively discussion of what went so badly wrong and what should be done in the future, but there is a general agreement that global banks under 'light-touch' regulation did not manage to act in ways that were consistent with their shareholders' interest (to put it mildly). In the years leading up to the autumn 2008 crisis, many banks grew rapidly and took risks that with hindsight were not well managed. When these risks turned bad – triggered by the problems in the US housing market – the damage turned out to be uncontainable for some and also exposed the extra risk represented by the interconnectedness of modern global financial services institutions. One notable quote came from Alan Greenspan, the former Chairman of the US Federal Reserve:

> *I made a mistake in presuming that the self-interest of organisations, specifically banks and others, were such that they were best capable of protecting their own shareholders and their equity in the firms . . . Those of us who have looked to the self-interest of lending institutions to protect shareholders' equity (myself especially) are in a state of shocked disbelief.*

These comments were made by Greenspan to a Congressional Committee in October 2008.[35] They are notable because Greenspan had been a lifelong believer in free markets and the leading advocate of light-touch regulation, and had been widely admired as such during the good years. His frank admission of a mistaken assumption about the behaviour of senior executives is particularly telling because it appears to cast doubt on one of the main foundations of Friedman's view of the corporate purpose – that society is best served by encouraging businesses to compete with each other within the law, with minimal further regulation.

The hugely expensive bailouts and nationalisations that resulted from the crisis have been followed by further revelations of questionable practice by banks: in the UK, for example, major banks were obliged by the courts to set aside billions of pounds to cover the expected cost of compensation for the mis-selling of Payment Protection Insurance (PPI) to large numbers of customers over a period of years.[36] This counted as 'mis-selling' because the products were unsuitable (i.e. of little or no value) to a number of groups – the self-employed, for example, or those with pre-existing health conditions. Most of the major banks were involved in this market, with strong pressure on staff to sell these profitable products wherever possible.

With hindsight, we can see that it should have been possible for senior managers to work out that this type of selling could eventually lead to claims against the bank that would outweigh any profits from the sales. Had this been done, some of the problems might have been averted. But there is perhaps something further to be said here: it hardly requires a degree in moral philosophy to work out that selling products to customers who quite foreseeably cannot benefit from them is an abuse of trust and something that a bank – or any other business – simply *should not do*. This is a clear example of the importance of the 'moral compass' mentioned earlier.

Reliance on regulators

The PPI example also leads to a further question about relying on regulations to govern the behaviour of companies: whether it is realistic to aim at regulations that completely rule out any bad or undesirable practice. This is difficult enough in its own right, but the risk is that increasingly detailed regulations will be taken by some as a list of things that may not be done, with the corollary that anything not expressly forbidden is potentially worth considering. This sort of cat-and-mouse game between regulators and regulated is an unhealthy use of energy and talent, partly because regulators will necessarily need time to absorb and respond to market innovations, but also because the quiet and insistent voice of the moral compass (*'we just shouldn't do this'*) may be drowned out entirely.

The PPI mis-selling scandal is not the only cause for concern – other reported problems have involved the mis-selling of interest rate hedging products, as well as the substantial fines imposed by US and UK regulators for attempts to manipulate the LIBOR inter-bank settlement rate. In 2014, some six years after the onset of the global financial crisis, UK and US regulators imposed fines totalling £2.6 billion on six prominent global banks in respect of attempts by traders to manipulate benchmark foreign exchange rates, whose levels are used every day to value a range of assets in world trade. Notably – and perhaps depressingly – this misbehaviour was reported by the UK's Financial Conduct Authority to have been going on between 2008 and 2013, that is to say *after* the injection of enormous sums of taxpayers' money into ailing banks in both countries.[37]

The prevalence of problems of this sort – whose consequences should have been all too predictable – in the industry may cause some to wonder whether the problems in some major banks are actually cultural at root, rather than arising from localised and temporary misbehaviour.

Moral reflection in ethical decision-making

The importance of active moral reflection in ethical decision-making in business would probably have come as no surprise to Adam Smith, the founder of the discipline of economics. Smith's 1776 work *The Wealth of Nations* was the first to set out clearly how markets work and how self-interested individuals competing in markets are guided by an 'invisible hand' to benefit society, even though this may be no part of their intention. Thus self-interest, mediated through the mechanism of the market, can be to the general advantage. But Smith's original discipline was not economics, but moral philosophy – his first major work, *The Theory of Moral Sentiments,* was published in 1759. The point here is that markets are best understood as very efficient systems for organising the supply of products and services to meet the demands of buyers. Beyond this very useful function, markets can offer no moral guidance, nor any guarantee that market outcomes will be ethically desirable. This gap can only be closed by the application of moral sense by actors in the market. In the 1930s this seemed to be very clear to bankers, as is evident in the famous statement made by J. P. Morgan Jr to a US Senate Sub-Committee in 1933:[38]

> I should state that at all times the idea of doing only first-class business, and that in a first-class way, has been before our minds. We have never been satisfied with simply keeping within the law, but have constantly sought so to act that we might fully observe the professional code, and so maintain the credit and reputation which has been handed down to us from our predecessors in the firm.

Of course, banking and the regulation of banking have become far more complex since the 1930s, but the basic sense of right and wrong is just as important today as it was then. The 2012 BBC Reith lecturer Niall Ferguson used one of his lectures[39] to express doubt about whether more complex and detailed regulation would provide an answer to the problems experienced in the financial services industry. It might be better, he suggested, to re-examine the approach described by Walter Bagehot's 1873 work *Lombard Street,* with a very powerful central bank exercising control based upon discretion, rather than detailed rules, and with the clear sanction of imprisonment for serious transgressions.

One further comment can be made in passing – it is not entirely clear that a greater stakeholder focus on the part of banks would have led to a very different outcome by 2008. Many of the banks badly damaged by the crisis were engaged in significant CSR programmes, as their websites at the start of 2009 made clear. With the benefit of hindsight, many stakeholders might have opted for more thoughtful and principled management of banks, rather than the benefits of bank CSR programmes. Increasingly, the phrase 'corporate social responsibility (CSR)' is being replaced by 'corporate responsibility (CR)'. If this signifies a more comprehensive assessment of a corporation's effect on society, routinely making full use of a moral compass, then this seems to be a welcome step forward.

Business ethics

The large-scale issues of CSR are to do with how a company should conduct itself within society; these questions certainly have an ethical aspect, as has been discussed, but they are not the whole of business ethics. Day-to-day decisions made by individual managers are not usually made on the basis of some detailed calculation of the consequences for shareholder value (however theoretically desirable that might be) and more general ethical considerations must play a part in resolving the dilemmas that sometimes arise in practice.

No single view of right or wrong

These questions can be complex, since there is no single view in general ethics of what makes something right or wrong. One school of thought emphasises **duties,** things that must be done (or refrained from) irrespective of the consequences. This deontological point of view holds that goodness or badness is evident only in the action itself: that, for example, lying is bad because it is bad in itself. By contrast, a **consequentialist** view of ethics holds that the goodness or badness of a proposed action is evident only in the consequences of that action: whether a lie is good or bad depends upon the consequences of that particular lie at the time. Utilitarianism, for example, is a consequentialist theory, in that it seeks to maximise the net happiness for everyone affected by a particular action ('the greatest good for the greatest number', as it is sometimes expressed). Both of the perspectives on CSR discussed in the previous section are also to some extent consequentialist, in that they are mainly concerned with an assessment of the effects of a firm's actions. We can also note that the idea of a moral compass typical of a duties-based approach to ethics – the sense that we just shouldn't do this – is one that is not reliant on any calculation of the consequences.

Both duties and consequences are plainly important in the way we deal with ethical issues in everyday life. Unfortunately, however, they are very different ways of reasoning, which can lead to contradictory outcomes in some cases. An exclusively duty-based view of ethics, for example, must sooner or later run into problems such as absolutism, or the difficulty of deciding which duty should take precedence over others in a particular situation. If, for example, both lying and killing are held to be inherently wrong, is it acceptable to lie in order to avoid a killing? And whatever answer is given, how do we know?

Informing our views

Nonetheless, duties and principles clearly do inform our views of how people should treat each other at work. An exclusively consequentialist view of ethics is likely to entail methodological problems of forecasting reliably what the consequences of an action may be and of deciding how to measure those consequences. Some forms of utilitarianism can be very unjust to small minorities, by allowing their unhappiness (i.e. as a result of some proposed action) to be offset by the increased happiness of a much larger number. Again, however, we can hardly deny that our assessment of the likely consequences of different actions plays a part in our view of acceptable and unacceptable behaviour in an organisation.

To return briefly to the earlier example of offshoring, a deontological approach to the ethics of offshoring would focus on aspects of the proposal that might be in breach of clear principles and duties. While no business can reasonably accept a general duty to keep existing employees on the payroll for ever, a contemplation of duties might cause a company to do as much as reasonably possible to soften the impact of the job losses, including the possibility of internal transfer, retraining, outplacement and more-than-minimum redundancy packages.

A utilitarian analysis would seek to identify all who would be affected – anywhere in the world – by the proposed offshoring decision and then assess the impact (positive or negative) on each person (or, more realistically, group). This would allow a sort of 'trial balance' of the consequences to be drawn up and an evaluation of the net impact on aggregate happiness. Necessarily in this method, the reduction in happiness for others, such as those who are made involuntarily redundant, is offset by the extra happiness created for some – those who get the offshore jobs, for example. Obviously, this is of little comfort to the former group, which illustrates one of the important criticisms of the utilitarian approach.

Ethical decision-making at work

How, then, are ethical choices to be made by people working for organisations? No simple and universal answer is available – ethical awareness is something that can be cultivated and the different perspectives will often help to shed light on a particular dilemma. Some perspectives may appear to be better suited to particular situations: whereas, for example, it is difficult to avoid some sort of consequentialist component in thinking about how a company should act, it is also clear that duty-based (or 'moral compass') arguments must also weigh heavily in thinking about the ethical treatment of people such as employees. The German philosopher Kant's view that we should always treat other people as ends in themselves and never simply as means is surely an important principle for ethical and decent HRM and one that would often be seen as more important than the prospect of short-term gain.[40]

Critical review and reflection

Provided companies comply fully with the laws of the land it is unfair to criticise them for behaving in a manner that benefits them most, even if this might be regarded as a breach of their social responsibilities.
To what extent do YOU feel able to justify this point of view as reasonable business practice?

Personal integrity and individual values are important elements in ethical decision-making at work, but the increasingly common company, professional or industry codes of conduct may also provide support and guidance (notice also the reference to the professional code in the 1933 quote from J. P. Morgan above). This is not to say that these ethical 'resources' will always provide clear and comfortable guidance – sometimes, people in organisations will experience tension between the conflicting demands of, say, their own personal values and the demands placed on them by their organisation. If these conflicts become intolerable and cannot be resolved through normal means, then an individual may decide to become a 'whistle-blower' in the public interest, by taking the high-risk approach of placing the problem in the public domain for resolution. Codes of conduct can help to reduce the risk of painful situations like this by providing a published set of values to which the individual can appeal, rather than taking the risk wholly personally.

A concept map outlining some issues of ethics at work is given in Figure 14.3.

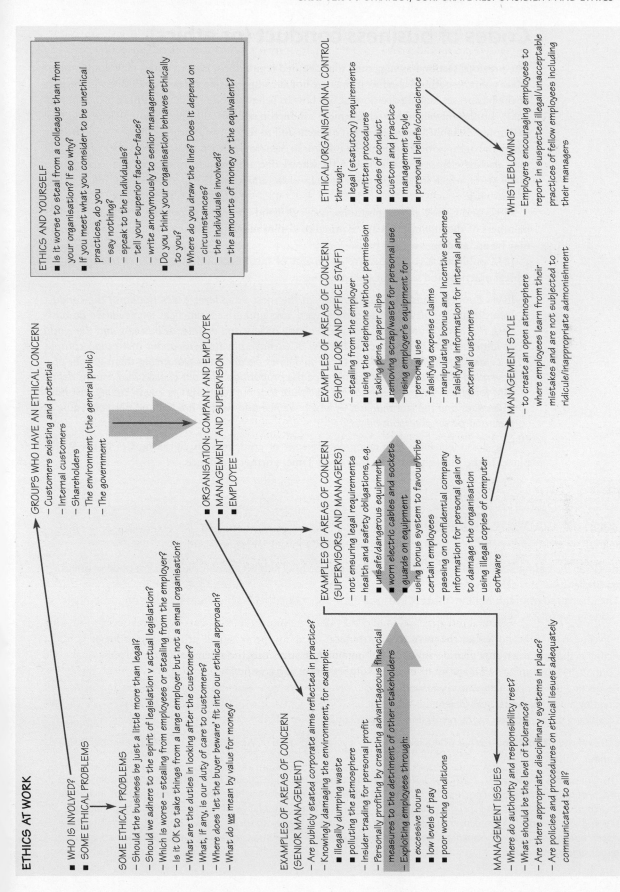

Figure 14.3 Concept map of ethics at work

Source: Copyright © 2008 The Virtual Learning Materials Workshop. Reproduced with permission.

Codes of business conduct (or ethics)

The previous section has suggested that detailed regulations, laws or codes may not by themselves guarantee ethical conduct if they are not accompanied by a clear moral sense on the part of the businesses making decisions about how to behave. Codes of conduct may, however, play a very important role in fostering ethical conduct in organisations, by sending clear guidance to employees about what is expected of them and to the outside world about the standards by which the organisation wishes to be judged. In some cases, concise and clear codes of conduct may also arise from a distillation of the knowledge and experience of the organisation over many years, which may be particularly helpful to junior or less experienced staff in their day-to-day work.

In US and Canadian organisations, codes of conduct are very common and in many cases members of the organisation are required to sign to indicate formally their acceptance. Codes may be updated on a regular basis.

IBM publishes a comprehensive document of business conduct guidelines relating to the ethical practices and values of the company.

> IBM's Business Conduct Guidelines are, at the most basic level, a description of the conduct we establish for all IBMers to comply with laws and ethical practices wherever we do business. It is a living document that we regularly review and update, as business and the world at large become more complex. But the BCGs have always been about more than compliance and ethics. By establishing these guidelines decades ago and giving them weight of a governing document, we have embraced the proposition that our choices and actions define IBM for others. And we have sought to ensure that our relationships – with clients, investors, colleagues and the communities in which we live and work – are built on our core value of trust and personal responsibility.[41]

The document includes a comprehensive set of guidelines on: Speaking Up; In the Workplace; In the Marketplace; On Your Own Time; Further Guidance.

Codes of conduct or ethics

In the UK an increasing number of organisations, of all types, also now publish a code of conduct or code of ethics. For example:

The Chartered Management Institute (CMI) has a Code of Conduct and Practice that is binding on all members. The code encapsulates, with supporting examples, six key principles:

- Behaving in an open, honest and trustworthy manner.
- Acting in the best interest of your organisation, customers, clients and/or partners.
- Continually developing and maintaining professional knowledge and competence.
- Respecting the people with whom you work.
- Creating a positive impact on society.
- Upholding the reputation of the profession and the institute.[42]

The University of Portsmouth has a detailed 'Ethics Policy' (as approved by Academic Council, 12 November 2013) and under 'Values' includes:

> The University's Strategy 2012-2017 includes a statement of values which should be reflected in all the policies and practices of the University. The Strategy states: 'We will be a socially responsible university, serious about inclusivity and committed to improving social mobility. We will maintain the highest levels of academic and professional integrity and will ensure that we deliver our obligations in relation to corporate social responsibility. Our strategy will be driven by values of equality, openness, tolerance and respect. We will demonstrate and expect of others ethical and responsible behaviours.[43]

An integrated approach

The late *Anita Roddick* suggested that business leaders should make ethics part of their heritage.

> We need to develop a corporate code of conduct, a formal, articulated and well-defined set of principles which all global businesses agree to live up to. A broadly kept code of conduct would shut down the excuse about the competition making ethical behaviour impossible once and for all. We must all agree not to compete in ways that destroy communities or the environment. We must all embrace the principles of socially responsible business, because the decisions of business leaders not only affect economies, but societies. Unless businesses understand that they have responsibilities they must live up to, in terms of world poverty, the environment and human rights, the future for us all is pretty bleak.[44]

According to *Philippa Foster Back*, OBE (Director, Institute of Business Ethics), the globalisation of business has raised questions of applying ethical values to the different cultures and societies in which organisations operate. The challenge for everyone concerned with ethics now is to ensure that values are embedded throughout an organisation. A code of ethics needs to be translated into reality through training and enforcement and driven from the top.[45]

McEwan summarises the separate histories of CSR, business ethics and corporate governance, and suggests a method of enquiry that attempts to integrate these different perspectives on business through three broad levels of enquiry:

- a **descriptive** approach that draws attention to the values and beliefs of people from different cultures and societies that influence their attitudes towards the various activities of business in their home countries and abroad;
- a **normative** approach that identifies sets of values and beliefs as a basis for making ethical decisions at the individual, group or senior management level in an organisation;
- an **analytical** approach that attempts to explore the relationship between these normative values and beliefs and other value-systems or ideologies, such as political or religious beliefs and culture or other social customs.[46]

A culture of ethics, integrity and compliance

Bennett points out that a culture of integrity focused on outstanding quality and business outcomes must be intentionally shaped and build on the values and principles of the organisation. This involves seven steps of: (1) designate a compliance owner; (2) implement written standards and procedures; (3) conduct appropriate training; (4) develop open lines of communication; (5) centrally manage all reports and allegations; (6) respond consistently and appropriately to alleged offences; (7) audit, monitor and adapt as needed. Bennett also points out the need for an integrated effort.

> Achieving an effective ethics and compliance programme requires more than simply adding rules and additional layers of controls. There must be an integrated effort that aligns financial and compliance requirements with the organisation's mission and values.[47]

Related legislation

As part of the growing attention to the concept of CSR there are a number of pieces of recent legislation that arguably relate to the concept of business ethics and organisational accountability. Although it is not in the scope of this book to provide detailed aspects of legal provisions, we should recognise the existence of such legislation, including the Human Rights Act 1998, the Public Interest Disclosure Act 1998, the Local Government Act 2000, the Freedom of Information Act 2000, the Corporate Manslaughter and Corporate Homicide Act 2007, the Bribery Act 2010 and the Equality Act 2010.

The **Human Rights Act 1998** came into force on 2 October 2000 and incorporates into English law rights and liberties enshrined in the European Convention on Human Rights. The provisions apply to the acts of 'public authorities' and make it unlawful for them to act in a way incompatible with a right under the Convention. The Act is designed to provide greater protection for individuals, and to protect them from unlawful and unnecessary interference. Everyone has the right to respect for their private and family life, their home and their correspondence. The Act has a significant effect on people both as citizens and at work.

The **Public Interest Disclosure Act 1998,** which has become known widely as the 'Whistleblower's Act', is designed to protect people who expose wrongdoing at their workplace, to provide reassurance that there is a safe alternative to silence and to provide a safeguard against retaliation. Employers need to establish clear internal procedures by which members of staff can raise any matters of personal concern.

The **Local Government Act 2000,** the so-called 'New Ethical Framework', requires all local authorities to provide codes of conduct to promote high standards of behaviour. The government has distinguished between general principles of conduct in public service and the code of conduct containing specific actions and prohibitions that demonstrate the principles are being observed.

The **Freedom of Information Act 2000** gives the public one simple right to access information held by public authorities. Under the Act, the public have a 'right to know'.

The **Corporate Manslaughter and Corporate Homicide Act 2007,** which came into force on 6 April 2008, clarifies the criminal liabilities of companies including large organisations where serious failures in the management of health and safety result in a fatality. For the first time, companies and organisations can be found guilty of corporate manslaughter as a result of serious management failures resulting in a gross breach of a duty of care.

The **Bribery Act 2010** consolidates and modernises the law on bribery and provides a more effective framework to combat bribery in both the private and public sectors. The Act creates a number of new offences relating to promising or giving an advantage or to bribes, and introduces anti-corruption regulations.

The **Equality Act 2010** covers areas of discrimination and bans unfair treatment and helps achieve equal opportunities in the workplace and in wider society.

Critical review and reflection

The harsh truth is that without EU intervention, government legislation and the threat of adverse press or television reports, the majority of organisations would give little regard to their social responsibilities or to business ethics.

To what extent do YOU support this contention? What has been YOUR experience of genuine concerns by organisations in general for their social responsibilities and ethical behaviour?

Ten key points to remember

1 Underlying the study of management and organisational behaviour is the nature of corporate strategy (or strategic management) for the organisation as a whole.

2 Strategy highlights the overall direction of an organisation, its goal, objectives and policy. The profit objective is not, by itself, a sufficient criterion for effective management.

3 The goals and objectives of the organisation may be pursued in accordance with an underlying ideology that determines the culture and conduct of the organisation.

4 Strategy gives rise to the consideration of organisational values and beliefs that draw attention to the importance of integrity and trust and ethical leadership.

5 The organisation cannot operate in isolation from interactions with its external environment and this gives rise to broader corporate social responsibilities.

6 Increasing attention is given to values and ethics and business. Ethics is concerned with the study of morality and understanding what makes things good or bad.

7 Two differing perspectives on ethics and corporate social responsibility, and how a business should act, are a shareholder-centred view and a stakeholder-theory view.

8 The scope of business ethics is very broad and gives rise to a number of questions including ethics and corporate purpose, and ethical decision-making at work.

9 An increasing number of organisations of all types publish a code of business (or professional) conduct, or ethics, which sets out their practices and values.

10 The globalisation of business highlights calls for an integrated approach to the application of ethical values. Related legislation arguably gives support to the importance of organisational accountability.

Review and discussion questions

1 Explain fully the nature, purpose and importance of corporate strategy.

2 Identify examples of objectives and policy in your own university or organisation. To what extent do you agree with Dryburgh's assertion that SMART objectives are really dumb?

3 To what extent do you believe profit maximisation is a realistic criterion for the effective management of a business organisation? What other indicators might be applied in terms of organisational performance and results?

4 Discuss critically the practical worth of value or mission statements and the extent to which they are likely to inspire members of staff. Support your answer with actual examples.

5 Explain fully the concept and ramifications of corporate social responsibility (CSR).

6 How would you attempt to explain the meaning and significance of organisational values and business ethics?

7 Compare and contrast the shareholder-centred and stakeholder approaches to social responsibilities for business. Which perspective do you tend to favour?

8 Comment critically on the code of ethics (or code of professional conduct) for your university or organisation; or if one does not exist, draw up your own suggested code.

9 Debate the extent to which you believe government legislation brings about a genuine advancement in the social responsibilities of organisations.

10 Give your own views on the importance of, and amount of attention you believe should be given to, corporate social responsibilities and ethical behaviour.

Assignment

a. Detail fully what you believe are the social responsibilities or obligations of your university (and/or other work organisation well known to you) and identify the major stakeholders.

b. Give specific examples of the ways in which the university has attempted to satisfy, and/or has failed to satisfy, responsibilities or obligations to these stakeholders.

c. Specify the extent to which attention has been given to values in the university, and to the principles, standards and expected practices or judgements of 'good' (ethical) behaviour.

d. Give your view on the code of conduct (or ethics) for your university.

e. Compare your observations with those of your colleagues and summarise what conclusions you draw.

Personal skills and employability exercise

Objectives

Completing this exercise should help you to enhance the following skills:

- Clarify the work values and beliefs that are important to you.
- Examine your sensitivity to, and dealings with, other people.
- Debate and justify with colleagues the nature of your values and beliefs.

Exercise

You are required to:
rate the following items according to the scale

5 (extremely important for me);
4 (very important for me);
3 (average importance for me);
2 (not important for me);
1 (I would oppose this).

What is required is your genuine beliefs and feelings about each item, not what others think or believe, but what you personally and honestly believe and feel about each item.

1	There should be clear allocation of objectives and accountability for them	____
2	We should be open and honest in all our dealings with each other	____
3	People's talents should be recognised, developed and correctly utilised	____
4	One should give acknowledgement and praise to those in authority	____
5	There are clear rules about what we should and should not do in getting the job done	____
6	Conflicts should be surfaced and resolved rather than allowed to simmer	____
7	The causes of problems should be directed away from oneself	____
8	Encouragement and support should be placed above criticism	____
9	Problems should be tackled and resolved in co-operation with others	____
10	What is right should be placed above who is right	____
11	Clear standard procedures should be in place for all important jobs	____
12	One should become visible and build up one's personal image	____
13	Equity and fairness should be applied to all, regardless of status or standing	____
14	Excellence should be our aim in all that we do, professionally and administratively	____
15	We give close attention to codes of conduct since this is what builds character	____

16 We should keep each other informed and practise open and friendly communication   _____

17 We know who should be making the decisions and refer decisions to the right person   _____

18 Everyone and their contribution should be treated with respect and dignity   _____

19 We should meet all our commitments to one another – we do what we say we will do   _____

20 One should form networks of support among those with influence   _____

21 There are clear reporting relationships – who reports to whom – and we stick to them   _____

22 People should take responsibility for their own decisions and actions   _____

23 Everyone should be committed to personal growth and lifelong learning   _____

24 Situations or events should be created so as to justify the advancement of one's goals   _____

25 Performance should be assessed against objectives and standards declared up-front   _____

26 Policies should be clear and not changed until there is proof that they need changing   _____

27 Everyone's needs should be given equal standing regardless of their position or status   _____

28 We should be committed to the service of others rather than ourselves   _____

29 Positive relationships should be established with those who have influence   _____

30 Warmth and affection should be demonstrated in our work relationships   _____

31 Individual productivity and performance should be encouraged and actively promoted   _____

32 We all know what our jobs are and we stick to our defined responsibilities   _____

33 Those from disadvantaged backgrounds should be helped to catch up with others   _____

34 One should expect to get support from those to whom we have given past support   _____

35 Goals should be challenging and stretch people to higher levels of achievement   _____

Source for the exercise: Misselhorn, A. *Head and Heart of Leadership*, (Reach Publishers, SA), (2012). p. 86. Reproduced with permission.

When you have completed the exercise, form into small groups to compare and discuss, frankly and openly, your ratings with those of your colleagues. Be prepared to justify your ratings but also listen with an open mind to the views of your colleagues.

Further information will be provided by your tutor.

Discussion

- How difficult was it for you to complete your ratings?
- How much agreement was there among members of your group? Did this surprise you?
- To what extent were you influenced to rethink your values or beliefs?

Case study
The Fairtrade Foundation

Over the last couple of decades, the ideals of fair trade have become prominent in UK retailing. The story of how this has come about shows how an organisation can make progress towards its own objectives through developing effective networks with other organisations, about the trade-offs that have to be managed along the way and about the realities of achieving improvements in business ethics.

The general concerns about unfairness in world trade are easy enough to set out. Firstly, the gap between the living standards of the richest and the poorest is distressingly wide and the scale of poverty enormous. The UN Development Programme pointed out in 2015 that although poverty rates halved between 1990 and 2010, there are still more than 1.2 billion people around the world – about one in five in developing regions – who live in extreme poverty.[48] Secondly, the fact that this gap is so wide is often felt to be something to do with the way in which international trade operates (although the definition of the actual problem is something on which experts differ sharply). Finally, there seems to be a growing sense that these are not just abstruse high-level policy problems, to be addressed by governments, experts and suchlike, but rather processes in which we *all* take

→

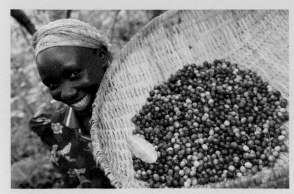

As the popularity of Fairtrade increases, is its growth sustainable or has commercialism resulted in a 'cleanwashing' of an idealistic movement?
Source: Simon Rawles/Alamy Images

part as a result of the choices we make when we buy and consume products and services. On the negative side, our demand for value for money in the shops may have unseen negative consequences for people in other countries who are in a much more parlous position than we are. More positively, consumer power may provide us with the means – if we take the trouble – to reduce the harm we do further along the supply chain and perhaps even create change for the better. The Fairtrade movement has sought to address these problems.

The Fairtrade movement is an international network of partners, who define fair trade as follows:

> *Fairtrade is about better prices, decent working conditions, local sustainability, and fair terms of trade for farmers and workers in the developing world. By requiring companies to pay sustainable prices (which must never fall lower than the market price), Fairtrade addresses the injustices of conventional trade, which traditionally discriminates against the poorest, weakest producers. It enables them to improve their position and have more control over their lives.*[49]

In the UK, the movement is centred around the Fairtrade Foundation, which was formed in 1992 by five prominent charities, later joined by the Women's Institute. Today, the Foundation has four main streams of activity:

- Providing independent certification of the trade chain and licensing use of the FAIRTRADE mark on products as a consumer guarantee.
- Help in growing demand for Fairtrade products and empowering producers to sell to traders and retailers.

- Working with partners to support producer organisations and their networks.
- Raising public awareness of the need for fair trade and the significant role of the FAIRTRADE mark in making trade fair.[50]

Launching the concept

As regular press reports make clear, Fairtrade in the UK has grown rapidly since its launch in 1992, from the first certified product (Green and Blacks' Maya Gold chocolate), through growth to include a wider range of products and then entry into the catering trade. Twenty years after launch, more than 4,500 Fairtrade products were on sale in the UK, with 2013 sales valued at £1.78 billon, up 14 per cent from the previous year.[51] For some years, percentage recognition of the Fairtrade mark has remained in the mid to high 70s,[52] a key factor in driving the growth of adoption by retailers. There is, however, plenty of scope for further growth: although the UK is an international leader in Fairtrade product penetration, these products still accounted for just 1.5 per cent of the overall UK food and drink market in 2013.[53]

The evolution of the Fairtrade approach has been the subject of a number of studies. *Davies*[54] suggests that three 'eras' can so far be distinguished:

- The 'solidarity' era (1970–90), in which sales were mainly in craft products, making use of alternative trading organisations such as not-for-profit and charity shops, specialist mail order and religious organisations. Product quality was inconsistent and sometimes poor, and branding very limited.
- The 'niche market' era (1990–2002), which saw a broadening of the range, with the growth of recognisable Fairtrade labelling and an appeal directed mainly at the ethical consumer, based upon public relations and press campaigns.
- The 'mass market' era (from 2002 onwards), distinguished by a rapid expansion of (mostly) food products into a wider range of mainstream outlets – most notably supermarkets, but also major chains of cafés and restaurants. Critically, Fairtrade decided to include large organisations in the scheme, allowing them to broaden the appeal to the mass-market customer.

In an earlier paper, *Jones et al.*[55] discussed some of the problems that had to be overcome when expanding into mass-market retail. For example, supermarkets need to secure adequate, consistent and regular supplies to maintain stocks, without which the growing consumer awareness will come to nothing. This is sometimes a challenge for smaller producers in the UK, but when the producer of the Fairtrade product lives in a remote part of a country with underdeveloped infrastructure, then the problem can be far greater. In the early stages, the willingness of a wider section of the market to pay a small price premium for a Fairtrade product was an area of uncertainty. Supermarkets had to play their part in consumer education in the early days via in-store leaflets and display materials and advertising campaigns.

Davies also addresses the question of how this development might continue in future, suggesting the possibility of more or less complete 'institutionalisation', in which the qualities of Fairtrade products become the norm for mainstream sales, rather than a specialised niche. Of course, this possibility only exists because Fairtrade products are now prominent in mass-market outlets. In future we may approach a tipping point where the average consumer will start to wonder why a particular brand on the supermarket shelf has *no* Fairtrade label. This could present a major management challenge for the Fairtrade Foundation: the label only works because it is widely recognised, understood and – above all – accepted as a trustworthy guarantee. That basic credibility is just as important for the supermarket retailer as for the consumer: if the reality starts to fall short of the promise in any respect, then things could quickly get difficult for the brand.

The issue of trust and credibility is becoming more complex for Fairtrade as its business grows: the FAIRTRADE logo has been joined in consumer consciousness by a number of other certification schemes. This increased emphasis on the ethics of products is in many respects a welcome development. For Fairtrade, it means greater competition for the public's attention, but it may also broaden the risk for the organisation and its image, since problems with any of these labelling schemes may damage credibility in ethical consumption more generally. Also, the range of issues covered by these schemes is more extensive than fair trade alone, raising the prospect of confusion about what exactly an individual label does guarantee and hence the risk of disappointment as a result of mistaken expectations.

Good or not; who decides?

As the Fairtrade movement has grown it has attracted criticism from both political wings. *Low and Davenport*,[56] for example, suggest that there are two dangers

inherent in this growth: that of appropriation of the organisation by commercial interests in the process that the authors call 'cleanwashing'; and the transformation of the Fairtrade message into one of 'shopping for a better world', in which the movement's original radical values are watered down. A different critique arrived from the Right in 2008 when the free-market-championing Adam Smith Institute published its report 'Unfair Trade'.[57] Acknowledging the good intentions of the movement, it argued that the Fairtrade approach was far less effective in reducing poverty than global free trade would be, if rich countries were to abolish the trade barriers and domestic subsidies that make it hard for poor countries to sell to them. In 2010, the IEA also suggested that the Fairtrade approach could only benefit some producers; in particular, Fairtrade seemed not to focus its efforts on the poorest countries, but rather on middle-income countries, where Fairtrade penetration was higher.[58]

Those who work under a hot sun for low rates of pay could be forgiven a degree of impatience with these theoretical arguments: does it really matter if some of the greatly increased number of buyers of Fairtrade products do not fully grasp or agree with the radical agenda of the early days? Is it really better for poor people to wait for the arrival of the benefits of true free trade, given the glacial progress of international negotiations towards that end? As Voltaire remarked, are we not in danger of letting the best be the enemy of the good? Those who benefit from the Fairtrade system seem to have little doubt of the improved benefits it brings.[59]

The Fairtrade movement has managed to achieve very rapid growth from a specialised niche into the mainstream. It has created and communicated a prominent brand identity that provides consumers with a specific guarantee about the value chain that has brought the product to the shelf. To achieve and sustain this credibility, the Fairtrade Foundation has had to specify and manage what happens upstream, in order to use the immense power of the supermarkets to bring these products to the mainstream market. Many supermarkets have enthusiastically joined in the process of consumer education about Fairtrade products, possibly for normal commercial reasons of self-interest. Yet they have undoubtedly helped the idea to become firmly established in the minds of their customers and thus to ensure that ethics stays on the consumer agenda, even in difficult economic times.

→

Tasks

1 Who are the stakeholders of the Fairtrade Foundation? Using Figure 14.2 as a starting point, identify examples of each type of stakeholder. Who are the most powerful? Who the most important? Identify areas where the interests of stakeholders conflict as well as those where they coincide.

2 Explain what you think Low and Davenport mean by the term 'cleanwashing' and why this might be a danger to the values of the Fairtrade Foundation.

3 With reference to the decision to include major supermarkets and other large-scale retailers in the scheme, discuss whether you think that 'good' acts can result from selfish motives or not. Present the arguments on both sides.

4 How do you think the Fairtrade Foundation should present its message during an economic recession, when Western consumers might well be more motivated by price than other considerations?

Notes and references

1. Johnson, G., Whittington, R., Scholes, K., Angwin, D., and Regnér, P *Exploring Strategy,* tenth edition, Pearson Education (2014).

2. Andrews, K. 'The Concept of Corporate Strategy', Irwin (1971), in Lynch, R. *Strategic Management,* sixth edition, Pearson Education (2012), p. 7.

3. Lynch, R. *Strategic Management,* sixth edition, Pearson Education (2012), pp. 459, 462.

4. Allen, R. S. and Helms, M. M. 'Employee Perceptions of the Relationship between Strategy, Rewards and Organizational Performance', *Journal of Business Strategies,* vol. 19, no. 2, 2002, pp. 115–39.

5. Stern, S. 'The Next Big Thing', *Management Today,* April 2007, p. 50.

6. Gratton, L. *Living Strategy: Putting People at the Heart of Corporate Purpose,* Financial Times Prentice Hall (2000), p. 18.

7. Schneider, S. C. and Barsoux, J. *Managing Across Cultures,* second edition, Financial Times Prentice Hall (2003), ch. 5.

8. See, for example, Hannagan, T. *Management: Concepts & Practices,* fifth edition, Financial Times Prentice Hall (2008), p. 396.

9. Reeves, R. 'The Trouble with Targets', *Management Today,* January 2008, p. 29.

10. Dryburgh, A., http://www.managementtoday.co.uk/features/1071164/dont-believe-it-its-smart-smart-objectives/ (accessed 8 June 2012).

11. See, for example, Brown, A. 'Organizational Culture: The Key to Effective Leadership and Organizational Development', *Leadership and Organization Development Journal,* vol. 13, no. 2, 1992, pp. 3–6.

12. Brech, E. F. L. (ed.) *The Principles and Practice of Management,* third edition, Longman (1975).

13. Lucas, E. 'Believe It Or Not, Values Can Make a Difference', *Professional Manager,* November 1999, pp. 10–12.

14. Cloke, K. and Goldsmith, J. *The End of Management and the Rise of Organizational Democracy,* Jossey-Bass (2002).

15. Gratton, L. *Hot Spots,* Financial Times Prentice Hall (2007).

16. Drucker, P. F. *The Practice of Management,* Heinemann Professional (1989), p. 59.

17. Mann, S., in conversation with Gidoomal, R. 'We Have to Be Proud of Our Integrity', *Professional Manager,* vol. 17, no. 5, 2007, pp. 18–21.

18. 'Creating a culture of integrity', *Governance & Compliance,* July 2014, pp. 26–8.

19. Yukl, G. *Leadership in Organizations,* seventh edition, Pearson Education (2010), p. 333.

20. 'Added values: The importance of ethical leadership', The Institute of Leadership and Management, June 2013.

21. 'Corporate Social Responsibility', Checklist 242, Chartered Management Institute, April 2013.

22. Pearce, G. 'Getting it straight', *Chartered Secretary,* August 2011, pp. 38–9.

23. Donaldson, T. and Preston, L. E. 'The stakeholder theory of the corporation: Concepts, evidence and implications, *Academy of Management Review,* vol. 20. no. 1, 1995, pp. 65–91.

24. Rollinson, D. *Organisational Behaviour and Analysis,* fourth edition, Financial Times Prentice Hall (2008).

25. Thanks to Ursula Wynhoven, https://www.unglobalcompact.org/news/381-09-05-2013

26. See, for example, Coyle, D. *The Economics of Enough: How to Run the Economy as If the Future Matters,* Princeton University Press (2011); and Skidelsky, R. and Skidelsky, E. *How Much is Enough? The Love of Money and the Case for a Good Life,* Allen Lane (2012).

27. Piketty, T. *Capital in the Twenty-First Century,* Harvard University Press (2014).

28. Sandel, M. *What Money Can't Buy: The Moral Limits of Markets,* Allen Lane (2012).

29. De George, R. T. *Business Ethics,* fifth edition, Prentice Hall (1999).

30. Friedman, M. 'The Social Responsibility of Business Is to Increase Its Profits', *New York Times Magazine,* 13 September 1970, pp. 32, 122–6.

31. Sternberg, E. *Just Business,* Little Brown (1994).

32. Cannon, T. *Corporate Responsibility,* Pitman (1994), pp. 32–3.

33. Sternberg, E. *Just Business,* Little Brown (1994).

34. RSA, *Tomorrow's Company – The Role of Business in a Changing World,* Royal Society for Arts, Manufactures and Commerce (1995).

35. *Guardian,* 24 October 2008, http://www.guardian.co.uk/business/2008/oct/24/economics-creditcrunch-federal-reserve-greenspan (accessed 8 August 2012).

36. Peston, R. 'The Big PPI Lessons For Banks', 9 May 2011, http://www.bbc.co.uk/blogs/thereporters/robertpeston/2011/05/the_big_ppi_lesson_for_banks.html (accessed 8 August 2012).

37. BBC News, 12 November 2014, 'Six banks fined £2.6bn by regulators over forex failings', http://www.bbc.co.uk/news/business-30016007; Ahmed, K. 'RBS boss admits – I cringed when I read forex chat room messages', BBC News, 12 November 2014, http://www.bbc.co.uk/news/business-30027544

38. A fuller version can be found at: https://www.jpmorgan.com/cm/ContentServer?pagename=Chase/Href&urlname=jpmorgan/about/culture_new/fcb (accessed 8 August 2012).

39. Full text at: http://www.bbc.co.uk/programmes/b01jmxqp/features/transcript (accessed 8 August 2012).

40. For a discussion, see De George, R. T. *Business Ethics,* fifth edition, Prentice Hall (1999).

41. Palmisano, S. 'IBM Business Conduct Guidelines', 2011, www.ibm.com (accessed 23 June 2012).

42. Chartered Management Institute, March 2011. For full details, see www.managers.org.uk/code

43. Available at: http://www.port.ac.uk/accesstoinformation/policies/humanresources/filetodownload,88682,en.pdf (accessed 23 November 2014).

44. Roddick, A. *Business As Unusual,* Thorsons (2000), p. 269.

45. Back, P. F. 'Taking a Proactive Approach to Ethics', *Professional Manager,* vol. 15, no. 3, 2006, p. 37.

46. McEwan, T. *Managing Values and Beliefs in Organisations,* Financial Times Prentice Hall (2001).

47. Bennett, M. 'Shaping the future', *Governance & Compliance,* June 2014, pp. 32–3.

48. http://www.undp.org/content/undp/en/home/mdgoverview/mdg_goals/mdg1/ (accessed 10 February 2015).

49. http://www.fairtrade.org.uk/what_is_fairtrade/faqs.aspx (accessed 10 February 2015).

50. http://www.fairtrade.org.uk/what_is_fairtrade/fairtrade_foundation.aspx (accessed 10 February 2015).

51. http://m.bbc.co.uk/news/business-26317759 (accessed 10 February 2015).

52. http://www.fairtrade.org.uk/FTDoc/Fairtrade-Annual-Impact-Report-2013–14.pdf (accessed 10 February 2015).

53. http://www.theguardian.com/money/2013/mar/02/fairtrade-taste-growing-britain (accessed 10 February 2015).

54. Davies, I. A. 'The eras and participants of fair trade: An industry structure/stakeholder perspective on the growth of the fair trade industry', *Corporate Governance,* vol. 7, no. 4, 2007, pp. 455–70.

55. Jones, P., Comfort, D. and Hillier, D. 'Developing customer relationships through fair trade: A case study from the retail market in the UK', *Management Research News,* vol. 27, no. 3, 2003, pp. 77–87.

56. Low, W. and Davenport, E. 'Has the medium (roast) become the message? The ethics of marketing fair trade in the mainstream', *International Marketing Review,* vol. 22, no. 5, 2005, pp. 494–511.

57. http://www.adamsmith.org/blog/international/unfair-trade (accessed 10 February 2015).

58. http://www.iea.org.uk/in-the-media/press-release/new-research-finds-fair-trade-movement-is-a-distraction-not-a-solution (accessed 10 February 2015).

59. See, for example, William Sutcliffe's 2004 *Guardian* article at http://www.guardian.co.uk/lifeandstyle/2004/aug/07/foodanddrink.shopping2 (accessed 10 February 2015).

CHAPTER 15
Organisational culture and change

A central feature of the successful organisation is the diagnosis of its culture, health and performance, and the ability of the organisation to adapt to change. It involves the applications of organisational behaviour and recognition of the social processes of the organisation. The manager needs to understand the nature and importance of organisational culture and climate, and the successful implementation and management of organisational change.

Learning outcomes

After completing this chapter you should have enhanced your ability to:

- detail the nature, types and main features of organisational culture;
- evaluate influences on the development and importance of culture;
- debate the importance and characteristic features of a healthy organisational climate;
- explain the nature and forces of organisational change;
- explore the nature of, and reasons for, resistance to change;
- examine the management of change, and human and social factors of change;
- review relationships between organisation culture and control.

Critical review and reflection

The socialisation of new members into an organisation's culture and climate is no more than a management control system and manipulation of the individual. It is therefore unethical and should be condemned.

How would YOU challenge the validity of this statement? What has been YOUR personal experience of socialisation into YOUR university or organisation?

Adapting to change

In order to thrive in an increasingly competitive, global environment with new technologies, an organisation must pay attention to its continual effectiveness and development. An underlying feature of the successful organisation is the ability to adapt to change. This involves the applications of organisational behaviour and recognition of the social processes of the organisation. No two organisations are the same. Each organisation has its own types of problems and most appropriate remedies. For an organisation to perform well and develop, the process of change must be in harmony with organisational culture. Successful management of change is dependent upon a culture of openness, participation and acceptance of new ideas. Sustained organisational improvement can only be achieved through involvement of people, who are the organisation.

> 'Rapid technological changes create huge opportunities for companies bold enough to seize them.
>
> (Attributed to Jeff Bezos, founder and CEO, Amazon)

Organisational culture

Although most of us will understand in our own minds what is meant by **organisational culture**, it is a general concept with many different meanings and difficult to define or explain precisely. There is also sometimes confusion over the difference between the interpretation of organisational culture and organisational climate (discussed below). Although people may not be aware consciously of culture, it still has a pervasive influence over their behaviour and actions. There is, however, no consensus on its meaning or its applications to the analysis of work organisations. A popular and simple way of defining culture is 'how things are done around here'. For example, *Atkinson* explains organisational culture as reflecting the underlying assumptions about the way work is performed; what is 'acceptable and not acceptable'; and what behaviour and actions are encouraged and discouraged.[1]

A more detailed definition from *Rachael Johnson*, Editor of *Governance & Compliance* magazine, is:

> In its broadest sense, our understanding of workplace culture is that it embodies the ethos and values of a particular organisation, which are expressed through the way it operates and the practices it undertakes. If the latter are deemed to be wrong, then the former needs to be addressed in order for any issues to be resolved effectively. Anything else would be superficial change and unlikely to have a lasting impact.[2]

The culture of an organisation is also often likened to the personality of an individual[3] (**see the Assignment at the end of this chapter**).

Relationship between culture and change

The pervasive nature of organisational culture means that if change is to be brought about successfully, this is likely to involve changes to culture. For example, *Stewart* makes the following comment on the relationship between culture and change:

> In recent years attention has shifted from the effects of the organization of work on people's behaviour to how behaviour is influenced by the organizational culture. What is much more common today is the widespread recognition that organizational change is not just, or even necessarily mainly, about changing the structure but often requires changing the culture too.[4]

A similar view is held by *Naylor*, who points out that: 'In the holistic system, any change will affect the culture and the culture will affect or constrain the change . . . Cultural change is intimately bound up with the process of organisational change.'[5]

However, although attention is often given to shifting the prevailing activities and atmosphere of an organisation to a brighter future, changing the ethos and culture of an organisation is not easy. In practice, organisations usually appear to alter their underlying ethos only on a gradual basis and the complexity of environmental pressures may itself hinder rapid change. Culture is often deep-rooted, and commitment to the objectives and policies of the organisation, people's cognitive limitations and their uncertainties and fears may mean a reluctance to accept a change in behaviour. Culture is reinforced through the system of rites and rituals, patterns of communication, the informal organisation, expected patterns of behaviour and perceptions of the psychological contract. (**Organisational change is discussed below.**)

A depiction of the way elements of culture can support and/or defend against change is given in Figure 15.1.

Critical review and reflection

It seems generally accepted that any organisational change will affect culture and that one of the main hurdles to effective adaption to change is the culture of the organisation. Culture and change are linked.

To what extent do YOU support this contention? How would YOU explain the interrelationship between organisational culture and change?

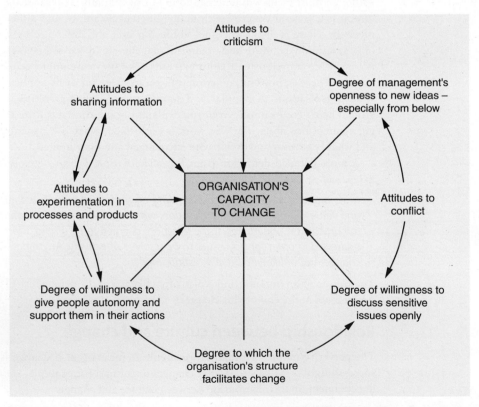

Figure 15.1 Organisational culture and change
Source: Senior, B. and Swailes, S. *Organizational Change*, fourth edition, Financial Times Prentice Hall (2010), p. 161, Pearson Education Ltd

Levels of culture

Schein suggests a view of organisational culture based on distinguishing three levels of culture, from the shallowest to the deepest: artefacts and creations; values; and basic assumptions.[6]

- **Level 1: Artefacts.** The most visible level of the culture is artefacts and creations – the constructed physical and social environment. This includes physical space and layout, the technological output, written and spoken language and the overt behaviour of group members.
- **Level 2: Espoused beliefs and values.** Cultural learning reflects someone's original values. Solutions about how to deal with a new task, issue or problem are based on convictions of reality. If the solution works, the value can transform into a belief. Values and beliefs become part of the conceptual process by which group members justify actions and behaviour.
- **Level 3: Basic underlying assumptions.** When a solution to a problem works repeatedly, it comes to be taken for granted. Basic assumptions are unconsciously held learned responses. They are implicit assumptions that actually guide behaviour and determine how group members perceive, think and feel about things.

Schein suggests that the basic assumptions are treated as the essence – what culture really is – and values and behaviours are treated as observed manifestations of the culture essence. See Figure 15.2.

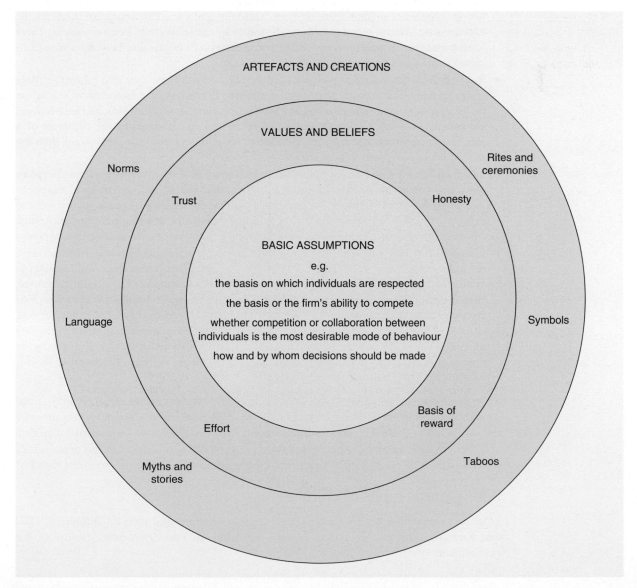

Figure 15.2 Schein's levels of culture

Source: Rollinson, D. *Organisational Behaviour and Analysis: An Integrated Approach,* fourth edition, Financial Times Prentice Hall (2008), p. 592, Pearson Education Ltd

Naylor suggests that seeing quite what forms organisational culture is difficult, and to make a start we need to recognise both the visible and invisible layers. On the surface is the visible layer made up of elements such as artefacts, symbols, languages, stories and activities, which can be collected, compared and assembled into a description of the organisation. Underpinning this 'visible culture' is the invisible layer of beliefs, values, norms, basic assumptions and understanding.[7]

Types of organisational culture

There are a number of ways to classify different types of organisational culture. Two common classifications are those by Handy and by Deal and Kennedy. Developing the ideas of *Harrison*,[8] *Handy* describes four main types of organisational cultures: power culture; role culture; task culture; and person culture.[9]

- **Power culture** depends on a central power source with rays of influence from the central figure throughout the organisation. A power culture is frequently found in small entrepreneurial organisations and relies on trust, empathy and personal communications for its effectiveness. Control is exercised from the centre by the selection of key individuals. There are few rules and procedures, and little bureaucracy. It is a political organisation with decisions taken largely on the balance of influence.

- **Role culture** is often stereotyped as a bureaucracy and works by logic and rationality. Role culture rests on the strength of strong organisational 'pillars' – the functions of specialists in, for example, finance, purchasing and production. The work of, and interaction between, the pillars is controlled by procedures and rules, and co-ordinated by the pediment of a small band of senior managers. Role or job description is often more important than the individual, and position is the main source of power.

- **Task culture** is job orientated or project orientated. In terms of structure, the task culture can be likened to a net, some strands of which are stronger than others, and with much of the power and influence at the interstices. An example is the matrix organisation. Task culture seeks to bring together the right resources and people, and utilises the unifying power of the group. Influence is widely spread and based more on expert power than on position or personal power.

- **Person culture** is where the individual is the central focus and any structure exists to serve the individuals within it. When a group of people decide that it is in their own interests to band together to do their own thing and share office space, equipment or clerical assistance, then the resulting organisation would have a person culture. Examples are groups of barristers, architects, doctors or consultants. Although it is found in only a few organisations, many individuals have a preference for person culture – for example, university professors and specialists. Management hierarchies and control mechanisms are possible only by mutual consent. Individuals have almost complete autonomy and any influence over them is likely to be on the basis of personal power.

Every organisation will have its own unique culture and most large businesses are likely to be something of a mix of cultures, with examples for each of the four types in varying areas of the organisation. Different people enjoy working in different types of organisational culture and they are more likely to be happy and satisfied at work if their attributes and personalities are consistent with the culture of that part of the organisation in which they are employed.

Four generic types of culture

From an examination of hundreds of business organisations and their environments, *Deal and Kennedy* categorise corporate cultures according to two determining factors in the marketplace:

- the degree of risk associated with the organisation's activities; and
- the speed at which organisations and their employees receive feedback on the success of decisions or strategies.

These factors give rise to four generic types of culture: the tough-guy, macho culture; the work-hard/play-hard culture; the bet-your-company culture; and the process culture.[10]

- **Tough-guy, macho culture** – an organisation of individualists who frequently take high risks and receive quick feedback on the right or wrong of their actions. Examples cited include police departments, surgeons, construction, cosmetics, management consulting and the entertainment industry. Financial stakes are high and there is a focus on speed. The intense pressure and frenetic pace often result in early 'burnout'. Internal competition and conflict are normal, stars are temperamental but tolerated. A high staff turnover can create difficulties in building a strong cohesive culture.

- **Work-hard/play-hard culture** – characterised by fun and action where employees take few risks, all with quick feedback. There is a high level of relatively low-risk activity. Examples include sales organisations such as estate agents and computer companies, mass-consumer companies such as McDonald's, office equipment manufacturers and retail stores. Organisations tend to be highly dynamic and the primary value centres on customers and their needs. It is the team that produces the volume, and the culture encourages games, meetings, promotions and conventions to help maintain motivation. However, although a lot gets done, volume can be at the expense of quality.

- **Bet-your-company culture** – where there are large-stake decisions with a high risk but slow feedback so that it may be years before employees know if decisions were successful. Examples include oil companies, investment banks, architectural firms and the military. The focus is on the future and the importance of investing in it. There is a sense of deliberateness throughout the organisation, typified by the ritual of the business meeting. There is a hierarchical system of authority, with decision-making from the top down. The culture leads to high-quality inventions and scientific breakthroughs, but moves only very slowly and is vulnerable to short-term fluctuations.

- **Process culture** – a low-risk, slow-feedback culture where employees find difficulty in measuring what they do. Typical examples include insurance companies, financial services and the civil service. The individual financial stakes are low and employees get very little feedback on their effectiveness. Their memos and reports seem to disappear into a void. Lack of feedback forces employees to focus on how they do something, not what they do. People tend to develop a 'cover your back' mentality. Bureaucracy results, with attention to trivial events, minor detail, formality and technical perfection. Process cultures can be effective when there is a need for order and predictability.

Criticisms of cultural typologies

Some writers are critical of the generic typologies of culture that suggest organisations have a single overriding cultural environment representative of management ideology and all stakeholders. The complex nature of organisations may give rise to many different cultures and overlapping and/or conflicting sub-cultures, including ways in which members of staff distinguish themselves within the organisation.

A notable critic of a unitary approach to a dominate culture imposed by senior management is *Smircich,* who uses the metaphor of a plant root. Culture is something that 'is' and has developed and spread (like plant roots), together with an organisation's history, structure and staff. It is culture that drives organisations and shapes their structure and interactions. Smircich views culture as usually defined hierarchically and is elevated as a critical variable that controls the nature of organisational life, and determines its performance and effectiveness.[11]

Martin contrasts an integrationist perspective of a single unified culture as a basis for organisational effectiveness with a differentiation or pluralistic perspective that views organisational culture in terms of diverse interest groups within their own objectives.[12] *Parker* also suggests that rather than a strong single culture, organisations possess multiple sub-cultures that may overlap or contradict each other. An organisation's culture may also be perceived differently in terms of either the formal or informal structure (**see Chapter 3**).[13]

Critical review and reflection

Attempting to analyse culture in terms of different levels or generic typologies is too simplistic and prescriptive. It serves no useful purpose in evaluating applications of management and organisational behaviour.
What do YOU think? How would YOU analyse the culture of YOUR own university or organisation?

Influences on the development of culture

The culture and structure of an organisation develop over time and in response to a complex set of factors. We can, however, identify a number of key influences that are likely to play an important role in the development of any corporate culture. These include history, primary function and technology, strategy, size, location, management and leadership, and the environment.[14]

- **History.** The reason and manner in which the organisation was originally formed, its age and the philosophy and values of its owners and first senior managers will affect culture. A key event in the organisation's history such as a merger or major reorganisation, or a new generation of top management, may bring about a change in culture. Corporate history can be an effective induction tool to assist a growth programme, and to help integrate acquisitions and new employees by infusion with the organisation's culture and identity.[15] Failure in mergers and acquisitions can arise from cultural clashes and failure to integrate different cultures.[16]

- **Primary function and technology.** The nature of the organisation's 'business' and its primary function have an important influence on its culture. This includes the range and quality of products and services provided, the importance of reputation and the type of customers. The primary function of the organisation will determine the nature of the technological processes and methods of undertaking work, which in turn also affect structure and culture.

- **Strategy.** Although a business organisation may pursue profitability, this is not by itself very clear or a sufficient criterion for its effective management. For example, to what extent is emphasis placed on long-term survival or growth and development? How much attention is given to avoiding risks and uncertainties? Or how much concern is shown for broader social responsibilities? The organisation must give attention to objectives in all key areas of its operations. The combination of objectives and resultant strategies will influence culture, and may itself be influenced by changes in culture. (**See also Chapter 14.**)

- **Size.** Usually larger organisations have more formalised structures and cultures. Increased size is likely to result in separate departments and possibly split-site operations. This may cause difficulties in communication and interdepartmental rivalries, with the need for effective co-ordination. A rapid expansion, or decline, in size and rate of growth, and resultant changes in staffing, will influence structure and culture.

- **Location.** Geographical location and physical characteristics can have a major influence on culture – for example, whether an organisation is located in a quiet rural location or a busy city centre can influence the types of customers and the staff employed. An example could be a hotel or restaurant. Location can also affect the nature of services provided, the sense of 'boundary' and distinctive identity, and opportunities for development.

- **Management and leadership.** Top executives can have considerable influence on the nature of corporate culture. Examples are the key roles played by Sir Richard Branson, Anita Roddick, founder of The Body Shop, and Marjorie Scardino and her change of style when she took over as the new chief executive of Pearson.

Her candour works . . . As an example of straight talking winning over a sceptical City and press, it is brilliant. As an example of just how much a company's culture can change under a new chief executive, it is breathtaking.[17]

Another example is *Louis Gerstner,* who remade the ossified culture of computing giant IBM bred by the company's success, rebuilt the leadership team and gave the workforce a renewed sense of purpose.[18] A further example is Harriet Green, who between 2012 and 2014 completely transformed the financial fortunes of travel operator Thomas Cook. Before her appointment as CEO, Thomas Cook was described by the Financial Times as 'a near-death experience'. Such was the impact of Harriet Green that after her sudden departure £360 million was wiped off the share price of the company.

However, all members of staff help to shape the dominant culture of an organisation, irrespective of what senior management feel it should be. Culture is also determined by the nature of staff employed and the extent to which they accept management philosophy and policies or pay only 'lip service'. Another important influence is the match between corporate culture and employees' perception of the psychological contract (**discussed in Chapter 1**).

- **The environment.** In order to be effective, the organisation must be responsive to external environmental influences. For example, if the organisation operates within a dynamic environment it requires a structure and culture that are sensitive and readily adaptable to change. An organic structure is more likely to respond effectively to new opportunities and challenges, and risks and limitations presented by the external environment. (**Recall the discussion on mechanistic and organic systems in Chapter 11.**)

The cultural web

In order to help describe and understand the culture of an organisation, *Johnson et al.* present a cultural web, which brings together different aspects for the analysis of organisational culture (*see* Figure 15.3).

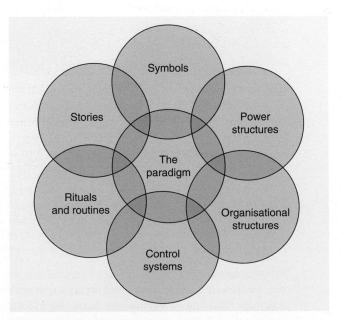

Figure 15.3 The cultural web
Source: Johnson, G., Whittington, R., Scholes, K., Angwin, D. and Regnér, P. *Exploring Strategy*, tenth edition, Pearson Education Ltd (2014), p. 156

- **Routine behaviours** – the ways in which members of the organisation behave towards each other and towards those outside the organisation and that make up how things are done or how things should happen.
- **Rituals** – the particular activities or special events through which the organisation emphasises what is particularly important; can include formal organisational processes and informal processes.
- **Stories** told by members of the organisation that embed the present and flag up important events and personalities, and typically have to do with successes, failures, heroes, villains and mavericks.
- **Symbols** – such as logos, offices, cars, titles, type of language or terminology commonly used, which become a shorthand representation of the nature of the organisation.
- **Power structures** – the power of the most powerful individuals or groups in the organisation, which may be based on management position and seniority, but in some organisations power can be lodged with other levels or functions.
- **Control systems** – the measurement and reward systems that emphasise what it is important to monitor, and to focus attention and activity upon, for example, stewardship of funds or quality of service.
- **Organisational structure** – which reflects power structures and delineates important relationships and activities within the organisation, and involves both formal structure and control and less formal systems.
- **The paradigm** of the organisation, which encapsulates and reinforces the behaviours observed in other elements of the cultural web.[19]

Culture and organisational control

A number of writers have referred to an alternative view of culture as a means of organisational control. For example, *Cartwright* sees culture as a system of management authority. When accepted by employees, cultural values increase the power and authority of management in three ways. Employees:

- identify themselves with their organisation and accept its rules when 'it is the right thing to do';
- internalise the organisation's values when they believe they are right; and
- are motivated to achieve the organisation's objectives.[20]

Egan refers to culture as the largest organisational control system that dictates how crazy or idiosyncratic people can be. Companies and institutions have both an overt and covert culture that influences both business and organisational behaviour.

> *The covert set can be quite dysfunctional and costly. Culture – the assumptions, beliefs, values and norms that drive 'the way we do things here' – is the largest and most controlling of the systems because it affects not only overt organisational behaviour but also the shadow-side behaviour . . . Culture lays down norms for the social system. In one institution you had to be an engineer to rise to the top. There was no published rule, of course, it was just the way things were. In one bank you could never be made an officer of the company if you wore polyester clothes. Culture tells us what kind of politics is allowed and just how members of an organisation are allowed to play the political game.[21]*

Watson refers to the cultural design of an organisation and the link between direct and indirect controls. In a highly centralised organisation with a tight bureaucratic structure and culture, there would be an emphasis on direct controls with prescribed rules and procedures, and a low level of psychological commitment from employees. In a less centralised organisation with a loosely bureaucratic structure and culture, there would be more attention to indirect controls with relatively loose rules and procedures, greater flexibility and discretion, and a culture of high-level commitment.[22]

Critical review and reflection

The idea that culture is a form of management control over the behaviour and identities of individuals is far too nebulous. It all depends on the personality and actions of immediate supervisors and/or senior managers.

What is YOUR considered opinion? To what extent do YOU believe your organisation's culture asserts control over YOUR behaviour?

Two different forms of culture

ACAS distinguishes two different organisational cultures and different ways of doing things:

- control culture with the emphasis on rules and procedures, control and compliance with precedent providing guidelines; and
- quality of working life culture with the emphasis on core values, with mission statements providing guidance and commitment via shared goals, values and traditions.[23]

Kershaw contrasts rules-based or values-based culture.

> In rules-based cultures, people follow the rules and procedures assuming they are in place for good reasons and will achieve results. Examples of this type of organisation are the emergency services and the military. However, some companies may have a rules-based bias as a result of the regulatory nature of the work they undertake, or even because of a particular management style. In value-driven organisations, there is a 'code of conduct' made up of a number of values that set out expected behaviours. People should understand the values of the organisation so that they know how to behave and perform to achieve objectives. . . Diverse organisations need a mix of 'command and control' and 'culture and values' to be successful.[24]

The importance of culture

Applications of organisational behaviour and effective management of people are dependent not only upon the nature of the industry or business, but also upon the characteristic features of the individual organisation – and its culture. The pervasive nature of culture in terms of 'how things are done around here' and common values, beliefs and attitudes will therefore have a significant effect on organisational processes such as decision-making, design of structure, group behaviour, work organisation, motivation and job satisfaction, and management control. With increasing globalisation, work organisations are becoming even more complex and internationally based. There is greater emphasis on the understanding and management of a diverse group of people from different nationalities into a coherent culture.

Reigle refers to culture as an important factor in successful technology implementation, innovation, mergers, acquisitions, job satisfaction, organisational success and team effectiveness, and to the importance of determining whether organisations exhibit organic or mechanistic cultures.[25]

Culture and work ethic

Culture can influence people's attitudes and behaviour at work. *Bunting* draws attention to the link between work ethic (**discussed in Chapter 1**) and culture, and the extent to which people have a choice over how hard they work. Although some people have no choice, for the vast majority of people there is a degree of choice but the choices are not made in isolation:

> *they are the product of the particular organisational culture of our workplaces, which promote concepts of success, of team spirit so that we don't let colleagues down, and a powerful work ethic. We are also influenced by a culture that reinforces that work ethic and its cycle of continual achievement and consumption as measures of self-worth.*

Bunting maintains that it is through work that we seek to satisfy our craving for a sense of control, mastery and security, and that clever organisations exploit this cultural context by designing corporate cultures that meet the emotional needs of their employees.[26]

The culture of the organisation is also important in determining the behaviour of managers and how well the organisation works. *Brodbeck* refers to a blame culture that exists in many organisations and where the brickbats fly more often than the bouquets. Such organisations are a very unhealthy environment in which to work. For example, an organisation may see low reports of errors as a healthy sign but in reality this is because individuals are worried about reporting mistakes. Improving the safety culture and a climate of proactive error management will encourage individuals to see the benefits when errors are pinpointed.[27]

The Core Partnership suggests that the kind of culture existing within an organisation can be gauged by the amount of time employees are expected to work past their core hours. This is often considered as an unwritten law. A culture that encourages bottom-sharing of new ideas contributes to employee morale.[28]

The competitive environment and concerns about job security have contributed to a prevailing work culture of 'presenteeism'. In many organisations working long hours is seen as a necessary feature of acceptable behaviour and career progression. Presenteeism does not necessarily imply physical presence at your place of work, but ready availability at most hours, including weekends and evenings, by email and mobile.

National cultural environment (**discussed in Chapter 1**) can have a noticeable effect on presenteeism. As the author experienced for himself in Australia, work-related activities are often undertaken comfortably away from the workplace, in local coffee houses for example, without concern about not being seen by management. This is in contrast to the typical work ethic throughout much of the USA, where again the author experienced the almost obsessive concern for always being seen about the place.

Culture and organisational performance

Culture is clearly an important ingredient of effective organisational performance. *Stanford* suggests that although people have difficulty in explaining why, intuitively they know that 'yes, of course' culture matters. It is an intangible asset that is both distinctive to that organisation and adds value to it (or diminishes value). Ten typical characteristics that form the typical organisation culture are: a story or stories, a purpose, a set of values, an attitude to people, a global mindset, a relationship network, a digital presence, a reputation, a customer proposition and a horizon-scanning ability. Although links between culture and business success are difficult to prove, Stanford maintains that even when there is a strong and healthy culture, a business cannot be successful if there is a flawed business model. However, with a strong and healthy culture there is less likelihood of a flawed business model.[29]

Hilton believes there is a stronger link and that companies succeed because of their culture. Most management systems, such as risk management, neglect the importance of culture and treat business as a mechanical operation when its outcomes depend fundamentally on the way people behave and interact.

> *The key to understanding any business is to understand its culture, yet often it is the most neglected and taken for granted part. Companies succeed because of their culture, they*

decline because of their culture and if there were to be any single reason advanced for the failure of two thirds of mergers and acquisitions, it would probably be the incompatibility in culture of the businesses.[30]

As *Clifton* points out, an organisation's culture, whether officially defined and promoted or just established organically, will determine a whole range of performance indicators. A happy and engaged workforce is widely acknowledged to outperform one where negativity and office politics thrive: 'Business leaders should re-evaluate the importance of culture when embarking on any change management programme focused on performance improvement.'[31]

Critical review and reflection

The extent to which an individual's needs and expectations at work are compatible with the culture of an organisation is probably the most important determinant of motivation and job satisfaction.

Are YOU able to challenge this assertion? How important is the culture of YOUR university to YOUR general state of well-being and to your studies?

National and international culture

With greater global competition, an understanding of national culture has become of increasing importance for managers. *Schneider and Barsoux* suggest that cultural beliefs and values influence the meaning of management and also show up differences in conceptions of organisations. National differences and cultural reasons raise concerns about the transferability of organisational structures, systems and processes, and question the logic of universal 'best practice'.[32] *Cheng et al.* also question the universality of theories of management and organisational behaviour on the grounds that they have not adequately addressed the factor of culture.[33]

According to *Francesco and Gold*, culture has recently been accepted as an explanation of organisational behaviour. One reason is the increase in competitiveness of nations and a second reason is that managers encounter different cultures in their contacts with people from other nations. However, there are limits to the use of culture to explain organisational behaviour, and the relationship between national cultural values and actual behaviour in organisations is complex.[34]

Menzies points out that understanding the culture of doing business in a particular country can give you the upper hand. While the cultural differences in doing business abroad represent one of the biggest barriers to efficient working, these barriers can be easily overcome by taking the time to understand the nuances of business culture, including different legal frameworks and local business culture and language.[35]

The CIPD points out that an increase in travel and technology and the international broadcasting of television channels has led to a blurring of some distinctions of culture. However, there are still clearly definable differences in culture between different countries and ethnic groups.

Although the outward signs of work (dress, technology, etc.) might be increasingly similar regardless of the country of origin, there are many ways in which people can be offended, and business propositions damaged, if there is not an understanding of the culture of the country in which the activities are being conducted.[36]

See the discussion on language as part of culture in Chapter 6, and culture as a contingent factor of leadership in Chapter 9. See also the case study on Brazil below.

A generic model of cultural categorisation

With the wide range of national cultures and regional variations, and a world of rapidly globalising business, *Lewis* draws attention to the importance of cross-cultural training and a generic model of cultural categorisation. His model classifies cultures under three main headings: linear-actives; multi-actives; and reactives (*see* Figure 15.4).

- **Linear-active people** tend to be task-orientated, highly organised planners who complete action chains doing one thing at a time. They prefer straightforward and direct discussion, adhere to logic rather than emotion, have faith in rules and regulations, honour written contracts and are process orientated.

- **Multi-active people** are emotional, loquacious and impulsive, and attach great importance to family, feelings and relationships. They like to do many things at the same time. Relationships and connections are more important than products. They have limited respect for authority, often procrastinate, are flexible and often change their plans.

- **Reactive people** are listeners who rarely initiate action or discussion. They concentrate on what is being said, listen before they leap and show respect. Reactives are introverts and adept at non-verbal communications. Silence is regarded as a meaningful part of discourse. Smalltalk is not easy and lack of eye contact is typical.[37]

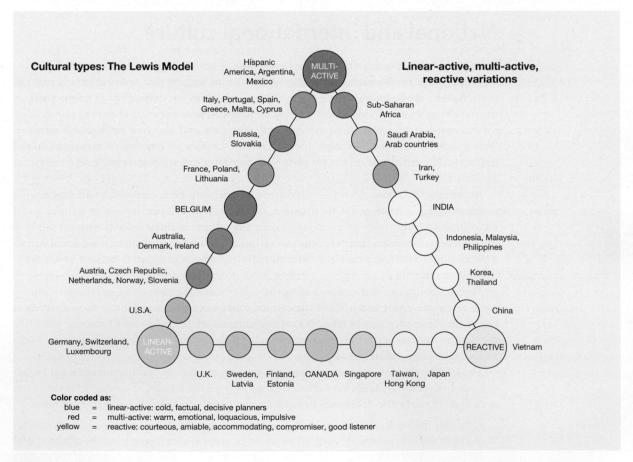

Figure 15.4 Cultural categorisation

Source: from The Cultural Imperative: Global Trends in the 21st Century, Nicholas Brealey (Lewis, R.D. 2007) © 2003 Richard Lewis. Reproduced by permission of Nicholas Brealey Publishing.

Case study
Brazil

Full of colour and rhythm, Brazil has become the new land of opportunity in South America. Currently the seventh largest economy in the world, Brazil is wrought by its diverse culture and geography. Its growing economy is a thriving fusion of Portuguese, African and indigenous Indian influences, all of which have left their mark on Brazilian society. When in Brazil to do business, having an understanding of the diversity of its society and the unique values and attitudes of its citizens will help you to develop better relationships and do business more successfully with your Brazilian colleagues.

Under its motto 'Ordem e Progresso', Brazilian culture is known for its hospitality, openness and traditional events, such as the carnival. The climate of Brazil comprises a wide range of weather conditions across a large area and a varied topography, but most of the country is tropical. It is important to appreciate that the Brazilian football team is a key component of national pride. As such you shouldn't schedule a business meeting during a soccer match and you should always comment about the game when on a conference call.

In Brazil family is at the centre of the social structure. Families in Brazil tend to be large and close-knit, providing members with security and connections. The importance of family is also evident in Brazilian business culture, where family members will often be found working for the same company, whether or not it is family-owned.

Relationships are one of the most important elements of Brazilian business culture. It is essential therefore to spend time getting to know your Brazilian counterparts, both personally and professionally. By cultivating close personal relationships and building trust, you will have a greater chance of successfully doing business in Brazil.

When you meet someone for the first time, it is polite to say 'muito prazer' (my pleasure). Expressions such as 'como vai' and 'tudo bem' are common forms of saying hello once you know someone and can demonstrate that you are making an effort to develop a relationship with a person. The use of titles and first names varies across Brazilian society. It is polite to address your Brazilian counterpart with their title and surname at the first meeting or when writing to them. Once you know them, it is common to use just first names, or else their title followed by their first name.

Advancing your company's relationship with a Brazilian company may rest upon your ability to gain trust. So, on your next meeting, remember to make eye contact, as this shows you are paying attention and are interested and honest. Make sure to accept any food or coffee that is offered to you, saying no can be seen as insulting. Do not show feelings of frustration or impatience as this will reflect poorly on you as an individual. Brazilians pride themselves on their ability to be in control, so acting in a similar fashion will improve your relationship with your Brazilian counterparts.

You should bear in mind that Brazilian companies tend to have vertical hierarchies, where managers at the top make most of the decisions. These positions tend to be dominated by men, but women are slowly gaining employment in executive roles.

Time in Brazil is approached in a flexible manner; punctuality and defined plans are not common. This carries over into business, which can result in negotiations taking much longer than scheduled. Meetings are also often delayed or cancelled without any prior warning.

Finally, Fique tranquilo, if Brazilians value any single trait, it's optimism and being able to solve problems. If the problem can't be fixed, you should just relax and forget about it. At the first signs of someone becoming stressed, a Brazilian will often say: Fique tranquilo (fee-kee kdang-kwee-loh), which means don't worry; it has a very calming effect.

Paola Fonseca, Manager at TMF Costa Rica

Source: This case was published originally in ICSA Global Outlook, a supplement to the May 2011 issue of *Chartered Secretary* magazine.

Critical review and reflection

The proliferation of definitions and explanations of culture, its anthropological origins and lack of clarity undermine its value to our understanding of organisational behaviour. It is too ambiguous a concept for the effective day-to-day management of the organisation.

Do YOU agree? What role do YOU think culture plays in the management of YOUR own university or work organisation?

Organisational climate

In addition to arrangements for the carrying out of organisational processes, management have a responsibility for creating a climate in which people are motivated to work willingly and effectively. Organisational climate is another general concept and difficult to define precisely. It is more something that is felt. It is often likened to our description of the weather and the way in which the climate of a geographical region results from the combination of environmental forces. Some of these forces are better understood than others. In a similar way that culture was defined simply as 'how things are done around here', climate can be defined as 'how it feels to work around here'.

Both culture and climate relate to the value-system of the organisation and both have an influence on the behaviour of its members. **Organisational climate** can be said to relate to the prevailing atmosphere surrounding the organisation, to the level of morale and to the strength of feelings of belonging, care and goodwill among members. Climate will influence the attitudes that members of the organisation bring to bear on their work performance and personal relationships. The extent to which employees accept the culture of the organisation will have a significant effect on climate. Whereas organisational culture describes what the organisation is about, organisational climate is an indication of the employees' feelings and beliefs of what the organisation is about. According to *Tagiuri and Litwin,* climate is based on the perceptions of members towards the organisation.

> *Organizational climate is a relatively enduring quality of the internal environment of an organization that (a) is experienced by its members, (b) influences their behavior, and (c) can be described in terms of the values of a particular set of characteristics (or attributes) of the organization.[38]*

Characteristics of a healthy organisational climate

Organisational climate is characterised, therefore, by the nature of the people–organisation relationship and the superior–subordinate relationship. These relationships are determined by interactions among goals and objectives, formal structure, the process of management, styles of leadership and the behaviour of people. Although similar types of organisations will share certain common features and norms, each organisation will have its own different and distinctive features. In general terms, however, a healthy organisational climate might be expected to exhibit such characteristic features as set out in Figure 15.5.

A healthy climate will not by itself guarantee improved organisational effectiveness. However, an organisation is most unlikely to attain optimum operational performance unless the climate evokes a spirit of support and co-operation throughout the organisation, and is conducive to motivating members to work willingly and effectively. *Gray* maintains from his research to have found a clear correlation between successful workplace outcomes and a range of climate characteristics and that a climate conducive to successful outcomes also tends to be

The extent to which members of staff believe there is:

- acceptance of the psychological contract between the organisation and its members
- managerial and leadership behaviour appropriate to the particular work situation
- mutual trust, consideration and support among different levels of the organisation
- easy access to senior staff with open channels of communication
- respect for individual differences, diversity, equality and inclusion
- attention to work environment and reduction of alienation or frustration at work
- genuine concern for flexibility and work/life balance
- opportunities for personal development and career progression
- democratic functioning of the organisation and opportunities for participation
- recognition of trade unions or staff representatives
- open discussion of conflict with attempt to avoid confrontation
- a sense of identity within the organisation
- a feeling of being a valued and appreciated member of the organisation

Figure 15.5 Characteristic features of a healthy organisational climate

conducive to individual happiness. The climate of an organisation has a significant impact on the quality and quantity of work that gets done and on the well-being of employees.[39]

Six dimensions of climate

Atkinson and Frechette of Forum Corporation maintain there is a direct correlation between organisational climate and financial results. A healthy climate increases employee motivation, catalysing more effective performance. Research by Forum identifies six dimensions that influence the work environment and employee motivation:

- **Clarity** – people's degree of understanding of the organisation's goals and policies, as well as the requirement of their job.
- **Commitment** – the expression of continuing dedication to a common purpose and to achieving goals.
- **Standards** – the emphasis management place on high-performance standards and the amount of pressure it exerts on teams to improve performance.
- **Responsibility** – the degree to which people feel personally responsible for their work.
- **Recognition** – the feeling that people are recognised and rewarded for doing good work, and that they receive accurate performance feedback.
- **Teamwork** – the feeling of belonging to an organisation characterised by cohesion, mutual support, trust and pride.

A corporate imperative now is to cultivate a positive organisational climate in a negative economic one. Successful leaders take pains to ignite a chain reaction that improves climate, increases motivation and enhances performance. Strong leaders have the motivation and influence skills to develop the workforce in these six measurable dimensions.[40]

Organisational change

Change is an inevitable and constant feature. It is an inescapable part of both social and organisational life and we are all subject to continual change of one form or another. Like it or not, change happens. Change is also a pervasive influence and much of the following discussion provides links with other topics in other chapters. The effects of change can be studied over different time scales, from weeks to hundreds of years, and studied at different levels. Change can be studied in terms of its effects at the individual, group, organisation, society, national or international level. However, because of its pervasive nature, change at any one level is inter-related with changes at other levels, and it is difficult to study one area of change in isolation.

At the individual level there could, for example, be a **personal transformational change** where circumstances have not changed, but because of some emotional or spiritual happening the individual was transformed or changed. This transformation may have some effect on the individual's behaviour and actions at work and relationships with colleagues. But our main focus of attention is on the management of organisational change. Organisational change can be initiated deliberately by managers, it can evolve slowly within a department, it can be imposed by specific changes in policy or procedures, or it can arise through external pressures. Change can affect all aspects of the operation and functioning of the organisation.[41]

Forces of change

An organisation can perform effectively only through interactions with the broader external environment of which it is part. The structure and functioning of the organisation must reflect, therefore, the nature of the environment in which it is operating. Factors that create an increasingly volatile environment include:

- uncertain economic conditions;
- globalisation and fierce world competition;
- the level of government intervention;
- EU influences and social legislation;
- political interests;
- scarcity of natural resources;
- rapid developments in new technologies and the information age.

In order to help ensure its survival and future success the organisation must be readily adaptable to the external demands placed upon it. The organisation must be responsive to change. Other major forces of change include:

- increased demands for quality and high levels of customer service and satisfaction;
- greater flexibility in the structure of work organisations and patterns of management;
- the changing nature and composition of the workforce;
- social and cultural influences such as diversity, equality and inclusion;
- conflict from within the organisation.

According to Dan *Wagner,* change is good:

> *It is the whole dynamic that creates successful companies in the first place, whether you are trying to do something differently or more efficiently, or something that leverages the technology that has become prevalent to do something better.*

And according to Duncan *Tait:*

> *It is always better to lead change than react to it, in my experience, because the later you leave it to react to change, the more severe your actions have to be.*[42]

Economic change in the EU

The European Commission points out that today all economic sectors face the permanent effects of economic change, which may be cyclical, structural or related to globalisation. In the past companies have had to change to adapt to specific events such as new technology or manufacturing process, but now change no longer constitutes a response to a specific crisis. Change has become permanent.

Economic change cannot be managed by preserving old practices but requires the development of common approaches and modern practices, and to generalise a proactive culture of anticipating change. In order to reflect the changed and changing environment, the EU is likely to face a number of challenges including finding the necessary skills to allow the European economy to remain competitive in the global market. The EU makes a range of funds available to Member States in order to support restructuring and works within a body of legislation, including information and consultation of workers on changes likely to affect them.[43]

Critical review and reflection

Continuing organisational change is inevitable. It is nothing new and a simple fact of life. There is no point in dwelling on the subject. It is easier just to accept the need to adapt to change as part of your working life.
To what extent are YOU in agreement? How readily are YOU able to adapt to change?

Planned organisational change

Change also originates within the organisation itself. Much of this change is part of a natural process of ageing – for example: as material resources such as buildings, equipment or machinery deteriorate or lose efficiency; or as human resources get older; or as skills and abilities become outdated. Some of this change can be managed through careful planning – for example, regular repairs and maintenance, choice of introducing new technology or methods of work, effective HR planning to prevent a large number of staff retiring at the same time, and management succession planning – training and staff development. However, the main pressure of change is usually from external forces. The organisation must be properly prepared to face the demands of a changing environment. It must give attention to its future development and success; this includes public-sector organisations and the armed forces.

A concept map of sources of organisational change is presented in Figure 15.6.

Most planned organisational change is triggered by the need to respond to new challenges or opportunities presented by the external environment, or in anticipation of the need to cope with potential future problems, for example uncertain economic conditions, intended government legislation, new product development by a major competitor or further technological advances. Planned change represents an intentional attempt to improve, in some important way, the operational effectiveness of the organisation.

The basic underlying objectives can be seen in general terms as:

- modifying the behavioural patterns of members of the organisation; and
- improving the ability of the organisation to cope with changes in its environment.

Behaviour modification

A programme of planned change and improved performance developed by *Lewin* involves the management of a three-phase process of behaviour modification:

- **unfreezing** – reducing those forces that maintain behaviour in its present form, recognition of the need for change and improvement to occur;
- **movement** – development of new attitudes or behaviour and the implementation of the change;
- **refreezing** – stabilising change at the new level and reinforcement through supporting mechanisms, for example policies, structure or norms.[44]

French et al. list eight specific components of a planned-change effort related to the above process (*see* Figure 15.7).[45]

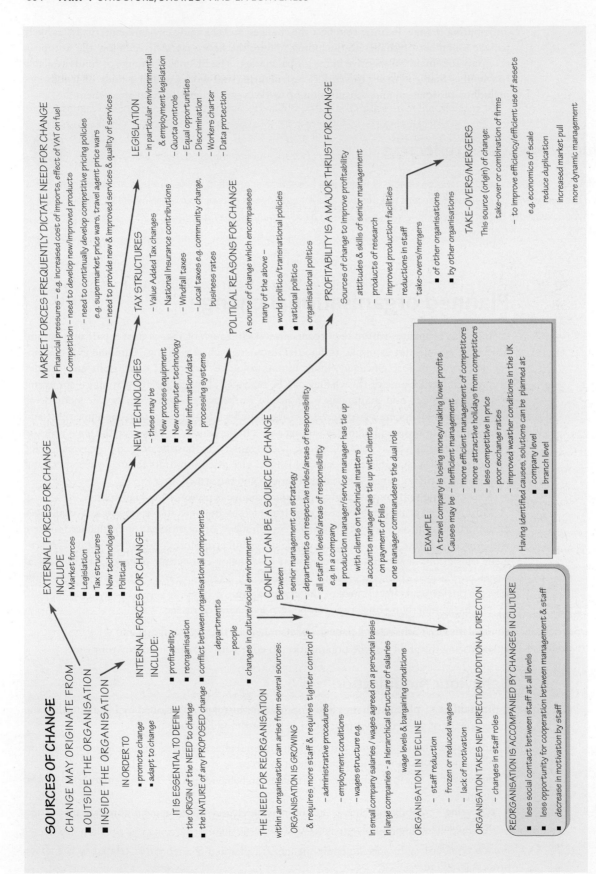

Figure 15.6 Sources of change

Source: Copyright © 2011 The Virtual Learning Materials Workshop. Reproduced with permission.

French, Kast and Rosenzweig refer to eight specific stages of a planned-change effort related to the above process.

- **Unfreezing** relates to the stages of (1) initial problem identification and (2) obtaining data.
- **Movement** relates also to stage (2) obtaining data; and stages (3) problem diagnosis, (4) action planning, (5) implementation, (6) follow-up and stabilisation, and (7) assessment of consequences.
- **Refreezing** relates also to stage (7) assessment of consequences; and (8) learning from the process.

Figure 15.7 Stages in a planned-change effort
Source: based on French, W. L., Kast, F. E. and Rosenzweig, J. E. *Understanding Human Behavior in Organizations*, Harper and Row (1985), p. 9.

Management and organisational behaviour in action case study:
MANAGEMENT 2020

HARRIET GREEN
CHIEF EXECUTIVE
THOMAS COOK

Harriet Green told the Commission about her personal 'transformation toolkit', which she has used to overhaul a number of organisations on different continents, including Thomas Cook.

'Driving transformation is a 24/7 job,' she said. 'Organisations are like living organisms and, when looking to transform them, you need to consider all elements, whilst addressing the most urgent priorities.' The critical three elements are:

The psychology: how people think, feel and act – in other words, the organisation's culture, values, ways of working and 'the way we get things done round here'.

The physiology: the systems and processes that underpin and connect the business, like nerve endings and blood flows.

And, finally, *its anatomy*: the organisational structure. Businesses need to create a lean, agile structure as befits a digitally enabled business, supporting fast decision-making, and reducing the layers of management between the CEO and customers.

Harriet believes a CEO must lead change in all three areas to truly transform the organisation. An effective CEO today needs to operate at the centre of the vortex – not from the top of the pyramid in a historical, hierarchical construct – and has to gather information from all the organisation's communities, both internal and external. *'Organisations are like living organisms and, when looking to transform them, you need to consider all elements, whilst addressing the most urgent priorities.'*

Harriet described some of the key 'tools' in her personal leadership toolkit that are helping her to drive the ongoing turnaround at Thomas Cook.

Investigate the problem

On her first day as CEO, Harriet sent a survey to everyone in the business asking what was wrong with it. In under a month, over 8,000 people had replied. Those at the frontline usually know what's not working and have a passion for fixing it.

Be visible

Communicate often, update the organisation regularly, and use different media, like video. Be available and reply quickly. Be visible, share honestly and celebrate success.

Be open

Ensure you are open to feedback from employees. At Thomas Cook, Harriet developed an 'Ask Harriet' email address, so employees could email in confidence on any issue. At its peak, Harriet received 200 emails a day and prides herself on replying to everyone.

Identify talent

Leaders need to identify their talented performers quickly. Engage with people across the organisation — meet the key players in every area, know their direct reports, and meet with up and coming talent. Identify quickly those who are not 'on the bus'—make decisions quickly. When transforming an organisation, moving at pace is essential—don't waste time trying to convert those managers and leaders who don't want to change and who make it clear that they will never support the new ways. Give everyone a fair chance to change but then take the tough decisions. Middle-management is often a big part of the problem—and also the solution. By engaging and fostering belief at the top and the bottom of the organisation, those in the middle who might be slower to change begin to feel the squeeze and move forward positively.

Build a winning team

Bringing in fresh talent, different industry experience and a different perspective is vitally important, as is identifying the skills and knowledge gaps early on. At Thomas Cook, Harriet personally recruited close to 80 people, believing that, when transforming the leadership of an organisation, the principle of 'a third, a third and a third' is usually the right balance: keep one-third of the original leadership team, promote one-third from within and bring in one-third to give fresh perspective and learnings from other industries, and then involve and engage them to work together as one aligned team.

Develop the culture

From the very start, focus on the culture. Develop and agree together the values and the ways of working. Create a strong code of conduct and involve the whole organisation. Everyone needs to clearly know what the organisation believes in, how it works and 'how we do things round here'. Together, these will create a culture and build trust. Every employee needs to see themselves and their beliefs reflected in the culture to succeed—like a flamingo looking into a pool. Develop clear leadership competencies to measure the performance of your leaders and enforce the code of conduct fairly and clearly for everyone without exception. Lead with integrity and by example every day. Be a role model.

Break down barriers

Silos and organisational politics have no place in transformations—build new teams, share best practice and encourage openness.

Celebrate success

Remember to take time to celebrate success—it's an important part of rebuilding belief, particularly in an organisation that's been through a tough time. Pride in the company, its performance, its products and its services is important for everyone.

Listen to stakeholders

Never stop listening to your customers. Never be so remote or so arrogant to think you can stop listening to any of your key stakeholders.

Source: 'MANAGEMENT 2020', Commission on The Future of Management and Leadership, Chartered Management Institute, July 2014, p.33, www.managers.org.uk/management2020. Reproduced with permission.

Tasks

1. Explain fully what you understand by transformational change. Give your own views on Harriet Green's 'transformation toolkit'.
2. To what extent do you believe sending a survey to everyone in the business is *ordinarily* likely to produce constructive and meaningful feedback? How well do you think this would work in your own university?
3. What particular problems do you foresee in attempting to 'create a strong code of conduct and involve the whole organisation'?

Transformational change

Organisations may be faced with the need for large-scale **transformational change** involving a fundamental shift in the culture, conduct of business and working practices of the organisation. Transformational change is often enacted over a **period** of time. The CIPD reports on the increasing demand for transformational change programmes as organisations emerge from the recession and once again seek more growth and development-orientated opportunities. Investment in change capability and capacity is essential for organisations wishing to have an ability to effect transformational change.[46] **See the Management and organisational behaviour in action case study.**

The challenge of e-business

Whatever the future of e-business, it will continue to bring tremendous change. One of the biggest changes for managers, especially within large organisations, is learning how to get to grips with an increasingly flexible workforce. As a result of the e-business environment many people can work at any time, anywhere and at any place. Many employees work at home but although the virtual office may help organisations to cut costs, it also poses many management challenges, including the challenge to put structures in place to ensure regular meetings take place. Flexible working calls for flexible managers. This means that the traditional line managers need to become leaders, coaches and facilitators. Given the accelerating rate of change, particularly with the Internet, it is essential that organisations invest in and develop their managers to succeed with this change.

Continuous organisational change and burnout

Rees and Rumbles point out that the pace and scope of change have been unprecedented and they examine the extent to which continuous organisational change leads to organisational burnout. Organisational causes of burnout include excessive workload, lack of autonomy and authority, insufficient reward, and disparity between personal and organisational values. Burnout may also have a 'spillover' effect on people's home lives. Rees and Rumbles question the extent to which organisations 'care' about the amount of stress that occurs during change and whether organisations can assess whether their human capital is close to burnout.

In terms of practical intervention, organisations must firstly have measures of measuring and evaluating organisational stress, and an understanding of the potential for organisational burnout. Organisations also need to determine how to get out of the burnout rut by becoming more resilient to change and engaging employees in a positive and productive manner in order to ensure long-term success. The involvement of managers in both preventing and dealing with the symptoms of burnout is paramount.[47] (**Organisational stress is discussed in Chapter 3.**)

Resistance to change

Despite the potential positive outcomes, change is often resisted at both the individual and the organisational level. Resistance to change – or the thought of the implications of the change – appears to be a common phenomenon. As long ago as 1970, *Toffler* wrote about the psychological dimension of 'future shock', and that people are naturally wary of change: 'Among many there is an uneasy mood – a suspicion that change is out of control.'[48]

Resistance to change can take many forms and it is often difficult to pinpoint the exact reasons. The forces against change in work organisations include: ignoring the needs and expectations of members; when members have insufficient information about the nature of the change; or if they do not perceive the need for change. Fears may be expressed over such matters as employment levels and job security, de-skilling of work, loss of job satisfaction, wage-rate differentials, changes to social structures and working conditions, loss of individual control over work and greater management control.

Change is reciprocal, and changing organisations will affect the nature of managerial work. *Lockhead* maintains that 'most successful organisations develop a culture that welcomes change and the opportunities it brings'.[49] However, according to *Crainer,* many managers refuse to accept the necessity of change. Instead of being proactive, change is often reactive, the last resort.

> *Research repeatedly shows that it is managers who are the chief stumbling block to making change happen. Changing organizational structures and managerial thinking challenges and undercuts traditional power bases . . . For the manager reared on the old functional certainties, the new world organization is very difficult to manage. Indeed, the vast majority of managers are neither trained nor equipped to manage in such an environment.*[50]

The impact of change on work organisations and their management draws attention to the importance of lifelong learning and self-development (**discussed in Chapter 5**).

Individual resistance

Some common reasons for individual resistance to change within organisations include the following:

- **Selective perception.** People's interpretation of stimuli presents a unique picture or image of the 'real' world. This can result in selective perception and lead to a biased view of a particular situation, which fits most comfortably into a person's own perception of reality, and can cause resistance to change. For example, trade unionists may have a stereotyped view of management as untrustworthy and therefore oppose any management change, however well founded the intention might have been. Managers exposed to different theories or ideas may tend to categorise these as either those they already practise and have no need to worry about, or those that are of no practical value and that can be discarded as of no concern to them.

- **Habit.** People tend to respond to situations in an established and accustomed manner. Habits may serve as a means of comfort and security, and as a guide for easy decision-making. Old patterns are seductive. Proposed changes to habits, especially if the habits are well established and require little effort, may well be resisted. However, if there is a clearly perceived advantage, for example a reduction in working hours without loss of pay, there is likely to be less, if any, resistance to the change, although some people may, because of habit, still find it difficult to adjust to the new times.

- **Inconvenience or loss of freedom.** If the change is seen as likely to prove inconvenient, make life more difficult, reduce freedom of action or result in increased control, there will be resistance.

- **Economic implications.** People are likely to resist change that is perceived as reducing either directly or indirectly their pay or other rewards, requiring an increase in work for the same level of pay or acting as a threat to their job security. People tend to have established patterns of working and a vested interest in maintaining the status quo.

- **Security in the past.** There is a tendency for some people to find a sense of security in the past. In times of frustration or difficulty, or when faced with new or unfamiliar ideas or methods, people may reflect on the past. There is a wish to retain old and comfortable ways. For example, in bureaucratic organisations officials often tend to place faith in well-established ('tried and trusted') procedures and cling to these as giving a feeling of security.

- **Fear of the unknown.** Changes that confront people with the unknown tend to cause anxiety or fear. Many major changes in a work organisation present a degree of uncertainty, for example the introduction of new technology or methods of working. A person may resist promotion because of uncertainty over changes in responsibilities or the increased social demands of the higher position.

Critical review and reflection

Some people actively thrive on new challenges and constant change, while others prefer the comfort of the status quo and strongly resist any change. It is all down to the personality of the individual and there is little management can do about resistance to change.

What is YOUR attitude to change? To what extent do YOU welcome and accept, rather than resist, change?

Organisational resistance

Although organisations have to adapt to their environment, they tend to feel comfortable operating within the structure, policies and procedures that have been formulated to deal with a range of present situations. To ensure operational effectiveness, organisations often set up defences against change and prefer to concentrate on the routine things they perform well. Some of the main reasons for organisational resistance against change are as follows:

- **Organisational culture.** Recall that the culture of an organisation develops over time and may not be easy to change. The pervasive nature of culture in terms of 'how things are done around here' also has a significant effect on organisational processes and the behaviour of staff. An outdated culture may result in a lack of flexibility for, or acceptance of, change.

- **Maintaining stability.** Organisations, especially large-scale ones, pay much attention to maintaining stability and predictability. The need for formal structure and the division of work, narrow definitions of assigned duties and responsibilities, established rules, procedures and methods of work, can result in resistance to change. The more mechanistic or bureaucratic the structure, the less likely it is that the organisation will be responsive to change.

- **Investment in resources.** Change often requires large resources that may already be committed to investments in other areas or strategies. Assets such as buildings, technology, equipment and people cannot easily be altered. For example, a manufacturer may not find it easy to change to a socio-technical approach and the use of autonomous work groups because it cannot afford the cost of a new purpose-built plant and specialised equipment.

- **Past contracts or agreements.** Organisations enter into contracts or agreements with other parties, such as the government, other organisations, trade unions, suppliers and customers. These contracts and agreements can limit changes in behaviour – for example, organisations operating under a special licence or permit, or a fixed-price contract to supply goods/services to a government agency. Another example might be an agreement with unions that limits the opportunity to introduce redundancies, or the introduction of new technology or working practices.

- **Threats to power or influence.** Change may be seen as a threat to the power or influence of certain groups within the organisation, such as their control over decisions, resources or information. For example, managers may resist the introduction of worker-directors because they see this as increasing the role and influence of non-managerial staff, and a threat to the power in their own positions. Where a group of people have, over a period of time, established what they perceive as their 'territorial rights', they are likely to resist change.

Perceptions and change

Although change is often resisted, *Cunningham* maintains that one of the greatest myths in management is the generalisation that people resist change. In fact people love change. The commonest reason for resistance is where people perceive a potential loss. For example, because of negative rumour-mongering, people may perceive that they will be worse off from a proposed change even if the opposite is in fact true. In a different context, changes that result, for example, in the loss of one's job can create real, fact-based resistance. While people welcome change that they want, they have to be careful about the pace of change. In a more general context people may be enthusiastic for change, for example in large organisations where some people want to see changes and improvements in communication.

> *What seems to get in the way is the continual chanting of the untrue generalisation that 'people resist change'. People resist some change – if they perceive that they are going to lose out. People welcome change that makes things better.*[51]

Managing change

The successful management of change is clearly essential for continued economic performance and competitiveness and is the life-blood of business success. New ideas and innovations should not be perceived as threats by members of the organisation. Efforts to maintain the balance of the socio-technical system will influence people's attitudes, the behaviour of individuals and groups, and thereby the level of organisational performance and effectiveness.

Many books and articles refer to the steps or actions to be taken to secure successful and sustainable change.[52] The CMI provides a thirteen-point action checklist for the implementation of an effective change programme:

1. Agree the implementation strategy.
2. Agree timeframes.
3. Draw up detailed implementation plans.
4. Set up a team of change champions.
5. Establish good programme management practices.
6. Communicate clearly.
7. Ensure participation and help to minimise stress.
8. Personalise the case for change.
9. Be prepared for conflict and manage it effectively.
10. Motivate your employees.
11. Develop skills.
12. Maintain momentum.
13. Monitor and evaluate.

The checklist aims to provide some generic guidance. It assumes a sound business case for change has been made, and the scope and objectives clearly defined. The detailed schedule for implementing change will vary according to both the type of organisation and the nature and scope of the changes planned.[53]

Toterhi and Recardo report that many business leaders continue to struggle with navigating their organisation through a change initiative. Despite increased awareness of change management processes, principles and practices, challenges from nine common blunders can significantly impede progress in achieving project goals:

Blunder 1. Accepting lucklustre leadership.
Blunder 2. Setting fire to perfectly good platforms.
Blunder 3. Treating change management as a separate workstream.
Blunder 4. Failing to align the organisation to support the change.
Blunder 5. Tolerating weak project management.
Blunder 6. Tolerating soft deadlines and weak metrics.
Blunder 7. Creating a convoluted plot.
Blunder 8. Failure to buy a warranty.
Blunder 9. Letting culture hold you hostage.

Toterhi and Recardo propose a road map of change, methodology, essential tasks and guidelines for change management.[54]

Minimising problems of change

People are the key factor in the successful management of change. If change is to work, it must change the perceptions, attitudes and behaviour of people. The effective management of change must be based on a clear understanding of human behaviour at work. Most people are not detached from their work but experience a range of emotional involvements through their membership of the organisation, and they feel threatened and disoriented by the challenge of change. Emotions such as uncertainty, frustration or fear are common reactions. It is understandable, therefore, that people often adopt a defensive and negative attitude, and demonstrate resistance to change. It is important to remember that change is a complex and powerful psychological experience, and that individuals react internally to change.

According to *Atkinson*, a major problem in driving change in organisations is dealing with and managing the resistance that will be encountered – but that resistance should be welcomed as a healthy response. Resistance is natural and should not be viewed only as a negative response to change. In the absence of really positive benefits from the proposed change, the 'default' response of resistance is acceptable.

> *It is unusual for any change not to attract some resistance. Even with foresight, pre-planning and all the apparent logic behind the need to change, you should expect some resistance as the norm. Recognise and welcome it as a healthy response and an opportunity to openly debate possibilities and treat resistance as a powerful ally in facilitating the learning process.*[55]

Taylor points out that one of the most stressful aspects of change is often the sense of loss of control that accompanies it. The individual can feel powerless and helpless. Many organisations spend a great deal of attention and energy focusing on the operational outcomes of proposed changes but often pay scant attention to enabling employees to adapt psychologically to the new situation.[56] *Reeves and Knell* suggest that 'knowledge leaders understand that change provokes an emotional response, that successful change involves allowing people to feel angry, resentful and afraid as well as excited, hopeful and energised'.[57]

Activities managed on the basis of economic or technical efficiency alone are unlikely to lead to optimum improvement in organisational performance. One of the most important factors in the successful implementation of organisational change is the style of managerial behaviour. Some members may actually prefer, and respond better, to a directed and controlled style of management. (**Recall, for example, the discussion on Theory X and Theory Y styles of managerial behaviour in Chapter 10.**) In most cases, however, the introduction of change is more likely to be effective with a participative style of managerial behaviour. If staff are kept fully informed of proposals, are encouraged to adopt a positive attitude and have personal involvement in the implementation of the change, there is a greater likelihood of their acceptance of the change.

- An important priority is to create an environment of trust and shared commitment, and to involve staff in decisions and actions that affect them. It is important that members of staff understand fully the reasons for change. Organisations should try to avoid change for the sake of change as this can both be disruptive and lead to mistrust. However, considerations of the need to change arising from advances in IT simply cannot be ignored. There should be full and genuine participation of all staff concerned as early as possible, preferably well before the actual introduction of new equipment or systems. Information about proposed change, its implications and potential benefits should be communicated clearly to all interested parties. Staff should be actively encouraged to contribute their own ideas, suggestions and experiences, and to voice openly their worries or concerns.

- Team management, a co-operative spirit among staff and a genuine feeling of shared involvement will help create a greater willingness to accept change. A participative style of managerial behaviour that encourages supportive relationships between managers and subordinates, and group methods of organisation, decision-making and supervision, are more likely to lead to a sustained improvement in work performance. There is an assumption that most people will direct and control themselves more willingly if they share in the setting of their objectives.

- As part of the pre-planning for new technology there should be a carefully designed 'human resource management action programme'. The action programme should be directed to a review of recruitment and selection, natural wastage of staff, potential for training, retraining and the development of new skills, and other strategies to reduce the possible level of redundancies or other harmful effects on staff. There should be full and meaningful consultation with trade unions and staff associations. Where appropriate, arrangements for greater flexibility or a shorter working week, and redeployment of staff, should be developed in full consultation with those concerned.

Critical review and reflection

The biggest difficulty with change is the associated fear and uncertainty. This is a natural reaction for most people. However, a participative style of management with full and open continuous communications throughout the change would noticeably minimise problems.

What is YOUR view? To what extent are YOU fearful and uncertain about organisational change?

Getting people to accept change

Anne Riches, an internationally recognised leader in neuro-scientific research, questions why some organisations struggle to change and applies an interesting approach to resistance to change based on a neuro-scientific understanding. Whether consolidating a merger, reengineering business processes, restructuring, changing value propositions, introducing new IT systems, relocating premises or changing the culture – all too often the process is derailed by the resistance of employees. Resistance to change is one of the most powerful drivers of human behaviour, and the key to dealing with it effectively is to understand both its physical and emotional components. Most organisations make two fatal errors when dealing with resistance. Firstly, they underestimate the strength of current patterns that employees are comfortable and familiar with. Secondly, they underestimate what will be required to change those patterns and deal with the automatic, though sometimes subtle, fight or flight responses that occur when employees interpret changes as threats.

The amygdala and The Almond Effect®

According to Riches, our brains are hard-wired to do three things: match patterns, resist or fight any threats to survival and respond first with emotion over logic. Our neural pathways and amygdalae are the key players in these reactions. The amygdala is an almond-shaped piece of the brain that triggers the 'fight or flight' reaction. Your brain has two amygdalae, and they play a fundamental role in ensuring your survival. Sometimes, though, the amygdalae set off a false alarm. This is what Riches calls The Almond Effect®. Put simply, you act without thinking and get it wrong. You can probably think of many times when this has happened, times when you said or did something in the heat of the moment and almost immediately afterwards regretted it.

At work, The Almond Effect often gets in the way. It is the reason why, all too often, human beings automatically react to change with resistance, even before they fully understand the nature of the change. The amygdala has activated the fear response based on previous memories of change (old neural pathways) associated with, for example, job losses, more work, new skills required, change of roster, cost cutting and so on. Stress hormones are released as part of the inbuilt flight/fight mechanism and show up at work as anger, anxiety, lethargy, poor performance and reluctance to change.

Mechanisms of change

Riches points out that people do not change behaviours easily. This is especially true in workplaces with cultures and histories that are slow and resistant to change. The nature and intensity of our motivation to change will differ in various circumstances but regardless of our reasons for wanting to change behaviours or thought patterns, we will have to create new neural pathways and then use them in preference to the old ones.

When we have to change, and even if we are strongly motivated to do so, we need to stay actively focused on changing our behaviours. If not, you may find yourself in a situation where the old behaviours are triggered automatically and reappear. Many managers seem to over-look this. They become frustrated and impatient with the time it takes for people to adopt change at work. They get tired of answering questions like: 'But what about . . . ?', 'What's wrong with the existing way?' and 'We've tried this before; what makes you think it will work this time?'. Many questions are rationally based, yet many more have an emotional basis.

It is worth remembering that:

- Humans are hard-wired for survival above all else.
- Our default thinking is habitual and self-perpetuating.
- Everyone is the product of their own experiences with different motivations and unique memories.
- Change can be frustratingly slow because it is hard brain work to rewire – even if it is logical and in the best interests.

Managers striving for commitment to change require people to respond to those emotion-based concerns even though they are under time pressures and deadlines. Failure to address the emotionally based questions results in delayed or failed change efforts. These questions are triggered by our amygdalae, which are concerned with anything that does not fit the existing patterns we know are 'safe'. **Successful change leaders know this.**[58]

Responsibilities of top management

The successful management of change is a key factor of organisational performance and effectiveness and should emanate from the top of the organisation. Top management have a responsibility for the underlying philosophy and attitudes of the organisation, for creating and sustaining a healthy climate and for establishing appropriate and supportive organisational processes. The successful implementation of change demands positive action from top management and a style of transformational leadership in order to gain a commitment to change. *Yukl* points out that, contrary to common assumptions, major changes are not always initiated by top management, who may not become involved until the process is well underway. However, large-scale change is unlikely to be successful without the support of top management.[59]

Leading IT change

A report published jointly by the CMI, the British Computer Society and the Change Leadership Network refers to challenges facing senior executives to ensure they are better prepared to lead technological change. Change always involves risk and on the basis of examination of ten detailed organisational case studies the report identifies five key challenges in obtaining best value from IT-enabled change:

- Creating transformational value rather than just implementing IT projects.
- Building capability for ongoing change. Being able to predict future business needs and how IT can help shape new business models and deliver the desired benefits.
- Creating a climate of open communication.
- Managing confidence and trust – understanding the impact of external changes.
- Building personal capability, learning and confidence.[60]

Change leaders

An interesting proposition is put forward by *Drucker*, who contends that 'one cannot manage change. One can only be ahead of it. Everyone now accepts that change is unavoidable.'

> But in a period of upheavals, such as the one we are living in, change is the norm. To be sure, it is painful and risky, and above all it requires a great deal of very hard work. But unless it is seen as the task of the organization to lead change, the organization – whether business, university, hospital and so on – will not survive. In a period of rapid structural change, the only

ones who survive are the Change Leaders. It is therefore a central 21st-century challenge for management that its organization becomes a change leader. A change leader sees change as opportunity. A change leader looks for change, knows how to find the right changes and knows how to make them effective both outside the organization and inside it. This requires:

1. *Policies to make the future.*
2. *Systematic methods to look for and to anticipate change.*
3. *The right way to introduce change, both within and outside the organization.*
4. *Policies to balance change and continuity.*[61]

Culture and change

Katzenbach et al. suggest that when a major change runs aground, leaders often blame their company's culture for pushing it off course. Too often culture becomes an excuse and diversion rather than an accelerator and energiser. Leaders see cultural initiatives as a last resort, except for top-down exhortations to change.

Must cultures are too well entrenched to be jettisoned. The secret is to stop fighting your culture – and to work with and within it, until it evolves in the right direction.[62]

Critical review and reflection

An organisation cannot develop, or change. It is the people comprising the organisation who determine the culture of the organisation, and who develop and change. The study of organisational culture and change should therefore concentrate priority on the actions, behaviour and effectiveness of individuals.

What is YOUR considered view? How realistic do YOU believe this contention to be?

Ten key points to remember

1 A central feature of the successful organisation is the diagnosis of its culture, health and performance, and the ability of the organisation to adapt to change.

2 Culture describes what the organisation is all about and helps to explain its underlying values and how things are performed in different organisations.

3 Culture is a general concept, and difficult to explain precisely. There are a number of ways to classify different types of organisational culture.

4 The culture of an organisation develops over time and in response to a complex set of factors. One view of culture is as a means of organisational control.

5 Culture has an important effect on the behaviour and actions of individuals, on the process of management and on organisational performance.

6 Organisational climate is based on the perception of members towards the organisation, and is the state of mutual trust and understanding among its members.

7 Organisations operate within an increasingly volatile environment. Change is a pervasive influence and an inescapable part of social and organisational life.

8 Planned organisational change involves a process of behaviour modification. Change is reciprocal and changing organisations may affect the nature of managerial work.

9 Change is often resisted at both the individual and organisational level. Resistance to change can take many forms and it is not always easy to pinpoint exact reasons.

10 The successful initiation and management of change must be based on a clear understanding of social factors and human behaviour at work.

Review and discussion questions

1 Explain how you would attempt to explain the concept of organisational culture. What factors do you believe influence the development of culture?

2 Discuss critically how you view the relationships between organisational culture and change.

3 To what extent do you believe the culture of an organisation can be likened to the personality of an individual?

4 What value do you place on different typologies of organisational culture?

5 Discuss critically the extent to which the climate within your own university has influenced the enjoyment of, and motivation towards, your course of study.

6 Explain fully how you see the main subject and focus of change.

7 Give specific examples of major change confronting management today and probable implications for your university and/or an organisation of your choice.

8 Explain fully why you think many people appear to exhibit a strong resistance to change. Where possible support your answer with actual examples.

9 Discuss critically your view of The Almond Effect® and a neuro-scientific understanding in overcoming individual resistance to change.

10 Explain fully what you believe are the most important features in the successful implementation and management of organisational change.

Assignment *Understanding your organisation's personality*

An important part of any manager's, salesperson's or front-line staff's role is to be an ambassador for the organisation. This means representing its values, its image and its style in a variety of situations.

In each case, you represent the personality not only of yourself, but of your organisation – and one of the most effective ways to explore the personality of your organisation is by describing it as if it were a person.

Ask yourself the following questions about your organisation:

* What gender would it be?
* How old would it be?
* Where would it live?
* Where would it prefer to holiday?
* What car would it drive?
* What interests or hobbies would it have?
* If it were to win the lottery, what would it do?

Source: Understanding Your Organisation's Image and Style, www.learningmatters.com

Compare and discuss your answers with colleagues. (Feedback may be given by your tutor.)

Personal skills and employability exercise

Objectives

Completing this exercise should help you to:

- Work together effectively in a small group.
- Evaluate organisational culture and its application to management and organisational behaviour.
- Undertake a critical review of the socialisation process.

Exercise

The socialisation of new members of staff into the culture of the organisation is an important aspect of management and organisational behaviour.

Working in small groups, you are required to undertake a detailed review of the socialisation of new members into the culture of your own university (or organisation). Comment critically, with supporting examples where possible, on the extent to which the socialisation process successfully addresses such topics as, for example:

- Design and nature of the induction programme
- Introduction to top management and key members of staff
- Expected patterns of behaviour
- Unwritten codes of behaviour, including dress codes
- Attempts to build cohesiveness among close working colleagues
- Mentoring relationships
- Responsibilities for human resource management
- Nature of discipline and grievance procedures
- Social facilities and activities
- Housekeeping arrangements such as canteen and refreshment facilities, car parking
- Opportunities for further studies, training and development, career progression.

Discussion

- How successfully did the socialisation process indoctrinate new members into the ways of the university or organisation and its cultural norms? What changes would you recommend?
- How much did you learn about the informal organisation or how things really work?
- To what extent did the socialisation process help generate an initial feeling of engagement with the university or organisation?

Case study
Changing priorities: ActionAid

The charity ActionAid was created by Albert Cecil Cole, a successful entrepreneur, in 1972. It was one of several philanthropic organisations (including Oxfam) either founded or supported by Cole, and in its first incarnation (as Action in Distress) its aim was to provide direct sponsorship of education; initially eighty-eight UK sponsors committed to the funding for eighty-eight children in India and Kenya. For the first ten years of its history it focused on creating similar long-term programmes of educational sponsorship in other African and Asian countries, but also gradually came to include projects related to health, sanitation and agricultural improvements in its range of activities. The educational sponsorship scheme is still a major part of its work: 60,000 children were sponsored during 2012, and the donors receive annual messages and photographs from their sponsored child together with reports from ActionAid staff on their progress.[63] Nevertheless, the organisation has changed considerably in its approach, structure and focus as the needs of developing countries themselves

Source: Marco Luzzani/Stringer/Getty Images

have changed. Such change is common in business organisations, which have to adapt to the market, but can be controversial and difficult for charities and other non-governmental organisations (NGOs) like ActionAid.

Charity, politics and human rights

The traditional model of organisations such as ActionAid, which attempt to address issues of poverty in developing countries, is a familiar one. It involves appealing to people's sense of altruism as a means of attracting both donors and workers. Money or effort is then directed at a specific problem, be it a major emergency (such as a flood or earthquake) or a more general issue (providing medical services, organising building projects, creating clean water supplies or shipping equipment and materials to where they are needed). The governments of most developed countries have also considered it important to contribute to such problems, and many earmark a percentage of national tax revenue for overseas aid. As a result of this, the governments of poor and developing countries have often found themselves heavily reliant on grants and loans from the developed world when trying to improve living conditions and reduce poverty. However well intentioned, aid does not necessarily lead to lasting change and, at worst, can result in a sort of dependency trap with money grants tied to the use of goods and services provided by the donor country. The traditional model of aid as charity and the responsibility of the developed world, even when it is effective on the ground, can be seen as having some important limitations and drawbacks.

The human rights-based approach (HRBA)[64] to issues of world poverty sees issues such as access to education as part of a wider picture – that of universal human rights. This is based on a very different philosophy from the familiar charity/aid approach. For example, if free basic education is considered as a universal human right by the international community (as it is under Article 26 of the United Nations Universal Declaration of Human

Rights)[65] then any government that fails to provide it is technically in breach of international law. NGOs that adopt the HRBA to their work believe that this means they have a responsibility to pressurise governments in the developing world to engage with these failures and to correct them. Furthermore, this pressure has to come from below. The people whose human rights are being breached should both understand that this is the case and be encouraged and enabled to campaign on their own behalf. Therefore the work of aid organisations has to include empowering and facilitating these campaigns, not simply providing materials or services.

From welfare to human rights activism

In its original form, ActionAid, like many charities and NGOs, adopted the 'traditional' model, which focused on providing the education that was seen as fundamental to enabling poor people to improve their situation. Educational programmes were organised and delivered locally, meaning that ActionAid developed a structure and system of governance that is largely decentralised and federalised:

> We are a federation. That means that every country has an equal share in decisions. The same applies to our work on the ground. ActionAid staff are local people, and we never impose our own solutions on the communities we work with.[66]

In the late 1990s ActionAid began a significant process of change. Firstly, it relocated its headquarters from London to Johannesburg and since 2003 it has been the only organisation of its kind that is based in a developing country. This move was one manifestation of a major ideological change: the adoption of the HRBA to its work. This new approach resulted from changing perceptions of how poverty could be alleviated on a sustainable basis, and involved a more controversial and overtly political attitude to development work.

In 2010 the organisation published a document that both consolidated its new philosophy and offered practical advice to its workers that would help embed a new way of working in its organisational culture and activities: *Action on Rights: Human Rights Based Approach Resource Book.*[67] This text was aimed at staff and was intended to offer both guidance and inspiration to programme workers. It gave a clear articulation of the new approach and traced its development back to the 1970s, telling three stories to illustrate three phases of change. The stories, about an education programme in Kenya, are summarised in a table that could be easily recognised by ActionAid workers, enabling them to understand the cultural change and to set it in a familiar context. For example, one extract from the table is about ActionAid's changing role:

Approach	Features of needs-based (with elements of welfare) approach to development	Features of a participatory-empowerment approach to development	Features of ActionAid's HRBA to development
ActionAid's role	Story 1 Direct implementation of basic services	Story 2 Working in partnership with the community and in some cases with government to meet the basic needs of poor and excluded people	Story 3 Working to empower rights holder organisations, build solidarity between rights holders and allies, and supporting campaigns to hold the state accountable to poor and excluded people

This represented a significant change: where previously the organisation had focussed on providing educational services to 'needy' populations, it was now focussing on helping these populations assert their right to publicly funded education.[68]

The resource book was used as part of a major initiative throughout the organisation to communicate and install the HRBA. This programme included training for key staff who could then run retreats and national training programmes for field staff in each country where ActionAid was operating. This intense communication and development programme was essential to achieving culture change:

Approaching development interventions as an instance of human rights work rather than need-based charitable work is a monumental shift in thinking and requires an overhaul of how staff and partners operate in the field. One could not expect such a transition to proceed easily or automatically.[69]

Longer-term support for the new strategy involved coaching, quality circles and a staff exchange programme. Workers had the opportunity to give feedback, which would, in turn, inform the organisation's strategy for the period 2012–17. The strategy, together with a further and more detailed resource book, was published in 2012.[70] One of the key purposes of these documents was to align the work of a decentralised organisation where power did not emanate from the top:

This resource book is designed to be relevant for all ActionAid staff and partners. It aims to help staff and partners design and implement local, national and international rights programmes that are aligned with our collectively agreed strategy. It aims to be relevant to programme specialists and policy analysts, to campaigners and communications staff, to managers and trustees, to frontline workers and fundraisers, to administrators and activists.[71]

Despite this effort, there is some evidence that grassroots staff were reluctant to abandon a 'service delivery' approach. Perhaps it is a measure of the organisation's growing confidence in the cultural change that has been achieved that ActionAid's International Education Team has felt able to reframe its approach by integrating service provision into the HRBA rather than seeing them as in opposition to each other.[72] Today ActionAid is viewed as one of the most progressive and radical NGOs working in the development sector. As Joanna Kerr, the Chief Executive, explains on the organisation's website:

The work we are doing is truly different because of the way we mobilise communities to defend their own rights.[73]

Tasks

1 Examine the culture change at ActionAid using Senior and Swailes' model (Figure 15.1). Which of the elements supported change, and which hampered it?

2 Using the concept of the cultural web (Figure 15.3), explain how ActionAid's management team used each of the elements to encourage the culture change that was needed when adopting the human rights-based approach (HRBA) to alleviating poverty.

3 What types of resistance to change might be expected in this case, and how could they be overcome? Examine the problem from the point of view of the following major stakeholders:

- Aid workers 'on the ground' in the host countries.
- The communities receiving ActionAid support.
- The governments of the countries where ActionAid is active.
- Sponsors and donors to the charity in the UK and other Western countries.

4 To what extent has ActionAid followed the CMI thirteen-point plan for the effective management of change? Explain your view.

Notes and references

1. Atkinson, P. E. 'Creating Cultural Change', *Management Services,* vol. 34, no. 7, 1990, pp. 6–10.

2. Johnson, R. 'Changing corporate culture', *Governance & Compliance,* June 2013, p. 3.

3. See, for example, Oswick, C., Lowe, S. and Jones, P. 'Organisational Culture as Personality: Lessons from Psychology?', in Oswick, C. and Grant, D. (eds) *Organisation Development: Metaphorical Explorations,* Pitman (1996), pp. 106–20.

4. Stewart, R. *The Reality of Management,* third edition, Butterworth–Heinemann (1999), p. 123.

5. Naylor, J. *Management,* second edition, Financial Times Prentice Hall (2004), p. 79.

6. Schein, E. H. *Organizational Culture and Leadership,* fourth edition, Jossey-Bass (2010).

7. Naylor, J. *Management,* second edition, Financial Times Prentice Hall (2004).

8. Harrison, R. 'Understanding Your Organization's Character', *Harvard Business Review,* vol. 50, May/June 1972, pp. 119–28.

9. Handy, C. B. *Understanding Organizations,* fourth edition, Penguin (1993).

10. Deal, T. E. and Kennedy, A. A. *Corporate Cultures: The Rites and Rituals of Corporate Life,* Penguin (1982).

11. Smircich, L. 'Concepts of culture and organizational analysis', *Administrative Science Quarterly,* vol. 28, no. 3, 1983, pp. 339–58.

12. Martin, J. *Cultures and Organizations: Three Perspectives,* Oxford University Press (1992).

13. See, for example, Parker, M. *Organizational Culture and Identity: Unity and Division at Work,* Sage (2000).

14. See, for example, Handy, C. B. *Understanding Organizations,* fourth edition, Penguin (1993); and McLean, A. and Marshall, J. *Cultures at Work,* Local Government Training Board (1988).

15. Kransdorff, A. 'History – A Powerful Management Tool', *Administrator,* October 1991, p. 23.

16. See, for example, Beckett-Hughes, M. 'How to Integrate Two Cultures', *People Management,* vol. 11, no. 5, 2005, pp. 50–1.

17. Blackhurst, C. 'Up Front at Pearson', *Management Today,* May 1997, pp. 50–7.

18. Gerstner, L. V. Jr Who Says Elephants Can't Dance? Inside IBM's Historic Turnabout, HarperBusiness (2002).

19. Johnson, G. et. al. *Exploring Strategy,* tenth edition, Pearson Education (2014).

20. Cartwright, J. *Cultural Transformation,* Financial Times Prentice Hall (1999), p. 34.

21. Egan, G. 'The Shadow Side', *Management Today,* September 1993, p. 37.

22. Watson, T. J. *Organising and Managing Work,* second edition, FT Prentice Hall (2006).

23. 'Effective Organisations: The People Factor', Advisory Booklet, ACAS, November 2001.

24. Kershaw, P. 'Culture and control', *Governance & Compliance,* July 2014, p. 4.

25. Reigle, R. F. 'Measuring Organic and Mechanistic Cultures', *Engineering Management Journal,* vol. 13, no. 4, 2001, pp. 3–8.

26. Bunting, M. *Willing Slaves,* HarperCollins (2004), p. xxiii.

27. Brodbeck, F. 'The More We Blame, the Less We Gain', *Professional Manager,* vol. 13, no. 6, 2004, p. 37.

28. The Core Partnership, 'A culture of openness and acceptance of new ideas may not be consistent', *Governance & Compliance,* June 2014, p. 35.

29. Stanford, N. *Organisation Culture: Getting it right,* The Economist/Profile Books (2010).

30. Hilton, A. 'Hearts and minds', *Chartered Secretary,* April 2011, p. 14.

31. Clifton, K. 'Values Added', *Manager,* Autumn 2012, p. 14.

32. Schneider, S. C. and Barsoux, J. *Managing Across Cultures,* second edition, Financial Times Prentice Hall (2003).

33. Cheng, T., Sculli, D. and Chan, F. 'Relationship Dominance – Rethinking Management Theories from the Perspective of Methodological Relationalism', *Journal of Managerial Psychology,* vol. 16, no. 2, 2001, pp. 97–105.

34. Francesco, A. M. and Gold, B. A. *International Organizational Behavior,* second edition, Pearson Prentice Hall (2005).

35. Menzies, J. 'Cultural advantage', *Global Outlook, Chartered Secretary,* May 2011, pp. 10–12.

36. 'International Culture Factsheet', CIPD, June 2013.

37. Lewis, R. D. *The Cultural Imperative: Global Trends in the 21st Century*, Nicholas Brealey (2007).

38. Tagiuri, R. and Litwin, G. H. (eds) *Organizational Climate,* Graduate School of Business Administration, Harvard University (1968), p. 27.

39. Gray, R. *A Climate of Success,* Butterworth–Heinemann (2007).

40. Atkinson, T. and Frechette, H. 'Creating a Positive Organizational Climate in a Negative Economic One', *Forum Corporation,* www.trainingindustry.com/media (accessed 8 October 2011).

41. For a discussion of change in relation to the complexities of organisational life, see Senior, B. and Swailes, S. *Organizational Change,* fourth edition, Financial Times Prentice Hall (2010).

42. In conversation with Saunders, A. 'How to cope with a changing world', *Management Today,* October 2012, pp. 52–5.

43. 'Adapting to change – The EU approach to restructuring', *Social Agenda: The European Commission's Magazine,* July 2011, pp. 15–20.

44. Lewin, K. *Field Theory in Social Science,* Harper and Row (1951).

45. French, W. L., Kast, F. E. and Rosenzweig, J. E. *Understanding Human Behavior in Organizations,* Harper and Row (1985).

46. 'Leading transformational change', Research report, CIPD, September 2014.

47. Rees, G and Rumbles, S. 'Continuous Organizational Change and Burnout', *International Journal of Knowledge, Culture & Change Management,* vol. 11, 2012, pp. 1–16.

48. Toffler, A. *Future Shock,* Pan (1970), p. 27.

49. Lockhead, Sir M. 'In My Opinion', *Management Today,* September 2008, p. 12.

50. Crainer, S. *Key Management Ideas: Thinkers That Changed the Management World,* third edition, Financial Times Prentice Hall (1998), pp. 144–5.

51. Cunningham, I. 'Influencing People's Attitudes to Change', *Professional Manager,* vol. 14, no. 3, May 2005, p. 37.

52. See, for example, Yukl, G. *Leadership in Organizations,* seventh edition, Pearson Education (2012).

53. 'Implementing an Effective Change Programme', Management Checklist 040, Chartered Management Institute, September 2014.

54. Toterhi, T. and Recardo, R. 'Managing change: Nine common blunders and how to avoid them', *Global Business and Organizational Excellence,* vol. 31, no. 5, 2012, pp. 54–69.

55. Atkinson, P. 'Managing Resistance to Change', *Management Services,* Spring 2005, p. 15.

56. Taylor, G. 'Managing the Situational and Psychological Pressures Brought About by Change', *Professional Manager,* vol. 16, no. 4, 2007, p. 14.

57. Reeves, R. and Knell, J. 'Your Mini MBA', *Management Today,* March 2009, pp. 60–4.

58. Material in this section reproduced with kind permission of Anne Riches, creator of The Almond Effect® and author of 'CLUES: Tips, strategies and examples for change leaders'. For further information see **www .AnneRiches.com**

59. Yukl, G. *Leadership in Organizations,* seventh edition, Pearson Education (2012).

60. Tranfield, D. and Braganza, A. *Business Leadership of Technological Change: Five Key Challenges Facing CEOs,* Chartered Management Institute (2007).

61. Drucker, P. F. *Management Challenges for the 21st Century,* Butterworth–Heinemann (1999), p. 73.

62. Katzenbach, J. R., Steffen, I. and Kronley, C. 'Cultural Change That Sticks', *Harvard Business Review,* vol. 90, July/August 2012, pp. 110–17.

63. ActionAid, **http://www.actionaid.org. uk/40th#campaigns** (accessed 16 March 2015).

64. Sometimes abbreviated to 'rights based approach' or RBA in the literature.

65. United Nations, **http://www.un.org/en/documents/ udhr/** (accessed 31 March 2015).

66. ActionAid, '40 Years of Fighting Poverty', **http://www. actionaid.org.uk/40th** (accessed 31 March 2015).

67. ActionAid, 2010, *Action on Rights: Human Rights Based Approach Resource Book,* available for download from **http://www.actionaid.org/sites/files/actionaid/hrba_ resourcebook_11nov2010.pdf** (accessed 10 April 2015).

68. Magrath, B. 'Global norms, organisational change: framing the rights-based approach at ActionAid', *Third World Quarterly,* vol. 35, no. 7, 2014, pp. 5–6. doi:10.1080/ 01436597.2014.926117

69. Ibid., p. 1.

70. ActionAid, 2012, 'People's Action In Practice: ActionAid's Human Rights Based Approach 2.0', **http://www. actionaid.org/sites/files/actionaid/1._peoples_action_in_ practice_final_20_07_2012.pdf** (accessed 10 April 2015).

71. Ibid., p. 11.

72. Magrath, op. cit., p. 10.

73. ActionAid, '40 Years of Fighting Poverty', op. cit.

CHAPTER 16
Organisational performance and development

Every work organisation is concerned with being effective. The ultimate survival of the organisation depends upon the attainment of its goals and objectives. The quality of management and commitment of staff to their work are central to the success of the organisation. Attention needs to be focused on managerial actions and behaviour and factors influencing levels of organisational performance and effectiveness.

Learning outcomes

After completing this chapter you should have enhanced your ability to:

- explain the crucial role of managers in work organisations;
- detail the attributes, qualities and skills of a successful manager;
- assess criteria for evaluating managerial effectiveness;
- evaluate the benefits of the learning organisation, and total quality management;
- assess the nature and importance of employee engagement and commitment;
- explore the nature and main features of management development;
- detail criteria for assessing organisational performance and effectiveness.

Critical review and reflection

Given a *forced-choice situation* most people would prefer to work for an effective organisation that offers long-term job security and consistent high wages rather than an organisation that is more about a happy place to work.

What do YOU think about this contention? To what extent is it true for YOU? Do you think YOUR view is likely to change over time?

The crucial role of managers

The underlying theme of this book has been the need for organisational effectiveness based on an understanding of organisational behaviour, the people resource and the role of management as an integrating activity. As mentioned earlier (**see Chapter 1**), whatever the nature of the work organisation it is through the process of management that the efforts of members of the organisation are co-ordinated, directed and guided towards the achievement of its goals. Management is the cornerstone of organisational effectiveness. Whatever the functions or activities within the organisation, there is a close relationship with the actions and behaviour of management.

The 'Quality of Management' is one of nine measures of success by which *Management Today* rates performance in its annual survey of Britain's Most Admired Companies. Other chapters of this book have emphasised the importance of management as an integrating activity that permeates every facet of the operations of the organisation. Recognition of the importance of effective management for organisational success is evidenced by the increasing attention given to the development of management skills and talent, discussed below.

A major survey undertaken by the Management Consultancies Association (MCA) and *Management Today* draws attention to the changing relationship between organisations and individuals. More and more work is outsourced, teams are dispersed across multiple locations, an increasing number of people work away from the organisations and greater empowerment is shifting responsibility to individuals. This shift of responsibility from the organisation to the individual begs the question: 'Are managers really necessary and what is the role of management?'

> *Ironically, a time when people appear to require less management is also a time when they want it more than ever. Half of all respondents to the MCA/MT survey felt their bosses spent insufficient time actually managing their staff, a figure that was highest among employees of large organisations and in the manufacturing, financial services and the public sector.*[1]

According to *Lucas,* global competition, particularly from the BRICK countries (Brazil, Russia, India, China and Korea), means that companies can no longer compete simply on price, and breaking the mould is more important than ever: 'Organisations need to be more creative in their approach to recognising, nurturing and turning innovative ideas into business reality – and managers are the key to that process.' Innovation, however, is not just about the big ground-breaking ideas of technological advances; it is often about small incremental changes to products, services or processes. Lucas reports on the crucial role of managers as the single most important factor in the success of innovation initiatives. This requires a leader and team with the ability and passion to turn ideas into business reality. Managers need to: provide focus for their teams; generate the energy to make change happen; be good at coping with ambiguity and uncertainty; create a culture where people feel safe to experiment; and be willing to give agenda time to innovation.[2]

Management practices and productivity

According to a report from the Advanced Institute of Management Research (AIM) and CMI, management practices are central to an understanding of the UK's competitive performance. Evidence from recent UK experiences is that productivity and performance are more influenced by what happens inside organisations than the economic and regulatory environments in which they operate. Productivity is linked closely to the adoption and utilisation of new management practices. Yet efforts to translate new management practices into improved performance are slower and less successful than some counterparts in France, Germany and the USA.

The report suggests that too easily commentators and consultants assume that a 'copycat strategy' will work. However, organisations need to do more than slavishly follow the latest 'big idea'. They need to adapt good practices to their own environment. But for true competitive advantage, organisations need to develop 'signature processes' that are difficult for rivals to replicate. Managers need to be alert and open to both developments in the wider world and the strengths and weaknesses of their own situation as they debate which practices might improve their competitiveness and how they might adopt them.[3]

Attributes and qualities of a manager

Whatever the role of the manager, or whether in the private or public sector, in order to carry out the process of management and the execution of work the manager requires a combination of technical competence, social and human skills and conceptual ability.[4]

As the manager advances through the organisational hierarchy, greater emphasis is likely to be placed on conceptual ability and proportionately less on technical competence (*see* Figure 16.1). (**See also the discussion on levels of organisation in Chapter 11.**)

- **Technical competence** relates to the application of specific knowledge, methods and skills to discrete tasks. Technical competence is likely to be required more at the supervisory level and for the training of subordinate staff, and with day-to-day operations concerned in the actual production of goods or services.

- **Social and human skills** refer to interpersonal relationships in working with and through other people, and the exercise of judgement. A distinctive feature of management is the ability to secure the effective use of the human resources of the organisation. This involves effective teamwork and the direction and leadership of staff to achieve co-ordinated effort. Under this heading can be included sensitivity to particular situations and flexibility in adopting the most appropriate style of management.

- **Conceptual ability** is required in order to view the complexities of the operations of the organisation as a whole, including environmental influences. It also involves decision-making skills. The manager's personal contribution should be related to the overall objectives of the organisation and to its strategic planning.

Although a simplistic approach, this framework provides a useful basis from which to examine the combination and balance of the attributes of an effective manager. For example, the extent of technical competence or conceptual ability will vary according to the nature of the organisation and the level at which the manager is working. However, major technological change means that managers at all levels of the organisation increasingly require technical competence in the skills of information communications technology.

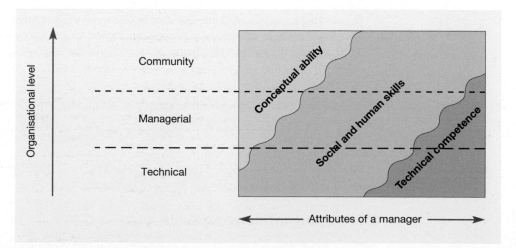

Figure 16.1 The combination of attributes of a manager

Critical review and reflection

Technical competence can easily be learned and not all managers require conceptual ability, but someone with poor social and human skills can never become an effective manager. These attributes are part of a person's personality and you cannot make a silk purse out of a sow's ear.

What do YOU think? To what extent do YOU believe training can make a real difference to management ability? How good are YOUR social and human skills?

The importance of management skills

In recent years, increasing attention has been given by the government to the importance of the supply and application of skills attainment. The UK Commission for Employment and Skills (UKCES) aims to raise UK prosperity and opportunity by improving employment and skills levels across the UK, benefitting individuals, employers, government and society. UKCES is leading major research into skills utilisation and the Treasury commissioned the Leitch Review of Skills, which reported in December 2006, to assess the required skills profile for the UK to achieve by 2020. The report recognises: that good management is a prerequisite to improving business performance; the high levels of demand for management skills; and the growing evidence base demonstrating the strong links between the impact of management skills and increased national competitiveness.[5]

Developing management skills for the future

A major study ('Management Futures') by the CMI, including a survey of 1,000 senior executives, has investigated how the world of work and management will look in 2018: 'The increased monitoring and surveillance of work on all levels will require organisations to ensure that they have many of the management skills such as interpersonal skills, building alliances, strategic planning and political skills that are needed in business today.'

The CMI foresees that the tasks of people within organisations will have a new focus. An increasingly flexible and transient workforce, and multicultural and remote teamworking, will require talented and prudent managers who excel in analysis, evaluation and, above all, good judgement.

Among the key findings are that:

The working population will be more diverse. Changing expectations of work and the impact of new technologies will require managers and leaders to develop a range of skills that focus on emotional and spiritual intelligence, judgement and the ability to stimulate creative thinking to improve productivity.

Among the recommendations to leaders and managers are the need to focus on individual employees and their needs when developing new technologies, to make organisations more human and to motivate people creatively.

A greater degree of emotional intelligence will be required by managers so that they can understand how people work and their likely reactions to change. They will also benefit from having the humility to accept that they are not always the ones with the best or most appropriate ideas.[6] (**Emotional intelligence is discussed in Chapter 4.**)

Developing influencing skills

According to *Mann*, few would argue that an integral role of management involves influencing people, especially in engaging and motivating employees without resorting to coercion, threats or manipulation. Influencing skills are wide ranging and overlap more general spheres of interpersonal and communication skills, assertiveness and self-presentation. Mann suggests key strategies that contribute to how well one can exert positive influence:

- **Listening skills** – As opposed to the use of authority, to really win hearts and minds you need to listen to the ideas, thoughts and complaints of staff.
- **Empowering skills** – Rather than telling staff what to do, empower them to develop their own strategies and skill base.
- **Respect** – Show respect to staff by considering their views and wishes, understanding their concerns and being sympathetic to issues in their private life.
- **Self-confidence** – Belief in your own abilities and strengths allows you to give people credit, accept responsibility for mistakes where appropriate and be decisive.
- **Nurturing skills** – Nurture your team's talent by awareness of individual skills and abilities, encouraging development and building on existing skill level.

Engaging managers use their spheres of influence to demonstrate appreciation of their team's efforts, listen to its opinions and ensure it feels supported.[7]

Growing emphasis on 'soft' skills

Management has become as much, if not more, about managing people than managing operations. Social and human skills that reflect the ability to get along with other people are increasingly important attributes at all levels of management. According to *Saunders,* the nature of management is changing and soft skills are on the rise. The stock of managers with the sharpest social and psychological skills is also on the rise because of today's lean, flat organisational structures. Octavius Black, CEO of MindGym, draws attention to the emotional side of work and claims that a degree in psychology would be a better training ground for managers.

> *We have done competitive advantage from strategy and from technology. What's left is competitive advantage from your people and the line manager is crucial to that. Get your people to flourish and your organisation will perform better.*[8]

Critical review and reflection

Octavius Black, as above, draws attention to the emotional side of work and claims that a degree in psychology would be a better training ground for managers.

What do YOU think? How well is YOUR course of study preparing YOU for a managerial role? How would YOU assess YOUR potential managerial skills?

Managerial effectiveness

The overall responsibility of management can be seen as the successful attainment of the given objectives of the organisation, upon which rests the ultimate survival of the organisation. There is therefore a clear and important need for effective management. And this need is just as strong in public-sector and voluntary organisations as in private-enterprise organisations. Indeed, it could be argued that in local government, for example, the accountability of public servants to elected members for their actions means that professional standards of management of the highest order are even more essential.

The importance of managerial performance and effectiveness has long been recognised by major writers such as *Drucker* who, originally in 1955, propounded that:

> *The manager is the dynamic, life-giving element in every business. Without their leadership 'the resources of production' remain resources and never become production. In a competitive*

economy, above all, the quality and performance of the managers determine the success of a business; indeed they determine its survival. For the quality and performance of its managers is the only effective advantage an enterprise in a competitive economy can have.[9]

Efficiency and effectiveness

Managerial efficiency can be distinguished from **managerial effectiveness. Efficiency** is concerned with 'doing things right' and relates to inputs and what the manager does. **Effectiveness** is concerned with 'doing the right things' and relates to outputs of the job and what the manager actually achieves. To be efficient the manager must attend therefore to the **input requirements of the job** – to clarification of objectives, planning, organisation, direction and control. But in order to be effective, the manager must give attention to the **outputs of the job** – to performance in terms of such factors as obtaining best possible results in the important areas of the organisation, optimising use of resources, increasing profitability and attainment of the aims and objectives of the organisation.

Effectiveness must be related to the achievement of some purpose, objective or task – to the performance of the process of management and the execution of work. Criteria for assessing the effectiveness of a manager should be considered in terms of measuring the results that the manager is intended to achieve. But **what is also important is the manner in which the manager achieves results and the effects on other people.** This may well influence effectiveness in the longer term. Managerial effectiveness results from a combination of personal attributes and dimensions of the manager's job in meeting the demands of the situation, and satisfying the requirements of the organisation.

Measures of effectiveness

Management involves getting work done through the co-ordinated efforts of other people. Managers are most likely to be judged not just on their own performance, but also on the results achieved by other staff.

> *Managers are successful if they create conditions for others to succeed.*
>
> *Ann Francke, Chief Executive CMI, Professional Manager, September/October 2012, p. 5*

The manager's effectiveness may be assessed in part, therefore, by such factors as:

- the strength of motivation and morale of staff;
- the success of their training and development; and
- the creation of an organisational environment in which staff work willingly and effectively.

The difficulty is determining objective measurement of such factors. Some possible indication might be given by, for example:

- the level of staff retention;
- the incidence of sickness;
- absenteeism;
- poor timekeeping; and
- accidents at work.

However, such figures are likely to be influenced also by broader organisational or environmental considerations, for example poor job security due to the economic climate, which are outside the direct control of the individual manager. In any case, there is the general question of the extent to which such figures bear a direct relationship to the actual performance of subordinate staff.

Other criteria of effectiveness

For some management jobs it might be possible to identify more quantitative factors that *may* give an indication of managerial effectiveness, including:

- meeting important deadlines;
- accuracy of work carried out by the department, perhaps measured by the number of recorded errors;
- level of complaints received from superiors, other departments, customers or clients, suppliers, the public;
- adherence to quality standards, for example the amount of scrap or waste material;
- keeping within agreed cost or budgetary control limits; and
- levels of output and productivity (*see* Figure 16.2).

Another broad, qualitative criterion of increasing significance today is in terms of perceived social accountability and the ethical behaviour of individual managers and the organisation as a whole (**discussed in Chapter 14**).

Composite list of basic qualities

Mintzberg refers to the many lists of the qualities of effective managers. These lists are usually short and incomplete as they do not include important aspects such as native intelligence, being a good listener or just having energy. For the 'sake of a better world' Mintzberg provides a composite list of fifty-two qualities (Figure 16.3): 'Be all fifty-two and you are bound to be an effective manager, if not a human one.' Mintzberg refers also to the romance of leadership that on the one hand puts ordinary mortals on managerial pedestals and on the other hand

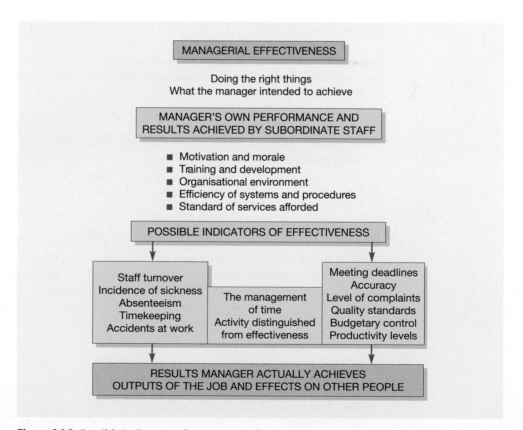

Figure 16.2 Possible indicators of managerial effectiveness

courageous	charismatic
committed	passionate
curious	*inspiring*
confident	
	visionary
candid	energetic/enthusiastic
reflective	upbeat/optimistic
insightful	ambitious
open-minded/tolerant (of people, ambiguities, and ideas)	tenacious/persistent/zealous
innovative	collaborative/participative/cooperative
communicative (including being a good listener)	*engaging*
connected/informed	supportive/sympathetic/empathetic
perceptive	stable
thoughtful/intelligent/*wise*	dependable
analytic/objective	fair
pragmatic	accountable
decisive (action-oriented)	ethical/honest
proactive	consistent
	flexible
	balanced
	integrative
	tall

Figure 16.3 Composite list of basic managerial qualities

Source: Henry Mintzberg, *Managing*, Financial Times Prentice Hall (2009), p. 197. Compiled from various sources; my own favourites in italics.

allows us to vilify them as they come crashing down: 'Yet some mangers do stay up, if not on that silly pedestal. How so?'

The answer is simple: 'successful managers are flawed – we are all flawed – but their particular flaws are not fatal, at least under the circumstances.'[10]

The 3-D model of managerial behaviour

However effectiveness is measured, managers are likely to be effective only if they adopt the most appropriate style of behaviour. A development of the Blake and Mouton Managerial Grid, discussed earlier (**Chapter 10**), is the three-dimensional (3-D) model of managerial behaviour suggested by *Reddin*. By adding a third dimension of managerial effectiveness to task orientation and relationship orientation, the 3-D model identifies eight possible styles of managerial behaviour:[11]

- **Task orientation (TO)** is the extent to which the manager directs both personal and subordinates' efforts through planning, organisation and control.
- **Relationship orientation (RO)** is dependent upon the manager's personal job relationships. This is characterised by consideration for subordinates' feelings, mutual trust and encouragement.

Figure 16.4 The four basic styles of managerial behaviour

The combination of TO and RO determines the manager's basic style of behaviour. The four possible basic styles (*see* Figure 16.4) are similar to those identified by Blake and Mouton in the Managerial Grid.

Apparent and personal effectiveness

Each of these four basic styles of management can be effective or ineffective depending on the situation in which they are applied. Effectiveness is defined by Reddin as:

> *the extent to which a manager achieves the output requirements of his position . . . Managerial effectiveness has to be defined in terms of output rather than input, by what a manager achieves rather than by what he does.*

Reddin distinguishes managerial effectiveness from (i) apparent effectiveness and (ii) personal effectiveness:

- **Apparent effectiveness** is the extent to which the behaviour of the manager – for example, punctuality, giving prompt answers, tidiness, making quick decisions and good public relations – gives the appearance of effectiveness. Such qualities may or may not be relevant to effectiveness.

- **Personal effectiveness** is the extent to which the manager achieves personal objectives – for example, power and prestige – rather than the objectives of the organisation.

Applying the third dimension of managerial effectiveness provides eight styles of managerial behaviour – four effective styles, which achieve output requirements, and four ineffective styles. For each of the basic styles – separated, dedicated, related or integrated – there is a more effective or less effective version. Effectiveness results from the appropriateness of a particular style of management to the demands of the situation in which it is applied.

Birkinshaw questions how one can become a better boss. Employees are looking for challenging work, space, support and recognition. But why do managers not do what they know they should? The busier you are, the more likely it is you will get into bad management: 'Lack of time and resources are only part of the story. The underlying problem is that many aspects of good management involve going against our natural instincts.' The hallmarks of a good manager include:

- the capacity to let go and to give power and freedom to others and allow others to make mistakes;
- giving credit to others and downplaying your own achievements – own your failures and share your successes;
- exercising self-control and the ability to regulate your own emotions and instincts. Be more attentive to your own shortcomings.[12]

Critical review and reflection

The philosophy and actions of successful managers should include acknowledgement of *mea culpa*, the admission of responsibility for their failings and a clear open apology for their mistakes.

Do YOU agree such behaviour would help improve the general quality and perception of management? To what extent are YOU able to accept openly responsibility for YOUR failings?

Management of time

Whatever the attributes or qualities of a successful manager, one essential underlying criterion is the effective use of time. With many managers who complain that they do not have sufficient time it may be more that they have failed to organise themselves or their work properly. Although currently a popular topic of attention, the importance of time management has long been recognised as an inherent feature of management. *Drucker,* writing in 1988, refers to time as the limiting factor for effective executives. Time is a unique resource – you cannot rent, hire, buy or otherwise obtain more time. The supply of time is totally inelastic; time is totally irreplaceable and everything requires time.[13]

According to the CMI, effective time management is simply making the best use of limited time towards achieving the best desirable goals.

> *Effective time management can help you to gain more control over your activities, increase your efficiency, improve your work/life balance and become proactive rather than reactive in preventing or dealing with problems. Getting to grips with time management should help to reduce work pressures so that you will feel more relaxed, and others will be more likely to perceive you as calm and well-organised.*

The checklist also refers to overwork as counterproductive, causing stress and a decrease in time efficiency. It is important to devote an adequate proportion of time to yourself and make time to play.[14]

Dryburgh suggests that, despite numerous courses, for many time management will remain a huge problem: 'There's a strange and slightly disturbing paradox about the time management industry – it is as big as it is because it doesn't work.'

> *Time management doesn't work because it assumes we are rational creatures when it comes to allocating our time. It assumes that we can work out, perfectly rationally, those things which are both urgent and important, and then concentrate our efforts there. The problem is that we are not rational. We avoid that which makes us uncomfortable (these tend to be the important things). We feel reluctant to do things differently, even when it is obvious to our rational selves that the old ways don't make sense any more. We find it hard to say 'no' to pointless requests.*[15]

Effectiveness and activity

For many managers, appearing always to be busy, a cluttered desk and a continual flurry of activity are outward signs of their effectiveness. The trouble is that such managers may be too busy 'doing' rather than **thinking about what they, and their staff, should be doing and how they should be doing it.** Activity may be a substitute for actual achievement. It is important therefore to distinguish effectiveness from activity. *Rees and Porter* suggest that:

> *Activity-centred behaviour is in any case much more likely to spring from incompetence and/ or insecurity rather than adroit political behaviour. Activity-centred behaviour is likely to aggravate the position of the manager in the long run rather than ameliorate it.*[16]

A similar point is made by *Hoyle and Newman*, who refer to the many people who are satisfied being busy but in their diligence and attention to detail mistake activity for achievement. Rather than the volume of work undertaken it is what work creates that is important. Attention should be focused on what is achieved and the end result.[17]

Managers' checklist

There are numerous popular time management techniques,[18] but still one of the most relevant approaches is that by *Stewart* who suggests that it is often salutary for managers to compare what they think they do against what happens in practice. Answers to the following questions will help managers decide what, if anything, they should check, and to review their effective management of time:[19]

1. Am I giving adequate attention to current activities, to reviewing the past and to planning for the future? In particular, am I giving enough thought to the future?
2. Am I dividing my time correctly between different aspects of my job? Is there, perhaps, one part of my job on which I spend too much of my time?
3. Have I changed what I am trying to do and how I work to allow for the effects of changes in my work?
4. Am I doing work that I ought to have delegated?
5. Who are the people that I ought to be seeing? Am I spending too much or too little time with any of them?
6. Do I organise my working day and week, as far as possible, according to priorities, or do I tend to deal with each problem as it turns up, or even as I think of it, without stopping to think whether there is something more important that I should be working on?
7. Am I able to complete a task, or am I constantly interrupted? If the latter, are all these interruptions an essential part of my work?

There are three questions that managers should ask of each of their activities:

- Should it be done at all?
- If so, when should it be done?
- Should it be delegated? (**Delegation is discussed in Chapter 13.**)

The nature of organisational effectiveness

The underlying theme of this book has been the need for organisational effectiveness based on an understanding of organisational behaviour, the people resource and the role of management as an integrating activity. Organisational effectiveness, however, is affected by a multiplicity of variables. For example, *Handy* identifies over sixty factors that impinge on any one organisational situation and that illustrate the complicated nature of the study of organisational effectiveness (*see* Figure 16.5).[20]

The democratic enterprise

According to *Gratton*, we have become accustomed to how contemporary organisations are structured, managed and run, but many more possibilities exist. Many people feel disconnected from their organisation and at times feel they have been treated unfairly and unjustly. Gratton refers to the 'democratic enterprise', that is organisations that are inspiring and meaningful, with the possibility for the individual and the organisation to create a win–win relationship and both benefiting but not at the expense of the other.

> *We are witnessing the emergence of a new way of looking at people and their role in organizations . . . More than at any other point in time, there is now a chance to create the Democratic Enterprise. Over the last decade it has become increasingly clear that through the forces*

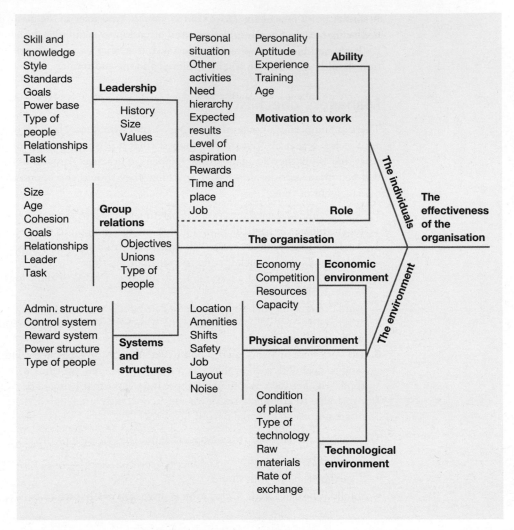

Figure 16.5 Some factors affecting organisational effectiveness
Source: From Handy, C. B. *Understanding Organizations*, fourth edition, Penguin Books (1993), p. 15. Copyright © Charles Handy, 1976, 1981, 1985, 1993, 1999. Reproduced by permission of Penguin Books Ltd.

of globalization, competition and more demanding customers, the structure of many companies has become flatter, less hierarchical, more fluid and virtual. The breakdown of hierarchies provides us with fertile ground on which to create a more democratic way of working.[21]

The learning organisation

A key factor in organisational effectiveness is the successful management of change, innovation and corporate renewal. Traditional views of managerial behaviour have placed emphasis on planning, organising, directing and controlling. However, increasing international competitiveness and the need for organisations to respond rapidly to constant change in their environment have drawn renewed attention in recent years to the concept of the **learning organisation**. It is associated with the concept of lifelong learning (discussed in Chapter 5). A central theme of the learning organisation is that **rapid learning is an essential ingredient of organisational performance and effectiveness**. It is therefore often associated with organisational development. The original idea has been around for many years, however, and was popularised in the 1960s–1980s by major writers such as Argyris.[22]

At its most basic, organisational learning can be seen in this sense:

in essence the aim is to create a culture for the continuous learning for all employees.[23]

Another significant contribution has been made by *Senge,* who defines the learning organisation as a place:

Where people continually expand their capacity to create the results they truly desire, where new and expansive patterns of thinking are nurtured, where collective aspiration is set free, and where people are continually learning how to learn together.[24]

Characteristics of the learning organisation

Senge maintains that organisations need to develop a culture of learning, and to instil 'people's commitment and capacity to learn at all levels in an organisation'. Senge suggests that there are five basic features of a learning organisation:

- **systems thinking** – the recognition that things are interconnected and organisations are complex systems;
- **personal mastery** – the competencies and skills associated with management including spiritual growth;
- **mental models** – the driving and fundamental values and principles of the organisation;
- **shared vision** – the importance of co-operation and a shared vision by team members;
- **team learning** – the two mutually complementary practices of dialogue and discussion, first separating them and then combining them.

Garratt views learning organisations as essentially liberating and energising and as crucial for organisational survival and growth. He refers to four characteristics of the learning organisation:

- It encourages people at all levels of the organisation to learn regularly and rigorously from their work.
- It has systems for capturing and learning information and moving it where it is needed.
- It values its learning.
- It is able to transform itself continuously.[25]

Lane et al. emphasise that training in the organisation's ICT skills is essential for corporate survival and should be part of a continuous learning culture. The learning organisation model will create a solid foundation on which continually to build. Lane *et al.* suggest that there is no accepted definition of the term 'learning organisation' but list some key attributes of this type of organisation:

- Learning organisations understand that teams are the fundamental learning unit – not individuals.
- Learning organisations develop a shared vision through which a singular purpose is established and learning is based on this purpose.
- Learning organisations place learning in the mainstream of their operations. Learning, quality and customers are all so important that they are everyone's job.
- A learning organisation has a culture that embraces questioning and change.
- Learning takes place in anticipation of change rather than just responding tactically to problems.
- In a learning organisation technology serves the workforce, not vice versa.
- Learning is intentional and focused on the strategy of the organisation, not reactive.
- Learning organisations structure their processes and systems so that learning and teaching are included in the day-to-day work role; consequently, learning is pervasive and change created from it is permanent.[26]

Concerns about implementation

Despite the apparent advantages that can flow from a learning organisation, there are concerns about its implementation and effectiveness, including questions about policies and procedures, necessary changes in behaviour and forms of assessment. It is also important to remember that learning starts with the individual and the impact of personality, ability and culture on the process of learning. (**Recall the discussion in Chapter 5.**)

Coopey believes that there are serious gaps in the learning organisation literature. He claims that writers have ignored the importance of control and political activity within organisations. He criticises the unitary view that is taken and the elitist model that is put forward. He points to research that shows that, in turbulence, political action increases, and concludes that the learning organisation may be destined to be a mechanism of management control, which will 'advantage some, but disadvantage others'. The effect of differential power, he believes, diminishes the potential for individual and collective learning.[27]

Critical review and reflection

Organisations have no separate identity of their own and do not exist without their members. The idea of a systematic, hierarchical and structured organisational learning approach is contrary to the instinctive individual process of learning.

To what extent do YOU believe that organisations, not just individuals, are capable of learning? Do YOU associate YOUR university with the concept of lifelong learning?

Total quality management

One particular approach to improved organisational performance and effectiveness is the concept of the Japanese-inspired **total quality management (TQM)**. There are numerous definitions of TQM. These are generally expressed in terms of **a way of life for an organisation as a whole, committed to total customer satisfaction through a continuous process of improvement, and the contribution and involvement of people.**

A major influence on the establishment and development of TQM was the work of *Deming*, who emphasised the importance of visionary leadership and the responsibility of top management for initiating change. Deming drew attention to the importance of pride in work and process control, and made constant reference to the importance of 'good management', including the human side of quality improvement and how employees should be treated.[28]

The successful organisation should as a matter of policy be constantly seeking opportunities to improve the quality of its products and/or services and processes. The organisation must also couple quality with a required level of productivity. According to the CMI, TQM is:

> *a style of managing which gives everyone in the organisation responsibility for delivering quality to the final customer; quality being described as 'fitness for purpose' or as 'delighting the customer'. TQM views each task in the organisation as fundamentally a process which is in a customer/supplier relationship with the next process. The aim at each stage is to define and meet the customer's requirements in order to maximise the satisfaction of the final consumer at the lowest possible cost.*

To be successful, the introduction of a TQM strategy involves the whole organisation in a major change with considerable research and planning, and a way of life that combines both the hard edge of quality with the soft side of cultural change.[29]

Implementation

If TQM is to be implemented successfully it must be seen as a total process involving all operations of the organisation and the active participation of top management. It demands a supportive organisational culture and a programme of planned management change. TQM places emphasis on the involvement of people as the key to improved quality. It involves changes to the traditional structure with greater emphasis on natural work groups, multidisciplinary working and team-based management. Attention must be given to effective education and training, empowerment and the motivation to take ownership of quality, and systems of communications at all levels of the organisation. A related successor to TQM is the balanced scorecard, discussed below.

Kaizen

An integral part of a total quality approach is the Japanese concept of **kaizen,** which means 'improvement', or is often interpreted as gradual progress of incremental change. In the work situation, kaizen was introduced in several Japanese organisations after the Second World War and is particularly associated with Toyota. It is not a methodology for large-scale change or the introduction of new processes, but focuses on the people aspect of improvement and the acceptance of change. The concept is based on a daily activity of continual evolutionary change, the elimination of waste and the belief that the individual workers know more about their own jobs than anyone else. Kaizen is a culture of continuous improvement as a way of life, involving the whole organisation and all its activities, and all members of staff from top managers to junior employees.

Cane suggests that the traditional kaizen approach embeds it in a hierarchical structure, although it gives considerable responsibility to employees within certain fixed boundaries. The approach:

- analyses every part of a process down to the smallest detail;
- sees how every part of the process can be improved;
- looks at how employees' actions, equipment and materials can be improved; and
- looks at ways of saving time and reducing waste.[30]

According to the Kaizen Institute, kaizen is the practice of continuous improvement based on guiding principles of: good processes bring good results; go see for yourself to grasp the current situation; speak with data, manage by facts; take action to contain and correct root causes of problems; work as a team; kaizen is everybody's business; and much more![31]

The balanced scorecard

The **balanced scorecard** (BS) is an attempt to combine a range of both qualitative and quantitative indicators of performance, which recognise the expectations of various stakeholders and relates performance to a choice of strategy as a basis for evaluating organisational effectiveness. Citing the work of *Kaplan and Norton* in a year-long study of a dozen US companies,[32] *van de Vliet* suggests that in the information era, there is a growing consensus that financial indicators on their own are not an adequate measure of company competitiveness or performance and there is a need to promote a broader view.

> The balanced scorecard does still include the hard financial indicators, but it balances these with other, so-called soft measures, such as customer acquisition, retention, profitability and satisfaction; product development cycle times; employee satisfaction; intellectual assets and organisational learning.[33]

Bourne and Bourne suggest most people think about the balanced scorecard in terms of key performance indicators (KPIs) and target-setting, but it is about aligning actions to strategy and showing people what is important. A well-constructed scorecard tells everyone in the organisation where it is going and what they are trying to achieve. It clarifies objectives and communicates them widely.[34]According to *Manager* magazine, the balanced scorecard has become well established as a system that draws data across multiple functions to produce as full a picture of organisational performance as possible. Referring to Kaplan and Norton, in order to reach a more balanced view of overall business performance, attention must also be given not only to financial measures, but also to ongoing investments in areas such as organisational capacity, customer/stakeholder objectives and internal processes.[35]

Critical review and reflection

Effective organisational performance is about quality of managers, inspired leadership and motivated staff. Concepts such as total quality management and balanced scorecard are just passing fads that offer little real long-term value.

What are YOUR views? To what extent do YOU think such concepts are of value to YOUR university and/or organisation?

Employee engagement and commitment

It is often said that people join organisations but leave their bosses. Among the factors that contribute to a healthy organisational climate is the extent to which members of staff have a sense of engagement with, and commitment to, their work, their managers and to the organisation. Genuine commitment requires not just a recognition or understanding of what the organisation expects, but an emotional and behavioural response from staff. The extent of their commitment will have a major influence on staff retention and level of work performance. For example, *O'Reilly* refers to the term 'organisational commitment' as 'typically conceived of as an individual's psychological bond to the organization, including a sense of job involvement, loyalty, and a belief in the values of the organization'.[36]

There are a number of underlying influences on the extent of employees' commitment to the organisation:

- People differ in their work ethic and the manner of their involvement with, and concern for, work and the extent to which they have an instrumental, bureaucratic or solidaristic orientation. Some people may well have a set attitude to work, whatever the nature of the work environment (**see Chapter 1**).
- People's behaviour and the level of their commitment are also influenced by the nature of the psychological contract and the degree to which it is perceived as fair by both the individual and the organisation.
- In terms of their relationship with the work organisation, employees may reasonably have the approach of 'what's in it for me?'. An important influence on the strength of commitment is the nature of the reward system and the satisfaction of needs and expectations at work in terms of economic rewards, intrinsic satisfaction or social relationships (**see Chapter 7**).

Importance of employee engagement

The CMI points out that interest in the concept of employee engagement has been growing in recent years, reinforced by pressures of economic recession.

For the organisation employee engagement can be a valuable resource of competitive advantage. It can improve performance, release innovation and creativity, lead to higher levels of customer service, facilitate the management of change, increase staff retention levels and boost interest in training and development. For the individual, engagement provides a sense of satisfaction in work, a feeling of belonging and the opportunity to develop and use personal skills and abilities to make a contribution that is valued and appreciated.[37]

The importance of **employee commitment and engagement** for business success, and the importance of people, have been highlighted in a report to the government by *Macleod and Clarke:*[38]

Business organisations function best when they make their employees' commitment, potential, creativity and capability central to their operation. Clearly having enough cash, and a sensible strategy, are vital. But how people behave at work can make the crucial difference between business and operational success or failure.

Employee engagement strategies enable people to be the best they can at work, recognising that this can only happen if they feel respected, involved, heard, well led and valued by those they work for and with.

Engaged employees have a sense of personal attachment to their work and organisation; they are motivated and able to give of their best to help it succeed – and from that flows a series of tangible benefits for organisation and individual alike.

Although improved performance and productivity is at the heart of engagement, it cannot be achieved by a mechanistic approach which tries to extract discretionary effort by manipulating employees' commitment and emotions. Employees see through such attempts very quickly; they lead instead to cynicism and disillusionment. By contrast, engaged employees freely and willingly give discretionary effort, not as an 'add on', but as an integral part of their daily activity at work.

Extracts from Macleod, D and Clarke, N. 'Engaging for Success: Enhancing performance through employee engagement', A report to Government, Department for Business, Innovation and Skills (2009).

Circle of employee engagement

De Vita maintains that employee engagement should not be written off as just another HR fad, but neither should it be viewed as a quick fix. Engagement relates to the core of a business – its values, culture and way of managing – and changing that is a tall order. But a truly engaged company is likely to be a 'great' one. As an example De Vita quotes the success of the John Lewis Partnership as a result of its co-ownership by employees combined with a collective management approach and the full engagement of employees.[39] The positive behaviour of a deeply engaged employee will rub off on clients, customers and colleagues. A highly engaged company is known to perform better, enjoy high staff retention, sustain long-term success, display energy, productivity and innovativeness and win regard as an attractive place to work. *See* Figure 16.6.

Engagement and the people factor

ACAS draws attention to people as the organisation's most important asset and describes employee engagement as the positive attitude or behaviour of someone at work. As well as being very valuable in their own right – in terms of performance, skills and creativity – individual employees bind every other aspect of working life together. The people factor is about:

- Creating a vision, or story, that everyone feels part of.
- Understanding what motivates and engages employees – is it pay, flexibility or having a say?
- Giving employees a voice – in one-to-one dialogue, team meetings and via employee representatives or trade unions.

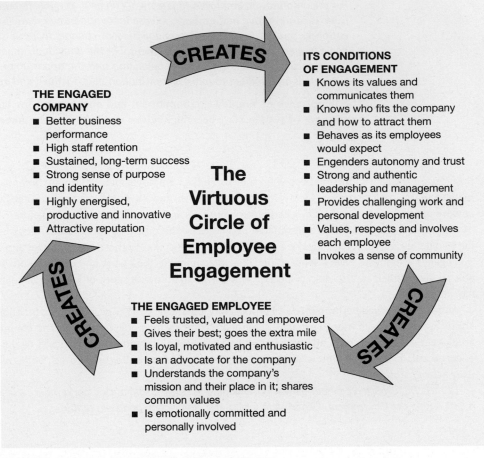

Figure 16.6 Virtuous circle of employee engagement
Source: De Vita, E. 'Get Engaged', *Management Today*, April 2007, p. 40. Reproduced from *Management Today* magazine with the permission of the copyright owner, Haymarket Business Publications Limited.

Making sure the way people behave supports organisational values on issues like equality and fairness at work.[40]

Critical review and reflection

Securing the engagement and commitment of staff is easy. Simply apply Herzberg's two-factor theory of motivation and give attention to first the hygiene factors and then the motivating factors.
To what extent would YOU support this contention? What is likely to determine YOUR level of engagement with and commitment to a work organisation?

A concept map of a summary of practical employee involvement is set out in Figure 16.7.

Investors in People

Investors in People (IIP) is owned by the UK government and managed nationally through the UK Commission for Employment and Skills as strategic brand owners. IIP specialises in highlighting and championing best practice in people management through a framework for assessment and accreditation. It is a flexible framework that organisations of any size or sector

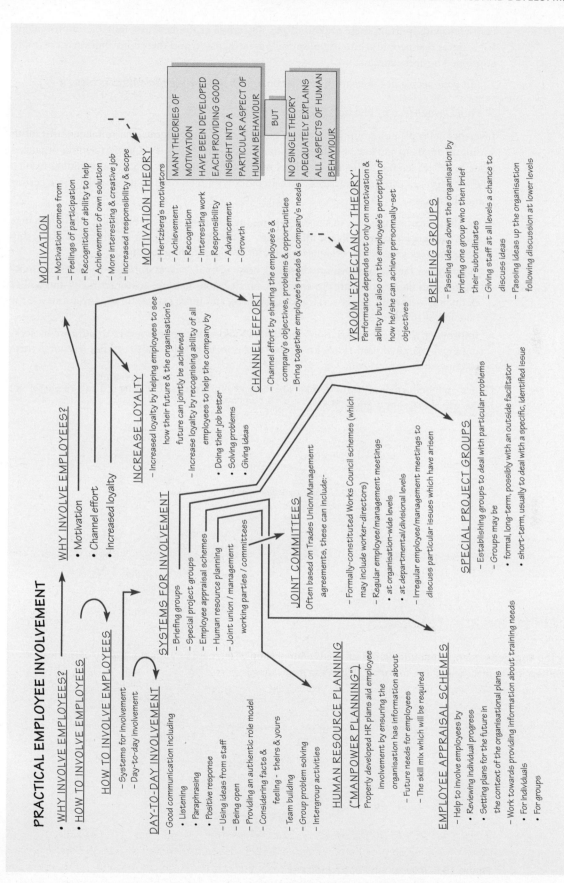

Figure 16.7 Concept map of practical employee involvement

Source: Copyright © 2011 The Virtual Learning Materials Workshop. Reproduced with permission.

can work with, putting their organisation's objectives at the heart of tangible improvement. IIP believes that people are an organisation's greatest asset, and their contribution is critical to continued business success.

Put your people at the heart of your vision and they'll use their talents to achieve it.

Paul Devoy, Head of Investors in People UKCES[41]

Investors in People point out that creating purpose in a fast changing environment whilst motivating through change have become essential skills for many roles. Outperforming organisations foster leadership skills at every level of the organisation to deliver outstanding results. The IIP Standard explores practices and outcomes within an organisation under three performance headings:

- **Leading:** creating purpose in a fast changing environment whilst motivating through change have become essential skills for many roles. Outperforming organisations foster leadership skills at every level of the organisation to deliver outstanding results.
- **Supporting:** for many, constant change is now normal. Successful organisations are moving towards flatter structures to enable faster decision-making, customer focus and agility. Reducing overheads, better service for customers and more successful organisations are the benefits of this approach.
- **Improving:** the best organisations are always looking for opportunities to improve by seeking every marginal gain. They know that every small change adds together to enable them to constantly outperform.

Under each performance heading there are three key indicators. The nine indicators are set out in the wheel diagram, Figure 16.8.

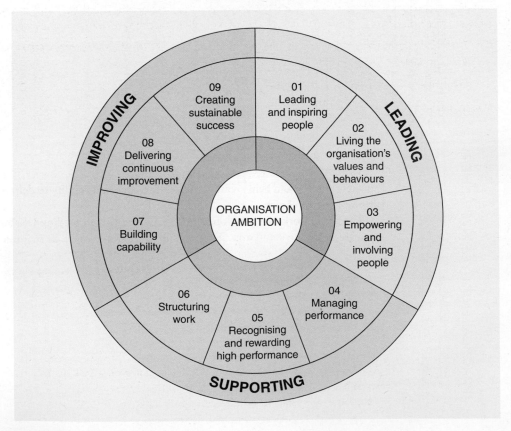

Figure 16.8 Investors in People indicators

Source: Investors in People, Copyright © Investors in People 2015

IIP: Vauxhall in Ellesmere Port

Uniting a workforce, transforming fortunes and securing a sustainable future for a car manufacturing plant.

What was the IIP motivation?

Vauxhall Motors is one of the biggest names in UK car production, employing over 4,300 people nationwide. Nearly half of them work at the company's manufacturing plant in Ellesmere Port, Cheshire. The future was looking bleak for Ellesmere Port. With Vauxhall's US owner General Motors losing money, there was a real risk the plant would close. But when GM needed to choose a plant to lead production of the new Astra, a lifeline emerged – as long as a new working agreement could be reached. Strongly focused on the 'people' end of the business, Managing Director Duncan Aldred sees IIP as a critical factor in Vauxhall's journey.

How has IIP helped?

Producing the Astra would require round-the-clock production, meaning big changes to working arrangements. Workers, unions and management had to co-operate to win the bid, listening to all voices to devise a mutually agreeable plan. It worked: 94 per cent of workers voted for a new four-year pay and conditions deal and the contract was secured. The senior leadership team applied IIP best practice to guide changes throughout the process and beyond. The framework was used to support development of key performance indicators, social responsibility strategy, succession planning and benchmarking. Today, Vauxhall UK has achieved the Standard across all UK sites.

What was the impact?

Production is due to start in 2015, securing all 2,100 existing jobs at the plant and paving the way to at least 700 new ones. Wider use of local suppliers will add further jobs locally. Meanwhile, Ellesmere Port is receiving a £125 million upgrade as it prepares to become a state-of-the-art 24/7 manufacturing operation.

> *The principles of Investors in People underpin every aspect of Vauxhall Motors' strategy, and Vauxhall is using the Standard to shape its future direction.*
>
> *Phil Millward, HR Director, Vauxhall UK*

Source: Investors In People content provided by the UK Commission for Employment and Skills. www.investorsinpeople.co.uk. Reproduced with permission.

The IIP Bronze, Silver and Gold levels highlight an organisation's standard of people management quality and help create a competitive edge in its ability to deliver a service and also as an employer of choice.

The framework was developed in collaboration with leading UK businesses and government to raise the standards of leadership and management. It is internationally recognised as a leading quality standard for people management and has proven to support businesses through times of change and economic uncertainty using recognised best practice.

The EFQM Excellence Model

Excellence is the goal for many organisations. EFQM (European Foundation for Quality Management) is a global not-for-profit organisation, based in Brussels. The EFQM Excellence Model is a business model that builds on the experience of previous models and is now adopted by organisations across the globe to strive for sustainable excellence.

The **EFQM Excellence Model** is a management framework used by over 30,000 organisations in Europe and beyond. The 'Model' takes a holistic view to enable organisations, regardless of size or sector, to assess where they are, help understand their key strengths and potential gaps

Figure 16.9 EFQM Excellence Model
Source: EFQM. Copyright © 2012 EFQM. The EFQM Excellence Model is a registered trademark of the EFQM. Reproduced with permission.

in performance across the nine criteria. It is based on the concept that an organisation will achieve better results by involving all the people in the organisation in the continuous improvement of their processes. The 'Model' is designed to be non-prescriptive. It is not a standard; it does not tell you what to do, but is there to provide guidelines.

Organisations are able to benchmark themselves against others both within and outside their sectors. The basic assumption is that excellent results in terms of performance, customers, people and society (the results) are achieved through leadership driving policy and strategy, people, partnerships and resources, and processes (the enablers). Innovation and learning are key to improving enablers that in turn improve results. (*See* Figure 16.9.)

The nine criteria of the 'Model'

Each of the nine criteria featured in the 'Model' are described as follows:

1. **Leadership.** How leaders develop and facilitate the achievement of the mission and vision, develop values for long-term success and implement these via appropriate actions and behaviours, and are personally involved in ensuring that the organisation's management system is developed and implemented.
2. **Strategy.** How the organisation implements its mission and vision via a clear stakeholder-focused strategy, supported by relevant policies, plans, objectives, targets and processes.
3. **People.** How the organisation manages, develops and releases the knowledge and full potential of its people at an individual, team-based and organisation-wide level, and plans these activities in order to support its policy and strategy and the effective operation of its processes.
4. **Partnerships and resources.** How the organisation plans and manages its external partnerships and internal resources in order to support its policy and strategy and the effective operation of its processes.
5. **Processes, products and services.** How the organisation designs, manages and improves its processes in order to support its policy and strategy and fully satisfy, and generate increasing value for, its customers and other stakeholders.
6. **Customer results.** What the organisation is achieving in relation to its external customers.

7. **People results.** What the organisation is achieving in relation to its people.
8. **Society results.** What the organisation is achieving in relation to local, national and international society, as appropriate.
9. **Business results.** What the organisation is achieving in relation to its planned performance.[42]

Management development

An environment of increasing business competitiveness, rapid change and technological innovations has highlighted the growing importance of **management development.** The 'Ability to Attract, Retain and Develop Top Talent' is another of the nine measures of success by which *Management Today* rates performance in its annual survey of Britain's Most Admired Companies. In particular, the general movement towards greater employee involvement and managing the people resource has emphasised an integrating rather than a controlling style of management. Managers need a balance of technical, social and conceptual knowledge and skills, acquired through a blend of education and experience. There is, therefore, a continual need for organisations to ensure the development of both present and future managers.

Reports from the Chartered Institute of Personnel and Development (CIPD) and the Chartered Management Institute (CMI) both draw attention to the importance of management development.

The CIPD has emphasised the crucial importance of management development to organisations' success, and to management capability as a driver for growth.

There is now a solid body of research evidence that shows that firms with a more-qualified management workforce and a dedicated programme of management development perform better and have more-sophisticated and higher-quality product market strategies.

Management and leadership skills play a crucial role in terms of economic enablers, skills investment, employee engagement and high-performance working practices. However, UK managers are generally less educated than their international counterparts and receive less management development. Part of the problem in improving management capability is resistance to change and identifying a clear causal link between management development and improvement in business performance. There is also still a distinct lack of recognition of the value of people management skills within management development in general.[43]

From a national survey of 4,500 managers, together with focus groups, interviews and case studies, the CMI reports on the business benefits of management and leadership development (MLD). Findings highlight considerable scope for improving the effectiveness of UK management and, by doing so, improving organisational performance. Higher-performing organisations invest 36 per cent more on MLD than low-performing organisations. The research indicated that in addition to a financial commitment to MLD, a range of associated factors is associated clearly with higher performance. A combination of commitment to MLD, alignment to business strategy and supporting HR practices explains as much as 32 per cent of the increase in people performance and 23 per cent in overall organisational performance.[44]

Critical review and reflection

Many top executives make the point that they have no formal management education or qualifications, and emphasise the importance of on-the-job experience. Many organisations waste time and money on the development of staff but then prevent them using their new ideas in practice.

What is YOUR view of management development? How do you think YOU can be best prepared for a potential managerial position?

Succession planning

Management **succession planning** aims to ensure that a sufficient supply of appropriately qualified and capable men and women is available to meet the future needs of the organisation. Such people should be available readily to fill managerial or supervisory vacancies caused through retirement, death, resignation, promotion or transfer of staff, or through the establishment of new positions. Succession planning should be related to the overall corporate strategy. According to the CMI, 'succession planning is more specific in its focus than talent management and tends to concentrate on key positions within senior management, including the chief executive officer and board members'.[45]

Baroness Kingsmill warns of the danger in replacing one leader with another from the same mould and the tendency of CEOs to recruit in their own image. It is inevitable that an organisational culture that centres on the leader develops. One of the downsides of succession planning is the danger that a single leadership type will prevail: 'A long-term commitment to talent development that encourages a mix of styles, capabilities and approaches can help to ensure that an organisation is responsive to change as well as resilient to crisis.'[46]

Planned career progression

Allied to management development and succession planning, there should be a programme of planned career progression. This should provide potential managers with:

- training and experience to equip them to assume a level of responsibility compatible with their ability; and
- practical guidance, encouragement and support so that they may realise their potential, satisfy their career ambition and wish to remain with the organisation.

Career progression should involve individual appraisal and counselling. However, care should be taken to avoid giving staff too long or over-ambitious career expectations. If these expectations cannot be fulfilled, staff may become disillusioned and frustrated.

Continuing professional development

In recent years, greater recognition has been given to the significance of lifelong learning and to **continuing professional development (CPD)**. Lifelong learning should, however, be the concern of all employees in the organisation and (despite the title) it is arguable that the concept of CPD should not be seen as applying only to professionals or managers as opposed to all employees.

Clearly, however, CPD does have particular significance for management development. A number of professional bodies have developed a competence-based CPD scheme for their members. For example, the CMI regards CPD as vital to a successful career and requires all members to make a commitment to their own professional development. Submission of a detailed CPD record is an integral and compulsory part of gaining the status of 'Chartered Manager'.

Self-development

An important part of the process of improving managerial or professional performance is self-development. This demands the ability to identify clearly real development needs and goals, to take responsibility for actions to reach these goals and to recognise opportunities for learning.

Self-development has to be self-initiated and continued throughout your working life. But if this is to be a realistic aim it requires an organisational climate that will encourage people to develop themselves and the active support of top management. People need sufficient authority and flexibility to take advantage of situations that are likely to extend their knowledge and skills. Superiors should be prepared to delegate new and challenging projects, including problem-solving assignments.

The future of management and leadership

Against the background of doldrums in the UK economy and shattered trust in business leaders, an all-party Parliamentary Group on Management formed the Commission on the Future of Management and Leadership with the CIM, launched in October 2013. Responding to the following major challenges is vital if UK management is improved in order to deliver success by the year 2020:[47]

- The UK lags behind many competitors on key economic indicators.
- Younger generations will drive new ways of working.
- Managers will need to be adequately trained.
- Technology demands better people skills.
- Globalisation will drive diversity and more cross-cultural working.
- Long-term sustainability is fundamental.

The report refers to the state of UK management and leadership today including:

- **Concerns about management effectiveness** – Good management is crucial to driving growth and productivity, but many of today's managers are simply not up to the job.
- **Ethics** – Four-fifths of workers do not think their manager sets a good moral example and less than a fifth are aware of their organisation's values.
- **Training is too little and too late** – UK managers are underqualified and many are left without the training and development they deserve to succeed in their jobs.

Top ten characteristics needed by managers

The evidence found that anyone can be a manager and anyone can be a good manager. The Commission identified the ten key characteristics of highly effective leaders and managers in the twenty-first century:

1. Clear sense of purpose.
2. Strong values and personal integrity.
3. Commitment to developing others through coaching and mentoring.
4. Champion of diversity.
5. Ability to engage and communicate across all levels.
6. Self-awareness and taking time to reflect.
7. Collaboration, networked and non-hierarchical.
8. Agile and innovative, technologically curious and savvy.
9. Personal resilience and grit.
10. Excellent track record of delivery.

We need managers who inspire and support their teams to succeed. These managers should be recruited not only for their technical skills they possess but also because they have the right attitudes, values and ethics. They should be managers who are assessed and paid not only on their results, but on how they achieve them.

Management and organisational behaviour in action case study
CEZ Distribution Bulgaria JSC

CEZ Distribution Bulgaria JSC is a part of the CEZ JSC, one of the largest energy companies in Europe, the market leader for Central and Eastern Europe. Some 2,700 employees work in the company and provide a continuous supply of quality electricity to 2.2 million customers.

The management and employees accepted the change, which became a priority for them, to meet the growing needs of its customers, to protect the interests of the shareholders, to respond to pressure from the external environment and to increase the efficiency of investment and implemented innovative solutions and technologies.

CEZ Distribution Bulgaria JSC adopted Investors in People as a global standard for best-practice people management. By engaging and developing people the company aimed to reveal and realize its potential to achieve its strategic goals. Covering everything from business planning and leadership to effectively managing and measuring results, Investors in People helped to get the outcomes strived for.

In 2013 the company's management team redesigned its vision and mission, and set clear strategic goals and relevant development priorities. The ongoing communication with and involvement of people in this process were of primary importance. The flexible framework of Investors in People helped the company to achieve its own unique business goals. On the way to achieving high recognition, corporate principles were very closely linked to the values of Investors in People, a strong leadership and management strategy was put in place and highly efficient people management practices were applied.

What was the impact?

The Investors in People Bronze accreditation is just the beginning of our journey of continuous improvement. We acquired a better understanding of change management for improving business performance through effective people management. The successful implementation of the organisational change improved team effectiveness. We had massive communication from and feedback to 2,500 employees.

The seven corporate values underpinned and aligned the competency model for each management level and people. They are in the hearts of people and a powerful driver for transformation in behaviour and performance. Clearly defined key performance indicators of top management to the first operational level were linked to the strategic objectives.

We have achieved a reduction in operating costs. The level of work accidents in compliance with health and safety requirements has been minimised. We have developed management and leadership competencies, and measured and improved team management effectiveness.

How did IIP help?

Investors in People gave us the courage to set high goals and achieve more and more. With a strong top management, focused on continuous improvement, clearly defined key performance indicators and corporate social responsibility, we went beyond the core Standard. Principles of IIP guide our work in one direction, allowing us to be more effective. We have focused our efforts on increasing the efficiency of people by providing learning that evolves their potential and improves their knowledge and skills. IIP is a standardised, outcome-based way of working that leads to better people management.

Source: Investors in People content provided by the UK Commission for Employment and Skills. www.investorsinpeople.co.uk. Reproduced with permission.

Tasks

1. Discuss what you think are key reasons for the successful improved performance of CEZ Distribution.
2. What do you see as the most effective way of obtaining both management's and employees' acceptance of change in the external environment?
3. Explain your view of the seven corporate values and principles of CEZ Distribution.

Organisational capabilities

Research from The Boston Consulting Group and twelve partner organisations, including the CMI, demonstrate clearly that organisational capabilities drive corporate success. Behavioural aspects, often seen as tangential, are vital differentiators – but only when they accompany structural capabilities such as superior organisational design and rigorous business process and controls. The study points out that although the world's best organisations may look like many of their competitors, under closer examination there are distinct combinations of winning attributes. The study developed a framework of twenty discrete organisational capabilities under six sub-categories: structural design, roles and collaboration mechanisms, processes and tools, leadership, people and engagement, and culture and change. (*See* Figure 16.10.)

Structural design

1. Organization structure
2. Role of the center
3. Layers and spans of control
4. Organizational cost-efficiency
5. Shared services, offshoring, and outsourcing

Roles and collaboration mechanisms

6. Role clarity
7. Cross-functional collaboration mechanisms
8. Informal/virtual networks

Processes and tools

9. Process excellence/optimization
10. Project management
11. Business analytics and information management

Leadership

12. Leadership performance
13. Leadership pipeline
14. Middle-management effectiveness

People and engagement

15. Recruitment and retention
16. Employee performance management
17. Employee motivation

Culture and change

18. Change management capabilities
19. Adaptability and flexibility
20. Culture

Description

- Reporting lines, including profit-and-loss accountabilities
- The corporate center's role with regard to involvement and leadership
- The number of reporting layers in the hierarchy; the number of people reporting directly to a manager
- The level of cost-efficiency enabled by the organization
- Internal service provider; cross-country relocation; subcontracting to other companies

- Understanding of the role's responsibilities in the organization
- Lateral coordination effort between functions or units
- Important but informal channels for reinforcing culture and communicating key information

- Processes optimized for high quality, short processing times, or low cost
- For example, roles, processes, and tools
- Skills, technologies, applications, and practices to drive business planning

- Capable and effective individual leaders and leadership teams
- Preparing for the next-generation leadership team
- Middle managers empowered to carry strategy into the organization

- Providing the necessary talent to meet strategic and growth goals
- Systems and processes aligned to ensure that goals are achieved
- The willingness to exert discretionary effort

- The organization's ability to manage change efforts
- A flexible structure that allows adapting to external challenges
- The set of shared values in an organization

Figure 16.10 Twenty vital organisational topics
Source: Organizational Capabilities Matter © 2012, The Boston Consulting Group (BCG).

All 20 organizational capabilities have an impact on overall performance – though clearly some have more influence than others. Even more interesting: there is a definite tilt towards behavioral factors – in particular leadership, employee engagement, and cross-functional collaboration.[48]

Critical review and reflection

There are varying measures of organisational performance that can be viewed at different levels, over different time spans and in different ways by competing interest groups. It is not realistic to establish clear universal criteria for the measurement of organisational success.

What are YOUR views? What specific measures of organisational effectiveness can YOU identify for YOUR university or organisation? How effective are these measures?

The future of the workplace

Management Today in association with Smart Technologies explored changes in how we work and the nature of the work environment. *Gyther* points out that the workplace is in a state of flux, which is down to a variety of factors: cost, carbon, technology, sustainability and culture.

> *People still accept that it's very important for an organisation to have a clear definition of what it is and how to go efficiently about achieving its aims, but how does the working environment play its part? The workplace is becoming more fragmented – people aren't working under the same roof as they were even 20 years ago.*

In addition to environmental concerns and globalisation, other issues raised in a round table debate included:

- How to get people to collaborate in real time across different parts of the world.
- The design of office space to be more open to encourage greater creativity.
- A danger that office design driven by technological development ignores the human cultural dimensions of work.
- With the move towards more flexible working and remote working, how will businesses that are built on the accumulation of the experience and skills of their people respond if those people are never together?
- The focus on interactive technology and bringing people together using technology.
- What is the speed of change of human behaviour to facilitate culture, organisation and a sense of belonging in a new set of environments? How to manage the transition of behaviour when everyone is stressed and insecure.
- The idea of a clean desk, the layering of technology, increased office size because of handling emails, the lack of reading.
- The dramatic change in work, which is now much more complicated. People working in different locations across different time zones but, at present, an extremely low understanding of virtual teaming.[49]

Successful organisations and people

The overall effectiveness of the organisation will be affected both by sound structural design and by individuals filling the various positions within the structure. Management will need to acknowledge the existence of the informal organisation that arises from the interactions of people working in the organisation. The operation of the organisation and actual working arrangements will be influenced by the style of management, the personalities of members and the informal organisation. These factors may lead to differences between the formal structure of the organisation and what happens in practice. *Stewart* found the relationship between people and organisation to be reciprocal.

> *People modify the working of the formal organization, but their behaviour is also influenced by it. It may make demands on them which they find an undue strain, so that they seek ways of modifying these pressures. The method of work organization can determine how people relate to one another, which may affect both their productivity and their morale. Managers, therefore, need to be conscious of the ways in which methods of work organization may influence people's attitudes and actions. Before behaviour is put down to individual or group cussedness, managers should look for its possible organizational causes.*[50]

Building an organisation involves more than concern for structure, methods of work and technical efficiency. The hallmark of many successful business organisations is the attention given to the human element; to the development of a culture that helps to create a feeling of belonging, commitment and satisfaction. Structure must be designed, therefore, so as to maintain the balance of the socio-technical system and the effectiveness of the organisation as a whole. Attention must be given to the interactions between both the structural and technological requirements of the organisation, and social factors and the needs and demands of the human part of the organisation.

The importance of people for organisational effectiveness is reinforced by a survey undertaken by the MCA and *Management Today*. The survey emphasises that the role of the organisation is social as well as economic and points to the desperate need for the basic, softer skills of managers in leadership, coaching and mentoring. Organisations need individuals they can trust, who are engaged in and committed to their work. If they want to survive, organisations need to recognise that they have to add value to their employees, that their social capital is just as important as their financial capital.[51]

People, diversity and organisational performance

An underlying consideration of the people element in work organisations of the future is attention to respect for individual differences and diversity (**discussed in Chapter 4**), and positive action on equality and inclusion. With increasing globalisation it is of greater importance to have a sound understanding of diverse countries and workforces. More than ever, effective organisational performance demands the successful management of diversity. For example, The Institute of Employment Studies, in conjunction with the CMI, emphasise the importance of diversity as a strategic priority for retaining and developing key people in the organisation.[52] And the CMI also reminds us that:

> *Many of us work in diverse environments, and even in more homogeneous workplaces, employees could well be dealing with clients from a variety of backgrounds, particularly in global businesses. Therefore, in the face of the trend towards greater diversity in both the workplace itself, and in the societies and markets that organisations serve, it is up to managers to make the most of this new, more diverse world that we all find ourselves in. Greater diversity, and the benefits that diversity bring, will only occur if there is genuine enthusiasm for the concept throughout the organisation. Actions taken to encourage greater diversity should not be tokenistic, isolated instances, but should be part of a broader mindset that sees diversity as an important part of any successful company.*[53]

A word of caution

Any student of management or reader of this book will realise there is no shortage of ideas on how to improve organisational performance. Understanding the latest concepts and pronouncements of leading writers is a part of a manager's development, and there clearly are potential benefits to be gained for both the individual and the organisation. However, as *Stern* reminds us, great ideas in business rise and fall, and favoured management styles and approaches come into and go out of fashion almost as fast as in the fashion industry.

> *Management is both science and art, and the trick of it lies in separating the good ideas from the bad, knowing when to be scientific and when to be artful . . . Here is Management Today's unfashionable contribution to the great fashion of management ideas: show a real interest in what people are doing for you. It matters.[54]*

Critical review and reflection

According to a senior researcher at the Work Foundation, there is no incontrovertible evidence that links company well-being to increased organisational performance.[55] So presumably attempting to establish clear links between the process of management and organisational effectiveness is a waste of time.

What is YOUR response to this assertion? How would YOU describe the relationship within YOUR own university and/or organisation?

Ten key points to remember

1 Every work organisation is concerned with being effective. The quality of management and commitment of staff are central to the success of the organisation.

2 Increasing attention is given to the attributes and qualities of a manager, to the development of social and human skills, and to the ability to work well with people.

3 There is a clear and important need for managerial effectiveness. Managers are judged not just on their own performance but on results achieved by other staff.

4 An essential ingredient of any successful manager is understanding the needs and expectations of staff, and the ability to work through and with other people.

5 A key factor in organisational effectiveness is the successful management of change and attention to the learning organisation and the continuous learning for all staff.

6 One approach to improved organisational performance is the idea of total quality management, associated with the concepts of kaizen and the balanced scorecard.

7 Among factors contributing to a healthy organisational climate is the extent to which members of staff have a sense of engagement with and commitment to their work.

8 Other important contributions to organisational effectiveness are the work of Investors in People and the European Foundation for Quality Management.

9 In an increasingly competitive environment, attention must be given to management development, the future of management and leadership, and succession planning.

10 The hallmark of many successful organisations is attention given to human and behavioural aspects and development of a culture of belonging, commitment and satisfaction.

Review and discussion questions

1 Give your own views on the importance and contribution of managers to organisational effectiveness. Support your answer with reference to your own university.

2 Explain what you see as the essential attributes, qualities and skills for a successful manager today.

3 What specific criteria and measures would you use to judge managerial effectiveness in any organisation of your choice?

4 Explain in your own words your understanding of what is meant by the learning organisation. To what extent is your own organisation a learning organisation?

5 Discuss the practical applications of total quality management and related concepts.

6 Give your views on the relevance of: (i) Investors in People; and (ii) the EFQM model for improved organisational effectiveness.

7 Explain fully those factors that have contributed to and/or detracted from your strength of engagement with and commitment to your university and/or any work situation.

8 Discuss the extent to which you believe there is a responsibility for your own continuous professional development and self-development.

9 Detail the questions you would ask, and the specific criteria you would apply, in attempting to evaluate the performance and effectiveness of your own university.

10 Give your own views on how you see the future of management and the nature of successful organisations.

Assignment

At Happy Training Company, people are asked who they would like as their manager:[56] 'Given how important a manager is to getting the most out of others, we let people choose theirs.'

- Detail fully what you see as the arguments for and against people choosing their own managers.
- To what extent does the type and nature of the organisation influence your views?
- Discuss if choosing your own manager would be appropriate to a university.
- How would *you* feel about choosing *your* own manager?
- If *you* were interested in a managerial career how would *you* feel about working in an organisation where people choose their own managers?

Personal skills and employability exercise

Objectives

Completing this exercise should help you to enhance the following skills:

- Participate meaningfully in a management development programme.
- Prepare for your future career progression.
- Take responsibility for your own self-development.

Exercise

You have recently been appointed to a trainee managerial position and selected for interview for an intensive management development training programme. You are pleased to have been invited for interview but unsure what to expect and nervous about your participation in the programme if selected.

- Explain fully how you can best prepare yourself for this development training programme.
- What questions might you expect to be asked?
- How would you explain benefits you have gained from your university course of study, including the balance between theory and practice?
- Detail the skills and abilities you would need to demonstrate.
- What form of exercises, activities and assessments might you expect?
- How would you expect to benefit from the programme?
- How might you best attempt to apply what you have learned on the programme in your actual work situation?

Discussion

- Explain how you see the relationship between university education and employability, and between off-the-job learning and on-the-job experience.
- How would you attempt to evaluate the effectiveness of the programme?
- To what extent should management development be suited to the individual or geared towards the needs of the particular organisation?

Case study
Co-operatives

Co-operatives are a distinctive form of organisation with a long history. The International Co-operative Alliance (ICA) website provides a definition:

Co-operatives are businesses owned and run by and for their members. Whether the members are the customers, employees or residents they have an equal say in what the business does and a share in the profits.[57]

While shareholder-owned firms may have emerged as the dominant model in producing goods and services in most markets today, co-operative organisations can often be found alongside them. Their combined importance is greater than many might realise: the European Commission's website reports that co-operatives:

are an important part of European economic life and industry; there are 250,000 co-operative enterprises in the European Union, owned by 163 million citizens (1 in 3 EU citizens) and they employ 5.4 million people.[58]

In the ICA's list of the world's top 300 co-operatives,[59] the importance of co-ops in banking and finance, retail, agriculture and a range of other sectors can clearly be seen, as well as the co-operative identity of some very well-known names around the world. The UK is not as strongly represented here as other EU Member States: the largest UK co-operatives, at positions 22 and 23 on the list, are the Co-operative Group and Nationwide Building Society.

Today's co-operatives are therefore not fading survivors of an archaic organisational form, but rather an interestingly different way of getting things done. The ICA estimates that more than 250 million people around the world are employed by co-operatives, including about 12 per cent of those employed in G20 nations.[60] This case looks at how organisations structured as co-operatives may behave differently and considers the implications of those special features for the markets of the twenty-first century.

A history of co-operation

Throughout human history, progress has been made by learning to co-operate; informal co-operation has been a feature of successful societies over the centuries. More formally defined co-operatives started to appear around the time of the Industrial Revolution: in the resultant urbanisation, working people had to rely upon buying food, rather than growing their own, and co-operative organisations grew up to protect the interests of workers

From humble beginnings in this nineteenth-century Lancashire store, the co-operative movement has inspired a form of business organisation that now accounts for up to 100 million employees around the world.
Source: Co-operative

against those of more powerful suppliers, who were often also employers.[61]

One of the key milestones in the history of co-operatives took place in 1844 in the north of England:

> In 1843, workers in the textile mills of Rochdale, England went on strike. When the strike failed, the millworkers began to look for other ways to improve their lives. Instead of calling for another strike or asking charitable groups for help, some of these people decided to take control of one of the most immediate and pressing areas of their lives. They believed they needed their own food store as an alternative to the company store. Twenty-eight people founded the Rochdale Equitable Pioneers Society.
>
> After saving money for over a year, these pioneers opened their co-op store at 31 Toad Lane on a cold December evening in 1844. Although the founders agreed to sell just butter, sugar, flour, and oatmeal, they also offered tallow candles for sale that night. They were forced to buy candles because the gas company refused to supply gas for the new group's lights. They bought candles in bulk and sold what they didn't use to their members.[62]

This venture was one of the earliest formal co-operative structures, whose founding principles are still an important statement of the values of the contemporary co-operative movement. The Rochdale principles (as they are now known) are set out below:[63]

1. Open membership.
2. Democratic control (one man, one vote).
3. Distribution of surplus in proportion to trade.

4. Payment of limited interest on capital.
5. Political and religious neutrality.
6. Cash trading.
7. Promotion of education.

These principles are an important clue to the distinctive nature of co-operatives today. Democratic control remains a cornerstone of the co-operative way of doing things: members must debate and then choose; the direction taken by the organisation will be the one chosen by the majority. Note the difference with shareholder-owned companies, in which 'votes' are proportional to the numbers of shares held, meaning that large institutional shareholders will usually outweigh private investors by a large margin. The third and fourth principles are also importantly distinctive: in a shareholder-owned company, rewards are proportional to shareholdings, but in a co-operative, rewards are determined by participation rates; in a co-op shop, the dividend is proportional to the amounts bought. As will be discussed below, the insight that co-operative members are better understood as users than investors is important in analysing members' motivation and behaviour.

Co-operatives and organisational behaviour

Co-operatives as organisational forms are of interest theoretically because of the effect of the unusual structure on incentives and behaviour. It is sometimes suggested, for example, that co-operatives are more likely than investor-owned firms to suffer from the 'problem of the commons' in economics: where the assets are in the hands of everyone but not in the hands of anyone, why should any member refrain from using the assets in ways that may damage them (i.e. overgrazing, in terms of the original problem)?

Other concerns have focused on the theoretical problems of co-operative decision-making by large numbers of members with diverse priorities and interests. *Borgen*[64] suggests that some of these perceived difficulties may result from a misleading assumption about the outlook and motivation of co-operative members: that they are akin to investors in a firm. If such an assumption were true, then analysing the decision-making problem in terms of property rights and agent/principal relationships would be justified. However, in his view, co-operative members are far more realistically understood as *users*, rather than investors: the fact that they have chosen to join suggests a strong interest in the output of the organisation. The member as user, then, will think differently from an investor and have a strong incentive to take part in decision-making.

Whatever the answer to these theoretical questions, there is certainly a strong continuing interest in co-operatives as a way of getting things done. A report by strategy consultants Booz Allen Hamilton[65] reviewed progress in the sector and suggested six distinctive features of co-operatives that allow these organisations to compete in the tough markets of today:

- **Consensual decision-making** – Co-operatives take a longer time in consulting members, but make up that time when it comes to implementation, in terms of both speed and quality.
- **Better communication** – Because of the stronger emphasis on member and employee communication, co-operatives find it easier to identify and draw upon the skills and enthusiasm of the organisation and also experience better customer loyalty.
- **Leadership development in the company and community** – Co-operatives have a long-term focus on developing a skill base, linked to a traditional commitment to education.
- **Long-range planning and experimentation** – Without the extreme pressure to deliver financial results that shareholder-owned companies often experience, co-operatives can think and invest over longer time scales and carry their membership with them.
- **Openness to learning best practices** – Co-operatives seem ready to learn from the experience of other co-operatives, often operating in different markets, but with important lessons and insights to offer.
- **The social dimension** – The co-operative model is particularly effective in assisting the development of emerging economies, by providing a model framework for entrepreneurship and management, which in turn can encourage a wider range of people to become involved.

Since the 2008–9 global financial crisis, co-operatives have often coped relatively well with the turbulent business conditions, possibly for some of the reasons discussed in the Booz Allen Hamilton report. The UK's Nationwide, for example, has grown successfully and is now the country's largest building society, having stood back from the trend towards demutualisation in the 1980s and 1990s.

Elsewhere in the sector, however, the picture has been less encouraging: the acute problems at the UK's Co-operative Bank (part of the Co-operative Group) hit the headlines in 2013 when a planned purchase of hundreds of branches from state-supported Lloyds Bank fell through.[66] In the following weeks, major problems emerged, many of which related to the bank's purchase of Britannia Building Society in 2009.[67] Although this crisis involved unusual problems of leadership and governance at the Co-operative Bank,[68] its underlying business problem of having taken on much more risk than it could manage was all too reminiscent of the much larger bank failures in 2008–9. By 2014, the Co-operative Group's ownership of its Bank had fallen to 30 per cent, with the cruel irony of the remaining share being held by US institutions, including hedge funds.[69] Furthermore, in March 2014 Euan Sutherland (formerly Chief Executive of B&Q) resigned as Chief Executive of the wider Co-op Group, suggesting that it was 'impossible' to overhaul the ailing business because of its complex governance structure.

What is to be learnt from this disappointing set of events? Perhaps no more than this: the co-operative model contains a number of distinctive features that should allow it to be the basis for a secure, trustworthy and successful provision of financial services. The ICA list of the top 300 co-operatives in the world[70] shows that this is very much the rule across a range of countries. The UK's experience with the Co-operative Bank shows that a poorly managed co-operative is unlikely to be successful, which is hardly surprising. Well-managed co-operatives abound and remain in business because of the quality of service that they provide.

In a sense, organisations have always had the prime purpose of facilitating people in working together and overcoming the problems that arise. The co-operative model may not have been the dominant business organisation so far, but it has developed a distinctive approach that works very well in some circumstances and promises much for the future.

Tasks

1 Figure 16.4 summarises the 3-D model of managerial behaviour proposed by Reddin. Explain which of the four main styles you consider to be most appropriate for managers in a co-operative business organisation. Would you recommend a different style for a shareholder-owned business or a public-sector organisation such as a prison or a local council? Give reasons for your answer.

2 It has been suggested that highly engaged employees facilitate improved business performance, and it might be expected that the workforce of a co-operative is very highly engaged. Using Figure 16.6, the virtuous circle of employee engagement, explain what might have gone wrong at the Co-op Group during 2009–14. To what extent was it a failure of management, and why do you think this?

3 Co-operatives exist in many business sectors (e.g. banking, agriculture, food retail and manufacturing). Most started on a small and local scale. Can you see any opportunities around you to create a co-operative, and how would you go about setting it up?

Notes and references

1. Czerniawska, F. 'From Bottlenecks to BlackBerries: How the Relationship between Organisations and Individuals Is Changing', Management Consultancies Association, September 2005.

2. Lucas, E. 'Switched On to Innovation', *Professional Manager*, vol. 16, no. 3, 2007, pp. 32–5; Mahden, M. in conversation with De Vita, E. 'Best Fit', *Management Today*, September 2008, p. 54.

3. 'Delivering the Promise of Management Practices', Advanced Institute of Management Research and Chartered Management Institute, November 2010.

4. Katz, R. L. 'Skills of an Effective Administrator', *Harvard Business Review*, September–October 1974, pp. 90–102.

5. Leitch Review of Skills: Prosperity for All in the Global Economy – World Class Skills, The Stationery Office, December 2006.

6. *Management Futures: The World in 2018*, Chartered Management Institute, March 2008; Handy, C. B. *Understanding Organizations*, fourth edition, Penguin (1993).

7. Mann, S. 'Cultivating influence', *Professional Manager*, January 2010, pp. 32–4.

8. Saunders, A. 'Rebuilding management's good name', *Management Today*, May 2011, pp. 44–6.

9. Drucker, P. *The Practice of Management*, Heinemann Professional (1989), p. 3.

10. Mintzberg, H. *Managing*, Financial Times Prentice Hall (2009), pp. 196–7.

11. Reddin, W. J. *Managerial Effectiveness*, McGraw-Hill (1970).

12. Birkinshaw, J. 'How to be a Better Boss', *Management Today*, September 2013, pp. 46–9.

13. Drucker, P. F. *The Effective Executive*, Heinemann Professional (1988).

14. 'Managing Your Time Effectively', Management Checklist 016, Chartered Management Institute, August 2011.

15. Dryburgh, A. 'Time management makes you efficient', *Management Today*, September 2011, p. 14. See also, Dryburgh, A. *Everything You Know About Business is Wrong*, Headline Book Publishing (2011).

16. Rees, W. D. and Porter, C. *Skills of Management*, fifth edition, Thomson Learning (2001), p. 22.

17. Hoyle, M. and Newman, P. *Simply a Great Manager*, Marshall Cavendish Business (2008).

18. See, for example, Claessens, B. J., van Eerde, W. and Rutte, C. G. 'A review of time management literature', *Personnel Review*, vol. 36, no. 2, 2007; and Forsyth, P. *100 great time management ideas from successful executives around the world*, Marshall Cavendish Business (2009).

19. Stewart, R. *Managers and Their Jobs*, second edition, Macmillan (1988), p. 123.

20. Handy, C. B. *Understanding Organizations*, fourth edition, Penguin (1993).

21. Gratton, L. *The Democratic Enterprise*, Financial Times Prentice Hall (2004), pp. xiii–xiv.

22. See, for example, Caulkin, S. 'Chris Argyris', *Management Today*, October 1997, pp. 58–9.

23. McKenna, E. *Business Psychology and Organisational Behaviour*, Lawrence Erlbaum (1994), p. 211.

24. Senge, P. M. *The Fifth Discipline: The Art of Practice of the Learning Organization*, Doubleday (1990).

25. Garratt, B. *The Fish Rots From The Head*, HarperCollins (1996). See also Garratt, B. *The Learning Organization: Developing Democracy at Work*, HarperCollins Business (2000).

26. Lane, T., Snow, D. and Labrow, P. 'Learning to Succeed with ICT', *British Journal of Administrative Management*, May/June 2000, pp. 14–15.

27. Coopey, J. 'Crucial Gaps in the Learning Organization: Power, Politics and Ideology', in Starkey, K. (ed.) *How Organizations Learn*, International Thomson Business Press (1996), pp. 348–67.

28. Deming, W. E. *Out of Crisis,* Cambridge University Press (1986); and *The New Economies for Industry,* Cambridge University Press (1993).

29. 'Total Quality: Mapping a TQM Strategy', Checklist 029, Chartered Management Institute, September 2011.

30. Cane, S. *Kaizen Strategies for Winning Through People,* Pitman (1996), p. 8.

31. www.kaizen-institute.com (accessed 27 October 2014).

32. Kaplan, R. S. and Norton, D. P. *The Balanced Scorecard: Translating Strategy into Action,* Harvard Business School Press (1996).

33. Van de Vliet, A. 'The New Balancing Act', *Management Today,* July 1997, pp. 78–80.

34. Mann, S. in conversation with Bourne, M. and Bourne, P. 'Insights into Using Strategy Tool', *Professional Manager,* vol. 16, no. 6, 2007, pp. 30–3.

35. 'On Balance', *Manager,* Autumn 2013, pp. 28–30.

36. O'Reilly, C. 'Corporations, Culture and Commitment: Motivation and Social Control in Organizations', in Steers, R. M., Porter, L. W. and Bigley, G. A. (eds) *Motivation and Leadership at Work,* sixth edition, McGraw-Hill (1996), p. 374.

37. 'Employee Engagement', Checklist 245, Chartered Management Institute, August 2011.

38. Macleod, D. and Clarke, N. Engaging for Success: Enhancing performance through employee engagement, A report to Government, Department for Business, Innovation and Skills (2009).

39. De Vita, E., 'Get Engaged', *Management Today,* April 2007, pp. 38–43.

40. 'The People Factor – Engage your employees for business success', ACAS, March 2014

41. www.investorsinpeople.org/about/benefits-of-iip (accessed 22 October 2014).

42. Material on EFQM Excellence Model reproduced with permission of European Foundation for Quality Management.

43. Rüdiger, K. 'Good Management – A New (Old) Driver for Growth', *Work Horizons,* CIPD, October 2011.

44. McBain, R., Ghobadian, A., Switzer, J., Wilton, P., Woodman, P. and Pearson, G. 'The Business Benefits of Management and Leadership Development', Chartered Management Institute, February 2012.

45. Stern, S. 'High Flyers: Low Risers', *Management Today,* June 2005, pp. 56–61.

46. Baroness Denise Kingsmill, 'How to pass the baton', *Management Today,* July/August 2010, p. 24.

47. 'MANAGEMENT 2020: Leadership to unlock long-term growth', The Commission on the Future of Management and Leadership, CMI, July 2014.

48. Roghē, F., Toma, A., Kilmann, J., Dicke, R. and Strack, R. 'Organizational Capabilities Matter', The Boston Consulting Group, January 2012.

49. 'The future of the workplace', *Management Today,* June 2011, pp. 57–60.

50. Stewart, R. *The Reality of Management,* third edition, Butterworth–Heinemann (1999), p. 125.

51. Czerniawska, F. 'From Bottlenecks to BlackBerries: How the Relationship between Organisations and Individuals Is Changing', Management Consultancies Association, September 2005.

52. 'Management Recruitment: Understanding Routes to Greater Diversity', Chartered Management Institute, June 2008.

53. 'Managing for Diversity', Checklist 152, Chartered Management Institute, February 2014.

54. Stern, S. 'The Next, Next Big Thing', *Management Today,* April 2007, pp. 50–3.

55. Mahden, M. in conversation with De Vita, E. 'Best Fit', *Management Today,* September 2008, p. 54.

56. Stewart, H. 'How to have a happy and productive office', *Management Today,* February 2012, pp. 38–42.

57. ica.coop/en/what-co-operative (accessed 16 February 2015).

58. http://ec.europa.eu/growth/smes/promoting-entrepreneurship/we-work-for/social-economy/cooperatives/index_en.htm (accessed 16 February 2015).

59. http://www.thenews.coop/49090/news/general/view-top-300-co-operatives-around-world/ (accessed 16 February 2015).

60. http://ica.coop/en/facts-and-figures (accessed 16 February 2015).

61. http://strongertogether.coop/food-coops/history-of-co-ops/ (accessed 16 February 2015).

62. Ibid.

63. http://www.cooperativegrocer.coop/articles/2004–01–09/co-op-principles-then-and-now-part-2 (accessed 16 February 2015).

64. Borgen, S. O. 'Rethinking incentive problems in cooperative organisations', Working Paper 2003-25, Norwegian Agricultural Economics Research Institute, 2003.

65. Lotti, R., Mensing, P. and Valenti, D. 'A cooperative solution', Booz Allen Hamilton Inc., 2006, http://www.strategy-business.com/resiliencereport/resilience/rr00034?pg=0 (accessed 16 February 2015).

66. http://www.telegraph.co.uk/finance/newsbysector/banksandfinance/10756341/Co-op-timeline-failed-deals-scandals-and-resignations.html (accessed 16 February 2015).

67. http://www.bbc.co.uk/news/business-27217198 (accessed 16 February 2015).

68. http://www.bbc.co.uk/news/uk-27305701 (accessed 16 February 2015).

69. http://www.theguardian.com/business/2013/oct/27/co-operative-group-retail (accessed 16 February 2015).

70. http://www.thenews.coop/49090/news/general/view-top-300-co-operatives-around-world/ (accessed 16 February 2015).

Academic viewpoint

Below you will find the title and abstract of a recent article in an academic journal that explores a topic relevant to the chapters in Part 4.

May, D. R., Luth, M. T. and Schwoerer, C. E. 'The Influence of Business Ethics Education on Moral Efficacy, Moral Meaningfulness, and Moral Courage: A Quasi-experimental Study', *Journal of Business Ethics*, no. 124, 2014, pp. 67–80. doi: 10.1007/s10551-013-1860-6

Abstract

The research described here contributes to the extant empirical research on business ethics education by examining outcomes drawn from the literature on positive organizational scholarship (POS). The general research question explored is whether a course on ethical decision-making in business could positively influence students' confidence in their abilities to handle ethical problems at work (i.e., moral efficacy), boost the relative importance of ethics in their work lives (i.e., moral meaningfulness), and encourage them to be more courageous in raising ethical problems at work even if it is unpopular (i.e., moral courage). Specifically, the study used a rigorous quasi-experimental pretest–posttest research design with a treatment ($N = 30$) and control group ($N = 30$) to investigate whether a graduate-level course in business ethics could influence students' levels of moral efficacy, meaningfulness, and courage. Findings revealed that participants in the business ethics treatment course experienced significant positive increases in each of the three outcome variables as compared to the control group. The largest increase was in moral efficacy, followed by moral courage, and finally, moral meaningfulness. These findings are discussed in the context of the current research on business ethics education and POS. Implications for future research are discussed.

Commentary

There is controversy surrounding the effectiveness of 'ethics' teaching in business schools and other educational institutions and the degree to which students take better decisions having studied business ethics. While ethical reasoning may improve, this does not of itself lead to ethical behaviour. This study attempts to quantify the results of ethics training by comparing a study group who have taken a course in ethics and a control group who have not. Results suggest that there was a positive effect and in particular the study noted an improvement in individual moral courage. Moral courage is important even where organisations have formal systems of internal whistleblowing, as standing up for an unpopular or apparently disruptive point of view is personally difficult and can lead to isolation and intimidation for the whistleblower. The authors suggest that elements of ethics education that provide individuals with the tools to challenge unethical action in a positive way are important for future ethics training.

The article might prompt you to consider some of the following questions

- Unethical behaviour can start at very junior levels in organisations; to what extent do you think low-level misbehaviour (petty pilfering, minor fraud on expenses claims, etc.) reflects a rejection of organisational power structures rather than the intention to behave badly?
- Given the need for individuals to develop moral courage, is ethical training more important for managers and leaders or for front-line staff?
- How far and how can ethical behaviour be integrated into organisational cultural norms by those with management responsibility?

Part 4 Case study
The Timpsons – solving life's little problems

Life can be full of little annoyances: the heel comes off your shoe; you get egg stains on your suit jacket; you lose a door key or lock yourself out of your car; your watch battery runs out; you need a passport-style photo for an ID card; you drop your mobile phone and crack the screen. This is scarcely end-of-the-world stuff, but annoying and frustrating nonetheless. You need a local service to fix it and you want it done quickly, but at the same time you probably would not want to pay a lot of money for the job. This is where Timpson can help you out. With over 1,400 stores located throughout the UK from the Highlands to Cornwall, the company has built a serious and successful business out of solving some of life's little problems.[1] This is the story of how the little things can add up to something big – not just in terms of the size of the business, but also in the way it is structured and managed.

The company did not start out in this direction; it has its origins in the industrial midlands in the mid-nineteenth century when William Timpson began to sell shoe laces as an 8-year-old boy. In 1870, at the age of 16, he opened his first shoe shop in Manchester and gradually built up a shoe retail and repair business before growing it into a shoe manufacturing company as well. The company flourished until the 1960s, when a combination of challenging business conditions and a family disagreement led to its being taken over by a larger conglomerate (United Drapery Stores), which in turn was bought by the Hanson Trust in 1983. This latter move gave John Timpson the opportunity to reacquire the family firm between 1983 and 1990, and having brought it back into his own control he decided against seeking external investment through a stock market flotation.

The fact that the company is wholly owned by John and his family means that he could make decisions that might otherwise have been unpopular with outside investors. For example, when profitability was falling in the late 1980s he was not threatened by hostile takeover bids that might have gained the support of shareholders and lost him the business once again. Certainly he had to make tough choices, such as the sale of its chain of unprofitable shoe shops in 1987 – made harder because they had been the core of Timpson since its foundation. However, the risks were taken with his own money and when he had the idea of combining shoe repair with key cutting, things began to turn a corner. Independence also allowed him to be opportunistic; taking up an employee's idea of adding watch repair to the range of services on offer, for example, or buying two businesses (dry cleaning and digital photography chains) that had gone into administration. By 2009 it was clear that the recession was in fact helping rather than damaging the company as people became more inclined to 'make do and mend', so while the shoe-making and retail trades suffered both from foreign low-cost manufacturing and a slump in sales, demand for shoe and watch repairs grew.

Today the business is back in the hands of the fourth and fifth generations of the Timpson family as John Timpson, William's great grandson, is Chairman and James Timpson (John's son) the company's Chief Executive. The two share a philosophy and outlook that has given the company a particular character and culture, although each man has made his own contribution to the Timpson way of doing business.

John Timpson has developed a distinctive philosophy that permeates the organisation and shapes its culture. He has published a number of books about managing, including guides to creating great teams, being a great boss, training people effectively and recruiting good staff. He writes for the business press, often participates in broadcasts about the world of work and runs a blog through the company website. His approach is often described as 'paternalistic' – a term that usually carries negative connotations, suggesting an autocratic 'father-knows-best' attitude to the workforce. However, his approach is anything but autocratic, and he freely admits that the staff are the ones who know best what customers want and how the business should operate. Certainly he has introduced a number of 'fatherly' perks for staff; they get a holiday on their birthday, there is a well-funded company hardship fund (loans are repaid in 99.8 per cent of cases) and there are significant bonus incentives for staff to sell above target in a business where the average transaction is probably below £10. He also thinks that it is vital that he spends more than half the working week out and about, visiting stores and chatting to staff. Not only does this make him a visible presence, reinforcing his view and ideas about business, but it also provides him with a valuable source of ideas, as he explained in 2009:

Source: © Andrew Paterson/Alamy Images

I met a guy called Glen Edwards, who was operating our shop in West Brom. Glen said 'I hope you don't mind but I'm doing a few watch repairs, because I used to do watch repairs', and I said 'how much are you taking?' He said '£120 this week.' Glen now runs the watch repair division. Our watch repair turnover last week was about £270,000, so that was pretty good.[2]

But his paternalism does not extend to wanting to control people; in fact his approach is quite the opposite. He is very keen to emphasise the importance of trust and autonomy – an insight that has led him to develop Timpson's distinctive 'upside-down' approach to management.

Managing upside down

One of the company's beliefs is that the front-line staff are the most important people to the business, and all others – managers, accountants, HR people – are there to support, not govern, the front line. Things that might seem to threaten a 'command and control' approach to managing do not bother John Timpson. For instance, writing on 27 June 2014 a few days before the right to flexible working was extended to all UK employees, he explained why he was not concerned about this new legislation and how he had come to be an upside-down manager. The key, he claims, is trust.

The simple trick is to trust every colleague who serves your customers with the authority to do it their way. Give them the freedom to do their job in the way they know best. You can't create great customer care through a set of rules. Personal service is produced by people who are allowed to use their initiative rather than following a process that tells them what to do. I should have cottoned on to this several years earlier when I read a book about Nordstrom, the US Department store chain with a reputation for heroic sales

clerks going well beyond the extra mile. In the middle of the book I saw a management chart that was upside down. Having seen the light, I told our shop colleagues they were free to do whatever they wanted as long as they followed two rules: 1) Look the part, and 2) Put the money in the till. I copied the Nordstrom chart and since then called our way of working 'Upside Down Management'.[3]

He goes on to explain that the idea did not immediately take root, and that it took over five years to change the company culture into one where rules largely went out of the window and staff were trusted to make everyday decisions about things that would normally be firmly controlled by management. It took some radical moves, for example:

To emphasise their freedom I said that anyone, even our newest recruit, could pay up to £500 to settle a customer complaint without reference to anyone else, and I let them treat our price list as a guide (they had my permission to charge whatever they wanted).[4]

As it turned out, the biggest challenge to upside-down management was the managers themselves.

The biggest task was to stop our managers issuing orders and persuade them to concentrate on giving praise, help and support, rather than policing a process. It isn't easy for managers to delegate authority while keeping responsibility; most executives do it the other way round.[5]

He is also of the view that modern management has made business life too complex, and managers should be ready to let go a bit:

Policies, governance, company rules, appraisals and budgets which often come with a generous sprinkling of company politics, can make work pretty stressful . . . Rigid managers don't do themselves any good by insisting that everyone sticks to the rules . . . Having the trust of your boss and being allowed to work in a way that suits you is a major contributor to wellbeing.

Along with the need to re-educate managers about their approach, there was also a problem relating to the staff, and the recruitment and training processes also had to undergo some major change in order to make upside-down management work.

The biggest lesson we learnt was about our people. Our upside down way of working only succeeds with the right characters. Our recruitment was all wrong; we were looking for cobblers and key cutters, when we should have been picking people with personality.

We can teach a guy with character how to cut keys but you can't put personality into a grumpy cobbler. Eventually upside down management worked so well in our shops (service got better and sales went up) I extended the principles to everyone else. Whatever the role in our business you are free to do your job the way you want.[6]

Mr Keen, Miss Ambitious, Mr Happy and Mrs Helpful – but no drongos!

The upside-down approach is not, however, all warm and cuddly. The business emphasises customer service and, as can be seen from the point about grumpy cobblers, Timpson needs a particular type of employee. The company website makes it clear that Timpson is looking for happy and helpful people who dress smartly, 'act the part' and put money in the till. Moody, scruffy, rude or unreliable people will not last long at Timpson; 'drongos' (as John and James call them) have to go and the company is pretty ruthless in getting rid of those whom it believes are holding the teams back. James Timpson describes it as a duty to get rid of bad workers as quickly as possible; fairly, honestly and legally yes, but quickly nevertheless. As Timpson has a waiting list of about 200 people seeking employment with it, for every drongo there is probably a replacement ready and waiting to join. This ruthlessness might be seen as the dark side of a paternalistic management philosophy, and it is no easy task to be a Timpson manager. Area managers must be prepared to confront underperformance and weed it out quickly. They get extensive training in disciplinary and dismissal processes (John Timpson has published a management guide on the subject), and anyone who is not comfortable with the approach is unlikely to get promoted. By contrast, the ambitious will find their career advancing very quickly, as James explained in an interview with *HR Magazine* in 2009:

if you are good then it will be a bloody quick promotion, and if you are crap then you'll leave.[7]

James is not particularly impressed by professional HR managers either, viewing them as potentially disruptive to the upside-down approach to running the business:

They try to take over. Every business we've taken over has had a bossy HR person. It's not the most important part of a business – HR is to support the front line; it is not there to tell staff what to do.[8]

The business may have over 3,000 employees but there are no more than seven members in the HR team, which comprises a head of people support and four regional HR specialists, a training manager and a dedicated health and safety officer; payroll is run from the company finance office. The people side of work is very much part of the local manager's job.

The Timpson Academy

Being unencumbered by the need to satisfy external investors and shareholders has left the Timpsons in a position to experiment with slightly unusual approaches to the business. One such has been James Timpson's initiative to give the chance of employment to people who often struggle to find a job – ex-prisoners. The idea stemmed from a visit he made to HMP Thorncross in Warrington, not far from the company offices in Manchester. He recalled the occasion during a press interview in 2013 saying that:

They gave me a guide, Matthew, who was about 18 and I really liked him. So I said 'when you're out, don't tell anybody, but I'll give you a job'. He's still with us today. He's brilliant.[9]

However, the early attempts to recruit more routinely from the prison were not altogether successful:

A third of people in prison are right for employment, a third have significant health problems which means they are not ready for employment and a third are people I would not want to have in my business. That's either because of the crimes they committed – we don't employ any sex offenders – or they are just bad bastards. I'd put them in shops and they'd nick money off us. They'd fight in the shop. Their drug dealer mates would be coming in. If it's going to go wrong it goes really wrong.[10]

The strategy had to become more focused and selective, and now the company employs two colleagues who visit prisons (they now work with about seventy institutions nationwide) to interview potential recruits and mentor them, giving the opportunity to develop the personal skills they will need for life on the outside. James explains that the successful recruits tend to have similar histories:

There's a similar pattern: in care or failed at school, got in with a bad lot, started drugs, drinking, nicking cars, got banged up. Most people we have have been to prison more than once. But they get to a stage where they want to get a job and be normal and stop the chaos.[11]

It is essential, James believes, to get people into the job as soon as they are released:

If you leave jail today you start working for us tomorrow. The longer the gap, the more likely it is there'll be problems. If recruits don't have anywhere to live we'll find somewhere and pay the deposit. They are pretty damaged these people. If you just expect them to turn up and work the next day it's not going to happen.[12]

In some cases prisoners, or 'foundation colleagues' as Timpson prefers to call them, nearing the end of their sentence will be recruited and work during the day on the ROTL (Release On Temporary Licence) scheme, and some are even managing shops:

They take the money, serve the customers, bank the money, lock the door and then go back to prison.

Three 'academies' based inside prisons additionally teach potential recruits the basics of key cutting, shoe and watch repair and customer service.

This might sound idealistic and philanthropic, and in many respects it is a socially responsible thing for any company to be doing. But there is also a business case. Prisons can be a source of talent, and as James observes:

I'd be mad to turn away profit because I don't want to employ someone who happens to have been to prison for a bit of their life.[13]

He also notes that they are very loyal, and prison life has disciplined them into being punctual. Not only that, but once on board the foundation colleagues show a similar retention rate to those recruited through more usual routes. Approximately 10 per cent of Timpson's workforce are ex-convicts, and for many of them the work is what enabled them to break out of the cycle of repeat offending, as one such colleague observed.

I think it's better what Timpson's doing than what the prisons are doing. I'd been to prison three times before I joined Timpson and I had no rehabilitation at all really. With Timpson they are giving you a career. If I'd just come out again I would have probably fallen back into the same routine. You go to job interviews and they ask you if you've got a criminal conviction and if you say yes you're immediately at the bottom of the pile. There's no rehabilitation for prisoners outside prison apart from companies like Timpson that are prepared to give you the chance.[14]

Scattering magic dust

The company website explains the Timpson approach in a short presentation called 'Magic Dust' (**http://www.timpson.co.uk/about/25/magic-dust**). It explains the components of its management philosophy in twenty-eight bullet points,[15] the last of which is 'Family Business'. Over the years it has won a number of awards and accolades, being placed highly in *The Sunday Times* and *Financial Times* '100 Best Workplaces' lists as well as gaining several awards for its work with prisoners and in re-settling ex-offenders.[16] For a low-tech, grassroots and unglamorous company, working upside down seems to be doing the trick.

Tasks

1. Use the information on organisation control strategies summarised in Figure 13.3 to examine the way in which Timpson is managed. Which control system best describes it, and what are the elements that contribute to the strategy?

2. What type of power do James and John Timpson exert within their company? Explain your view with reference to a model of power from Chapter 13.

3. To what extent can the paternalistic nature of Timpson's organisational culture be described as ethical? Use concepts from Chapter 14 to explain your view.

4. Which of Handy's organisational cultures in Chapter 15 best fits Timpson?

5. Analyse the way in which change to an 'upside-down' model was resisted by managers, and explain how John Timpson was able both to effect a cultural change and to make it stick.

6. Can Timpson be described as a 'learning organisation'? Use the ideas in Chapter 16 to explain your view.

Notes and references

1 Timpson website, **http://www.timpson.com/** (accessed 9 March 2015).

2 Teather, D. 'John Timpson, the cobbler who is showing his rivals a clean pair of heels', *Guardian*, 3 April 2009, **http://www.theguardian.com/business/2009/apr/03/john-timpson-interview** (accessed 10 March 2015).

3   Timpson, J. 'Flexible working boosted my business', *Telegraph*, 27 June 2014, http://www.telegraph.co.uk/finance/businessclub/management-advice/10930476/John-Timpson-In-25-years-I-want-to-say-HS2-was-a-good-idea.html (accessed 10 March 2015).

4   Ibid.

5   Ibid.

6   Ibid.

7   Davis, G. 'View from the Top: Interview with James Timpson managing director of Timpsons', *HR Magazine*, 21 December 2009, http://www.hrmagazine.co.uk/hr/interviews/1015064/view-top-interview-james-timpson-managing-director-timpsons (accessed 11 March 2015).

8   Ibid.

9   Osborne, A. 'Timpson has key to giving ex-convicts a second chance', *Telegraph*, 22 August 2013, http://www.telegraph.co.uk/finance/newsbysector/retailandconsumer/10266250/Timpson-has-key-to-giving-ex-convicts-second-chance.html (accessed 10 March 2015).

10 Osborne, 2013, op. cit.

11 Ibid.

12 Ibid.

13 Warren, C. 'An ex-offender could be your best employee', *People Management*, 5 August 2013, http://www.cipd.co.uk/pm/peoplemanagement/b/weblog/archive/2013/08/05/an-ex-offender-could-be-your-best-employee.aspx (accessed 10 March 2015).

14 Osborne, 2013, op. cit.

15 See diagram below.

16 Timpson website, http://www.timpson.co.uk/about/81/awards (accessed 11 March 2015).

APPENDIX Review of personal skills and employability

The contents of this book have drawn attention to the importance of features that relate to the development of your personal skills and employability. Referring back to the diagram **on page xxiii** consider carefully the following *examples*:

- Self-awareness and confidence – *for example*:

  be mindful of how your attitudes, beliefs and values impact on others; admit to your perceptual bias, distortions and errors; recognise the nature of your work orientation and work ethic; acknowledge your strengths and shortcomings.

- Relationships with others – *for example*:

  demonstrate respect and empathy towards other people; display awareness of social interactions and influences; accept formal hierarchical and organisational relationships; acknowledge different individual needs and expectations at work.

- Communication and presentation skills – *for example*:

  be able to converse well with other people; be sensitive to non-verbal communications and body language; contribute meaningful participation in class and seminar activities; present clear, coherent and persuasive reports and other written documents.

- Working in groups and teams – *for example*:

  work constructively and harmoniously with colleagues; accept group consensus and decision-making; recognise the roles you perform best and the contribution you make; accept the importance and impact of the informal organisation.

- Dealing with difficult situations – *for example*:

  accept conflict as a reality of management and organisational behaviour; be able to cope with potentially stressful work situations; display support and empathy in responding to practical or emotional needs of colleagues.

- Influencing others and leadership – *for example*:

  interrelate well with working colleagues; recognise how your own values and beliefs impact on others; be mindful of the attributes and qualities required of an effective leader; judge your readiness for a leadership role.

- Coping with and managing change – *for example*:

  acknowledge the continuous pace of change; adapt to the changing face of the workplace and need for flexibility; accept the increasing importance of communications information technology within work organisations.

- Observing ethical behaviour – *for example*:

  honour corporate social responsibilities and codes of conduct; respect the role, status and authority of senior members of staff; recognise pluralistic approaches to power; demonstrate ethical values and behaviour.

- Working in multicultural organisations – *for example*:
  embrace the impact and benefits of diversity; understand the pervasive influence of organisation culture; be able to work harmoniously with people of different ethnic origin, gender, age, sexual orientation, religious beliefs or social class.
- Displaying managerial potential – *for example*:
  prioritise effectively your time; accept the need for lifelong learning and personal development; participate actively in management development programmes; accept responsibility for your self-development and career progression.

Use these examples to reflect upon the extent to which you have enhanced your awareness and knowledge of such features, and are better prepared to demonstrate your personal skills and employability, and aid your career progression.

Remember to update your personal profile.

Concluding exercise

Definitions of organisational behaviour (OB) generally relate to improving organisational performance and effectiveness. Accordingly, underlying your study of OB has been the interrelationship with that of management and the social and human skills that reflect the ability to work well with other people. The development of personal skills in management and leadership plays a crucial role in terms of both your future career employability and continued contribution to organisational success.

Exercise: how good are you at managing and leading at the same time?

In the below table there are two lists of different attributes. For each attribute in both columns rate yourself using the scale below. Where possible rate yourself in a particular situation or job context.

How well do the following attributes describe your behaviour? Rate each item: always (5); mostly (4); sometimes (3); seldom (2); never (1).

Column A	Column B
Quick to recognise problem situations that require attention and action	Willing to hear and consider alternatives from others, even if they are different to one's own
Know where one is headed and the results to be achieved	Good at listening to others and taking seriously what they have to say
Work to high standards of efficiency and effectiveness – get the job done well and on time	Take an interest in individuals and their abilities and what makes them tick
Focus on one issue at a time, giving full attention to reaching a conclusion	Favour listening and understanding to talking
Aware of what is and what is not important and focus on priorities	Handle conflict and disagreements with patience and try to find the answer to suit both parties
Think clearly and logically, working through problems in an orderly and logical manner	Aware of one's own strengths and weaknesses and how one comes across to others

Column A	Column B
Gather facts and information before drawing conclusions	Work well in a team and with others; can be described as co-operative and a team player
Work out, beforehand, the best way to tackle a problem or do the job	Know when to be tough and push hard and when to ease back when dealing with others
Fix problems and also prevent their recurrence by removing the cause	Consider who to involve and the best way to involve them before taking action
Follow up to check and rectify things if they have gone wrong	Explore what people feel and how they will react before taking action

Scoring

To score your own balance between 'managing' and 'leading', you can do so by adding up all the scores you gave yourself for those attributes in Column A and the scores you gave yourself for those attributes listed in Column B. The attributes listed in Column A are typically management orientation and the attributes listed in Column B are typically leadership orientation.

There is no one universal mixture of management + leadership behaviour. It will depend on the situation and the people involved. But we all have natural preferences that could lead us to a particular approach to a given situation regardless of the circumstances.

Key questions

1. What did you score?
2. How might you need to change your management + leadership mix to match a particular situation?

Source: Adapted and reproduced with permission from Hugo Misselhorn, M.O.D. Consulting. August 2014. hugomodc@iafrica.com

Glossary

Ability Generally defined as a stable characteristic of a person's capacity for physical or mental performance.

Accountability The ultimate responsibility that managers cannot delegate. While managers may delegate authority, they remain accountable for the decisions and actions of their subordinates.

Action-centred leadership A theory of leadership that focuses on what leaders do. It states that the effectiveness of a leader is dependent upon meeting three areas of need within the work group: the need to achieve the common task, the need for team maintenance and the individual needs of group members.

Action learning An approach to management development that involves a small self-selecting team undertaking a practical, real-life and organisational-based project. The emphasis is on learning by doing with advice and support from tutors and other course members.

Adhocracy A flexible, loosely structured, adaptable, organic and informal form of organisation.

Adjourning The adjourning or disbanding of a group because of, for example, completion of a task, or members leaving the organisation or moving to other tasks.

Adoption phase A range of choices relating to the introduction of new technology into organisations consisting of initiation, progression/feasibility, investment decision, and planning and systems design.

Agenda-setting A constant activity of managers involving a set of items, or series of agendas, relating to aims and objectives, plans, strategies, ideas, decisions to be made and priorities of action in order to bring about desired end results.

Aggression A physical or verbal attack on some person or object.

Alienation Refers to the detachment of the person from their work.

Alienative involvement Where members are involved against their wishes. There is a strong negative orientation towards the organisation.

Anthropology The study of the cultural system, that is human behaviour as a whole and the science of humankind.

Attitudes Can be defined as providing a state of 'readiness' or tendency to respond in a particular way. They are learned through life and are embodied within our socialisation process.

Attribution theory The way in which individuals make sense of other people's behaviour through attributing characteristics to them by judging their behaviour and intentions on past knowledge and in comparison with other people they know.

Authoritarian (autocratic) style of leadership Where the focus of power is with the manager. The manager alone exercises decision-making and authority for determining policy, procedures and the allocation of work, and has control of rewards or punishments.

Authority The right of subordinates to take action or make decisions that the manager would otherwise have done.

Away days An approach to management development that uses activity-based exercises undertaken away from the workplace. The main objective is often building team spirit and working relationships.

Baby-boomers A generation and age group at work born between 1946 and 1963 and typified by a search for security.

Balanced scorecard An attempt to combine a range of both qualitative and quantitative measures of performance that recognise the expectations of various stakeholders.

Behaviourism A school of psychology developed out of research studies into learning that is interested in the study of behaviour and those actions that could be observed, measured and controlled.

Brainstorming (thought showers) Where a group adopts a 'freewheeling' attitude aimed at generating as many ideas as possible. The focus is on freedom of expression and the quantity of ideas rather than quality.

Bureaucracy A form of structure found in many large-scale organisations. Bureaucracy is based on specialisation of tasks, hierarchy of authority and decision-making, systems of rules and regulations and an impersonal orientation from officials.

Bureaucratic organisations Authority is based on the acceptance of the law of formal rules and procedures, and on impersonal principles.

Bureaucratic orientation An individual's orientation to work in which he or she regards it as a central life issue. There is a sense of obligation to the work of the organisation.

Calculative involvement Where attachment to the organisation is motivated by extrinsic rewards.

Chain of command The number of different levels in the structure of the organisation; the chain of hierarchical command.

Charismatic organisation An organisation in which authority is legitimised by belief in the personal qualities of the leader and the leader's strength of personality and inspiration.

Classical approach The organisation is thought of in terms of its purpose and formal structure and this approach aims to identify how methods of working can improve productivity. Emphasis is placed on the planning of work, the technical requirements of the organisation, principles of management and the assumption of rational and logical behaviour.

Classical conditioning A theory on learning developed by Pavlov, using dogs. Pavlov found that instinctive reflexes could be 'conditioned' to respond to a new situation and new stimulus.

Coaching A supportive relationship aimed at creating understanding, direction and action. Coaching uses deductive techniques and the coach does not have to be an expert in the subject.

Coercive power Based on fear and the subordinate's perception that the leader has the ability to punish or bring about undesirable outcomes for those who do not comply with the directives (e.g. withholding promotion or privileges).

Cognitive theories of learning Theories of learning that identify how and why people learn, taking individual factors into consideration, and not simply the behaviour demonstrated through the learning process.

Community level The level within an organisation that is concerned with broad objectives and the work of the organisation as a whole.

Conceptual ability The ability to view the complexities of the operations of the organisation as a whole, including environmental influences, and the ability to make decisions.

Concertive control A system of control not exercised by managers but by the value consensus of the team to a system of normative rules.

Conflict Present where there is an incompatibility of goals arising from opposing behaviours at the individual, group or organisational level. Particularly, conflict is behaviour intended to obstruct the achievement of some other person's goals.

Constructive behaviour A positive reaction to the blockage of a desired goal through problem-solving or compromise.

Content theories of motivation These theories attempt to explain those specific things that actually motivate the individual at work and are concerned with identifying people's needs, the strength of those needs and the goals they pursue in order to satisfy those needs.

Contingency approach An extension of the systems approach to management that implies that the structure of an organisation and its success are dependent upon the nature of tasks that are undertaken and the nature of environmental influences. There is, therefore, no one best way to structure or manage organisations; rather, it must be dependent upon the contingencies of the situation.

Continuing professional development (CPD) The process of planned, continuing development of individuals throughout their career.

Control By their very nature control systems are concerned with regulation of behaviour and improvement in performance. Control is not only a function of formal organisation but also organisational behaviour and interpersonal influence.

Corporate social responsibility This concept gives rise to how a company should conduct itself within society, and different views on what a business is for and how it should act. Social responsibilities arise from the interdependence of organisations, society and the environment.

Corporate strategy This formalises the objectives and policy of an organisation and serves to describe its sense of purpose together with its direction and scope over the long term.

Creativity The application of imaginative thought, which may lead to new ways of seeing things, and results in innovative solutions to a problem or the initiation of change.

Decentralisation Where specific delegation is given to sub-units or groups within an organisation such that they enjoy a measure of autonomy or independence.

Decision-making (decision theory) approach An approach to management that focuses on managerial decision-making and how organisations process and use information in making decisions.

Delegation The process of entrusting authority and responsibility to others throughout the various levels of the organisation, and the creation of a special manager–subordinate relationship.

Democratic style of leadership Where the focus of power is more with the group as a whole than with the manager. Leadership functions are shared with members of the group and the manager is more part of a team.

Differentiation Describes the difference in cognitive and emotional orientation among managers in different functional departments with respect to goal orientation, interpersonal relations and formal structure.

Displaced aggression When aggression is displaced towards some other person or object than that which is perceived as the source of frustration; that is, a 'scapegoat' is found for the outlet of frustration.

Diversity The recognition of individual differences and that people are not homogeneous. Focuses on the multiplicity of visible and non-visible differences among people.

EFQM (European Foundation for Quality Management) Excellence Model A management model that enables organisations to assess their key strengths and potential gaps in performance across a set of nine criteria.

E-learning Learning via information and communications technology.

Electronic panopticon Use of information technology to monitor and record the work of employees.

Element functions Activities within an organisation that are not directed towards specific and definable ends but are supportive of the task functions and an intrinsic part of the management process.

Emotional intelligence The sum of a range of interpersonal skills that form the public persona, including the emotional qualities of individuals.

Employee commitment (and engagement) Typically conceived as an individual's psychological bond to the organisation including a sense of job involvement, loyalty and a belief in the value of the organisation.

Empowerment Where employees are allowed greater freedom, autonomy and self-control over their work, and the responsibility for decision-making.

Equity theory A theory of motivation that focuses on people's feelings of how fairly they have been treated in comparison with the treatment received by others.

Ethics The study of morality – practices and activities that are considered to be importantly right and wrong, together with the rules that govern those activities and the values to which those activities relate.

Expectancy theory A theory of motivation based on the idea that people prefer certain outcomes from their behaviour over others. Motivation is a function of the relationship between effort, level of performance and rewards related to performance.

Expert power Based on the subordinate's perception of the leader as someone who is competent and who has some special knowledge or expertise in a given area. This power is based on credibility and clear evidence of knowledge or expertise.

External environment (and environmental factors) The external factors outside of the organisation that can influence and affect the performance of it, the major environmental factors being technical, economic, social and governmental.

Extrinsic motivation Related to tangible rewards such as salary, promotion, working conditions and fringe benefits. These tangible rewards are often determined at the organisational level and may be outside the control of individual managers.

Fixation When an individual is frustrated but persists in a form of behaviour that has no adaptive value and actions are continued that have no positive results.

Flat hierarchical structure An organisation that has broad spans of control and few levels of authority.

Flexible working arrangements A range of flexible working practices designed to help employees balance work and home life.

Formal groups Formal groups are created to achieve specific organisational objectives and are concerned with the co-ordination of work activities. Group members have defined roles and the nature of tasks to be undertaken is a predominant feature of the group.

Formal organisation A planned co-ordination of the activities of a number of people for the achievement of some common, explicit purpose or goal, through the division of labour and function, and through a hierarchy of authority and responsibility.

Forming The initial formation of a group and the first stage in group development.

Frustration A negative response to the blockage of a desired goal resulting in a defensive form of behaviour.

Functional relationships The formal relationships within an organisation between people in a specialist or advisory position and line managers and their subordinates. These occur when a person offers a common service throughout all departments of the organisation.

Functions of leadership This focuses attention on the functions of leadership, rather than the personality of the leader, and how the leader's behaviour affects and is affected by the group of followers. This approach to leadership believes that the skills of leadership can be learned and developed.

Generation X A generation and age group at work born between 1964 and 1980 and typified by, after the slog, the rewards.

Generation Y A generation and age group at work born between 1980 and 1995 and typified by travel first, then a career.

Globalisation In broad terms, organisations integrating, operating and competing in a worldwide economy.

Goal theory A theory of motivation based on the premise that people's goals or intentions play an important part in determining behaviour. Goals guide people's responses and actions and direct work behaviour and performance, leading to certain consequences or feedback.

Group Any number of people who interact with one another, are psychologically aware of one another and who perceive themselves as being in a group.

Group norm Codes and practices developed by a group that group members consider to constitute proper group behaviour.

Groupthink The tendency within a group to 'drift along' towards decisions that may be inappropriate or unquestioned due to various in-group pressures.

Halo effect When the perception of a person is formulated on the basis of a single favourable or unfavourable trait or characteristic and tends to shut out other relevant characteristics of that person.

Hierarchy Clearly delineated levels of management authority as a means of co-ordination and control.

Hierarchy of needs A theory of motivation developed by Maslow, which states that people's behaviour is determined by their desire to satisfy a progression of physiological, social and psychological needs.

Human relations approach A management approach based on the consideration of and attention to the social factors at work and the behaviour of employees within an organisation. Particular importance is paid to the informal organisation and the satisfaction of individuals' needs through groups at work.

Hygiene (maintenance) factors Factors within a job that serve to prevent dissatisfaction. They are related to the job environment, are extrinsic to the job itself and include job security, working conditions and salary.

Idiographic approaches Approaches to the study of personality that focus on understanding the uniqueness of individuals. These approaches regard personality as a process that is open to change.

Informal groups Serve to satisfy the psychological and social needs of the group members and are not necessarily related to tasks to be undertaken. Informal groups are based on personal relationships and membership can cut across the formal structure of an organisation.

Informal organisation An organisation arising from the interaction of people, their psychological and social needs, and the development of groups with their own relationships and norms of behaviour, irrespective of those defined within the formal structure.

Information technology A term used to cover the application of computers, computer networks and telecommunications to the retrieval, storage and transmission of information.

Inspirational (visionary) leadership Leadership associated with the concept of creating a vision with which others can identify, getting along with others and inspiring through personal qualities or charisma.

Instrumental orientation An individual's orientation to work in which he or she regards it as a means to an end and not as a central life issue.

Integration Describes the quality of state of collaboration that exists among departments required to achieve unity of effort by the demands of the environment.

Intelligence The ability for constructive thinking, adaption, reasoning and problem-solving.

Interactionist perspective A view that believes conflict is a positive force and necessary for effective performance. This approach encourages a minimum level of conflict within a group in order to encourage self-criticism, change and innovation.

Internal environment Relates to the culture and climate of an organisation and to the prevailing atmosphere surrounding the organisation.

Intrinsic motivation Related to psychological rewards such as achieving appreciation, positive recognition and being given the opportunity to use one's ability. These psychological rewards can usually be determined by the actions and behaviour of individual managers.

Introduction phase The second main phase in the adoption and introduction of new technology into an organisation. This involves working on the technology and the associated organisational changes with a view to making them effective.

Investors in People (IIP) Owned by the UK government and specialises in highlighting and championing best practices through ten indicators for people management success.

Job satisfaction An attitude or internal state that is associated with, for example, a personal feeling of achievement either quantitative or qualitative.

Johari window A simple framework for looking at self-insight that classifies behaviour in matrix form between what is known–unknown to self and what is known–unknown to others. It is used frequently to help individuals in a T-group experience.

Kaizen A Japanese concept of a total quality approach based on continual evolutionary change with considerable responsibility to employees within certain fixed boundaries.

Knowledge management The promotion and formalisation of learning within the workplace with the aim of aligning training with the needs of the business.

Laissez-faire (genuine) style of leadership Where the manager consciously makes a decision to pass the focus of power to members of the group, allowing them freedom of action. The manager has observed that the members of the group work well on their own and does not interfere.

Lateral relationships Formal relationships within an organisation that exist between individuals in different departments or sections, especially between individuals on the same level.

Leadership A relationship through which one person influences the behaviour or actions of other people.

Leadership Grid® A grid that compares the varying styles of management based on the concern for production against the concern for people.

Learning A change of a relatively permanent kind that may result in new behaviours and actions or new understanding and knowledge gained through a formal process or spontaneously and incidentally through life experiences.

Learning organisation An organisation that encourages and facilitates the learning and development of people at all levels of the organisation, values the learning and simultaneously transforms itself.

Legitimate power Based on the subordinate's perception that the leader has a right to exercise influence because of the leader's role or position in the organisation. This power is based on authority and related to a person's position within an organisation.

Lifelong learning Changes and learning that continue throughout life, and take place in a variety of ways and range of situations.

Line and functional organisation A means of making full use of specialists while maintaining the concept of line authority. Creates an informal type of matrix structure.

Line relationships A formal relationship within an organisation between individual positions where authority flows vertically down through the structure.

Management The process through which efforts of members of the organisation are co-ordinated, directed and guided towards the achievement of organisational goals.

Management development Concerned with improving both the effectiveness of individual managers and management performance as a whole. Managers need a balance of technical, social and conceptual knowledge acquired through a blend of education and experience.

Managerial effectiveness Concerned with 'doing the right things' and relates to the outputs of the job and what the manager actually achieves.

Managerial efficiency Concerned with 'doing things right' and relates to inputs and what the manager does.

Managerial Grid® *See* Leadership Grid®.

Managerial level The level within an organisation that is concerned with the co-ordination and integration of work at the technical (organisational) level.

Managerial roles Organised sets of behaviour associated with a manager. Arise as a result of the formal authority, status and activities of a manager.

Matrix structure Where there is a two-way flow of authority and responsibility within an organisation due to the vertical flow of authority and responsibility from the functional departments and the horizontal flow of authority and responsibility from project teams.

Mechanistic system A rigid system of management practice and structure that is characterised by a clear hierarchical structure, specialisation of task, defined duties and responsibilities, and knowledge centred at the top of the hierarchy.

Mentoring A supportive and challenging relationship in which the mentor offers advice, guidance and support. The mentor is typically an expert in an area or a leader within an organisation.

Mission statement Sets an organisation's purpose, guiding values and principles, and the way in which it intends to achieve its objectives, while recognising the interests of other stakeholders.

Moral compass Lack of moral awareness in business and public affairs – the absence of an intuitive sense of right and wrong.

Moral involvement Based on the individual's belief in, and value placed on, the goals of the organisation.

Motivation The driving force within individuals by which they attempt to achieve some goal in order to fulfil some need or expectation.

Motivators (growth) factors Factors within a job that, if present, serve to motivate the individual to superior effort and performance. These factors are related to the job content of the work itself and include recognition, personal growth and sense of achievement.

Myers–Briggs Type Indicator (MBTI) A personality test that identifies sixteen types of personality based on individuals' extroversion or introversion and their cognitive functions of thinking, feeling, sensation and intuition.

Neo-human relations A management approach developed by such writers as Maslow, Herzberg and McGregor, which adopts a more psychological orientation than that of the human relations approach.

Network-building Involves individuals interacting with others and establishing a network of co-operative relations. These networks are outside of the formal structure and provide a means of exchanging information on a wide range of topics.

Neuro-linguistic programming (NLP) The name originates from three disciplines that all have a part to play when people are communicating with others: neurology, linguistics and programming. NLP emphasises the significance of the perceptual process, and ways in which information is subjectively filtered and interpreted.

Nomothetic approaches Approaches to the study of personality that focus on people in general through the analysis of group data. These approaches claim that personality is largely inherited and resistant to change.

Normative power A form of power that relies on the allocation and manipulation of symbolic rewards (e.g. esteem and prestige).

Norming The third stage of group development during which members of the group establish guidelines and standards and develop their own norms of acceptable behaviour.

Objectives (organisational) Objectives set out the specific goals of the organisation, the aims to be achieved and the desired end results.

Open-systems model The organisation is viewed as an open system that takes inputs from the environment and through a series of activities transforms or converts these into outputs to achieve some objective.

Operant conditioning A theory of learning developed by Skinner showing the effects of reward and punishment and demonstrating that responses in behaviour are learned because of their outcomes.

Operationalisation A stage in technology introduction when the workforce can have direct impact on such aspects as working practices, tasks, decisions about methods, and tools and techniques.

Organic system A fluid and flexible system of management practice and structure that is characterised by the adjustment and continual redefinition of tasks, a network structure of control, authority and communication, and where superior knowledge does not necessarily coincide with positional authority.

Organisation structure The pattern of relationships among positions in the organisation and among members of the organisation. It defines tasks and responsibilities, work roles and relationships, and channels of communication.

Organisational behaviour The study and understanding of individual and group behaviour and patterns of structure in order to help improve organisational performance and effectiveness.

Organisational behaviour modification (OBMod) The application of learning principles to influence organisational behaviour. It can be seen as a form of operant conditioning or reinforcement theory.

Organisational climate Relating to the prevailing atmosphere surrounding the organisation, to the level of morale, and to the strength of feelings or belonging, care and goodwill among members. Organisational climate is based on the perceptions of members towards the organisation.

Organisational culture The collection of traditional values, policies, beliefs and attitudes that constitute a pervasive context for everything we do and think in an organisation.

Organisational goals Something that the organisation is striving to achieve, a future expectation, a desired future state and something towards which the activities of the organisation are directed in an effort to attain this state.

Organisational ideology Based on the beliefs, values and attitudes of the individuals, this determines the culture of the organisation and provides a set of principles that govern the overall conduct of the organisation.

Organisational stakeholders Those individuals or groups who have an interest in and/or are affected by the goals, operations or activities of the organisation or the behaviour of its members.

Organisational sub-systems The interrelated sub-systems of an organisation: tasks, technology, structure, people and management. These sub-systems need to be co-ordinated to ensure that the activities of an organisation are directed towards the achievement of aims and objectives.

Organisations Structures of people that exist in order to achieve specific purposes, common aims and objectives by means of planned and co-ordinated activities.

Parkinson's Law The concept of the 'Rising Pyramid' and the idea that 'work expands so as to fill the time available for its completion'.

Path–goal theory A contingency model based on the belief that the individual's motivation is dependent upon expectations that increased effort to achieve an improved level of performance will be successful.

Perception The dynamic and complex way in which individuals select information (stimuli) from the environment, interpret and translate it so that a meaning is assigned that will result in a pattern of behaviour or thought.

Perceptual defence When people select information that is supportive of their own point of view and choose not to acknowledge contrary information. They avoid or screen out certain stimuli that are perceptually disturbing or threatening.

Performing The fourth stage of group development during which the group concentrates on the performance of the common task.

Personal (informal) power Power that derives from the individual and is in the eye of the beholders who believe that person has the ability to influence other people or events to make things happen.

Personal transformational change Where circumstances have not changed but because of some emotional or spiritual happening the individual was transformed or changed.

Personality An individual's unique set of characteristics and tendencies that shape a sense of self, and what that person does and the behaviour they exhibit.

PESTEL analysis A technique for analysing the general external environment of an organisation in terms of the political, economic, socio-cultural, technological, environmental and legal aspects.

(The) Peter Principle Concerned with the study of occupational incompetence and hierarchies, and the idea that 'in a hierarchy every employee tends to rise to their level of incompetence'.

Pluralist perspective Where a work organisation is viewed as being made up of powerful and competing sub-groups with their own legitimate loyalties, objectives and leaders.

Policy (organisational) Developed within the frame of the objectives and details, the 'how', 'where' and 'when' in terms of the course of action that must be followed to achieve the objectives.

Positive organisational behaviour The study and application of positively oriented human resources and psychological capacities that can be measured, developed and effectively managed for performance improvement in today's workplace.

Positive psychology The scientific study of what makes life most worth living.

Postmodernism A more recent view of organisations and management that rejects a rational, systems approach and accepted explanations of society and behaviour. Postmodernism places greater emphasis on the use of language and attempts to portray a particular set of assumptions or versions of the 'truth'.

Power The level of control or influence a person holds over the behaviour of others, with or without their consent.

Private-enterprise organisations Organisations owned and financed by individuals, partners or shareholders accountable to their owners or members. The main aim is of a commercial nature such as profit, return on capital employed, market standing or sales level.

Privatisation The transfer of business undertakings from state (government) control to the private sector. The extent of state ownership, and the balance between commercial and social interests.

Process theories of motivation Concerned with how behaviour is initiated, directed and sustained, that is the actual process of motivation.

Project team A team set up as a separate unit on a temporary basis for the attainment of a particular task. When the task is completed the team is disbanded or members reassigned to a new task.

Projection Attributing or projecting one's own feelings, motives or characteristics to other people. Projection is a distortion that can occur in the perception of other people.

Psychological contract An unwritten contract between employers and employees that covers a series of mutual expectations and satisfaction of needs arising from the people–organisation relationship.

Psychology The study of the personality system, that is human behaviour, traits of the individual and membership of small social groups.

Psychometric (psychological) tests Tests that assess an individual's typical responses to given situations based on his or her choices and strength of feeling; or that assess an individual's ability to perform effectively under standard conditions, including aptitude and ability.

Public-sector organisations Organisations created by the government and include, for example, municipal undertakings and central government departments that do not generally have profit as their goal but have political purposes.

Qualities (traits) approach to leadership This assumes that leaders are born and not made. Leadership consists of certain inherited characteristics, or personality traits, which distinguish leaders from their followers. Attention is focused on the person in the job and not the job itself.

Radical perspective A perspective on organisations that challenges the traditional view of conflict, and sees organisations in terms of disparity in power and control.

Rational–economic concept of motivation Based on the belief of earlier writers such as F. W. Taylor that employees want, more than anything else from their employer, the highest possible wages for their work and are motivated by their economic needs.

Referent power Based on the subordinate's identification with the leader. The leader exercises influence because of perceived attractiveness, personal characteristics, reputation or charisma.

Regression When an individual is frustrated and reverts to a childish or primitive form of behaviour, for example sulking, crying or tantrums.

Remunerative power A form of power that involves the manipulation of material resources and rewards (e.g. salaries and wages).

Responsibility Involves an obligation by a subordinate to perform certain duties or make certain decisions and having to accept possible reprimand for unsatisfactory performance.

Responsible leadership An organisation's approach to governance, social responsibilities and business ethics.

Reward power Based on the subordinate's perception that the leader has the ability and resources to obtain rewards for those who comply with directives (e.g. pay or promotion).

Risky-shift Where a group decides to take a riskier course of action rather than the more conservative or safer option.

Role The expected pattern of behaviours associated with members occupying a particular position within the structure of the organisation.

Role ambiguity This occurs when there is a lack of clarity as to the precise requirements of the role and the individual is unsure what to do.

Role conflict Arises from inadequate or inappropriate role definition and results in a person behaving in a way that may not be consistent with their expected pattern of behaviour.

Role expectations Indicate what the person is expected to do and their duties and obligations.

Role incompatibility Arises when compliance with one set of expectations makes it difficult or impossible to comply with the other expectations. The two role expectations are in conflict.

Role incongruence This arises when a member of staff is perceived as having a high and responsible position in one respect but a low standing in another respect.

Role overload When an individual faces too many separate roles or too great a variety of expectations and is unable to meet all expectations satisfactorily.

Role set Comprises the range of associations or contacts with whom the individual has meaningful interactions in connection with the performance of their role.

Role underload When the prescribed role expectations fall short of the individual's own perception of his or her role.

Rusty halo effect Where general judgements about a person are formulated from the perception of a negative characteristic.

Scientific management Developed by F. W. Taylor, this classical approach to management advocates the breaking down of work processes into discrete tasks to find the 'one best way' of performing each task in terms of scientific procedures. Increased productivity is rewarded by financial rewards.

Self-established roles Where formal expectations are specified loosely or in very general terms, and members have the opportunity to determine their own role expectations.

Self-fulfilling prophecy The essence of the prophecy is that simply because it has been made, this will cause it to happen. People strive to validate their perceptions irrespective of the actual reality.

Servant leadership A philosophy based on ethical responsibility of leaders; a spiritual understanding of people and empowering people through honesty, respect, nurturing and trust.

Shared and distributed leadership As opposed to hierarchical leadership, this gives recognition to the sharing of leadership function, power and decision-making through all levels of the organisation.

Shareholder-centred view Sees the directors of the company as agents of its owners and duty bound to act so as to maximise the interests of those owners.

Situational (or contingency) approach to leadership Where the person who is best suited to lead in a particular situation takes on the role of leader. The importance of the situation is the focus and the person who is seen as the most suitable leader is appointed by the group.

Social action A study of organisations in which the organisation is considered from the standpoint of the individual. Individual goals, interpretation of the work situation in terms of the satisfaction sought and the meaning that work has for them are used as a basis for explaining behaviour.

Social and human skills Abilities related to interpersonal relationships in working with and through other people, and the exercise of judgement.

Social-enterprise organisations Set up in response to community, social or environmental concerns and bring together aspects of both the private and public sectors.

Social exchange theory A fundamental feature of human interaction that gives rise to the exchange of social and material resources.

Social identity theory A means of understanding the psychological basis of intergroup discrimination. Individuals are perceived as having not just one 'personal self' but a number of 'selves' derived from different social contexts and membership of groups.

Social learning theory Based on the premise that people learn by observing and interacting with others, and through imitation.

Social loafing (Ringelmann effect) The tendency for individuals to expend less effort when working as a member of a group than as an individual.

Sociology The study of the social system, that is social behaviour, relationships among social groups and societies, and the maintenance of order.

Sociometry A method of indicating the feelings of acceptance or rejection among members of a group.

Socio-technical system A sub-division of the systems approach that is concerned with the interactions between the psychological and social factors and the needs and demands of the human part of the organisation and its structural and technological requirements.

Solidaristic orientation An individual's orientation to work in which group activities are most important. There is an ego involvement with work groups rather than with the organisation itself.

Span of control The number of subordinates who report directly to a given manager or supervisor.

Staff relationships These formal relationships within an organisation arise from the appointment of personal assistants to senior members of staff. Someone in a staff position usually has little or no direct authority in his or her own right but acts as an extension of his or her superior.

Stakeholder theory A business is for its stakeholders and the actions of management should be designed to balance stakeholder interests.

Stakeholders (organisational) *See* Organisational stakeholders.

Stereotyping The tendency to ascribe positive or negative characteristics to a person on the basis of a general categorisation and perceived similarities. It occurs when an individual is judged on the basis of the group to which it is perceived that person belongs.

Storming The second stage of group development, which involves members of the group getting to know each other and putting forward their views.

Strategic rewards Based on design and implementation of long-term policies and practices to support closely and advance both business and employee aspirations.

Stress A source of tension and frustration that tends to arise when an individual feels that a certain situation should not exist.

Succession planning Related to overall corporate strategy and aims to ensure a sufficient supply of appropriately qualified men and women to meet future needs of the organisation.

Systems approach (view) A management approach that attempts to reconcile the classical and human relations approaches. Attention is focused on the total work of the organisation and the interrelationships of structure and behaviour. The organisation is viewed within its total environment and emphasises the importance of multiple channels in interaction.

Talent management A strategic approach to gaining competitive advantage through such indicators as improved retention and succession planning of high performers, and making the organisation attractive to work in.

Tall hierarchical structure An organisation that has narrow spans of control and a relatively large number of levels of authority.

Task function (within organisations) The basic activities of the organisation that are related to the actual completion of the productive process and directed towards specific and definable end results.

Team role A pattern of behaviour, characteristic of the way in which one team member interacts with another, where performance facilitates the progress of the team as a whole.

Technical competence Relates to the application of specific knowledge, methods and skills to discrete tasks.

Technical level The level within an organisation that is concerned with specific operations and discrete tasks, with the actual job or tasks to be done and with the performance of the technical function.

Technology approach A sub-division of the systems approach that emphasises the effects of varying technologies on organisation structure, work groups and individual performance and job satisfaction.

Telecommuting Where staff work from home with a computer network and telephone.

Theory X A theory towards human nature and behaviour at work that assumes that most people are lazy, have an inherent dislike of work and must be coerced, controlled and directed through a central system of organisation and the exercise of authority, and that motivation occurs only at the lower levels of needs.

Theory Y A theory towards human nature and behaviour at work that assumes that most people enjoy work, are creative, can exercise self-direction and control and want to accept responsibility, and that motivation occurs at the higher as well as lower levels of needs.

Total quality management (TQM) An approach to quality within an organisation that is committed to total customer satisfaction through a continuous process of improvement, and the contribution and involvement of people.

Total rewards Encompasses all aspects of work valued by employees including learning and development opportunities and working environment in addition to pay and benefits.

Traditional organisations An organisation in which authority is legitimised through tradition, custom and a long-standing belief in the natural right to rule or is possessed through the 'traditional' procedure.

Transactional analysis (TA) Originally developed by Eric Berne, this is a popular way of explaining the dynamics of interpersonal communication, which assumes that individuals store all events and feelings ever experienced and that the personality has three ego states: Child, Adult and Parent.

Transactional leadership Based on legitimate authority within the bureaucratic structure of the organisation. The emphasis is on the clarification of goals and objectives, work tasks and outcomes, and organisational rewards and punishment.

Transformational change Involves a fundamental shift in the culture, conduct of business and working practices of an organisation, and often enacted over a period of time.

Transformational (or creative) leadership Based on the objective of transforming the performance or fortunes of a business. The emphasis is on generating a vision for the organisation and the leader's ability to appeal to the values of followers in attempting to create a feeling of justice, loyalty and trust.

Type A personality Individuals who thrive on hard work and long hours, and exhibit characteristics such as a high need for achievement, extreme competitiveness, impatience and aggressiveness. Type A personalities are more vulnerable to heart attacks.

Type B personality Individuals who exhibit the opposite characteristics from Type A and who are less vulnerable to heart attacks.

Ultimatum game An economic behavioural game that can arguably be related to the concept of equity theory.

Unconscious bias Our preferred people preferences. The subtle, unconscious behaviours that are hard-wired into us and difficult to eliminate altogether.

Unitarist perspective Where a work organisation is viewed as an integrated and harmonious whole, with managers and other staff sharing common interests and objectives.

Virtual teams Teams where the primary interaction among members is by some electronic information and communication process.

Withdrawal When an individual is frustrated and 'gives up' or resigns him- or herself to the situation.

Index